ICONS OF THE AMERICAN COMIC BOOK

ICONS OF THE AMERICAN COMIC BOOK

From Captain America to Wonder Woman

Volume Two

Randy Duncan
and Matthew J. Smith, Editors

GREENWOOD ICONS

 GREENWOOD

AN IMPRINT OF ABC-CLIO, LLC
Santa Barbara, California • Denver, Colorado • Oxford, England

Library of Congress Cataloging-in-Publication Data

Icons of the American comic book : from Captain America to Wonder Woman / Randy Duncan and Matthew J. Smith, editors.
     p. cm. — (Greenwood icons)
  Includes bibliographical references and index.
  ISBN 978-0-313-39923-7 (hardcover : acid-free paper) — ISBN 978-0-313-39924-4 (ebook)
1. Comic books, strips, etc.—History and criticism. I. Duncan, Randy, 1958– II. Smith, Matthew J., 1971–
  PN6710.I27 2013
  741.5'9—dc23   2012034779

ISBN: 978-0-313-39923-7
EISBN: 978-0-313-39924-4

17 16 15 14 13   1 2 3 4 5

This book is also available on the World Wide Web as an eBook.
Visit www.abc-clio.com for details.

Greenwood
An Imprint of ABC-CLIO, LLC

ABC-CLIO, LLC
130 Cremona Drive, P.O. Box 1911
Santa Barbara, California 93116-1911

This book is printed on acid-free paper ∞
Manufactured in the United States of America

Contents

Lee, Stan

For more than 40 years Stan Lee has been America's best-known comic book writer and a worldwide comics celebrity. He has become associated with the superhero concept in general and in particular with **Marvel Comics** characters such as **Hulk, Spider-Man,** and the **X-Men**. His very name has become a recognizable brand, and a variety of comic book companies have paid him for the privilege of having the Stan Lee charisma associated with their superheroes. Lee has also been a creator, consultant, or spokesperson for numerous superhero projects in film, television, and online.

HISTORY

A good deal of misinformation about Stan Lee has been disseminated by Stan Lee himself. By all accounts, including his own, Lee has a terrible memory, and when he cannot recall something he is liable to give the most interesting answer that comes to mind. Even in cases when he does remember the facts, if they do not make for a good story, Lee's natural inclination is to embellish those facts. For example, his official biography says he won the *Herald-Tribune*'s "Biggest News of the Week" writing contest three weeks in a row, but researchers for his unauthorized biography found that he actually won seventh place and two honorable mentions (still not shabby out of thousands of entries) (Lee and Mair 2002, 14; Raphael and Spurgeon 2003, 6). In a *Tampa Times* interview Lee declared, "I learned to read by reading comic books" (Raphael and Spurgeon 2003, 41). However, young Stanley Lieber, as he was known then, was an avid reader years before the first comic books appeared on the scene.

Stanley Martin Lieber was born in New York City in 1922 to Jack and Celia Lieber, immigrants from Romania. His father, a garment cutter, was often out of work during the Depression. After living in a couple of locations in upper Manhattan, the Lieber family moved to a one-bedroom apartment in the Bronx. Stanley attended De Witt Clinton High, a few years behind other comics notables **Will Eisner** and **Bob Kane**. Stanley was praised by his

(Associated Press)

teachers, popular with his classmates (*A&E Biography: Stan Lee* 1995), and apparently quite the extrovert—his nickname was Gabby (Raphael and Spurgeon 2003, 7). When he graduated in 1939 he had to get a job to help support the family. Stanley had alternately daydreamed about being an actor, an advertising copywriter, a lawyer, or a novelist, but for a brief time it seemed he might follow his father into the garment industry. He got a job as an office boy at a trouser manufacturing shop, but he so disliked the impersonal environment and mindless tasks that when he was fired his initial anger soon turned to relief. But he needed a job, and he was soon presented with the opportunity that would define his career.

Stanley had an uncle, Robbie Solomon, who worked at Timely Publications, a pulp magazine publisher that the year before had begun dabbling in comic book publishing and had some success with characters such as the Human Torch and Sub-Mariner. Timely owner Martin Goodman, who already had a number of relatives working for him, was married to one of Stanley's cousins. Uncle Robbie set up an interview at the Timely Comics operation. Editor Joe Simon interviewed Stanley and hired him on the spot to be an assistant, erasing stray marks on the artwork, picking up lunch, and whatever else was needed, for eight dollars a week.

Joe Simon and **Jack Kirby**, the editor-in-chief and the art director, were the heart of Timely Comics. When Stanley joined the company in late 1940, Simon and Kirby were about to launch what would prove to be a very successful a new title, **Captain America** *Comics*. Simon and Kirby kept Timely sales booming throughout 1941 with other superheroes, such as the Young Allies and the Vision. Office gofer Stanley Lieber wanted in on the action. He began his professional writing career with a two-page text piece, "Captain America Foils the Traitor's Revenge," in *Captain America Comics* #3 (1941). These text pieces, which were included in order to qualify the comics for cheaper postal rates, were often unsigned, but young Stanley proudly signed his with his new nom de plume—Stan Lee. Decades later Lee would claim he created the pen name because he was saving his real name for the serious writing he intended to do some day. While he would occasionally use other pen names (including "S. T. Anley" and "Neel Nats") to make it appear Timely had a larger writing staff, Stan Lee became Stanley Lieber's professional name, and some 30 years later he made it his legal name.

Lee continued to write the text pieces, but he also began to get assignments for backup features such as the five-page "Headline" Hunter, Foreign Correspondent story in *Captain America Comics* #5 (1941). It was not long before Lee was making less coffee and writing more scripts, and even creating characters. Probably the first superhero Lee created was Jack Frost (*USA Comics* #1, 1941), whose appearance and powers resemble the Iceman character Lee and Kirby would use in the X-Men decades later. The same year Lee also created the Witness, Father Time, and the Destroyer, who proved to be one of his most enduring Golden Age creations.

Captain America Comics was a huge hit for Timely, but when Simon and Kirby felt they were not getting the 25 percent of the profits they had been promised, they let **DC Comics** know they might be available. DC offered them a very generous contract. Goodman found out and promptly fired them. Simon and Kirby left Timely in late 1941, and 18-year-old Stan Lee became the editorial director and main writer. He was young to be the boss, but most of the talent entering the industry those days was very young, and Lee had enthusiasm and charisma that set him apart. Artist Dave Gantz said Lee "had energy and was young, tall, and good-looking" and referred to him as "the Orson Welles of the comic book business" (Raphael and Spurgeon 2003, 26).

Lee was essentially running the successful Timely Comics operation until he enlisted in the Army in November 1942. He was assigned to a Signal Corps unit and remained stateside for the duration of the war. Lee's official designation was "playwright," but he spent his time writing instruction manuals, scripting training films, and creating posters (a task at which he got to put his seldom-used drawing skills to use). Lee had a relatively enjoyable Army experience—he was far from the fighting and got to put his creativity to work in interesting ways. He wrote a marching song for the Army Finance Department and trained their payroll officers with cartoon-heavy manuals featuring his creation Fiscal Freddy. He also continued to write comic book scripts for

Timely. With free room and board and two sources of income, Lee was able to buy his first car while in the Army.

When he mustered out of the Army in fall 1945, Lee picked up where he had left off as editor and chief writer at Timely (his friend Vince Fargo had been taking care of editorial duties in his absence). Despite his heavy writing load, usually two or three scripts a week, he also enjoyed being a single young man in New York. Apparently Lee was never the type of writer who was consumed by his job. As he explains it, "Being the ultimate hack, I would start doing my thinking when I sat down in front of the typewriter, and not a minute before" (Lee and Mair 2002, 57).

Early in his career Lee made some attempts to establish rapport with his readers, and there were some glimpses of the Stan Lee persona that would come to the forefront in the 1960s. In *Mystic Comics* #5 (1941) he directly addresses the readers with a two-page text piece that gives background information on the various characters in the book and explains why they were chosen for the anthology. In 1947 Lee wrote an unusual little booklet, *Secrets behind the Comics*, with the help of one of his best friends, artist Ken Bald. Lee directly addressed the reader with a snappy, informal style, and just a dash of the bombast for which he would later become famous ("Never before have you read a book like this! It will amuse and astound you!"). *Secrets* really did reveal behind-the-scenes information about creating comic books and ended with an invitation for aspiring creators to submit their work directly to Lee, but the publication was probably intended to promote the image of the comic book industry in general, and Timely Comics in particular. Not that comic books seemed to need much promoting in the late 1940s.

Timely, likely most of the comic book industry, was thriving at the end of the 1940s. However, Goodman began cost-cutting measures because he wanted to reallocate some of his resources to what he saw as the more profitable distribution end of the business. In 1950 he directed Lee to fire the "bullpen" of staff artists who worked in house. Lee continued to work with most of the same artists, but now they were freelancers who were paid by the page rather than on salary. The transition was easy to manage because Lee had accumulated a large inventory of finished but unpublished stories. Goodman used the money he saved to start a nationwide magazine distribution business, Atlas News Company, in 1951. Goodman's comic book publishing company, which frequently changed names, became known as Atlas during this era due to the Atlas globe of the covers of the books. In the mid-1950s the company moved from the spacious office in the Empire State Building to a less expensive space in a new Park Avenue office building.

Lee's new office was cramped and windowless, but his mandate from Goodman was the same as it had always been—copy any idea that was popular. Lee spent most of the 1950s writing humor (e.g., *Millie the Model*, *The Adventures of Pinky Lee*, and *My Friend Irma*) and Westerns (e.g., *Gunsmoke*

CAN'T HIT A HOME RUN EVERY TIME

Not every Stan Lee supervillain was as malevolently magnificent as Doctor Doom. After living with and studying kangaroos, Frank Oliver developed a prodigious leaping ability, so when he undertook a life of crime it was only natural that he called himself the Kangaroo. Leap Frog's jumping ability was the result of electric springs in the soles of the flippers he wore on his feet. Stilt Man had a suit of armor with telescopic legs that allowed him to tower over his opponents. The heroes he fought usually just wrapped something around his legs and tripped him. A sentimental favorite with many fans is the alliteratively but laughably named Paste Pot Pete. Changing his name to the Trapster did not hide the fact that he was attempting to fight superheroes by shooting paste at them. No one trembled in fear when these villains arrived on the scene.

Western and *Frontier Western*). The company had always had a penchant for following trends, but during the Atlas era it often verged on outright plagiarism. When **Little Lulu** began appearing in comic books in 1948, Lee soon mimicked her with *Little Lizzie* (1949). There was *Homer Hooper* (1953), a red-headed, love-struck teen with a large H on his sweater who was nearly a direct copy of Archie Andrews. When Harvey had a hit with *Casper the Friendly Ghost* (1952), Lee answered with *Homer the Happy Ghost* (1955). Even one of Lee's most acclaimed creations from the 1950s, *The Black Knight* (1955), with magnificent artwork by Joe Maneely, was in inspired by the sort of content EC Comics had been using in their "New Trend" title *Valor* (1955).

Because science fiction and horror were so prevalent and popular in movie theaters during the 1950s Atlas naturally started churning out work in those genres. The Comics Code Authority had banned the use of supernatural monsters such as vampires and werewolves, but science fiction creatures were still fair game. Movies such as *The Creature from the Black Lagoon* (1954), *Them!* (1954), and especially *Godzilla, King of the Monsters* (1956) were clearly the inspiration for the monsters that began appearing in Atlas titles such *Strange Tales*, *Tales of Suspense*, and *Tales to Astonish* beginning in 1959. The most memorable of these creatures were the creative collaborations of Lee and Jack Kirby, who had returned to the company in the late 1950s.

In the early 1960s Lee was still creating science fiction monsters such as Fin Fang Foom (1961, with Jack Kirby) and Tim Boo Ba (1962, with **Steve Ditko**). Lee did not feel much affinity for these characters. That lack of engagement reinforced that he had been writing and editing comic books for two decades, and it was a job he had always intended to leave eventually. One of the most often repeated stories in the Stan Lee legend (and as with all such stories, it should be viewed as part of the conscious crafting of that legend) is that Lee told his wife, Joan, about his discontent and that he was considering quitting. She advised him that he should start writing the kind of stories he wanted to write and the worst that could happen is that Goodman would fire him, which is what he wanted anyway.

Lee was still contemplating his wife's advice when boss Martin Goodman told him that DC Comics was having success with their new superhero team, Justice League of America, and that Lee should try a superhero team title. Lee teamed with artist Jack Kirby to create *Fantastic Four* (1961). For the first few issues the book seemed a lot like a typical Atlas science fiction or monster title with superheroes inserted, but by 1962 the superhero team had evolved into a family and, for a time, *Fantastic Four* truly became, as was proclaimed on the cover for years, "the world's greatest comic magazine."

Stan Lee was reinvigorated and, in collaboration with Kirby, Ditko, and other Atlas artists, began creating a universe of superhero characters that were both quirky and contemporary. Hulk was a reimaging of the Frankenstein monster, with a touch of Jekyll and Hyde, for the Atomic Age. **Iron Man** translated the Cold War tensions of the 1960s into the superhero milieu. The mutant X-Men had to deal with the stigma of otherness. Arguably Lee's most significant creation (or co-creation with Ditko) was Spider-Man. Nerdy teenager Peter Parker, who is plagued by bullies, has trouble impressing girls, and is always in need of money, is the Everyman superhero. Yet, he also displays rare nobility by continually sacrificing his own happiness in order to protect people who seem to fear or hate him. Spider-Man became Lee's favorite character, and it showed. Peter Parker/Spider-Man's personality is perhaps more purely the creation of Stan Lee than anything else that came out of his collaborative work during the Marvel era. Lee continued to write the Spider-Man newspaper strip long after he had relinquished scripting chores on the comic book, though increasingly ghost writers have been doing the strip under his name.

With bold concepts and bravura artwork provided by the likes of Kirby and Ditko, with Lee adding wry humor mixed with elements of soap opera melodrama, Marvel comics of the 1960s were a breath of fresh air in an industry that had grown stale. The work attracted a growing number of enthusiastic fans. Because it was Lee's voice that spoke to the fans through captions in the stories and on the Bullpen Bulletins promotional page, Stan Lee became almost as well known, and well liked, as the superheroes themselves. And when the characters made the transition to other media, Lee went with them. Beginning with the *Spider-Man* animated series (1967–1970) Lee got a consultant credit, and pay, for virtually every cartoon featuring a Marvel character. Yet the artists with whom Lee had co-created the Marvel characters were not receiving the same recognition and financial rewards. It was a disparity that would continue to grow, causing rifts in Lee's professional relationships and tarnishing his legacy.

Stan and Jack

For serious fans and historians of American comic books, the most problematic aspect of Stan Lee's career is his relationship with Jack Kirby. At the very beginning of his career Lee was just an "office boy" who assisted Kirby and partner Joe Simon when they were running the operation at Timely Comics, but he stepped into their roles as editor and art director when they were fired. By some accounts Kirby suspected it was young Lee who had told publisher Martin Goodman that Simon and Kirby were moonlighting for DC, which led to their firing. If in fact Kirby harbored some resentment toward Lee, it must have been galling for him to go back to Goodman's company 16 years later, hat in hand, and ask Editor-in-Chief Lee for work. Kirby's options for comic book work were limited for a number of reasons. He had temporarily burned his bridges at DC due to a financial dispute with editor Jack Schiff, and the number of smaller publishers had been reduced due to a combination of the Comics Code restrictions on content, increasing competition from television, and a cyclical correction of the industry's overexpansion in the early 1950s. Kirby was a godsend for the former Timely Comics (most recently Atlas), which was in 1958 essentially nameless, severely reduced in size, and barely limping along on inventory stories. Lee and Kirby would soon turn the company's fortunes around, first with their moderately successful monster comics, and then with the introduction of the Fantastic Four.

The murky origins of the Fantastic Four are indicative of the conflicting perceptions and claims that would come to characterize the Lee and Kirby collaboration. Lee has repeatedly said that because he was considering quitting anyway, he was throwing caution to the winds and creating the kind of off-beat characters he would be interested in writing. Lee's two-page typed synopsis for the first issue, which has been reprinted in a number of venues (Thomas 1998, 5–6), seems to support his version. Kirby denied he ever saw such a synopsis and, after his bitter split with Marvel, claimed the team was totally his idea. The brainy Reed Richards, the gruff and tough Ben Grimm, the brash Johnny Storm, and the girl-next-door Sue Storm certainly seem similar to the character archetypes (a brain, a brawler, a hot-head, and a clean-cut all-American boy) developed in the Simon and Kirby kid gangs and brought to adulthood in the Challengers of the Unknown just four years before the creation of the Fantastic Four.

Which man should receive credit for a particular concept or character is difficult to determine due to the then-unconventional manner in which Lee worked with his artists in general, but Kirby in particular. Because he was responsible for writing so many titles each month and did not want to leave his freelance artists sitting idle while he finished complete scripts, Lee gradually transitioned into a collaborative model that became known as the Marvel method of producing comic books. As Marvel writer and editor Roy Thomas describes the process: "The artists were given a story line [*sic*], which might be anything from a few sentences to in quite a few cases two or three pages . . . a general plot line" (Thomas in *Comics on Trial* 2011, n.p.). Lee tended to give the artists a good bit of latitude in how they developed the idea because, as he put it, "no matter how they drew it, even if they didn't do it as well as I might have wanted, I was conceited enough to think I could fix it up by the way I put the dialogue and the captions in" (Lee in *Comics on Trial* 2011, n.p.). The more he worked with artists and the more confidence he had in their abilities, the less detailed the plot synopsis he would give them. Lee had a great deal of confidence in Kirby and often gave him very little instruction. Consequently, Kirby came to feel he was essentially creating the stories. Lee, however, believed that putting in the dialogue was where characterization occurred: "I would like to feel that the style I gave the stories by putting the dialogue in was quite important. After all, the manner of speech is really what gives the characters their personality" (Lee in McLaughlin 2007, 93). And even in the late 1960s, as he became less involved in crafting plots, Lee's contributions "had a lot to do with determining the final tone of the Marvel books, their mix of ardent philosophizing, hothouse sentimentality, brazen salesmanship, and rhetorical cheek" (Hatfield 2012, 86).

In fleshing out Lee's plots Kirby often introduced supporting characters without consulting Lee, and in drawing the first issue of the famous Galactus trilogy he introduced a herald who sought out suitable planets for the ravenous Galactus to consume. Initially Lee thought the seemingly naked silver man riding a surf board through space was too bizarre, but he quickly became taken with the audacity of the idea, and after a few issues of writing the Surfer's dialogue, doing what he considered to be the work of creating the character's personality, the Surfer became one of his favorites. In 1968 Lee decided the character was popular enough to be featured in his own series. Kirby was not consulted about it nor asked to draw the strip. The move probably stung even more because, unaware of the plans for the character, Kirby had been working on a Silver Surfer origin story for a forthcoming issue of *Fantastic Four* when he found out the first issue of the new series featured a very different origin concocted by Lee. It was one of the most significant but certainly not the only instance in which Kirby felt he had been disrespected or even betrayed.

Kirby also became resentful that Lee was increasingly in the spotlight while it seemed that he continued to toil (and to his way of thinking, doing the lion's share of the work) in the shadows. In the latter half of the 1960s Marvel and its growing stable of characters became something of a pop culture phenomenon, and the mainstream press starting paying more attention. As a result, Stan Lee became a celebrity beyond the comics community. When reporters went to the Marvel office they found Lee; Kirby was at home in his studio, hunched over the drawing board. While Kirby could be overly serious or even come off a bit glum, Lee was "witty, charming, and eminently quotable" (Evanier 2008, 141). And Lee had the spiel down pat, having already honed his pitchman skills in converting readers into avid fans.

By the end of the 1960s Lee and Kirby's working relationship had become strained nearly to the breaking point, and in early 1970 Kirby received what he considered to be an onerous contract from Marvel's new owners. He left to work for rival DC Comics.

Years later at Jack Kirby's funeral, Lee sat quietly in the back of the room and at the end of the service departed "without saying much of anything to anyone" (Evanier 2008, 211). Perhaps it is now impossible to accurately assess Lee and Kirby's individual contributions to the creation of the Marvel Universe (though each man certainly has passionate advocates who make claims for his genius), yet, "The two men, it becomes clear, did their best work in a state of artistic synergy, making art as a team that was better than anything they could do apart" (Heer 2003).

The Stan Lee Brand

In the 1970s Lee's career began taking a distinctly different turn. He was spending less of his time in the office and more of it giving media interviews and on the college lecture circuit. Lee gradually developed a new look that he felt better suited his new lifestyle. The young man with the severely receding hairline was now a middle-aged man with a full head of hair (a toupee at first, and then a transplant) (Raphael and Spurgeon 2003, 158). He grew a mustache, began wearing tinted glasses and casual clothes, and, of course, always had a ready smile to complete the persona. He appeared in magazine ads and a television commercial. On January 5, 1972, he even played Carnegie Hall. Unfortunately, "A Marvel-ous Evening with Stan Lee at Carnegie Hall" was a mishmash of readings and musical performances from guests. The evening did not let Lee's personality shine through, and young fans quickly became restless. Despite this high-profile flop, the new corporate owners (Perfect Film, later Cadence Industries, had bought Marvel in 1968) viewed Stan Lee as one of the company's greatest assets, and his star continued to rise.

When Martin Goodman retired in1972 he made his son Chip the publisher. Lee was frustrated by what he saw as Chip's failure to understand the comics business but determination to meddle in editorial decisions. Lee pressured the executives at Cadence to ease the younger Goodman out of the company, and Lee was named president and publisher (Ro 2004, 179). Soon, at the direction of new editor-in-chief Roy Thomas, "Stan Lee presents" was added to the credits page of every Marvel comic book.

Lee and his family moved to Hollywood in 1980. While totally disconnected from the company's comic book production, Lee was still on the Marvel payroll, tasked with pitching Marvel characters for television and film projects. Stan Lee's personality had shined through in a comic book industry full of introverted writers and artists, but in Hollywood nearly everyone was a charismatic huckster. He had limited success on Marvel's behalf—many Marvel characters were optioned, but only a few low-budget movies were produced, and only one of those, *Howard the Duck* (1986), got a theatrical release in the United States. When control of Marvel changed hands in the wake of the company's 1996 bankruptcy, Avi Arad was in control of film and television deals for Marvel properties. Arad was at the helm for *Blade* (1998), the first successful movie based on a Marvel character; Lee, as his contracted stipulated, still got a producer credit, but had no real input and even his cameo appearance was left on the cutting room floor.

Lee would never again be Marvel's Hollywood point man, but a new contract he negotiated in 1998 assured that he would always get a production credit and a share of the profit. Marvel still considered the Stan Lee name to be a valuable product. The promotion and subsequent success of the big-budget 2002 *Spider-Man* movie brought Lee back into the spotlight because he was so associated with the character in the public imagination. Lee used his high-profile moment in Hollywood as a springboard to a string of projects for the small screen. He was executive producer and writer for the risqué cartoon *Stripperella* (2003–2004), which aired for one season on Spike TV. He was the executive producer and host of two seasons of *Who Wants to Be a Superhero?* (2006–2007) on the Sci Fi Channel. He later lent his name to and co-hosted *Stan Lee's Superhumans* (2010–2011) on the History Channel.

Of course the Stan Lee name is most marketable within the comic book industry, and once Lee had a contract that allowed him to work for Marvel's competitors, he started getting offers. The 13 titles in the *Just Imagine* series reimagined the origins and characterizations of DC's best-known icons, beginning with *Just Imagine Stan Lee with Joe Kubert Creating Batman* (2001). In 2010 Lee had a hand in the conception and plotting of three new titles for BOOM! Studios; all of the comics have Lee's distinctive signature on the cover. In 2012 there was *Stan Lee's Mighty 7* limited series for Archie Comics. Lee's co-authors did the heavy lifting on all these projects, but to the publishers the actual stories were probably not nearly as important as being able to put the Stan Lee name on the cover.

Lee continues to maintain his celebrity status outside the world of comics with cameos in movies, guest appearances as himself on television shows, and books such as *Stan Lee's How to Draw Comics* (2010) and *Stan Lee's How to Write Comics* (2011). Lee is chairman and CEO of POW! Entertainment, Inc., which he founded to market the intellectual properties he has created since the disastrous collapse of a previous corporate venture of his, Stan Lee Media, in 2001. POW! is not only generating new projects and forging media partnerships (most notably with the Walt Disney Company), but seeking to perpetuate the Stan Lee legend with the documentary *With Great Power: The Stan Lee Story* (2010).

IMPACT ON COMICS

Stan Lee helped revitalize the comic book industry in the 1960s. In the previous decade attacks on the industry, such as **Fredric Wertham**'s *Seduction of the Innocent*, convinced much of the public that comic books were vile at best, and probably a danger to children. On the other hand, by the end of the decade many comic book readers were convinced the Comics Code Authority, an industry self-regulation effort, had made comic books safe and dull. The offbeat but very human characters Lee had a hand in creating at Marvel shook up the staid superhero genre.

Most of the dynamic superhero action, many of the soap opera situations, and, in the case of Kirby, the grandeur of mythic figures and sweeping epics, might have come from the fertile imaginations of the artists with whom Lee worked, but it was Lee's dialogue and captions that really established the tone that set Marvel apart. Skills Lee had developed during all those years of grinding out hack work were being applied with a new verve. Spider-Man's wisecracks reflected decades of writing funny animal and humor comics. The soap opera plots of career girl titles such as *Nellie the Nurse* feed into the melodrama of Peter Parker's personal life.

Perhaps just as important as the characters with whom the readers could identify was the rapport those readers felt with Stan Lee. In the Stan's Soapbox column and even in captions within the stories, he directly addressed readers in his friendly, jaunty style. From the covers to the credits to the ads, Lee's tongue-in-cheek hyperbole permeated the books. He gave himself (Smilin' Stan, Stan "The Man" Lee) and other Marvel creators (Jolly Jack Kirby, Jazzy Johnny Romita) nicknames, and thus personalities. A "seamless continuity of script and hype, all composed or tweaked by Lee, created a single, consistent voice: his" (Hatfield 2012, 68).

Lee's writing style, which could be corny and clever in the same panel, influenced many future comic book writers, but there is a single sentence that has resonated with fans and is likely to be an enduring part of Lee's legacy. In writing the "voice over" narration that appears in the final panel of the first Spider-Man story (*Amazing Fantasy* #15, 1962) Lee succinctly expressed what has become the raison d'être of the superhero: "With great power there must also come—great responsibility."

IMPACT ON AMERICAN CULTURE

Stan Lee had a role in creating characters such as Spider-Man, Hulk, and X-Men that have been part of American popular culture for nearly 50 years, their images appearing everywhere from Underoos to blockbuster movies. While many comic book characters have become known across the globe, very few people know the names of the writers and artist who created these characters. Stan Lee, however, established himself as the architect of the Marvel Universe. The process began in the 1960s as he did scores of interviews and appearances to hype the new line of Marvel superheroes, and culminated in the mid-1970s with four mass market paperbacks, beginning with *Origins of Marvel Comics* (1974), published by Simon and Schuster. Reprints of key Marvel stories were preceded by Lee's reminiscences about his inspiration for the characters. While he presented himself as the primary creator of the characters, he repeatedly acknowledged the contributions of the artists with whom he collaborated. "Heading the list of such artists who have helped create what has come to be known as the Marvel Age of Comics is Jolly Jack Kirby" (Lee 1976, 12). Yet, it was Lee's name on the cover, and it was Lee who became the first true celebrity to emerge from the comic book industry.

Lee has also had a growing presence in other media. In 1982 he began narrating the animated series *The Incredible Hulk* and *Spider-Man and His Amazing Friends*. He began his onscreen cameo appearances as a jury foreman in the 1989 made-for-television movie *The Trial of the Incredible Hulk*, and has appeared in virtually every Marvel-based movie since then, well over a dozen, and more every summer. When Lee appeared as himself in the movie *Mallrats* (1995) perhaps only comic book **fanboys** knew who he was, but with continued appearances as himself in popular shows such as *Entourage* (2010), *The Big Bang Theory* (2010), and *Chuck* (2011), he bolsters his status as America's best-known comic book creator. His hosting the reality shows *Who Wants to Be a Superhero?* and *Stan Lee's Superhumans* has further cemented the association of Stan Lee with superheroes.

In 2008, Stan Lee became the only comic book creator to ever be awarded a National Medal of the Arts by the president of the United States in recognition of his contributions to American culture.

SUMMARY

Stan Lee is not a tortured genius (see **Chris Ware**). He is not an eccentric genius (see **Alan Moore**). In fact, he is probably not a genius; just a smart guy with a talent for using language and a knack for self-promotion. As the front man for Marvel Comics, Lee extrapolated his natural characteristics into a persona with a recognizable look (mustache, gray at the temples, tinted glasses, and an upbeat smile) and more than one catch phrase (e.g., "Excelsior!", "Face front, True Believers!"). He became the comic book industry's only true celebrity and the creator most associated with the superhero concept. Lee is very aware that he has become the face of the American comic book industry, and more than that, a featured "character" in the story of the industry that is being created by fans and scholars. As he told one interviewer in 2005, "I have to act 'iconish' all the time, so that the public isn't disappointed." But in typical Stan Lee fashion he quickly chuckled and undercut his serious observation with, "That's why every minute of the day I have to be totally magnificent" (Lee in McLaughlin 2007, 212).

See also Ditko, Steve; Doctor Doom; Fantastic Four; Hulk; Iron Man; Kirby, Jack; Marvel Comics; Spider-Man; Thing, The; X-Men

ESSENTIAL WORKS

Lee, Stan (w), and Jack Kirby (a). *Fantastic Four* #41–#50 (1965–1966) and *Fantastic Four Annual* #3 (1965) reprinted in *Fantastic Four Vol. 5 (Marvel Masterworks)*. New York: Marvel Comics, 2011.

Lee, Stan (w), and John Romita (a). *Amazing Spider-Man* #41–#50 (1966–1967) and *Amazing Spider-Man Annual* #3 (1966) reprinted in *Amazing Spider-Man Vol. 5 (Marvel Masterworks)*. New York: Marvel Comics, 2010.

FURTHER READING

Fingeroth, Danny, and Roy Thomas, eds. *The Stan Lee Universe*. Raleigh, NC: Two-Morrows Publishing, 2011.

Raphael, Jordan, and Tom Spurgeon. *Stan Lee and the Rise and Fall of the American Comic Book*. Chicago: Chicago Review Press, 2003.

Randy Duncan

Lex Luthor

Of all the villains **Superman** has fought, Lex Luthor is his most implacable and, despite Luthor's lack of superpowers, most dangerous foe. For nearly 75 years Luthor has attempted to humiliate and kill Superman. Lex Luthor is Superman's archnemesis. Due to his multiple appearances in movies and animated series and his central role in the *Smallville* television series, Luthor is one of the best-known villains in all of popular culture.

HISTORY

In *Action Comics* #23 (1940), his first appearance, Lex Luthor is a mad genius intent on using his "scientific miracles" to make himself the "supreme master of the world" by manipulating nations into war and making his grab for power once they are weakened. With his secret lair in a colossal dirigible, Luthor is a combination of Jules Verne's *Robur the Conqueror* (1886), an inventor who attempts to use his airship to become master of the world, and Adolf Hitler, who was beginning his conquest of Europe as **Jerry Siegel and Joe Shuster** were creating the first Luthor story. Superman thwarts the villain's plans, and when the great dirigible crashes to the ground in flames, that seems to be the end of Lex Luthor. However, Luthor returns and gradually morphs from a would-be world conqueror into more of a mob boss seeking money. Luthor and Superman clashed so many times that Luthor began to be identified as an archnemesis and the relationship became competitive, but it was not yet personal. At first, his attempts to kill Superman were not motivated by envy or hate; it was simply that Superman was an obstacle to his goals.

This Golden Age version of Luthor was not destined to be *the* Lex Luthor. Decades later, when comic book writers and editors put more emphasis on maintaining a consistent character history, the early Superman adventures were explained away as the exploits of the Superman of Earth-Two, and his archenemy Lex Luthor was retroactively changed to Alexei Luthor of Earth-Two. Alexei Luthor was killed by another Superman villain, Brainiac, in *Crisis on Infinite Earths* #9 (1985).

Luthor first had red hair, and then gray hair until he was mistakenly drawn as bald in the Superman newspaper strip, and that look was carried over into his next comic book appearance, *Superman* #10 (1941). His baldness became a key plot point in a Silver Age revamping of his origin. *Adventure Comics* #271 (1960) provides a back story for Luthor. He is a brilliant young scientist living in Smallville, Superboy's hometown. Lex is a great admirer of Superboy, and the two become friends. However in using his superbreath to blow out a fire in Lex's lab, Superboy inadvertently destroys a groundbreaking, irreproducible scientific breakthrough and drenches Lex with chemicals that make him permanently bald. Lex is convinced Superboy deliberately destroyed his work because he was afraid Lex's genius might eclipse his own fame. Lex vows, "Superboy will regret the day he decided to steal the glory of Luthor!"

In his quest to have his genius recognized and exact revenge on Superman, Luthor becomes "the foremost comic book mad-scientist supervillain" (Coogan 2006, 67). He invents not only exotic weapons, often powered by kryptonite, but a teleportation machine, a time machine, and a superstrong metal he calls Luthorite. He operates from elaborate secret lairs on mountain tops or under the sea, and no matter how many of these secret hideouts Superman destroys, Luthor always has more in reserve that he can go to when he inevitably escapes from prison.

Mad scientist Luthor began to change into more of a conventional supervillain. In the *Super Friends* cartoon of the late 1970s he wore a costume—a high-collared purple spandex bodysuit with crisscrossed green bandoliers (the leggings would later be green). The costume was then used in the comic books for a few years. The cover of *Action Comics* #544 (1983), the 45th anniversary of the title, proclaimed the introduction of the new Luthor. He appeared in a purple and green high-tech battle suit that allowed him to mimic many of Superman's powers and shoot various forms of kryptonite energy blasts. Luthor no longer had to fight Superman through his machines, minions, and machinations; they could now go toe to toe.

In *The Man of Steel* (1986), the limited series that totally rebooted Superman's continuity, the mad scientist with a personal grudge version of Luthor was replaced by a radically different villain—a ruthless tycoon. In the issue in which he is introduced, Luthor lets a terrorist threaten the guests on his yacht so that he can see Superman, who recently arrived in Metropolis, in action. One of those guests, the mayor, deputizes Superman to arrest Luthor for reckless endangerment. Luthor is indignant: "You can't arrest me. I'm Lex Luthor. I'm the most powerful man in Metropolis!" "No, you're not, Lex" answers the mayor, with Superman standing behind him, "Not anymore." Luthor is soon released from jail, but he has been humiliated and upstaged by Superman. The admiration the people of Metropolis once had for him now seems to be focused on Superman. Luthor vows to commit his considerable resources to killing Superman.

AN EVIL FOR ALL SEASONS

In his first appearance, soon after Hitler had begun his conquest of Europe, Lex Luthor was a tyrant whose quest for more power threatened to plunge all of Europe into war. After World War II when people lived in fear of a nuclear holocaust, Luthor was an inventor of superweapons. Just a few years before the movie *Wall Street* (1987) expressed the love-hate relationship America had developed with corporate greed, Luthor was reinvented as an unscrupulous businessman. At the dawn of a new century, as ideological polarization and cynicism about the political system were reaching a crescendo, Luthor became a conniving politician. A decade into the 21st century, as intellectuals advocated a postmodern perspective distrustful of clear-cut distinctions between good and evil, Luther became a roguish Übermensch using his will power (and a power ring) to create the reality he desired. It seems that Lex Luthor is a malleable villain, responsive to the zeitgeist, who becomes what we fear.

In the new continuity Superman had never been Superboy and Lex Luthor had never lived in Smallville. A new backstory for Luthor was fleshed out over time. He was raised by an alcoholic, abusive father in Suicide Slum, the poorest section of Metropolis. His parents' death in a car accident, which he arranged, left him as the beneficiary of a life insurance policy he had secretly taken out on them. He used that money and his intelligence to climb out of poverty and build what eventually became Lexcorp, a huge aerospace company with lucrative defense contracts. At first this tycoon Luthor simply hired scientists to create his anti-Superman weapons, but gradually he took a more active role in the lab, and elements of the pre-reboot brilliant mad scientist reappeared. It was not long before Luthor donned an updated version of his battle suit in order to take the fight to Superman in person.

The tycoon version of Luthor was overweight and balding when he was first introduced. However, Luthor upgrades himself by transferring his mind to a cloned body in which he pretends to be his own son. When his cloned body rapidly degenerates, leaving him helpless, Luthor sells his soul to a devil in return for a young, vigorous body. The deal has the added benefit that Luthor is able to blame all his past crimes on the clone that he claims had taken his place.

The best-known versions of Lex Luthor are those presented in the various Superman movies and the *Smallville* (2001–2011) television series. Luthor was played by Gene Hackman in three feature films, starting with *Superman* (1978). This Luthor has no personal history with Superman. He claims to be a criminal mastermind, but he comes off as little more than an egomaniac surrounded by buffoonish henchmen. In *Superman Returns* (2006) Kevin Spacey's Luthor seems a bit more intelligent, but for the most part he mimics Hackman's broad, hammy performance. In *Smallville*, Luthor has a friendship with Clark Kent (who will eventually become Superman) that gradually turns to enmity. Much of young Luthor's villainy seems to stem from simultaneously competing with and vying for the love of his ruthless and manipulative billionaire father.

Lex Luthor's history has fluctuated—alternating back and forth between growing up in Smallville and growing up in Metropolis, with stories combining elements of both backgrounds. Different versions of Luthor have appeared simultaneously in different media. One constant, although the motivations might vary, is that Luthor hates Superman.

In some versions Luthor seems to be xenophobic, hating Superman for being an alien. More often he hates what this outsider has done to humanity—making them feel inferior, but also making them dependent on him so that they will never reach their full potential. Luthor truly considers Superman to be a threat and he sees himself as a hero trying to remove Superman for the good of humanity.

After Luthor became a more fully developed character, there has always been an element of personal jealousy and envy. Luthor, who is increasingly portrayed as the most intelligent human in the DC Universe, is convinced he would have been the most remarkable man in Metropolis, probably the entire planet, if Superman had not come to Earth. In fact, he is convinced he is Superman's superior, but the ignorant masses cannot see that because they are awed by Superman's flashy costume and powers. That is why simply killing Superman is not enough to appease Luthor; he wants to humiliate him first. He wants Superman to acknowledge his superiority.

IMPACT ON COMICS

Luthor appeared on the scene during the primitive stage of the superhero genre when the conventions were still being formulated. His repeated appearances in *Action Comics* and *Superman* helped establish the supervillain, and particularly the archenemy character type.

Lex Luthor has always helped sell comic books. Whenever he appeared to match wits with Superman, it was an event. While in some contexts Luthor remains the villain readers loved to hate, in other contexts he can be the sort of antihero protagonist readers can root for against more vile villains. In some of his more recent depictions he is even a character they can admire for his ingenuity, determination, and self-confidence. In 2010–2011 Luthor became the protagonist in *Action Comics*, which usually features Superman, and he had a popular year-long run outwitting a number of his fellow supervillains, conning the powerful evil god Darkseid, and even facing down Death when she comes to claim him after a seemingly fatal fall.

IMPACT ON AMERICAN CULTURE

Luthor has had a cultural presence far beyond his comic book appearances. In the Columbia serial *Atom Man vs. Superman* (1950) Luthor, in the guise of the Atom Man, threatens Metropolis with a device that can disassemble and reassemble a person's atoms. It is vintage mad scientist Luthor. This was his first appearance on the big screen. From 1978 to 2006 Luthor was the villain in four Superman feature films. Luthor first appeared in animation in *The New Adventures of Superman* (1966) and has been in more than a dozen animated series since then. He is a character in half a dozen video games. There are action figures of Luthor in his Super Friends costume, his battle suit, and even his prison grays.

Lex Luthor is the American dream gone bad. On the one hand, he is a self-made man. The Suicide Slum version of his origin is a classic Horatio Alger story in which he rises out of poverty to the pinnacle of success through determination, intelligence, and hard work. Yet, Luthor also tips the scales in his favor through murder, deceit, and a ruthless disregard for anyone who stands in his way. And once he is a success, as a businessman who puts profit above people, Luthor is "the neurotic extreme of capitalism" (Peeples 2005, 85).

SUMMARY

In the first season of *Smallville* Lex tells Clark (who will one day become Superman), "Our friendship is going to be the stuff of legend" ("Hug" 2002). While their relationship did not remain friendly, it certainly became the stuff of legend. Lex Luthor has become an indispensable part of the Superman mythos. Superman stands as a beacon that calls us to be the best that we can be, while Luthor serves as a warning about the hazards of giving in to our baser instincts.

See also Siegel, Jerry and Joe Shuster; Superman

ESSENTIAL WORKS

Cornell, Paul (w), Gail Simone (w), Pete Woods (a) et al. (a). *Superman: The Black Ring, Volumes 1 & 2*. New York: DC Comics, 2011.
Superman vs. Lex Luthor. New York: DC Comics, 2006.

FURTHER READING

Batchelor, Bob. "Brains versus Brawn." In *The Man from Krypton*, ed. Glenn Yeffeth. Dallas: BenBella Books, 2005.

Coogan, Peter. *Superhero: The Secret Origin of a Genre*. Austin, TX: MonkeyBrain Books, 2006.

Gersh, Lois H., and Robert E. Weinberg. *The Science of Supervillains*. Hoboken, NJ: John Wiley & Sons, 2005.

"Hug." *Smallville*, season 1, episode 11. February 5, 2002.

Peeples, Gustav. "God, Communism, and the WB." In *The Man from Krypton*, ed. Glenn Yeffeth. Dallas: BenBella Books, 2005.

Randy Duncan

Little Lulu

Little Lulu is a young girl with corkscrew curls, always attired in a little red dress with a white collar and with a little red beret on her head. She originally appeared in captionless single-panel cartoons in the *Saturday Evening Post*, but soon spread to advertisements, various forms of children's toys, an iconic electric billboard on Manhattan's Times Square, animated films, and finally to her own comic books.

HISTORY

Little Lulu made her debut in the *Saturday Evening Post* on February 23, 1935, with a wordless single-panel cartoon depicting the little curly-haired girl strewing banana peels instead of flower petals at a wedding. Created by Marge Henderson Buell (1904–1993), who signed her work "Marge," Lulu replaced the magazine's previous regular cartoon panel, *Henry*, a wordless panel about a little boy. Since the magazine wanted something similar from Buell, she gave them a girl instead, later explaining to a reporter, "I wanted a girl because a girl could get away with more fresh stunts that in a boy would seem boorish" (Jacob 2006).

It is also possible, however, that Buell created a girl character instead of a boy because, as a female cartoonist, she related more to girls. By 1929 she had already produced two ongoing syndicated strips, *The Boy Friend* and *Dashing Dot*, both, as their names suggest, starring women. A brief survey of female cartoonists will show that most of them have produced comics and cartoons that star female figures.

Buell's panel ran in the *Post* until December 30, 1944, at which time Lulu became a spokesperson for Kleenex tissues, and also finally graduated from single panels to comic strip form. Despite her early fame and popularity, Little Lulu is perhaps best known from her comic books, which ran from 1948 until 1984. *Marge's Little Lulu* was published in *Dell Four Color Comics*, Dell's one-shot try-out line, for 10 issues before getting her own monthly title at Dell and later Gold Key Comics. Aside from her credit on the covers, Buell also approved the rough drafts of the strips that Dell regularly sent to her. Most of the comic books were scripted by John Stanley, who also provided layouts. Stanley's layouts were penciled and inked by Irving Tripp and various other artists. Although Buell stopped drawing Lulu in 1947, she retained control over her curly-haired character. In 1950, Little Lulu debuted as a daily strip in the *Chicago Tribune*, and was syndicated by the Chicago Tribune–N.Y. News Syndicate until 1969. Buell retired in 1972, and her name was removed from the title of the comic books, which became simply *Little Lulu.*

John Stanley, a brilliant writer and artist who also created his own characters for comic books like *Thirteen Going on Eighteen* and *Melvin the Monster*, fleshed out the Little Lulu universe, or "Luluverse." Buell had already given Lulu her pudgy friend, Tubby, originally named "Joe," but Stanley added an entire cast of characters: Lulu's teacher, Mrs. Feeney, and the truant officer, Mr. McNabbem, as well as her parents, Mr. and Mrs. Moppet (Yes, Lulu's last name described the character), Lulu's best friend, Annie, and Alvin, the even littler boy whom Lulu babysits and to whom she tells stories about Witch Hazel and the poor little girl who gets lost in the forest while picking beebleberries. Tubby got his own comic book, *Marge's Tubby*, from 1952 to 1961, and acquired a little cousin, Chubby, who looked like a miniature version of himself.

The comics featured recurring themes: One prefeminist recurring theme was the Boys' Club. Tubby and the neighborhood boys used an upended wooden crate as a clubhouse, upon which they hung a sign that read, "No Girls Allowed." In issue after issue, spunky Lulu devised plans to break into the clubhouse, only to be kept out by the boys in issue after issue. Actually, Stanley's scripts were often feminist back in the days before anyone had ever heard the term *women's liberation.* In *Four Color* #97 (1946), Tubby enters a contest to build a model airplane. When Lulu offers to help, he snorts, "*Girls* can't make nothing but *fudge*!" Lulu answers, "How about Joan of Arc and Madame Curie?"

Another recurring theme was the "Spider" stories. Tubby, always convinced that Lulu's father was a master criminal, would disguise himself as "The Spider" in order to solve a crime that always turned out to not be a crime at all. These stories always end with Tubby walking away, saying, "The 'Spider' spins again!"

One such five-page story from *Little Lulu* #81 (1955) bore just that title: "The 'Spider' Spins Again." Lulu's father has just shaved off his mustache. He says to his wife, "Makes me look *younger*, don't you think?" But when Tubby walks in with Lulu, he has a different reaction. He says, "Lulu, I hate to tell you this, but I feel it's my duty. . . . your *pop* is *guilty* of something!" He reasons, "He shaved his mustache off 'cause he doesn't want to be *recognized* by the *police*!" Tubby further decides, "He prob'ly walked out of the *bank* he works for with a *lot of money*!" When Lulu counters that her father does not work for a bank, Tubby answers, "He did something *else* then!" and leaves, to come back in disguise with a false mustache, a grass skirt, and a fright wig on his head.

THOSE LITTLE GIRLS IN THEIR RED DRESSES

For some unknown reason, little girls in red dresses with white collars proliferate in the pages of comic books and strips. The trend was probably started in 1924 by Harold Grey's *Little Orphan Annie*, who appeared in American newspapers for 86 years. Answering readers who may have wondered whether Annie owned only one dress, Grey drew one strip in which Annie is doing her laundry, hanging her dresses on the clothesline to dry. Every dress is an identical little red dress with a white collar!

Orphan Annie was followed by *Little Annie Rooney*, another red-clad orphan, in 1927. Ernie Bushmiller's *Nancy* started as a character in her aunt *Fritzi Ritz*'s strip in 1933, but starred in her own title by 1938, wearing a red dress and white collar. Lulu was a relative latecomer to the red dress club in 1935, and people occasionally confuse her with Nancy, although one has but to read the strips to see how much they differ. Harvey's Little Audrey and Little Dot both wear red dresses, although Little Dot's dress is covered with black polka dots. Only Little Lotta has no red dress, perhaps because none could be found in her size.

In an effort to get Mr. Moppet out of the house, so he can look for the stolen money he is convinced is hidden there, Tubby decides, "*Old* people are like *cats*, Lulu—they can climb *up* trees pretty good, but they can't climb *down* again so good!" So he climbs to the top of a tree in Lulu's back yard and hollers, "*Help! Help! I can't get down! Help!*" Lulu's father comes running to the rescue, climbs the tree, and his foot gets stuck on a branch. So there he is, dangling by one foot from the tree, yelling "*Help!*" while Tubby runs back into the house: "*Now* I have *plenty* of time to search the house for that *money!*" and Lulu runs to a cop for help. Tubby looks out a window and sees the police emergency van approaching the house, sirens screaming, and thinks they've come to arrest Mr. Moppet. "Gosh! The *police*! They've got some *nerve*! This is *my* case! I'll work *fast* and maybe I can find the money before *they* do!"

The police have stuck a ladder up the tree and gotten Mr. Moppet down, and while they hold him, Tubby comes running out of the house: "*Stop! Stop! Let him go! He's innocent! I searched the house from top to bottom and didn't find a thing!*" Naturally the police—and Mr. Moppet—stare uncomprehendingly at Tubby in his strange disguise. What is this weird kid talking about? The cops walk away carrying their ladder, and Tubby tells Lulu, "See that, Lulu? One word from *me* and they *let him go!*" In the next-to last panel, Mr. Moppet returns to his bedroom to find it has been ransacked, and in the last panel Tubby walks down the street proudly saying, "The 'Spider' spins again!" while a dog, frightened by his getup, runs away from him.

IMPACT ON COMICS

Little Lulu comic books were published all over the world, and translated into such languages as French, Greek, Spanish, Norwegian, Finnish, Swedish, Dutch, Japanese, Arabic, and Portuguese. In Brazil, the comic book was called "Luluzinha" and in Holland she was "Lieve Lulu." From 1944 to the present, there have been well over 100 Little Lulu items manufactured. She has been turned into dolls, bobbleheads, and paper dolls; she has appeared in Little Golden Books and on greeting cards, candy, handbags and backpacks, scarves, towels, glass tumblers, wrapping paper, banks, and children's soaps and shampoo.

By the 1940s, Little Lulu's popularity had inspired other comic book publishers to come up with their own plucky little girl characters, always with the prefix "Little" in front of their names. Little Iodine, by Jimmy Hatlo, ran in American newspapers from 1943 to 1985, and was published in comic book form by Dell from 1949 to 1962. In the 1950s, Archie Comics published Lil' Jinx from 1954 well into the 1970s, and Harvey Comics produced three little girl characters, each of whom had her own comic book: Little Audrey (1952), Little Dot (1953), and Little Lotta (1955). Although the little girl characters were all cute and sassy, they never inspired Lulu's enthusiastic fan following or multiple product spin-offs.

From 1982 to 1992, Jonathan Merril edited and published a bimonthly fanzine dedicated to Little Lulu comics as scripted by John Stanley, "The Stanley Steamer." In 1992, Ed Buchman started a Little Lulu fanzine called "The HoLLywood Eclectern," and since then fans of the comic book have met every year at San Diego's **Comic Con International**, where they perform plays adapted from vintage Little Lulu comic book stories.

In 1994, Lulu's attempts to crash the boys' club inspired a group of women within the boys' club of the comics industry to form a national nonprofit organization called Friends of Lulu, aimed at encouraging female participation in comics as creators and as readers. Friends of Lulu was open to both men and women. They held Lulucons within various comic conventions, and sponsored awards such as the Lulu of the Year and the Women Cartoonist Hall of Fame. The organization lasted for 17 years, closing in 2011 after losing its nonprofit status.

IMPACT ON AMERICAN CULTURE

As a spokesmodel, the resourceful little girl showed the magazine and newspaper reading public, in comic strip form, how Kleenex tissues could solve all their problems for a period of 16 years. She appeared on buses and subway placards and until 1965, on Times Square in an iconic 35-foot-high billboard, composed of 24,000 flashing neon lights with 10-foot-tall letters. The lights formed pre–digital-age animated cartoon images: Tubby sneezes, Lulu pulls out a Kleenex tissue for him, and Tubby blows his nose.

During World War II Little Lulu became a pinup, painted on the nose cone of American bombers. From 1943 on, she starred in animated cartoons for both film and television. The earliest cartoons were produced from 1943 to 1948 by Fleischer Studios, renamed Famous Studios, for Paramount. All in all, Paramount produced 27 animated Little Lulu cartoons. Lulu's voice was provided by Mae Questel, who had previously been the voice of Betty Boop. In the 1950s, the animated cartoons were syndicated to television, and in the 1980s they were released on home video. In the 1970s, Lulu starred in two half-hour live-action television Saturday morning specials, played by Lauri Hendler, and from 1995 to 1999, she appeared on HBO in the *Little Lulu Show*, with Tracy Ullman providing her voice.

Lulu, Tubby, and all their friends live in single-dwelling houses, in stereotypical middle-American two-parent households, in which the father goes out to work and the mother stays at home. Lulu and her friend Annie play with dolls, as is expected of good little middle-American girls, but this does not prevent Lulu from fighting for equality with the boys. Thus, although the sign on the boys' clubhouse reads "No Girls Allowed," she never takes "No" for an answer. When Tubby tells her he wants to be both a fireman and president of the United States, she says, "I think maybe *I'll* be President of the United States!" Tubby shouts, "*You?*" and Lulu answers, "Why not? Why *shouldn't* a *girl* be President?" Tubby offers, "Tell you what—maybe I'll let *you* be th' *First Lady*!" and Lulu counters, "*Nothing doing! I'll* be the President! *You* c'n be the *First Lady*!"

SUMMARY

Little Lulu is ever the optimist, believing that if she works hard enough for something, she will gain it—and she does, whether it is quarters earned by supplying umbrellas to grown-ups in the rain, or getting back her doll carriage wheels *and* the silver loving cup prize after Tubby and the boys have put the wheels on their wagon for the soap box race. She takes seriously the American belief that in this country all people are equal, and anyone can grow up to be president. If any of the kids in the Little Lulu comics do ever grow up to be president, I would put my money on Little Lulu, who epitomizes the traditional "can-do" American attitude.

See also Dell Comics

ESSENTIAL WORKS

Marge. *The Little Lulu Library*. Scottsdale, AZ: Another Rainbow Publishing, 1985.

FURTHER READING

Cabarga, Leslie, ed. *The Harvey Girls*. Milwaukie, OR: Dark Horse Books, 2009.
Robbins, Trina. *From Girls to Grrrlz*. San Francisco: Chronicle Books, 1999.
Robbins, Trina. *The Great Women Cartoonists*. New York: Watson Guptill Publications, 2001.

Trina Robbins

Lois Lane

Since her debut alongside **Superman**, Lois Lane has been alternately positioned as a girlfriend and a professional nemesis. But more than this, she is a character that has displayed tenacity and talent, and has risen above the sexist whims of editors both actual and fictional to become an award-winning journalist who is fiercely respected within the DC Universe, and an influential icon in the real world.

J. P. Williams notes that "analysis of the significance of popular culture in contemporary society requires an understanding of the importance of fictional characters as embodiments of cultural values and concerns" (Williams 1990, 103). Therefore, Lois Lane is culturally relevant; as a character that has been a staple of the *Superman* mythos since 1938, she has reflected, and potentially influenced, societal attitudes towards women—particularly unmarried career women—for over 70 years. This makes her a unique marker of changing American ideas about gender, perhaps even more so than her contemporary, the larger-than-life, Amazonian superhero **Wonder Woman**.

HISTORY

Like Superman and his alter ego, Clark Kent, Lois Lane has been around since the inaugural issue of *Action Comics* in 1938. Though she may lack a trademark costume, her perpetual moxie, as well as staying power and ability to evolve era to era, makes her, as much as any superhero, a recognizable icon in her own right. Like other female reporters embedded in the American cultural consciousness—from Rosalind Russell's Hildy Johnson in the film *His Girl Friday* (1940) to Dale Messick's comic strip heroine Brenda Starr, to television's Murphy Brown (1988–1998)—she is a fictional character that has inspired real-world women toward professions in journalism.

Lois was co-created by writer **Jerry Siegel** and illustrator **Joe Shuster**, and modeled on the feisty film character Torchy Blane who featured in a number of eponymous films during the 1930s. The image of the female reporter in the 1930s and 1940s was inspirational and exciting—and provided meaty roles for actresses, who enjoyed the opportunity to play aggressive, independent, and ambitious professionals rather than simply love interests or femmes fatales.

Like many real-life female reporters of her day, Lois Lane's career started as a "sob sister" writing for the lovelorn column. Anxious to tackle more challenging material, she tried to scoop the hard-hitting stories assigned to her journalistic rival, Clark Kent. Though her editor continued to insist that such work was too important for "a girl," Lois made continued efforts to prove her worth as a newspaperwoman. Considering Clark's secret identity as Superman allowed him to both secure and write a story before Lois's article could ever see print, in the early days of the comic she worked much harder than him for much less recognition.

Lois, created to be both love interest and foil to the hero, is often in need of rescuing due to her reckless attempts to report a story. But she's no damsel in distress. Rather, her attempts at proving herself to her sexist male co-workers lead her to the trouble she is so famous for getting into. She fearlessly goes the extra mile, even at danger to herself, and she does it without superpowers.

While brave, saucy, assertive, driven, passionate, and tenacious, Lois is also known to be temperamental, competitive, reckless, cynical, irritating, and impulsive. She's quick to throw a verbal insult or a physical punch—and in later comics her back story was modified so that she no longer was the daughter of parents who owned and maintained a farm, but an army brat trained in combat technique by her general father.

Lois Lane received her own comic book title in 1958 that ran for over 137 issues before ending in 1974. Though this was seemingly a step towards establishing her identity as independent from Superman, the title reinforced her "true" position in his story. Rather than being *Lois Lane, Reporter* (reporter being a title afforded Lois's pop culture contemporary, Brenda Starr) she was *Superman's Girl Friend, Lois Lane*. The series was a combination of adventure and romance, and generally detailed Lois's schemes to convince or trick Superman into marrying her and/or revealing his secret identity. Amidst fantastic transformations, Lucille Ball-esque escapades, superpowers, catfights, and "imaginary" tales, "*Superman's Girl Friend Lois Lane* was a wildly entertaining, cleverly written, and beautifully illustrated comic, and its heroine, while often portrayed as irritating, had a genuinely endearing quality" (Madrid 2009, 68).

As pop culture must reflect the changing social landscape in order to remain relevant, by the late 1960s and early 1970s the concerns of the women's movement could not help but find their way into Lois Lane's comic, and in 1972, Lois Lane embraced the cultural moment by quitting her job at the *Daily Planet* in favor of a more autonomous freelance career. While much of the dialogue was contrived and stereotyped, with talk about "woman power" and "chicks sticking together," it was the most independent Lois had been in years—and certainly as good as the representation of feminist politics in comics of the era would get. In fact, Lois had gone from being denied a story in the

1940s because her editor suggested it was "too important for a girl" to being in a position to choose her stories (and get paid for it).

Lois would continue to evolve in both the comics as well as live-action and animated media (see below). In the 1980s, the Superman mythos was revamped after the seminal *Crisis on Infinite Earths* series, most notably through John Byrne's acclaimed miniseries *The Man of Steel*. The iconic "love triangle for two" was changed as well, and Lois and Clark became friends, then lovers, rather than Lois and Superman. Her career was always front and center, and as she respected his superhero duties, he respected her work. The rivalries of the past became genuine affection, leading Lois and Clark to begin dating in earnest and eventually become engaged. Of course, their relationship could not proceed without requisite melodramatic bumps in the road including the death and return of Superman, and the reemergence of an aggressive old flame.

In the 1990s, the seminal *Superman: The Wedding Album* issue allied with the television series *Lois & Clark: The New Adventures of Superman* to finally have the long-sparring, long-loving Clark Kent and Lois Lane tie the knot. Though television and comics each had their own take on the courtship, engagement, and ultimately, ceremony, the pair were finally wed nearly 60 years after they had first met, and with Lois now sharing Clark's secret. Each character has evolved to be worthy of the affection of the other, and they have become one of the most recognized and loving couples in both comics and popular culture at large.

By the 2010s, Lois has become what DC comic book writer Gail Simone calls "the best, most dogged, most determined and fearless reporter in the DCU" (Brady, 2007). Even though she and Clark are no longer wed in the revamped continuity of the "New 52," her status as executive producer of the Planet Global Network underscores her iconic status as an independent career woman.

IMPACT ON AMERICAN CULTURE

Lois Lane has appeared as a character in film and radio serials, television series, and movies and has been referenced in popular culture from the 1979 hip hop single, "Rapper's Delight," by the Sugarhill Gang to 1990s *Seinfeld* episodes.

She was in a series of animated cartoons in the early 1940s produced by Max Fleischer Studios. Lois was voiced by Joan Alexander—who had also voiced the character on the *Superman* radio show. The radio series ran from 1940 to 1951.

Noel Neill was the first woman to play Lois Lane on screen, and starred opposite Kirk Alyn's Superman in the movie serials. In the first season of the

"I AM CURIOUS (BLACK)!"

Civil rights was addressed in *Superman's Girl Friend Lois Lane* #106 (1970) titled "I Am Curious (Black)!" Written by Robert Kanigher, the story involves Lois's attempts to report on the "nitty-gritty" of Metropolis's predominately black neighborhood "Little Africa." No one will speak to her, as they are mistrustful of "Whitey"—as she is referred to by an activist. At her behest, Superman uses his Plastimold machine to transform her into a black woman for 24 hours so that she can complete her investigation and story (which Lois is sure will win her a Pulitzer Prize). Lois learns many, many "lessons" about racial prejudice and ends up befriending the very activist who misjudged her for *her* color. When he is wounded protecting her, Lois discovers they are the same blood type and saves his life by donating her blood. When he discovers Lois is actually white, they seal their friendship with a handshake, and the issue ends with a panel depicting a well-intentioned, yet very contrived, white hand shaking a black hand. There is also a scene in which Lois asks Superman if he would marry her if she were black. He does not answer.

television series *Adventures of Superman* (1952–1958), as well as the movie *Superman and the Mole Men* (1951), she was played by Phyllis Coates. During an extended break in shooting, Coates was offered another job, and when the television series returned Noel Neill was asked to reprise the role. She starred as Lois until the series' cancellation in 1958.

Again, though Lois of the comics has always been a professional, she has been less recognized as an emblem of feminist ideas than Wonder Woman. Perhaps this is because they were created with different intentions, although their fates have often paralleled each other with each era's incarnations. For example, both Lois and Wonder Woman underwent radical transformations in terms of their fashion style and career during the second wave of feminism—even as their feminist politics themselves were both stereotyped and compromised.

Margot Kidder's embodiment of Lois in 1978's *Superman: The Movie* allowed audiences to see a more nuanced, liberated, and indeed, feminist vision of the character. It was a generosity afforded by era, writing, medium, and Kidder's innate fire. She has said the women's movement informed her characterization of Lois, and that because of the relative paucity of female reporters at that time, "You could not NOT portray [Lois] as a feisty, independent woman." By portraying Lois as the feminist she can be—hardworking, talented, and dynamic—Kidder became THE quintessential face of the character, just as Lynda Carter had done for Wonder Woman (Stuller 2010, 141).

Lois Lane would later be played by Teri Hatcher in the *Moonlighting*-esque television series *Lois & Clark: The New Adventures of Superman* (1993–1997). In fact, that series was originally meant to be called *Lois Lane's Daily Planet* (Rossen 2008, 192). The character was voiced by Dana Delany in *Superman: The Animated Series* (1996–2000), in which Lois first used "Smallville" as a nickname for Clark Kent. The moniker was subsequently used in comics, and evolved into a term of affection in both comics and on the series *Smallville*. Other animated versions have been voiced by actresses Anne Heche, Kyra Sedgwick, and Christina Hendricks.

Lois Lane was played by Erica Durance on the long-running television series *Smallville* (2001–2011). (And on an intriguing side note, the makers of *Smallville* had allegedly once pitched a series on Lois Lane that completely ignored Clark Kent.) She first appeared in the season four premiere, "Crusade," when she came to Smallville to investigate the disappearance of her cousin, Chloe Sullivan (Allison Mack). Prior to Lois's debut, Chloe had served as a proto–Lois Lane—she was both editor and reporter of her high school newspaper, studied journalism at Metropolis U, worked at the *Daily Planet* newspaper. On *Smallville*, Lois and Clark further reflected changing gender roles in American culture. Their depiction of the iconic relationship is the most equal partnership to date—and one that is based on love, friendship, practical and emotional support, and mutual respect.

Kate Bosworth portrayed a rather dour version of the reporter in the 2006 film *Superman Returns*. As a single mother and Pulitzer Prize winner, hers was an interesting take on the character. But ultimately, it lacked the fire of other interpretations. Oscar-nominated actress Amy Adams appears as Lois Lane in Zack Snyder's *Man of Steel* (2013).

Many of the actresses that have portrayed Lois have appeared in cameo roles in later Superman properties. Phyllis Coates played mother to Teri Hatcher's Lane on *Lois & Clark,* and Hatcher in turn played mother to Erica Durance's incarnation of the character on *Smallville*. Noel Neill had cameos as Lois Lane's mother in *Superman: The Movie* and Lex Luthor's dying lover and benefactor in *Superman Returns*.

SUMMARY

Over the years Lois Lane has reflected conflicting cultural concerns regarding women and sex and gender roles. She evolved from a trouble-making career girl who mocked Clark Kent and tried to steal his assignments (though she had good reason for both), to a woman obsessed with marrying Superman, to an independent, well-respected journalist and the equal partner of Clark Kent, both personally and professionally. And while she may be the most important character in Superman's mythos other than himself, she is more than the longest surviving significant other in comics and popular culture. Lois Lane's name has become synonymous with investigative journalism, making her an influential icon in her own right.

See also Siegel, Jerry and Joe Shuster; Superman; Wonder Woman

ESSENTIAL WORKS

The Adventures of Superman. Producer Whitney Ellsworth. Starring George Reeves, Phyllis Coates, Noel Neill, and Jack Larsen. 1952–1958. Burbank, CA: Warner Home Video, 2005–2006. Film.

Hamilton, Edmond, et al. *Superman: Daily Planet*. New York: DC Comics, 2006.

Siegel, Jerry (w), and Joe Shuster (a). "Superman." *Action Comics* #1 (June 1938). National Allied Publications. Reprinted in *Superman: The Action Comics Archives Volume 1*. New York: DC Comics, 1998.

Superman: The Movie. Director Richard Donner. Starring Margot Kidder and Christopher Reeve. 1978. Film.

FURTHER READING

Jones, Gerard. *Men of Tomorrow: Geeks, Gangsters and the Birth of the Comic Book*. Cambridge, MA: Basic Books, 2004.

Stuller, Jennifer K. "Feminist Analysis: Second Wave Feminism in the Pages of Lois Lane." In *Critical Approaches to Comics: Theories and Method*, edited by Matthew J. Smith and Randy Duncan, 235–51. New York: Routledge, 2011.

Stuller, Jennifer K. *Ink-Stained Amazons and Cinematic Warriors: Superwomen in Modern Mythology*. New York: I. B. Tauris, 2010.

Williams, J. P. "All's Fair in Love and Journalism: Female Rivalry in *Superman*." *Journal of Popular Culture* 24 (1990): 103–12.

Jennifer K. Stuller

Mad

A comic book that became a magazine, *Mad* was the brainchild of **Harvey Kurtzman**, an editor who worked for **EC Comics**. It began publication in 1952 and has been published continuously since. *Mad* became a cultural institution, with its basic message that "The media is lying to you, and we are part of the media" (National Public Radio 2004). This message transformed U.S. culture, influencing artists and performers and also inspiring regular folk to social action.

HISTORY

According to Harvey Kurtzman, he created *Mad* "out of desperation" (Kurtzman 1991, 41). Needing to make more money and work faster, he turned to what he knew: humor and parody. Inspired by college humor magazines, he began writing and drawing stories that lampooned comic books, classic tales, and the common media of the day. He made fun of superheroes, cowboys, and other stereotypes, and in the process he ended up creating a cultural institution that transcended comics and made a huge impact on U.S. society.

The Early Days of *Mad*

Mad was one of the later publications to come from EC Comics, a publishing company more known for gruesome horror, shocking science fiction, and harrowing war comics. Harvey Kurtzman was one of EC's editors, and he was in charge of the war comics. He spent long hours researching in order to create realistic tales, leaving him exhausted and also limiting the amount of comics he could create. Because the only way he could make more money to take care of his family and pay his mortgage was to produce more comic books, Kurtzman pitched new ideas to publisher Bill Gaines. Gaines thought that the humor material had the most potential and suggested Kurtzman put together

(Photofest)

a comedy publication. Accounts vary on who came up with the title *Mad*, but it arose from a brainstorming session with Gaines, Kurtzman, and Al Feldstein, the other editor on staff. (Actually, at first the comic book was called *Tales Calculated to Drive You Mad*, but the *Mad* part was most prominent in the title.) At first Gaines felt that the comic book would not be profitable, but he thought it was funny and knew he could use profits from the horror books to keep the enterprise afloat.

Sales from the first issue were poor, but those figures were not known until issue #3 had been published. Starting with issue #4, which featured the superhero parody "Superduperman!" sales picked up and a meteoric rise in popularity occurred. *Mad* became one of the most popular comic books on the racks. By then its comic style had been established, with tons of gags crammed into every page. Stories included numerous foreign words and phrases, particularly Yiddish and Polish terms such as *furshlugginer* and *potrzebie*. Kurtzman wrote every story for the first 23 issues, with art provided by a stable of outstanding artists, including Will Elder, Wally Wood, and Jack Davis, who reveled in opportunities to draw their own gags in every available space.

From Comic Book to Magazine

Comic books were greatly affected by an anticomics movement that linked them to juvenile delinquency and other social ills. **Frederic Wertham**'s popular book *Seduction of the Innocent* added to this furor, and a Senate subcommittee was formed to investigate the comic book industry. The results of these hearings had a profound effect on EC Comics and *Mad*. Every book EC published was subject to a newly made Comics Code Authority, and most of their titles were not publishable under the new guidelines.

In order to avoid having to scrap his entire line of books, and also to appease Kurtzman who had been offered work on a prominent magazine, Gaines decided to turn their most popular remaining title, *Mad*, into a larger-sized, glossy magazine with more pages. Kurtzman had desired this promotion for years. As a magazine, *Mad* would be exempt from the new Code, and Kurtzman would have more leeway in what he could write and draw. *Mad* also added new writers to contribute to the magazine, including television pioneer Ernie Kovacs, funnyman Roger Price, and book editor Bernard Shir-Cliff, all fans of the comic book. The new *Mad Magazine* was a hit, and soon it became the sole EC publication, after lagging sales and many conflicts with the Comics Code Authority had forced Gaines to stop publishing comic books.

Those conflicts were costly in terms of legal fees, and soon Gaines found himself bereft of funds and seeking a new distributor for his magazine. Kurtzman saw this time as an opportunity to get more control of the business and issued an ultimatum to Gaines that he wanted a 51 percent controlling share of *Mad*, or he would walk away from the magazine he created and wrote. Gaines felt he had no choice but to reject that offer and replaced Kurtzman with Al Feldstein. Kurtzman, it turns out, had an offer to create a new humor magazine from a young publisher who was gaining notoriety and success with *Playboy*, Hugh Hefner, and he took some of his *Mad* colleagues with him. Gaines and Kurtzman's relationship was never the same after that rift.

Mad under Feldstein

Under Feldstein's editorship, *Mad* went in a different direction. The magazine became less political; they just made fun of everyone from politicians to hippies to communists. Also, the magazine began to cater to younger readers in particular, and Feldstein tried his best to give them what they wanted and on time. Popular features such as "Spy vs. Spy," "The Lighter Side of . . . ," "Snappy Answers to Stupid Questions," and the "*Mad* Fold In" ran frequently. Fake advertisements, movie and television parodies, and skewed views of everyday life filled the magazine. The advertisements in particular so closely resembled their source material that *Mad* eventually angered some advertisers. The magazine solely depended on its subscription and newsstand sales to fund its production and did without selling ad space within the magazine from 1957 until 2001 (44 years!). This situation was very rare in the publishing world but also not much of a problem because of a large readership. Feldstein's reign as editor was marked by colossal growth: the magazine's audience multiplied eight times at its peak popularity in the 1970s. By the time he retired in 1985, that number had dropped some, but his 29-year tenure could not be called anything but a success.

Feldstein recruited new artists and writers, including Sergio Aragones, Dave Berg, Paul Coker, Nick DeBartolo, Mort Drucker, Duck Ewing, Stan Hart, Al Jaffee, Don Martin, Norman Mingo, Paul Peter Porges, Antonio Prohias, and Angelo Torres. Many of these talented creators were dedicated and contributed to the magazine for decades, becoming known as "The Usual Gang of Idiots." Clearly, *Mad* had a self-deprecating view of itself. Jokes that the magazine was cheap and that it was also constantly overcharging for its poor contents were prevalent. Publisher Bill Gaines was constantly portrayed as a fat, dirty, penny-pinching, lazy dictator. *Mad* insolated itself from criticism by making fun of itself as much as it did celebrities, parents, politicians, ad-men, teachers, and social situations.

Mad after Gaines

Longtime publisher Bill Gaines died in 1992. There was a serious question of whether it would continue without the man who had been a part of producing it from the very beginning. A full-page ad of Alfred E. Neuman shedding a tear ran in the *New York Times*, simultaneously eulogizing Gaines and announcing that the magazine would carry on without him.

Mad came to be more under the governance of Warner Brothers, the company that then owned the magazine, and in particular under **DC Comics**, the logical subsidiary to look after this property. The magazine was "revamped" in 1997 to be edgier and appeal to a more mature, sophisticated audience. A number of the older contributors began to die or retire, so today there is more of a rolling bunch of creators producing the magazine. Editor or co-editor since 1985, John Ficarra has kept *Mad* going, but like most contemporary magazines, it has been losing its readership over the years. However *Mad* has also branched out into other media. It lent its name to the sketch comedy series *MadTV* that ran for 14 seasons on the Fox television network as well as a weekly animated series that began in 2010 on Cartoon Network. A constant

MAD'S MAD MASCOT

When people think of *Mad* magazine they think of the smiling, vacant face of Alfred E. Neuman. He has appeared on almost every cover since 1955 playing a wide range of characters, from Yoda to Voldemort, Justin Bieber to Uncle Sam. He has run for U.S. president every election since 1956 under the slogan, "You could do worse, and always have!" (Reidelbach 1991, 138). However, this character, which is so associated with the magazine, was not created by anyone working for *Mad*. And originally he was not even called Alfred E. Neuman.

The name Alfred E. Neuman appeared in the magazine long before the character did; it referred to a joke swiped from an old radio show. The character first appeared on the cover of *Mad* as part of the artwork on a fake catalog cover on issue #21. When the comic book became a magazine, his face appeared in an emblem emblazoned with his famous motto, "What—me worry?" and it has been there in some shape or form ever since. At first, the *Mad* staff called him Melvin Coznowski, Mel Haney, or the "What—Me Worry Kid." It was not until issue #29 that the name was connected with that famous, freckled face.

The boy's face originally appeared in a series of advertisements for painless dentistry from the 1890s. There were two major legal disputes over who owned the image, but in the end *Mad* prevailed to keep their mascot. He has become so closely associated with the magazine that once a letter from Auckland, New Zealand, bearing nothing but his face somehow made its way through the mail to the *Mad* editorial offices in New York City (Markstein 2001, 2).

presence in young people's lives for almost 60 years, *Mad* continues to make an impact and make people laugh.

IMPACT ON COMICS

Mad's impact on comics is both obvious and subtle. Most obviously, it spawned scores of imitations and has greatly affected the look and feel of satire comics since. Some of the imitators had titles such as "*Whack, Unsane, Bughouse, Crazy, Eh!, and Nuts*" (Reidelbach 1991, 24). EC even got into this racket, producing their own *Mad* imitation, *Panic*, which was edited and written by Feldstein. Even decades after its initial publication, it has spawned imitators, including **Marvel Comics**' *Not Brand Echh* and later *What the-?*, both greatly influenced by the *Mad* style.

Part of the reason for its strong presence in comics is that *Mad* cultivated strong work from its creators, who moved into other venues. Joe Orlando was a longtime EC employee, but eventually he moved into an editorial position at DC Comics where he started a humor comic *Plop!* that owed obvious debts to *Mad*, and not simply because it employed prominent *Mad* artists Basil Wolverton, Wally Wood, and Sergio Aragones. Other magazines also poached *Mad* artists to bolster their content, such as when *Cracked* recruited long-time artists John Severin and Don Martin. Regarding independent comics, the most prominent project to come from a *Mad* alumnus must be *Groo the Wanderer*, a long-running series drawn by Sergio Aragones about a brainless, accident-prone, cheese-dip-loving barbarian.

More subtly, *Mad* had a profound effect on comics creators who in turn have influenced many others. Underground comix legend **Robert Crumb**, renowned for his ground-breaking works, has stated that the cover to *Mad* issue #11 "changed the way I saw the world forever" (Kitchen and Buhle 2009, iv). Pulitzer Prize winner **Art Spiegelman**, who created *Maus*, similarly credits the comic book version of *Mad* as giving him the inspiration to use cartoon animal comics to tell a mature, powerful, and graphic Holocaust history (National Public Radio 2004). Surprisingly, *Mad* has also played a part in one of the most celebrated superhero comics narratives. *Watchmen* creators **Alan Moore** and Dave Gibbons found the magazine a common influence, and in the spirit of the parody "Superduperman!" they turned the idea of super-heroes on its head (Jensen 2005, 2). Only instead of playing this skewed view for laughs, they wove a dramatic tale.

IMPACT ON AMERICAN CULTURE

Just as *Mad* had an impact on comic books, it also had a huge impact on U.S. culture as a whole. According to *Time*'s Richard Corliss, it was groundbreaking—the first publication whose purpose was to parody all other forms of entertainment. Furthermore, he added, "To say that this became an influential manner in American comedy is to understate the case. Almost all American satire today follows a formula that Harvey Kurtzman thought up" (Kitchen & Buhle 2009, vi). This statement seems to be borne out in *The Simpsons* producer Bill Oakley's statement that "basically everyone who was young between 1955 and 1975 read *Mad*, and that's where your sense of humor came from" (Ortved 2009, 273). It would be difficult to imagine satirical programs like *Laugh-In*, *Saturday Night Live*, or *The Daily Show*, all highly influential shows themselves, without the existence of *Mad* and its Usual Gang of Idiots.

The list of *Mad*'s fans includes many cultural icons, from rock star Jimi Hendrix to powerhouse directors George Lucas and Steven Spielberg ("*Mad*

Magazine: A Semi-secret History" 2011), political activist Tom Hayden, and leading art figure Andy Warhol (Moldstad 2011, 5). Almost certainly, however, its greatest influence lay with its effect on common people. *Mad* encouraged people to think for themselves and question authority figures, the media, and rules in general. Valuing individuals' rights and also accepting social diversity were implicit messages within the comics. Many people who read them as children grew up to lead and participate in the political movements of the 1960s and 1970s. Inadvertently, Harvey Kurtzman planted the seeds of social revolutions that would transform America.

SUMMARY

For almost 60 years *Mad* has made its readers laugh and think. By ridiculing television shows, movies, parents, teachers, politicians, and even itself, the magazine has communicated the message that it is best for people to think for themselves, to look beyond the surface of things. It has been a feast for the eyes, featuring artwork by accomplished and highly skilled artists who cram each page full of jokes in the words and pictures.

In a sense, *Mad* is a news magazine for kids. It gives younger readers access to things they could not otherwise see. Popular R-rated movies and other media are parodied and presented in G-rated form, but without dumbing down the content. Children can keep up with various aspects of U.S. culture, including current events, because of *Mad*. Additionally, they are exposed to a humorous voice that allows them to pierce through the pomposity and pretentiousness of everyday life.

When *Mad* first appeared, there was nothing like it, and readers flocked to gaze at the great art and zany stories. It influenced so many people that today there are many things that share its satirical slant, including websites, television programs, and movies. *Mad* is one of those rare works that has not just reflected but also shaped American society. It is not only iconic; it may be the most influential comics publication ever.

See also EC Comics; Kurtzman, Harvey

ESSENTIAL WORKS

Kurtzman, Harvey (w), and Wally Wood (p). "Superduperman!" *Tales Calculated to Drive You Mad* #4 (Apr.–May 1953), E.C. Comics. Reprinted in *Mad About the Fifties*. New York: Little, Brown, 1997.

The Usual Gang of Idiots. *MAD for Decades: 50 Years of Forgettable Humor from MAD Magazine*. New York: Sterling Publishing, 2007.

FURTHER READING

DeBartolo, D. *Good Days and Mad: A Hysterical Tour Behind the Scenes at Mad Magazine*. New York: Thunder's Mouth Press, 1994.
"The Idiotical: The Official Blog of *Mad Magazine*." http://mad.blog.dccomics.com/. Accessed July 25, 2011.

Stergios Botzakis

Maus

Maus in many ways has had more impact on both the history of comics and defining what a comic can be or do than, say, **Superman**. It changed the way the world looked at the art form, and allowed comics to come out from behind the cape and into the mainstream of "serious" literature. This groundbreaking work took 13 years to complete and established comics as an art form comparable to film and literature, with its serious subject, complex shifts in time, and narrative structure. *Maus* won a Special Pulitzer Prize in 1992, the first comic ever to do so, along with a myriad of awards from industry, popular, and scholarly associations.

This nonfiction comic depicts the personal historical tale of **Art Spiegelman**'s Holocaust survivor father, Vladek, as well as the conflicted relationship between father and son. The comic is nearly 300 pages long, comprised of now-iconic animal cartoons and hand-written text. Released as one hardback volume in 1996, this animal fable of the Holocaust begins in mid-1930s Poland and ends in modern-day New York. Vladek's survivor's tale is framed by his current interactions with his son, the author and illustrator of the comic.

HISTORY

The first "Maus" strip was published in 1972 in *Funny Animals*, an underground comix publication by Apex Novelties. Counterculture comics or comix became increasingly popular in the late 1960s and early 1970s. Spiegelman lengthened the work as a serial in *RAW* magazine, which he co-edited with his wife Françoise Mouly (who also appears in the comic). In 1986 the first volume of the collected story was published as *Maus: A Survivor's Tale* (subtitled *My Father Bleeds History* in subsequent printings), and in 1991 the second volume, *Maus: A Survivor's Tale II: And Here My Troubles Began* was released. The two volumes have been collected into one graphic novel as *The Complete Maus: A Survivor's Tale*.

Maus is often considered a graphic representation of an oral history, which is as complex as it is contradictory. The comic is based on the oral interviews recorded by Spiegelman with his father. An oral history is rarely left as an audio recording, but is instead transcribed and edited by the recorder along with his observations and descriptions. Spiegelman, as a cartoonist, used the medium with which he was most familiar to present his father's story. According to Joshua Brown, "Spiegelman's use of language is remarkable in its exactitude and lack of bravado. The language has the peculiar mix of confusion and clarity of spoken words—because, indeed, the dialogue is based on Spiegelman's interviews with his father" (Brown 1988, 96). Though *Maus* is not what one traditionally thinks of as an oral history, Spiegelman's methods and fidelity to the spoken language create an authenticity or naturalization that is from the oral history tradition, despite or perhaps because of its graphical approach.

A great deal of research was required to translate verbal descriptions into accurate depictions of WWII Europe. Spiegelman visited Auschwitz twice while doing research for *Maus*, and he had a local history of Sosnowiec (the area in Poland his parents are from) translated into English. He spoke with other Holocaust survivors and used their sketches of concentration camps as a basis for his own strips. Converting oral history into an authentic graphic representation was a difficult undertaking that required a great deal of effort to create the "historical understanding" (Brown 1988, 102) that is necessary, particularly for Holocaust literature.

IMPACT ON COMICS

Maus broke barriers for comics by entering the realm of academia, mainstream popular culture, and classrooms. Its serious subject matter defied the labels of silly or inconsequential. The visual style and metaphor of the comic are cartoons, making the work accessible to a larger audience than a darker more realistic style. Spiegelman uses animals as a metaphor. Jews are presented as mice, Nazis as cats, Poles as pigs, Frenchmen as frogs, and Americans as dogs. According to Joshua Brown, "By drawing people as animals, Spiegelman evokes the stratification of European society. . . . When you read *Maus*, you don't tend to identify the characters as animals. You decipher human beings, and then the metaphor takes hold" (Brown 1988, 108). The choice of animals for each group is informed by the stereotypes of the era, among which is the Nazi concept of Jews as "vermin" that Spiegelman turns on its head by making the mice empathetic protagonists. Interestingly, when characters are attempting to pass as something they are not in the text they wear masks of other species. An iconic self-portrait of Spiegelman from volume II, chapter 2, is an illustration of the human Art with a mouse mask on, surrounded by the emaciated bodies associated with concentration camp victims (201). This controversial portrait brings to light issues that many scholars and artists have with profiting from Holocaust-related artwork, as well as the artist's own feeling of not really being a proper Jew because he does not share his father's experiences and fears of the Holocaust.

Along with the complicated animal metaphor, Spiegelman steps away from several traditional comics conventions in his books. He breaks or bleeds panels, creates polyptych pages and montages, and incorporates photographs into *Maus*. By breaking the rules, whether the conventions of the medium or self-created rules like metaphor, Spiegelman breaks down the assumptions the reader creates from stereotypes, form, and even narrative. Bleeding panels create visual impact and emphasis on details that would normally be lost in a scene; Spiegelman uses this technique infrequently. It is not until the end of *Maus* that the visual narrative is complicated with deteriorating adherence to the comics aesthetic. One method that breaks Spiegelman's established visual style is the polyptych, which uses several panels to form a larger picture on a page. This singular polyptych in *Maus* creates an image of an old Vladek among the photos of his family (276). The preceding page's montage layout of panels and illustrated "photographs" further complicates the visual aesthetic, breaking down both narrative and form.

Spiegelman also includes photographs of his dead mother and brother in the comic (102, 165), the first as a sample from a previous work incorporated into the "present" storyline of the comic and the second as a tribute. However, it is the third photograph that by far breaks the most conventions of comics: a photograph of his father in a camp uniform, which breaks loose from the panel and visually "lays" on top of the comic (294). This emphasizes the importance of the image and the depth of the comic in a visual manner. In discussing the use of photographs in *Maus*, Marianne Hirsch states, "The power of the photographs . . . is not in their evocation of memory, but in their status as fragments of a history we cannot assimilate" (Chaney 2011, 41). By loosening the animal metaphor and deconstructing the medium, Spiegelman allows for "crystalline ambiguity" (Witek 2007, 194), humanity, and a focus on the "arbitrariness" of both artistic expression and historical horror (Ewert 2000, 101).

Maus continued to break comics conventions with the release of a CD-ROM in 1994 that provided readers with extras on the creation process, the original interview recordings with Vladek, videos from Spiegelman's visits to Auschwitz, and sketches by survivors. This is the first digital, interactive, behind-the-scenes extra for a comic book. By providing much of the source material for *Maus* to the general public, the work broke yet another convention of not only comics but of biography and historical studies. Spiegelman treated his reading public as equals and provided additional material to be digested alongside *Maus*. According to Paul John Eaken, the CD-ROM provided a clear understanding for those not previously invested in comics to learn about the creation process and to better understand that *Maus* is not a

THE SIMPSONS, SPIEGELMAN, AND MAUS

The Simpsons, in the episode "Husbands and Knives" (19.7, November 18, 2007), featured guest appearances from three renowned comics artists: Alan Moore (*Watchmen*), Art Spiegelman (*Maus*), and Dan Clowes (*Ghost World*). In the episode the three form the League of Extraordinary Freelancers, complete with ripped shirts and bulging muscles, to fight Comic Book Guy, who is tearing up his competitor's store at which they are book signing. Spiegelman dons his "maus" mask as depicted in his comic book, then declares that "Maus is in the house," with a martial arts punch. The episode concludes with the three artists levitating over the city of Springfield as an asteroid hurtles to Earth, at which point they decide they would rather go to a benefit for comics artists than save Springfield.

Guest starring on *The Simpsons* is a status symbol for celebrities and pop icons, as the show is the longest running sitcom in television history and an American culture staple. Famous bands like U2, the Red Hot Chili Peppers and the remaining Beatles; actors including Elizabeth Taylor, Tom Jones, and Kim Basinger; and entertainment personalities Larry King and Conan O'Brien have been included on the show. Pop culture icons have guest starred as their characters including Leonard Nimoy as Spock, Lucy Lawless as Xena, David Duchovny as Mulder, and Gillian Anderson as Scully. Spiegelman and his fellow cartoonists join these ranks; however, it is their artistic work that is iconic and recognizable in the episode, not the artists themselves.

biography with illustrations but a comic with graphics central to the narrative and the historical accuracy of the work (Chaney 2011, 15). The content from the CD-ROM was used at various institutions to supplement units on the Holocaust, as they added *Maus* to reading lists. Unfortunately, the CD-ROM only works on an outdated platform, which limits its current use. However, in 2011 the original CD-ROM was updated as a DVD-R extra to the *MetaMaus* book in which Spiegelman further explores the creation and legacy of *Maus*.

IMPACT ON AMERICAN CULTURE

Maus has been widely celebrated by both the comics industry as well as the larger public. It has won dozens of awards including major industry prizes like the Eisner Award (1992), Harvey Award (1992), and the Max & Moritz Prize (1990). In 1992 *Maus* became the only comic book ever to win a Pulitzer Prize. The committee decided on the Special Awards and Citations Pulitzer because it was unsure of where *Maus* should be categorized. In fact *Maus* has been the cause of much confusion and controversy over the years as booksellers and newspapers are uncertain of the work's status. *Maus* has been listed under fiction with the *New York Times* and has won several awards as fiction. However, Spiegelman has asked for a correction on several occasions, as *Maus*, like the majority of his work, is a nonfiction memoir (Doherty 1996, 69).

After its Pulitzer win *Maus* reaped a plethora of positive reviews and prompted op-ed pieces in the pages of the major metropolitan dailies including the *New York Times*, *Chicago Tribune*, and *L.A. Times*, which is "a sure sign of its status as a cultural as well as a literary event" (Doherty 1996, 71). The combination of "inherent audacity" (Doherty 1996, 70) and "serious form of pictorial literature" (Langer 1991) created "an epic story told in tiny pictures" (*New York Times*) that entered *Maus* into the "national lexicon" (Doherty 1996, 71) of American culture. With its historical win, *Maus* brought comics and Holocaust literature into the forefront of the public eye in the early 1990s. Its presence is still felt in American culture as *Maus* joins the ranks of iconic comics, recognizable for its imagery, themes, and historical precedent.

The themes and values addressed in *Maus* are hardly comical or childish, as a graphic novel addressing the Holocaust. These themes include family and survivor's guilt, memory and history, survival, race and class, high art and low culture, and power and warfare and are often connected with American values and ideals. American culture has assimilated and lauded individuality, equality, and pragmatism, and though *Maus* does not deliberately evoke these values, it cannot help but be informed by them. Early in the work, long before Vladek is confined to a concentration camp, he speaks of learning English in order to go to America (16); "the dream of America, while never spelled out, implies a society redeemed by an alternative social vision—a vision of radical social mobility and opportunity" (Rosen 1995, 253). The American dream that Vladek has is that in which an individual can find equality and comfort. Perhaps the easiest correlation between the themes in *Maus* and American values and culture is that of survival and pragmatism. "Vladek is a born survivor, but not a born Survivor" (Doherty 1996, 81), and his innate ability to persevere through practicality makes him a survivor though his personality "flaws" do not allow him to become a stereotype of a Holocaust Survivor. Even the use of different styles of English throughout *Maus* brings forth the value of survival, as English, even Vladek's broken English, was a contributing factor to his survival as he pragmatically used his knowledge.

Maus has joined the canon in several areas including Holocaust studies, comics studies, and personal histories. Spiegelman's biographical work is incorporated into a variety of compilations in Jewish and Holocaust studies including *Bearing Witness*, *Holocaust Literature*, *Ethical Diversions*, and *Utter Silence*, bringing the alternative comic into mainstream academic study. Additionally, *Maus* is an iconic comic that contributed to the emergence of comics, especially alternative comics as a literature with its own language, conventions, and styles, much like viewing film as literature (Hatfield 2005). The incorporation of *Maus* into a variety of disciplines has opened up the possibility of comics studies as a valid field of discourse, challenging the stigma associated with comics.

However, Spiegelman stated that "the one thing specific to my work has been that I wasn't interested in teaching anybody a damn thing" (Witek 2007, 192). Yet, *Maus* has been widely introduced into English literature, history, and art classrooms as early as middle school and as late as college. In 2009 *Maus* was chosen by the Young Adult Library Association as one of its recommended titles for all students (the list is revised every five years and used by educators and librarians across the country). In an interview with Susan Jacobwitz, Spiegelman stated he is careful to stay "close to things small and true" (Witek 2007, 159); by only discussing his father's experiences he stays authentic and keeps *Maus* from becoming a political platform. Spiegelman is grateful for *Maus* remaining in print, even as a "Holocaust for Beginners" book, though he cautions educators, stating, "I never intended it as a teaching tool. . . . I don't think it replaces the various histories that are around" (Witek 2007, 158). Despite or perhaps because of Spiegelman's reluctance to make grand overtures both in the text itself and in his many interviews, *Maus* has become a standard addition to reading lists across the country, removing much of the stigma associated with comics in the education system and further popularizing comics in the classroom.

SUMMARY

Maus is an iconic comic that challenged critics, scholars, and the American public to revise their concept of what a comic can be and do. Breaking comics conventions, creating complex metaphor and authentic language, *Maus* has been an innovator of the comics form and its perception in American culture. The first and only comic to earn a Pulitzer Prize, *Maus* brought alternative comics into the forefront of popular culture, academia, and the comics industry. Bringing the comics art form into the discourse of serious literature, *Maus* has become iconic not only in the culture of comics but also in Holocaust literature, academia, and the popular press. With themes and values addressing the Holocaust, memory, oral history, equality, and pragmatism, *Maus* entered classrooms across the country as a teaching tool. It brought a variety of new eyes and minds to the comics art form; its popularity derived from the mix of simple cartoons and the complex, personal narrative of father and son. Its popularity can be seen in its impact on American culture from classrooms to popular television programs.

See also RAW; Spiegelman, Art

FURTHER READING

Geis, Deborah R. *Considering Maus: Approaches to Art Spiegelman's "Survivor's Tale" of the Holocaust.* Tuscaloosa: University of Alabama Press, 2003.

Marcuse, Harold. University of California, Santa Barbara, "Maus Questions and Resources." http://www.history.ucsb.edu/faculty/marcuse/classes/33d/33dTexts/maus/MausResources.htm. Accessed July 12, 2011.

Spiegelman, Art. *MetaMaus: A Look into a Modern Classic.* New York: Pantheon, 2011.

Tanya D. Zuk

Marvel Comics

Marvel Comics is one of the largest comic book publishers in the world and has a long and rich history. Marvel's characters are iconic because they are instantly recognizable around the world. **Spider-Man, Captain America, Iron Man**, the **Hulk**, the **Fantastic Four**, the **X-Men, Blade**, Daredevil, Thor, and the Avengers are ingrained in our popular consciousness. From the very beginning, Marvel Comics created characters that stood out as different from typical superhero fare. Stories were set in the "real" world (often in New York, the home of Marvel's offices) with its characters having real-life problems. The talent that has passed through the Marvel offices over the past 70 years is a who's who of sequential art royalty: to name a few, Bill Everett; Otto Binder; Tarpe Mills; Gil Kane; John Romita, Sr.; Joss Whedon; Brian Michael Bendis; Denny O'Neil; Roy Thomas; John Buscema; **Steve Ditko**; Marv Wolfman; Jim Starlin; Steve Gerber; and **Alex Ross**. The names most associated with Marvel Comics are **Jack Kirby** and the man known as "Mr. Marvel," **Stan Lee**.

HISTORY

The origins of Marvel Comics began in the late 1930s as the imprint Timely Comics. The publisher, Martin Goodman, was previously active in the pulp magazine industry, publishing Westerns, sports, science fiction, and detective thriller stories, including *Marvel Science Stories* (the first to use *Marvel* in the title). The first issue of *Marvel Comics* appeared in 1939. *Marvel Comics* #1 (renamed *Marvel Mystery Comics* by issue #2) featured the Human Torch and Prince Namor, the Sub-Mariner. The Human Torch was a Frankenstein-like android who burst into flames when coming into contact with oxygen. The Sub-Mariner was a half-human prince from the underwater city of Atlantis. As writer **Grant Morrison** points out, "Timely's big innovation, which was to serve the embryonic Marvel [Comics] well and help distinguish it from DC, was to [have its superheroes] come down from Olympus and give voice to the elements themselves by personifying the forces of nature as heroes" (Morrison 2011, 28). In this case, fire and water!

MUSICAL MARVEL

Marvel had experimented with musical comics as far back as 1954 with *World's Greatest Songs*, which illustrated some of the popular songs of the day, but the "results were just so strange" (Daniels 1993, 75). In the 1970s Marvel produced comics based on the Beatles and KISS. In 1994 the Marvel Music imprint was launched with the first issue of *Alice Cooper: The Last Temptation* written by Neil Gaiman and illustrated by Michael Zulli. The imprint published several prestige graphic novels based on the music or lives of musicians such as the Rolling Stones, Bob Marley, KRS-One, Mary Stuart, and, oddly, Billy Ray Cyrus. The imprint was discontinued in 1995, but that same year America's supreme publisher of comics teamed up with America's greatest band, the Grateful Dead, to produce a series of backstage passes featuring Marvel characters for the band's 1995 summer tour.

From the first comic Marvel heroes, such as the Sub-Mariner (the first Marvel antihero), were different. The Human Torch protected humanity and sought assimilation (eventually becoming police officer Jim Hammond), while the Sub-Mariner had an uneasy relationship with humans who he felt did not respect the ocean or its creatures. The Sub-Mariner was not always a protector of humanity, and oftentimes fought against them. *Marvel Mystery Comics* #8–#9 (1940) featured one of the first big crossover battles in comics with the Sub-Mariner fighting the Human Torch.

At Timely Comics, Goodman hired the man who would play a pivotal role in the history of Marvel Comics, Stanley Lieber (Lee), who was Goodman's wife's cousin. Lee quickly rose from being a general office boy to writing comic scripts. Others who worked for Timely during this period included Bob Wood, Syd Shores, Otto Binder, Bill Everett, and Alex Shomburg (who did over 100 covers).

With the publication of *Captain America Comics* #1 in 1941 by Jack Kirby and Joe Simon, Timely hit its stride. Here was a character dressed up in the American flag fighting real-life villains like Hitler months before America entered the war. After America entered the war, patriotic superheroes and heroines were the norm. Other Timely patriotic heroes included Mr. Liberty (renamed Major Liberty), the Destroyer, Jap Buster Johnson, the "female Captain America Miss America" (Miller 1967, 1), and the Patriot. Comics during World War II were big business, and millions of comics sold every month. Comics provided those in the service and on the home front a morale boost, as adults as well as kids regularly read them. Some of the other characters that Timely created included Tommy Tyme, Blonde Phantom, the Vision, the Blazing Skull, Pinto Pete, 3X's (Marvel's first team of adventurers), the Fighting Hobo, the Angel (one of the first heroes with a mustache), and Electro and Microman (early versions of Iron Man and Ant-Man) (Olshevsky 1980, A-55, 58).

After World War II ended, superhero comics gradually faded. **Romance,** crime, Westerns, horror, science fiction, comedy, sports, and "funny animal" comics rose in popularity. *Marvel Mystery* and, briefly, *Captain America Comics* became horror anthologies.

In the early 1950s Timely Comics became Atlas Comics and continued publishing romance and Western titles, but followed trends and upped its output of monster, war, humor, horror, science fiction, crime, and suspense titles as each genre became popular. Atlas was the "secret king of pre-code horror," producing some of the best horror titles in the history of comics (Carter 1992, A-88). Atlas even got into the act of publishing 3-D comics titles (3-D movies were all the rage briefly during the 1950s). These included *3-D Action* and *3-D Tales of the West*. Other comics produced had titles like *Girls' Confessions*, *All True Crime*, *Sports Action*, and *Homer the Happy Ghost*. By far the most popular titles produced featured the Western, war, and horror genres. Some of the horror titles included *Menace, Strange Stories of Suspense, Marvel Tales, Strange Tales*, and *Adventures into Weird World*. Artists and writers who worked with Atlas during this period were some of the best in the business and included Joe Maneely; John Romita, Sr.; John Buscema; Russ Heath; Dick Ayers; John Severin; Bob Brown; and Bernie Krigstein.

Atlas briefly tried to revive the superhero genre with the "big" three: Human Torch, Captain America, and the Sub-Mariner. Instead of fighting Nazis, the enemy was now communists, spies, and saboteurs. However, this was short-lived as superheroes fighting communists did not resonate with the public at this time.

In addition, there was backlash against comics spurred in part by the publication of **Fredric Wertham**'s 1954 *Seduction of the Innocent*, which argued that comics were a major cause of juvenile delinquency. After congressional hearings were held, the comics industry developed the self-censoring Comics Code. Sales declined so much that it was necessary in 1957 for Stan Lee to let nearly everyone on staff go. "I was the one who had to fire the staff. It was the toughest thing I ever did in my life" (Lee quoted in Hajdu 2008, 327). In 1957 Atlas output went from publishing 85 titles to 16 (Hajdu 2008, 327). The most crippling blow came when Atlas had to distribute their books through Independent News, owned by rival National Periodical Publications (DC Comics), and the distributor limited Atlas to eight books a month. Goofy monster, Westerns, and romance/humor comics survived. The company nearly went out of business during the period known historically as "the Atlas implosion."

Stan Lee was at a crossroads in the early 1960s; he had always wanted to write the great American novel and was growing weary of working in comics, but his wife suggested that he should write a comics story that he himself would want to read. Consequently he created the *Fantastic Four* (1961) with artist Jack Kirby, and it ushered in the "Marvel Age of Comics." The Fantastic Four featured a newly revamped Human Torch. Here was a group who lived in New York and had real problems. Lee perfected the soap opera–style plots that became a Marvel trademark, and Kirby's dynamic art grabbed readers' attention. Other heroes soon followed, including Ant-Man, the Hulk, Spider-Man, Thor, Iron Man, Sgt. Nick Fury, Dr. Strange, Daredevil, and the Silver Surfer. In addition to the Fantastic Four, other team books included the Avengers and the X-Men. Marvel also successfully brought back Golden Age Timely characters the Sub-Mariner and Captain America (apparently Atlanteans age slowly, and Cap was frozen in a block of ice for decades).

Despite publishing superhero fantasy stories, Marvel Comics experimented with realism not seen before in comics. One could read 1960s Marvel Comics and get an understanding of the times. For example, the *X-Men* dealt with civil rights, and Cold War and Atomic Age fears appeared in the *Hulk* and *Iron Man*. Marvel added an African hero, **Black Panther**, and an African American hero, Falcon, to their universe of characters. Real-life lessons were found in the pages of *Amazing Spider-Man* and *Journey into Mystery* featuring Thor. In a rarity at the time for superheroes, Daredevil, Professor X, and Donald Blake (Thor) had physical disabilities.

While Marvel heroes were often grounded in realistic social and personal problems, they also led lives of fantastic adventure. The Marvel storytellers began to expand the scope and grandeur of their universe with multi-issue, epic storylines such as the Sentinels story arc in the pages of the *X-Men* (1965) and the Galactus trilogy in the pages of the *Fantastic Four* (1966). Among the legendary creators who worked for Marvel in the 1960s were Steve Ditko (co-creator of Spider-Man and Dr. Strange), John Buscema, Don Heck, Roy Thomas, and two of the most influential artists in the history of comics—**Neal Adams** and **Jim Steranko**.

The 1970s continued to be a prolific and successful period for Marvel. The company expanded beyond its own roster of characters and began licensing characters from literature, film, and television. Robert E. Howard's Conan and Kull characters were successfully brought to life on the comics page by writer Roy Thomas and artists John Buscema and Barry Windsor-Smith. The company adapted blockbuster films like *Star Wars*, *Planet of the Apes*, and *Star Trek*, and television programs such as *Battlestar Galactica*.

In 1971 Marvel published a story without the approval of the Comics Code that is considered a milestone by many comics historians. Stan Lee wrote a story about the horrors of drug abuse in the pages of *Amazing Spider-Man* #96–98 (1971). Also groundbreaking was the death of Peter Parker/Spider-Man's girlfriend Gwen Stacy in *The Amazing Spider-Man* #121–#122 (1973). One scholar argued that this story was so potent that readers learned "about the true nature of life and death" from this comic storyline (Blumberg 2003).

NO-PRIZE NOW PRIZED

In 1964 when Stan Lee asked readers to define what the Marvel Age of Comics meant to them, he assured them that "there will be no-prizes, and therefore, no losers." The phrase "no-prize" became an inside joke at Marvel and soon, in typical bombastic style, Lee declared the No-Prize was awarded for "meritorious service to the cause of Marveldom." There was literally no prize other than recognition in the letters page of one of the Marvel comic books, but when Lee announced they would be awarded to readers who pointed out continuity errors, more and more fans began scrutinizing the comics and reporting errors in hopes that Lee or another Marvel editor might respond to them on the letters page with a "consider yourself No-Prized." In 1967 the nonexistent prize became slightly more tangible when Marvel started sending out empty envelopes emblazoned with "Congratulations! This envelope contains a genuine Marvel Comics NO-PRIZE which you have just won!" These envelopes have become prized collector's items.

As the Comics Code started to relax, Marvel introduced edgier antihero characters like the **Punisher**, Ghost Rider, and **Wolverine**, as well as political and social satire in the stories of Howard the Duck. Marvel produced black-and-white magazines that did not have Code approval, but the relaxed Code allowed zombies, vampires, werewolves, demons, and other monsters to become popular comic book forms as well. One of the high points was *Tomb of Dracula* by Marv Wolfman and Gene Colon. This series set a standard for excellence in sequential art storytelling because of its complicated narrative and tasteful art.

Perhaps the most important series during the 1970s was Marvel's "reboot" of the X-Men in *Giant Size X-Men* #1 and *Uncanny X-Men* #94 (both 1975). This was a brand new X-Men much different from the 1960s version but with the same goal of providing storytelling that argued for equality of everyone regardless of race or gender. The new X-Men had an African woman, an Asian, a Native American, and a blue-skinned German, among others, making the X-Men one of the most diverse collections of superheroes in the history of comics. Chris Claremont and John Byrne became the creative team with #108 (1977), and their classic run on the X-Men is still considered one of the high points of Marvel Comics' history.

Marvel began to document and mythologize its own history with *Origins of Marvel Comics* (1974), *Son of Origins of Marvel Comics* (1974), *Bring On the Bad Guys* (1976), and *The Superhero Women* (1977). Marvel also collaborated with its main competitor, **DC Comics**, by producing the team-up of the decade—*Superman vs. The Amazing Spider-Man* (1976). During the

1970s, some of the talent who rose to prominence at Marvel included Archie Goodwin, Gil Kane, Jim Starlin, George Perez, Steve Englehart, Gary Friedrich, Mike Ploog, and Steve Gerber.

The 1980s saw Marvel expanding into more licensed properties like James Bond, Transformers, and G.I. Joe. The 1980s started with a huge X-Men event known as "The Dark Phoenix Saga," a powerful tale of loyalty and sacrifice that is considered the quintessential X-Men story and one of the greatest superhero stories ever told. Writer/artist Frank Miller had an influential run on *Daredevil*, making the character almost an antihero, which affected the storytelling Brian Michael Bendis and Ed Brubaker would re-create two decades later. Marvel introduced a younger version of the X-Men in the New Mutants, and Wolverine received his first solo title with much success. The original five X-Men were reunited in the pages of *X-Factor*, and a second version of the Avengers was introduced as the West Coast Avengers. The company also introduced one of its most critically acclaimed series, *The 'Nam* by Doug Murray and Michael Golden. The series was based on the Vietnam Conflict, written from the point of view of the soldiers, and praised by critics and veterans for its realistic portrayals of the war.

Under the editorship and writing of Jim Shooter (with artists Mike Zeck and Bob Layton), Marvel produced a major crossover event that set the standard for all crossovers to follow. *Marvel Super-Heroes Secret Wars* (1984–1985) was a 12-issue limited series featuring all the major Marvel heroes and villains in an epic struggle against the godlike Beyonder. Writer Mark Grunewald's limited series *Squadron Supreme* (1985–1986) was a tale in which the superheroes have taken over the world and eliminated crime by forcing everyone to behave. This series is often considered to be in the same vein as **Watchmen** or *The Dark Knight Returns* for its examination of how the existence of superheroes might change the world.

In 1982, Marvel began publishing graphic novels with *The Death of Captain Marvel*. The company began its creator-owned imprint, *Epic Comics*, publishing comics and graphic novels without the approval of the Comics Code and selling to the direct market of comic book stores. The themes were more mature and allowed writers and artists room to be creative. Epic also published licensed titles like *Hellraiser*. The Epic imprint brought in a plethora of great talent including J. M. Dematteis, Chuck Dixon, Jo Duffy, Ann Nocenti, Ted McKeever, and Harlan Ellison. French artist Moebius worked with Stan Lee on the Silver Surfer tale *Parable*. The famous manga epic *Akira* by Katshuiro Otomo was first published in America by Epic in 38 volumes. The company also broke new ground in 1988 by publishing the very first computer-generated graphic novel, *Iron Man: Crash*.

In 1986 Marvel introduced its "New Universe" line of titles in an attempt to create characters and storylines separate from the Marvel Universe proper. Some of the characters and titles included *Star Brand*, *Kickers Inc*, and *D.P.7*.

While the storylines were often very good, the "New Universe" titles never found sufficient readers, and the line was cancelled in 1989.

Perhaps the biggest event during the 1980s was the marriage of Peter Parker/ Spider-Man to longtime love interest Mary Jane Watson in 1987. While Peter married M. J. in *Amazing Spider-Man Annual* #21, Spidey married her in a ceremony presided over by Stan Lee at New York's Shea Stadium on June 5, 1987, in front of a live audience and televised to the world.

The 1990s started out very promising with the rise of new talent like **Todd McFarlane**, who injected new life into the *Amazing Spider-Man* series, which brought in new fans. Writer Kurt Busiek and artist Alex Ross teamed to produce the four-issue prestige series *Marvels* in 1994. Busiek's innovative story told the history of the Marvel Universe through the eyes of photographer Phil Sheldon, and Ross's beautiful painted artwork made *Marvels* a fan favorite.

All this success early in the 1990s did not shield Marvel from one of its darkest periods, as the company filed for Chapter 11 bankruptcy in late 1996. Billionaires Ronald Perelman and Carl Icahn fought over the company in the courts, as documented in Dan Ravi's *Comic Wars* (2002). Neither Perelman nor Icahn gained control of the company, and Marvel managed to bounce back.

Increasingly in the 1990s crossovers became bigger, spanning numerous titles with multiple writers and artists. One of the most controversial was the Spider-Man "Clone Saga," which temporarily revamped Peter Parker's world. Other major events included *Onslaught*, *Age of Apocalypse*, and *Heroes Reborn*. With stiff competition from upstart publisher **Image Comics**, the collapse of the speculator market, and a disastrous experiment with self-distribution, Marvel was in financial trouble in 1996. In an attempt to decrease operating costs and increase sluggish sales, *Heroes Reborn* saw Marvel outsource production of four of their most important titles (*Fantastic Four*, *Avengers*, *Captain America*, and *Iron Man*) to the studios of popular Image creators Jim Lee and Rob Liefeld. All the titles were rebooted, starting with issue #1 and presenting revamped version of the characters. The gimmick increased sales but left many longtime Marvel fans disgruntled. After 13 issues Marvel resumed production of the books and rejoined the characters to their previous continuity.

Toward the end of the decade, changes in management occurred as Joe Quesada, Ike Perlmutter, Bill Jemas, and Avi Arad took on upper-level management positions at Marvel and helped bring the company out of the bankruptcy slump. The Marvel Knights Imprint was introduced, showcasing characters like Ghost Rider, Daredevil, Captain America, and the Punisher, among others, in edgy stories designed specifically for an adult audience.

The 2000s and beyond has been a period of rapid growth and change for Marvel (McLaughlin 2002). Some important talent during the postmillennium included Brian Michael Bendis (who became one of Marvel's most popular writers), Warren Ellis, Grant Morrison, Steve Epting, Jonathan Hickman, Mike Allred, Neil Gaiman, Ed Brubaker, Mark Millar, and Garth Ennis.

The very successful *Ultimate* line was introduced in 2000 to bring in new readers who might like to read comics but did not want to wade through 50 years of continuity. With the *Ultimate Spider-Man* and *Ultimate X-Men*, Marvel received both critical and fan acclaim, and writers Bendis and Millar became superstars. The line was soon expanded to include *Ultimate Fantastic Four* and *The Ultimates* (a version of the Avengers).

The company unsuccessfully tried to bring back the Epic imprint but finally opted for the more limited creator-owned Icons imprint. The Max line imprint was introduced as one with mature content, while Marvel Adventures was created as an all-ages line. Marvel entered the digital age by offering digital access to its comics through its website.

The biggest crossover event of the decade was *Civil War* (2006–2007), which many saw as a post-9/11 statement on the state of civil liberties in the United States. Enhanced humans were required to give up their secret identities and register with the government. The *Marvel Zombies* series showcased characters as gut-munching zombies in an attempt to keep up with the craze for all things undead in popular culture. Other crossover events included *Fear Itself*, *House of M*, *Disassembled*, *Secret Invasion*, and *Dark Reign*. The year 2012 brought a huge crossover event between the Avengers and the X-Men, pitting Marvel's two most popular teams against each other.

There were also numerous deaths, including the death and subsequent resurrection of Captain America and the resurrection of his long-dead partner Bucky Barnes. The Fantastic Four's Human Torch was also killed off and reborn. Ultimate Spider-Man/Peter Parker died and was replaced by the multi-racial Miles Morales.

In 2009, Marvel was bought by Disney for $4 billion, thus further solidifying Marvel's role in the world of comics and popular culture. Because Disney intends to aggressively license the "treasure trove of over 5,000 characters" and exploit them across multiple media platforms, even more Marvel characters are likely to become iconic.

IMPACT ON COMICS

Perhaps Marvel's innovation that impacted the comics industry the most was the "Marvel Method" of producing stories that was developed during the 1960s, when Stan Lee, Jack Kirby, and Steve Ditko created the Marvel Universe as we know it today. Using the Marvel Method, the writer (usually Lee) would provide a basic outline, and the artist would then plot and draw the story based on the outline, oftentimes adding secondary characters. Later the writer would fill in the dialogue. This was truly a collaborative process and completely opposite of the way it was done before by just giving the artist a full script he or she followed exactly.

From Marvel's beginnings in the 1940s as Timely Comics, it reached out to its audience to gauge what they would like to read. Early issues of *Daring Mystery Comics* and *Marvel Mystery Comics* "carried advertisements . . . awarding a total of $25 to readers who sent in the best 100-word essays on their favorite characters." This input led to the cancellation of several titles and helped dictate "the direction Timely would take in 1940 and 1941" (Olshevsky 1980, A-55). Timely also held a contest for the best 100-word dialogue between the Human Torch and the Sub-Mariner. Timely responded to those who wrote in with a letter and "obviously valued its rapport with the readers" (Olshevsky 1980, A-61).

Lee and the Marvel editors would often talk to readers by addressing them as "True Believers" and "Heroes," making reading Marvel Comics a unique experience. Lee "even gave the Marvel writers and artists 'pet' names, which further personalized the public's perception of Marvel" (Weiner 2008, 12). As editor Lee would often ask readers their opinions and encouraged questions and correspondence (a policy Marvel still maintains to this day). What was even more distinct, however, were the "No-Prize" awards (see sidebar) given out to those who found errors in the comics. The result of this was that readers were made to feel that they were truly part of the comics experience. In the 1960s Marvel even created a fan club, the Merry Marvel Marching Society (MMMS), further cementing reader loyalty with the company. Marvel briefly created the Friends of Ol' Marvel (FOOM) in the 1970s with its own publication. In the 1990s, some fans co-opted what began as a derogatory term for obsessive Marvel followers and began proudly referring to themselves as Marvel Zombies.

Marvel also used hyperbole to promote and market itself to great effect. For example, the company sometimes referred to itself as Marvel Pop Art Productions in the mid-1960s. The Marvel Bullpen is known as the House of Ideas (one of the most effective marketing slogans the company came up with). Stan Lee used iconic phrases that are now part of the vernacular including "'Nuff Said," "Hang Loose," and "Excelsior!"

The Marvel Bullpen page that appeared in all the comics provided chatty insider information that fostered good will between fans and company. The most prominent and engaging aspect of the Bullpen page was Stan's Soapbox, a column in which Lee dispensed folksy philosophy with a relentlessly upbeat tone. From 1983 to 1994 the company published *Marvel Age*, a publication that kept fans up to date on happenings within the company. Marvel has continued to cultivate a connection with fans on its website, which features video podcasts, discussion boards, up-to-date information on its comics, and characters in various media (games, film, etc.).

The storytellers who produce Marvel comic books have always injected a dose of real life (marriage, children, etc.) in the characters, in contrast to the relatively static DC heroes, and have brought into focus the historical issues of the time, whether it is war, drug abuse, or the debate over civil liberties. Although there are those who are critical of the way Marvel has portrayed female heroes (Glicksohn 1974), the company always maintained that through strong characters they were equalizing gender, race, and sexual orientation. Some of the strong female protagonists are the Invisible Woman, Ms. Marvel, Mystique, Night Nurse, Rogue, and Storm. Marvel created some of the earliest African American superheroes, including Luke Cage, Blade, the Falcon, and Black Goliath. Key gay characters include Northstar, Rawhide Kid, and Sunfire.

IMPACT ON AMERICAN CULTURE

Marvel Comics is a publisher that is a true American success story. Its pages are filled with the hard work and creative efforts of a long list of iconic storytellers. The history of Marvel literarily exemplifies the American Dream, that fame and fortune can come to a company that perseveres and never gives up. Marvel went from being a "second-string publisher in the 1940s" (Olshevsky 1980, A-46) to implosion and near death in the 1950s. Conversely, the 1960s saw Marvel become the number one comics publisher in the world with its iconic cast of characters. During the 1970s and 1980s, Marvel steadily grew, but the 1990s brought Marvel into bankruptcy. The company recovered in the 2000s to once again dominate the comics world.

Marvel has gone beyond just a comic and book publisher to licensing its characters for toys, video games, and films. One reason Marvel characters remain popular is because of the blockbuster films and successful animated series that feature its characters. Captain America was the first Marvel character adapted for film with a Republic serial in 1944. Marvel characters first appeared in animated television programming when *Marvel Super-Heroes* originally aired during the latter half of 1966. The show featured five of Marvel's leading characters on a rotating basis and employed limited animation produced from the artwork in the comics. *The Incredible Hulk* live-action television series in the late 1970s/early 1980s redefined how to successfully bring a comic character to the small screen. The 1998 *Blade* feature film was Marvel's first success on the big screen. Soon other Marvel characters, such as the Fantastic Four, Spider-Man, and Iron Man, were appearing in successful film franchises. With the 2000 release of the *X-Men* film, Marvel characters became synonymous with the summer blockbuster film. In addition to working with major film companies (mostly for distribution), Marvel Studios produces its own direct line of animated movies (Marvel Animation) and works to produce and finance its own feature films, including *Iron Man 1* and *2* (2008 and 2010), *Incredible Hulk* (2008), *Thor* (2011), *Captain America* (2011), and *The Avengers* (2012).

Marvel Comics also helped redefine a new paradigm by creating comics that were not just for children but that adults could enjoy as well. Stan Lee's early writing often employed a higher level of vocabulary but with enough action to satisfy kids. Lee and other Marvel writers/artists occasionally gave lectures at universities, which brought a higher level of respectability to sequential art.

SUMMARY

Marvel is one of the most successful comic book companies in history. Marvel's characters grapple with real-world problems in a fictional universe in which their adventures are interconnected. From its early days as Timely Comics, Marvel's characters inhabited the same universe. Like everyday people, the Hulk was just as likely to encounter Spider-Man or Captain America (sometimes in the same issue). While Marvel characters have a common touch that makes them relatable, they also have a nobility about them (even the villains like **Dr. Doom** and Magneto are complex and not your standard "run-of-the-mill" criminal). Some villains were capable of doing great good. Conversely, sometimes heroes are not always what they seem and can have a dark side, such as Hank (Ant-Man) Pym's personality disorder and Tony (Iron Man) Stark's battle with alcoholism.

In 2012, Marvel Comics had come full circle with the 600th issue of *Fantastic Four*, the title that originally ushered in the Marvel Age of Comics in 1961. Marvel characters have truly become transmediated in popular culture through television, trading cards, role-playing games, movies, clothing, video games, music, action figures, fan films, prose novels, children's books, the Internet and, of course, comics and graphic novels. Marvel's own website and use of social media is a great example of how to create an interactive experience for fans who want to keep up to date or need a bit of quick reference information about a character. Stan Lee has often quipped that he wanted Marvel to be a wonderland like Disney. With Disney's recent acquisition of Marvel, this just might be possible.

See also Black Panther; Blade; Captain America; Ditko, Steve; Doctor Doom; Fantastic Four; Hulk; Iron Man; Kirby, Jack; Lee, Stan: The Punisher; McFarlane, Todd; Spider-Man; Steranko, James; The Thing; Wolverine; X-Men

ESSENTIAL READING

Lee, Stan (w), Jack Kirby (p), and Steve Ditko (p). *Origins of Marvel Comics*. New York: Simon and Schuster, 1974.

Simon, Joe (w), Jack Kirby (p), and Carl Burgos (p). *The Golden Age of Marvel Comics Volume 1*. New York: Marvel, 1997.

Thomas, Roy (w), John Bryne (p), and Jim Starlin (p). *Women of Marvel: Celebrating Seven Decades*. New York: Marvel, 2011.

FURTHER READING

Defalco, Tom. *Marvel Chronicle: A Year by Year History*. New York: DK, 2008.

Marvel website, http://www.marvel.com.

Sanderson Peter. *Marvel Universe*. New York: Henry N. Abrams, 1998.

Thomas, Roy. *Stan Lee's Amazing Marvel Universe*. New York: Sterling Books, 2006.

Robert G. Weiner

McCloud, Scott

Scott McCloud is a comic book artist, inventor, theorist, and leading advocate of visual literacy. He is best known for his comic book *Zot!* and his nonfiction books exploring the visual conventions of the comics medium, including *Understanding Comics*, *Reinventing Comics*, and *Making Comics*. It is Scott's willingness to challenge traditional conventions, experiment with new tools, and take risks in moving comics forward that makes him an icon of the medium.

HISTORY

Scott McCloud (originally spelled McLeod) was born in 1960 in Boston and grew up in the nearby town of Lexington. The son of an engineer and an encouraging mother, Scott was the youngest of four children, with a penchant for fine art and science fiction. By the age of 14, Kurt Busiek (who in his own right has a successful career as a comics writer) introduced Scott to comic books. At first he thought they were way too campy for his tastes, but after some urging by Kurt, Scott came to appreciate their style and design. By 15, Scott knew that his life's work (in one way or another) would be spent in the comics industry.

Growing up, Scott and Kurt dabbled in comics, writing and illustrating their own self-published books. One such piece was "The Battle of Lexington." It was Scott's first attempt at experimenting with unusual panel sizes and layouts, something he would revisit in future comics. After high school, the pair went to Syracuse University in New York where Scott graduated with a Bachelor of Fine Arts in Illustration. From there, his first "real" comics job was working in the production department at **DC Comics** in Manhattan, a position he obtained as a result of a portfolio class in college. This was the beginning of a long and prosperous career in the comics industry.

(Scott McCloud)

IMPACT ON COMICS

A modest beginning in the industry begat for Scott McCloud a long and fruit-ful career marked by critical acclaim, awards, and the moniker of one of the most important individuals in contemporary comics. His reach, though, is not just found in print comics. Rather, Scott's impact on the industry is found in his inventions and theoretical work as well.

The Iconic Artist

Scott McCloud's first major published work was *Zot!*, a 36-issue comic book series begun in 1984 with Eclipse Comics. The incentive for *Zot!* came from two divergent sources: Dick Calkins's classic *Buck Rogers* comic strip and Osamu Tezuka's *Astro Boy*. It was a superhero story wrapped in the artistic styling of manga that harkened back to the Golden Age of comics. Its themes were a postmodern critique on society and were done mostly in response to the ever-growing dark storylines of most mid-1980s superhero comics. Critics praised Scott for the groundbreaking comic. In 1985 he won the Jack Kirby Award for Best New Series as well as the Russ Manning Award for Most Promising Newcomer. Although the comic ended in 1991, McCloud brought it back to the digital frontier with *Zot! Online*.

Throughout his career, Scott worked on an eclectic collection of comics, some as writer and some as artist. For instance, *Destroy!!* (Eclipse Comics) was a giant-sized one-shot comic that came on the heels of the highly successful *Zot! Destroy!!*'s premise was straightforward: to show as much violence and destruction as possible in each and every panel. *Destroy!!* became more than just a parody of superhero comics; it was about the relationship between cover and content. As Scott notes on his website: "I got the idea when I first heard people complaining about a **Marvel** comic called *SuperBoxers* and claiming that it was 'nothing but senseless violence from beginning to end.' I thought this sounded cool, but was disappointed, upon acquiring a copy, to discover that *SuperBoxers* included a plot, characterization, and other distractions. It wasn't PURE. *Destroy!!* was my attempt to get it right" ("Destroy!!" 2011).

In the 1990s, Scott scripted and worked on several different titles, including issues of the popular *Justice League Adventures* and issues #2–#13 of *Superman Adventures*. However, some comics—self-admittedly—were not as successful as others. The computer-generated comic book *The New Adventures of Abraham Lincoln* did not quite meet fan (and critic) expectations due in part to its digital artwork. Regardless, Scott's digital experiments became a method he explored further with the launch of his website in 1998 (http://www.scottmccloud.com) and with his nonfiction work *Reinventing Comics*.

In 2004, Scott scripted and did layout for a three-part series from DC called *Superman: Strength* and is currently working on a new graphic novel entitled *The Sculptor* (Scott McCloud, 2011).

The Artist as Inventor

A polymath in his own right, Scott McCloud is more than just an artist and writer. He is also an inventor who is willing to take risks in order to move the comics industry forward. As he notes on his website, "I've had a weird career. Not everything I do takes the form of a graphic novel or webcomic. Sometimes I just come up with ideas that take on a life of their own" ("Inventions" 2011). Some of his inventions include the Creator's Bill of Rights, the Big Triangle, and the Infinite Canvas.

The Creator's Bill of Rights had its origin in November of 1988 when Scott attended a two-day gathering of artists. With his colleagues, the group discussed a creative manifesto for comic book artists. At a follow-up meeting held that July, Scott replaced the manifesto with the first draft of what he dubbed the Creator's Bill of Rights, a document that espoused the rights owed artists in the production of comic books. Scott's early work on the document shows his passion and commitment to the medium and artist alike, marking his foray into the field as an icon of the industry.

DEFINITION OF TERMS

Scott McCloud's iconic and oft-cited definition of comics comes from his 1993 award-winning work, *Understanding Comics*. In it he builds on Will Eisner's early work in the medium, ultimately describing comics as "juxtaposed pictorial and other images in deliberate sequence, intended to convey information and/or to produce an aesthetic response in the viewer."

The Big Triangle was first presented in *Understanding Comics*. The triangle contains a visual vocabulary (pictures, words, symbols, etc.) in one map, allowing readers to see the relationship between image and word. Scott's work on the relationship between word, thought, and meaning is groundbreaking, and the results contribute to the larger body of knowledge surrounding the way in which viewers make meaning from what they see.

One of Scott's more radical inventions comes from *Reinventing Comics*. In it, he argues that digital comics could lead to the creation of an Infinite Canvas: the idea that the computer screen is just a window looking *at* the comic rather than the screen acting as a page or panel. The Infinite Canvas challenges artists to think more globally about where and when readers encounter the storyline. Rather than consider the traditional X-axis (width: reading panels from left to right) and Y-axis (height: reading the page from top to bottom), Scott argues for the inclusion of a Z-axis in digital comics (depth: moving *into* the panels as scenes). This allows for a dyadic relationship with the comic, one that interacts with the readers as much as they wish.

It is this verve for looking at the medium through a new perspective, pushing both the theoretical and technological boundaries of what is possible—and what is not—that make Scott's work paramount for scholars and creators alike. Scott is not afraid to take a chance with technology, utilizing new concepts to help solve old problems, or use the medium to help solve problems *of* the medium. This is what makes Scott McCloud more than just a comics artist, but rather an artist *and* a theorist of the medium.

IMPACT ON AMERICAN CULTURE

Instinctually, Scott McCloud always knew how comics functioned. Friends would ask him how panels functioned and he would explain it to them, quickly jotting his answers down and saving them for work on a future project. From those notes came a trio of highly successful nonfiction works that impacted the way comic book artists, writers, and scholars worldwide thought about the medium.

The Inventor as Theorist

In 1993, Scott published the canonical *Understanding Comics*, a deconstruction of the visual iconography we see in comics. Scott presented his argument antithetically to traditional monographs: he writes in the form of a comic. And why not? If Scott's argument is that comics are capable of doing anything, then his books needed to show that.

In *Understanding Comics*, Scott develops a now oft-cited definition of comics that expands upon **Will Eisner's**, as well as explores a working theory of *how* comics function. *Understanding Comics* provides a historical grounding for the idea of comics, develops a working vocabulary of comic elements, and integrates theories of psychology, communication, and visual communication into a cohesive, accessible format available to both scholars and the general public alike.

Understanding begins by noting the lack of critical attention to the comics medium: "At one time or another virtually all the great media have received critical examination, in and of themselves. But for comics, this attention has been rare, Eisner's own *Comics and Sequential Art* being a happy exception" (McCloud 1993, 6). In understanding the comics medium, Scott integrates semiotic theory with Gestalt psychology, borrowing the term *closure* to explain how the lack of specific imagery between the panels (frames) functions as a prompt for readers to know that action took place there. Closure plays on the common understanding of readers and helps facilitate the transactional experience of the visually mediated communication act. In other words, between panels we assume time and action exist based on what we *do*, not what we see.

One indication of Scott's insight and contribution to the theoretical aspects of comics is the extraordinary impact *Understanding Comics* has on readers and scholars. In 1994, the book won the Eisner Award, the Harvey Award, the Alph'art Award at Angoulcme, and a *New York Times* Notable Book award. It has been translated into 16 languages and excerpted into textbooks and edited collections of all kinds. Icons of the comics industry like Will Eisner, **Neil Gaiman, Alan Moore,** and **Art Spiegelman** praised *Understanding Comics* for its groundbreaking work in the medium. Likewise, scholars were both supporting and refuting Scott's work, engaging in a discussion of new visual rhetorics. In a personal e-mail, Scott reflects back, modestly noting, "It seems to have changed some minds, so that's gratifying" (McCloud 2011).

In 1998, Scott launched his website, http://www.scottmccloud.com, and began his foray into digital comics, including such works as *My Obsession with Chess, Zot! Online,* and *I Can't Stop Thinking*. The latter was an appendix to his next book, *Reinventing Comics*, which was published in 2000 as a follow-up to *Understanding Comics*.

Reinventing Comics arrived when the web was becoming popular for more than just finding information; it was becoming an interactive forum for fans and artists alike. In *Reinventing Comics*, Scott argued how comics and industry needed to evolve into this new space, perhaps changing altogether what we knew comics to be. To do this, he argues for 12 different "revolutions" in the way comics (as we know them) are created, distributed, and perceived by readers. Scott explores them as art and literature and explicates the diversity and understanding of the industry. From there, he challenges readers to think about developing new advances into the design, production, and the distribution of comics. The Infinite Canvas became the cornerstone of the book's concluding chapters.

Unlike *Understanding Comics*, though, *Reinventing Comics* received more than its share of critical scrutiny—even from Scott himself: it is not as fluid and reader-friendly as *Understanding Comics* and has some theoretical flaws. To this, publisher Gary Groth wrote a two-part review in 2002 entitled "McCloud Cuckoo-Land" for *Comics Journal* (#232 and #234). Groth did not look upon the book favorably and discounted its predictions. Ever the eternal optimist, Scott took up the challenge and responded to Groth's claims (which appeared in issue #235). The Groth-McCloud debate is part of the contemporary history of the medium—one that represents old guard versus new guard, as Salon.com remarked.

Understanding Comics explores how comics function as a medium, both visually and psychologically. And *Reinventing Comics* takes a serious look at the industry and its digital future. With the publishing of *Making Comics* in 2006, Scott gives an inside look at how comics are made. *Making Comics* covers the basics for up-and-coming artists, including choosing the right moment to reveal to readers, framing, word and image relationships, creating realistic characters and worlds for readers, styles and genres, and using the right tools for storytelling.

With its release, Scott extended chapter 5 onto his website, provided how-to videos on YouTube, and a program for displaying facial expressions in a comic-like face (called the Grimace Project). To promote his book, Scott and his family (wife Ivy and daughters Winter and Sky) went on a 50-state tour, blogging about their year-long adventure, giving presentations, seminars, and book signings.

Finally, 2008 saw the release of a descriptive guide from Scott called the "Google Chrome Comic." An instrument for journalists and users, the comic synthesizes interviews conducted with Chrome engineers with the technical specs on the search engine into a user-friendly document. The piece was highly sought after by consumers, especially on the heels of Scott's *Making Comics* tour.

As an artist, Scott made his mark telling visual stories, but as a theorist Scott used his talents to try to help those outside of the medium understand its full potential and capabilities.

The Theorist as Speaker and Teacher

Since 1994, Scott McCloud has made a name for himself as a talented and insightful speaker on such topics as comics, visual communication, innovations, storytelling, and media evolution. He has spoken at colleges and universities the world over, including Harvard, Indiana University, MIT, Ohio State University, Savannah College of Art and Design, and the Shanghai International Schools.

Apart from higher education, Scott has lectured and consulted with some of the major corporations in the world (Google, Pixar, Microsoft, Adobe), government-related agencies (DARPA, National Cancer Institute), and museums (Smithsonian). In addition, Scott is a mainstay at conferences like SXSW, **Comic-Con International,** the Disney Comic Writers Seminar, and the Chicago Humanities Festival.

Scott is also much more hands-on than one might think. His personality and motivation to engage young creators have him offering 1-, 2-, 3-, or 5-day seminars on comics and storytelling. Using hands-on exercises, Scott works with participants to help them focus their ability to communicate visually. Such seminars have been held at MIT, the Boston Arts Academy, and at the Sydney Opera House.

SUMMARY

From artist to theorist, inventor to teacher, Scott McCloud is an icon of the comics discipline. His career began at a time when traditional modes of creating comics were the norm, but as he grew, so did the medium. Scott embraced the digital frontier, realizing that change is not only inevitable, but also indicative of progress. His work—sometimes cerebral and other times not—seemingly bridged the visual gap, allowing others to see how this progress can be admirable and even necessary for the comics industry.

Within Scott McCloud is the essence of a renaissance student and teacher: one who is constantly seeking knowledge, experimenting with industry innovations, and trying to figure out how comics work and where they can grow in the future. And rather than keep these secrets to himself, Scott shares his talent and insight with others, hoping it will take root and grow in others.

Scott is never stagnating, nor is he without projects. For every one project that he finishes, he plans for 10 more (McCloud 2011). And perhaps this is what captivates and draws audiences into his work: the idea that there is always something new from the iconic Scott McCloud just around the corner.

See also Eisner, Will; Kubert, Joe; Spiegelman, Art

ESSENTIAL WORKS

McCloud, Scott. *Making Comics: Storytelling Secrets of Comics, Manga and Graphic Novels*. New York: HarperCollins, 2006.

McCloud, Scott. *Reinventing Comics: How Imagination and Technology Are Revolutionizing an Art Form*. New York: HarperCollins, 2000.

McCloud, Scott. *Understanding Comics: The Invisible Art*. New York: HarperCollins, 1993.

McCloud, Scott. *Zot! 1987–1991: The Complete Black and White Collection*. New York: HarperCollins, 2008.

FURTHER READING

Chute, Hillary. "Scott McCloud: Cartoonist." *The Believer*, April 2007. http://www.believermag.com/issues/200704/?read=interview_mccloud.

Hanson, Scot. "Scott McCloud: A Comics-Format Interview." *Kairos* 14, no. 1 (November 2008.) http://www.technorhetoric.net/14.1/interviews/hanson/index.html.

Spurgeon, Tom. "CR Sunday Interview: Scott McCloud." *Comics Reporter*, September 14, 2008. http://www.comicsreporter.com/index.php/cr_Sunday_interview_scott_mccloud.

Alec R. Hosterman

Todd McFarlane

Todd McFarlane rose to prominence in the late 1980s due to his distinctive artistic style. He became one of the true "superstar" comics creators of the 1990s after providing art for **Marvel Comics'** *Incredible Hulk*, *Amazing Spider-Man*, and *Spider-Man* titles. He later co-founded **Image Comics** with a group of other ex-Marvel creators, launching his own original creation, Spawn, in the process. He has also developed his own line of toys along with a film and animation studio.

HISTORY

Todd McFarlane was born in Alberta, Canada, in 1961. Although he became a fan of comics in high school and began to draw superheroes as an amateur in his teenage years, he nurtured a dream to become a professional baseball player. This led to his being awarded a baseball scholarship to Eastern Washington University, where he earned a general studies degree with an emphasis on graphic arts, communications, and art.

However, McFarlane maintained his love of comics, and working at a comic book store helped him to fund his college education. When his college baseball eligibility ended and no Major League teams sought him out, he continued to draw comic book characters. Determined to find a job in the industry, McFarlane repeatedly submitted his artwork to comic book editors. Today, he claims to have collected more than 700 rejection letters in the process, before catching his first big break.

That break came when McFarlane accepted an offer from Marvel's Epic Comics imprint to pencil "Slash," an 11-page backup story in *Coyote* #11 (1985). Shortly afterward, McFarlane married his high school sweetheart, Wanda, in July 1985. At the same time, he continued to make a name for himself in the comics industry, penciling several issues of Marvel's *Incredible Hulk*, along with a handful of books for **DC Comics** including *Infinity, Inc.*, *Detective Comics*, and *Batman: Year Two*.

But it was with Marvel that McFarlane really hit the big time. His distinctive style—which incorporated lavishly rendered textures, intricate line work, and slightly exaggerated physical characteristics—marked him out as an important talent. He was soon given the task of penciling Marvel's flagship title, *Amazing Spider-Man*, from issue #298 onwards. It was this series that ultimately launched McFarlane's career into the stratosphere.

McFarlane's run on *Amazing Spider-Man* with writer David Michelinie was a high-profile comic that earned the artist a huge fan base, while at the same time giving McFarlane the chance to draw one of the best-known American superheroes as well as many of the classic **Spider-Man** villains.

The series gained a unique visual identity as a result of McFarlane's contribution. While his artwork has been known to polarize readers—with some people put off by the exaggerated, caricatured appearance of the characters and his obvious flexibility when it comes to accurate anatomy—others were won over by the cinematic framing, kooky poses, high level of detail, and over-the-top rendition of rippling musculature, all of which made him a perfect fit for Spider-Man.

Particularly noteworthy additions were the wide "bug-eyed" approach to Spider-Man's eyepieces, the extremely detailed webbing on his costume, the tweaked and slightly more stylized design of the Spider on his chest, the more "spidery" poses, and the new, more three-dimensional take on his webs, which editor Tom DeFalco dubbed "spaghetti-webbing" due to the tangled appearance of its multiple strands.

This novel take on the character drew a lot of attention to the series. And McFarlane was perhaps a harder-working artist than people give him credit for, inking his own pencils for most of his run, even at times when *Amazing Spider-Man* was shipping biweekly. Michelinie's opinion of his co-creator was also glowing, with the writer openly praising his collaborator's storytelling abilities, his art style, his lack of ego, and his professionalism (DeFalco 2004).

McFarlane barely had time to get to grips with the series before it reached its landmark 300th issue, which provided the debut of one of the title's most enduring villains: Venom.

Venom is perhaps the perfect example of a character who gained instant popularity in the 1990s due to his simple characterization and striking appearance, but who reveals himself to be a little lacking in depth once you scratch the surface of his personality. A deranged carbon copy of Spider-Man in his black costume—albeit with a sinister grin slapped on—the villain had an even more exaggeratedly muscular physique than McFarlane's take on Spider-Man provided.

Nevertheless, Venom still proved hugely successful with readers, leading to numerous return appearances. He also starred in several of his own limited series that cast him as a violent antihero, as well as appearing in 2007's blockbuster movie *Spider-Man 3*.

(AP/Wide World Photos)

The Michelinie/McFarlane partnership continued for almost two years and 28 issues before the team finally parted company. McFarlane's decision to leave didn't reflect any animosity towards his writer, but a growing sense of dissatisfaction with his lack of control over his own work.

Early signs of McFarlane's outspoken beliefs in creator's rights mixed with the creator's desire to grow as an artist and as a nascent writer, and as he started to skip issues of *Amazing Spider Man*, it became clear that Marvel was going to have to do something to appease the hot young artist or risk losing him completely. Therefore, in 1990, Marvel gifted him with a new project that McFarlane could both write and illustrate: the "adjectiveless" *Spider-Man* title. The first issue alone justified the economic rationale for Marvel giving McFarlane his own series, with sales that were counted in the millions and with multiple cover variants issued to cash in on the popularity of McFarlane's name. Unfortunately, commercial success didn't automatically equate to critical acclaim for McFarlane's new venture, and many found the artist's attempts at writing to be clumsy, unsophisticated, and pretentious. This was perhaps unsurprising, given that McFarlane the artist was an experienced draftsman, whereas McFarlane the writer was just starting out.

Stories also became darker in tone than *Amazing Spider-Man* readers might have been used to. McFarlane pitted the hero against drug addicts, child abusers, and demonic killers, and the dark and often downbeat stories were seen by some as ill-fitting for a character who had traditionally been so light and airy.

The introduction to the collected edition of McFarlane's first story, "Torment," details some of the headaches that editor Jim Salicrup experienced in working with writer-artist Todd McFarlane. Compromises had to be made, including the enforcement of more costume changes (albeit minor alterations) across the entire line of other Spider-Man comics, limitations on the villains that McFarlane could use in his stories, and disagreement over how the role of Spider-Man's love interest, Mary Jane, should be handled. The letters' pages during McFarlane's run on *Spider-Man* show a surprising amount of public disagreement between Salicrup and McFarlane as they responded to their fans' missives. However, they also show McFarlane as a canny artist, with some of his comments showing real insight into the direction that the industry was taking.

The extreme, adult themes of one *Spider-Man* storyline, "Perceptions," which dealt with police corruption, child rape, and murder, led certain stores to stop stocking the series, and this generated further tension between McFarlane and his editorial superiors. In retrospect, it's perhaps surprising that Marvel let the artist get away with so much, but it's also surprising that McFarlane stayed around so long after his stint on *Amazing Spider-Man*. Any concerns that the artist might have had about not owning his work weren't really addressed by giving him his own solo title, as it was still a work-for-hire assignment on a company character. And it was becoming increasingly obvious that McFarlane had done about as much as he could with Spider-Man on a visual level.

The problems eventually came to a head just over a year into McFarlane's run on *Spider-Man*. After a couple of frankly disposable issues in which a black-suited Spider-Man aided a band of downtrodden, homeless mutants in a fight against Morbius, the living vampire—showing hints of the sort of direction in which McFarlane would later take *Spawn*—the cracks started to show. McFarlane was starting to require help in order to meet his art deadlines, and he missed an issue with #15. His final issue in the series, #16, is a poor testament to the contribution he made to the history of the Spider-Man character and is possibly the weakest of his entire run.

It's surely not the finale that McFarlane would have wanted, but clashes with the series' new editor Danny Fingeroth ensured that his position was soon untenable with Marvel, and he left the company under something of a cloud by forming a breakaway publisher with a group of other Marvel creators.

Taking a six-month hiatus from Marvel in August 1991 when his first daughter was born, McFarlane took the opportunity to form plans to start his own publishing company. Having grown frustrated with the limited creative

MCFARLANE'S SPAWN

When black ops soldier Al Simmons is sent to Hell for his bloody deeds, he becomes a pawn of the Dark Lord Malebolgia, who needs a soldier capable of leading Hell's army in the final battle against Heaven. Desperate to return to Earth to protect his family and take revenge on the friend who betrayed him, Simmons agrees to become Malebolgia's general. His scarred body is reanimated, and he returns to Earth as the grotesque but powerful Hellspawn (or Spawn), imbued with a hell-born energy that allows him to do virtually anything he can imagine. As Spawn regains memories and the principles of his former life, he begins using his powers against the forces of evil. Yet he is constantly plagued by his "guardian demon," and knows that once his mystic energy is depleted he must return to Hell to fulfill his bargain.

Spawn is a savage adolescent fantasy, equal parts sexy and gory. Todd McFarlane and the artists who followed him filled splash pages and double-page spreads with bravura art that did not leave much room for story. Even McFarlane has admitted that much of the success of the comic was probably attributable to his ability to draw Spawn's huge, flowing, and really cool-looking cape.

control afforded by mainstream comics publishers, he grew determined to create a company in which artists could hold greater influence over their characters.

Learning that several other prominent Marvel artists felt the same way, McFarlane—along with Jim Lee, Rob Liefeld, Jim Valentino, Erik Larsen, Marc Silvestri, and Whilce Portacio—formed Image Comics, a corporation that would publish books for each artist's individual comic book company. This gave each of the artists control over the destiny of their own characters, as well as allowed them to benefit financially from their creations, including when it came to licensing and merchandising.

McFarlane's signature creation was Spawn, a character who owed a certain debt to Spider-Man and Venom, even if it was based on a sketch that the artist had drawn back in his teenage years. A lithe, athletic, and muscular figure, the hero (whose alter ego was named after a baseball buddy from McFarlane's earlier life, Al Simmons) was encased in a black, shifting, liquid costume which, like Venom's costume, also happened to be alive, with white and red markings and big, white bug-eyes. The webbing of Spider-Man may have been replaced with heavy chains, but there was no denying the inspiration, even when the tone of the book was substantially darker.

Spawn #1 (1992) sold over a million copies, and the book remained a flagship Image title for some time to come. Image itself made waves in the comics industry with its emphasis on its creators' ownership of the series that they wrote and illustrated. The Image Comics ethos was a clear reaction against McFarlane's experiences with the Big Two, and he hammered his point home with the help of Dave Sim in *Spawn* #10, a story in which the hero encounters a prison full of recognizable Marvel and DC superheroes—including Spider-Man—in a clear attack on companies that have exploited characters without the involvement of the original creators.

IMPACT ON COMICS

Of all McFarlane's achievements, it was co-founding Image Comics that had the most profound effect on comics, proving that the stranglehold of DC and Marvel could be broken and that a more modern approach to creators' rights could be forged. It was for this reason that **Wizard Magazine** in May 2008 rated "The Launch of Image Comics" as the biggest event to rock the comics industry between 1991 and 2008.

However, McFarlane's long and as-yet-unresolved legal battle over the Miracleman/Marvelman character—to which McFarlane claims he bought the rights as part of a deal with Eclipse comics in 1996, despite opposition from comics luminaries including **Neil Gaiman**, who maintains that rights to the character were not part of the deal—has been used by some to argue that McFarlane isn't as respectful of creators' rights as he might claim.

Unfortunately, the innovations that McFarlane made in the field of creators' rights and the high sales generated by his output didn't always translate to artistic success, with his books' style-over-substance approach and emphasis on art over story feeding an industry trend that some would argue almost signaled the death-knell of the comics industry in the 1990s.

Nevertheless, when it comes to Spider-Man, McFarlane's bug-eyed, kooky approach has become one of the defining ways of depicting the character, a now-standard look that has been imitated by countless subsequent artists—including Erik Larsen, who followed McFarlane on *Amazing Spider-Man*. Most fans would agree that no one has ever pulled it off as effectively as McFarlane did.

McFarlane's other series such as *Spawn* still remain interesting from a historical point of view. However, their shallow excesses make for a difficult read in comparison to today's more sophisticated, writer-oriented comics, and McFarlane eventually became less and less involved with *Spawn* comics in any meaningful way, taking a more managerial than hands-on approach to Image's output as time passed, instead launching his own multimedia projects.

McFarlane lists his artistic influences as including comics artists John Byrne, George Perez, and Marshall Rogers, along with Michael Golden, Art Adams, and Walter Simonson. His influence can be felt on many artists of the 1990s and 2000s, particularly those who followed him on the *Spawn* title such as Greg Capullo and David Finch.

IMPACT ON AMERICAN CULTURE

The success of *Spawn* drove McFarlane to branch out into the toy market, resulting in an avalanche of *Spawn* action figures being released through the artist's own toy company that he formed in 1994. Intricately detailed and highly articulated, McFarlane's action figures—which eventually encompassed other characters, as well as real-life sports stars and personalities from the video game, film, and music industries—became well-loved and highly sought after by collectors.

Spawn was also adapted into a live-action movie in 1997, as well as an HBO animated series the same year. McFarlane won an Emmy and a Gold DiVi award for the HBO series and the *Spawn* motion picture DVD, respectively. He is working on a sequel to the live-action *Spawn* film that he claims has a darker tone than the original.

McFarlane has also worked in the music industry, helping create award-winning music videos for such groups as Korn and Pearl Jam. The "Freak on a Leash" music video from Korn's *Follow the Leader* album won a Grammy and two MTV Video Awards.

And in January 1999, McFarlane made one of his most infamous decisions by purchasing a baseball, Mark McGwire's 70th home run ball from the 1998 season, for a record $3 million.

However, McFarlane will probably be best remembered as one of the founders of Image Comics. A "David and Goliath" story still being discussed today, the launch of Image teaches us that creators can seize control of their own creations, can play an active role in managing the business of comics, and can find success without the backing of large corporations like Marvel and DC.

SUMMARY

Todd McFarlane remains a name that polarizes the comics industry. Some see him as the arrogant upstart artist who thought he was bigger than the iconic characters on which he was given his first big breaks in the late 1980s. Others praise him as the man who stood up to DC and Marvel and showed them that he could break away from them and compete with them on their terms, changing the face of creators' rights and challenging the industry with the creation of Image Comics, still Marvel and DC's closest competitor after 15 years. Others may even point to him as the very embodiment of the comics boom and subsequent bust of the 1990s, which almost led to the collapse of the market altogether.

Yet, regardless of these perceptions, there are some things about McFarlane that are impossible to deny: his work was and remains incredibly popular, and he used his talents to become one of the leading comic book creators of the decade, ultimately positioning himself at the head of an empire that still enjoys a healthy business producing comics, toys, animated features, and video games.

See also Hulk; Image Comics; Spider-Man

ESSENTIAL WORKS

McFarlane, Todd (w, p, i). "Questions." *Spawn* #1 (May 1992), Image Comics. Reprinted in *Spawn Origins Volume 1*, Image Comics, 2009.

McFarlane, Todd (w, p, i). "Torment: Part One." *Spider-Man* #1 (August 1990), Marvel Comics. Reprinted in *Spider-Man: Torment*, Marvel Comics, 2011.

Michelinie, David (w), and Todd McFarlane (p, i). "Venom." *Amazing Spider-Man* #300 (May 1988), Marvel Comics. Reprinted in *Spider-Man Legends Volume 1: Todd McFarlane*, Marvel Comics, 2001.

FURTHER READING

DeFalco, Tom. *Comics Creators on Spider-Man*. London: Titan Books, 2004.

Khoury, George. *Image Comics: The Road to Independence*. Raleigh: TwoMorrows Publishing, 2007.

"Todd McFarlane Complete Biography." Spawn.com, http://spawn.com/info/todd/bio.long.aspx. Accessed 31 July 2011.

Dave Wallace

Milestone Comics

Founded in 1993, Milestone Comics was an independent publisher of superhero comics with a specific focus on ethnically diverse characters, the most successful of which were the titular African American heroes of *Icon*, *Hardware*, and *Static*.

The Milestone line of superhero comics premiered in February 1993 with the launch of *Blood Syndicate*, *Icon*, *Hardware*, and *Static*. Milestone was founded and owned by four young African American creators, Dwayne McDuffie, Denys Cowan, Michael Davis, and Derek T. Dingle, with the express purpose of developing complex, ethnically diverse characters. All four of the founders had experience within the comic book and publishing industry—in particular McDuffie was a prolific and well-respected writer who had worked for both **Marvel** and **DC Comics**, and Cowan was a popular artist who had developed a strong fan following for his work at both of the major publishers. The Milestone founders believed that minorities had been underrepresented and/or misrepresented in the superhero genre, and the explicit goal of Milestone was to create an independent superhero universe that reflected the ethnic and racial diversity of the real world.

HISTORY

Emerging in the early 1990s amid a wave of creator-owned, independent comic book publishing enterprises, Milestone distinguished itself through a unique cooperative distribution agreement with DC Comics. According to the arrangement, Milestone remained an independently owned and controlled publisher whose series would be printed and distributed by DC. This corporate alignment represented a new business model between comic book publishers. A crucial aspect of the deal was that Milestone would not relinquish any of the legal or creative rights to their work. Milestone insisted on three basic points: (1) that they would retain total creative control, (2) that they would retain all copyrights for characters created under the Milestone banner, and (3) that they would have the final say on all merchandising and licensing deals pertaining to their properties (Brown, 2001, 29–31). The Milestone/ DC contract, which was finalized in May 1992, is comparable to the standard relationship between independent film production companies and major Hollywood studios. Much like large film studios who pay small independent production companies a creative service fee and a share of the royalties in exchange for the distribution rights of a movie, DC Comics in effect licensed the characters, editorial services, and creative content of the Milestone series for an annual fee of $500,000 to $650,000 and a share of the profits. In addition to printing and distributing the series, DC was also responsible for promoting the Milestone titles within the pages of their regular comics, in all marketing materials, at conventions, and in any other advertising materials. By entering into a partnership with DC, which is a subsidiary of the multimedia conglomerate Time-Warner, Milestone became an immediate presence in the comic book industry. Their titles were guaranteed to be produced and distributed on time, automatically appeared in all the major retail ordering catalogues, were granted better shelf space in comic specialty stores, and were made available in convenience, grocery, and regular book stores. DC also served as Milestone's licensing agent for other media and ancillary products and helped to arrange lucrative deals like Milestone trading cards and the *Static Shock* cartoon that aired on the WB Network from 2000 to 2004. The arrangement also meant that the Milestone characters were kept alive after the company officially folded in 1997 through occasional appearances in DC books, and most recently a select few have been integrated into the larger DC universe. Most notably, Dwayne McDuffie's 2008 to 2009 run as the writer for DC Comics flagship title *Justice League of America* saw most of Milestone's major characters introduced into mainstream continuity through a cross-over story arc. This paved the way for new Milestone-derived titles when DC Comics rebooted their entire catalogue of series in 2011.

Set primarily in the fictional city of Dakota, the Milestone universe centered on several superheroes of color following a chemical catastrophe known as "The Big Bang," which resulted in a range of characters developing superpowers. The four initial series, *Blood Syndicate*, *Icon*, *Hardware*, and *Static*, were later joined by *Xombi*, *Shadow Cabinet*, and *Kobalt*. Each of the series featured ethnically diverse characters within the traditional formula of superhero comics. The original four series, for example, were variations on conventional stories. *Hardware* followed the exploits of Curtis Metcalf, a brilliant African American scientist and inventor who developed a powerful mechanized suit (much like Marvel's **Iron Man**) that allows him to fight crime and wage a war against his corporate employer's evil empire. *Blood Syndicate* was a variation on the classic superteam type of story that saw a superpowered street gang band together to protect their turf and ultimately deal with larger-scale threats. *Icon* was Milestone's flagship title about Augustus Freeman, an alien who crash-lands in America in the era of slavery and eventually assumes

COVER STORY

When issue #25 of Milestone's most popular series, *Static*, appeared on comics stands in 1995, the cover art was only partially visible through a heart-shaped hole in an otherwise all-black shield. This special anniversary issue featured a storyline that involved the high-school-aged Virgil (Static) Hawkins losing his virginity with his steady girlfriend Daisy. The cover art, by Zina Saunders, depicted a tender moment of Virgil and Daisy kissing on a couch. Scattered around the room was Virgil's Static mask, a strip of condoms, and a sex manual. Despite the autonomy granted to Milestone in their contract with DC Comics, DC insisted on enforcing their rule of not depicting sex on the cover of comic books. The partially censoring cover panel was an awkward compromise between the two publishers. Ironically this contentious portrayal of sex in *Static* is generally regarded as one of the most responsible and sensitive treatments of the topic in comics. For an industry that routinely depicts seminude men and women posed erotically and beating each other up on the cover of their books, drawing the line at an image of two committed individuals intending to practice safe sex seems an odd choice.

the persona of Icon, a **Superman**-like character, when a teenage girl, Raquel Ervin, challenges him to stand up as a symbol for African Americans. Raquel also takes on the role of Rocket, Icon's sidekick, and serves as his political conscience. Raquel is also notable for her eventual teenage pregnancy that allowed the book to delve into uncharted social issues within a comic book. And Milestone's most popular series, *Static*, followed the exploits of Virgil Hawkins, a wise-cracking teenager who discovers he has electrical powers and sets out to fight crime like his favorite comic book heroes while he also struggles with the challenges of adolescent life from bullies to first loves to, in a particularly controversial storyline, losing his virginity. By placing African American heroes at the forefront of conventional superhero stories, Milestone was able to not just present an array of ethnically diverse heroes and role models, but also to question the traditionally WASPish realm of superheroics and earlier misguided attempts to construct heroes of color that had been firmly rooted in racial stereotypes.

Unfortunately, Milestone Media, Inc. fell victim to industry changes and economic fluctuations in the market and, like many other small, creator-owned publishers, had to close their doors in 1997. The glut of new comics publishers that came to prominence in the mid-1990s (e.g., **Image**, Broadway, Penthouse) flooded the market with series that were generally regarded as having inferior stories, derivative characters, and undependable delivery schedules. Milestone had always struggled to distinguish itself from the other publishers, but ultimately failed to secure a strong enough presence to avoid the economic implosion that occurred when the comics bubble burst.

IMPACT ON COMICS

All of the Milestone titles sought to balance traditional superhero stories with real-world issues and concerns. Like most superhero stories, the Milestone characters had to routinely battle supervillains and alien invaders. But unlike most mainstream superhero series, the Milestone stories also incorporated themes of systemic racism, economic and political disenfranchisement, and gang warfare. The structure of Milestone's flagship title, *Icon*, allowed the series to function as a commentary on America's history of racial problems in general, and the comics industry's reliance on ethnic stereotyping in particular. Through flashbacks readers learned that Augustus Freeman, the alien who would become the hero Icon, was raised in the American South during slavery and eventually had a personal share of many major African American experiences from the Civil War to civil rights, and a variety of political perspectives from being an American expatriate living in Paris to being a wealthy Republican during the Reagan era.

Within *Icon*, Milestone also introduced a 1970s-style blaxploitation hero, Buck Wild, complete with a huge Afro and cheesy ghetto exclamations, as a means to critique the earlier stereotype of African American heroes in comics. When Buck Wild dies in *Icon* #30, Icon himself delivers a eulogy that succinctly summarizes the complex history of blaxploitation stereotypes in comics:

> Years before I arrived, Buck Wild was already there, fighting the good fight. Although we may, from our current perspective, have found him crude and ill-informed, we cannot deny his importance. Intentions count as much as actions. And Buck was nothing if not well-intentioned. He spent his life fighting for what is right, all the while struggling with questions of identity and public perception that we still do not have answers for. He reinvented himself time and again, searching for a comfortable way to present himself to the world. And while we winced on occasion at his embarrassing speech and demeaning behavior, more often we cheered him on. . . . Because whatever else he was, he was always a hero. A hero for those of us who had no heroes. Were it not for him, we wouldn't be here today. . . . And for all his failures, he died as he lived, trying to do what was right. Let us hope that when our day is done, history remembers us as kindly as it remembers him. (McDuffie 1995, 6–7)

In one well-written and self-referential speech, the Milestone agenda of celebrating a balance of ethnic diversity and advancement, remembering and reconsidering past stereotypes, and calling for a new era of ethnic heroes is made clear.

IMPACT ON AMERICAN CULTURE

Milestone's unique relationship with DC Comics has meant that their characters still remain viable properties for DC and their parent corporation Time-Warner. And the racial barriers that Milestone challenged helped establish the market potential for ethnically diverse characters that have become far more prevalent in recent years at the two major companies, DC and Marvel. Similarly, the Milestone titles helped to attract a far more diverse audience to comics that continue to celebrate the diversity pioneered by Milestone through various online communities. Founding partner Dwayne McDuffie, in particular, who continued his prolific work as a writer of superhero fiction for animated television series such as *Justice League Unlimited* and *Teen Titans* and in comics with an award-winning run on the series *Justice League of America*, helped keep the inclusive spirit of Milestone alive long after the company folded. When McDuffie suddenly passed away in 2011, the numerous media tributes and celebrations of his career that appeared far beyond just the narrow confines of the comic book publishing world served as a testament to the profound and lasting influence of the Milestone agenda of multicultural superheroes.

SUMMARY

Milestone's unique identity as a mainstream African American comic book publisher brought a great deal of media attention to their titles. Feature stories about the company in magazines like *Black Enterprise* and *Ebony* in particular helped draw new readers to the medium from a larger cultural background and to highlight the traditional lack of diversity in comics. The short-lived success of Milestone changed the industry's perspective on ethnicity in the superhero genre and helped pave the way for future characters of color. Many fans also credit Milestone's emphasis on racially diverse heroes as instigating a larger array of new ethnically identified characters at both DC Comics and Marvel, and as inspiring a less stereotypical approach to long-existing characters such as Marvel's Luke Cage and Black Panther. Most recently several of the Milestone characters have reemerged within the pages of DC Comics' *Justice League of America* and *The Brave and the Bold*. The groundbreaking ethnic focus of the Milestone characters and their enduring popularity with fans made it almost a forgone conclusion that at least a few of them would return to print. Significantly, the 2011 relaunch of the entire DC

Universe included the integration of Milestone's fictional Dakota, with Static receiving his own new ongoing series *Static Shock*. Despite Milestone's short, five-year existence the company and its characters made an indelible mark on the business and the fantasy of superhero comics.

See also Black Panther; DC Comics

ESSENTIAL WORKS

McDuffie, Dwayne, and M. D. Bright. *Icon: A Hero's Welcome*. New York: DC Comics, 2009.
McDuffie, Dwayne, and Denys Cowan. *Hardware: The Man in the Machine*. New York: DC Comics, 2009.
McDuffie, Dwayne, and Robert Washington. *Static Shock: Trial by Fire*. New York: DC Comics, 2000.

FURTHER READING

Brown, Jeffrey A. *Black Superheroes, Milestone Comics, and Their Fans*. Jackson: University of Mississippi Press, 2001.
Singer, Marc. "'Black Skins' and White Masks: Comic Books and the Secrets of Race." *African American Review* 36 (2002): 107–19.

Jeffrey A. Brown

Miller, Frank

Frank Miller is a prolific American comic book writer and artist whose graphic novels have had a significant impact on the comics industry. He is best known for his dark stories that deal with themes of violence, death, destruction, and the pointlessness of life. The culmination of work created throughout his legendary career has transcended comic books into popular movies, whether that be in direct adaptation of his works such as *300* or his influence upon the *Batman* franchise.

HISTORY

Frank Miller was born in Olney, Maryland, on January 27, 1957. He grew up in Montpelier, Vermont, with six brothers and sisters (George 2003, 72). Miller's parents valued discipline and hard work. His mother, a nurse, juggled working a night shift and raising seven children. Despite a comfortable, middle-class upbringing, Miller never felt that he belonged (George 2003, 15).

Miller's artistic life began at a very young age, even though he was not born into an artistic family. In fact, he recalls completing his first comic book at age six, which he gave to his mother. Growing up, Miller knew without question that he wanted to become a comic book artist. He read comics like *Superboy* and *Amazing Spider-Man*, and admired artists like **Jack Kirby**. By age 15, Miller's interest in comics waned though he continued to draw. Miller never received any formal training in art, and he attributed his learning to reading and working in the field. He took a job as a receptionist at an art gallery featuring the work of Thomas Wood, but claims it had no influence on his artistic life. He would later admit, though, that he explored other artists and approaches and tried to absorb those styles (George 2003, 16).

Miller's career began in New York in 1978, with freelance contributions as a penciller to Gold Key's *The Twilight Zone*. Miller eked out a living, as he also began drawing for major companies like **DC Comics** and **Marvel Comics**,

(AP Photo/Joel Ryan)

working as an artist for DC anthologies and Marvel titles like *Spectacular Spider-Man* and *John Carter: Warlord of Mars* (Lambiek 2007).

Miller's big break came in 1979 when he was chosen to take over art chores on *Daredevil* from Gene Colan. *Daredevil* began its run in 1964 with creators **Stan Lee** and Bill Everett. Daredevil's alter ego is Matt Murdock, a New York lawyer who is struck blind in a freak childhood accident that leaves him with preternaturally heightened senses, including a "radar sense" that helps him perceive the world around him. Following the murder of his father by gangsters, Murdock becomes obsessed with justice. Though the title had run more than 15 years, it was not one of Marvel's top tier books, but Miller would change all of that.

After drawing 10 issues of the adventures of Matt Murdock, blind lawyer by day and radar-augmented hero by night, Miller assumed writing duties as well, developing his own style akin to the film noir of cinema (Lambiek 2007). His approach proved to be quite popular, to the point that it was often parodied, most successfully by Kevin Eastman and Peter Laird, whose *Teenage Mutant Ninja Turtles* referenced many of the tropes in Miller's *Daredevil* run. During this run, Miller created the popular character of Elektra, the remorseless assassin who had a romantic past with Daredevil. In addition to Daredevil and Elektra projects, Miller worked on a project involving the character **Wolverine** at this time, providing art for the fan-favorite X-Man's first limited series.

In 1983, Miller created his first graphic novel, *Ronin*, for DC. Heavily influenced by Japanese manga, *Ronin* helped secure Miller's credentials as an emerging force in the industry. It is notable for its experimentation with comic form and the fact that it was published as a creator-owned comic, one of the first for DC, who traditionally claimed copyright over any series it published. In 1986, DC also published Miller's seminal work, *Batman: The Dark Knight Returns*. Miller redefined the legendary character and "introduced more adult-oriented storytelling to superhero comics" (Lambiek 2007, para. 4). The tale focused on an aging Batman, who comes out of retirement to resume his war on crime. The *Dark Knight*, along with **Alan Moore** and Dave Gibbon's **Watchmen**, would signal a turn toward innovation in the superhero genre in particular and the overall comic book industry. These works transformed comics by proving that illustrated tales of men in tights could rise to the level of serious, adult art.

After crafting a new origin tale for the Caped Crusader in *Batman: Year One* (1987), Miller signed on with **Dark Horse Comics** to work collaboratively with other artists, mostly as a writer. He also began a short stint in Hollywood as a scriptwriter around the same time, contributing scripts to *Robocop 2* (1990) and *Robocop 3* (1993). Both projects had strong ties to the *Robocop* comics he previously penned. Unfortunately, Hollywood proved very frustrating for Miller. Unhappy with the outcome of the *Robocop* films, he returned to writing graphic novels and vowed not to allow anyone to adapt one of his stories to film ever again.

Miller began working on his famous crime noir series, *Sin City*, in 1993 (Lambiek 2007, para. 6). Now working under his own Legend imprint for Dark Horse, Miller had a newfound level of freedom that provided him the opportunity to finally do what he loved. *Sin City*, produced in black and white, featured extremely high contrasts and stark backgrounds to tell its story. Influenced by expressionist film and by other artists, like **Will Eisner**, who brought expressionism into comics, Miller tried to create more of a psychological presence in this and other works (George 2003, 23). Miller and his wife, colorist Lynn Varley, published *300* in 1998. *300* is stylized very similarly to *Sin City*, but with the addition of color. Still, *300* featured *Sin City*-like high contrast levels and powerful silhouettes. Also like *Sin City*, *300* proved popular in print and on film.

In 2005, Lynn Varley divorced Frank Miller. The two did not have any children. Coming off the success of the *300* movie, Miller continued to write and draw, especially the *Sin City* series. In 2011, he produced the controversial graphic novel *Holy Terror*, which featured a Batman stand-in doling out violent justice to terrorists of Middle Eastern origin. Miller was unapologetic for his politically incorrect depiction, another in a string of commentaries that mark him as one of the most opinionated and controversial figures in the industry.

IMPACT ON COMICS

Miller combines several artistic elements including line, light sourcing, illumination, and shadows. Also on display is Miller's masterful use of negative space to create silhouettes, which he would employ throughout his career. Because of printing limitations, especially during Miller's early years as a comic book artist, much of his published work does not appear extremely detailed. He learned to remove details that could potentially take away from the overall message, especially considering a lot of his work would be vividly colored in by a separate artist. According to Miller, he has worked on making his drawings serve the purpose of telling the story, instead of using details that might obscure it (George 2003, 19).

Miller is an important creator because of how he experimented with the form. His work follows in Will Eisner's legendary footsteps with the way he uses the page as a unit of composition. Like Eisner, Bernie Krigstein, and a few others, he translates cinematic techniques into the comic book art form. Creators such as Eisner may have brought film noir style to the comics page much earlier, but Miller revitalized the style first in *Daredevil* and then in *Sin City*. Also, he has developed a minimalist style of stark black-and-white composition that seems to be influenced both by woodcut novelists like Franz Masereel and Lynd Ward and the dramatic silhouettes of newspaper cartoonist Milton Caniff.

Miller also played a role in introducing American audiences to manga. Themes and characters in both his runs on *Daredevil* and his creator-owned *Ronin* were heavily influenced by Japanese comics. When First Comics began to reprint Kazuo Koike and Goseki Kojima's *Lone Wolf and Cub* in translation in 1987, Miller provided the covers for the American editions, using his cachet to help bring a curious audience to a style of comics storytelling that has gone on to become one of the most visible areas of growth in the medium in the last several decades.

IMPACT ON AMERICAN CULTURE

Frank Miller is clearly one of the top writers and artists of the superhero genre of comics and graphic novels. His work has spawned a renewed interest in superheroes, not just in the comics industry, but also in films. Certainly, his 1986 contribution of *Batman: The Dark Knight Returns* helped contribute to a wider cultural appreciation for comics as an artform, as it, along with **Art Spiegelman**'s *Maus* and Alan Moore and Dave Gibbons's *Watchmen,* became hallmark works in the maturation of the medium. The approach to Batman laid out by Miller in *The Dark Knight Returns* influenced the launch of Tim

ELEKTRA

Frank Miller created Elektra as a femme fatale to confront Daredevil. Debuting in *Daredevil* #168 (1981), she is revealed to be the college sweetheart of Daredevil's alter ego, Matt Murdock. But the trauma of watching her father killed before her eyes drove her out of Matt's loving embrace and towards the life of a professional assassin. At the end of Elektra's inaugural story arc, Miller killed off the character, having rival assassin Bullseye run her through with one of her own weapons, a three-pronged knife called a sai. However, the red-garbed ninja proved to be too popular to kill off for long, and Miller resurrected her later. Elektra would go on to become one of Marvel's marquee female characters, including appearing in a pair of ongoing series, numerous miniseries, and starring in 2003's *Daredevil* feature film and 2005's *Elektra*, as portrayed by Jennifer Garner.

Matthew J. Smith

Burton's *Batman* (1989) film franchise and its subsequent revitalization a generation later when Christopher Nolan launched his trilogy with *Batman Begins* (2005). That film specifically borrows a number of concepts directly from Miller's *Batman: Year One*.

Films based on Miller's works have become iconic in their own right. Miller's decade-long discontent with Hollywood faded when director Robert Rodriguez presented a short film based on Miller's *Sin City*. Undeniably impressed, Miller approved a full-length film, which was released in April 2005. *Sin City* was extremely successful on many levels, furthering Miller's already brilliant career and paving the way for more successful adaptations.

Sin City adapted three of Frank Miller's *Sin City* graphic novels: the original first book, now subtitled *The Hard Goodbye*, along with *That Yellow Bastard* and *The Big Fat Kill*. The setting is something like the Gotham City that Miller created in *Batman: Year One*, only more disturbing. The city is ruled over by a wealthy and corrupt family that uses the police force as its own private army. Rodriguez meticulously reproduced Miller's static image-framing choices to the point that he actually insisted that Miller take a co-directing credit on the film. When the Directors Guild of America told Rodriguez he could not do that, he resigned from the guild, and did it anyway. As critic John Scalzi (1995) notes, he was right to do so. Miller turns out to be absolutely critical to this film, both as a writer and as a visual stylist. Until *Sin City*, no film has ever managed to carry over the feel of a graphic novel as completely as this film does or made it act in the service of the film medium as effectively.

The plot follows a *Pulp Fiction*–style multiple storyline. In one narrative, lowlife Marv, perfectly acted by occasional real-life lowlife Mickey Rourke, seeks revenge for the death of prostitute Goldie, who showed him kindness. In another, aging cop Hartigan, played by an aging Bruce Willis, is unwilling to let a senator's pedophile son continue unimpeded in his wickedness, regardless of the consequences. Another tale has death row escapee Clive Owen aiding an exceptionally well-armed brothel in covering up the death of a dirty cop, while fighting IRA mercenaries. This entirely unbelievable pastiche could only come from the pages of a comic book. But Rodriguez and Miller do one better—they transform celluloid into a moving, living, breathing, and, above all, bleeding incarnation of the ink and words much beloved by adolescents everywhere.

Miller's next iconic film contribution, *300* (2006), is a blood-dark account of the ancient battle of Thermopylae. Greece in the 5th century B.C. is a land truly favored by the gods, bathed in rich, harmonious dark chocolate, beige, and gray colors. The film's hero, King Leonidas (Gerard Butler), has lived his entire life to fight this battle against the Persians. Messengers from the Persian army arrive in Sparta, arrogantly offering either capitulation or annihilation. Leonidas kills the messengers. But political opportunism rules the Spartan council, which insists that Leonidas consult the Oracle. The Oracle refuses to release the Spartan army to its ruler as no battle can occur during an upcoming religious celebration. So Leonidas has little choice but to venture forth with 300 of his best warriors as "bodyguards." He chooses to engage the Persians in the Thermopylae pass, a narrow corridor between the steep cliffs of the Aegean Sea. Here the vast numbers of the enemy count for little since only a few can go up against Sparta's best at any one time. A succession of charges by Persian forces—everyone from slave warriors to an elite guard called the Immortals—is slaughtered by the 300. At this point, Xerxes (Rodrigo Santoro) appears, a bejeweled, depraved giant carried on a high tower by his slaves. The god-king tries unsuccessfully to seduce Leonidas in a homoerotic passage as the ancient world stands still. But it is a deformed and pathetic creature, Ephialtes (Andrew Tiernan), an outcast Spartan, who betrays the 300 by showing Xerxes a hidden path leading behind Spartan lines. Ephialtes' betrayal dooms the 300, but they die "beautiful deaths."

300 grossed nearly $130 million in its first ten days of release, and a great deal of its success is due to its graphic novel creator, Frank Miller. Though Miller did not direct *300*, director Zach Snyder reportedly made a creative decision: he asked himself, what would Frank do? Thus, *300* is slavishly faithful to Miller's 1999 comic book. For example, in adapting Miller's take on

Spartan battle gear, Snyder and costume designer Michael Wilkinson strip the warriors down to essentials: a helmet, shield, red capes, loin cloths and sandals in warm colors. All the rest is highly masculine flesh. The Persians, by contrast, are dressed in all sorts of jewels, peacock blue, gold, purple, black— a pastiche of exotic, foreign, and decadent costumes.

300 also tells the Thermopylae story without a trace of irony. The movie depicts Sparta and the Spartans in all their proud, martial, vicious, nasty, unsentimental, and egalitarian glory. In addition, Snyder clearly portrays the Spartans as "the good guys." The Spartans are believers in human freedom who oppose the Persians because the Persians demand nothing but submission to a false god-king. In other words, recounting the story of Thermopylae is tantamount to telling a story of Western civilization taking a stand against rampaging Eastern barbarians.

Frank Miller finally stepped into the role of solo directing with *The Spirit* (2008), based on the urban crime-fighter created by Miller's mentor and comic book innovator Will Eisner in 1940. Despite Miller's style keeping in step with the winning formula of *Sin City* and *300* and the participation in the project of big-name stars like Samuel L. Jackson, the film proved to be a critical and commercial failure. While this filmmaking experience may have cast some doubt on Miller's abilities to operate in Hollywood mode, it has certainly not spoiled the impression he has made on American culture.

SUMMARY

Frank Miller has become an iconic creator because of his distinctively hard-boiled approach to comics. His tough guys are able to endure harm that would humble any ordinary man. They are enveloped in violent worlds that demand violent responses to murderous threats. The settings are dark, urban jungles where one must keep moving to keep alive. Heavy shadows punctuate a world where there are black and white, literally on the page and figuratively in the virtues of his characters. Presiding over this dystopian vision is Miller: artist, storyteller, icon.

See also Batman; DC Comics; Marvel Comics; Teenage Mutant Ninja Turtles

ESSENTIAL WORKS

Miller, Frank (w, a). *Frank Miller's Sin City: The Hard Goodbye*. Milwaukie, OR: Dark Horse, 2005.

Miller, Frank (w, p), Klaus Janson (i), and Lynn Varley. *Batman: The Dark Knight Returns*. New York: DC Comics, 1986.

FURTHER READING

Eisner, Will, and Frank Miller. *Eisner/Miller*. Milwaukie, OR: Dark Horse, 2005.
George, Milo. *The Comics Journal Library, Volume Two: Frank Miller*. Seattle: Fanta-
    graphics Books, Inc., 2003.

Rod Carveth

MLJ/Archie

Other than devoted, long-time comic book historians and collectors, few Americans realize one of their most revered humorous pop cultural icons, **Archie Andrews**, originated from an obscure company that was primarily interested in shoot-'em-up pulp magazines and superhero comics. In fact, it is difficult to imagine how any reader in 1941 could have connected an Andy Hardy/Henry Aldrich–type fabulous teen success story with Louis Silberkleit's Columbia Publications pulp firm and with the related MLJ Comics, founded in 1939 by Silberkleit and two business partners, John Goldwater and Maurice Coyne. In retrospect, the stunning success and iconic nature of Archie and his extensive retinue could not have come from more unlikely origins.

HISTORY

Columbia Publications published numerous pulp and (later) digest magazines for more than a quarter century until 1960, when Silberkleit's firm abruptly abandoned magazine fiction in favor of expanding what had become a remarkably successful comic book line under the Archie Series label. It is fair to say that of the 10 major pulp magazine publishers pumping out fiction at various times during Columbia's 1934–1960 existence, collectors generally find Columbia the least memorable, in contrast to the success of the Archie Series comics. The pulp company—often referred to as "Double-Action" or "Blue Ribbon" because of cover logos—almost never had collectible cover artists or long-running series characters.

In fact, just as Archie was unassumingly introduced in a six-page backup story in *Pep Comics* #22 (1941), Columbia had its only fling with a genuine pulp hero—the Black Hood, who originated in MLJ Comics in 1940. He appeared in three now extremely rare pulp magazines late in 1941 and early in 1942 before retreating back to the Golden Age comic books. MLJ, though, had dozens of heroic characters in its early comics of 1939–1942 vintage. They just were not destined for anywhere near the success of Archie Andrews and his female friends, Betty Cooper and Veronica Lodge.

(The Digital Comic Museum)

Archie, of course, was far from unique during his early years. He had dozens of competitors through the 1950s, but very little in the way of successful commercial competition after that. Patsy Walker, a female protagonist in the wacky Archie manner, debuted three years later, in **Marvel**/Timely's *Miss America Comics* #2 (1944). At about the same time, National Comics (**DC**) brought forth its first teen strip, *Buzzy*, which was obviously designed to capitalize on the growing popularity of Archie.

Archie even had competition within his own publisher's ranks. In fact, MLJ debuted Wilbur Wilkin, similar to Archie, three months earlier in *Zip Comics* #18 (1941), and created female doppelganger Ginger Snapp in *Zip Comics* #35 (1943). Ginger remained primarily a backup strip, but Wilbur's original incarnation enjoyed a moderately successful 87-issue run of his own title from 1944 to 1959. Unlike the creations from National Comics (DC), Fawcett Publications, and Martin Goodman's Marvel/Timely Comics, the MLJ superheroes and other "serious" characters were just successful enough to keep the firm alive long enough to see the Archie characters develop into what would become a multimillion-dollar property.

MLJ stood for the initials of founders Maurice Coyne, Louis Silberkleit, and John Goldwater, who went on to become one of the most important figures in the comic book industry as the primary creator of Archie along with cartoonist Bob Montana. Most of the significant pulp publishers—with the notable exceptions of Popular Publications and Munsey Publications—eagerly jumped into the comic book field when they saw how successful National Comics became with **Superman**, who debuted in *Action Comics* #1 (1938) and **Batman**, who first appeared in *Detective Comics* #27 (1939). Columbia/MLJ was no exception. The firm's first comic book was *Blue Ribbon Comics* #1 (1939), quickly followed by *Top-Notch Comics* #1 (1939), *Pep Comics* #1 (1940), and *Zip Comics* #1 (1940). All four titles were heavily promoted in 1940 in the Columbia pulps, since there was a certain degree of crossover interest. Teenagers often read pulp magazines, and adults, particularly members of the military, occasionally would pick up comic books. The publisher surely knew this, or there would have been no reason to promote the new comic book line in the pulps.

Blue Ribbon Comics #1 was named after Columbia's *Blue Ribbon Western* and *Blue Ribbon Sports* pulp titles. Early on, Blue Ribbon was not really a superhero comic, although two little-known superheroes soon appeared in backup stories, Bob Phantom in #2 (1939) and the Fox in #4 (1940). *Blue Ribbon* #4 appeared a full five months after #3 (1940), a timeline hiccup that was common in several of Silberkleit's pulp titles. *Blue Ribbon*'s early cover features were Rang-A-Tang the Wonder Dog in #1–#2 and #6–#8 and Corporal Collins in #3–#5. This would not have surprised any readers at the time; in November 1939 the only superheroes with their own titles were National's Superman and Centaur's short-lived Amazing Man, although other eponymous superhero titles would soon appear.

The Goldwater-guided editorial crew, however, apparently realized that features like Rang-A-Tang and Corporal Collins would seem pedestrian on covers in contrast with early Golden Age superheroes such as Blue Beetle, Green Mask, Black Terror, the **Flash**, Human Torch, and **Green Lantern**, to name only a few of the dozens that sprang forth in the wake of Batman's success. Thus, even though Rang-A-Tang and Corporal Collins held their own features in *Blue Ribbon Comics* through the end of the title's run with #22 (1942), the covers were soon given over to the supernatural hero Mr. Justice, who debuted in #9 (1941), and the **Captain America** knockoff Captain Flag, who took charge in #16 (1941). Another superhero, the Inferno, ran in #13–#22, making *Blue Ribbon* a genuine Golden Age superhero anthology for a brief time and giving those issues a special cachet with collectors and historians.

In contrast, *Top-Notch Comics* began with a little-remembered superhero feature, the Wizard, who continued throughout the title's run through #27 (1942). The Wizard acquired a costumed aide, Roy the Super Boy, in #8 (1940), not long after **Robin** the Boy Wonder joined Batman in *Detective Comics* #38

(1940). If you detect a bit of copycat syndrome here, you would be right. *Top-Notch*'s best-remembered feature, the Black Hood, debuted in #9 (1940) as the cover feature and held the cover spot through #27 along with 13- and 14-page features, which were among the meatiest ever offered by MLJ. The Black Hood ultimately lasted longer than any MLJ superhero except the Shield.

You get an idea how quickly MLJ abandoned most of its superheroes by the way the firm converted *Top-Notch Comics* into a largely humorous title called *Top-Notch Laugh Comics* with #28 (1942), making it the first title from a successful Golden Age publisher to convert from heroes to humor. However, MLJ did retain the Black Hood in shortened strips through the end of the title's run with #45 (1944). The title became *Laugh Comix* for #46–#48 and then emerged as *Suzie* with #49 (1945), which ran through #100 (1954). Suzie, who debuted in *Top-Notch Laugh* #28, was one of the first working-girl strips originally created for comic books, as opposed to the many such characters in comic strips.

Pep Comics and *Zip Comics* were considerably more successful among MLJ's "Big Four," in large part because the two titles had far stronger and more colorful cover superhero features in the Shield and Steel Sterling, respectively. *Pep Comics* #1 has always enjoyed the distinction of being the home of the first flag-costumed, patriotic superhero in comics, the Shield, who was given a kid partner, Dusty the Boy Detective, in #11 (1941)—two months before the appearance of *Captain America Comics* #1 (1941), by far the most heralded of all patriotic hero comics, and his kid sidekick Bucky, who debuted along with Cap. It seems likely that the sidekick craze of the early Golden Age was spurred by Batman's partner, Robin, particularly since *Detective Comics* had one of the highest circulations of any Golden Age title and all competitors surely saw this landmark title.

The Shield also boasts another distinction—he was the only MLJ superhero to survive well into the Archie era. The Shield and Dusty ran continuously until they last appeared in *Pep* #65 (1948), although they permanently gave up their cover-featured status with #49 (1944). In fact, the Shield was the only nonhumor feature in *Pep* beginning with #61 (1947), when the title went bimonthly after two full years of quarterly status. Archie Publications assumed there was enough historical interest in the Shield that they introduced a reprint volume of the first 10 *Pep* stories in 2002. The Shield, under a different identity and different origin, was even Archie's first Golden Age revival at the dawn of the Silver Age, with the two-issue run of the awkwardly titled "Double Life of Private Strong" in 1959, conveying the adventures of the supergenius Lancelot Strong, a.k.a. the Shield.

Pep Comics also has the distinction of publishing the first superhero death in comics, that of the Comet in #17 (1941), and the superhero "birth" of his brother, the Hangman, in the same issue. During the dawning of serious comic book collecting in the 1960s, some comic book hunter-gatherers were more intrigued by *Pep* #17 than they were by *Pep* #22 (1941)—long since immortalized as the debut of Archie.

Zip #1 introduced one of MLJ's most dynamic heroes, the colorfully named Steel Sterling, and he was featured until the end of *Zip*'s run with #47 (1944). Steel Sterling and the Black Hood, who briefly had his own title, clearly rank as two of MLJ's top three characters along with the Shield. *Zip* featured two other colorful heroes, Black Jack in #20–#35, and the Web in #27–#38. But they, along with most of MLJ's superheroes, were gone by the end of 1943. Collectors shudder when they realize that MLJ experimented with a rather silly costumed hero, the Red Rube, in #39 (1943) through #47. It is noteworthy that the Red Rube was one of the few costumed heroes not revived by the firm during the mid-1960s superhero craze, then again under various imprints in the 1980s and 1990s.

MLJ tried a superhero anthology titled *Jackpot Comics* on a quarterly basis from #1 (1941) through #9 (1943), featuring Steel Sterling, Black Hood, Mr. Justice, and the military strip Sergeant Boyle in all issues. But there was a backup interloper beginning in #4 (1941–1942)—Archie! Indeed, the story in #4 is apparently the second or third Archie story to hit the stands in the wake of his introduction in *Pep* #22. But, in a dismaying portent for fans of superhero strips, *Jackpot* became the all-humorous *Jolly Jingle Comics* with #10. Before the *Jackpot* experiment, though, MLJ produced the sporadically published *Shield-Wizard Comics* #1 (1940) through #13 (1944), which featured the eponymous heroes and their sidekicks. MLJ also published *Special Comics* #1 (1941–1942) before converting the title to *Hangman Comics* with #2 (1942) through #8 (1943). The title then became *Black Hood Comics* with #9 (1943–1944) through #19 (1946), published on a quarterly basis. Just as *Top Notch Comics* was converted from a superhero title to a humor title in 1942, Black Hood's title became another home for Archie's gang with the transition to *Laugh Comics* #20 (1946). MLJ was the first successful comic book publisher to abandon the vast majority of its superheroes en masse in favor of humorous strips led by the Archie gang.

The MLJ logo disappeared forever following *Archie* #18 (1946). *Archie* #19 (1946) bore the logo "An Archie Magazine." Likewise, "An Archie Magazine" was first bannered on *Black Hood* #17 (1945–46) and *Pep* #56 (1946). This is noteworthy since Archie was not yet anywhere near the iconic figure he became while appearing in more than 400 issues of various titles from Archie Magazines in the 1950s. MLJ/Archie, in fact, produced only 27 comic books with 1946 dates, according to the issue-by-issue database established by noted comics historian Dan Stevenson. Of these 27 issues, Archie and his retinue appeared in only 12 issues—*Archie* #18–#23, *Pep* #56–#59 and *Laugh* #20–#21. Goldwater and Co. clearly envisioned Archie as the firm's flagship character by 1946, but wartime paper issues and other financial concerns still constricted Archie's soon-to-become explosive growth.

GINGER

A little more than a year after Archie Andrews appeared from MLJ Comics, the firm created perhaps the first wacky teenage girl in a six-page backup strip in *Zip Comics* #35 (1943). Yet who remembers Ginger Snapp? Archie has appeared in more than 7,000 issues, but Ginger was an Archie series backup except for 10 seldom-seen issues of her own title in 1951–1954.

Ginger's primary beaus were named Tommy and Ickky. That is right, Ickky! The colorless guys who sought Ginger's affection were not nearly as interesting as the two gorgeous girls competing for Archie's affection. In fact, Ginger was so little known, even during her "prime," that publisher L. B. Cole's Star Publications came up with their own Ginger Snapp in four issues of *School Day Romances* in 1949–1950 until, apparently, the Archie Series editors objected.

Ginger was the first comic book teen girl (not comic strip teen femme) and may have been inspired by the success of radio's Judy Foster in *A Date with Judy*. Ginger debuted the year before the far more successful creations of Timely's *Patsy Walker* and Quality's *Candy*. Suzie, a loony backup character in MLJ's *Top-Notch Laugh Comics*, was successful enough to convince MLJ's editors to change the title to *Suzie Comics* with #49 (1945). Ginger, orphaned when *Zip Comics* was discontinued in 1944, became a backup strip in *Suzie Comics*. In 1951, Archie Publications began publishing Ginger in her own title. She appeared essentially quarterly until the title ended with #10 in 1954, thus relegating Ginger to backup status again.

Ginger was a kind redhead, though definitely an opportunist. On the cover of *Ginger* #4 (1952) she says, "No, Biff, I'm not going to the prom with you— I'm going with Ickky because he's such a gentleman, so noble, so sweet" and in a thought bubble, she continues, "and because he just got a new, sleek, red convertible!"

Ginger's stories were nonetheless often truly funny. For example, in "Saved by the Belle" in #1, a burly fellow named Monk bullies Ickky into staying away from Ginger. She gains revenge and defends Ickky's pride by forcing Monk to pony up outrageous bucks for a date, causing Monk to relinquish Ginger to Ickky. "She's expensive! She thinks I'm the Marshall Plan!" Monk says to the nerd. In "The Love Seat" in *Ginger* #3 (1952) Monk and Ickky inadvertently kiss in the dark when they think the other is Ginger after the power has failed. It is doubtful the Comics Code Authority, established shortly after Ginger's title was discontinued in 1954, would have approved these shenanigans!

After wartime paper restrictions ended, the Archie boom was to emerge in full force during the late 1940s and early 1950s. Meanwhile, most of Columbia's 1946–1960 fiction magazines involved the Western genre, but there were also significant contributions to the mystery, science fiction, sports, and romance genres. By that time, however, the pulps were essentially dead and Archie's pals 'n' gals had taken center stage, retaining their pop-cultural prominence to this day.

IMPACT ON COMICS

Beginning in the late 1950s, Dan DeCarlo became an icon for more than four decades for his work on Archie and related characters. It is DeCarlo, far more than any other artist, that modern fans think of when the term "iconic" is used in relation to MLJ/Archie.

Many readers today have never heard of any other MLJ comic book characters, even though Archie did not truly flower until after World War II, when the Golden Age superhero comics were on the wane. Superman, Batman, Captain America, **Captain Marvel** . . . they all appeared well before Archie in the comic books, where all five of these icons originated. Even Americans who have seldom if ever followed the comics know these names. But who outside the comic book–collecting community remembers the Shield, the Web, or Steel Sterling?

All of the Archie superheroes failed dismally during a short-lived mid-1960s revival in *The Fly* and *The Mighty Crusaders* titles. The revival of *The Black Hood*, *The Shield* and *Steel Sterling* was even less successful under the Red Circle imprint of the 1980s and when DC tried publishing the MLJ heroes under the Impact! Comics imprint in the early 1990s under a licensing agreement. Indeed, the only commercially successful Archie Series hero during the Silver Age and beyond was the moderately successful Fly, created by Joe Simon and **Jack Kirby**, who ran in 39 issues of his own title beginning in 1959. Yet, the company is attempting a revival of their superheroes as the New Crusaders in 2012.

By far the most successful Archie Series innovation was Bob Bolling's Little Archie, relating the often hysterical adventures of the Archie crowd as young grade-schoolers. Little Archie debuted in 1956 with the surprise appearance of his own title and ran 180 issues through 1983, in addition to appearing in numerous other comics. Beyond the Silver Age years of the 1960s, Archie came up with several pop-cultural successes with their own titles, most notably famed Archie artist Dan DeCarlo's Sabrina the Teenage Witch, and the licensed **Teenage Mutant Ninja Turtles** and Sonic the Hedgehog. In recent years, Archie has gone on to explore even more progressive representations with its introduction of Kevin Keller, an openly gay character in the Archie narrative universe.

MLJ did accomplish one long-lasting commercial feat—the creation of the digest line—the success of which no other comic book publisher has come even remotely close to matching. With the establishment of the direct market and comic book specialty shops, comic books essentially disappeared from public view, but Archie's digest format, begun in 1973, found a home among the candy and tabloids lining grocery store checkout lines, and is the only comic book most Americans ever see.

IMPACT ON AMERICAN CULTURE

MLJ's most enduring impact on American culture centers around Archie Andrews and his friends from Riverdale High School. The *Archie Andrews* radio program aired on various networks from 1943 to 1953. Archie and the gang were featured in half a dozen different animated television shows from 1968 to 1974, and many of those were collectively put into syndication as *The Archies*. A real-life band, the Archies, was created to play the songs for *The Archie Show* cartoon (1968–1969), and the group had a bubblegum pop hit with the song "Sugar, Sugar." The punk band Jughead's Revenge released half a dozen albums before a lawsuit brought by Archie Comics forced them to disband. In 1990, NBC tested the waters for an Archie television series with the live-action movie *Archie: To Riverdale and Back Again*, which looked in on the gang 15 years after graduating from high school. The move was poorly received, and the series never materialized. In 2010 the U.S. Postal Service issued a stamp that showed Archie sharing an ice cream soda with Betty and Veronica.

Writer **Harvey Kurtzman** and artist Will Elder famously parodied the Riverdale gang in the "Starchie" story in a 1954 issue of *Mad Magazine*. Then in the early 1960s Kurtzman and Elder paired to create the Goodman Beaver stories for the humor magazine *Help!* This more ribald parody of Archie prompted legal action from Archie Comics. Archie characters have made unsanctioned "guest appearances" in cartoons such as *The Simpsons* and *Family Guy*. Archie has also had some unusual crossovers in his own comic books. The Marvel Comics antihero the **Punisher** was undercover at the Riverdale prom in *Archie Meets the Punisher* (1994), and the Riverdale teens had a four-part adventure with the rock band KISS beginning in *Archie* #627 (2011).

Two Archie spinoff characters, Sabrina and Josie, became better known in their television and film incarnations. Sabrina began her television career rather inauspiciously in *Sabrina and the Groovie Goolies* cartoon, which was renamed *Sabrina the Teenage Witch* in the second season and ran until 1974. By 1977 she was popular enough to get equal billing with America's favorite teen in *The New Archie and Sabrina Hour* cartoon. A 1996 live-action made-for-TV movie proved successful enough to launch the live-action television series *Sabrina the Teenage Witch*, which ran from 1996 to 2000. *Sabrina: The Animated Series* ran for 65 episodes beginning in 1999, and *Sabrina's Secret Life* aired as part of various CBS cartoon blocks from 2006 to 2011.

The 16-episode run of the animated series *Josie and the Pussycats* began in 1970. Two years later the show was revamped as *Josie and the Pussycats in Outer Space*, and 16 episodes ran during the 1972–1973 season. The producers put together a real-life bubblegum pop group, which included a young Cheryl Ladd, to sing the songs written for the show. The group cut an album and six singles for Columbia Records. In 2001 Universal Pictures and MGM released *Josie and the Pussycats* as a feature film starring Rachael Leigh Cook, Tara Reid, and Rosario Dawson. Most viewers did not seem to appreciate the movie as a spoof, and it was a box office bomb.

Perhaps one of the most fondly remembered MLJ characters is **Katy Keene**, the original creation of cartoonist Bill Woggon. "The Pin-Up Queen," as she was known, made a significant impact on millions of young girls in her own title, with #1–#62 from 1949 to 1961 plus numerous specials and dozens of backup appearances in other Archie titles. Hundreds, perhaps even thousands, of youngsters enjoyed seeing their fashion concepts reproduced in the Katy Keene stories by Woggon, who drew them all. Several artists contributed to a Katy Keene comeback in the 1980s, but the series was only moderately successful.

SUMMARY

The Shield was America's first flag-costumed patriotic superhero, and Katy Keene still holds a special place in the hearts of many of her former readers, but the Archie characters were MLJ's only truly significant contributions to comics history. For more than 70 years readers have been entertained by the antics of the clumsy but likable 17-year old who just cannot decide between Betty and Veronica.

See also Archie Andrews; Katy Keene

ESSENTIAL WORKS

Castiglia, Paul, ed. *The Shield: America's First Patriotic Comic Book Hero*. New York: Archie Comic Publications, 2002.
Uslan, Michael, and Jeffrey Mendel. *The Best of Archie*. New York: Archie Comic Publications, 2011.

FURTHER READING

Benton, Mike. *Super Hero Comics of the Golden Age*. Dallas: Taylor Publishing Company, 1992.
Phillips, Charles. *Archie: His First 50 Years*. New York: Abbeville Press, 1991.

Michelle Nolan

Moore, Alan

Alan Moore is marked as one of the most maverick, unpredictable, and defiant writers in the Anglophone comics world. He is also something of a cult legend; a bearded, drug-using, snake-worshipping, anarchist magician, who pours vituperative scorn on the crass commercialism of mainstream comics companies while crafting esoteric word-worlds from his home in the English East Midlands. Moore was notoriously at the forefront of the "British invasion" of the American comic book mainstream in the mid-1980s, blazing a trail through superhero comics that introduced new levels of formal complexity and political realism to the genre. He went on to wreak similar havoc with the clichés and limitations of horror/crime fiction and pornography with the epics *From Hell* and *Lost Girls*, before returning to the world of superheroes with his own America's Best Comics imprint in order to counteract the dark, cynical, revisionist paradigm he himself helped inculcate. While increasing disdain for the American industry has led him to a shift away from comics in favor of intermedia performance, prose fiction, and magical ritual, Moore remains one of the most influential and highly regarded writers in the field. What distinguishes him as a comics icon has been his commitment to ceaseless experimentation with the unique potential of the medium, subverting orthodoxies, transmuting genres, and fiercely resisting standardization.

HISTORY

Alan Oswald Moore was born on November 18, 1953, in Northampton, England, where he has resided all his life. He was born into a working-class family, his father, Ernest, working for the local brewery and his mother, Sylvia, for a printer, once Alan and his brother were old enough to be cared for by their maternal grandmother. The family lived in public housing in an area of relative deprivation called the Burroughs, a neighborhood later designated for slum clearance as part of the city's 1960s redevelopment. Moore's parents had a dread of illiteracy, which still afflicted their community, and so taught him to read at the age of four. He joined the library soon after, and began reading voraciously, particularly seeking out stories with a fantastic element; the myths and legends, fairy tales, and ghost stories that stimulated his imagination.

Moore first picked up American superhero comics at a market stall and was captivated by their bold colors, fantastic scenarios, and remarkable characters, a far cry from traditional, black-and-white British weeklies. He eventually gravitated away from clean-cut **DC Comics** superheroes towards the "gritty, streetwise realism" and more marginalized, complex characters of the Silver Age **Marvel Comics** revolution, of greater relevance to a time of profound social and cultural change (Moore 1983, 45). The intense and dynamic artwork of **Jack Kirby** and **Steve Ditko** inspired the creation of his first comics, the extremely small press ballpoint-on-notepaper *Omega Comics*, produced and sold at his Spring Lane Primary School.

Unlike most children from his background, Moore passed the Eleven Plus, a selective exam taken by all pupils at the end of primary school (at the age of eleven), which determined the nature of their further education and future career prospects. Moore gained entry to the boys-only Northampton Grammar School, where he encountered a strict regime of discipline and conformity that activated his dissident antiauthoritarian politics. Although his academic performance deteriorated in this stultifying environment, he continued to read insatiably, his tastes shifting towards work that experimented with form, defied convention, and challenged social taboos. This ranged from the cosmic horror of H. P. Lovecraft to the groundbreaking science fiction published in *New Worlds* magazine under the editorship of Michael Moorcock, via the visceral avant-garde outpourings of Beat writers like Allen Ginsberg and William Burroughs. He also discovered the irreverent satire and absurdist humour of **Harvey Kurtzman**'s *Mad*, and was blown away by his first exposure to the exuberantly transgressive "bigfoot" cartooning of **Robert Crumb** on the front cover of British underground paper *Oz* (Moore 1998, 73).

These influences converged in his contributions to *Embryo*, a rebellious, mimeographed poetry magazine self-published with fellow pupils, which was later banned from the grammar school. Moore not only submitted poems but produced the majority of the magazine's graphic content, emulating the contemporary pop psychedelia of **Jim Steranko** and **Neal Adams**, as well as underground comix artists like George Metzger and Vaughn Bodé. It was such progressive comics that galvanized early British fandom, and in his late teens Moore became increasingly involved in the fan scene, attending the second U.K. comics convention in 1968, and contributing articles, illustrations, comics, and short stories to fanzines. His first professionally published work was an advertisement in the underground paper *Cyclops* in 1970 for science fiction and fantasy bookshop Dark They Were and Golden Eyed, which also sold comics, comix, and drug paraphernalia, revealing the crossover between fans and hippies. Moore himself embraced the hippie counterculture, growing

(Redferns)

his hair long and becoming so inspired by Tim Leary's romanticization of the LSD dealer that he became one himself, leading to his expulsion from school in 1971 without qualifications or job prospects beyond low-paid, unskilled labor.

However, the countercultural experience that left an indelible mark on Moore's politics and creative practice was his involvement with the Northampton Arts Lab. One of a number across the United Kingdom, the lab aimed to create a participative, experimental, and autonomous cultural space, challenging disciplinary specialization by encouraging work across different media. Moore was stimulated by the group's nonconformist attitude, socialized creative practice, and disdain for the art establishment, but especially by this holistic approach. As well as contributing to Arts Lab publications, he ventured into music and theater, participating in poetry readings and collaborative multimedia performances. This performative aspect, which taught him the rhythm and effect of language, had a huge impact on his sonorous and fluid literary style, while also driving his "method" approach to characterization and attempts to inhabit his characters' speech and physicality.

Enthused by the vernacular accessibility, taboo-breaking satire, and do-it-yourself impulse of underground comix, Moore turned to the underground press as a radical cultural space similar to Arts Lab. He contributed comics to the local monthly *anon, Alternative Newspaper of Northampton* (1974–1975) and the Oxford-based *Backstreet Bugle* (1978–1980), with fervid, densely stippled artwork and anthropomorphic characters inspired by Crumb and S. Clay Wilson. He moved on to regular strips in the music magazine *Sounds* (1979–1983) and local paper the *Northants Post* (1979–1986) under the pseudonyms Curt Vile and Jill de Ray, as he was still claiming unemployment benefits. Ultimately he concluded that he lacked the talent to become a successful cartoonist and decided to focus instead on a career as a freelance comics writer.

Moore first broke into mainstream British comics in 1980 with a series of "Future-Shocks" and "Time-Twisters" in IPC's *2000 AD*, a cutting-edge science fiction anthology with an antiestablishment streak. Working on these two- to five-page shorts taught him the basic craft of comics writing, how to construct and cohere necessary story elements satisfactorily and effectively in a small amount of space. His success was awarded with three ongoing series for the title, *Skizz* (1983), *D. R. & Quinch* (1983–1984), and *The Ballad of Halo Jones* (1984–1986). At the same time he was making similar progress at Marvel U.K., which was starting to solicit original British material to accompany its U.S. reprints, moving from uncredited *Dr. Who* and *Star Wars* back-up strips to a stint on *Captain Britain* (1982–1984). During this period Moore was part of a wider generation of upstart young creators who were stirring up British comics, challenging hack practices and stale conventions. He addressed this cohort in his outspoken articles in Marvel U.K.'s *The Daredevils* that railed against the degeneration of **Stan Lee**'s revolution into mindless repetitive formulas and the woeful representation of women in comics (which he tried to remedy with the predominantly female cast of *Halo Jones*). Nowhere was this insurgency more evident than in the groundbreaking independent anthology *Warrior*, set up by Dez Skinn to target older readers, which offered an unprecedented degree of creative freedom and copyright ownership. Moore contributed three series to the title: *Marvelman*, a dramatic updating of a whimsical 1950s superhero, with Nietzschean undertones; *The Bojeffries Saga*, a surreal working-class horror sitcom; and *V for Vendetta*, a noir thriller about a masked anarcho-terrorist's insurrection in a fascist future Britain. Although *Warrior* collapsed after only 26 issues (lasting from 1982 to 1985), Moore's work for the magazine earned him fan recognition, critical acclaim, and multiple Eagle awards, as well as attention of American publisher DC, for whom he would produce his best-known comics.

In 1983 Moore was contacted by Len Wein, editor of the revived *Saga of the Swamp Thing*, to ask if he wanted to write the poorly selling series. After drafting a 10-page treatise anatomizing the character and identifying its flaws, Moore began his three-year spell (1984–1987) in the same way he had tackled *Captain Britain*—by immediately killing off the protagonist, negating prior continuity, and conceptually rebuilding the character from scratch. Indeed, in his first full-length issue, #21 "The Anatomy Lesson," Moore had the Floronic Man dissect the **Swamp Thing** to discover it was not actually a human-plant monster hybrid, but an entirely vegetable creature, deeply connected to the natural world via "the green." This revision facilitated the exploration of environmentalist politics, ecosophical questions, and gothic intertexts that characterized Moore's run, as well as released the potential of Steve Bissette and John Totleben's lushly textured artwork and elaborate, organic page layouts.

As a result of his *Swamp Thing* success, Moore was selected to come up with a treatment of the Charlton superheroes acquired by DC. Moore's proposal to insert these characters into a realistic 1980s world was deemed too extreme, and so he and artist Dave Gibbons were offered the opportunity to create entirely new characters, in a 12-issue limited series that would become Moore's most celebrated work, **Watchmen** (1986–1987). Building on *Marvelman*, which was eventually republished and completed with Eclipse as *Miracleman* (1985–1989), *Watchmen* further explored the geopolitical, technological, and cultural consequences the actual existence of superheroes would effect. It radically deconstructed the conventions of the genre, by probing the likely (dubious) ideology, morality, and psychology of masked crime fighters, remorselessly picking apart each superhero archetype. Moore intended the series to function not only as an antiauthoritarian critique of hero-worship, but as a "fabulous analogy" for the effect of growing nuclear arsenals on humanity, with the plot alongside a ratcheting up of Cold War tensions that reflected the hawkish reality of the Reagan-Thatcher period (Hull 1986). However, more than anything Moore wanted to use *Watchmen* as a textbook to demonstrate the level of formal complexity possible in comics, and the clean lines, flat color, and uniform grid of the artwork belie a self-consciously ornate and reflexive narrative structure, as well as a treasure trove of telling background details and repeated symbolic motifs.

Watchmen established Moore as one of DC's star writers, and at the same time he produced several back-up strips and one-shots featuring their well-known character properties, including notable **Superman** and **Green Lantern** Corps stories. Of greatest impact on DC Universe continuity was his definitive **Batman/Joker** story *The Killing Joke*, published in 1988 with art by Brian Bolland. Under DC, Moore also reprinted and completed *V for Vendetta* as a 10-issue miniseries (1988–1989), with David Lloyd's artwork colored and resized to appeal to the American audience. However, he became increasingly unhappy with his treatment by the publisher, falling out with the company over issues of creator rights. He particularly objected to the fact that *Watchmen* was kept continuously in print, rendering the contractual copyright reversion clause he had fought for meaningless.

In the end, Moore resolutely decamped to the emergent new wave. In 1988 he had also established his own imprint, Mad Love, with his wife Phyllis and their mutual lover Debbie Delano. It was set up in order to self-publish

AARGH! (Artists Against Rampant Government Homophobia), a benefit anthology for gay rights activists in the face of the Thatcher government's introduction of discriminatory legislation, known as Clause 28. Moore went on to collaborate on one-off projects with the likes of **Harvey Pekar** and Bryan Talbot, contribute to cutting-edge titles like *RAW*, and pursue the most non-commercial projects he could find, such as "Shadowplay: The Secret Team," a caustic history of illegal CIA operations featured in the Christic Institute's *Brought to Light* exposé (1989), which brought him under British government surveillance. He intended to use Mad Love to publish the equally singular work *Big Numbers*, about fractal maths, chaos theory, and a shopping mall development; however, his working relationship with artist Bill Sienkiewicz collapsed after only two issues, shortly followed by the dissolution of his marriage and Mad Love.

Two works begun in this period that did eventually see completion were *From Hell* (1989–1996) and *Lost Girls* (1991–2006), both initially serialized in Steve Bissette's alternative horror anthology *Taboo* and equally epic in scope, length, and ambition. *From Hell*, a reinterpretation of the historical Jack the Ripper murders, subverted the traditions of whodunnit detective fiction by focusing less on the forensic details of the horrific crimes and more on the multifaceted social, political, and cultural context in which they occurred. It offered a dense reading of Victorian London as not only a network of physical spaces but a web of social relationships inflected by gender, race, class, sexuality, morality and religion, science and technology, a city with layers of historical, mythological, and symbolic meaning.

Lost Girls aimed to similarly challenge conventional notions of pornography. It united well-loved characters from children's literature, Alice from *Alice in Wonderland*, Wendy from *Peter Pan*, and Dorothy from *The Wizard of Oz*, in an Austrian spa in 1913. The comic depicted them as three grown women of different ages and classes who engage in extended and diverse hardcore sexual scenarios, while also sharing the stories of their childhood sexual awakening—eroticized reinterpretations of their origin texts. *Lost Girls* combined Melinda Gebbie's delicate, ethereal artwork with exploration of proscribed sexual practices, and a narrative that uses the growing shadow of World War I to make "a passionate argument for the freedom of the sexual imagination and passionate argument against war as a complete failure of any sort of imagination" (Moore in Baker 2007, 74). As a result, it contested the aesthetic, moral, intellectual, and political standards of contemporary porn. On completion it received a mixed reaction from critics and fans, but did succeed in arousing its creators to the extent that they became lovers and were married in 2007.

In 1993, on his 40th birthday, Moore announced he was becoming a ceremonial magician. That same year he had made an unanticipated return to superhero comics with work on **Todd McFarlane's** *Spawn*. This was the first of a number of projects for brash, creator-owned indie companies **Image** and Awesome, that ran alongside his larger, ongoing epics. These included the Kirby pastiche *1963* miniseries (1993), and stints on Jim Lee's *WildC.A.T.s* (1995–1997) and Rob Liefeld's *Supreme* (1996–2000). In 1999, in the wake of Awesome's collapse, Moore launched his own Wildstorm imprint, America's Best Comics (ABC), to provide work for creators left stranded. Moore developed a whole line of titles from a list of interesting names found in one of his workbooks, but Wildstorm was bought out by DC before the first comic hit the shelves. Not wanting to break his contract with the artists involved, Moore ended up once again working under the auspices of the corporate giant he loathed.

The ABC line, especially flagship title *Tom Strong*, aimed to counteract the grim and gritty superhero trend of the post-*Watchmen* era and restore a sense of innocence and wonder. In the case of *Tom Strong* (1999–2003) this involved looking to the superhero's pulp fiction and newspaper strip precursors (while unconsciously providing the American mainstream's first interracial family). With *The League of Extraordinary Gentlemen* (1999–) the intertextual net was cast far wider, focusing on a band of heroes swiped from Victorian romance, horror, and adventure fiction, but set in an alternative steampunk world inhabited by a vast array of characters from novels, children's literature, television, theater, and film. *The League* tests the very definition of comics, expanding on the use of fictional back matter in *Watchmen* to incorporate prose appendices, mock adverts, and games in the vein of British boy's story papers. This was extended even further in *The Black Dossier* to include maps, postcards, cutaways, and inserts (including the glasses needed to read a 3-D sequence), as well as lengthy prose parodies of writers ranging from William Shakespeare to Jack Kerouac. Other ABC titles written by Moore included *Top 10* (1991–2001), a superhero/cop drama amalgam, and anthology series *Tomorrow's Stories* (1999–2002).

However, it was ABC's *Promethea* (1999–2005) in collaboration with artist J. H. Williams III that combined Moore's re-revision of the superhero with his new magical practice. In *Promethea* Moore used a superheroine who personified creativity and the power of storytelling to explore aspects of the occult, particularly Hermetic Qabalah, as well as his own conception of Ideaspace, an immaterial dimension composed of all fantasy, imagination, and thought, traversable through magical ritual. In the series a young Sophie Bangs, researching the history of the character Promethea from folklore to comic books for a college project, ends up being trained by earlier versions to actually become the latest incarnation of the goddess and bring about Apocalypse. The reader moves with Sophie on her journey from the alternate reality of a retro-futurist New York through the various spheres of Immateria, this realm of stories. Yet Moore uses the title not only to expound his philosophy of magic, but as a metafictional commentary on comics themselves, contrasting the sterile

MOORE ON FILM

Moore has always emphasized comics' unique qualities and attempted to move beyond cinematic paradigms, highlighting the greater degree of reader agency in this more intimate medium. He has become increasingly irritated by DC's optioning of his comics for screen adaptations, contributing to his acrimonious relationship with the company. Moore regards translation of an existing work into a different medium as conceptually redundant, in distinction from his own appropriation of other fictions to create something new.

- *Return of the Swamp Thing* **(1989)** featured lines of butchered dialogue from Moore's run.
- *From Hell* **(2001):** Moore publicly distanced himself from the Hughes brothers' film as a distinct entity from his comic.
- *The League of Extraordinary Gentlemen* **(2003)** added other characters, leading to a lawsuit from different screenplay writers that was settled out of court. Outraged, Moore decided to decline all future payments from film adaptations and insist they go instead to his collaborators.
- *Constantine* **(2005):** Moore demanded his name not appear on this *Hellblazer* adaptation.
- *V for Vendetta* **(2005):** After it was announced that Moore was excited about the film at a press conference, he threatened to withdraw *The League* from Wildstorm and take his name off all his DC Comics without a public apology, retraction, and signed assurance his name would not appear on the movie. This contributed to his severance of all contact with DC and the demise of ABC.
- *Watchmen* **(2009):** Moore was uncredited on this attempt to adapt a work both he and initial director Terry Gilliam deemed unfilmable.

predictability of the Five Swell Guys superhero team, and the facile cynicism of trendy Weeping Gorilla comics inside the narrative, with the imaginative formal experimentation of *Promethea* itself. This included one issue that was a continuous circular frieze, another incorporating the photography of Jose Villarubia, a final chapter that worked as both a comic book and two giant posters, and a celebrated double-page sequence on a Möbius strip.

In 2003 Moore announced his retirement from comics, following a raft of disputes with DC over editorial interference, censorship, and film adaptations of his work (see sidebar). So disillusioned was he with the industry, that he decided to abandon the medium almost entirely. Over the next few years he wrapped up all the ABC titles, apart from *The League*, co-owned with artist

Kevin O'Neill, which he took to alternative publishers Top Shelf and Knock-about. In some ways his trajectory came full circle, with a renewed focus on the work in other media such as prose, poetry, journalism, performance, and illustration he had pursued throughout his comics career in the Arts Lab vein. In 2009 he initiated his own countercultural magazine, *Dodgem Logic*, named for an unrealized fanzine project from his early 20s.

In "Writing for Comics," an article for the *Fantasy Advertiser* written at the height of his post-*Watchmen* fame, Alan Moore offered advice to the aspiring comics scribe. He began by reproaching the stagnation of the mainstream comics industry and its retrograde formulism, and asserting the need for comics to undergo a "process of almost continual change," a consistent challenging of the underlying assumptions and unwritten laws restricting the development of the medium (Moore 2003, 2). This critical and subversive drive characterizes his entire approach to comics storytelling. As Jochen Ecke points out, Moore himself provides an astute alchemical analogy of this approach as a process of "solve and coagula," taking things apart in order to put them back together in improved form, a method lauded in his dismantling of the superhero genre, but equally present in his wider innovations in content and form (Ecke 2011, 109).

Moore's 1988 article was especially critical of comics that were entirely plot driven, with no interesting idea behind them and no relevance to contemporary life. Moore's own work has explored unconventional and challenging ideas from quantum mechanics to mysticism, but also addressed socially relevant themes such as racism and unemployment in a thought-provoking fashion, often through the prism of futuristic or fantastic estrangement. Informed by his lifelong anarchism, his comics have consistently confronted topical political issues. Indeed, his work of the 1980s can be read as a sustained critique of the policies of the Thatcher and Reagan administrations from feminist, antimilitarist, queer, class-conscious, and ecological perspectives. While later works perhaps lack the outspoken radicalism of the emphatically antiauthoritarian *V for Vendetta*, comics like *Lost Girls* and *The League* maintained a strong antiwar, anti-imperialist political slant pertinent to the era of Bush and Blair.

However, relevance for Moore is not just a matter of an "unavoidable political element," but a certain realism, in terms of the construction of a convincing social totality (Moore in Baker 2007, 46). Detailing his storytelling approach he asserts that "the job of a writer is to conjure a sense of environmental reality as completely and unobtrusively as possible . . . a sense of a completely realized and credibly detailed world" (Moore 2003, 20–22). For Moore this has meant extensive planning, often systematically mapping the distinct diegesis of each work to a level of detail that may never manifest on the page. It has also meant increasing amounts of research, moving from his construction of a recognizable Louisiana in *Swamp Thing* through reference to road maps, photographs, music, and slang, to the intense historical reading that went into *From Hell*, backed up by lengthy footnote appendices. Such exhaustive world building gives Moore's work a richness that is matched by "a depth of characterization rarely found in the medium," using his performative experience to give each character distinct gait, gestures, expressions, accent, and voice, while also incorporating a greater diversity of characters in terms of age, gender, race, and sexuality (Millidge 2011, 12).

Moore's *Fantasy Advertiser* piece additionally insisted on formal experimentation, focusing on techniques that drew on comics' unique potential rather than looking to cinematic precedents. These included complex, nonlinear narrative structures that made use of the audience's ability to read at their own pace and flip back and forth through the pages at will. Moore also highlighted the potential for amplification of meaning in the divergence between verbal and visual elements, or through the inclusion of incidental background details. His comics have often self-reflexively examined the medium's peculiar faculty for representing time through spatial arrangement of panels, often exposing a tension between the narrative transitions between panels and the conceptual content of the page as a whole in order to explore notions of simultaneity and recurrence. Yet Moore's works have also abandoned some of the most familiar comics devices, with *V for Vendetta* and *From Hell*, for instance, relinquishing captions, thought balloons, and sound effects in the quest for realism. In the afterword included in the 2003 Avatar republication of *Writing for Comics*, Moore forcefully derided some of the techniques seen as the signature of his celebrated DC titles, such as clever panel transitions that used overlapping dialogue or synchronicity of images, or captions overloaded with purple prose, and reiterated the need for continuous progress to avoid the creative torpor that comes with a readily identifiable style.

Moore's work can be seen to have evolved, particularly in his move away from the mainstream superhero genre, in terms of increasingly unconventional content and atypical form and format. Yet, most identifiable has been an intensifying intertextuality. Moore's comics have always included numerous allusions, quotations, and eyeball kick references to other works from a range of media, including films, novels, pop music, visual art, television, and, of course, comics. However, with series like *The League* this has increased to the level of focusing specifically on the appropriation, combination, and recontextualization of other fictional worlds, "to see what new fictions are generated when you collate two old ones" (Moore in Chris Murray 2011, 9) The dense webs of intertextual reference in Moore's later output also bring to the fore the metafictional quality present in much of his oeuvre, the way his works call attention to their own fictionality through the use of mise-en-scene comics-within-comics, self-aware characters, creator cameos, and self-conscious reference to genre conventions, established formulas, and reader cultures within the narrative itself. With his growing interest in magic as the power of creativity and story telling, Moore's comics have become ever more self-conscious, critical, and idealist stories about stories.

IMPACT ON COMICS

Alan Moore has been credited with bringing a literary sensibility to comics. Even before he became interested in the manipulation of language as a magical practice, Moore demonstrated his appreciation for the "fine craft of wordsmithing" in his comics writing, mobilizing the resonant qualities of rhythm, phrasing, and stylistic devices like alliteration and assonance, while also trying to capture naturalistic dialogue (Moore 2003, 39). *From Hell* in particular situated him as part of a wider cohort of English writers with an interest in psychogeography, including Iain Sinclair and Peter Ackroyd, and he has become increasingly prominent on the U.K. literary circuit, for instance giving talks on William Blake and readings of William Burroughs.

However, Moore has always approached comics writing with a visual awareness developed from his own cartooning experience. His infamously lengthy and meticulous scripts, which go into intense detail about character, setting, mood, lighting, and point of view in each panel, are based on his own rough thumbnail breakdowns, used to help provide a workable layout and visual structure for each page. While this could be seen as a form of auteurism, Moore has always endeavored to genuinely collaborate with his co-creators, not only writing to their perceived strengths but engaging in extensive dialogue and exchange of ideas, sometimes outside of editorial mechanisms, in opposition to the conventional hierarchical and alienating division of labor in the mainstream industry.

Yet, ironically, it has been Moore as the celebrity comics auteur of the 1980s who has had the greatest impact on the field. His real-world dethroning of the superhero led to a new revisionist trend of violent, psychotic antiheroes that became the genre standard in turn. *Watchmen*'s publication coincided with the release of equally somber superhero title **Frank Miller**'s *Batman: The Dark Knight Returns*, as well as the first volume of **Art Spiegelman**'s critically acclaimed alternative comic *Maus*, and shared the extensive media hype of the "Kapow! Shazam!! Comics Grow Up" variety that surrounded these "Big Three" adult titles (see Sabin 1993, 87–95). While Moore has won countless Kirbys, Harveys, and Eisners throughout his career, nothing has matched the publicity, sales, and critical approbation of *Watchmen*, which garnered numerous accolades worldwide including the only Hugo ever awarded to a comic book. Despite initially relying on direct comics shop distribution, the series' success was also concurrent with the emergence of "graphic novel" as a promotional term, and the targeting of the broader book store market, being immediately repackaged by DC as a glossy trade paperback collected edition. These wider contextual factors contributed to a somewhat equivocal reevaluation of comics as a form of literature, commensurate to the novel in terms of cultural value and legitimacy, and *Watchmen* was often cast as the prime example.

Swamp Thing had an equally important impact on the American mainstream, with its issue #29 (1984) being the first DC comic published without the Comics Code Authority seal of approval, following objections to a double-page zombie spread and incest storyline. In later episodes the seal was replaced with the masthead "For Mature Readers," initiating a ratings system that several DC freelancers, including Moore, objected to and petitioned against. However, the success of Moore's run in many ways also facilitated the creation of Vertigo in 1993, a DC imprint, then edited by Karen Berger, that brought together the darker, more complex horror and fantasy titles aimed at an older readership. These included *Hellblazer*, a series featuring the street-smart, working-class magician John Constantine, created by Moore and his *Swamp Thing* collaborators. Many Vertigo titles featured the work of writers who had followed in Moore's footsteps as part of the so-called British invasion of American comics, such as **Neil Gaiman**, **Grant Morrison**, Jamie Delano, Warren Ellis, Garth Ennis, and Mark Millar (both Gaiman and Millar citing Moore as the direct inspiration for their careers as comics writers).

At the height of his celebrity, Moore was mobbed at conventions. His subsequent withdrawal from the limelight, abandonment of the mainstream, and pursuit of almost willfully challenging and esoteric works alienated some fans, while others, on the other hand, disapproved of his work on Image's garish, violent superhero titles. Although Moore has contributed to a widening of the comics audience, and intentionally confronted misogyny and patriarchy with works like *From Hell* and *Halo Jones*, there has also been significant critical discussion on fan message boards and blogs of the repeated graphic portrayal of violence against women, specifically rape, in his work. Moore's confrontational relationship with publishers, which has included disputes with Marvel U.K., IPC, and DC over issues of copyright ownership, remuneration, unauthorized reprints, censorship, and editorial interference, has equally antagonized some of his collaborators, notably Alan Davis. However, for many, Moore, fondly dubbed the Magus, remains a fearless comics visionary who refuses to compromise his artistic integrity for commercial concerns.

IMPACT ON AMERICAN CULTURE

Alan Moore's prominence in wider American culture has declined somewhat since the dizzy heights of Watchmania, when he made numerous TV appearances, was profiled in *Rolling Stone*, and his reintroduced smiley face became the emblem of acid house rave culture. However, despite his increasing distaste for celebrity and reluctance to give interviews to corporate media, his enduring cult status was affirmed with an appearance on *The Simpsons* in 2007. Moore's ventures away from the comics medium into other fields, particularly music and performance, have resulted in projects that are less accessible to audiences outside of the United Kingdom, although many are available in different formats. Moore's site-specific, spoken-word performances, developed from his magical experiences, have been released on CD and adapted to comics form by Eddie Campbell and collected in *A Disease of Language* (2005). U.S. publishers, such as Caliber Press and Avatar, have also produced comics adaptations of his lyrics, prose fiction, and theatrical work. His 1996 novel *Voice of the Fire*, comprised of 12 stories that form almost geological strata of his native Northampton, faced other difficulties in translating to a wide audience, as a result of a literary density and localism he promises will only be intensified in his next novel, *Jerusalem*. Yet, as Gary Spencer Millidge asserts, Moore, particularly with his deconstruction of the superhero in *Watchmen* and *Miracleman*, has had an unmistakable influence, not only on the field of American comics, but on television shows such as *Heroes* and films like M. Night Shyamalan's *Unbreakable* (Millidge 2011, 80). Ironically, Moore has strongly criticized and distanced himself from the film adaptations of his own work, which have, nevertheless, raised his public profile once again (see sidebar).

As an outsider and an anarchist, Moore, like many of his peers in the British invasion, has always maintained "a degree of critical distance and ironic detachment" that has allowed him to challenge traditional American values and institutions, and particularly to "deconstruct the superhero as a project of American mythology" (Murray 2010, 35). His dystopian superhero narratives have muddied the genre's simplistic Manichean morality by bringing out the chauvinist and oppressive aspects of such characters, and aligned this authoritarian, militarist ideology with the realities of American imperialism. Moore has equally come to view the practices of the U.S. comics industry, in terms of questionable business practices, venal competitiveness, and exploitative labor relations, as consistent with this unscrupulous foreign policy. If he takes any inspiration from America, it is from the anarchist and anarcho-syndicalist traditions of Emma Goldman, Murray Bookchin, and the Wobblies, and the joyfully rebellious culture of the 1960s psychedelic movement, a politics and creative vision that combine in his relentless struggle against established conventions and conservative orthodoxies and commitment to the "idea of progressive comic books" (Moore in Baker 2007, 44).

For Moore this means comics that not only constantly push the envelope in terms of storytelling, form, and content but that can change the world. While many academic readings of his work have placed it in a postmodernist idiom, Moore himself has always insisted his work is part of an avant-garde tradition of subversive culture with a social purpose. He insists that comics are a useful tool "in the arsenal of people who are seeking social change" (Moore in Killjoy 2009, 52), an accessible popular medium that can potentially transform consciousness as "propaganda for a state of mind ... [for] ... the way you see the world" (Moore in Baker 2005, 28). The utopian aspect of his work derives from this belief in the magical, perception-altering power of language and imagination. Significantly, *V for Vendetta* has become a touchstone for dissident protest movements around the world, with masks based on the film adaptation used by anonymous hacktivists, Occupy protesters, and Egyptian activists of the Arab Spring. Moore's ongoing connection to such radical social movements, dating from his own involvement in local antifascist activism in the 1970s, was demonstrated by his 2011 pledge to contribute to an Occupy benefit anthology, following Frank Miller's virulent criticism of the protests.

SUMMARY

In *V for Vendetta*, the protagonist V describes his violent actions as *Verwirrung*, a period of chaotic destruction that facilitates the emergence of a new society of mutual aid and voluntary order, or *Ordnung*. In many ways Moore too assimilates Russian anarchist Mikhail Bakunin's dictum that "the passion for destruction is a creative passion" (1971), advocating that only the persistent and insubordinate dismantling of every venerable convention, tried-and-true method, and time-honored approach will release the potential of the comics medium. As a result Alan Moore is iconic as a resolute iconoclast.

See also From Hell; Killing Joke, The; Watchmen

ESSENTIAL WORKS

Moore, Alan (w), and Eddie Campbell (p, i). *From Hell*. Marietta, GA: Top Shelf, 1999.
Moore, Alan (w), Dave Gibbons (p, i), and John Higgins. *Watchmen*. New York: DC Comics, 1987.
Moore, Alan (w), and David Lloyd (p, i). *V for Vendetta*. New York: DC Comics, 1989.
Moore, Alan (w), and Kevin O'Neill (p, i) *The League of Extraordinary Gentlemen: The Black Dossier*. New York: America's Best Comics, 2007.

FURTHER READING

di Liddo, Annalisa. *Alan Moore: Comics as Performance, Fiction as Scalpel*. Jackson: University Press of Mississippi, 2009.
Khoury, George. *The Extraordinary Works of Alan Moore: Indispensable Edition*. Raleigh, NC.: TwoMorrows Publishing, 2009.
Millidge, Gary Spencer. *Alan Moore Storyteller*. Lewes, U.K.: ILEX, 2011.

Maggie Gray

Morrison, Grant

Of all the writers comprising the British invasion of American comic books, Glasgow-born Grant Morrison (b. 1960) is the most dizzyingly postmodern, fiercely countercultural, and unabashedly psychedelic. He has won every major U.S. comics award many times in many categories for his writing. Although his best-known creator-owned work remains *The Invisibles* for DC's Vertigo imprint, he is perhaps more adored for his work-for-hire runs on titles like *Animal Man*, *Doom Patrol*, *JLA*, and *All-Star Superman*. The Scottish writer was raised in a poor Glasgow neighborhood by progressive activist parents. He grew up watching sci-fi TV shows like *The Prisoner* and characterizes his teen years as rebellious. He was a "straightedge" (no drinking, drugs, or smoking) punk rocker, enamored with the DIY ethos and viewed anyone over age 23 as "old." A voracious reader, Morrison devoured American comics, though he claims to have possessed a stronger interest in the homegrown British scene at that time. Outside of comics and before breaking into the industry, he deeply admired the dark conceptual fiction of H. P. Lovecraft, studied books about magic, listened to indie records, played in his supercharged power-pop band The Mixers, and watched foreign cinema.

HISTORY

At the tender age of 17, Morrison broke into comics with Edinburgh magazine *Near Myths*, one of the first British alternative comics. He created, wrote, and drew a strip called *Gideon Stargrave*, which established his interest in science fiction with a strong literary bent. Indeed, the eponymous character is based on J. G. Ballard's story collection *The Day of Forever*. Morrison spent nearly a decade on the dole before being able to make a living from comics, and the poverty he endured is, he admits, reflected in some of his angrier deconstructions of the superhero genre—for instance, *Captain Clyde*, a newspaper strip about an unemployed Glasgow superhero published in the *Govan Press*. Morrison laid the groundwork for many of his Vertigo plots and characters with his work on *Starblazer*, a monthly black-and-white British small-format

(Getty Images)

comics anthology. Despite failing to interest **DC Comics** in a proposal for a series teaming up the Justice League of America and Jack Kirby's New Gods, Morrison focused on writing comics exclusively. He penned stories for *Warrior* and in 1986 found work with Marvel U.K., writing strips in *Doctor Who Magazine* and in *Spider-Man and Zoids* (a toy tie-in series). He also contributed to the *Future Shocks* series in weekly British comics anthology *2000 A.D.* Despite such prodigious output, the following year, 1987, is considered Morrison's breakout, especially given his Gen X–influenced, superhero-deconstructing *Zenith* storyline, which debuted in *2000 A.D.* and established him as one of the top British comics writers.

The title character (a.k.a. Robert McDowell) of this roughly four-part epic is a self-absorbed, bored pop star battling extradimensional villains. Zenith does not fight evil for selfless reasons or abstract concepts like truth and justice; rather, he possesses ulterior motives that benefit him and boost his album sales. Thematically, *Zenith* lays the foundation for ideas and concepts Morrison would explore to a greater degree as his career progressed, particularly in his landmark works for DC Comics—*Arkham Asylum*, *Animal Man*, *Doom Patrol*, and *The Invisibles*, and in his sociological, prose-only examination of superhero comics, *Supergods*. These themes include nonlinear narratives, the tenuous relationship between creators and creations, the possibility of multiple realities and cosmologies, and the sensitive link between mental and physical processes.

Indeed, in the wake of *Zenith*'s success in England, and no doubt spurred on by **Alan Moore**'s success in turning a previously third-tier title, *Swamp Thing*, into a bestseller, DC Comics editors arrived in London to scout for talent, meeting with Morrison (and, interestingly, Morrison's peer and a soon-to-be-writing-legend **Neil Gaiman**). Morrison pitched them *Arkham Asylum* and an *Animal Man* story, both of which DC accepted. American comics would never be the same. By this time, Morrison had studied Moore's **Watchmen** and **Frank Miller**'s *The Dark Knight Returns* and was already formulating a different approach to comics. Morrison's first major success in the United States was *Arkham Asylum: A Serious House on Serious Earth* (1989), illustrated by Dave McKean, the publication of which benefitted enormously from the simultaneous release of the Tim Burton-directed *Batman* movie. *Arkham* is a heavily symbolic work influenced by everyone from *Alice in Wonderland* author Lewis Carroll to psychologist Carl Jung, British occultist Aleister Crowley, French filmmaker Jean Cocteau, and French playwright Antonin Artaud, among others. Morrison intended *Arkham* to be highly artistic and akin to an experimental film, in contrast to the more "realistic" superhero adventures in the *Watchmen/Dark Knight* mode. The genesis for the graphic novel, originally published in hardcover and paperback versions, comes from a few paragraphs in a *Who's Who: The Definitive Directory of the DC Universe* entry about **Arkham Asylum**. In it, we learn about the hospital's tragic founder, Amadeus Arkham. Morrison extrapolates from this bit of information to conjure a tale chock-full of literary allusions and references, and in which the hospital's administrator, inspired by Arkham's diary, interprets **Batman** as an evil entity who must be destroyed. The administrator releases the patients and prepares for a violent showdown with Batman. Ultimately, the flashback-laden book manages to relate a story that addresses the nature and meaning of dreams, unreality, mirror imagery, and Tarot cards while satisfying readers looking for a Batman-beats-up-the-bad-guys plot. *Arkham* was hailed as an instant classic and is today still considered to be among the very best Batman stories ever told, abetted in no small part by McKean's visionary art and Gaspar Saladino's evocative lettering. (Interestingly, Alan Moore dismissed the book in an interview, which leads many to believe there is an ongoing feud between the two comics-writing giants. It is hard to determine if this feud actually exists.)

After *Arkham*, Morrison earned greater praise for his run on *Animal Man*, an obscure and rarely used DC character (secret identity: Buddy Baker) created by Dave Wood and Carmine Infantino in 1965. Morrison is credited with relaunching and revitalizing the Animal Man character (and later the Doom Patrol superhero team) in the same way Moore and Gaiman revamped the once-little-known U.S. comics characters **Swamp Thing** and Sandman, respectively. A vegetarian and animal-rights supporter, Morrison instilled these same values in Baker, a first for American comics. As a result, at one point during Morrison's run on the title, Animal Man assists an eco-terrorist group in rescuing a dolphin pod, then attempts to drown a fisherman by casting him into the ocean. (A dolphin rescues the fisherman.) However, *Animal Man* is less a political series than a postmodern one in Morrison's artful hands. Indeed, *Animal Man* crystallizes his major themes—the nature of reality, the role of the hero in a cynical world, and the inherent limitations of U.S. genre comics.

If *Animal Man* allowed Morrison to address animal-rights issues and metatextual concerns, *Doom Patrol*, about a team of superhero misfits who only enhance their feelings of alienation and psychological trauma whenever they use their powers, gave him free rein to explore various literary and visual-arts methods—surrealism, Dadaism, William S. Burroughs's cut-up technique (whereby a text is broken into pieces, then rearranged to create a new, often nonlinear text)—within the superhero format. If this did not push comics boundaries enough, Morrison went so far as to introduce a character, Flex Mentallo, designed to parody Charles Atlas fitness ads, once de rigueur in American comics dating back to the 1940s. (In 1996, Morrison and Quitely produced a *Flex Mentallo* four-issue miniseries.) In addition, Morrison's *Doom Patrol* is infamous for its many challenging, subversive, comics-referencing moments, including a dream sequence satirizing 1960s-era **Marvel Comics' Stan Lee/Jack Kirby**-style rock-'em-sock-'em fight sequences, specifically the battle royal from a *Fantastic Four* story called "This Man . . . This Monster." In a standalone one-shot issue titled *Doom Force Special* published in 1992, Morrison spoofed the bombastic, intellectually faint storytelling approach of then-popular *X-Force* artist Rob Liefeld. Morrison would also simultaneously send up Marvel Comics' brutal **Punisher** character and reference an old **Superman's** pal Jimmy Olsen story ("The Bearded Boy") in *Doom Patrol* issue #53 (1992), titled "The Beard Hunter"—allusions within parodies within dream sequences. Although criticized as bordering on, if not being completely, unintelligible to anyone but the staunchest comics collectors, *Doom Patrol* won a cult following and much critical adulation. *Doom Patrol* co-creator and original writer Arnold Drake believed only Morrison treated the characters to their truest, fullest expression (Johnston 2007).

Morrison's masterpiece of conspiracy-adventure comics and longest work to date remains *The Invisibles*, about a secret globe-spanning group of very odd heroes (including a Brazilian transsexual shaman named Lord Fanny and

MORRISON AS COMICS CHARACTER

Morrison has no problem appearing in comics that he himself writes. He first appeared as a comics character with a cameo in *Animal Man* #14 (1989). He confronts Buddy Baker at the end of issue #25 and spends most of #26 (1990) talking at length with the hero about the arbitrary creator and his creations and the link between reality and fiction. Morrison later appears among the Seven Unknown Men of Slaughter Swamp in the *Seven Soldiers* miniseries (2005). In that same series, Morrison, wearing a DC Comics logo tie clip, appears in the final chapter and narrates the concluding events. Morrison also appears in an issue of *Simpsons Comics*, fighting with another comics writer, Mark Millar, over the title of "Writer of X-Men" (2003).

a Liverpool soccer hooligan who may or may not be a/the Buddha) battling mental fascism and psychic oppression via a number of different tactics—magic, time travel, astral projection, tantric sex rituals, immersion tanks, Monarch butterfly hunting, and more. The Invisibles' enemies are the Archons of Outer Church, interdimensional alien gods who have, unbeknownst to everyone, enslaved the human race. Drawn by various artists between 1996 and 2000, *The Invisibles* marks Morrison's first creator-owned project since *Zenith* and stands as the high-water mark of the psychedelic narrative in mainstream comics. However, in addition to its tripped-out plots, *The Invisibles* is thickly layered with vast, near-encyclopedic references to film, pop music, tabloid tattle, American historical events, and outré science. Above all, the series digs deeply into the notion of conspiracy theories and disinformation memes, ideas first fictionally elaborated on by extreme sci-fi writer Philip K. Dick, whose groundbreaking novel *VALIS* looms large in the evolution of *The Invisibles*, and postmodern U.S. literary superstar Thomas Pynchon, whose *The Crying of Lot 49* outlines many of the ideas that Morrison expands upon and explodes. Like his previous works, the Vertigo-published series is self-referential and playfully ironic. The difference is in the chaotic scope and sheer density of *The Invisibles*, whose only competition in terms of obsessive scholarship is Alan Moore's structured, premeditated, and labyrinthine Jack-the-Ripper saga *From Hell*.

Even as he blew minds wide open with *The Invisibles*, Morrison continued to take on work-for-hire assignments. He was tasked with revamping the Justice League of America, featuring every major DC Comics character—Superman, Batman, **Wonder Woman**—characters virtually synonymous with American comics. Indeed, Morrison's run on *JLA* (1997–2000) was a significant commercial success. Critics credit it for changing the direction of superhero comics from cynical realism à la *Watchmen* to wide-eyed, "wide-screen" action. After his run was collected in four volumes, in addition to the graphic novel *JLA: Earth 2*, Morrison would leave DC for Marvel. From 2001 to 2004, he began writing the top **X-Men** title, *New X-Men*, followed by two limited series, *Marvel Boy* and *Fantastic Four: 1234*.

While at Marvel, Morrison launched creator-owned Vertigo projects like the lukewarmly received *Seaguy*, about a superpowerless hero in a scuba suit with a cigar-smoking tuna fish for a sidekick, and the more ambitious, better-reviewed, darkly psychedelic *The Filth*, about a pornography-obsessed sex addict who also belongs to a secret organization waging war against hordes of "anti-people." Perhaps his most affecting and unanimously praised work during the early 2000s is *We3*. Drawn by Frank Quitely, *We3* marks Morrison's return to his animal-rights platform, yet in a larger and more profound sense as the graphic novel tells an emotional—and often wordless—escape tale about a trio of weaponized lab animals who encounter humans along the way—with mixed reactions. It was because of triumphs like *We3* that Morrison was voted as the number two favorite comic book writer of all time by Comic Book Resources in 2006. (Morrison even beat Neil Gaiman, voted number three, and was only topped by writing deity Alan Moore.)

Despite the success of and acclaim for his creator-owned Vertigo work, Morrison was and is still referred to by industry editors as the "revamp guy." He once again rekindled interest in obscure DC characters with *Seven Soldiers of Victory*. Morrison also collaborated on *52*, a weekly comic book series that ran for a year (hence the number 52). But his most enduring hired-gun achievement of the late 2000s is his 12-issue series *All-Star Superman* (again with Quitely), which won many awards—Eisner for Best New Series 2006, Best Continuing Series Eisner 2007, and several U.K. Eagle Awards. *All-Star Superman* also won three Harveys in 2008 and an Eisner for Best Continuing Series in 2009. Since this massive achievement, Morrison has relaunched and written *The Authority* and *WildC.A.T.s* for the DC imprint WildStorm, along with *Batman*, *Batman and Robin*, *Batman Incorporated*, and *Final Crisis* (a cosmic adventure series relying on Jack Kirby's New Gods characters) for DC Comics. For Vertigo, Morrison has produced another surreal superhero escapade, *Seaguy 2: The Slaves of Mickey Eye*, as well as the series *Joe the Barbarian*, in which the young protagonist suffers from diabetes and, in a hypoglycemic state, hallucinates his adventures in a fantasy realm while in the real world he looks for soda.

In addition to his celebrated and widely appreciated comics work, Morrison is a playwright, short-story writer, journalist, travel writer, and TV screenwriter. A member of the Writer's Guild of America, he has penned screenplays for Dreamworks Animation SKG and for a handful of video games, including *Predator: Concrete Jungle* and *Battlestar Galactica*. He reportedly records music with his band, which includes his wife and manager Kristan.

IMPACT ON COMICS

Morrison's iconic status stems from his dual reputation, his unparalleled achievement in both creator-owned and mercenary endeavors. On the one hand, he is uniformly considered to be a very challenging writer unafraid to introduce avant-gardism, experimentalism, and strong postmodern elements of metatextuality, metafiction, and pastiche. (Metatextuality is intertextual discourse, in which one text makes critical commentary on another text. Metafiction is fiction that self-consciously addresses the devices of fiction, thereby exposing the fictional illusion. Pastiche, finally, is a literary composition borrowing from the style or content of several other different works.) Morrison is not the first to employ such techniques, but he is arguably the first comics author to push them as far as they can go, particularly in the case of *The Invisibles*. Moreover, his ability to cobble together a vast array of literary and mythic archetypes and historical figures into a single storyline has rarely, if ever, been matched. Moore and Gaiman remain his only close rivals in this arena.

On the other hand—and quite unlike Moore and Gaiman—Morrison enjoys an enviable status within the mainstream comics community as a master conceptualizer and perhaps the single most important iconic (as well as obscure) comics character revamper of the last 15 years. No other author has had the same level of success in taking stale or forgotten properties, brushing off the corrosion or dust, and presenting them newly polished for readers to admire and read in awe. Nowhere is this more apparent than in Morrison and Quitely's *All-Star Superman*, in which Morrison attempted to present the essential elements of the Man of Steel. Indeed, *Time* magazine's Lev Grossman ranked *All-Star Superman* third in his "Top 10 Graphic Novels of 2007" list. Grossman praised Morrison for expertly and acutely writing a character that, because of his invincible powers and upright moral code, is difficult to flesh out.

As a result of these very different, somewhat opposing, achievements, Morrison's approach to writing comics can be (over)simplified as twofold. First, in his creator-owned Vertigo projects, he takes narrative risks while constantly striving to formally innovate and to deconstruct the elements of storytelling that readers often take for granted—linearity, scene-cutting and transitions, creative whims—and to unmask the clichés many comics fans are often too eager to swallow—say, gratuitous fight scenes. For this reason, Morrison is arguably more responsible than any other comics writer for defining the Vertigo brand and house style. However, when working with corporate characters like Superman, Morrison instead indulges readers, embracing their desire for spectacle and wonder and awe while really only tweaking the basic template—or some might call it "formula"—just enough so that everything is fresh and nothing is rendered too alien for fans to accept. His fingerprints are everywhere upon the DC Universe of the last 15 years. Thus, Morrison holds the rather unusual distinction of being adored by superhero comics fans and sequential-art critics alike.

IMPACT ON AMERICAN CULTURE

Morrison's work in other media is significant. His playwriting has resulted in two productions performed by Oxygen House at the Edinburgh Fringe. More recently, his sociological, historical, and cultural examination of superhero comics titled *Supergods: What Masked Vigilantes, Miraculous Mutants, and a Sun God from Smallville Can Teach Us about Being Human* is already considered a landmark piece of scholarship. Kirkus Reviews called *Supergods* "as thorough an account of the superhero phenomenon as readers are likely to find, filled with unexpected insights and savvy pop-psych analysis" (2011). Morrison's nonfiction debut was listed as number one in *Wired* magazine's 2011 list of "10 Books That Will Fry Your Mind This Summer." Amazon named *Supergods* among the Best Books of the Month for July 2011, saying it "succeeds at being a great history of comic books over the past century, but it's an even more convincing exploration of humankind as a whole" (2011).

Morrison was also the subject of a 2010 feature-length documentary, *Grant Morrison: Talking with Gods*. The film closely examines Morrison's life, career, and seemingly infinite imagination, offering sit-down interviews with Morrison and his many collaborators in the industry. The film enjoyed a limited U.S. theatrical release, followed by a DVD release. Though not widely reviewed, *Talking with Gods* is popular among fans and praised in comics blogs. He makes a cameo appearance in a video for the song "Art Is the Weapon" by popular U.S. emo-rock band My Chemical Romance.

SUMMARY

Morrison is the definition of the iconic creator in the American comics industry, one who manages to walk an interesting line between maverick genius and crowd-pleasing blockbuster writer. A practitioner of chaos magic, he claims to have been abducted by aliens in Kathmandu and to have communicated with demons. These experiences have heavily influenced his scripts, especially *The Invisibles*. That he almost died of an infection during the writing of that series causes his fans to consider him an almost-martyred artist who nearly died for his comics work. Morrison proves that a true creative talent in comics can have his cake and eat it, too. That he continued to write controversial titles for British comics companies up until the mid-1990s speaks to his commitment to his native industry—and to his subversive nature, given that these titles included *The New Adventures of Adolf Hitler* and autobiographical anti–Margaret Thatcher rumination *St. Swithin's Day*. Morrison follows his muse in true iconic fashion.

See also Arkham Asylum; DC Comics; Gaiman, Neil; Moore, Alan

ESSENTIAL WORKS

Morrison, Grant (w), Frank Quitely (p), and Jamie Grant (i). *All-Star Superman Vol. 1* and *Vol. 2*. New York: DC Comics, 2007 and 2009.

Morrison, Grant (w), Chas Truog (p), and Doug Hazlewood (i). *Animal Man Books 1–3*. New York: DC Comics, 1999–2002.

Morrison, Grant (w), and various artists (p, i). *The Invisibles Volume 1–7*. New York: DC Comics, 1999–2002.

FURTHER READING

Callahan, Timothy. *Grant Morrison: The Early Years*. Edwardsville, IL: Sequart Research & Literacy Organization, 2007.

Morrison, Grant. *Supergods: What Masked Vigilantes, Miraculous Mutants, and a Sun God from Smallville Can Teach Us about Being Human*. New York: Spiegel and Grau, 2011.

Jarret Keene

Mr. Natural

As a reluctant guru, **Robert Crumb**'s Mr. Natural cajoled others—physically and mentally—to fulfill their potential and to resist the temptations of consumerism dominating American culture. Mr. Natural is not only one of the prominent faces of the underground comix movement alongside Fritz the Cat and the **Fabulous Furry Freak Brothers**, but as one of the enduring figures of the 1960s, his reach extends beyond comics.

First emerging in underground newspapers in 1967, the irrepressible Mr. Natural appeared in numerous comic series well into the 1990s: from *Zap Comix* to *Uneeda*, *Hup*, *Bijou Funnies*, *Mystic Funnies*, and on to his own comic book series, *Mr. Natural*. A collection of stories, *The Book of Mr. Natural: Profane Tales of That Old Mystic Madcap*, was published by **Fantagraphics** in 1995, and a second edition, printed in 2010, became readily available in the graphic novel sections of mainstream bookstores.

Mr. Natural reminds us—in funny and serious ways—that American society's swing toward commercialism in the 20th century imperils our planet. One of Mr. Natural's signature moves was a swift kick to his disciple's or opponent's rear; as an iconic character, Mr. Natural will continue to apply that gesture to our culture into the future.

HISTORY

R. Crumb created the first Mr. Natural strip, "Mr. Natural: The Zen Master," for *Yarrowstalks No. 1* in 1967, a Philadelphia underground newspaper. Flakey Foont appeared two issues later, beginning his role as Mr. Natural's primary acolyte. Also in 1967, another underground newspaper, *The East Village Other*, began publishing Mr. Natural strips as well, including "Mr. Natural Meets God" and "Mr. Natural Repents."

Mr. Natural's move to the national stage occurred in the influential series *Zap Comix* in 1967, shortly followed by his own comic, which ran for three issues from 1970 to 1977. In 1976, Crumb began a weekly series of Mr. Natural strips in the *Village Voice*, but discontinued it when, as he wrote in the final installment, "I . . . I guess I'm just not cut out for this regular strip business. . . . I thought I could do it. . . . I was attracted by the economic security. . . . A regular weekly gig for that kind of money looked real good. . . . But . . . I can't handle it" (Crumb 2008, 41). Committed to a mental institution by Flakey Foont, Mr. Natural was left to languish there for years.

In an interview on National Public Radio's *Fresh Air*, Crumb cited the mysticism he experienced under the influence of LSD combined with the cartoon stereotypes he recalled of little old men with long white beards as the origin of Mr. Natural. He commented that he didn't "invent anything out of whole cloth. It all has antecedents from the popular culture, all of it" (Gross 2005). In the *R. Crumb Checklist*, Don Fiene argued the forebear of Mr. Natural was not Prof. O. G. Wottasnozzle from Elzie Segar's *Popeye* strip, as Harvey Pekar suggested, but rather a character created by Gene Ahern, "the 'little hitchhiker,' who wore a long white beard and a smock and always kept asking the question: 'Nov shmoz ka pop?'" (Fiene 1981, vi). He points to similar occurrences of the phrase in Crumb's comics that demonstrate his awareness of this character: "For instance, in the third panel of 'Hey Boparee Bop,' in the book *Head Comix*, Av and Gar say the words 'Smock hock d'pop!' [In] 'Av 'n Gar,' a character identified as 'the local acid head' says 'Shmock hock d'pop.' Finally, in a drawing published for the first time in *The Complete Fritz the Cat*, on page 74, but drawn probably in 1966 or 1967, Fritz, as the 'Evil Hypnotist' says: 'Nov shmoz k' pop'" (Fiene 1981, v–vi). In his smock, Mr. Natural also resembles Richard F. Outcault's main character in "The Yellow Kid," one of the first popular American comics characters at the turn of the 20th century.

In *Mr. Natural* #1 Crumb himself created a humorous, apocryphal past for Mr. Natural. According to "The Origins of Mr. Natural," the first record of Mr. Natural is a photograph from 1908, when he was 35 or 40, as guessed at in the photo, making him close to 100 years of age when he achieved fame in the 1960s. Mr. Natural had many vocations in his youth: running liquor, selling a wonder drug (actually ordinary tap water), as a lecturer, a magician in vaudeville, and a well-known band leader in the Chicago area. After giving away his accumulated wealth, he rode the rails and drove taxi in Afghanistan, before retreating to Death Valley in 1955. In 1960, the first group of followers created the Mr. Natural Fan Club of America. By the mid-1960s, he was touring colleges and universities and was "already coming into his own as a recognized powerful force on this planet, a great religious leader, and a living model of Godlike perfection for all of Humanity to emulate" (Crumb 1970, n.p.).

Mr. Natural has lived an eventful life. A significant highlight has to be when Mr. Natural told God in "Mr. Natural Meets God" that heaven was corny and outdated, for which he was thrown out of heaven—Mr. Natural had been struck by a car—and condemned to hell. In "Mr. Natural Repents," he showed remorse, agreeing to undergo three weeks of chastisement, including rolling a heavy ball up hill with a smaller ball chained to his ankle. Another noteworthy event occurred in "Mr. Natural's 719th Meditation." In this story, he falls into deep meditation in the desert. The world changes around him: first a new highway, then a teeming city, is built around him. When a policeman shouts at him to move, he subconsciously summons the power to wipe out the city. Over time, the ruins disappear, the desert returns to its original state, and Mr. Natural wakes up. Most importantly, in a nine-month-long series in the *Village Voice*, we witness the events that led up to Mr. Natural's involuntary commitment. Following a series of curt exchanges with a naïve acolyte, Billy Bob, Mr. Natural falls into a deep hole on hike. There he has a very intense battle with the imp Pizuzu, scourge of the ancient Chaldeans, as a result of which he remembers the secret of life: hang loose. He defeats the imp and rises out of the hole determined to start a commune. Exuberant, he seeks out Flakey Foont to share the good news with him. Foont, used to Mr. Natural's troublesome antics, however, believes he has finally lost his mind. Consequently, Flakey and his girlfriend commit Mr. Natural to a mental institution.

Mr. Natural was a barometer for the 1960s and 1970s. His ascent as ersatz guru paralleled the rise of gurus in American popular culture, for example the Beatles and their short-lived association with Maharishi Mahesh Yogi, who introduced transcendentalist meditation to the West. The story "Mr. Natural Meets the Kid" parodies Guru Maharaj Ji, a boy from India, who claimed to have direct communication with God. Mr. Natural's oppositional character mirrored the counterculture of the era, spurning material possessions and popular entertainment. That resistance to possessiveness extended to relationships, Mr. Natural's lack of boundaries in his sexual interactions with women reflecting the acceptance of open relationships during the era. Such cultural phenomena waned, however, and Mr. Natural, perhaps, lost the pulse of American culture, unable or unwilling to respond to the nihilism of the punk movement, to the corporatization of the Reagan era, or to the giddiness of the dot.com revolution.

IMPACT ON COMICS

As part of R. Crumb's stable of characters, especially those appearing in the early issues of *Zap Comix*, Mr. Natural made significant impact on underground comix. He was not the first character to slice away at American hypocrisy—**Harvey Kurtzman**'s *MAD* was populated by such figures—but Mr. Natural surfaced at the right time to cut deeper. He was at the head of the pack in critiquing American greed, its obsession with celebrity, and its puritanical views on sexuality.

The iconic *Zap Comix*, of which Mr. Natural was a founding cast member, heralded a new style. Crumb stood out for his archaic style, evoking a nostalgia that belied the no-holds-barred content. Characters like Mr. Natural

STAR TREATMENT

Lucas Neff, star of *Raising Hope*, a comedy on the Fox Network, donned a Mr. Natural T-shirt on an early episode. The Mr. Natural Walking Tee, available from R. Crumb's website, depicts Mr. Natural, strolling, hands behind his back. Neff has also worn a "Keep on Truckin'" T-shirt on the show.

are easy to laugh at—even as he tortures the likes of Flakey Foont—while the events depicted in his relationship with Cheryl Borck, who dubbed herself Devil Girl, may cause one to flinch. Frank L. Cioffi writes that Crumb's comics "contain images that resonate with iconography of 1950s advertising and children's cartoons, but the stories they tell and the words being used to tell them go in directions that oppose the often conventionalized, homey, if sometimes wackily exaggerated images." Mr. Natural, for example, "a small bearded man robed in white, suggests a sage, yet his pseudo-solomonic utterances ('Keep on Truckin'!') form a disconnect with this image" (Cioffi 2001, 111).

Appearing as the women's movement was gaining traction—perhaps in response to it—much of *Zap Comix* was considered misogynist and racist. Trina Robbins argues that Crumb opened the door to comics that expressed violence toward women, with Mr. Natural, through his relationship with Devil Girl, making a significant contribution to that controversial body of work. Robbins wrote that because Crumb was a cultural hero, "his comics told everybody *else* that it was okay to draw this heavily misogynist stuff. The phenomenon of the underground commix of the seventies, so full of hatred toward women, rape, degradation, murder, and torture, I really believe can be attributed to Crumb having made this kind of work stylish" (Beauchamp 1998, 41–42). Youth, in any case, embraced both Crumb and Mr. Natural. The Natch quickly became a mascot for youth who adorned themselves with Mr. Natural patches.

IMPACT ON AMERICAN CULTURE

Though R. Crumb has been approached on numerous occasions to develop media projects based on Mr. Natural, Mr. Natural has never been the subject of a TV show, an animated cartoon, or a daily newspaper strip. Disappointed in the X-rated Ralph Bakshi film based on his character Fritz the Cat, Crumb has refused offers to create movies or television series based on his characters. Without Crumb's permission, a pornographic film, *Up in Flames*, was produced in 1973 featuring Mr. Natural and Gilbert Shelton's Fabulous Furry Freak Brothers.

Mr. Natural has been extensively marketed, sometimes without Crumb's approval. On the official R. Crumb website one can purchase sets of postcards and Mr. Natural T-shirts. A website, "Keep On Truckin' Apparel" (http://www.kotapparel.com/index.php), sells Mr. Natural Organics, images of Mr. Natural printed on organic cotton T-shirts. Tennis shoes, coffee cups, lighters, cufflinks, whistle tins, patches, and buttons have been produced, and in 1993 he was made into a squeak-toy. Crumb recently released a 12-inch-tall statue of Mr. Natural made of light-colored sandstone and hand-carved in Bali, based on a 4-and-a-half-inch statue of Mr. Natural released in 1984. Businesses have been named after Mr. Natural, including a tattoo parlor in Virginia and a music school in San Francisco's Haight-Ashbury.

Mr. Natural resists the majority of American values, though his father, whom Mr. Natural takes Flakey Foont to meet, acts out the pioneer value of good vs. bad. Immediately after meeting Flakey, Mr. Natural's father gives him a boot to the behind. Later in the story we find out that his father believes that "th' old ways is th' best ways!!" (Crumb 1973, n.p.). Clearly his father believes you must share this value or you are one of the bad guys, worthy of being thrown down the stairs as Foont was. Mr. Natural pays no heed to government or formal law. The individual is preeminent and the determiner of his or her rights. Mr. Natural through his actions counters the American value of identifying success by accumulating power, status, wealth, and property. In numerous strips he tries to persuade Flakey Foont and Shuman the Human to forego each of these things. In fact, Mr. Natural deplores success, even his own. Just as he gains in popularity, he abandons everything and heads back to his refuge in the desert. Mr. Natural, as exemplified in "Mr. Natural's 719 Meditation," does not believe in the kind of progress in which the growth of cities encroaches on the natural world. He will do everything in his power to turn back the tide of such expansion. For the most part Mr. Natural satirizes the American value of hard work. Yet late in his career, in *Mystic Funnies* #1, in response to Flakey's disappointment that Mr. Natural can be "cynical and opportunistic" (Crumb 1997, n.p.), Mr. Natural points out a waitress of 35 years and a businessman beloved by his employees as examples of saints.

Throughout his long existence, Mr. Natural has taught us to ask our own questions, to seek our own answers, to recognize what can be destructive in our world—media, addiction, laziness, the trap of material possessions, and the loss of open space and its transformative calm.

SUMMARY

Mr. Natural has a long and perhaps checkered past, both in comic fiction and fact. As satire of the shallow attempts at spiritual growth prevalent in the 1960s and 1970s, Mr. Natural will remain an illuminating emblem of the era. Making fun of those who seek out help before they help themselves will continue to be relevant as we appear to still be capable of being duped by individuals or organizations that claim to provide the answers to all our questions.

Mr. Natural's legacy, however, is problematic. It is said that he is R. Crumb's most likable character. And so it goes in early appearances in *Yarrowstalks*, the *East Village Other*, and the first four issues of *Zap Comix* in which the Natch is as charming as a Zen koan, challenging, unpredictable, irascible, poised to slap a follower—usually the hapless Flakey Foont—the moment his mind veers toward laziness or selfishness. He nudges, pushes, shoves us to make up our own mind, to make our own decisions. He's a libertarian extraordinaire. Yet a number of events make Mr. Natural's popularity questionable: the molestation of Big Baby in "On the Bum Again, Part One," for which he was imprisoned, along with Big Baby. The cover of *The Complete Crumb Comics: Volume 7* addresses this notorious comic, showing Mr. Natural in a baby bonnet dancing with Big Baby, a baby bottle, and a baby powder can, with a caption declaring, "Relax! Believe it or not she's over eighteen!" (Crumb 1991/2009, cover). Mr. Natural's violent treatment of Devil Girl in a number of stories, actions that those who don cozy cotton Mr. Natural T-shirts may have repressed or chosen to ignore, may be difficult to reconcile as well.

In many ways, Mr. Natural represents the superego, the best of human nature—self-reliance, independence, compassion, a sense of timelessness and universality. The events mentioned above, however, make it obvious that Mr. Natural is as vulnerable to the excesses of the id as anyone. A remarkably complex cartoon character, Mr. Natural will make readers laugh or cringe—or both at the same time—for generations.

See also Crumb, Robert; Fabulous Furry Freak Brothers; Fantagraphics; *Zap Comix*

ESSENTIAL WORKS

Crumb, R. "Mr. Natural in Death Valley." *Zap Comix* #0, Apex Novelties, 1968. Reprinted in *The Complete Crumb Comics Volume 4: Mr. Sixties!* Seattle: Fantagraphics, 2009.

Crumb, R. "Mr. Natural: I Am the Greatest." *Mr. Natural* #2 (1971), Apex Novelties. Reprinted in *The Book of Mr. Natural: Profane Tales of That Old Mystic Madcap*. Seattle: Fantagraphics, 2010.

Crumb, R. "Mr. Natural Meets the Kid." *Zap Comix* #7, Apex Novelties, 1974. Reprinted in *The Complete Crumb Comics Volume 10: Crumb Advocates Violent Overthrow*. Seattle: Fantagraphics, 1997.

FURTHER READING

George, Milo, ed. *The Comics Journal Library, Volume 3: R. Crumb*. Seattle: Fantagraphics, 2004.

Hatfield, Charles. *Alternative Comics: The Emerging Literature*. Jackson: University Press of Mississippi, 2005.

Crag Hill

Sacco experimented with a number of nonfiction genres, including an account of his travels with the band Miracle Workers during a 1988 European tour, a history of U.S. and British bombing campaigns during World War II, a biographical piece about his mother's experiences as a girl during World War II in Malta, and a story chronicling his reaction to the start of the first Gulf War.

In search of a new project in 1991, Sacco decided on a comic about the situation in the Middle East. He saw the comic as an opportunity to discuss issues from the Palestinian point of view because he felt their story deserved more attention. He chose journalism as his vehicle because he did not want to be "an intifada tourist" bent on satisfying his own curiosity (Powers 1995, 102).

IMPACT ON COMICS

Palestine established journalistic storytelling as a genre of nonfiction comics, and Sacco adapted the conventions of reporting to the comics form. This graphic novel not only tells the stories of the Palestinians Sacco interviewed, but follows the creator's own journey to find his journalistic voice.

Comics scholars discuss the impact of comics journalism within the larger framework of independent or alternative comics. Making the case for alternative comics as literature, Charles Hatfield (2005) noted that long-form comics, in particular, are "capable of supporting ambitious, disarmingly original and questioning work" (163).

Palestine tackled serious subject matter, representing the realities of life in the Palestinian territories, often in gruesome detail. Sacco's nonfiction graphic novel is appropriately situated within the influential body of work produced in the last 25 years that demonstrates there is nothing inherent in the form that relegates it to the production of juvenile fantasy literature. The key difference, however, is Sacco's self-identification as a journalist. *Palestine* develops the "vocabulary" of journalistic storytelling in comics form.

As the writer/artist of *Palestine*, Sacco determines the way in which text and images work together to tell the story. However, he cannot ignore the narrative conventions of journalism, particularly regarding who is telling the story. Like much mainstream reporting, Sacco's graphic novel is a blend of the past and the present. Sacco uses his interview subjects' words to re-create their experiences both textually and visually. In addition, he records events as an eyewitness.

A skillful interviewer, Sacco obtains details that provide him with material for visual storytelling. He noted, "(W)hen I was telling someone's story as a flashback, I relied on the answers to the 'visual' questions I had asked to render the episode satisfactorily" (Sacco 2007, xxii). He also visits many of the locations in order to provide a visual reference for his drawings. He demonstrates this technique in a story titled "The Boys: Part One." Panels that show

FOOTNOTES IN GAZA

A decade after he traveled to the Middle East to gather material for *Palestine*, Joe Sacco returned to the Gaza Strip. He made two trips between November 2002 and March 2003 to conduct research for his graphic novel *Footnotes in Gaza*. This time, as he is reminded when his application for press credentials is denied, his primary focus is not "real-time" news. Instead, his interest is in a massacre in Kahn Younis in November 1956 during which the Israelis, during a brief occupation of the Egyptian-ruled Gaza Strip, killed 275 Palestinian civilians.

Journalists and historians both record the past—it is just that journalists have access to sources while events are still relatively fresh in their minds. Sacco's challenge was to piece together a narrative from 1956 through records and through recollections of those who survived. As he did in *Palestine*, Sacco captures his own search for information in the present, using it to reconstruct images of the past. As he writes in his introduction, "The past and the present cannot be so easily disentangled."

him and his guides are juxtaposed with Sacco's re-creation of the events in 1987, drawn from the same angle.

Sacco experiments with different techniques for signifying the past. In some stories, such as "The Bucket," he introduces his sources and includes the question or questions that begin the narrative of past events. Then he embeds panels depicting the past in the interview scene, using captions to designate quotes that narrate the past. When he shifts back to the present, his subjects' voices are captured in word balloons. This subtle difference serves to remind the reader which images Sacco sees and which images he creates through the words of others.

In a later chapter of *Palestine*, he uses the same technique of differentiating time through the use of captions and word balloons, but he does not alternate between present and past. Sacco chooses three Palestinians to narrate an account of life in Ansar III, the largest Israeli prison. The images all depict the past. He uses small drawings in inset panels to signal who is speaking (journalists would refer to photos this size as "mug shots").

For one story, "Moderate Pressure, Part II," Sacco places his panels on black pages as another way to signal the shift from present to past. He continued to employ this technique for later works, most notably *Safe Area Goražde*.

These techniques represent a hybrid visual-textual form of journalistic attribution. They help readers distinguish between Sacco's first-person accounts and the information from others (signified in print news with direct and indirect quotes and in television news with voice-overs). This distinction is essential in journalism, because it allows readers to determine how much credence to give accounts of events based on *who* is telling the story. In fact, the practice of including sources with opposing views in a news story is a convention of journalistic storytelling that acknowledges the often interpretive nature of news narratives—at least on the part of the sources.

However, conventions of mainstream reporting require journalists themselves to remain outside the story they report. The prohibition against editorializing—that is, including the journalist's opinions in the story—and the practice of writing in the third person are meant to signal the journalist's objectivity. Even in television coverage, the use of "I" is generally limited to statements of information, such as "I can see" or "I am told" (Fox and Park 2006, 48).

Palestine is first-person reporting, however, and Sacco employs a "stream of consciousness" approach as he breathlessly shares his impressions and thoughts with the reader. This changes as *Palestine* unfolds. Sacco's eyewitness reports adhere more and more closely to the rules of reporting. He shifts the focus from himself to the people he interviews, gradually removing himself from the narrative, and he increasingly disciplines both text and image.

Sacco begins *Palestine* by foregrounding his presence both visually and textually, refusing to retreat behind the invisible language of reporting in print journalism, where the reporter's own voice is never evident. Nor does he distance himself from events the way script and camera techniques in television news do. He is part of the action, rather than standing in the foreground.

Sacco also draws himself at work. He drinks tea with his sources, inspects the scars on the back of a man interrogated by Israelis, shoots photos of poor living conditions in Jabalia, and summons the courage to cover a demonstration in Ramallah that quickly turns violent. The images are accompanied by Sacco's internal monologue. For example, he shares his thoughts during the demonstration: "I don't want to get too close. . . . I promised mom I'd be careful. . . . besides I'm shaking like a . . . leaf" (Sacco 2001, 121).

However, readers see less and less of Sacco as *Palestine* continues. He appears in the background or off to the side in the panels. He talks less and listens more. Adopting a motif that would become common in comics journalism, Sacco draws himself with a notebook and pencil. The metonymic image of hands holding a notebook is all that is required to signify Sacco as reporter. This device first appears in the appropriately titled "Getting the Story," about halfway through the graphic novel.

The reporting becomes more systematic. Instead of recording chance meetings in the market or during a taxi ride, Sacco makes a list of stories he wants to cover. Sacco's increasingly focused reporting also is reflected in the page design of the graphic novel. Initially, the pages of *Palestine* are chaotic. Images and panels overlap. The sequential order is not always clear. Further into the graphic novel, however, the design changes. The text no longer rambles across the page, panels become more rectangular, and pages are designed in easy-to-follow grids. This signifies Sacco's acceptance of the narrative boundaries of journalistic storytelling. By adhering, albeit gradually, to journalistic conventions of reportorial distance, Sacco moves from a story he conceived initially as autobiographical to "something more journalistic" (Gilson 2005, 80).

Sacco's later work carries forward this more disciplined approach. In *Safe Area Goražde*, he employs many of the storytelling techniques he developed in *Palestine*. Black page borders signify the narratives by others of past events. He is a subdued presence in the graphic novel, and his interviews and the stories they tell are much more purposeful.

Even in shorter pieces, such as "Up! Down! You're in the Iraqi Army Now" for *Harper's* in April 2007, Sacco largely adheres to the convention of the unseen, omniscient narrator expected in mainstream journalism, never introducing himself to the reader either textually or visually. He appears in the background in several panels, but the readers cannot pick him out unless they know how Sacco draws himself. It is not until the final two pages that Sacco shifts to first person and draws himself interviewing Iraqi soldiers.

With so few creators working in this highly specialized genre of nonfiction comics, it is difficult to say yet how Sacco has influenced other comics journalists. Certainly his success, and the attention it has focused on the genre, has raised the profile of other works. As the study and production of comics are incorporated into university curricula, a new generation of creators may cross disciplinary boundaries to learn journalistic storytelling in the comics form. And when they do, Sacco's work will be their textbook.

IMPACT ON AMERICAN CULTURE

Sacco's *Palestine* is linked to the broader culture in two key ways. First, like the New Journalism to which it has been compared, *Palestine* expanded the debate on the nature of journalistic storytelling. Second, *Palestine* can be read as a work of media criticism.

While comics scholars such as Hatfield have analyzed comics journalism as a form of literature, Rocco Versace (2007) and others tie comics journalism specifically to the New Journalism of the 1960s and 1970s. In addition to New Journalism, this style of writing has been called narrative journalism, literary journalism, and creative nonfiction. In a longer form, it has been classified as the nonfiction novel. New Journalism is characterized by the use of fiction techniques such as dialogue, description, and a narrative voice that places the writer in the scene, rather than as an omniscient observer.

Sacco makes use of the same fiction techniques, but he employs both text and image. Versace argues that the New Journalists and comics journalism challenged mainstream reporting's claim of objectivity by foregrounding the interpretive nature of all journalistic storytelling. The comics form allows journalists "to foreground their role as reporter . . . visually as well as textually" in several ways: the artwork calls attention to reporting as a creative process; the images of journalists in their own stories reinforce their presence; the page layouts remind readers of the journalist's role in determining narrative structure; and visual details produce a more "layered" story than prose alone (Versace 2007, 115–21).

Versace's views echo an earlier piece by Kristian Williams (2005), published in *Columbia Journalism Review*, where the author argues that comics journalism is "inherently subjective" because of the combination of text and image (52). Williams concludes that by rejecting objectivity simply through the choice of the comics form, journalists open up possibilities in journalistic storytelling and provide options for readers by providing interpretive reporting.

Both Williams and Versace, however, discount the powerful influence of journalistic conventions on both the practice and reception of reporting. Sacco's *Palestine* is not about his disregard of the practices of mainstream journalism. Rather, it is about his struggle to resolve the tensions between the conventions of mainstream journalism—which he learned in college—and the form of comics, which is read as a creative work, rather than reportorial.

The debate over New Journalism tried, unsuccessfully, to resolve whether such works can still be considered journalism. The boundary between journalism and literature may be artificial, but works such as *Palestine* that occupy this territory "between" are useful as a way to examine our own understanding of journalists and the stories they tell.

Not only does Sacco's comics journalism provide a rich entry into the debate about the nature of journalism, but Sacco uses *Palestine* to criticize journalism by questioning its purpose. Journalism reveals problems, but it seldom provides solutions. Reporting is voyeuristic, the very trap Sacco vowed not to fall into when he settled on the story of the Palestinians as a project.

This is a theme that Sacco returns to frequently. At first, Sacco is confident about his reasons for his visit. In "Blind Dates," a man he interviewed says, "You write something about us? I showed you, you saw! You tell about us?" Sacco's aside to the reader: "Of course of course! I'm off to fill my notebook! I will alert the world to your suffering!" (Sacco 2005, 10).

As he continues to seek material for his comic, though, Sacco begins to doubt his mission. In the story "Law," a man asks, "What good does it do, your coming here to write about these things?" (Sacco 2001, 161). Sacco does not record his reply, if indeed he had one. Later, in "Pilgrimage," a woman asks him, "How are words going to change things?" After fumbling for an answer, Sacco looks away and says to Sameh, who is translating, "Tell her I don't know what to say to her" (Sacco 2001, 243).

The relentless misery that Sacco so gleefully sets out to uncover early on in *Palestine* begins to weigh on him—an occupational hazard of journalism that usually goes untold. In "Pilgrimage," a chapter-long story, Sacco muses that his guide, Sameh, has "heard every blow and humiliation described twice, once by the person telling me, and again when it comes out of *his* mouth as translator" (Sacco 2001, 219). Later in the chapter, he draws Sameh weeping.

These tears—which Sacco, as a journalist, is not allowed to shed—suggest that this narrative distancing of the journalist may be a denial of what is journalism's most powerful purpose—telling true stories that make a difference.

SUMMARY

In *Palestine*, Joe Sacco's training as a journalist in college in the 1980s and his talent as an artist come together in a pioneering work of comics journalism. He spent several weeks with the Palestinians in winter 1991–1992, learning about their lives, gathering details that would find their way into a nine-issue miniseries published from 1993 to 1995. Sacco established the vocabulary for comics journalism, experimenting with ways in which to represent the building blocks of reporting, such as eyewitness accounts of events and interviews, in the comics form. Not only is *Palestine* among the ranks of the nonfiction comics that have achieved acclaim outside of comics fandom, but Sacco's work is considered a part of the literary journalism movement that reemerged in the 1960s and 1970s. *Palestine*, like the works of other literary journalists, makes an important contribution to the debate about the nature and purpose of journalism.

In *Palestine*, readers see how Sacco adapts the professional norms of journalism to the comics form. At the same time, he struggles to resolve the tensions that this adaptation creates. Ultimately, however, Sacco wants us to accept *Palestine* as a work of journalism.

See also Fantagraphics; Sacco, Joe

ESSENTIAL WORK

Sacco, Joe. *Palestine*. Seattle: Fantagraphics Books, 2001.

FURTHER READING

Marshall, Monica. *Joe Sacco*. New York: Rosen Publishing Group, 2005.
Powers, Thom. "Joe Sacco Interview." *Comics Journal* 176 (1995): 88–109.
Versace, Rocco. *This Book Contains Graphic Language: Comics as Literature.* New York: Continuum, 2007.

Amy Kiste Nyberg

Plastic Man

Plastic Man, the "Pliable Prankster," sprang into action in *Police Comics* #1 (1941) and was quickly hailed as one of the most madcap and unique superheroes in the Golden Age of comics. Created for Quality Comics by writer and artist Jack Cole as part of a superhero anthology title, Plastic Man's debut adventure was a six-page story buried in the middle of the comic book. Other characters featured in that premiere issue included Firebrand, the Human Bomb, and Phantom Lady, but they were all soon eclipsed by Cole's creation. His creativity and imagination attracted so many readers that Plastic Man was promoted as the cover's featured hero by the fifth issue. Soon the hero was appearing in 15-page stories, which were longer than the typical Superman and Batman tales of the era, and he earned the opening position in *Police Comics*. While many other heroes populated the comic book, Plastic Man was the undisputed star of the title for most of its 102-issue run. Although he was not comics' first elastic hero, Plastic Man's success led to a number of similarly stretchable superheroes, such as Mr. Fantastic and Elongated Man. Although Cole left the character in the 1950s, his slapstick tone and offbeat humor have continued as his hero's defining characteristics. The superhero has been revived a number of times over the decades, but these attempts have never been commercially successful. Still, because Plastic Man is a favorite figure of many comics creators and fans, he has bounced back in a variety of titles, television programs, and toys.

HISTORY

It is ironic that comics' most lighthearted superhero was devised by the depressive Jack Cole, who was largely self-trained. Cole entered the industry in 1937 and was soon considered a "triple threat" for his skills as a writer, artist, and editor. He started working for Harry "A" Chesler before moving on to Lev Gleason Publications where he toiled on such superheroic characters as Daredevil (no relation to the **Marvel Comics** character). In late 1940, Cole was hired by Quality Comics publisher Everett "Busy" Arnold for its new line of superhero comics. Cole would remain at Quality Comics for the rest of his comic book career. Among his first assignments was assisting **Will Eisner** on *The Spirit*. He learned much about how to compose a story both narratively and artistically from his apprenticeship alongside Eisner. His most notable creation during this period was Midnight, a Spirit knock-off who was partnered with a talking monkey. Busy Arnold had requested a clone of the popular hero in the event that Eisner got drafted into the Army during World War II. Later, Cole and Lou Fine were the primary ghost artists on *The Spirit* when Eisner entered military service.

A few months after his creation of Midnight, Cole was inspired to create Plastic Man after seeing some circus sideshow freaks. He initially intended to name his character the "India Rubber Man," but Busy Arnold suggested that "Plastic Man" would be more appropriate since it suggested the substance that was reshaping the modern world. In his 1941 origin story, "Plas" (as he was nicknamed by his friends) was introduced as a crook named "Eel" O'Brian (his true name "Patrick" would not be revealed until years later) who was cracking a safe at the Crawford Chemical Works. His gang of criminals is discovered by a guard and flees in a hail of bullets. O'Brian's fate is forever altered when a stray shot bursts a large chemical vat and he is showered with acid. Abandoned by his fellow thieves, an injured and desperate O'Brian runs for miles through a swamp and into the mountains before he falls unconscious. Upon awakening, he learns he has been discovered by some kindly monks who have tended to his wounds and shielded him from the police. Inspired by their generosity and belief that he deserves a second chance, O'Brian immediately vows to reform his criminal ways. Only then does he discover that his physical body has been as transformed as his soul. The acid has affected him so that he is now like a human rubber band—a man who can stretch his shape into any form he can imagine. He looks into a mirror and exclaims, "What a powerful weapon this would be . . . against crime! I've been *for* it long enough! Here's my chance to atone for all the evil that I've done!" Upon his recovery, he returns to his old gang as "Eel" O'Brian and then captures them as Plastic Man. He maintained his malicious persona to gather information on criminal activity through his underworld connections. In later stories Plas was an FBI agent. He concealed his identity by remolding his face into the more attractive hero. Plastic Man's costume was a red rubber suit with yellow and black stripes that stretched along with his various contortions. He also wore large wrap-around goggles instead of a traditional mask. One of the recurring fun features of the stories was Plas transforming himself into some character, vehicle, or object. Readers soon learned to spot the hero in his various disguises by his signature suit, which was retained no matter the form.

Plastic Man's superpower made him capable of stretching every atom of his body into any shape he desired. He seemed totally unbreakable, and his

OFFSPRING

Plastic Man is not the only stretchable superhero in the DC Comics roster. In 1999, Mark Waid (w) and Frank Quitely (a) introduced readers to Offspring—Plastic Man's son. Debuting in *The Kingdom: Offspring* #1, a spin-off of the noncontinuity miniseries *The Kingdom* (which was itself a sequel to *Kingdom Come*), Offspring is actually Ernie O'Brian, who is treated as a joke by his family, friends, and foes. He wears a predominantly white outfit, with black areas that resemble a design similar to a soccer ball.

Although this version of the character did not exist in mainstream DC Comics continuity, it is later revealed in the pages of *JLA* that Plastic Man does have a son named Luke "Loogie" McDunnagh—his illegitimate child by "Angel" McDunnagh. This version of Offspring has a unique set of powers of his own: he can change his color and mass as well as manipulate his shape. Plastic Man asks Batman to scare his son straight after the youth falls in with a gang. Offspring is also briefly a member of the Teen Titans. He also made appearances in DC's *52*, a limited weekly series that began in 2006.

shape-shifting was limited only by his own overactive imagination. Every story presented Plas manipulating himself into an endless variety of forms as he fought crime. He could disguise himself as a chair, boat, automobile, lasso, snake, blimp, parachute, or whatever popped into his mind. He could change his features to impersonate anyone and never stretched exactly the same way twice. He was also known for his mercurial sense of humor. Plastic Man was apparently invulnerable as bullets bounced off him, and he could even be flattened by a steamroller without any harm. However, he could be affected by intense temperatures. Great heat made him melt while freezing cold would make him stiffen like a board.

In *Police Comics* #13 (1942) Plastic Man was joined by one of the most unique sidekicks in comic book history—Woozy Winks, a bumbling, overweight man with a strange superpower of his own. After saving a wizard from drowning, he was rewarded by a spell that caused the forces of nature to protect him from harm. Initially he employed his new invulnerability for crime before he was reformed by Plastic Man. This power was ignored in later stories and Woozy was presented as Plas's inept friend and assistant. He was usually depicted as wearing a green outfit with large black polka dots and a wide-brimmed straw hat. Woozy's personality was based on that of Lou Costello, a popular comedian of the era, and his body echoed Popeye's pal Wimpy mixed with filmmaker Alfred Hitchcock. Woozy Winks's chubby body and bulbous nose offered a fine artistic contrast to the tall, slender Plastic Man who sported a pointy nose and a body that seemingly jutted out at all angles.

Other than Woozy, Cole never developed a recurring supporting cast or rogues' gallery. The villains were a unique array of bad guys with names like Doctor Erudite, the Sinister Six, Madam Brawn, Mister Morbid, Wriggles Enright, and Spadehead. One of the more notable of these foes was Amorpho, an alien blob of protoplasm that faced Plastic Man in *Police Comics* #21 (1950). Like Plas, Amorpho was a shape shifter that could assume the appearance of anything or anyone it encountered. It needed vast amounts of salt for sustenance and began a crime spree to replenish itself. Amorpho eventually assumes Plastic Man's form and a battle erupts before the hero ties him in knots and forces him to return to outer space. Another bizarre antagonist was Cyrus Smyth, a deceased 17th-century alchemist whose brain has been transplanted into the body of a dying Army pilot. He is further transformed into a giant that must walk on its hands since the body he possesses is paralyzed below the waist. He swallows Plastic Man whole, but is choked to death when Plas climbs out of his stomach and lodges himself in the giant's windpipe! Many of Cole's villains would meet a form of justice that was outside the bounds of the normal judicial system or superhero code.

IMPACT ON COMICS

Jack Cole's Plastic Man adventures were bizarre concoctions of wit, whimsy, and vaudeville shenanigans that were meshed with a surrealistic art style. His boldly expressive drawings with their humorously exaggerated bodily features in the early issues evolved into elegant expressionism. During this era, comic book artists were expected to master all aspects of the visual form: drawing, inking, and lettering. Cole was a master at all three. His brushstrokes and strong contrasts between light and dark played against a constant variety of viewpoints. The stories flow logically (no matter how wacky the plot) and are a wonderful blend of the written word and sight gags. The reader is continually engaged by pages that are bursting with a vitality that is absent from many other Golden Age superheroes' exploits. Cole's Plastic Man stories may be seen as a predecessor to *Mad*, which launched in 1952 with its own anarchic spirit. The tremendous popularity of Plastic Man allowed the hero to headline his own comic book starting in 1943. Cole was at the peak of the comics industry in the postwar years. He was earning the top rate for comic books (about $35 per page) as well as occasional sales bonuses. However, his insistence on total creative control was causing him to burn out. When he was told that the demand for Plastic Man stories necessitated his taking on assistants and ghost artists, Cole is said to have burst into tears. Cole abandoned his signature character in 1950, although Plastic Man remained in print until 1956 when *Police Comics* became a straight police procedural.

Cole's career continued to advance even after he left Plastic Man behind and wrote a variety of crime comics. In the early 1950s, he was contacted by a young man named Hugh Hefner, who had grown up reading *Plastic Man* and called it "the most hallucinogenic comic book of its time" (Spiegelman and Kidd 2001, 113). Hefner signed Cole to an exclusive contract with his new men's magazine named *Playboy*, where he became the leading cartoonist. A few years later Cole launched a newspaper comic strip titled *Betsy and Me*. In 1958, Jack Cole committed suicide for reasons that have never been revealed. He left two suicide notes—one for his wife and the other to Hugh Hefner. In the letter to Hefner he wrote, "When you read this I shall be dead. I cannot go on living with myself & hurting those dear to me" (Spiegelman and Kidd 2001, 121–22). At the coroner's inquest, Dorothy Cole testified that, in her letter, her husband did explain why he killed himself. The contents of that note were never made public. Dorothy did not maintain contact with Cole's family or friends after his death. She remarried approximately a year later.

Cole's death may have robbed the comics of one of its true greats, but Plastic Man has continued on. In 1956, while the comics industry was seeing increased competition from television and the decline of the superhero genre, Quality Comics ceased operations. Many of its properties, such as Blackhawk, G. I. Combat, and Plastic Man were sold to **DC Comics**. Unfortunately, the elastic hero was shelved for a decade. After a one-shot appearance in the *Dial H for Hero* feature in *The House of Mystery*, Plastic Man was revived in a 1966–1968 Silver Age series written by Arnold Drake. This version of Plastic Man, however, was said to be the son of the 1940s hero. As a child he had drunk a bottle of the same acid that gave "Eel" O'Brian his powers. Without Cole's input, however, the series was an uninspired mix of campy humor and TV parodies. A revival by Ramona Fradon was briefly attempted in 1976. *Adventure Comics* became Plastic Man's new home beginning in 1980 with art by Joe Staton. Over the following decades DC Comics incorporated Plastic Man into its mainstream superhero universe with varying results. Phil Foglio presented a somewhat darker version of the character in a 1988–1989 miniseries. Many of the most prominent creators in comics today have found ways to include Plastic Man in their work recently. Among the most notable are Grant Morrison, who added Plas to the Justice League of America in the late 1990s and revealed O'Brian had a son named Luke (who took the name Offspring when he began his own heroic career); **Frank Miller**, who featured him in both *All-Star Batman and Robin, the Boy Wonder* and *Batman: The Dark Knight Strikes Again*; and Alex Ross, who frequently includes him in various covers and stories showcasing the JLA. Perhaps the most successful revitalization of Plastic Man occurred in a 2004–2006 series written and drawn by Kyle Baker. Unlike previous revival attempts, which did not employ Cole's cartoony style or humor, Baker's version of Plas was much more in step with the hero's Golden Age roots. Here, O'Brian was again an FBI operative who acted as a double agent. Woozy Winks was rescued from comics limbo to assist his old buddy. The stories were humorous and often featured exaggerated versions of other classic DC Comics characters. Baker's series was critically praised and won the 2004 Eisner Award for Best New Series, but it was canceled after 20 issues. Since that time, Plastic Man has continued to make guest appearances throughout the DC Universe.

IMPACT ON AMERICAN CULTURE

Just as no comics panel could fully contain Plastic Man, he bounced from the comic book pages themselves onto the television screen many times over the years. He made his animated debut in a 1973 episode of the Saturday morning staple *Super Friends* and gained his own series in 1979. Titled *The Plastic Man Comedy/Adventure Show*, it featured Plas fighting crime as he was assisted by two new characters: his blonde girlfriend Penny and a somewhat politically incorrect Hawaiian fellow named "Hula Hula." In a subsequent season, Plas and Penny married and were joined by their son "Baby Plas." Beginning in 2008, Plastic Man was a recurring guest on *Batman: The Brave and the Bold*. In this animated series, Batman is involved in Plas's origin, having caused the acid accident during the robbery and later helping him become a superhero.

Plastic Man has been immortalized as an action figure many times. He was featured in Kenner's popular Super Powers line of toys in 1986. In 1999, when DC Comics started its own toy company, DC Direct, Plastic Man was one of the first characters commissioned. Toy versions of the character associated with the TV programs *Justice League Unlimited* and *Batman: The Brave and the Bold* (as well as a Heroclix gaming figure) have also hit toy store shelves in recent years.

On April 19, 1999, the *New Yorker* featured Plastic Man gawking at a Picasso painting on its cover. That issue ran a biography of Jack Cole by **Art Spiegelman**, which would be expanded two years later into the book *Jack Cole and Plastic Man: Forms Stretched to Their Limits!*

SUMMARY

Plastic Man was one of the signature creations of the Golden Age of comic books. His anarchic personality, unlimited flexibility, and offbeat adventures were a perfect showcase for the unique talents of Jack Cole. This hero, who refused to be contained by any comics' panel, brought an unrestrained sense of humor and imagination to the superhero genre. Although Plastic Man has endured for decades, few subsequent writers or artists have been able to match the wit and whimsy of Cole's 1940s stories. Perhaps the best statement discussing the stretchable sleuth's iconic status in comics comes from historian Peter L. Mayer who stated, "Plastic Man was one of the wackiest, zaniest characters to pop out of the pages of a comic book, a golden persona from a golden age. And Plas is a personification of Jack Cole—a vivid yellow, red, and black embodiment of a comic art genius" (1999, 9).

See also DC Comics; *Mad*

ESSENTIAL WORKS

Baker, Kyle. *Plastic Man: On the Lam!* New York: DC Comics, 2005.
Cole, Jack. *The Plastic Man Archives, Volume 1.* New York: DC Comics, 1999.

FURTHER READING

Amash, Jim, and Mike Kooiman. *The Quality Companion: Celebrating the Forgotten Publisher of Plastic Man.* Raleigh, NC: TwoMorrows Publishing, 2011.
Cole, Jack. *Betsy and Me.* Seattle: Fantagraphic Books, 2007.
Cole, Jack. *Classic Pin-Up Art of Jack Cole.* Seattle: Fantagraphics Books, 2010.
Spiegelman, Art, and Chip Kidd. *Jack Cole and Plastic Man: Forms Stretched to Their Limits!* San Francisco: Chronicle Books, 2001.

Charles A. Coletta

Pogo

Walt Kelly's Pogo is not just the charismatic little possum who lounges in the shady glades of Georgia's Okefenokee. For mid-century Americans, Pogo and his "downhome" companions provided an astute perspective on human affairs and a warmly soothing state of mind. To know Pogo, or as "Pogo-philes" have put it over the years, to "Go Pogo," is to embrace generous tolerance and affable idealism. Like his titular critter, Kelly's animal ensemble valued humor over hatred, preferred camaraderie to conflict, and exuded thriving diversity rather than divisiveness. As an amalgamation of children's nursery rhymes, Disney-esque vitality, and Kelly's own political acumen, the anthropomorphic cast laughed, sang, and played away our failings and iniquities with special aplomb. With admirable humility and quirky wit, Pogo and pals brought fresh, hilarious awareness to wide-ranging issues such as the arms race, McCarthyism, civil rights, and the environmental movement. Yet, the strip—in all its multitudinous forms—never lost its joyful emphasis on the transcendent powers of love and friendship.

Pogo evolved physically across genres, but the charm of his good fellowship was a latent element of Kelly's concept all along. Among the most important comic strips of the 20th century, Pogo's influence quickly grew from early appearances in funny animal comics of the late 1940s to the successful newspaper strip and paperback compendiums of the 1950s, 1960s, and 1970s (Harvey 1999, 102). Looking backward, very few comic book heroes—super or otherwise—have attained so high a level of artistry or admiration as Walt Kelly's Pogo. Comparable marsupial role models are simply too scarce.

HISTORY

Of all the icons here surveyed, few have had as many stutter-starts and reboots as Pogo, but not a single one ever rang false. The first of Pogo's avatars appeared, appropriately enough, for Christmas 1941, in the premiere issue of *Animal Comics*. Fresh from a fruitful journeyman period as a Disney animator, Kelly envisioned a series of anthropomorphic Southern pastorals focusing primarily on Albert the Alligator, a devious trickster who periodically indulged in devouring his friends and neighbors. Pogo served as Albert's foil, a "genial soul who's willing to go along with anyone. He is not naïve, however, nor is he wishy-washy, he does stand up for himself and others when necessary" (Thompson 1990, 10). In early appearances, Pogo was upstaged by the equally sweet African American urchin, Bumbazine, the only human to ever appear amidst Kelly's menagerie. Some see Kelly's early removal of Bumbazine, a stereotypical "pickaninny" hold-over from Dixie humor, as the creative turning point of Kelly's concept. Substituting an animal for a caricatured minority, Kelly moved the entire oeuvre closer to allegorical fable (Thompson 1990, 8). Still, early Bumbazine tales are rife with antic adventure, remediating elements of folksy humor, children's bestiaries, vaudeville sketches, circus stunts, and antebellum comedic traditions lifted from showboats, Chautauquas, and minstrel routines. At the same time, Kelly's screwball send-up channeled Uncle Remus, Thornton Burgess, and Uncle Wiggily—also featured in *Animal Comics*—as Albert, Bumbazine, and Pogo laughed each other silly.

Emphasis eventually shifted from cold- to warm-blooded beasts, but the powerful contrast between Pogo and Albert's personalities would remain. In the strip's later incarnations, their differences still spark a poignant synergy that stands alongside America's greatest comedic duos. As Kelly described it, "Pogo is the warm hearted little guy we would all like to think we are. Albert is closer to what we think of the other fellow" (Kelly and Crouch 1984, 50). In their Albert-centric phase, *Pogo* stories would enjoy regular installments in nearly every issue of *Animal Comics* from 1942 to 1947. These were followed by two lively "Albert the Alligator and Pogo Possum" specials in *Dell's Four Color* series in 1946 and 1947 that led to the full-fledged *Pogo the Possum* **Dell** comic book that ran for 16 issues from 1949 until 1954. These contained well-crafted tales of chicanery among the swamp folk and boasted richly colored covers that stand among the most lavish examples of the time. A Dell *Pogo Parade* compendium of early *Animal Comics* reprints appeared in 1953, and aside from a few appearances in other titles like *Our Gang* and *Santa Claus Funnies*, the jovial possum's comic-book legacy was fairly finished by the mid-1950s.

Other print habitats would prove more extensive and enduring. In fact, as a syndicated newspaper strip, *Pogo* would claim its largest audience and give Kelly a public forum in nearly 300 papers, including a nationwide readership of well over 35 million by 1952. The newsprint *Pogo* also began somewhat humbly, as a feature special to the *New York Star* from October 4, 1948, through January 28, 1949. After barely four months, the *Star* folded and Kelly sold *Pogo* for syndication, where it quickly gathered steam as a cleverly relevant, especially artsy funny animal series loaded with "juicy brush strokes and hysterical folk poetry" (Marlette quoted in Kelly and Crouch 1989, 5).

(Digital Comic Museum)

As Kelly refined his material and expanded his cast, its ensemble nature became uniquely cheery. Early characters like the ever-oblivious turtle, Churchy LaFemme, and Howland the know-it-all Owl were paired with a revised Albert the Alligator who was now "warm hearted and generous, but he doesn't really like to let anybody know it for fear they'll think he's soft" (Kelly and Crouch 1984, 50). Other creations like the trusty hound Beauregard, the sweetly skunky Hepzibah, the misanthropic Porkypine, and the boisterous promoter P. T. Bridgeport (Kelly's ursine homage to P. T. Barnum) would fill out Pogo's cast alongside the itinerant foxes, wildcats, rabbits, moose, raccoon, dogs, cats, moles, chickens, mice, bugs, frogs, and assorted creatures of the American countryside who wandered across Kelly's stage. The arrival of the three Bat Brothers in March 1951 signaled one of *Pogo*'s most popular gags, a quasi-Greek chorus whose disinterested commentary on the passing show could bounce from existential irony to raucous belly laughs in a single frame. In one press release, Pogo himself declares, "Confusion seems to be a way of life in the Okefenokee Swamp that we live in. We try to do things right but they turn out a little upside down or inside out. So as Porkypine says, we don't take life too seriously 'cause it ain't nohow punishment'" (Kelly and Crouch 1984, 67).

Foremost among many familiar Pogoisms is the expression "We have met the enemy and he is us," introduced in a 1971 campaign to commemorate Earth Day. The story focuses on Pogo and Porkypine, natural swamp dwellers, who move gingerly through the "beauty" of their own "forest primeval" because of the rubbish humans have left behind. Revising Oliver Hazard Perry's declaration of victory over England in the 1813 Battle of Lake Erie, Kelly turns its bravura force inwards on itself, forcing readers to recognize their potential for apathy vis-à-vis environmental issues. As one of many cautionary ironies in *Pogo*, the surprising reversal of humanistic animals scolding people who behave like beasts chagrined earnest readers. Its fanciful frolics laced with heavy dollops of satire, *Pogo* would become the unofficial voice of the Left, centered on the promotion of social responsibility and personal liberty.

Kelly's heady commentaries were also crucial to Pogo's iconic status. Just as Charles Schulz explored loneliness and failure through the epiphanies of children, Kelly attacked the mendacity of American politics through his animals' naiveté. Pogo's creator promoted a jocund popular image, loading his press releases with self-parody, but he was, without doubt, a man of stern social responsibility and deep disregard for opportunists who endangered the public for their own self-interest. In a 1952 article for the *Chicago Review* entitled "Pogo's Politics," Kelly asserted that the average American "sees no connection between bustling onto a bus ahead of others who have been waiting longer than he and the swinging of a bloody sword against a child's head in some town in a country impossible to spell. It is only the dirty foreigners and associated villains (members of the opposition political party, or opposing [sic] church), whom he can readily identify as the enemy" (Kelly 1955, 15). From such a mind came *Pogo*'s endless stream of bizarre inversions, as if Kelly, like his great influence Lewis Carroll, sought solace in exploring the utter nonsense of human endeavor.

When Kelly deployed farce and satire against forces that he feared might stunt or abuse our freedoms, the results were thrilling. The most famous example came in 1953 with the arrival of the terrible Simple J. Malarkey, a fearsome feline lambaste of Senator Joseph McCarthy. As Bill Watterson observed about Kelly's treatments of McCarthy, Khrushchev, Spiro Agnew, and J. Edgar Hoover, "One thing, anyway, is clear: Pogo's swamp had true evil in it" (Kelly and Crouch 1989, 13). As the McCarthy and Hoover episodes would show, *Pogo*'s best weapon against the suppression of liberty was conversation: "It was a strip where characters talked and talked, inevitably misunderstood each other, and argued. It was a wonderful, rich parody of what passes for communication between human beings. The word balloons were

THE LANGUAGE OF POGO

Pogo's plots, gags, dialogue, and even its unique lettering were flooded with double and triple entendres, overloaded meanings, and mixed metaphors. Its grammar was purposely scrambled into suggestive signs that tempted brave readers to dig ever deeper into the encrypted truths underneath. Enduring examples include the ever-changing titles on Pogo's half-sunken skiff, the Gothic font attached to the preachy perspectives of Deacon Mushrat, the histrionic circus-poster graphics of P. T. Bridgeport's bombastic balloons, and, most famously, the syllabic deconstructions of familiar melodies, jingles, and songs. The gleeful dynamics of these nonsensical tunes were so captivating that "many Pogophiles whose parents taught them 'Deck Us All with Boston Charlie' and whose grandchildren are learning the song today" have elevated *Pogo's* language to a holiday tradition (Kelly and Crouch 7, 1984). Kelly even illustrated an official songbook and performed on the banjo-jammy album *Songs of the Pogo*, which brought a "hep" new dimension to the strip's already riotous musical vocabulary.

filled with puns, obscure references, inside jokes, utter nonsense, and once in a while, quiet wisdom" (Watterson quoted in Kelly and Crouch 1989, 12).

As the newspaper strips gained momentum, Kelly began to build Pogo's most enduring stage. In 1951, he released the first of nearly 40 paperback compilations, mostly through Simon & Schuster. Publishing an average of two volumes a year, these affordable editions had staying power well beyond ephemeral comic books or disposable newspaper funnies. They allowed readers to collect and study *Pogo* repeatedly in its entirety. Some books in the series do little more than reprint daily sequences, but others such as 1953's *The Pogo Papers* and 1968's *Equal Time for Pogo* reintroduce suppressed material that some editors, "quivering with courage" in Kelly's estimation, would not print. Whenever he was censored, Kelly acquiesced enough to provide "Bunny rabbit" substitutes featuring bunches of "cute little rabbits enacting very tame and quiet gags" (Goulart 2000, 73).

With no need for sweet bunnies, unfettered paperbacks like 1954's *Stepmother Goose* or 1966's *Pogo Poop Book* pushed the popular possum in surprising directions. Kelly meticulously conformed the newspaper stories to new page space, but also added lengthy segments of new material that included uncensored poems, songs, fairy tales, and stories. These miscellanies became remarkably complex, almost schizophrenic texts through which Kelly indulged audiences young and old. As a past master of children's cartooning and Christmas comics like Dell's *Santa Claus Funnies*, *The Brownies*, *Our*

Gang, and *Fairy Tale Parade*, Kelly provided children's stories in Pogospeak that celebrated sweetness and innocence.

The same books, however, included shrewd commentaries on the Army-McCarthy hearings, the John Birch Society, and the Ku Klux Klan. These wicked little parodies are even more sharply conceived than the news strips and, at times, rival the most skeptical elements of world satire. The *Pogo Stepmother Goose* offers a silly two-page revamping of Simple Simon the Pieman involving Albert and Churchy, but this is followed by the harrowing 20-page "The Trial and the Tarts," a fuming assault on the McCarthy affair that features the vicious polecat Malarky ruling over a kangaroo court described in terms of the final trial scene from *Alice in Wonderland* wherein a strangely cross-dressed Pogo portrays Carroll's plucky heroine.

Despite the chilling qualities of such strange meditations on abuse and corruption, *Pogo* remained a warm, hopeful facet of American comedy from his humble comic book birth in 1941 until the strip's official conclusion in 1975. Until that time, Pogo's inimitable charm, modest wit, and steadfast disposition could quiet the most irascible rabble-rousers. Kelly always framed Pogo in verdant, lively strokes of anthropomorphic fancy and nonsensical wordplay that churn with gleeful inventiveness and satiric power. Today, his efforts have assured the little critter with a huge heart his place among the highest achievements in American cartooning and the world's most beloved animal characters.

IMPACT ON COMICS

Kelly and Pogo garnered multiple accolades and awards including the National Cartoonist Society's prestigious Reuben Award in 1951, and its Silver T-Square for a lifetime of Extraordinary Service in 1972. Kelly was also the first cartoonist to contribute to the Library of Congress and an early entry into the National Cartoon Museum's Hall of Fame. Numerous archival editions and reprints of Pogo's legacy exist and the early Albert-focused tales are included in Michael Barrier and Martin Williams's pioneering *Smithsonian Book of Comic-Book Comics*. Thomas Andrae's exhaustive biography of Kelly and a definitive series of *Pogo* newspaper reprints appeared in 2011 and 2012. Even the eclectic album *Songs of the Pogo* has been reissued on CD with expansive critical commentary. Cartoonists and animators from diverse quarters of contemporary comics also pay frequent homage to the "impollutable opossum." Chief among these are **R. Crumb**, Harvey Pekar, Matt Groening, Lynn Johnston, Dave Sim, Michael Fry, Patrick McDonnell, Bill Watterson, and Jeff Smith, whose Smiley Bone shares not only Albert the Alligator's devil-may-care attitudes but also his signature vest and cigar. Arguably, even Charles Schulz's Snoopy owes a bit of his limitless imagination and effusive spirit to his swampy cousin down Okefenokee way.

Palestine

Palestine is a nine-issue comic book miniseries, later republished as a graphic novel, chronicling the experiences of comics journalist Joe Sacco and of the people he met during a trip to the Middle East in winter 1991–1992. Although not the first comic to be considered a work of journalism, *Palestine* set the standard for creators in this nonfiction comics subgenre. In *Palestine*, Sacco experiments with first-person journalistic storytelling, establishing both graphic and textual journalistic conventions that have been used in other journalistic comics.

HISTORY

Published by **Fantagraphics,** the first issue of the miniseries *Palestine* appeared in 1993, and the final issue in 1995. In 1996, it won an American Book Award. The graphic novel *Palestine*, which collects all nine issues of the comic, appeared in 2001, after the publication of Sacco's second book-length journalistic work, *Safe Area Goražde*. A 2007 deluxe hardcover edition included background information about the making of *Palestine*, with notes and illustrations by Sacco as well as an interview with the author.

Sacco's journalism education began in high school in Beaverton, Oregon, when he joined the staff of the student newspaper at Sunset High School. He majored in journalism at the University of Oregon, graduating in 1981 (Marshall 2005; Powers 1995). He began to hone his cartooning skills at the same time, drawing cartoons for student newspapers in high school and college. He combined his interest in comics and journalism with an editorial position at the *Comics Journal* beginning in 1986. The publisher of the *Comics Journal*, Fantagraphics, also became Sacco's comics publisher (Powers 1995; Groth 2001).

As is typical of many alternative comics creators, Sacco handles both the writing and artwork chores for his comics. *Palestine*, like most of his work, was published in black and white, although the original miniseries had color covers.

IMPACT ON AMERICAN CULTURE

From the 1950s through the 1970s, Pogo remained one of the nation's most beloved comic strips, yet Kelly kept a tight grip on the licensing of his fuzzy protagonist. Aside from the Dell comics, newspaper features, and paperbacks, his merchandising included a few scarce premiums and one television adaptation, NBC's half-hour *Pogo Special Birthday Special* from May 1969. Kelly seemed to conceive of his characters as public servants, as in the fascinating 1961 brochure *Pogo Primer for Parents (TV Division)* created for the U.S. Department of Health's Children's Bureau Headliner Series.

What Pogo lacked in commercialization, he more than made up for in promotional campaigns and campus lectures. For road shows, chalk talks, and charity appearances, there has never been a busier possum. For more than 15 years, Kelly toured his characters with a "killer lecture schedule" providing every campus newspaper with original site-specific material to commemorate his visits (Kelly and Crouch 1989, 152). The most famous of these tours involved Pogo's entry into the 1952 presidential campaign, when official "I Go Pogo" shirts and buttons became a hip collegiate fashion trend and some 500,000 turned out at various stumping events (Kelly 1972, 52). Pogo's public remained resilient, and the most devoted Pogophiles still maintain an Official Pogo Fan Club. These loyal Pogo lovers have compiled collector's guides and newsletters, enjoyed frequent Pogofests, and circulated literate fanzines like *The Okefenokee Star* and *Fort Mudge Most*. In recent years, Pogophilia has invaded cyberspace where websites like igopogo.com and pogopossum.com offer comprehensive updates on the people's possum. It seems appropriate that Walt Kelly's *Pogo* has endured as a communal icon, inspiring the same group-centered lessons, discussions, and debates that energized the comics.

Though *Pogo* could exude darker tones, mirth always prevailed in Kelly's world. In fact, *Pogo*'s primary function was always the celebration of freedom, the perpetuation of kindness, and the exploration of imagination. It is also worth noting that *Pogo* enjoyed a revival through the Los Angeles Times Syndicate from 1989 to 1992, with art by Neal Sternecky and scripts by Larry Doyle for much of the four-year run. Less political and more nostalgic, the resuscitated *Pogo* was a competent straightforward gag strip. Though it lacked Kelly's inimitable magic, its presence in many papers spoke to the nationwide desire to somehow rekindle those glorious heydays on the Okefenokee when a possum, an alligator, and their pals happily decked us all with Boston Charlie.

SUMMARY

All told, Pogo and his cohorts filled comic books, newspapers, and paperbacks with a humor so forgiving of folly and so filled with ingenuity, it rivals

Franklin, Twain, Rogers, or Barry's contributions to American comedy. Rooted in animal fantasy and nonsensical wordplay, *Pogo* could leap from cuddly farce to piercing critique in a heartbeat, and its general message of compassion, thoughtfulness, and optimism frequently exposed the most pernicious assaults on American ideals. From his earliest appearances as Albert's scruffy sidebar snack to the heights of his popular 1952 presidential race, Pogo's parade of songs, games, jokes, and generally good times have happily taught us all to shake hands with our own internal enemies.

See also Bone; Dell Comics

ESSENTIAL WORKS

Kelly, Walt. *The Complete Daily and Sunday Comic Strips Volume 1: Through the Wild Blue Wonder*. Seattle: Fantagraphics, 2011.
Kelly, Walt. *The Pogo Papers*. New York: Simon & Schuster, 1952.
Kelly, Walt. *The Pogo Stepmother Goose*. New York: Simon & Schuster, 1954.
Kelly, Walt. *Ten Ever-Lovin' Blue-Eyed Years with Pogo 1949–1959*. New York: Fireside, 1976.

FURTHER READING

Andrae, Thomas. *Walt Kelly: The Life and Times of the Creator of Pogo*. New Castle, PA: Hermes Press, 2011.
Kelly, "Mrs. Walt," and Bill Crouch, Jr. *Outrageously Pogo*. New York: Fireside, 1985.
Kelly, "Mrs. Walt," and Bill Crouch, Jr. *Phi Beta Pogo*. New York: Fireside, 1989.
Kelly, "Mrs. Walt," and Bill Crouch, Jr. *Pogo Even Better*. New York: Fireside, 1984.

Daniel F. Yezbick

The Punisher

After his wife and two children are gunned down by mobsters in New York City's Central Park, Vietnam War veteran Frank Castle arms himself to combat the underworld as the Punisher. A controversial character in **Marvel Comics'** fictional universe in that not only does the Punisher not possess any superpowers, he is frequently portrayed as an antihero. His methods, actions, and sentiments are starkly contrasted to those of such noble superheroes as **Spider-Man** and **Captain America**. Despite this, the Punisher has remained one of Marvel Comics' most popular characters since the mid-1980s. He encapsulates ongoing social anxieties about urban crime and symbolizes the distinct American ideal of individualistic vigilantism. Indeed, the Punisher serves as an ideological mirror, reflecting back both the writers' and the readers' attitudes about the American criminal justice system.

HISTORY

Writer Gerry Conway created the Punisher as Marvel Comics' version of Mack Bolan, a.k.a. the Executioner, the protagonist of a series of action-adventure novels written by Don Pendleton that began in 1969 with the book *War against the Mafia*. By the time the Punisher first appeared in *Amazing Spider-Man* #129 (1974), 16 *Executioner* novels had been published. In a costume designed by artist John Romita, Sr., the Punisher debuts as a former U.S. Marine duped by the villainous Jackal into believing the Friendly Neighborhood Wall-Crawler was a murderer. The cover to the issue misleadingly billed the Punisher as "the most lethal hired assassin ever!" Not truly a mercenary, the Punisher more accurately described himself on the final page of his introductory story as "just a warrior . . . fighting a lonely war." He fought a war against the mob for very personal reasons. As first revealed in *Marvel Preview* #2 (1975), one day while on military leave, he took his family to the park for a picnic. As fate would have it, they stumbled upon a mob execution, and to eliminate the witnesses, the mobsters fired upon the family. Only the father managed to survive.

(AP Photo/Marvel Comics)

Looked at from a different perspective, even the father died; he became resurrected as the Punisher, determined to rid the country of organized crime all by himself. The origin is deliberately similar to that of Mack Bolan, who became the Executioner after the Mafia brought about the death of Mack's family. Other similarities with the Executioner include the Punisher's favored means of transportation—a specially outfitted battle van—as well as the recounting of his exploits in a "War Journal."

Throughout the late 1970s and early 1980s, the Punisher mostly appeared as an infrequent guest star in *Amazing Spider-Man*. For a couple of 1982 issues of *Daredevil*, though, writer/artist **Frank Miller** used the Punisher as an opponent of—and figure of ideological contrast to—his main protagonist. The Punisher's willingness to kill suspected criminals put him at odds with Daredevil's desire to honor the due process of law. After that, writer Bill Mantlo depicted the Punisher as an unhinged psychotic in *Spectacular Spider-Man* #82 (1983), shooting at unarmed civilians for such transgressions as littering and traffic violations, all in the name of maintaining law and order. After his arrest, a judge deems the Punisher incapable of understanding the criminal charges against him. He is carted off to a mental institution, convinced that it is the criminal justice system that is insane, not he.

The Punisher's real name remained unrevealed until the first issue of his eponymous limited series. According to *The Punisher* #1 (1986), the man who wore the skull-emblazoned costume was Frank Castle. Written by Steven Grant, the issue also explained away the Punisher's psychotic behavior from Bill Mantlo's story: when last incarcerated in Rikers Island Prison, the Punisher's food had been laced with hallucinogenic drugs. Courtesy of his enemies, Frank had a bad trip. He recovered, however, and resumed his war with a newfound determination as well as unexpected popularity among comic book readers.

The five-issue limited series sold way beyond expectations. It sold so well that Marvel approved the production of an ongoing title for the character. *The Punisher* #1 (1987), written by Mike Baron with art by Klaus Janson, was the comic book industry's bestselling title that month (Elliott 1987, 27). The Punisher's heyday had officially dawned. From the late 1980s until the mid-1990s Marvel fed its readers a cornucopia of Punisher publications: graphic novels, limited series, one-shot specials, reprints, interpublisher crossovers (where the Punisher even teamed up with **Archie!**) to go along with three ongoing titles (*The Punisher*, *The Punisher War Journal*, *The Punisher War Zone*) and *The Punisher Armory*, a comic book that provided descriptive illustrations of the Punisher's equipment and weaponry. During this period, the character also made guest appearances in numerous other Marvel comic books like *The 'Nam* and, once again, *Amazing Spider-Man*.

Without question, the Punisher became one of Marvel Comics' franchise properties, in no small part due to the character's personification of Americans' anger and anxiety about crime. Between the late 1960s and the late 1980s, the violent crime rate in the United States had tripled (Bureau of Justice Statistics). Many felt crime had become an epidemic, and the topic dominated the national discourse of the 1980s. Television news programs documented it. Commentators and politicians railed about the justice system's inability to curb it. Volunteer organizations like Curtis Sliwa's Guardian Angels patrolled against it. And citizens like New York City subway shooter Bernhard Goetz became controversial heroes by confronting it. Corollary to the rising crime rate of the 1980s, the United States correctional system no longer focused on rehabilitating its prisoners (Miller 2011). That suited the majority of Americans just fine because they wanted criminals punished. The Punisher then was an alluring fantasy figure for its time: he offered criminals the ultimate form of punishment. In that vein, Punisher comic books offered its readers catharsis and identification: the satisfaction of reading the demise of fictitious criminals at the hands of someone who, like the readers, had no superpowers but the resolve of retribution.

While the Punisher's readers vicariously enjoyed their hero's brand of justice over the years, Marvel's presentation of the character vacillated, particularly on whether the Punisher *was* a hero. In some stories, the Punisher refused to kill anyone in cold blood. In others, he murdered unarmed targets without hesitation or compunction. Steven Grant, author not only of the inaugural Punisher limited series but also the Punisher graphic novel *Return to Big Nothing* (1989), depicted the character as a paranoid loner, ultimately classifying him as a "clinical psychotic—someone who has a complete disconnection from his emotions" (Witterstaetter 1989, 6). On the other hand, Mike Baron, who wrote over 80 Punisher issues as well as 3 Punisher graphic novels, somewhat softened the hardest edges of his protagonist, endowing him with a wise-cracking attitude and long-term allies, like computer hacker Microchip. Baron defined the Punisher as an "existential hero," someone seeking to control his environment and define life on his own terms (Zimmerman 1988, 7). And then there's writer Eliot Brown: in the editorial page of *The Punisher Armory* #1 (1990), he described the Punisher as "that dangerous sort of criminal who believes he knows how to frame his own justice, ignoring the laws of other men."

Marvel's writers also disagreed on other aspects of the Punisher, like the kind of opponents the character could—or should—confront. The two villains he most often faced were the Kingpin, the Marvel Universe's iconic crime lord, and Jigsaw, a gangster seeking vengeance against the Punisher for the mutilation of his face. The two foes suited the Punisher's modus operandi and capabilities as a former Marine with access to an assortment of small arms weaponry, because going up against mobsters was one thing and going up against megalomaniacs with extraordinary superpowers was something else. Whether the Punisher encountered other prominent Marvel Comics supervillains—and was an evenly matched opponent against them—depended on the inclinations of his writers. For instance, Mike Baron seldom used supervillains during his run on *The Punisher* because he felt they violated the book's film noir realism (Zimmerman 1988, 5). When he did use them though, like the time **Dr. Doom** appeared in *The Punisher* #29 (1990), he made clear that the Punisher was outclassed. Similarly, from 2004 to 2009, Garth Ennis eschewed supervillains altogether for the *Punisher* series he wrote under Marvel's "explicit content" MAX imprint. However, Ennis also wrote 1995's out-of-continuity *Punisher Kills the Marvel Universe* one-shot in which—as the title indicates—the Punisher kills every Marvel Comics superhero and supervillain. The second *Punisher War Journal* volume, written by Matt Fraction, paraded a slew of costumed crooks for the Punisher to confront, including Stilt-Man, Hate-Monger, the Rhino, and Kraven the Hunter. The Punisher even participated in Marvel's "Civil War" (2006), "World War Hulk" (2007), "Secret Invasion" (2008), and "Dark Reign" (2009) crossover events. Perhaps Rick Remender got in the last word on how the Punisher fares against

THE PUNISHER'S REIGN

The following lists Punisher comic books published at the zenith of the character's popularity, between 1987 and 1995:

- *The Punisher* (104 issue series launched in 1987)
- *The Punisher: Assassin's Guild* (1988 graphic novel)
- *The Punisher War Journal* (80-issue series launched in 1988)
- *The Punisher: Intruder* (1989 graphic novel)
- *The Punisher: Return to Big Nothing* (1989 graphic novel)
- *The Punisher Armory* (10-issue series launched in 1990)
- *Punisher: The Prize* (1990 graphic novel)
- *The Punisher: Kingdom Gone* (1990 graphic novel)
- *The Punisher: No Escape* (1990 graphic novel)
- *Punisher: P.O.V.* (4-issue 1991 miniseries)
- *The Punisher: War Zone* (41-issue monthly series launched in 1991)
- *Punisher: Bloodlines* (1991 graphic novel)
- *Ghost Rider/Wolverine/Punisher: Hearts of Darkness* (1991 graphic novel)
- *The Punisher: Blood on the Moors* (1991 graphic novel)
- *The Punisher: G-Force* (1992 graphic novel)
- *Punisher: Die Hard in the Big Easy* (1992 graphic novel)
- *Punisher/Captain America: Blood & Glory* (3-issue 1992 miniseries)
- *Punisher/Black Widow: Spinning Doomsday's Web* (1992 graphic novel)
- *The Punisher 2099* (34-issue series launched in 1992)
- *Punisher: The Ghosts of Innocents* (2-issue 1993 miniseries)
- *Spider-Man/Punisher/Sabretooth: Designer Genes* (1993 graphic novel)
- *The Punisher: Origin Micro Chip* (2-issue 1993 miniseries)
- *Wolverine and The Punisher: Damaging Evidence* (3-issue 1993 miniseries)
- *Batman/Punisher: Lake of Fire* (1994 graphic novel)
- *Punisher/Batman: Deadly Knights* (1994 graphic novel)
- *The Punisher: A Man Named Frank* (1994 graphic novel)
- *The Punisher Meets Archie* (1994 one-shot)
- *The Punisher: Empty Quarter* (1994 graphic novel)
- *Ghost Rider/Wolverine/Punisher: The Dark Design* (1994 graphic novel)
- *The Punisher: Year One* (4-issue 1994 miniseries)
- *Punisher Kills the Marvel Universe* (1995 one-shot)

superpowered opponents: at the conclusion of a no-holds-barred fight in *Dark Reign: The List—Punisher* (2009), Wolverine's son, Daken, ruthlessly decapitates the Punisher and then discards his dismembered remains into the streets like so much trash.

Captain America actually called the Punisher a "murderous piece of trash" as the World War II icon pummeled the former Vietnam War Marine in *Civil War* #6 (2006). Years earlier, though, the two combat veterans stood at attention and saluted each other in a display of mutual respect at the end of their 1992 *Blood and Glory* miniseries. Cap's diametrically opposed actions exemplify the kind of contradictory reactions Marvel's fictional universe has towards its resident vigilante. Depending once again on the writers' whims, Marvel's other crime fighters have either shunned the Punisher like a pariah or been grateful for his help. Even Spider-Man, who has encountered the Punisher more times than any other character, could not decide if he was unbothered by the Punisher's tactics (see 1974's *Giant-Size Spider-Man* #4) or disgusted by them (see 1990's *Amazing Spider-Man* #331).

Although the writers could not come to a consensus on certain aspects of the Punisher, none of them lost sight of the fact that he was a Vietnam War veteran. But unlike Captain America, the Punisher did not have a super soldier serum running through his veins that kept him eternally young. That meant by the dawn of the 21st century, the Punisher was fighting crime as a man in his 50s at the very youngest. Even for comic books, that stretched credibility. Rick Remender fashioned a solution: after the death of the Punisher at the hands (or claws) of Daken, the Legion of Monsters, a group that includes a vampire, a werewolf, and a mummy, stitched together the Punisher's body parts to resurrect him as a sort of Frankenstein's Monster. Then, during a five-issue span when his comic book was officially retitled *Franken-Castle* (2010), the Punisher was endowed with the magical power of a piece of the Bloodstone, which both regenerated and rejuvenated him.

With a younger man's body, Frank Castle resumed his old vendetta. And the Punisher's lonely war went on.

IMPACT ON COMICS

The Punisher limited series was one of a handful of titles—chief among them, Frank Miller's *Batman: The Dark Knight Returns* and **Alan Moore** and Dave Gibbons's **Watchmen**—whose popularity ushered in a more grim and gritty era of superhero comic books starting in the late 1980s and extending well into the 1990s. This new era featured bleak—sometimes nihilistic—stories and depicted graphic violence committed by morally ambiguous protagonists, many of whom showed no qualms about killing criminals. Antiheroes like Spawn and Lobo became fan favorites.

At the same time the Punisher was influencing the kind of comic book stories being told, the character also paved the way for *how* those stories were being told. That is because a narrative device utilized in Punisher stories since the mid-1970s became en vogue by the late 1980s: first-person captions. The prevalent comic book storytelling devices at the time of the Punisher's first appearance were thought balloons and third-person omniscient narrators. Gerry Conway introduced the Punisher's subjective "War Journal" narration in *Marvel Preview* #2 (1975) to emulate Mack Bolan's War Journal narration from Don Pendleton's *Executioner* novels. A decade later, comic book writers largely abandoned the use of thought balloons and omniscient narrators in favor of first-person narration due to, again, the popularity of comic books already using first-person captions—like *The Punisher*—and the need to cater to an older reading audience who could process—and appreciate— more sophisticated storytelling techniques.

IMPACT ON AMERICAN CULTURE

Of Marvel Comics' entire catalog of properties, the Punisher is arguably the most cinematically translatable, as he seamlessly fits within the popular film genre that glorifies characters dispensing individualistic brands of justice. This includes films like *Dirty Harry* starring Clint Eastwood (1971), *Death Wish* starring Charles Bronson (1974), *Commando* starring Arnold Schwarzenegger (1985), and *Die Hard* starring Bruce Willis (1988). Little surprise then that three unconnected Punisher movies were filmed over a 20-year period. The first, produced by New World Pictures in 1989 on a modest budget, starred Swedish muscle man Dolph Lundgren as an ex-cop who, while hiding out in the city sewers, wages war against organized crime. Due to New World's financial problems, this first Punisher film's release excluded American theaters. It debuted in the United States via the home video market. In the second *Punisher* film, produced by Artisan Entertainment and distributed by Lions Gate in 2004, actor Thomas Jane portrays Frank Castle as an FBI agent who seeks revenge against mobster Howard Saint, played by John Travolta, for the murder of his family. Its Tampa, Florida, setting aside, the movie drew direct inspiration from several Punisher comic books, particularly 1994's *Punisher: Year One* miniseries and Garth Ennis's "Welcome Back, Frank" story from the Marvel Knights volume of *The Punisher* published in 2000. The third Punisher film, titled *Punisher: War Zone*, was jointly produced by Lionsgate and Marvel Studios and released in 2008. It matched the Punisher (Irish actor Ray Stevenson) against his longtime comic book nemesis, Jigsaw (English actor Dominic West).

None of the Punisher films enjoyed any notable success at the box office. In fact, *Punisher: War Zone* ignominiously became the lowest money-grossing film featuring a Marvel Comics character to date (Box Office Mojo). The biggest impact the Punisher has had on American culture then has been on youth fashion because of the most noticeable part of the Punisher's costume: his chest skull logo. Adorned on black T-shirts, the Punisher logo becomes not only a signifier of death but also a provocative fashion statement worn by rebellious youths all over the country. Case in point: prototypical "angry young man" rapper Eminem appeared on the cover of the June 2009 issue of hip-hop magazine *XXL* with a Punisher logo on his bare chest. The magazine's appearance on the newsstands coincided with the release of the *Eminem/Punisher* digital comic book.

SUMMARY

Originally created as a Mack Bolan analogue, the Punisher uses his experience as a Vietnam War veteran to wage a one-man war against crime. Motivated by the murder of his family, he is the iconic solitary vigilante, that alluring figure within America's cultural mythology that embodies a frontier brand of individualistic justice. But what the Punisher signifies beyond that depends on his writers and his readers. For some, he is a force of righteousness, remedying the failings of the judicial system by killing criminals who deserve to die. For others, the Punisher is a dangerous antihero whose self-absorbed, lethal tactics isolate him from Marvel Comics' noble superheroes, the majority of whom uphold the due process of the law. From this point of view, the Punisher demonstrates the selfish recklessness of vigilantism.

The Punisher, then, simultaneously evokes divergent American ideals, reminding readers of the contradictory principles that compose the national cultural identity. In doing so, he becomes one of the most controversial characters in the history of superhero comic books.

See also Captain America; Marvel Comics; Miller, Frank; Spider-Man; *Watchmen*

ESSENTIAL WORKS

Grant, Steven (w), Mary Jo Duffy (w), Mike Zeck (p), Mike Vosburg (p), and John Beatty (i). *The Punisher* #1–#5 (Jan.–May 1986), Marvel. Reprinted in *The Essential Punisher: Vol. 1*. New York: Marvel Comics, 2006.

Grant, Steven (w), Mike Zeck (p), and John Beatty (i). *The Punisher: Return to Big Nothing*. New York: Marvel Comics, 1989.

Miller, Frank (w, p), Roger McKenzie (w), and Klaus Janson (p, i). *Daredevil* #183–#184 (June–July 1982). Marvel. Reprinted in *The Essential Punisher: Vol. 1*. New York: Marvel Comics, 2006.

FURTHER READING

Marvel Comics. "The Punisher." http://marvel.com/characters/bio/1009515/punisher. Accessed on June 22, 2011.
Tipton, Scott. "Happiness Is a Warm Gun." http://www.comics101.com/archives/comics101/61.php. Accessed on June 29, 2011.

Keith Dallas

RAW

RAW magazine (1980–1991) was the premier English-language showcase for avant-garde and international comics in the 1980s and a harbinger of the graphic novel boom of the early 21st century. It was co-edited by future *New Yorker* art editor Françoise Mouly and her husband, veteran underground cartoonist **Art Spiegelman**, whose seminal graphic novel **Maus** was first serialized in *RAW*. *RAW* promoted the idea of comics as a serious adult literary and artistic form by publishing formally innovative contemporary comics, translating the work of established international cartoonists, and reprinting underappreciated works by early-20th-century artists. Its wide-ranging subject matter and styles highlighted the medium's versatility, and its attention to design and printing brought an art-world sensibility to comics.

HISTORY

RAW magazine emerged from co-editor Françoise Mouly's experiments in printing and her burgeoning interest in comics, as well as from Art Spiegelman's editorial work with the underground quarterly *Arcade* (1975–1976) and his dissatisfaction with existing venues for publishing comics for adults. A former architecture student from France, Mouly met Spiegelman in 1976 while exploring American comics as a way to improve her fluency in English. Before Mouly discovered *Arcade* and was introduced to Spiegelman, she had searched in vain for the English equivalent of European magazines like *Pilote*, *Spirou*, and *Métal Hurant* that featured comics. After marrying Spiegelman in 1977, Mouly learned printing at a Brooklyn vocational school while doing freelance coloring work for Marvel Comics. She bought her own printing press, and shortly afterwards, Mouly began publishing an annual *Streets of Soho Map and Guide* that provided a source of income and funding for her other early projects under the "Raw Books" imprint. After a 1978 European tour during which she and Spiegelman met many future *RAW* contributors, Mouly began making prints, ephemera, and postcard-sized mailbooks featuring the work of American and European cartoonists. These experiences increased Mouly's interest in comics

and publishing, and she first considered small-press book publishing before deciding upon a magazine as more efficient and more manageable. As the genre-oriented sci-fi/fantasy magazine **Heavy Metal** began to publish French comics in English translation in the late 1970s, Mouly likewise set out to introduce European comics to an American audience. Despite Spiegelman's earlier frustrations with editing the underappreciated *Arcade*, by January 1980 Mouly had persuaded him to work on at least one issue of a new magazine of comics, graphics, and illustrated writing (Kartalopoulos, "The Magazine").

Though *RAW* would explore the intersection between comics and other visual and literary arts, its primary intent was, in Mouly's words, "to make it manifest how good comics could be" (Kartalopoulos, "Part One"). Subsidized by profits from Mouly's Soho map, *RAW* was meant to fight the prejudice against comics as lowbrow and ephemeral by presenting work that was "beautiful," "moving," and "powerful," according to Mouly (Kartalopoulos, "The Magazine"). Besides highlighting comics as a serious medium, the magazine was also intended to bridge cultural and artistic gaps by bringing together artists and writers from around the world under one umbrella.

The first volume of *RAW* (issues #1–#8, 1980–1986) focused on showing a wide range of visual work that hadn't been published before. It emerged as a highbrow and experimental counterpoint to the more entertainment-oriented *Arcade* and **Robert Crumb**'s low-art underground *Weirdo* (1981–1993). Under Spiegelman's hands-on editorial direction, *RAW* nurtured a new generation of alternative cartoonists, many of whom were students (Kaz, Mark Newgarden, Drew Friedman), teachers (Jerry Moriarty), or alumni of New York's School of Visual Arts, where Spiegelman taught. Other contributors, including Heinz Emigholz and Patricia Caire, were associated with the avant-garde Collective for Living Cinema in Lower Manhattan, where Spiegelman gave a series of lectures on comics. The magazine drew some of its talent from veterans of underground comics, including Bill Griffith, Kim Deitch, Justin Green, and Robert Crumb, though *RAW* used their work sparingly and went beyond the familiar underground content of sex, drugs, and violence. *RAW* also introduced American readers to high-quality work in translation by prominent international cartoonists such as France's Jacques Tardi, Spain's Javier Mariscal, the Netherlands' Joost Swarte, Argentina's José Muñoz, and Japan's Yoshiharu Tsuge.

Moreover, throughout its run, *RAW* reprinted a judicious selection of comics from the turn of the century through the 1940s, including work by Winsor McCay, George Herriman, Milt Gross, Boody Rogers, and Basil Wolverton. Spiegelman considered this archival project central to making a magazine that would not become dated and to "creating a common denominator that wasn't temporal" (Kartalopoulos, "The Magazine"). Many of the early-20th-century artists that appeared in *RAW*, including less well-known cartoonists like Fletcher Hanks, benefited from the exposure and later went on to be collected in archival editions from publishers such as Fantagraphics, with which *RAW* had grown up.

The early *RAW* presented contributors' work to its best advantage through an innovative format and impressive production values. Establishing the format of the first eight issues, *RAW* #1 was oversized (10 1/2″ × 14 1/4″) to showcase its artwork. As with subsequent issues, the first issue was prepared to exacting standards on quality paper; according to a 1985 *Village Voice* article, Mouly approved just 3,500 of about 5,000 copies of *RAW* #1. Despite its relatively large printings, which reportedly ran as many as 7,500 copies, the first volume became a hybrid of the mass market and was handmade with such features as a full-color image pasted onto the cover (#1) and a hand-torn cover (#7). At a time when Tribeca's Printed Matter was first bringing widespread attention to publications made by artists, *RAW* magazine emerged as an art object in its own right, with varied paper stocks and extras like tipped-in comic booklets and trading cards with bubble gum (#2). Full-color covers were painstakingly created using elaborate hand-cut color separations, and the cover for #3 with a Gary Panter illustration even won a 1981 *Print* magazine design certificate. Consequently, *RAW* attracted artists who wanted to see their work published in the best possible way.

Through 1986, *RAW*'s generous size and attractive presentation encouraged experimentation over narratives and shorter over longer works; content followed format. Because most of *RAW*'s early pieces were one or two pages, lengthier entries tended to stand out. Some noteworthy examples from the first volume include Francis Masse's topsy-turvy "A Race of Racers" (#4), Charles Burns's creepy "The Voice of Walking Flesh" (#4), an excerpt from Jacques Tardi's *It Was the War of the Trenches* (#5), and Crumb's biographical "Jelly Roll Morton's Voodoo Curse" (#7).

However, by far the most important work to appear in *RAW* was Spiegelman's own epic Holocaust memoir *Maus*, one chapter of which was included as a small-format supplement from issues #2–#8 and as a regular feature in the final three issues. Spiegelman's plans to do a book-length comic about his parents' experiences as Jews in Poland during World War II predated plans for *RAW*. In fact, in 1978, Spiegelman first wrote down an outline for *Maus* as a proposal for Casterman, the French publisher of the monthly *À Suivre*. *RAW* provided Spiegelman with a venue for his developing story as well as a deadline for installments of *Maus* between work on *RAW*, weekly stints with Topps Chewing Gum, and freelance illustration work. *Maus*'s inclusion as a booklet allowed it to be produced on a more intimate scale and signaled its separateness from the rest of the magazine as an ongoing narrative.

Though comics were *RAW*'s focus, many issues also featured illustrated nonfiction pieces. In fact, issue #1 opened with an illustrated translation of an essay about criminal necrophilia by protosurrealist French author Alfred Jarry, who was the subject of a later comic by Bill Griffith (#4). Other topics of prose pieces included urban life, consumer culture, and Reaganomics. Spiegelman comments, "If we'd known more writers, we might have had more literary content, although probably dealt with it more visually" (Kartalopoulos, "The Magazine").

After the 1982 release of its third issue, *RAW* began to publish a series of "RAW One-Shots," stand-alone forerunners of today's graphic novels, with a body of work by individual magazine contributors in various formats. These books, printed in editions of at least 2,000–3,000 copies, featured comics or illustrated prose pieces and gave special attention to the work's physical presentation. For instance, the first of these, Gary Panter's *RAW*-sized *JIMBO*, was printed on newsprint, and its covers were made of corrugated cardboard, finished with black binding tape and a two color sticker. A planned edition of French cartoonist Jacques Tardi's work never materialized, but later large-format works included Sue Coe and Holly Metz's *How to Commit Suicide in South Africa* (1983) and self-described paintoonist Jerry Moriarty's *Jack Survives* (1984). Digest-sized hardcover books by Panter (*Invasion of the Elvis*

Zombies), Charles Burns (*Big Baby*), and Coe (*X*) followed. The books were as enthusiastically received as *RAW* itself and have since become collectors' items. The One-Shots were sold through bookstores and not just comic shops, increasing their circulation and promoting comics in mainstream publishing.

With the 1986 publication of the first volume of *Maus* by Pantheon Books, Spiegelman and Mouly began their joint partnership with commercial publishers. Pantheon and later Penguin continued the *RAW* One-Shots, but Spiegelman and Mouly lost some of their creative control as they had to conform to industry production standards. Pantheon's reprinting of material from the first three issues of *RAW* in *Read Yourself Raw* (1987) brought a retrospective note to the magazine, but *RAW* itself was revived by Penguin in 1989 after a three-year hiatus.

Even with Spiegelman and Mouly still at the helm, *RAW* was a very different magazine under Penguin. Because of large-scale commercial production, its print runs increased dramatically, starting with 40,000 copies of the first issue. It became *Maus*-sized, reduced to a digest format, but it also grew in length to 200 pages, allowing it to show more work by more artists and reorienting it toward extended narratives, even though not many artists were making long-form comics yet. The shift from a visual emphasis to more of a narrative focus helped to inspire some of *RAW*'s most memorable storytelling experiments in comics, including Richard McGuire's time- and space-bending "Here" (vol. 2, #1) and **Chris Ware**'s superhero satire "Thrilling Adventure Stories" (2.3). According to *RAW* associate editor and cartoonist Richard Sikoryak, there was talk of making a fourth issue with Penguin as a full-color comics anthology, which would have been the first of its kind, but daunting technical challenges, a perceived lack of cooperation from the publisher, and even Spiegelman and Mouly's waning interest led to those plans being scrapped (Kartalopoulos, "The Magazine").

Despite *RAW*'s expansion and its mainstream distribution, it ended its run in 1991 after three issues with Penguin and the publication of volume two of *Maus*. By that time, other venues and publishers for English-language comics with literary and artistic aspirations had begun to emerge, including **Dark Horse Comics** and Drawn & Quarterly. Four years later, RAW Books and Gates of Heck co-published the surrealist chain-story *The Narrative Corpse*, originally conceived in 1990 for *RAW*. In 2000, the RAW imprint was revived by HarperCollins for Spiegelman and Mouly's "Little Lit" series of children's comics for a new generation of readers.

IMPACT ON COMICS

In just over a decade, *RAW* showed that comics should be taken seriously and that comics could memorably and distinctively present long-form narratives. The magazine launched Spiegelman's Pulitzer Prize–winning *Maus*, the most

NEW YORK STATE OF MIND

In 1993 Françoise Mouly became the art editor of the *New Yorker*, and Art Spiegelman became a contributing editor and staff artist for the magazine. Soon, a variety of *RAW* alums, including Chris Ware, Adrian Tomine, and Ivan Brunetti, were contributing interior art and covers for the prestigious magazine. Spiegelman himself contributed some controversial and acclaimed covers, from "The Kiss," showing a Hassidic Jewish man and a black woman kissing at a time those communities were engaged in violent conflict in the Crown Heights section of Brooklyn, to the black-on-black image of the Twin Towers that graced the September 24, 2011, issue. For a time, Speigelman was also the comix editor at *Details* magazine. The couple became so influential that fellow cartoonist Ted Rall complained that Spiegelman and Mouly had a stranglehold on cartooning assignments in America and seeing that the best work went to their clique of *RAW* contributors and Baby Boomer friends.

critically acclaimed graphic novel to date, which demonstrated that comic books could be great works of literature. Moreover, *RAW* introduced the work of many of today's most respected comics artists, from Lynda Barry to Chris Ware, to a larger audience. *RAW* is also largely responsible for inspiring the widespread interest that brought comics and graphic novels into bookstores, libraries, museums, and classrooms by the early 21st century. Internationally, *RAW* and *Maus* encouraged a broadened approach to comics that moved beyond genre fiction (Kartalopoulos, "The Magazine"). In retrospect, *RAW* fulfilled its mission of bringing together like-minded creators to demonstrate what was possible in making and publishing comics, and it validated their work as part of commercial culture.

IMPACT ON AMERICAN CULTURE

Throughout its run, *RAW* displayed its countercultural roots through its often satirical responses to current events and contemporary politics. Just as the undergrounds of the late 1960s and early 1970s showed a revulsion for Richard Nixon and the Vietnam War, *RAW* reacted against what its creators saw as the retrogressive policies and politics of the conservative Reagan administration. *RAW* #5 featured an audio flexi-disc of Doug Kahn's satirical sound collage "Reagan Speaks for Himself," accompanied by a Sue Coe illustration, with clips from a 1980 Reagan interview spliced together to make him sound senile, politically out of touch, and indifferent to poverty, violence, and predatory corporate greed.

The sole American manufacturer of soft vinyl records refused to produce the Reagan record on moral and legal grounds, leading *RAW* to cry foul to its readers and to have the disc manufactured overseas. More important, the incident raised the specter of censorship, which *RAW* confronted again in issue #5 when it published Pascal Doury's sexually explicit "Theodore Death Head." Anticipating obscenity complaints and possible legal ramifications for distributors and retailers, the magazine censored itself, removing offending genitalia from the comic and offering them as a mail-in sheet of stickers that readers could apply themselves. This calculated incident highlighted the lack of clear standards for obscenity in American publishing and the perils of self-appointed culture police.

Never shying away from potential controversy, *RAW* also addressed issues of America's history of racism and sought to intervene in global issues of racial inequality. For instance, the magazine ran Drew Friedman's "Comic Strip" in issue #2 despite Spiegelman's concern that it perpetuates racist stereotypes, while defending its prejudices in an addendum about the making of the strip. Later, Sue Coe's *How to Commit Suicide in South Africa* challenged the Reagan administration's lack of an official position on apartheid and advocated boycotting companies that did business in South Africa.

RAW also reflected fears about nuclear disaster and nuclear war in the wake of the 1979 Three Mile Island accident and at the height of the Cold War. Panter's "Jimbo" strips responded to nuclear anxieties by depicting the horrors encountered by the survivors of a nuclear explosion or atomic bomb, and his first one-shot was made to resemble something that might have survived a nuclear attack. *RAW* #8 also included an extended excerpt from Paul Boyer's book *By the Bomb's Early Light* that critiques American scientists' and politicians' post-Hiroshima rhetoric of fear. Thus, even as *RAW* was a product of its time, it also worked to shape readers' attitudes toward late-20th-century America.

SUMMARY

The brainchild of New York underground cartoonist Art Spiegelman and his wife and co-editor Françoise Mouly, *RAW* was from the start a groundbreaking graphics magazine and the premier anthology of its day for experimental and international comics. From 1980 to 1991, the sporadically published *RAW* helped to develop innovative cartooning talent outside of mainstream comics and assembled a stylistically diverse body of work that explored the formal and narrative capabilities of comics as a medium. By providing a common venue for cutting-edge cartoonists, *RAW* created a virtual community of contemporary artists and became the center of an international comics avant-garde. With lavish production values unprecedented in a comics publication, *RAW* also promoted the idea of comics as a serious art form. Moreover, through its forays into book publishing and especially its serialization of Spiegelman's landmark *Maus*, *RAW* influenced the developing concept of the graphic novel as an artistically and commercially viable form.

See also Maus; Spiegelman, Art

ESSENTIAL WORKS

McGuire, Richard (w, a). "Here." *RAW* vol. 2, #1 (1989). Reprinted in *An Anthology of Graphic Fiction, Cartoons, and True Stories*, edited by Ivan Brunetti, 88–93. New Haven, CT: Yale University Press, 2006.

Spiegelman, Art (w, a). *The Complete Maus: A Survivor's Tale*. New York: Pantheon, 1996.

Ware, Chris (w, a). "Thrilling Adventure Stories." *RAW* vol. 2, #3 (1991). Reprinted in *An Anthology of Graphic Fiction, Cartoons, and True Stories*, edited by Ivan Brunetti, 364–69. New Haven, CT: Yale University Press, 2006.

FURTHER READING

Hignite, Todd. *In the Studio: Visits with Contemporary Cartoonists*. New Haven, CT: Yale University Press, 2006.

Kartalopoulos, Bill. "A RAW History: Part One," 64.23.98.142/indy/winter_2005/raw_01/index.html. Accessed October 19, 2011.

Kartalopoulos, Bill. "A RAW History: The Magazine," 64.23.98.142/indy/winter_2005/raw_02/index.html. Accessed October 19, 2011.

Spiegelman, Art, and Françoise Mouly, ed. *Read Yourself Raw*. New York: Pantheon, 1987.

Witek, Joseph. *Art Spiegelman: Conversations*. Jackson: University Press of Mississippi, 2007.

Michael W. Hancock

Richie Rich

Richie Rich is a fictional character created by Alfred Harvey and Warren Kremer for Harvey Comics in 1953. He debuted in *Little Dot* #1 and was dubbed "the poor little rich boy." Richie is the only child of fantastically wealthy parents and is the world's richest boy. Richie Rich was Harvey Comics' most popular character, eventually starring in over 50 separate titles.

HISTORY

As the 1950s opened, comics were enjoying unparalleled popularity. Part of the reason for that popularity was a shift from the crime-fighting and Nazi-fighting heroes of World War II (**Superman, Batman, Captain America, Wonder Woman**) to more of an emphasis on horror and sexual innuendo. In 1954, facing pressure from parents' groups and legislators, the Comics Magazine Association of America (CMAA)—a self-regulatory body governing what was at that point one of the most popular forms of entertainment among young people—adopted a Comics' Code (Hajdu 2008). Among the Code's 41 specific provisions were prohibitions against the use of the words "horror" or "terror" in the comic magazines' covers, all scenes of horrors, excessive bloodshed and other types of gore, depictions of zombies, instances of disrespect toward law and order, and vulgarity and profanity. In adopting such a stringent code, the comic book industry hoped to ward off federal legislation, which it successfully did. Overnight, a number of comic book companies either changed their lineup of titles or dispensed with belonging to the CMAA.

Harvey Comics was a comic publisher founded in 1941 by Alfred Harvey (later joined by brothers Robert and Leon) when he bought out Brookwood Publications. Harvey Comics started out publishing comic books that featured a combination of characters it inherited from Brookwood, licensed characters such as the Green Hornet and Joe Palooka, and its own original characters. Among the areas the publisher specialized in were comics of horror and terror.

RICHIE RICH TITLES

Below is a selection of the variety of titles starring Richie Rich. In addition to these, numerous additional titles, several of them one-shots, have starred Richie and his supporting cast.

- *Richie Rich* (1960–1991)—254 issues; (1991–1994)—28 issues
- *Richie Rich and . . .* (1987–1990)—11 issues
- *Richie Rich and Cadbury* (1977–1991)—29 issues
- *Richie Rich and Casper* (1974–1982)—45 issues
- *Richie Rich and Dollar* (1977–1982)—24 issues
- *Richie Rich and Gloria* (1977–1982)—25 issues
- *Richie Rich and His Girlfriends* (1979–1982)—16 issues
- *Richie Rich and Jackie Jokers* (1973–1982)—48 issues
- *Richie Rich Bank Book* (1972–1982)—59 issues
- *Richie Rich Billions* (1974–1982)—48 issues
- *Richie Rich Cash* (1974–1982)—47 issues
- *Richie Rich Diamonds* (1972–1982)—59 issues
- *Richie Rich Digest* (1986–1994)—42 issues
- *Richie Rich Digest Stories* (1977–1982)—17 issues
- *Richie Rich Digest Winners* (1977–1982)—16 issues
- *Richie Rich Dollars and Cents* (1963–1982)—109 issues
- *Richie Rich Fortunes* (1971–1982)—63 issues
- *Richie Rich Gems* (1974–1982)—43 issues
- *Richie Rich Gold and Silver* (1975–1982)—42 issues
- *Richie Rich Inventions* (1977–1982)—26 issues
- *Richie Rich Jackpots* (1972–1982)—58 issues
- *Richie Rich Million Dollar Digest* (1980–1982)—10 issues; (1991–1994)—12 issues
- *Richie Rich Millions* (1961–1982)—113 issues
- *Richie Rich Money World* (1972–1982)—59 issues
- *Richie Rich Profits* (1974–1982)—47 issues
- *Richie Rich Riches* (1972–1982)—59 issues
- *Richie Rich Success Stories* (1964–1982)—105 issues
- *Richie Rich Vaults of Mystery* (1974–1982)—47 issues
- *Richie Rich Zillionz* (1976–1982)—33 issues
- *SupeRichie* (1976–1979)—14 issues

In response to the new CMAA code, Harvey Comics eliminated a number of titles that would not meet code muster and increasingly focused on the children's market instead. Even before the Code's institution, Harvey was licensing a few popular newspaper comic strip characters, such as Sad Sack, and animated characters, such as Casper the Friendly Ghost and Little Audrey, from Famous Studios, but in 1959 the company bought the rights to the entire line of characters created by Famous Studio (by then renamed Paramount Cartoon Studios).

A key to Harvey Comics' success was Warren Kremer, best known for his creation of the most well-known original characters at Harvey Comics, including Richie Rich. Starting in 1948, Kremer brought his distinct vision to comics, one heavily influenced by the animation studios of the day. Key to Kremer's style was the introduction of greater depth of field within his panel compositions. This added mass and greater realism to his images. This approach would go on to influence other comic artists across the industry.

Kremer either designed or came to define the look of many of Harvey's most popular characters: Casper the Friendly Ghost, Hot Stuff, Joe Palooka, Little Audrey, Little Max, Richie Rich, and Stumbo the Giant. Kremer also contributed animation storyboards, and did most of the covers for the Harvey titles. Over a period of 35 years, his influence—most prominently in his role as art editor—on the company and its properties was considerable. Joining Kremer's contributions to the Richie Rich legacy were other illustrators, including Ernie Colón, Sid Couchey, Dom Sileo, Ben Brown, Steve Muffatti, and Joe Dennett. Writers included Sid Jacobson, Lennie Herman, Stan Kay, and Ralph Newman.

In 1953, Harvey Comics debuted *Little Dot* (a comic book about a little girl obsessed with polka dots). The series' two back-up features would go on to be popular features in their own right: *Little Lotta* (a little girl obsessed with eating) and *Richie Rich*. Yet it was a few years before Richie got a shot at his own series. Tentatively, he starred in two issues of *Harvey Hits*, #3 in 1957 and #8 in 1958, but those were the only comics Richie headlined during the 1950s.

It took until November 1960 before Richie got his own title, but that was the start of something significant. The stories evolved from initially poking fun at the family's implausible wealth to more adventure yarns. Richie's popularity caught on thereafter. While other Harvey characters may have had multiple titles to their credit (e.g., Sad Sack), none matched Richie Rich for sheer variety. Richie's eponymous title ran 254 issues (1960–1982; 1986–1991) followed by a second volume of 28 issues (1991–1994). Beyond that were a host of spin-off series starting with *Richie Rich Millions* (1961–1982) and *Richie Rich Dollars & Cents* (1963–1982). More than 50 titles would go on to feature the so-called Poor Little Rich Boy. (See sidebar for even more embarrassment of riches.)

Richard "Richie" Rich, Jr., is, unsurprisingly, the wealthiest child in the world, with a $100,000-a-week allowance to prove it. He appears to be approximately eight years old and wears a waistcoat, a white shirt, a giant red bow tie, and blue shorts. He lives in the town of Richville and is even depicted as attending a local school.

His family is richer than any robber baron or aristocracy one can imagine. And yet, instead of the jaded, greedy family one might expect, the Riches are a happy family, in contrast to troubled real-life wealthy families such as the Vanderbilts. The Riches also give generously to others. A subtle message seems to come from the series: the less one worries about money, the more one can focus on what really counts, namely, developing meaningful relationships.

The plots of most Richie Rich tales involve a group of friends, a familiar trope in Harvey Comics. Richie's confidants include his dog, Dollar; his girlfriend, Gloria Glad; and his cousin, Reggie Van Dough. The stories often focus on Richie solving some problem with his seemingly endless supply of money. For instance, in one story Richie's gang gets into a spot of trouble when they break a store window while playing baseball. Richie steps up to save the day by simply buying the owner a whole new store! Many Richie Rich stories also center around his fascination with the latest in new technology, as Richie has the financial means to buy any new device he wishes.

Harvey Comics thrived during the 1960s, but with the decline in the children's market following the end of the Baby Boom came a decline in the interest in the children's comics market. Consequently, after a slow, inexorable sales decline, Harvey Comics ceased publishing in 1982 as founder Alfred Harvey retired.

In 1986, Alan Harvey, Alfred's oldest son, resurrected Harvey Comics and resumed focusing on a few core titles, digests, and reprints ("From the Ashes," 1985). In 1987 Harvey unsuccessfully sued Columbia Pictures for $50 million, claiming that the iconic Ghostbusters logo used in the 1984 film was too reminiscent of Casper. Unfortunately for Harvey, they failed to renew the copyrights on Casper, and the suit was thrown out. The revival was short-lived because Harvey sold to Jeffrey Montgomery's HMH Communications in 1989, and the company was renamed Harvey Comics Entertainment (HCE). After a few years of publishing reprints, HCE ceased publishing in 1994, but Montgomery optioned Richie Rich and Casper for two feature films: *Richie Rich* premiered in 1994, and *Casper* in 1995 (Arnold 2002).

In 2010, **Dark Horse Comics** began publishing *Harvey Comics Treasuries*, which included Richie Rich adventures. Ape Entertainment published an edition of *Richie Rich* in 2011. The first printing sold out, and a second printing was announced. For the Ape Entertainment comic, Richie is an altruistic adventurer who travels the world trying to make life better for the poor with the aid of his faithful butler, Cadbury, and his robot maid, Irona. The press release from Ape Entertainment describes the latest version of Richie Rich as "Part James Bond Jr. and part Indiana Jones with Donald Trump's bank account; Richie Rich is an altruistic adventurer who travels the world helping the less fortunate" (http://www.comicbookresources.com/?page=article&id=32372).

IMPACT ON COMICS

Richie Rich may have appeared in more individual American comic books than any other character, neck-in-neck with **Archie Andrews** (Markstein 2008). Numerous supporting characters were added to Richie's cast over the years: his parents, Richard and Regina Rich; their butler, Cadbury; his girlfriend, Gloria Glad; his buddies, Freckles and Pee-Wee Friendly; and his snobbish cousin and rival, Reggie Van Dough.

In the mid-1980s, **Marvel Comics** showed interest in licensing some of Harvey's properties. When negotiations proved fruitless, Marvel asked former Harvey writer/artist Lennie Herman to create *Royal Roy* under its Star Comics imprint in 1985. Ironically, Warren Kremer, who drew Richie Rich, drew Royal Roy. Harvey sued for copyright infringement, but the Royal Roy comic ended after six issues and the lawsuit was dropped.

IMPACT ON AMERICAN CULTURE

In November 1980 Richie began appearing in an animated cartoon produced by Hanna-Barbera and sharing a Saturday morning show initially with Scooby-Doo. ABC kept him on the air until 1984, teaming him with such other stars as Pac-Man and a cartoon version of Little Rascals. *The Richie Rich Show* is faithful to its comic book counterparts, except that Richie, Reggie, and Gloria appear to be about 12 years old instead of 7 or 8 as in the comics. Also, Richie's trademark waistcoat and blue shorts were replaced by a red sweater with an "R" and full-length slacks. Richie Rich was voiced by Sparky Marcus. His redhead girlfriend Gloria was voiced by Nancy Cartwright (who does the voice for Bart Simpson), with Dick Beals as Reggie Van Dough, William Callaway as Professor Keanbean, Joan Gerber as robot maid Irona and Regina Rich, Christian Hoff as Freckles and Pee-Wee, Stanley Jones as Cadbury and Mr. Rich, and Frank Welker as Dollar.

For most of those aged 7–24, the character of Richie Rich is best known from the 1994 movie starring Macaulay Culkin as the lead character (in Culkin's final role as a child actor). The film, produced by Silver Pictures Davis

Entertainment and released by Warner Brothers under its Family Entertainment label, was critically panned, and the box office receipts were disappointing. The film cost $40 million and generated only a bit over $38 million in revenues. The movie did, however, make $125 million in the home video market. It would be sad to think that the importance of the character of Richie Rich is as a rather forgettable film character. The story of how Richie Rich developed says a lot about comic book history in the 1950s.

Cartoonist Peter Kuper used Richie Rich as a means to criticize President George W. Bush and his administration when he created comics and animated shorts of "Richie Bush, the Poor Little Oligarch" in the early 2000s. Kuper cast stylized versions of the president, his cabinet, and family as characters with a Richie Rich-like look, mocking the president's wealth and his policies. In 2004 U.S. Customs seized copies of one comic book containing the satire, claiming it pirated copyrighted material, but the Comic Book Legal Defense Fund successfully lobbied for the book's release.

SUMMARY

Why the appeal of Richie Rich? The reason may lie in the fact that Richie has money and the power that money brings, but he does not exploit or obsess over it. Both he and his friends around him just take it for granted that he is one of the wealthiest people around. His friends like Richie just because he is just a regular person in the neighborhood.

Richie Rich's appeal to children could be seen as twofold. His character appeared at the time of the Baby Boom. As Baby Boom children grew up in an affluent age, they were aware of—and in awe of—the power of money. Thus, Baby Boom children adopted Richie Rich as a goal to aspire to—a person of great wealth and power. At the same time, Richie's nonchalance about his wealth meant wealth was not associated with snobbery or elitism. Richie was one of their own. This dual appeal was likely the reason that Richie Rich lasted so long as a character and in so many venues.

It is unclear as to whether the reboot of Richie Rich by Ape Entertainment will generate enough excitement among young readers to make the comic a success. Still, few titles in the history of comics have been as popular as Richie Rich.

See also Dark Horse Comics; Little Lulu

ESSENTIAL WORK

Carbaga, Leslie, ed. *Harvey Comics Classics Volume 2: Richie Rich, the Poor Little Rich Boy.* Milwaukie, OR: Dark Horse Comics, 2007.

FURTHER READING

Arnold, Mark. "Harvey Comics History." *The Harveyville Fun Times!* http://web
.archive.org/web/20080724205323/http://home.att.net/~thft/harveyhist.htm. Accessed December 26, 2011.

Hajdu, David. *The Ten-Cent Plague.* New York: Farrar, Straus, and Giroux, 2008.

Markstein, Don. *Don Markstein's Toonopedia.* 2008. http://www.toonpedia.com.
Accessed December 26, 2011.

Rod Carveth

Robin

Easily one of the most recognizable superhero characters worldwide, Robin "the Boy Wonder" serves as **Batman**'s sidekick and crime-fighting partner. Usually depicted as a joking acrobat in bright colors in contrast to Batman's darker and more stoic persona, the Robin character injects youth and humor into Batman's crime stories. Since the character's debut in 1940, many different young men have joined the Bat-family of heroes to serve as the Dark Knight's squire. Though Robin began as the junior half of the "Dynamic Duo," he would later lead other teen heroes in the Teen Titans and Young Justice, and ultimately became as popular a solo hero as Batman's assistant. Today Robin serves as a valuable marketing property and media staple in films, television, and video games featuring the Batman mythos.

HISTORY

In *Detective Comics* #38, Batman creators **Bob Kane and Bill Finger**, along with teenage assistant and inker Jerry Robinson, introduce audiences to "the sensational character find of 1940," Robin, the Boy Wonder. In the metastory *Real Facts Comics* #5 (1946), Kane asserts that the impetus to create Robin came from a reader's letter asking for Batman "to have someone who can share the secret of his identity." Young Dick Grayson watches in horror as criminals murder his circus acrobat parents, only to be taken in as a ward by millionaire Bruce Wayne who suffered a similar tragedy. Swearing by candle light to aid Wayne's war on crime, Grayson becomes Robin. Adding a light-heartedness to Batman's adventures, the laughing daredevil Robin offered snappy comebacks to criminals even as he spent more than a few stories as "Robin, the boy hostage" whom Batman had to repeatedly rescue. Originally merely a lure for the dollars of young readers, Robin helped double the sales of Batman comics (Daniels 2004, 37). He also appeared in solo stories in *Star-Spangled Comics* #65–#130 (1947–1952) with Batman as a near-ubiquitous guest star. Still, Grayson grew into his own and even banded with other teenage sidekicks to form their own superhero team, the Teen Titans. But after 44

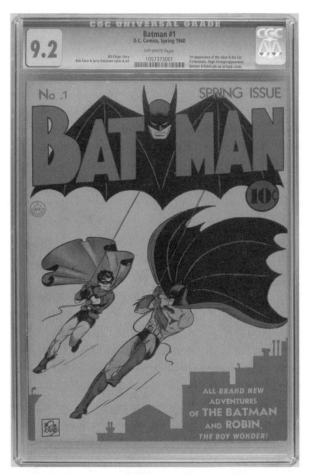

(AP Photo/Heritage Auctions)

years of publication, writers saw the need for a change as Grayson began to chafe at being the backside of "Batman and—." He went off to college only to spend more time leading the Teen Titans and less as Batman's "Teen Wonder." In *Tales of the Teen Titans* #44 (1984), Grayson abandoned the Robin role in favor of a new identity inspired both by Batman and **Superman**. As Nightwing, Grayson often took leadership roles in crises and even led the Justice League for a time. He protected his own city south of Gotham, called Blüdhaven, until it was destroyed in a supervillain attack. Even though most of the superhero community recognize Grayson as the original Robin grown into Nightwing, to the larger world, Batman seems to maintain only one Robin.

Jason Todd, the second Robin, possesses a checkered past both within comics and in the real world. First introduced as a virtual clone of Dick Grayson in the form of a teenaged circus performer in *Batman* #357 (1983), Todd received a new origin after the series *Crisis on Infinite Earths* (1985) reorganized **DC Comics'** continuity. Growing up as a tough street kid, Todd earned his role as Batman's new partner by stealing the tires from the Batmobile. Unlike Grayson, though, Todd's Robin failed to sit well with fans. To pour salt on the wound, as Nightwing, Grayson distanced himself from Batman for a time due to feelings of betrayal from being replaced by a new Robin whom Wayne chose to legally adopt as a son. Whether out of feeling that Todd had stolen Grayson's position or disliking Todd's more rebellious and rage-fueled attitude, fans ultimately decided to end Todd's time as Robin rather violently. DC Comics controversially allowed fans to call a 900 number and pay to vote on the future of the character. The 1988 "Death in the Family" storyline revealed that outcome as the **Joker** viciously beat Todd before blowing him up. Todd's life ended thanks to a margin of less than 100 votes (O'Neill 1988). The images of Batman holding Todd's bloody corpse and the presence of his costume in memorial in the Batcave remain iconic parts of the character's history.

After Todd's death, a concerned admirer by the name of Tim Drake notices Batman becoming much darker and violent without a Robin to balance him. Having deduced Grayson's (and by extension, Batman's) secrets, he confronts the two heroes and becomes the third Robin in 1989's "A Lonely Place of Dying" story arc. Unlike Todd, who could be read as an interloper to Grayson's role, Drake was written into Grayson's origin as the Drake family posed for a photo with the Flying Graysons minutes before their murders. Trained by Batman, Nightwing—a big brother of sorts—and a host of other DC Comics characters, Drake became a prominent hero and adopted his own costume distinct from the one used by previous Robins. Like Grayson, Drake proved sociable and founded his own team of Teen Titans as well as their precursor team, Young Justice. Drake also broke from tradition in that he was largely raised by wealthy parents and initially took the mantle without being an orphan. However, this changed when Drake's father was killed in Brad Meltzer's *Identity Crisis* (2004). Drake, perhaps the most intellectually sophisticated of the Bat-family, struck out on his own as much as he partnered with Batman. He appeared in his own *Robin* titles (1991–2009) and the follow-up *Red Robin* (2009–2011).

During Jeph Loeb and Jim Lee's storyline "Hush," readers were shocked when *Batman* #617–#618 (2003) seemingly revealed the villain Hush to be a resurrected Jason Todd. Though initially just a red herring for fans, the positive reception to Todd's reappearance led to a resurrection thanks to the reality-altering events of the *Infinite Crisis* series (2005–2006) Todd, deeply affected by his death and rebirth, became the Red Hood, a reference to the Joker's previous criminal moniker. Still seeing himself somewhat as a heroic crusader, Todd violently did away with many criminals before Batman thwarted him. Later, audiences learned that Todd suffered some traumatic event—presumably child abuse—that led him to a life of crime before meeting

Batman. Though Batman attempted to heal Todd by making him Robin, placing him in violent situations and ordering the red-haired Todd to dye his hair black to maintain the public image of a single Robin likely exacerbated the emotional damage. As such, Todd retains a contentious relationship with Batman and the other Robins whom he sees as Batman's favored "children."

When Bruce Wayne apparently died in *Final Crisis* (2009), the Batman family went through further shake-ups. Though Todd explosively reappeared to seize the Batman identity, Grayson won the cowl as the new Batman while Drake lost the Robin mantle to newcomer Damian Wayne, Bruce's illegitimate son. *Batman* writer Grant Morrison had previously surprised fans by taking the out-of-continuity graphic novel *Batman: Son of the Demon* (1987) and inserting the sexual encounter between Batman and Talia al Ghul and the resultant child into mainstream continuity. As the son of Wayne and the grandchild of Ra's al Ghul, Batman's arch-nemesis, Damian was raised in secret by his mother to be a warrior and possesses an aristocratic and violent personality at odds with previous versions of Robin—particularly with Drake, who consequently became the solo hero Red Robin in response.

With the reboot of the DC Universe in 2011, Grayson returned to being Nightwing and Damian remains Robin but as Wayne's partner. After the relaunch, the Robin moniker now identifies characters who have served as Batman's partner in a sort of crime-fighting internship. The characters apprentice with Batman for an unspecified period of time before leaving the nest as their own heroes.

Beyond the mainstream DC Comics continuity, Robin continually reappears in a variety of ways. One motif saw a teen Bruce Wayne adopt a Robin costume as a way to hide his identity while he trained to become Batman such as in John Byrne's *Superman & Batman: Generations* (1999). DC also introduced the concept of "Elseworlds" stories wherein characters were set in new situations and environments. Specifically, the Batman-Robin partnership seems to work in any genre or setting including pirate ships, feudal Japan, and even the far future where a robot serves as "Robin, the Toy Wonder." Regardless of how the character is portrayed, Robin provides Batman an emotional connection with which to share the burden of his crime-fighting career.

IMPACT ON COMICS

The introduction of Robin changed Batman comics irrevocably. With the advent of Robin, editorial pressure changed much of the Batman character from a gritty vigilante more in line with pulp crime stories into a superhero who no longer killed criminals (Levitz 2011, 112). The introduction of a boy partner shifted the tone of these stories with more lighthearted banter and

GIRL-WONDER?

While his most recognizable sidekicks have been dark-haired teenaged boys, the Dark Knight employed other crime fighters-in-training as his Robin:

- Stephanie Brown appeared first as the Spoiler, a masked vigilante thwarting the crimes of her criminal father, the Cluemaster. Later dating then-Robin Tim Drake, Brown assumed the mantle of Robin when Drake abandoned the role. Her tenure ended badly when she disobeyed Batman and caused a violent gang war in Gotham City that led to her controversial torture and presumed death. Fans later questioned if Batman truly counted her as Robin as her death never earned her a memorial in the Batcave. Brown would later return as the new Batgirl with Batman's blessing.
- Carrie Kelly became the Robin of the future in Frank Miller's *Batman: The Dark Knight Returns* (1986). Aiding the aged revolutionary Batman, she appeared in her own Robin costume with green-tinted sunglasses as a mask. In Miller's sequel, *The Dark Knight Strikes Again*, Kelly fought crime as Batman's second-in-command as the new Batgirl. Although these stories occur outside mainstream continuity, Kelly in many ways influenced the creation of Tim Drake as she idolized Batman, sought out his partnership, and would later be regarded by Wayne as his child.

led to a more personable Batman who worked with the Gotham police. DC Comics spent decades since negotiating the dark and brooding Batman with the joking "Caped Crusader" image joined by laughing sidekicks.

The impact of teen hero sidekicks—the majority of which were boys—likely contributed to the shifting of comic books to a mainly adolescent audience. Though he was not the first sidekick, Robin's success arguably led to the emergence of many more teen sidekicks and instituted a generic convention for teen heroes: the Human Torch's Toro (1940), Captain America's Bucky (1941), Green Arrow's Speedy (1941), among many others. Like Robin, these teens often grew up and would become heroes in their own right, sometimes replacing their fallen mentors. Thus Robin began the legacy hero lineage that continues through both DC Comics and rival Marvel Comics. Dick Grayson's assumption of the Batman cowl as well as stories showing Drake or Damian Wayne as the Batman of the future create a sense of timelessness around the characters, implying that no matter who wears the masks, there will always be a Batman and Robin for audiences to enjoy. Furthermore, while many of the major characters like Superman and Batman have experienced relatively little character change or evolution, Robin and other teen sidekicks have aged somewhat in time with their fans. This later contributed to DC's continuity problems in trying to reconcile the disparate ages between certain characters.

More so than any other comic book character, Robin serves to evince a particular zeitgeist. The history of DC Comics may in fact be referenced by Robin as each generational age seems to have its own Robin character: the Golden Age (young Dick Grayson), the Silver Age (teen Grayson), the Bronze Age (Jason Todd), the Dark Age (Tim Drake), and the Modern Age (Damian Wayne). According to comic book writer Devin Grayson, "To see Batman do something heroic is inspiring on an almost archetypal level. To see ROBIN do something heroic is inspiring on a PERSONAL level" (Grayson 1998, emphasis in original). This personal connection allows fans to put themselves in the position of working alongside Batman without taking over for the hero. For many, Robin serves as the participatory gateway through which to enjoy Batman's mythos.

IMPACT ON AMERICAN CULTURE

Robin can be found anywhere one finds Batman, including comic books, television shows, films, video games, and much more. Robin exists as a media entity inextricably linked with Batman and shares nearly as much ubiquity in American culture. Popularly, the Robin known to most audiences is Dick Grayson, thanks to his live-action and cartoon appearances. The highly campy *Batman* television series (1966–1968) starring Adam West as Batman and Burt Ward as Robin made Robin as recognizable as his mentor with an explosion of marketing materials. This series also popularized Robin's grossly overused catchphrase "Holy [anything]!" in American vernacular. After the show ended, cartoons like *The Super Friends* featured Robin as a fulltime member again spouting "Holy!" in front of any noun imaginable. Decades after the show's cancellation, this catchphrase maintains its association with Robin in popular culture.

Though actor Chris O'Donnell played a live-action Robin in Joel Schumacher's disappointing films *Batman Forever* (1995) and *Batman & Robin* (1997), the character remains a more valuable staple in animated projects. *Batman: The Animated Series* (1992–1995) and *The New Batman Adventures* (1997–1999) used the Grayson character, eventually aging him into his Nightwing persona and introducing Tim Drake to media audiences as something of a mash-up of the Todd and Drake Robins. As a star character, Robin appeared in the animated programs *Teen Titans* (2003–2006) and *Young Justice* (2011–), which both prominently featured the Dick Grayson version of Robin. Jason Todd appeared in the adaptation of the story of his postdeath return in direct-to-video animated film *Batman: Under the Red Hood* (2010).

The well-known partnership of Batman and Robin also invites some criticism and humorous jibes, however. Famously, psychologist **Fredric Wertham** denounced the characters' perceived homosexual and pedophilic relationship in his attack on the comic industry in *Seduction of the Innocent* (1954). Wertham also called attention to the questionable morality of putting a minor in harm's way. Decades later, Bruce Wayne's questionable predilection for adopting young, damaged boys—particularly one named "Dick"—and putting them into brightly colored and at times revealing costumes remains the source of many jokes in popular culture. Such juxtaposition certainly served to make Batman look more masculine by comparison. Additionally, *Saturday Night Live* offered a particularly memorable series of animated shorts called "The Ambiguously Gay Duo" in direct allusion to the West and Ward partnership in *Batman*. Audiences also continue to poke fun at how the Dark Knight hides in the shadows but his teen partner wears bright colors like some sort of distracting bull's-eye for criminals (particularly after the well-publicized death of Jason Todd). The graphic novel *Brat Pack* (1990) by Rick Veitch explicitly engages with the violence, sexual abuse, and pedophiliac implications of teen sidekicks. Nonetheless, despite the potentially ludicrous nature of the team-up, Batman and Robin stand as the most well-known superhero team in America and beyond.

SUMMARY

After 70 years together as the "Dynamic Duo" of crime fighters, Batman and Robin stand out as ubiquitous superhero characters. As the seminal archetype that inspired many more sidekicks in future comic books, Robin brought light to Batman's darkness such that audiences of all ages could appreciate the character. For each generation and age of comic book history, there is a Robin that reflects the points of view of younger fans and invites them into the comics medium. While Dick Grayson remains the primary Robin in popular culture, the long-standing histories of Jason Todd and Tim Drake, and now Damian Wayne, continue to feed to a repository of stories so large that it even rivals that of Batman.

See also Batman; Joker; Kane, Bob and Bill Finger

ESSENTIAL WORKS

Morrison, Grant (w), and Andy Kubert (p). *Batman and Son*. New York: DC Comics, 2008. [Reprinting *Batman* #655–#658.]

Starlin, Jim (w), and Jim Aparo (p). *Batman: A Death in the Family*. New York: DC Comics, 1988. [Collecting *Batman* #426–#429.]

Wolfman, Marv (w), George Perez (w), Jim Aparo (p), and Tom Grummett (p). *Batman: A Lonely Place of Dying*. New York: DC Comics, 1990. [Reprinting *Batman* #440–#442 and *New Teen Titans* #60–#61.]

FURTHER READING

Bissette, Stephen P. *Teen Angels & New Mutants: Rick Veitch's* Brat Pack *and the Art, Karma and Commerce of Killing Sidekicks*. Encino, CA: Black Coat Press, 2011.

Brooker, Will. *Batman Unmasked: Analyzing a Cultural Icon*. New York: Continuum, 2001.

Medhurst, Andy. "Batman, Deviance, and Camp." In *The Many Lives of the Batman: Critical Approaches to a Superhero and His Media*, edited by Roberta E. Pearson and William Uricchio, 149–63. London: Routledge, 1991.

Kane Anderson

Romance Comics

At one time, comic books depicting romantic relationships were some of the most popular on the newsstands. Primarily consumed by young women from the late 1940s to the mid-1970s, romance comics capitalized on formulaic stories of courtship, marriage, heartbreak, and redemption. Though no longer published in the United States, mid-20th-century romance comics continue to be some of the most unique and iconic examples of American comic books.

HISTORY

The romance genre of comic books, designed primarily for girls and young women, was, somewhat ironically, driven by a male creative team. Joe Simon and **Jack Kirby** led what would become a publishing craze (albeit somewhat short-lived) with *Young Romance* #1 in 1947, published by Prize Comics, an imprint of Crestwood Publications. Inspired by romantic stories in the pulp magazines of the 1930s and 1940s, confessional magazines, and teen humor titles such as *Archie*, Simon and Kirby opened up the comic book medium to a whole new audience of readers—women. These early Simon and Kirby romance comic book stories included themes of dating, marriage, jealousy, and divorce.

Romance comics gained a large following during the late 1940s and early 1950s. For every comic book that was on the newsstand between 1949 and mid-1950, approximately one out of four was a romance comic (Nolan 2008, 63). Publishing company after publishing company jumped on the bandwagon, and soon, almost every comic book outfit was putting out some type of romance comic. Each publishing company used various gimmicks to make their titles stand out on the newsstand. One company, American Comics Group, produced stories that were complex and plot-driven, while another publisher, Ace, put out stories that were more generic in tone. Yarns woven by Fox were pulp-like and a little on the dodgy side, while St. John published accounts of romance that were down to earth, and embellished by the stylings of legendary artist Matt Baker.

The genre continued to swell in popularity, and became so profitable in the eyes of publishers that in the second half of 1950 the market became over-saturated, leading to near collapse. Titles were swiftly culled, and once the industry emerged from what comic book historian Michelle Nolan has coined the "Love Glut," only around 30 remained of the 147 romance titles that had been on the market just months prior (Nolan 2008, 62).

Despite fewer issues on the newsstand after the "Love Glut," romance comics continued to feature stories dealing with raw tales of human emotion. It was not long; however, before the genre hit another rough patch. In 1954, the industry changed with the creation of the Comics Code Authority—a self-regulatory body that censored the content of all comic books destined for the newsstand. Romance comics were not exempt from the restrictions of the Comics Code, and they too had to be altered to fit the new regulations. The stories before the implementation of the Comics Code were rather adult and often intermingled with themes of crime. "Nightmare Romance!" from Avon's *Romantic Love* #7 (1951) is a typical example of a pre-Code crime-infused romance story. In the tale, Fran Edwards, owner of a modeling agency, is duped into hiring a man named Wayde, who ends up forcing the models to double as party girls for his own monetary gain. Ignorant of Wayde's extra-curricular activities with the models, Fran falls in love with him. Upon find-ing out Wayde's scandalous deeds, Fran vows to keep his secret. Eventually though, she goes to the police when she finds out that he has also been cheat-ing on her with one of the models. During the climax of the story, Wayde is hunted down by the police and shot dead, but not before beating Fran up for involving the law. Not escaping punishment herself, Fran is also shot during the altercation. While in the ambulance, Fran prays for God's forgiveness for getting wrapped up in the sins of lust and passion.

Most scholarship to date discusses the impact of the Comics Code on the horror and crime genres, but the romance genre was equally affected. After the advent of the Comics Code, romance comics lightened up considerably on the crime and adult-oriented themes, and salacious covers with promises of lusty interior stories such as "Nightmare Romance!" were abolished. The mid- to late 1950s saw a surge in stories of domesticity, and the newly formed concept of the "teenager" began to be embraced by both popular culture and romance comics alike.

As youth culture evolved in the decades after World War II and the baby boomers grew into teenagers, romance comics also evolved. Titles from **DC** and **Marvel** such as *Falling in Love*, *Heart Throbs*, and *Our Love Story* revolved around youth activities—concerts, dancing, and the life of college coeds. Fashion began to play an increasingly important role, and the real-life designs of the 1960s and 1970s, from bell bottoms to hot pants and go-go boots, were heavily present in the pages of romance comics. Trends and tra-ditions in 20th-century dating, courtship, and marriage were also reflected

(Digital Comic Museum)

in the pages of romance comics—such as the growing importance of the automobile.

Surprisingly, quite a few romance stories were told from a male character's perspective. For the most part, however, these mid-20th-century romantic tales were told from the point-of-view of female characters, as written by men such as Dana Dutch of St. John fame, and Richard Hughes, editor and writer for the American Comics Group. Unlike superhero comics, most romance stories were noncontinuous one-shot-type stories with new (but archetypal) characters in each. Some exceptions include DC's "Reach for Happiness" series in *Secret Hearts*, which ran for a staggering 29 consecutive issues and the 22-issue-long "3 Girls—Their Lives—Their Loves" arc from *Heart Throbs*. In an attempt to be seen as more "relevant," publishers began to introduce stock characters such as hippies, swingers, and student protestors in their late 1960s and early 1970s issues. Cultural events such as the Woodstock Festival, as well as the rise of the women's movement and society's shifting views towards race and the war in Vietnam, were also incorporated into the romance stories.

A unique feature of the romance genre was the advice column. Most often run by a "love expert," these columns gave readers a chance to ask their burning questions concerning dating, marriage, and etiquette. Though occasionally editorial snippets made their way into the romance advice columns, they were primarily devoted to solving the mysteries of young love for a generation eager for expert advice. Readers as young as nine years old sought help concerning romance, parents, friendship, health, and beauty. The columnists (most often pseudonyms for various editors) had likeable personas such as "Ann Martin, Counselor-at-Love" and "Julia Roberts, Romance Counselor" and served as beacons of morality for confused adolescents. The advice columns promoted engagement with the comics and today remain textured documents of midcentury domestic life and youth culture.

IMPACT ON COMICS

Devoted primarily to a female readership, romance comics were an innovation in the comic book industry. Though women certainly read and enjoy other genres, romance comics were a cultural space designated for primary consumption by young women. The themes and elements of romance comics did occasionally make their way into superhero titles and targeted the same demographic. DC titles such as *Adventure Comics* (featuring **Supergirl**), *Superman's Girlfriend Lois Lane*, and *Wonder Woman* were all heavily influenced by romance comics in the late 1960s and early 1970s. Linda Danvers (Supergirl), **Lois Lane**, and Diana Prince (**Wonder Woman**) were no strangers to tears, fashion, and heartbreak. Advertisements for the aforementioned titles frequently ran in romance comics and played up on the similarities between them and the love comics. Romantic elements were also incorporated into Marvel's superhero comics starting in the 1960s under the guidance of **Stan Lee**. Every month, characters such as **Spider-Man**, Daredevil, Thor, and **Iron Man** dealt with romantic issues and subplots. John Romita, one of the most prolific romance artists at DC, enjoyed great success on Marvel's *Amazing Spider-Man* because of his talent for drawing beautiful women that was honed during his tenure drawing romance comics.

While romance comics undoubtedly had loyal fans (as evidenced by healthy sales numbers and the legions of readers who wrote in to the advice columns), there never emerged a distinct fan culture as occurred with the superhero comics genre. Like magazines, romance comics were a disposable part of girl culture—read and loved, but ultimately, thrown away. Today, among comic book and comic art collectors, romance comics are highly sought after, but remain primarily unknown to the mainstream. Though the genre has many fans, there still are some who view romance comics as outdated remnants of American culture. Recent revivals such as *Marvel Romance Redux* (2006), which featured old romance stories with rewritten dialogue in a silly and satirical manner, reveal a modern attitude that romance comics are a waste of serious attention.

IMPACT ON AMERICAN CULTURE

Like other comic book genres, romance comics mirrored the changes going on in society concerning issues of race and equality during the late 1960s and throughout the 1970s. Romance comics were often on the forefront of the four-color medium, forging the way for societal change. When it came to racial integration and the women's movement, romance comics helped to challenge prevailing values of the time. One such story, "Black + White = Heartbreak!" from *Girls' Love Stories* #159 (1971) told the trials of a young white woman, Margo, and her African American fiancé, Chuck, who are unable to convince their friends and families that their love is stronger than color. The increasing momentum of the women's movement (usually referred to "women's lib" in the romance comics) also became an important theme during the 1970s. With stories such as "Give Me Liberty or Give Me Love!" from *Young Love* #92 (1972) and "The Movement or My Heart!" as featured in *Our Love Story* #18 (1972), "Libbers," or women fighting for equal rights, were depicted not as plain Jane man-haters, but as likeable young women with forward-thinking attitudes. Though many of the stories and titles may seem somewhat humorous to today's reader, they no doubt served to educate and inspire young women navigating the world of dating and marriage in the sanctioned norms and mores of romantic life.

Romance comics fell very much in line with prevailing attitudes of the American value system during their heyday. Traditions of marriage and family were held strong, as were ideals of effort, hard work, and optimism. As a generalization, in romance comics, those who worked hard and were generally good would find romance. Those who were evil or willingly did others harm found themselves spurned and alone. The American dream of prosperity was never far from the minds of romance comic book characters. Romance comics not only entertained but educated young readers in culturally acceptable dating and courtship practices through sequential stories, advertisements, and expert advice.

Though superhero comics continue to dominate the industry, romance comics have had a lasting legacy on American popular culture through a most unexpected mode—fine art. Pop artist Roy Lichtenstein swiped images from romance comics for many of his most famous paintings including "Drowning Girl," whose imagery came from the story "Run for Love" (*Secret Hearts* #83, 1962) and which hangs today in the Museum of Modern Art in New York. Over the years, art scholars have maintained that Lichtenstein's derivative

ROMANCE COMIC ADVICE COLUMNS OF THE 1960S AND 1970S

In an age when experts were held in the highest regard, it is no surprise that romance comics doled out advice to their adolescent audience. Composed primarily by editorial staff using pseudonyms, the advice columns gave the romance comics a personal touch. Below are the names of the columnists, their columns, and the titles those columns appeared in, divided by publishing company.

Charlton
- Buck Mason—"Buck's Bag" (*Teen Confessions, Time for Love*)
- Dr. Harold Gluck—"Canteen Corner" (*Time for Love*) and "Teenage Troubles" (*Career Girl Romances, I Love You, Love Diary, Sweethearts, Teen-Age Love, Time for Love*)
- Jeanette Copeland—"Just Jeanette" (*Hollywood Romances, Just Married, Love and Romance, Romantic Story, Secret Romance, Sweethearts, Teen-Age Love*)
- Jennifer White—"Jennifer's Corner" (*Secret Romance, Teen Confessions*)

DC
- Ann Martin—"Ann Martin, Counselor-At-Love" (*Secret Hearts*)
- Barbara Miles—"From Barbara Miles, with Love" (*Girls' Love Stories, Heart Throbs*)
- Carol Andrews—"To You . . . From Carol Andrews" (*Falling in Love*)
- Donna Fayne—"Like It Is!" (*Heart Throbs, Love Stories*)
- Jane Ford—"As Jane Ford Sees It . . ." (*Young Love*)
- Jill Taylor—"You Can Be Beautiful!" (*Falling in Love, Girls' Love Stories, Heart Throbs*)
- Julia Roberts—"Julia Roberts, Romance Counselor" (*Girls' Romances*)
- Laura Penn—"Laura Penn . . . Your Romance Reporter" (*Young Romance*)
- Lynn Farrell—"Telling It the Way It Is . . . to Lynn Farrell" (*Heart Throbs*)
- Marc—"Marc—On the Man's Side" (*Young Love*)
- Page Peterson—"Do's and Dont's [*sic*] of Dating" (*Young Romance*)
- Paul—"Paul—The Other Side" (*Falling in Love, Young Romance*)

MARVEL
- Suzan—"Suzan Says" (*My Love* and *Our Love Story*)

paintings from romance comics elevated the medium and brought comic books critical attention. However, looking retrospectively, the dismissal of the source material negates their impact on millions of young midcentury readers, and the creators who produced the romance comics.

Lichtenstein's paintings do highlight what is perhaps the most iconic image associated with the romance comic book genre—a beautiful young woman with a tear-stained face. This imagery, based on the romance covers of the 1960s and 1970s, has become synonymous with the genre, and has been used for merchandise ranging from T-shirts to address books—all revered for their kitschiness. Though iconic, the aforementioned crying woman representation has perhaps turned off those modern readers who are more accustomed to the fierce "girl power" iconography that has been a mainstay of popular culture for the past two decades.

The romance comic book genre is not widely known among the general public, as the vast majority of people have only come into contact with romance comics through Lichtenstein's work or unknowingly via the previously mentioned kitschy merchandise. Romance comics are primarily remembered by either the people who read them as children or by comic book fans who admire the highly skilled artistic merits of the creators. Those who encounter romance comics in other ways sometimes view the genre with pity and contempt because they reflect an era before the women's movement was a generally accepted part of American culture and when marriage was seen as the ultimate goal in a woman's life. Varying degrees of snarkiness are directed towards romance comics, and when not the object of disgust, they are often outright forgotten in favor of other comic book genres. Scholarship on romance comics has been rather limited, but the body of literature available is a robust one, though small in comparison to scholarly works based on the adventures of superheroes. It is a genre that continues to offer a plethora of interesting source material, and is a genre that this author and other scholars continue to explore. As romance comic books and the original art pages from the comics are sought after by collectors, they are increasingly becoming more valuable.

SUMMARY

Romance comics were popular because they were easily obtained by teenagers and young adults with disposable incomes, so the question becomes, *why are they not published anymore?* Though there is no hard and fast reason for the demise of the genre, there are a couple theories that attempt to explain why it no longer exists in its original form. It is often pointed out that the restrictions of the Comics Code prohibited the types of stories and themes that could keep readers engaged, such as adultery and violence. Also cited are changing societal norms and a readership that outgrew the genre, as well as the rise of the television soap opera and Harlequin-style romance novels.

Today, romance comics may be an easy target for teasing and misappropriation, but when we put into perspective their importance to a generation of young adults and the American experience, it is easy to understand why they were so loved. Romance comics remain an iconic part of our American visual culture and give us a glimpse into the lives of teenagers and young adults from the 1940s through the 1970s. Characters with vulnerabilities, doubts, shortcomings, and insecurities made them easy to identify with and are the hallmarks of the appealing genre. Gone but not forgotten, romance comics, with their innumerable kisses and tears, continue to stand as a time capsule of midcentury domestic and cultural life.

See also Archie Andrews; Lois Lane; Supergirl; Wonder Woman

ESSENTIAL WORKS

Colletta, Vince (p). "A Teen-Ager Can Also Love!" *Teen-Age Romance* #77 (September 1960), Marvel. Reprinted in *Marvel Romance*. New York: Marvel, 2006.
Dutch, Dana (w), and Lily Renee (p, i). "Was I Too Young for Love?" *Teen-Age Romances* #1 (January 1949), St. John Publishing Company. Reprinted in John Benson, ed., *Romance Without Tears*. Seattle: Fantagraphics, 2003.
Roth, Werner (p), and Vince Colletta (i). "Black + White = Heartbreak!" *Girls' Love Stories* #163 (November 1971), National Comics Publications [DC Comics]. Reprinted in part on *Sequential Crush*, February 19, 2010, http://sequentialcrush .blogspot.com/2010/02/black-white-heartbreak.html.

FURTHER READING

Benson, John. *Confessions, Romances, Secrets and Temptations: Archer St. John and the St. John Romance Comics*. Seattle: Fantagraphics Books, 2007.
Nodell, Jacque. Sequential Crush. http://sequentialcrush.com.
Nolan, Michelle. *Love on the Racks: A History of American Romance Comics*. Jefferson, NC: McFarland, 2008.
Scott, Naomi. *Heart Throbs: The Best of DC Romance Comics*. New York: Simon & Schuster, 1979.

Jacque Nodell

Rorschach

Rorschach is one of the main protagonists in the landmark superhero miniseries and subsequent graphic novel *Watchmen* (1986–1987). He is a grim-and-gritty character who adopts an uncompromising stance toward crime and criminals. The character's moral rigidity and extralegal methods allow the creators of *Watchmen*, **Alan Moore** and Dave Gibbons, to explore the pros and cons of vigilante-style justice. As numerous commentators have pointed out, Rorschach is loosely based on a Charlton Comics character, the Question, who first appeared in *Blue Beetle* #1 (June 1967). The Question was created by the gifted comics writer-artist **Steve Ditko**, who in the same year came up with an analogous character, Mr. A, for the comics magazine *witzend* #3. While it seems evident that Moore and Gibbons are broadly unsympathetic to Rorschach's dogmatic approach to crime fighting, he is arguably one of the book's only heroic figures. The now-iconic character was memorably portrayed in the 2009 film version of *Watchmen* by the actor Jack Earle Haley.

HISTORY

Watchmen is set in an alternative universe where costumed vigilantes have been active since the late 1930s and where the most popular comic book genre is pirate stories. As the book opens, Richard Nixon is serving out his fourth term as president of the United States, and the country is on the brink of all-out nuclear war with the Soviet Union. The year is 1985. Following urban protests and civil unrest in the mid-1970s, the practice of costumed crime fighting has been banned. Most would-be heroes have retired, with the exception of those who operate outside the law (Rorschach) or as government-sanctioned agents (the Comedian). The only true superhero is Doctor Manhattan, whose God-like powers are the result of an accident at a nuclear physics lab that exposed a research scientist, Jon Osterman, to a life-altering "intrinsic field experiment." The others are more or less ordinary men and women who dress up in colorful costumes to fight crime—as well as their own inner demons.

With the obvious exception of the book's mass-murdering criminal mastermind, Rorschach is arguably the most psychologically disturbed of all of the major *Watchmen* characters. His fanatical perspectives on crime, punishment, and society, and his unstinting reliance on physical coercion, clearly mark him as an antisocial personality with sociopathic tendencies. It is not accidental that his costume primarily consists of a mask that resembles the famous Rorschach inkblot tests that became a popular diagnostic instrument for psychologists in the post–World War II period. The most peculiar aspect of his costume is the fact that the mask's inkblot patterns are in constant motion. Apart from the mask, his costume consists of a brown overcoat, a hat, and boots. Despite his lack of superpowers and sophisticated weaponry, and his relatively small frame, Rorschach strikes terror into the heart of the criminal underworld, whose denizens appreciate the lengths to which he will go to extract information and avenge wrongdoing. The character demonstrates a single-minded commitment to an Old Testament form of justice that casts a stark light on the capacity of the police and public officials to maintain a lawful and peaceable social order.

Character Biography

Rorschach was born in 1941; his given name is Walter Joseph Kovacs. He is the only child of Sylvia Kovacs, a prostitute, and "Charlie," one of her clients. After severely injuring two teenaged bullies as a child, he was placed in the Lillian Charleton Home for Problem Children for a number of years, where he excelled at boxing and gymnastics. He decided to become a costumed crime fighter after reading about the tragic, real-world case of Kitty Genovese, whose brutal murder in 1964 might have been prevented if neighbors had responded to her cries for help. At first, Rorschach merely assaulted wrongdoers and left them for the authorities, instead of killing them. He eventually adopted a more radical approach. During the late 1960s and early 1970s he worked in tandem with the mild-mannered Daniel Dreiberg, the second Nite Owl. Their partnership came to a close when so-called costumed adventuring was banned under the 1977 Keene Act, although they start working together again during the second half of the *Watchmen* story arc.

Rorschach's methods evolved—or, rather, devolved—once he investigated the kidnapping of a young girl and found her bones being chewed on by the kidnapper's two German shepherds. The barbarity of the crime scene provoked him into a state of permanent murderousness, and from this point forward his worldview could be described as a kind of unblinking, right-wing nihilism. Given the severity of his outlook, it seems more than a little plausible that he would be unwilling to either retire or cooperate with the authorities following the passage of the Keene Act. In a sense, "Walter Kovacs" died with the girl, and the Rorschach persona became his all-consuming identity. After this point, the only time the mask slips off is when he is resting in his grungy apartment or pacing New York's gang-ridden streets while carrying a "The End Is Nigh" placard.

It is in this alarmist, plainclothes guise that the reader is first introduced to Rorschach—on the very first page of *Watchmen*'s inaugural issue—although it isn't revealed for several issues that the redheaded sign-carrier is at the same time an outlaw vigilante. In fact, Rorschach plays a leading role in almost all 12 issues of the limited series. His importance is reaffirmed in the final issue, whose closing panel offers a close-up of his private diary, which, if published, promises to reveal the truth about Ozymandias's epochal conspiracy. It is Rorschach who initially figures out that the Comedian's murder was not a random act, and he is also on hand when the archvillain is finally confronted. While the miraculous Doctor Manhattan offers a much more engaging and unpredictable personality, and the Nite Owl a far more sympathetic everyman type, Rorschach presents a compelling portrait of comic book vigilantism pushed to an extreme, albeit logical conclusion. He is not intended as a role model—far from it—but by the end of the series the reader gains a deeper appreciation for how someone motivated by a raw sense of justice could travel so far from the boundaries of civilized conduct.

Origins

The English comics writer Alan Moore originally conceived of *Watchmen* as a superhero murder mystery based on the Charlton Comics heroes of the 1960s, to which **DC Comics** acquired the rights in the mid-1980s. DC's editors encouraged Moore to use new characters, so as to preserve the Charlton stable for future, ongoing stories. Moore had already established himself as an up-and-coming comics writer for his contributions to the U.K. comics magazines *2000 AD* and *Warrior*, and for his work on DC's **Swamp Thing**. His friend Dave Gibbons was also becoming known in the industry for his polished, tightly organized artwork, much of which was featured in the pages of *2000 AD*, the home of Judge Dread and other iconic English comics characters.

Rorschach was loosely inspired by the Charlton character the Question, who was perhaps the most ruthless of all of Charlton's costumed crime fighters. Working out of the fictional Hub City, the Question donned a pseudoplastic facemask to obscure his features from lawbreakers, police officers, and the general public. As with Rorschach, his mask was the lynchpin of his costume, and he similarly sported an overcoat and broad brim hat. The Question was the creation of Steve Ditko, who played a significant role in the Silver Age through his work on such iconic **Marvel** characters as **Spider-Man** and Doctor

WHO IS THE QUESTION?

A number of characters in Ayn Rand's 1957 novel *Atlas Shrugged* pose the mysterious question, "Who is John Galt?" It is many pages into the novel before Galt reveals himself and gives a very long speech in which he articulates Rand's philosophy of Objectivism, including his declaration that because a thing is what it is (A is A), there are no moral gray areas and "in any compromise between good and evil, it is only evil that can profit" (part 3, chapter 7).

Ten years later, Steve Ditko's superhero the Question declares, "Honest men don't deal with known thieves. It can only lead to corrupting that which is honest!" (*Mysterious Suspense* #1, 1968). The Question first appeared in a backup story in *Blue Beetle* #1 that was advertised on the cover of the comic with a banner that asked, "Who is the Question?" Surely it was no coincidence that this query echoed the question so central to *Atlas Shrugged*. Ditko was a devotee of Rand's Objectivism and the Question was his first attempt to embody that philosophy in a superhero. The Question shows criminals no mercy and has no sympathy for anyone who compromises their principles. The Question was the template for Rorschach, and Rorschach's attitudes and actions are certainly consistent with Objectivism. At the end of *Watchmen* when Nite Owl pleads with Rorschach to go along with a cover-up—"This is too big to be hard-assed about! We have to compromise."—Rorschach responds: "No. Not even in the face of Armageddon. Never compromise."

Randy Duncan

Strange. Ditko is a reclusive and by now legendary figure in the comics industry. He famously refuses to give interviews, and he avoids comics conventions. From the 1960s onwards his comics have tended to reflect his longstanding engagement with the ideas of Ayn Rand and her Objectivist philosophy, which stresses the pursuit of self-interest and the moral underpinnings of laissez-faire capitalism. He seems to have valued the relative autonomy he enjoyed at Charlton Comics as both a writer and artist, particularly in comparison to Stan Lee's more hands-on editorial regime at Marvel Comics. That said, at one time or another Ditko worked, mostly as a freelancer, for almost all of the major comics companies, from DC and Marvel, to **Dark Horse** and Eclipse. Although he retired from mainstream comics at the end of the 1990s, he continues to occasionally release self-published comics, essays, and editorial cartoons.

Rorschach bears a familial resemblance to another masked Steve Ditko character from the mid-1960s, Mr. A, who originally appeared in the pages of

Wally Wood's independent comics magazine *witzend*. Ditko retains the rights to this character and has published a number of stories featuring Mr. A over the past several decades. Mr. A's alter ego is Rex Graine, a crusading newspaper reporter known for his fedora hats and unbending moral code. He sees the world in strictly black-and-white terms and kills without remorse when innocent lives are at stake. He also takes the time to carefully explain his actions, and principles, to both rogues and readers. While Mr. A stories are usually crime adventures, they can also be read as pointed allegories that advance the Objectivist cause. As with the Question, Mr. A is implacable in his opposition to all forms of criminal behavior, and he views the slightest transgression or prevarication as the start of a very slippery slope. Along with certain visual touches, Rorschach shares with both the Question and Mr. A an unrelenting commitment to truth telling and a willingness to sacrifice even his own life to uphold his fundamental convictions. It is precisely this aspect of Rorschach's character that is put to the test in the 12th issue of the *Watchmen* miniseries. In fact, it is this sense of stubborn morality that turns Rorschach into a true hero at the end of Moore and Gibbons's story.

Vigilante Politics

The rights and wrongs of vigilantism has been a popular theme in comic books from their inception. To the extent that they operate outside of the law, superheroes in general can be considered vigilantes, although they often cooperate with the authorities, at least from time to time. Characters like the Question, Mr. A, and Rorschach tend to be more scornful about the criminal justice system than most costumed avengers, even if they retain a romantic attachment to the flag, the Constitution, and the *idea* of the law. In *Watchmen* as in many other superhero stories, there is an unresolved tension between the more moderate or optimistic perspective of figures like Nite Owl, who believes that the system can be reformed and that people are fundamentally good, and the more extreme or pessimistic views of a Rorschach, who only sees rot and decay and who fears that, indeed, the "end is nigh." The stark contrast between **Superman** and **Batman**, two of the earliest superheroes, can be expressed in precisely these terms. In superhero comics, moral conflicts and dilemmas are often hashed out between superheroes rather than between heroes and villains. Villainy gives superheroes something to fight about, not only to fight against.

Vigilantism comes in many different forms, in other words. There is a significant difference between the vigilante who seeks to right a specific wrong, or who works alongside legally constituted authorities, and the more hardcore vigilante who is engaged in an ongoing, murderous, and essentially lawless war against lawlessness. Rorschach is obviously on the lone wolf end of the vigilante spectrum. He is, as they say, beyond the point of no return. It is difficult to imagine how his journey could end in any other way except violently; there is no happy ending for these kinds of characters. The job of a Rorschach is to show the reader what can happen when a violent, psychologically scarred individual places the abstract concept of justice above all other considerations. He encapsulates an entire worldview, and offers a useful contrast with other kinds of characters. _Watchmen_ would have been arguably a much less engaging story without Rorschach and his raw-meat ideology.

Rorschach's obvious counterpart in mainstream comics is Frank Castle, a.k.a. the **Punisher**, whose survival over a period of several decades reflects the commercial imperatives of serial fiction rather than the otherwise compelling logic of the character and his social environment. While the Punisher was introduced into the Marvel Universe in the mid-1970s and is based on an earlier pulp fiction character, the Executioner, who dates to the late 1960s, he only caught fire with readers during the Reagan administration, with the 1986 publication of the limited series _Circle of Blood_. In the real world, anyone who took up arms against violent criminals would sooner or later be severely maimed, killed, or locked up for life. However, since the Punisher represents a lucrative revenue stream, both in comics and on the big screen, his inevitable bad ending has been deferred in the interests of milking the not inconsiderable audience for vigilante-based entertainment.

IMPACT ON COMICS

Rorschach's single-minded approach clearly resonated with many _Watchmen_ readers. Along with the Punisher, and arguably the **X-Men's Wolverine**, Rorschach helped push superhero comics in a darker, less hopeful direction than had been the case in the Silver Age. These characters both reflected and responded to the growing disenchantment of the general public in the 1970s and 1980s, as urban decay, violent crime, and mounting evidence of corruption at the highest levels served to undermine the social consensus and optimism of the postwar period. Longtime comics fans often bemoaned the rise of so-called grim and gritty superheroes, but they proved popular with newer readers. It is possible that Rorschach and his counterparts provided a sort of catharsis for an audience that was becoming increasingly skeptical about the capacity of public institutions to address deep-rooted social problems. In recent years there has been something of a swing of the pendulum in the other direction, as comic book creators and fans have once again embraced a more light-hearted approach to superhero storytelling. In the closing decades of the 20th century, however, the lone wolf pessimists reigned supreme.

IMPACT ON AMERICAN CULTURE

The impact of Rorschach and similar vigilante characters can be discerned in the wider culture, as well as in the world of comics. Vigilante movies proved particularly popular and even ubiquitous in the 1980s and 1990s, and the genre continues to flourish at the box office. Many reviewers and moviegoers were enthused by Jack Earle Haley's performance in the *Watchmen* movie, and by the vengeful character he portrayed, even if they found fault with the film as a whole. Some critics complained that the film was overly faithful or deferential to the source material and failed to work on its own terms. At the same time, *Watchmen* screenings grossed over $100 million in the United States alone, and the movie is considered a commercial success by the motion picture industry. The film spawned action figures; two video games; an animated "motion comic"; an animated adaptation of *Tales of the Black Freighter*, the fictional comic book that plays an important role in the *Watchmen* universe; and a pair of viral videos that provided back story for major plot points. Several versions of the film have been released on DVD and Blu-Ray, including an ultimate collector's edition, and a director's cut. The success of the film also helped promote sales of the graphic novel, which remains a bestselling title on Amazon.com and other Internet sales outlets. There are over a million copies of the graphic novel in print.

For many readers—and viewers—Rorschach is the true hero of the *Watchmen* story. The character provides an especially vivid example of our culture's romantic infatuation with extreme vigilantism. He is emblematic of a kind of contemptuous if principled rejection of the political system and the social order that is by definition immoderate and unreasoning. He speaks to that part of the electorate, and inner selves, that has lost all hope in the American dream.

SUMMARY

Rorschach is a compelling if problematic fictional character whose very existence raises troubling questions about the capacity of our laws, institutions, and elected representatives to make things right. While he is obviously disturbed, he is also a man of stubborn conviction. Moore and Gibbons did a great job of fashioning an unlikely and unlikable masked hero whose politics are very different from his creators' but who nevertheless has something important to say. Rorschach's obdurate search for the truth plays a pivotal role in propelling the *Watchmen* narrative forward and in uncovering a malignant conspiracy that eventually results in the death of millions of New Yorkers. Few if any readers of *Watchmen* are likely to emulate his actions. But his political pessimism, and his take-no-prisoners sensibility, resonate with a surprisingly large number of people.

See also Moore, Alan; *Watchmen*

ESSENTIAL WORKS

Gibbons, Dave, with Chip Kidd and Mike Essl. *Watching the Watchmen*. London: Titan Books, 2008.
Moore, Alan (w), and Dave Gibbons (a). *Watchmen*. New York: DC Comics, 1995.

FURTHER READING

Di Liddo, Annalisa. *Alan Moore: Comics as Performance, Fiction as Scalpel*. Jackson: University of Mississippi Press, 2009.
Kaveney, Roz. *Superheroes! Capes and Crusaders in Comics and Film*. London: I. B. Tauris, 2008.
Van Ness, Sara J. *Watchmen as Literature: A Critical Study of the Graphic Novel*. Jefferson, NC: McFarland, 2010.
White, Mark D., ed. *Watchmen and Philosophy: A Rorschach Test*. Hoboken, NJ: Wiley, 2009.

Kent Worcester

Ross, Alex

Alex Ross is one of the most iconic artists in the field of sequential art. His realistic portrayals of characters revolutionized comic art. Ross carved a niche for himself and built a large fan base since coming onto the comics scene in the early 1990s. He has collaborated with other sequential art heavyweights like Kurt Busiek, Mark Waid, Paul Dini, and Jim Krueger.

HISTORY

Nelson Alexander Ross was born January 22, 1970, in Portland, Oregon, but spent his formative years in Lubbock, Texas. He currently lives in Illinois. Ross grew up in a spiritual environment as his father Clark is a minister. In addition, young Alex found solace in the colorful adventures of super-heroes whose godlike powers he found fascinating. His father, Ross states, laid "the moral framework that allowed him to appreciate the routinely good deeds performed by the likes of Superman and Spider-Man" (Ross Biography, 2011). According to his mother Lynette (also an artist), Alex was already drawing by the time he was three (FAQ 2011).

After Ross graduated from Lubbock High School, he moved to Chicago (when he was 17) to attend the American Academy of Art. His time there was beneficial: "I learned where I was as an artist and what kind of discipline I'd already learned. Here I was, drawing from a model for the first time and realizing I could represent the model. Not everyone in the class could do that. It was important to make that discovery" (Ross Biography, 2011). Ross's artistic inspirations include George Perez, Bernie Wrightson, and **Jack Kirby**, whom he calls "more or less, the Picasso of comics" (Khoury "Interview" 1999). Outside of comics, he finds the work of Salvador Dali, Andrew Loomis, and most importantly Norman Rockwell to be inspiring. It is Rockwell's realistic "slice of life" style that influences Ross the most. He likes to apply the "photorealism" of Rockwell's drawings to comics (Ross Biography, 2011). While studying at the Art Academy, it occurred to Ross that painted comics would be an interesting way to illustrate them.

Ross has drawn nearly every major character from the two big mainstream comic publishers, **DC** and **Marvel**. DC comics published a beautiful hardcover, *Mythology: The DC Comics Art of Alex Ross*, showcasing his work for the company in 2003 and again in 2010 when it published *Rough Justice: The DC Comics Sketches of Alex Ross*. He has also done other comics work including *Spawn, Battle of the Planets*, and even heroes based upon Indian mythology like the Ramayana. While Ross illustrates the occasional full storyline, he is most known for comics and graphic novel cover artwork.

The series *Terminator Burning Earth* published in 1990 by Now Comics is usually credited as being Ross's first published work. Other early work was featured in Marvel/Epic's 1992 *Hellraiser* series. Ross's big break came when writer Kurt Busiek saw some of his work and invited him to collaborate on Marvel Comics' now legendary series *Marvels* (1994). It is this series that made Ross a household name in the comics' world. Ross and Busiek created a tale that spanned the history of the Marvel Universe, but told it from the point of view of an ordinary person. Ross's painted characters and Busiek's insightful writing brought a new authenticity to mainstream superhero comics. In the introduction to the graphic novel, **Stan Lee** was glowing in his praise of the work: "I've never read anything like the stories on the pages ahead, nor have I ever seen anything surpassing the spectacular artwork which brings each episode to life" (Lee 2008, 5).

Ross continued his success by teaming up with writer Mark Waid for DC's *Kingdom Come* (1996). Like *Marvels*, this series took a more realistic approach to presenting superheroes in a possible future. This particular story has special significance for Ross, as his father Clark Ross was the model and inspiration for the character of minister Norman McCay.

Ross contributed to other important comics and graphic novels including *Uncle Sam* (1997), *Superman: Peace on Earth* (1999), *Batman: War on Crime* (1999), *Wonder Woman: Spirit of Truth* (2011), *Absolute Justice* (2009), *Astro City* (1995), *Avengers/Invaders* (2007), and *Captain America* (2008). In addition to doing artwork for projects, Ross takes an active role in creating original storylines and concepts that other writers and artists build upon. In 1999 Ross and writer Jim Kreuger created the magnificent *Earth X*, for Marvel Comics, featuring unique versions of Marvel characters in a dystopian future where everyone possessed superpowers. *Earth X* spawned five more volumes including *Universe X* and *Paradise X*, both in two volumes, and the *Earth X Trilogy Companion*. The series featured major and minor characters from Marvel's history. The impetus for the *Earth X Trilogy*, according to Ross, "began with a fat **Spider-Man**." He had been asked by **Wizard** *magazine* to create a "series of sketches showing my interpretation of the future Marvel Universe" (Ross, Kreuger and Reinhold 2008, 10). In 2001 Graphitti Designs produced a limited-edition (6,000 signed copies) oversize box containing a

WEST TEXAS TALENT

Alex Ross went to Lubbock High School, the same school as rock pioneer Buddy Holly. Lubbock and West Texas are known for having a wealth of musical talent including Mac Davis, Waylon Jennings, Jimmie Dale Gilmore, Joe Ely, Butch Hancock, Terry Allen, Legendary Stardust Cowboy, Sonny Curtis, Ralna English, Tommy Hancock, and Pat Green. Meat Loaf also briefly made his home in Lubbock. In addition to musicians, Lubbock and West Texas have also been the home to others like comics artist Will Terrill and artists Stacy Elko, Jim Johnson, and Paul Milosevich. X-Men villain Fred Dukes/the Blob is from Lubbock.

Ross attended weekend art classes at Texas Tech University, home to the Red Raiders. Other famous people who attended Texas Tech include Governor Preston Smith; musician John Denver; actors Barry Corbin and G. W. Baily; would-be presidential assassin John Hinckley, Jr.; and cartoonist Dirk West.

hardcover of *Earth X*, a poster, and two CDs that included music, spoken word, and video.

He worked again with Jim Kreuger for the series *Justice* (2005), about the Justice League, and *Project Superpowers* (2008). The latter brings back numerous public domain characters from the Golden Age of comics, including Dare Devil (called the Devil), Fighting Yank, the Green Lama, and the Black Terror. Ross created the storyline for *Invaders Now,* with a new version of the Invaders set in the present day, but featuring Golden Age greats Steve Rogers Super Soldier, Captain America (Bucky), the Human Torch, Toro, the Sub-Mariner, and the original Vision.

IMPACT ON COMICS

Alex Ross is highly regarded by the general public, fans, and those within the industry. Writers like working with Ross and consider it an honor to have a cover drawn by him. He received numerous Eisner awards during the years 1994, 1996–2000, 2004, and 2010. The Eisner is the comic industry's equivalent of a Grammy or Oscar. Some of the award-winning titles include *Marvels, Uncle Sam, Kingdom Come, Superman: Peace on Earth,* and *Batman: War on Crime.* A few of the categories Ross won are for best painter, best limited series, and best publication design. In addition, he won best cover artist in 1996–1998 and 2000 (*Comic Book Awards Almanac* 2007). In 1998 Ross also won the "Comic Book Award" from the National Cartoonists Society. He has won the prestigious Harvey Award, known for recognizing some of the best work in the comics industry.

His work on graphic novels like *Marvels* and *Kingdom Come* brought many new readers to comics as well as astonishing those who had read comics for years. Ross's work on these and other graphic novels garnered him fan nominations and awards. His work earned him seven award nominations (1994–2000) for the *Comics Buyer's Guide* Fan Awards for Favorite Painter and 17 nominations for Favorite Cover Artist (1995–2011). He has also occasionally been nominated for *Wizard* Readers Award for Favorite Action Figure Line and has often won in the Favorite Painter category. From this it is obvious that comics fans love Alex Ross.

Before Alex Ross broke into the comics industry, comics characters were not drawn with much realism. Even today many artists prefer traditional drawing methods or use computer programs to hone their art. Like Arthur Suydam, Jon Muth, Bill Sienkiewicz, and Simon Bisley, Ross uses paint to create comics characters. He often employs friends and family as models for characters like Captain Marvel, Superman, the Spectre, Uncle Sam, and Galactus. In the supplementary material in graphic novels like *Marvels* and *Kingdom Come*, readers can see photos of Ross's models and sketches. Like **Neal Adams**, Ross works in a style that one might call "realistic comic art." His work has brought praise from those within and outside of the comic industry. For example, in 2002 the publication *Chicago* listed Ross as one of the "eight men and women whose achievements have made Chicago a better place" (2002, 52). The magazine *Illustration* regards his work as significant: "Alex Ross' fantastic painted images have gained him a legion of fans, from comic book lovers to those who never opened a comic but simply admire his incredible paintings of the world's greatest superheroes" (Gagliardo 2009, 106).

George Khoury, writing in the *Jack Kirby Collector*, stated: "Who can forget the first time they saw an illustration by Alex Ross? He is quite possibly the most popular artist to arrive on the comics scene since the Neal Adams experience of the late Sixties. He blew us away with his romanticized vision of the Marvel Universe in *Marvels*. *Kingdom Come* caused shockwaves throughout the industry and fandom for its sheer power and epic storytelling" (Khoury 1999). Ross's painted style has been an inspiration for other comic artists and companies to follow. For example, Brad Parker's painted art, featured prominently in *Green Lantern: Fear Itself* (1999), is similar in tone and style despite both having unique characteristics.

IMPACT ON AMERICAN CULTURE

Alex Ross is an intensely private person. He does grant occasional interviews and sometimes attends comics conventions. While he appreciates his fans, the artist prefers to let his art speak for itself. It is obvious from his prolific output that Ross works tirelessly. He puts a great deal of care into his paintings regardless of the subject, which is why he only intermittently does full graphic novels or comic book issues. Ideas for plots, stories, and artistic renderings flow from his mind.

Alex Ross's artistic endeavors go beyond the comics world into movies, television, music, and toys. This is unusual for an artist working in the comics industry. On the *Flash Gordon* (1979) special edition DVD, he was interviewed about the history and influence of the character. He also did the cover artwork. For the December 2001 issue of *TV Guide*, Ross created four interconnected covers featuring individual cast members from the television show *Smallville* and one for Superman. When the first *Spider-Man* movie came out in 2002, *TV Guide* (April/May) published four issues featuring the webslinger on the cover. One featured Ross's work. The artist's reputation for excellence continued to get him work as he was asked to design the promotional poster for the 74th Academy Awards in 2002 with the tagline "The Gold Knight Returns" (a tribute to **Frank Miller**'s *Batman: The Dark Knight Returns*). There were rumors that Hollywood was trying to tempt Ross away from doing traditional comics work. His work was also featured in M. Night Shyamalan's film *Unbreakable* (2000). More people worldwide have seen Ross's art than probably any other comic book artist. In 2004, his paintings were featured in the opening credits of *Spider-Man 2*, giving Ross universal exposure.

The heavy metal band Anthrax are huge comic book fans, and Ross did artwork for several of their albums including 2004's *Music of Mass Destruction*. He designed the cover for the crossover video game *Mortal Kombat vs. DC Universe Kollector's Edition*. In 2011 it was announced that Ross would be painting the covers for the HBO series comic book tie-in of George R. R. Martin's *Game of Thrones*. Another unique way Ross's work has permeated popular culture is through toys, head busts, statues, and action figures based upon his artistic designs. These include *Batman: Black & White*, *Kingdom Come*, *Justice*, the **Thing**, Justice League, Captain America, and Flash Gordon, among many others. He has the distinction of being one of the few comics artists to have multiple lines of action figures based solely upon his work.

The artist has written the occasional book foreword including *Rocketo Journey to the Hidden Sea* (2006) by Frank Espinosa and *Kimota! The Miracleman Companion* (2001) by George Khoury. Ross calls **Alan Moore**'s *Miracleman* "the best comic I ever read backwards" (Ross 2001, 5). In addition, Alex Ross is the focus of several special volumes devoted to his work and artistic achievements. Wizard Entertainment published the *Alex Ross Millennium Edition* in 1999 and revised versions in 2003 and 2009. Dynamite Entertainment produced *The Dynamite Art of Alex Ross* in 2011, highlighting his cover work on characters like the Green Hornet, Red Sonja, and the series *Project Superpowers*. In the fall of 2011, the Andy Warhol Museum in Pittsburgh opened the exhibit *Heroes and Villains: The Comic Book Art of Alex Ross* comprising "5,500 square feet of gallery space" (Kowalski 2011). While comic art has been featured in conventional art galleries before, it is rare when a specific artist's work is featured exclusively.

Ross's effort, optimism, and hard work show that success is an attainable goal. "Ross's career offers [an] important message: follow your dream" (Ross Biography, 2011). His work teaches us that one can be successful through perseverance and a genuine belief in one's self and one's abilities, even if you come from a modest background.

SUMMARY

Very little about Ross's career is not iconic. His roots come from the American heartland firmly planted within the Judeo-Christian background. Ross is one of the finest examples of someone who pursued the American dream through hard labor. He has been called the "Cecil B. DeMille of comics" (Khoury 2001, 2). Like DeMille's films, Ross's work is epic in scope and style with a "cast of thousands" of heroes coming together for the common good. Ross himself took the altruistic lessons he learned from his father and the heroes he loves by donating his work for auctions, with proceeds going to the Twin Towers Fund, UNICEF, and the Make a Wish Foundation. In addition, he painted covers for both Marvel and DC's benefit comics for those who suffered because of 9/11. "When I began donating the art to charity, it was because I felt a public gesture like that would allow people to see how these heroes can be inspirational," Ross explains. "I've always wanted people to understand that these heroes offer lessons that can benefit all of us" (Alex Ross Articles 2011). This shows the artist's patriotic and civic duty by wanting to give something back to a world and culture that has blessed him.

See also DC Comics; Marvel Comics

ESSENTIAL WORKS

Ross, Alex (p), and Kurt Busiek (w). *Marvels*. New York: Marvel, 2010.
Ross, Alex (p), and Paul Dini (w). *World's Greatest Superheroes*. New York: DC Comics, 2010.
Ross, Alex (p), Mark Waid (w), and Todd Klein. *Kingdom Come*. New York: DC Comics, 2008.

FURTHER READING

Lewis, David A. "New Jerusalem Postponed: Revelation and Darnall & Ross's *Uncle Sam.*" *International Journal of Comic Art* 12, no. 1 (Spring 2010): 337–54.

Ross, Alex, and Chip Kidd. *Mythology: The DC Comics Art of Alex Ross.* New York: Pantheon, 2005.

Ross, Alex, and Wizard Entertainment. *Alex Ross: Millennium Edition: Wizard Alex Ross Special Edition.* Congers, NY: Wizard Entertainment, 2003. Official Site, http://www.alexrossart.com/.

Robert G. Weiner

Sacco, Joe

Joe Sacco (1960–) is a comics journalist whose best-known works include long-form comics about conflict in the Middle East and the war in Bosnia. Among his books are **Palestine**, first published as a nine-issue miniseries between 1993 and 1995; *Safe Area Goražde* (2000); and *Footnotes in Gaza* (2009). Sacco both writes and draws his own work, which is published in black and white. His work has won acclaim from both the comics and journalism communities, and he is considered by many to be the world's leading comics journalist.

HISTORY

Joe Sacco was born in Kirkop, Malta, on October 2, 1960, the son of Leonard and Carmen Sacco. He has an older sister, Maryanne. The family moved to Australia when Sacco was one year old and relocated to California when Joe was 12. They lived in Los Angeles before moving to Beaverton, Oregon, a Portland suburb, in 1974. There Joe attended Sunset High School, graduating in 1978. At the University of Oregon, he earned a degree in journalism, finishing in three years.

Sacco began his journalism career writing for a trade publication of the National Notary Association. Bored by the work, he stayed a little over a year before trying a number of other jobs, none of which suited him any better. He moved to Malta in 1984, where he broke into comics by writing romance comics. He returned to the United States in 1985, settling in Portland, where he co-founded an alternative magazine, the *Portland Permanent Press*, with Tom Richards. It folded in 1986.

The *Comics Journal* offered Sacco a job, and he relocated to be near their offices in California. He returned to Portland but continued to work for **Fantagraphics**, editing a comic for the publisher he retitled *Centrifugal Bumble-Puppy*. The editorial work did not pay well, so Sacco also took a part-time job at the public library.

When Fantagraphics pulled the plug on *Bumble-Puppy*, Sacco launched his own comic, *Yahoo*, which Fantagraphics agreed to publish. Six issues

(AP Photo/Khalil Hamra)

appeared between 1988 and 1992. The second issue of *Yahoo* documented the six-week European tour in 1988 of the band Miracle Workers, where Sacco experimented with the first-person, documentary style that he would hone in later works. After the tour ended, Sacco stayed in Berlin for five months, picking up illustration work drawing posters and album covers. He returned to the United States briefly, then moved back to Berlin.

While there, he completed a story titled "When Good Bombs Happen to Bad People," a nonfiction historical comic. The story covered the British bombing of Germany, 1940–1945; the U.S. Bombing of Japan, 1944–1945; and the U.S. bombing of Libya in 1986. Searching for his next project, he decided to visit the Palestinian territories, staying for two months in the winter of 1991–1992. Sacco compiled the material that became the nine-issue miniseries *Palestine*, published between 1993 and 1995.

Twenty years after earning his degree, Sacco began to receive the recognition for his reporting that had been his goal as a newly minted journalism school graduate. *Palestine* had received some early critical recognition, earning an American Book Award in 1996. It was not until the series was collected and republished in 2001, however, that *Palestine* attracted widespread attention. By that time, his second major piece of long-form comics journalism, *Safe Area Goražde*, had been published.

Sacco started on *Goražde* in fall 1995, after finishing the final issue of *Palestine*. More prepared for the task at hand, Sacco secured a letter from a publisher, which entitled him to press credentials and a trip into Bosnia with a U.N. convoy. He spent six weeks in Sarajevo before traveling on to Goražde, a designated "safe area" for Muslims in the midst of hostile Bosnian Serb territory.

Sacco made three trips to Bosnia in the mid-1990s to report on the situation there for *Safe Area Goražde*, published in 2000. Unlike *Palestine*, *Goražde* was intended to be published as a single work. Readers can trace Sacco's progress on the comic because of Sacco's practice of dating his pages. He began drawing the prologue in June 1996, and the last page is dated March 2000. He won a Guggenheim Fellowship in fine arts in April 2001, which provided him with funding to continue his work in comics journalism. He published two more books based on his material from Bosnia, *The Fixer* (2003) and *War's End* (2005).

In addition, Sacco continued to publish shorter work in magazines, including illustrations for a piece in *Harper's* magazine written by Chris Hedges. A trip in spring 2001 was the impetus for Sacco's next long-form comics journalism project, *Footnotes in Gaza*. As part of their report, Hedges and Sacco included some historical context about a massacre of civilians in Khan Younis in 1956. The material was cut from the published article. Sacco wrote, "To me, the story of the Khan Younis killings was not so easily dispensable" (*Footnotes* 2009, ix). He decided to return to Gaza to research the events of 1956, making two trips between November 2002 and March 2003. *Footnotes in Gaza* was published in 2009. Unlike his earlier work, *Footnotes* combined historical research with reportage. He interviewed Palestinians who lived through the 1956 massacres in Kahn Younis and Rafah. Using this oral history, coupled with scant documentary evidence, he tried to piece together what happened. In addition, he chronicled his efforts to gather this information, juxtaposing current events with those of 1956.

Events depicted in *Footnotes* were more relentlessly brutal than his earlier work, and crafting the 418-page book took its toll on Sacco. He commented: "But I think I need to go in another direction after this book. What am I going to do after this? Keep detailing massacres? For me, personally, I think I'm not going to get anything out of it anymore. I've come to the end of that" (Chute 2011).

Sacco's *Footnotes* won an Eisner Award in the Best Writer/Artist-Nonfiction category in 2010. The book also won the $10,000 Ridenhour Book Prize in 2010, given in honor of Ron Ridenhour, a Vietnam veteran who helped expose the My Lai massacre. The award is presented by the Nation Institute and the Fertel Foundation.

Sacco turned his attention to other types of stories, returning to his birthplace to document Malta's efforts to deal with Africans who set off from Libya's coast in an effort to reach Europe, but ended up on Malta. The two-part story, titled "The Unwanted," was published in the *Virginia Quarterly*

Review in Winter 2010 and Spring 2010. Closer to home, he teamed up again with Hedges for "City of Ruins," illustrating the article, which was published in *The Nation* on November 22, 2010. His scenes of Camden, New Jersey, are hauntingly similar to those of Palestinian refugee camps. Sacco has made reference to a larger book project on postindustrial America with Hedges. The French magazine *XXI* commissioned and published a Sacco story on farmers in India who belong to the Dalit, the "untouchable" caste. Sacco reissued his shorter work in the collection titled *Journalism*, published in 2012.

IMPACT ON COMICS

Joe Sacco took the genre of comics journalism and made it his own. No one else working in this nonfiction genre has come close to achieving the success Sacco enjoys. The skills required for a comics journalist—the ability to tell a story through the complex combination of text and image in the comics form, plus the training in journalism—mean that few have followed in his footsteps so far. Among those who have been compared to Sacco are Ted Rall, Peter Bagge, and Josh Neufeld.

What distinguishes Sacco's work from that of other creators of nonfiction comics is not his subject matter nor his first-person narrative, but his decision to tell his stories journalistically. Sacco did not start out to be a comics journalist. *Palestine* was intended to be an autobiographical account, but it turned into "something more journalistic" (Gilson 2005, 80). Reviewers and scholars link Sacco's work to that of literary journalists. In many ways, Sacco's artwork accomplishes more easily the description and attention to what "New Journalist" Tom Wolfe termed the "status details" of people and their surroundings. Sacco, too, uses dialogue rather than quotations and constructs scenes. Sacco cites George Orwell, Michael Herr's *Dispatches*, and the early work of Hunter S. Thompson as influences.

Sacco's challenge goes beyond that of prose journalists, however. Once Sacco decided on a journalistic approach to storytelling, he had to meld the conventions of comics with the conventions of reportage. He developed and refined the "language" of journalism for the comics medium in a number of ways. Captions and word balloons substitute for quotations and attribution. Information is presented in a variety of forms, from text-heavy exposition to images with no text at all. He uses a number of techniques to signal when he relied on a source's account of an event he had not witnessed himself, such as embedding the panels on black pages. The motif of Sacco with pencil and notebook in hand emphasizes his journalistic purpose. Even the "blank" glasses came to signify Sacco as a stand-in for the reader.

Much of Sacco's work is also considered investigative reporting. The labor-intensive process of producing long-form comics journalism makes it ill-suited

JOE SACCO

Joe Sacco's artwork is easily recognizable, but readers of his graphic novels would be hard pressed to recognize Sacco from his self-portrait. In the tradition of Superman's alter ego, mild-mannered reporter Clark Kent, the Sacco-drawn Sacco is a slightly built man, usually shorter than those around him. He always looks as if he is trying not to take up too much space in the panel. His buck teeth protrude slightly from his thick lips, and his nose is topped by even thicker glasses.

What is most striking about the image of Sacco, however, is his eyes—they are invisible behind the lenses. Perhaps this signifies Sacco's journalistic objectivity. Sacco can see out, but his own reactions to what he sees remain a mystery to readers. Maybe Sacco wants readers to identify with him, to literally put themselves in his place and imagine it is their eyes seeing the scenes that Sacco so carefully crafts. Or it could be that he finds it too difficult to draw his own eyes behind those thick glasses.

for reporting on current events. It took Sacco four years to complete *Footnotes in Gaza*. This explains Sacco's concentration on issues such as conflict in the Middle East, the wars in Bosnia and Iraq, and illegal immigration and poverty in the United States.

Choosing such topics also permits Sacco some leeway in blending genres, which links him to other creators of nonfiction comics. The best-known example is **Art Spiegelman**'s *Maus*, which has been analyzed as biography, autobiography, memoir, history, and Holocaust narrative. Sacco is, by turns, a journalist, an autobiographer, and a historian. This is most evident in *Footnotes in Gaza*, in which Sacco's history project is woven into first-person reportage of life in the Gaza strip.

Sacco's proximity to the underground and alternative comics scene in Portland, Oregon, no doubt helped shape his work. He has said in a number of interviews that his main influences include **Robert Crumb** and Harvey Pekar. Underground comics pushed the boundaries of the comics form at a time when mainstream comics languished under the restrictions of the comic book industry's self-regulatory code. While underground artists are best known for their transgressive treatment of topics such as sex and drugs, this movement in the 1970s also inspired a new generation of creators—helped by changes in comic book distribution and retail sales.

If the comics form can encompass memoir, travelogue, essay, political commentary and satire, biography, autobiography, and history—why not journalism?

IMPACT ON AMERICAN CULTURE

Joe Sacco has successfully crossed over into "mainstream" nonfiction publishing. *Footnotes in Gaza* was published by Metropolitan Books, an imprint of Henry Holt. Initially, comics buyers ignored his work; sales of the last of the nine issues of *Palestine* barely hit 2,000. Sacco commented: "I would never have lasted if comics remained in comic-book stores. My work didn't start to do well until I had, you know, a book out that was in a bookstore" (Adams 2011).

Bookstores carried *Safe Area Goražde*, and mainstream critical attention bolstered sales. Sacco points to the review in the *New York Times Book Review* as the turning point: "Certainly after that, everyone started being interested in it" (Adams 2011). Now, of course, not only is his work reviewed in the *New York Times*, it is also published there. Sacco's story "Portrait of the Cartoonist as a Dog Owner" appeared in the *New York Times Sunday Book Review* on August 13, 2010.

Sacco's elevated status is recognized in two areas: he wins praise for his abilities as a comic book artist and, perhaps more telling, he is honored for his achievements in journalism. For example, the website touting the University of Toronto speaker series for spring 2011 notes that guest speaker Sacco "is one of the world's premier comic book artists and is widely recognized as a central figure in bringing graphic novels and sequential art into the cultural mainstream." Sacco's page on the Arthur C. Carter Journalism Institute at New York University's online archive "Primary Resources" observes in its description of *Footnotes in Gaza*: "Having already established his reputation as the world's leading comics journalist, Sacco (*Safe Area Goražde*) is now making a serious case to be considered one of the world's top journalists, period."

Not only has Sacco won acceptance of *his* comics journalism, he has broken ground for mainstream culture to recognize the potential of comics journalism in general. For example, independent comics journalist Dan Archer was among those awarded a Stanford University Knight Journalism Fellowship in 2011. The prestigious fellowship carries a stipend of $60,000 plus expenses. According to his biography page on the Knight Fellowship website, Archer's project was "to promote comics journalism as a legitimate, innovative way of news storytelling."

Sacco's work also may serve to highlight issues of transparency and credibility in the debate about journalism and its practice. Scholar Richard Todd Stafford observed in his analysis of Sacco's work that Sacco "shows a sophisticated reflexivity towards issues of journalistic credibility" (2011). By using the comics form, Sacco foregrounds the role of the journalist in the creation of the news story. In addition, his depiction of the reporting process and his candid discussion of the limitations of the reporter as both an observer and as an interpreter of others' accounts of events caution readers against blind acceptance of the "facts" of journalism. At the same time, Sacco insists the importance of the journalist's role is to not lose sight of the "essential truth" of the story (Sacco 2010, 116).

SUMMARY

Joe Sacco established comics journalism as a genre of nonfiction comics. His skill as a cartoonist, combined with his training as a journalist, allows him to navigate the difficulties of adhering to the storytelling conventions of both. Sacco's approach to journalism is similar to that of literary and investigative journalists. The first-person approach allows Sacco to deftly blend autobiography, journalism, and, oftentimes, history into compelling stories. His interests in history and politics draw him to global conflict, and he does not shy away from depicting the lives of his subjects in all their brutal detail. Sacco's work reaches an audience beyond the regular comic book reader, winning acceptance for comics as journalism.

See also Fantagraphics; *Palestine*

ESSENTIAL WORKS

Sacco, Joe. *Footnotes in Gaza*. New York: Metropolitan Books, 2009.
Sacco, Joe. *Palestine: The Special Edition*. Seattle: Fantagraphics Books, 2007.
Sacco, Joe. *Safe Area Goražde: The Special Edition*. Seattle: FantagraphicsBbooks, 2011.

FURTHER READING

Marshall, Monica. *Joe Sacco*. New York: Rosen Publishing Group, 2005.
Versace, Rocco. *This Book Contains Graphic Language: Comics as Literature*. New York: Continuum, 2007.

Amy Kiste Nyberg

The Sandman

Neil Gaiman's *The Sandman* tells the story of Dream, also known as Morpheus, third eldest of the Endless—seven siblings who embody fundamental abstractions of human existence. They are, in order of age: Destiny, Death, Dream, Destruction, the twins Desire and Despair, and the youngest, Delirium, formerly known as Delight. Morpheus's tale begins when a group of occultists seeking immortality attempts to capture Death, but ensnares Dream instead.

The first arc of *The Sandman* tells of Dream's escape and return to power, but that escape is only the beginning of the journey he will undertake: over the seven-year run of the series, Dream of the Endless undergoes a process of substantial transformation and humanization. In the course of telling Dream's story, and the stories of those both directly and indirectly touched by it, *The Sandman* helped to transform the landscape of American comic books.

HISTORY

In 1987, **DC Comics** editor Karen Berger gave a practically unknown British author named Neil Gaiman the chance to write a monthly comic. Two years prior, Gaiman, then working as a film critic, had sent **Alan Moore**, who was writing DC's *Swamp Thing*, a note and a copy of a book he had co-written. Moore enjoyed the book, contacted Gaiman in response, and the two went on to become friends. When Gaiman sent Moore a *Swamp Thing* script he had written, Moore mentioned him to Berger, and when Berger attended the 1986 U.K. Comic Art Convention, Gaiman introduced himself and later sent her the script he had sent to Moore. In the interim, Gaiman began his friendship and collaboration with artist Dave McKean, and so it was that the two of them met with Berger and Dick Giordano, then vice-president of DC, in 1987. Berger and Giordano had gone to the United Kingdom looking for talented writers and artists to recruit; they were impressed with Gaiman and McKean and offered them the chance to tackle something from the DC archives.

Gaiman chose to resurrect Black Orchid, and he and McKean got to work immediately. DC liked the resulting miniseries enough to publish it in the more expensive Prestige format. McKean was also assigned to draw **Grant Morrison**'s *Arkham Asylum*, and Gaiman was offered a monthly comic. Eager for a more flexible character to work with, Gaiman suggested the Sandman, one of the oldest characters in the DC stable. *The Sandman* began publication in 1989 and ran for 75 issues until 1996.

The first character bearing that name appeared in the 1930s and subsequently went through various incarnations, including Wesley Dodds and Hector Hall—both of whom would eventually intersect with Gaiman's new Sandman—and Garrett Sanford, the first Sandman said to dwell in the world of dreams. It was this idea that intrigued Gaiman, so he kept that, and changed everything else about the character. Gaiman's Sandman is no crime fighter, but the embodiment of dreaming itself and the keeper of the Dreaming—an ever-changing realm inhabited by various dreams, mythological creatures, mysterious beings, and the occasional dreamer. Morpheus is a combination of rock star bravado, god-like power, and adolescent angst (see *Brief Lives*, for example, where he stands on a balcony, generating the rain that soaks him after a broken heart), but we are told in "Season of Mists" that, of all the Endless, only Destiny is as "conscious of his duties," as "meticulous in their execution" (Gaiman et al. 1992, *Season* 23). Morpheus is also, as attested by Frank McConnell, "the human capacity to imagine meaning, to *tell stories*: an anthropomorphic projection of our thirst for mythology" (McConnell 1996, *Dreams* 4). This would once have been heady stuff for a monthly comic. If it seems to us less so, we have, in part, Gaiman's *Sandman* to thank.

When we meet Dream, he has been summoned and imprisoned by a group of occultists led by Roderick Burgess, in the year 1916. He escapes from Burgess's son 72 years later, exacting a nightmarish revenge before setting off to reclaim his instruments of power. When Dream begins to repair the damage done as a result of his capture, he seems to think only in terms of restoring order to his realm, and to believe that he will be left to carry out his duties just as he did before. Instead, Dream is drawn, slowly but surely, out of his isolation and into responsibility for past actions, and for relationships past and present.

"The great storytellers," as McConnell writes in his foreword to *The Kindly Ones*, "have always wanted to tell us as much about the business of storytelling as about the stories themselves" (McConnell, *Kindly* 1996, 9). This emphasis on the stories we tell both to and about ourselves comes into focus as the reader begins to glimpse important facets of the protagonist's character, and comes to understand through his wounded pride, his vengeful spirit, and his callousness towards those he loves who, not just what, Dream is. We begin to see as early as "24 Hours" that *The Sandman* is a story about stories—how they define us, constrain us or grant us freedom, how we both need and need to be wary of them. But, if the earliest issues feel like a fairly straightforward action/horror comic, the clear turning point is "The Sound of Her Wings" (Gaiman et al. *Preludes*), in which Dream, having regained his freedom and

SOME OF *THE SANDMAN*'S MANY AWARDS

Eisner Awards

- Best Writer—Neil Gaiman (1991–1994)
- Best Continuing Series (1991–1993)
- Best Graphic Album: Reprint—*The Doll's House* (1991)
- Best Single Issue/Single Story—"Season of Mists," *The Sandman* #22–#28 (1992)
- Best Artist/Penciller/Inker or Penciller/Inker Team (1994—P. Craig Russell for "Ramadan," *The Sandman* #50; 1997—Charles Vess for "The Tempest," *The Sandman* #75)
- Best Publication Design—Dave McKean for *Season of Mists* (1993)

Other Awards

- World Fantasy Award for Short Fiction—Neil Gaiman and Charles Vess for "A Midsummer Night's Dream," *The Sandman* #19 (1991)
- British Fantasy Award for Best Anthology/Collection—*The Wake* (1998)
- Best Graphic Album: Reprint and Best Archival Collection/Project—*Absolute Sandman, vol. 1* (2007)

his artifacts of power, falls into a malaise. Death attempts to bring him out of the doldrums and suggests that they spend the day together while she works. "The Sound of Her Wings" was introspective and light on both horror and action, but it gave readers some big clues into Dream's psyche and introduced one of the series' most popular characters. Wearing all black, sporting Egyptian-themed makeup and jewelry (the Eye of Horus, a symbol associated with protection, power, and the afterlife, and the ankh, linked to life and deities of the afterlife), Death was an immediate fan favorite, and eventually had her own spin off. In "The Sound of Her Wings," we see Morpheus's respect for his sister, and the bond between them. We see also that Dream is not quite the same as before he was taken, but has been affected by his time in captivity in ways that he cannot yet understand. Finally, we see two other concerns that will pervade the rest of the series: Dream's sense of duty or responsibility, and his tenuous grasp on the finer points of interpersonal relationships. These are the factors that largely shape all of what followed.

IMPACT ON COMICS

Reception for *The Sandman* was immediately and overwhelmingly positive. Gaiman and *The Sandman* received praise from writers of all stripes—Norman

Mailer, Stephen King, Clive Barker, and Harlan Ellison, to name a few—and by the second year of its run, *The Sandman* had already begun to distinguish itself as something truly noteworthy. The series and its various spinoffs won numerous awards for both writing and visuals, including Gaiman's four Will Eisner Comic Industry Awards (sometimes referred to as the comics industry Oscars) for Best Writer. Perhaps most controversially, "A Midsummer Night's Dream" (*The Sandman* #19) won the 1991 World Fantasy Award for Best Short Fiction. This was the first and last short story in comic book form to win that honor, as comics are now ineligible, allowed only in the Special Award Professional category.

The Sandman also played a pivotal role in altering the way comics are published. In 1990, after much critical praise and press attention (especially a mention in *Rolling Stone*'s 1989 "Hot Issue"), DC put out a collection of *Sandman* stories initially entitled simply *The Sandman*, later *A Doll's House*, to capitalize on the publicity. Sales were good enough to warrant collecting the first arc (as *Preludes and Nocturnes*) and the first set of short stories (as *Dream Country*). These titles all met with such success that DC went on to publish every *Sandman* storyline in collected form, facilitating the rise of the graphic novel format.

Just as significantly, *The Sandman* was a part of the comics industry's British Invasion. In the late 1980s and early 1990s, Gaiman and other U.K. artists—e.g., Jamie Delano, Peter Milligan, and Grant Morrison, all following in the footsteps of earlier artists like Alan Moore, Dave Gibbons, and Brian Bolland—shook up the comics industry by creating darker, more complex stories, and drawing the focus away from superhero-themed titles. When DC created the Vertigo imprint in 1993, it was with these more mature titles in mind. *The Sandman* was Vertigo's flagship title, drawing a readership ranging from die-hard comics fans to those who read only *The Sandman*. It also garnered a large following of female readers, and readers older than DC's usual demographic. The quality of its storytelling and artwork, and the expanded audience it brought in, surely helped to make *The Sandman* the bestselling title on the Vertigo roster.

Gaiman has said that, early in its run, *The Sandman* was outselling any horror comic since the 1970s. This may have been due, in part, to issues like the horrifying "24 Hours" (in Gaiman et al., *Preludes*), in which a madman wreaks havoc on a diner full of innocent (and not-so-innocent) people. By that time, Gaiman had certainly made good on the promise of the earliest ads, which played up the title as a horror comic, promising to "show you terror in a handful of dust" (Bender 1999, 18). Yet Gaiman said from the start that *The Sandman* would not always be a horror comic, but would "be as varied and unpredictable as dreams themselves, . . . [following] the human subconscious wherever it may go, even into the darker realm of internal mythologies" (Gilmore 1997, 10). This depth is, arguably, the reason that *The Sandman*

SPINOFFS AND CONTINUATIONS (A VERY PARTIAL LIST)

- *Death: The High Cost of Living* (1993) and *Death: The Time of Your Life* (1996): two 3-issue limited series written by Neil Gaiman, featuring Dream's charismatic elder sister.
- *The Little Endless Storybook* (2001): Jill Thompson's depiction of the Endless as toddlers.
- *Lucifer* (2001–2006): A monthly series written by Mike Carey, continuing the story of *The Sandman*'s Lucifer.
- *The Sandman: Book of Dreams* (1996): co-edited with Ed Kramer. An anthology of original short stories, each somehow featuring the world of *The Sandman*.
- *The Sandman: The Dream Hunters* (1999): Neil Gaiman's illustrated novella, in which he creates a new myth, inspired by elements of Japanese folklore.
- *The Sandman: Endless Nights* (2003): A graphic novel of collected short stories, one for each of the Endless. Written by Neil Gaiman.
- *The Sandman Presents* (1999–2004): A collection of limited series by various authors and illustrators featuring secondary characters from *The Sandman*.

has had such an enduring effect. It has been over 15 years since the end of *The Sandman*, but far from having faded into comics history, it continues to be one of Vertigo's most lucrative properties, so much so that they chose to publish it in both trade editions and deluxe Absolute editions—oversized, archival-quality books with bonus features and retouched or recolored art. In March 2011, Vertigo announced volume 5 of the *Absolute Sandman* series, which will collect Gaiman's later entries into *Sandman* lore: *Endless Nights*, *The Dream Hunters*, and *Sandman Midnight Theater*. Through the ongoing popularity of these collected volumes, *The Sandman* continues to be a presence in the American comic book scene. To quote Terry Pratchett, Gaiman's *Sandman* "left the comics world shaken, and it'll never be quite the same" (Pratchett 2008, xii).

IMPACT ON AMERICAN CULTURE

At the height of *The Sandman*'s popularity, there was also a fair amount of other Sandman-related merchandise: statues, T-shirts, tarot cards, posters. Some of this merchandise made its way into the culture in more ways than one—one of Mike Dringenberg's posters of The Endless was regularly seen on *Roseanne* (ABC, 1988–1997), where it hung on the bedroom door of Sara Gilbert's character, Darlene. Gaiman himself has appeared on television, albeit in animated form, on the children's program *Arthur*; and in January of 2011, he recorded an episode of *The Simpsons*. For over a decade, there were attempts at a *Sandman* movie, but as of 2007, that seems to have been shelved indefinitely. In November of 2010, it was reported that Warner Brothers TV, a sister company to DC Entertainment, was acquiring the rights in the hopes of creating a television show.

But the greatest measure of *The Sandman*'s impact on American culture may be the sheer volume of writing it has inspired. Gaiman co-edited a volume of *Sandman*-inspired short stories *(The Sandman: Book of Dreams)*, and spinoffs written by other authors have focused on minor characters (e.g. *Petrefax and Merv Pumpkinhead*) as well as more important secondary characters (*Lucifer*). Perhaps this should not be surprising of a character also known as "The Prince of Stories." In addition to the Endless-related fiction that has proliferated in its wake, *The Sandman* has also been embraced by academics. One collected volume of academic papers includes discussions of everything from Gaiman's literary influences to female power to Borges, while other texts offer in-depth analyses of the series, some accompanied by Gaiman's own words, in the form of lengthy interviews with him.

SUMMARY

It is no surprise that *The Sandman* has so thoroughly engaged readers over the years. Gaiman wanted to lead his readers to expect a different, more ambitious type of story than many were accustomed to from more traditional American comics. He accomplished this by bringing together influences as diverse as the DC catalog, New Wave science fiction, and the Wizard of Oz. He wove familiar stories from religion and mythology (figures from Judeo-Christian, Hindu, and Norse stories appear in varying capacities) together with poetry and music (T. S. Eliot, Lou Reed, and Tori Amos, to name a few), and everyday life. Careful readers of the early confrontation between Morpheus and his captors might, for example, have noticed that Morpheus quotes Shakespeare's *A Midsummer Night's Dream*. Later, Shakespeare himself becomes a character, and his relationship with his son serves as a parallel for Dream's own family dynamics, just as his plays shed light on both the plot of the series and the nature of the creative process.

While the reader begins to understand Morpheus's character early on, his self-knowledge comes a bit more slowly, and with dire consequences. Over the course of 76 issues, the Prince of Stories begins to tell a new story about himself, one that is equal parts redemption and tragedy. After Morpheus has taken his sister's hand, clearing the way for a new Dream, the librarian of the Dreaming (Julian) says that Morpheus died because there was only so much he could allow himself to change (Gaiman et al., *The Wake 1997*, 59). This may be true, but much of the power of *The Sandman* lies in the extent to which Dream does change. We watch as he learns to see others as more than obstacles or duties, comes to take his interpersonal relationships as seriously as he takes his duties as the Lord of Dreams, and becomes capable of showing mercy, grief, and love. We watch as he is destroyed, not because he remains static, but precisely because the changes he makes make him vulnerable. Heady stuff, indeed, for a monthly comic, but it is this substance—this resonance—that makes *The Sandman* iconic.

See also Gaiman, Neil

ESSENTIAL WORKS

Gaiman, Neil (w), and P. Craig Russell (p, i). "Ramadan." *The Sandman #50*. Reprinted in *Fables and Reflections*. New York: DC Comics, 1994.

Gaiman, Neil (w), William Shakespeare (w), and Charles Vess (p, i). "A Midsummer Night's Dream." Reprinted in *The Sandman #19* in *Dream Country* (1991). New York: DC Comics.

Gaiman, Neil (w), Brian Talbot (p), and Mark Buckingham (i). "Orpheus." *The Sandman Special*. Reprinted in *Fables and Reflections*. New York: DC Comics, 1994.

FURTHER READING

Bender, Hy. *The Sandman Companion*. New York: Vertigo/DC Comics, 1999.

Sanders, Joe, ed. *The Sandman Papers*. Seattle: Fantagraphics Books, 2006.

Wagner, Hank, Christopher Golden, and Stephen R. Bissette. *Prince of Stories: The Many Worlds of Neil Gaiman*. New York: St. Martin's Press, 2008.

Candace E. West

Scott Pilgrim

Scott Pilgrim is the epitome of the "Generation Y" slacker turned good. He leads an action-packed yet also somewhat mundane existence, filtering his life and his romantic experiences through the lens of 1980s and 1990s video games, Japanese manga, superhero comics, and indie rock. Over the course of a series of six books by Bryan Lee O'Malley, the Toronto-dwelling 20-something proves his worth as a boyfriend and as a human being by exuberantly fighting off seven "evil exes" to win the love of his new girlfriend, Ramona Flowers, while also coming to terms with his own emotional baggage and becoming a more mature and self-confident person as a result.

HISTORY

In 1998, a Canadian Indie rock band called Plumtree released a single called "Scott Pilgrim." An upbeat but also bittersweet love song built around the lyric "I'll fight you for a thousand years," it was this song that ultimately inspired cartoonist and musician—and Plumtree fan—Bryan Lee O'Malley to create a series of six graphic novels based around a character who must literally do battle with his girlfriend's seven exes to win her love.

Having already published the understated coming-of-age tale *Lost at Sea* with American independent comic book publisher Oni Press in 2003, O'Malley followed it a year later with the first Scott Pilgrim book, *Scott Pilgrim's Precious Little Life*. The book introduced Scott as a 23-year-old Canadian slacker who plays bass guitar for ramshackle Indie rock band Sex Bob-omb in Toronto, who lives with a sometimes irritating yet always loyal gay friend and roommate Wallace Wells, and who has recently begun an eyebrow-raising relationship with a young Chinese Canadian high school student, Knives Chau.

Soon, however, Scott's life changes when he encounters an enigmatic Amazon.ca delivery girl called Ramona Flowers. Falling for her instantly, he manages to convince her to go on a couple of dates despite still being romantically involved with Knives. As his love life grows more complicated and complex,

CLASSIC VIDEO GAME REFERENCES IN SCOTT PILGRIM

- Scott's band Sex Bob-omb is named after the enemy Bob-omb from Nintendo's *Mario Bros.* franchise, while rival bands Crash and the Boys and the Clash at Demonhead are named after other games available for the company's NES console. Other bands, such as Kid Chameleon and Sonic & Knuckles, are named after games available for Sega's Genesis console.
- The fights between Scott and Ramona's evil exes imitate numerous elements of Capcom's hugely popular 1990s beat-em-up *Street Fighter II.*
- Scott's climactic battle with Gideon Graves in the final *Scott Pilgrim* volume includes several homages to Square Soft's role-playing game *Final Fantasy VII.*
- The color sequence that opens the fourth *Scott Pilgrim* volume culminates in an imitation of the title screen of Sega's *Sonic the Hedgehog 2.*
- In the fourth *Scott Pilgrim* volume, Scott dreams he lives in the world of Nintendo's *Legend of Zelda.*
- The title page for the fifth *Scott Pilgrim* volume imitates the logo of Taito's *Double Dragon* series.
- Gideon Graves's logo is an inverted version of the Triforce logo from Nintendo's *Zelda* franchise.
- Conventions such as enemies turning into coins, a character's head representing an "extra life," gaining experience points for achieving certain milestones, and the use of measurement bars to represent quantities such as cash, thirst, or pee are also drawn from the generic conventions of 1980s and 1990s video games.

Ramona places more obstacles in Scott's path by revealing to him that he must defeat seven of her ex-lovers in physical combat if he wants to prove himself a serious romantic contender.

It's from here that the book departs from the relative realism of the earlier sections of *Scott Pilgrim's Precious Little Life*, throwing Scott into a video game–style battle with Matthew Patel. The first of Ramona's "evil exes," Patel deploys legions of fireball-throwing vampire angels in his fight with Scott, before being ultimately beaten by a "dragon punch" move that Scott learned from video game *Street Fighter II.* Defeated, Patel obligingly turns into a pile of loose change, in the manner of so many video game enemies, leaving Scott to wonder what future battles with the evil exes will bring.

Despite these kinds of fantastical touches, which O'Malley gradually ramps up as the series of books progresses—with the sixth book containing some truly psychedelic sequences—the writer-artist also manages to keep certain elements of Scott's life grounded in a sense of realism. Over the course of the six volumes, O'Malley develops Scott and his supporting cast to the point that readers become as invested in seeing how certain relationships play out as they are in whether Scott can defeat each of the evil exes in turn.

O'Malley adds depth to Scott by gradually revealing his history with his own ex-girlfriend, Envy Adams, as well as hinting at other past relationships in sometimes oblique ways. Scott's romance with Ramona also takes some unexpected twists and turns, including a surprise break-up at a crucial juncture that challenges readers' expectations of the series' formula up to that point.

Secondary characters also receive a significant amount of attention from O'Malley, with the gradually revealed subtleties of Scott's relationship with bandmate Kim Pine adding layers to his personality, with Wallace Wells undergoing his own journey between the lines of the series, and with Sex Bob-omb's lead singer Stephen Stills revealing surprising elements concerning his own romantic relationships towards the end of the series.

But it's the mixture of the mundane and the fantastical that makes Scott so resonant with a generation that has grown up steeped in the fantasies of video games, rock superstardom, popular science-fiction movies, and escapist comics. Character-based soap opera rubs shoulders with bizarre excursions into subspace superhighways and epic video game–inspired fights, culminating in a climax in which Scott's relationship with Ramona, his fighting prowess, and his belief in his own self-worth are all tested in a clash with the evil ex that holds most power over Ramona, Gideon Graves.

IMPACT ON COMICS

Scott Pilgrim is arguably the first character to truly reflect the interests and cultural experiences of a generation of comics readers who grew up in the late 1980s and 1990s. Countless references to American popular culture—as well as the increasingly globalized popular culture of other nations—are sprinkled throughout the series of *Scott Pilgrim* graphic novels, but they are far more than mere set dressing. Instead, they form an integral part of Scott's worldview, meaning that readers that grew up with the same cultural touchstones would immediately feel kinship with the slacker-turned-hero.

While the *Scott Pilgrim* series captured a significant comics-reading audience that was more used to American superheroes, it also crossed over to a larger, more mainstream audience. This was partially due to the book's format. Like *Lost at Sea*, the book was published in a small, squarebound, black-and-white format that imitated the style of popular Japanese manga comics—including *shonen manga* such as *Dragonball Z*, which also included extreme fight scenes reminiscent of popular beat-em-up video games.

The angular, high-energy visual style of Japanese manga books was also adopted by O'Malley in drawing the series. Although the relatively crude style of his illustrations in the first volume was developed and improved upon by the time the final volumes were published, the books still resolutely stuck to simple, easily-recognizable character models and heavy linework that enabled it to stand out from the seemingly more finessed work that was becoming increasingly popular in contemporary American superhero comics.

The series made innovative use of comics devices such as narrative captions and flashbacks, presenting them in a stylized yet accessible manner. Bold, declarative captions were used to impart important information about characters—sometimes humorously and sometimes simply to convey a character's back story or personality without resorting to heavy amounts of expository dialogue. And flashbacks were often presented in a cruder, childlike art style, both to differentiate them from the modern-day action and to convey a sense that the past incarnations of Scott were less mature than the older version that readers were used to in the present day.

Along with these innovations, the series also incorporated storytelling conventions from outside comics, most notably from video games. An apparently arbitrary but nonetheless enjoyable "points" system was employed throughout, with characters receiving experience points for certain achievements. And a more comedic use of video game devices was sometimes used for one-off gags, such as the "pee bar"—modeled on an energy bar from beat-em-up games—that indicated to readers that Scott was desperate to relieve himself.

Video games cast their influence not just on these individual details, but also the structure of the books. Each book can be seen as acting as a "level" of a video game, with each of Ramona's evil exes functioning as an "end of level boss."

Music also played an important role, especially given that many of the series' subplots revolved around Sex Bob-omb's quest for musical success. O'Malley used his pacing and panel layouts to convey a sense of musical rhythm, and used different styles of text to suggest the sound of the music being played by the various bands featured in the series. Given the notorious difficulty of conveying music in comics, it is a credit to O'Malley's skill that he managed to describe the punk-edged indie-rock sounds of Sex Bob-omb so effectively to his readers.

Innovative and experimental conventions such as those employed in *Scott Pilgrim* soon found their way into more mainstream comics whether by direct influence or parallel inspiration such as Matt Fraction's *Uncanny X-Men* and Paul Cornell's *Wisdom* series for Marvel.

Given the way in which the *Scott Pilgrim* series captured the generation-Y zeitgeist, it is perhaps unsurprising that the series was successful, especially with readers of a similar age to O'Malley. However, considering the relative

newness of the character, it is nonetheless impressive that the comics community has so emphatically taken him to heart.

The United Kingdom's *Empire* magazine rated Scott Pilgrim 40th in a list of
the greatest comic book characters, while Scott was ranked as the 85th greatest comic book character of all time by *Wizard Magazine* and the 69th greatest comic book hero of all time by IGN. All are considerable achievements for
a character that only made his debut in 2004, and are testament to his impact
on the world of comics.

IMPACT ON AMERICAN CULTURE

As a relative newcomer to the world of comics, it is perhaps not surprising
that the *Scott Pilgrim* series reflects American culture as much as it is a contributor to it.

Scott's worldview is constantly filtered through a prism of various cultural
influences, making it sometimes difficult to decide whether the books accurately
reflect the reality of the character's world or whether the fantastical elements
of the series are meant to indicate that Scott's outlook has been so colored by
movies and video games that he cannot tell the difference between what is real
and what is not. Does the emotional baggage of Ramona's exes *really* manifest
itself as supervillains that Scott has to fight to the death, or is that merely the
only way that the media-saturated Scott can rationalize his feelings?

Along with specific elements of pop culture, the *Scott Pilgrim* series also
reflects wider American culture, notably when it comes to multiculturalism.
O'Malley is careful to include a diverse mix of different races and religions
among his cast, without ever feeling the need to highlight these elements as
particularly significant to the plot. There are also elements that will be of
more parochial interest to Toronto inhabitants, with local Toronto landmarks
and shops faithfully re-created in Scott's world.

Also notable in terms of Scott's wider cultural impact is the fact that
O'Malley's series was adapted into a movie in 2010. *Scott Pilgrim vs. The
World*, starring Michael Cera and Mary Elizabeth Winstead, condenses the
story of all six graphic novels into a single film, directed by British director
Edgar Wright. Wright was the perfect choice to helm the *Scott Pilgrim* movie,
given his experiences of directing British sitcom *SPACED*. Like Scott Pilgrim,
the characters of *SPACED* viewed the world through a filter that aggregated
various elements of pop culture including comics, movies, and music to the
point at which the events of their real lives were virtually indistinguishable
from the fantasies that colored their perceptions. Being steeped in so many elements of geek culture—as well as having helmed music videos—gave Wright
the innate grasp of pop culture and music that adapting Scott Pilgrim's adventures to film required, with the director's stylish editing techniques making

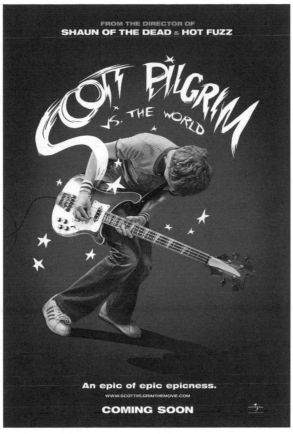

(Photofest)

him adept at transposing narrative conventions such as O'Malley's idiosyncratic captions and flashbacks smoothly onto film.

However, arguably the most faithful adaptation of O'Malley's graphic novels came with the *Scott Pilgrim vs. The World* video game, available on the Playstation Network and on Xbox Live. This adaptation gave developer and publisher Ubisoft the chance to turn the comics' video game appropriations back on themselves, allowing Scott's life to literally play out as a 1980s scrolling beat-em-up video game.

Along with these high-profile multimedia exploits—which also included an animation airing on Cartoon Network's *Adult Swim*, also voiced by Michael Cera—Scott's likeness has been used on merchandise including T-shirts, dolls, mugs, posters, and even authentic "Todd Ingram wristbands" modeled on those sported by Ramona's third "evil ex."

In all likelihood, the *Scott Pilgrim* books' greatest contribution to American culture has to be in presenting a thoroughly modern and media-literate love story that also carries a powerful message about self-belief and earning power through maturation and growing self-confidence. Although many readers focus on the love story between Scott and Ramona, it is Scott's maturing view of himself and his growing self-confidence that really define the series. While taking control of his relationship in book 4 might earn Scott the "power of love," it is when he "levels up" again in book 6 that Scott earns the "power of understanding," allowing him to empathize with others and also to come to terms with his own emotional baggage.

While some of Scott's past relationships might be depicted as morally questionable—with the baggage of his past experiences represented by his evil double, Nega-Scott—it is by coming to terms with that baggage and adopting a mature and positive outlook towards his latest relationship in spite of past difficulties that he truly proves his worth.

SUMMARY

Scott Pilgrim rocketed to popularity because he is essentially a direct analogue for his target audience. He is honest, occasionally lazy, often too hard on himself, frequently unconfident about his relationships, but he has good intentions and a pure heart. He has also lived through and absorbed most of the same pop culture that his target audience would have experienced and enjoyed, with his adventures containing frequent references to music, movies, video games, and comics that they would recognize and appreciate.

As well as allowing Scott's audience to feel "in on the joke," this cultural literacy has helped fans to feel that the books are being written by somebody who really understands their viewpoint. That is not a product of cynical calculation: O'Malley, as a relatively young creator, born in 1979, really is in tune with the thoughts and feelings of the generation that have bought and enjoyed his work, and Scott's huge popularity despite his relative newness as a character is testament to that.

Combined with the relentlessly positive message of the series, the innovative approach to storytelling, the human soap-opera, and the high-energy fight scenes, it is easy to see how Scott Pilgrim has become an instant success and earned his place as one of comics' most iconic characters.

See also Wizard

ESSENTIAL WORKS

O'Malley, Bryan Lee. *Scott Pilgrim's Finest Hour*. Portland, OR: Oni Press, 2010.
O'Malley, Bryan Lee. *Scott Pilgrim's Precious Little Life*. Portland, OR: Oni Press, 2004.

FURTHER READING

O'Malley, Bryan Lee. Official Bryan Lee O'Malley Website. http://radiomaru.com/. Accessed July 31, 2011.

Oni Press. Official Scott Pilgrim Website. http://www.scottpilgrim.com. Accessed July 31, 2011.

Dave Wallace

Sgt. Rock

Sgt. Frank Rock is the leader of Easy Company, a designated company within the American Army serving in Europe against the Nazis during World War II. Sgt. Rock is readily identified by his rank, specifically the stripes on his helmet, as well as his well-worn, dirty uniform. Often he is also depicted as wearing two belts of .30-caliber ammunition, which is both practical as well as talisman-like. He also carries a Thompson submachine gun and several hand grenades. He is often quiet and has a calming effect on troops around him, especially when the fighting is at its most intense. He is unshaven, not as a form of disrespect, but due to the fact that he is often in the thick of the fighting against a stubborn enemy that will not quit. Despite a lack of officers present in the unit, Rock is clearly officer material if he wants it. Yet, he is content to serve as the immediate leader and confidant of his men.

HISTORY

Sgt. Rock was the creation of one of the strongest creative teams in war comics: Robert Kanigher writing and **Joe Kubert** illustrating. The first appearance of a Sgt. Rock–like character was in the **DC Comics** mainstay *Our Army at War* #68 (1959). In this first story, the unnamed sergeant was like a prize fighter, as he would not quit, regardless of the situation, be it a boxing bout or combat. This aspect of his "never say die" attitude was one that often figured into the stories. No matter how difficult the fighting was, Rock was there helping his men to persevere and defeat the enemy. While the fighting was extreme, Rock was cool and almost detached. In some regards, the comparison of Rock to the movie characters portrayed by John Wayne (specifically Sgt. Stryker in the movie *Sands of Iwo Jima* from 1949, a decade before Rock was introduced) is readily apparent. Over a few months, the character slowly took form. In "The Rock of Easy Company" (*Our Army at War* #81, 1959), Sgt. Rocky (as he was first called in this story) was seen as the steadfast squad leader that everyone could rely on to get things done. Soon after, Sgt. Rock took his final and familiar role of the squad leader that served as a model of comic book war stories for decades after.

The idea was to create a squad that was of average troops with Rock as their squad leader. In this regard, the reader could see Rock substituting for their relatives who might have fought in any theater in World War II. He fought mostly in the European theater, and within that area mostly in France. The stories were mostly nondescript early on, as were the military units. It has become somewhat of a parlor game to identify Rock's unit, as he fought everywhere.

Over the years, Rock became one part of a unit of recognizable characters. His loyal second-in-command was the giant of a man, Bulldozer Nichols, who carried a .30-caliber machine gun into combat (a 31-pound weapon usually served by a crew of four!). In addition, there were Wildman, a former school teacher with fiery red hair and a beard that gave him a wild appearance; Ice Cream Soldier, who never seemed to melt under pressure during the fury of combat; Short-round, Junior, and Archie, who were mere grunts who met the need for assistance; Little Sure Shot, an Apache Indian who put his wilderness and shooting skills to deadly effect against the Germans; and Jackie Johnson, an African American who joined the group later on but still proved his worth as a steadfast soldier in combat. The use of Jackie was important, as he was introduced into *OAAW* #113 in 1961, when integrated units were common, but the memories of segregated units from World War II still existed.

There were additional characters that were used from time to time throughout the series' run (both as *Our Army at War*, and later *Sgt. Rock*), which was from 1958 through 1988. Most were in the stories as replacements or as a driver for the story. Some of the stories discussed battle fatigue or other forms of combat-related stress or mental breakdown, such as the story "So Long, Scribbly" (*Sgt. Rock* #408), or the many stories that featured soldiers who doubted their abilities in combat such as "The Rock and the Wall" (*Our Army at War* # 83, 1959). The stories served as a metaphor for the realities that are encountered by soldiers of any army during the fog of war, or through the indoctrination of propaganda. The central idea here is that while soldiers may have their doubts concerning killing, their enemy is one that will hit innocents as well as fight in an ungentlemanly manner. To that end, Rock was the moral barometer of the fighting. He would get men to overcome their fears and fire on an enemy, but also remind his own troops of the need to defeat an enemy that is ruthless.

Sgt. Rock also met several other characters that later were given their own series, including Johnny Cloud (a Navajo who was a pilot), Mademoiselle Marie (a Maquis operative who assisted the Allies in fighting the Germans), and even the crew of the Haunted Tank, led by Jeb Stuart, who is in turn guided by the ghost of the Confederate general of the same name. The Losers

PLASTIC SOLDIERS

Sgt. Rock has had several versions of toys made through license. They include a small 3-3/4″ figure that was produced in the early 1980s by Remco, and more recently larger 12″ figures done through Hasbro toys as part of the G. I. Joe line. Ironically, the figures were done to emulate the toys that were based off the popular Marvel themed war comic, *G. I. Joe*. Since then, DC Direct has also introduced a 6″ figure, a limited 12″ edition, and even a "Kubrick" (or Lego-like) style Sgt. Rock. These figures often had nondescript or no enemy figures, such as the infamous Iron Major to fight against Rock. In addition to Rock, members of his supporting cast have also been cast in plastic, including Mademoiselle Marie, Little Sure Shot, Wildman, Bulldozer, and Jackie Johnson.

and the Haunted Tank were other war features that were part of the DC line, also created by Kanigher and Kubert. Many of these chance meetings allowed Kanigher and Kubert to tie in other comic stories or characters, not uncommon with the DC line of the 1960s.

Sgt. Rock served in his role as the quintessential combatant well into the 1980s. Even during the unpopular Vietnam War, Rock was a part of DC Comics' stable of characters. However, his name became a derisive way of describing a Vietnam soldier who was careless in his actions while looking for personal glory, as was noted in Tom Engelhart's *End of Victory Culture*. By the early 1970s, the stories in the Sgt. Rock comics often told of the futility of war, or served in fictional story form as a protest for the real actions of the U.S. Army in places like My Lai, Vietnam, where innocent civilians in the village were killed by U.S. soldiers during the Tet Offensive of 1968. This was exemplified in the story "Head-Count" (*OAAW* #233, 1971). In the story, the replacement John Doe kills all German-looking people in the French town of Alimy—an anagram of My Lai—and is eventually killed. But was he a villain or a killer? The point was that it is in the perception of the combatant, and that the war is full of moral dilemmas that Rock seemed to avoid more often than not. In fact, the slogan of the DC Comics released from this era exemplified this attitude: "Make war no more." Sgt. Rock often questioned the actions of combat and the point of all the bloodshed.

Also by the 1970s, *Our Army at War* became *Sgt. Rock*. In these later comic books, the stories became more thematic and focused on location (for example, in Italy while the fighting south of Rome bogged down) or on aspects of injustice during the war, such as the treatment of African American soldiers at home and overseas. By the early 1980s, the war comic genre as a whole was changing and losing ground and sales, and in 1988, Sgt. Rock was finally retired. This retirement was not permanent, as he has appeared in several stories, and was revived in the new DC *Men of War* title that was part of the DC relaunch in the fall of 2011. In this new series, the character of Rock is Joe Rock, grandson of the original Sgt. Frank Rock.

IMPACT ON COMICS

Sgt. Rock was not the first, but he was the most common stereotype of the strong, silent sergeant that made the Army work during World War II. While officers gained the glory, Rock was often shown shying away from any sort of glory and would often state, "I was just doing my job." He was also used as a model for many other war comics with a no-nonsense soldier who got things done.

The formula of the mixed-race and -ethnicity unit of war stories really was perfected by the Sgt. Rock stories. The immediate emulation of the Sgt. Rock stories was by **Marvel Comics**, when they introduced *Sgt. Fury and His Howling Commandos* in 1963. While Rock was serious and the stories had some levity, the Fury stories were often more focused on humor and characterization. Kubert was also imitated by many other comic book artists when it came to the war stories. Artists from several other publishers (in particular Charleton Comics) ripped off Kubert's style of art for the war comics. Kubert was also popular enough that he was brought in to take over from **Will Eisner** in the comic book illustrations that accompanied the U.S. Army supplemental manuals. *PS Magazine* is still produced by the Army, and Kubert's illustrations decorated the interior art well into the 2000s.

The Sgt. Rock character was recognizable to the extent that he has been featured in other comics. In 2003, Kubert teamed up with writer Brian Azzarello to create a graphic novel that told of Easy Company in the Ardennes during the Hürtgen Forest campaign. Entitled *Sgt. Rock: Between a Rock and a Hard Place*, the new story incorporated more "realistic" language and violence that was shocking but was more reflective of the violence of real combat. The story featured a murder within the combat zone, and was well received. The success of this graphic novel spawned a six-issue miniseries entitled *Sgt. Rock—the Prophecy*, in which Easy Company was sent into Lithuania to rescue a Jew from both the Germans and the communists, as he is seen by many as a prophet. Finally, in 2008, Billy Tucci took the main characters from Easy Company, and wrote a new miniseries entitled *Sgt. Rock—The Lost Battalion*, in which Easy assists in the rescue of the lost battalion of Texans from the 36th Infantry Division. To that end, Rock and Easy Company fight alongside the fabled 442nd Regimental Combat Team, the Japanese Americans who distinguished themselves in Italy and southern France. As of the fall of 2011, Sgt. Rock was reintroduced when DC Comics relaunched their entire line of comics starting at issue #1 of the new *Men of War* series. Sgt. Joe Rock (grandson of the original Frank Rock) is now fighting in Afghanistan, but the simple concept of courage under fire still remains.

IMPACT ON AMERICAN CULTURE

For many comic book readers who grew up in the 1950s and early 1960s, Rock's heroics were part of the society that worshipped the World War II veteran and often wanted to emulate Rock's strength under the pressure of combat. These same readers later became the soldiers who fought in Vietnam, where the opinion of the combat troops was drastically different. These same soldiers would note how someone in combat who sought glory or acted foolishly was trying to act like Sgt. Rock (e.g., gain glory but at risk of death). In some regards, Rock became the prototype of the strong action hero that is often emulated in action movies today. His strength and external coolness belie internal struggles that are never shown to others.

He has been repeatedly referenced in movies and TV shows, such as *Buffy the Vampire Slayer* and *Angel*. Rock was part of the *Justice League* cartoon (parts two and three of the "Savage Time" arc), and there have been several attempts to bring the story of Easy Company to the movie screens. Some actors associated with the project included Bruce Willis and Arnold Schwartzenegger, but as of 2011, the story still is merely fantasy and speculation in the minds of the general public.

SUMMARY

Sgt. Rock was not the first hardboiled sergeant that was featured in comic books, but he has served as a major comic book character for decades. He is still instantly recognized by many comic book readers, and his popularity has ensured constant emulation, imitation, and reinvention. His character, and that of his unit, symbolized the mixed ancestry of the United States, where soldiers overcame their differences to defeat a common enemy. Sgt. Rock has been a lasting character that continues to maintain popularity in the 21st century.

See also DC Comics; Kubert, Joe

ESSENTIAL WORKS

Kanigher, Robert (w), and Joe Kubert (a). *DC Showcase Presents: Sgt. Rock Volume 1*. New York: DC Comics, 2007.

Kanigher, Robert (w), and Joe Kubert (a). *DC Showcase Presents: Sgt Rock Volume 2.* New York: DC Comics, 2008.

FURTHER READING

Conroy, Mike. *War Stories: A Graphic History.* New York: Collins Design, 2010.
Engelhart, Rob. *The End of Victory Culture.* New York: Basic Books, 1995.
Schelly, Bill. *Man of Rock: A Biography of Joe Kubert.* Seattle: Fantagraphics Books, 2008.

Cord A. Scott

Sheena, Queen of the Jungle

Sheena, Queen of the Jungle is one of the earliest and most influential heroines in the history of comics, getting her start as a recurring character in every issue of *Jumbo Comics* from 1938 to 1953. The series has subsequently been reimagined many times in comics, animated cartoons, television, and film in the decades since its initial run. The original series and character were created by **Will Eisner** and S. M. "Jerry" Iger, and their studio's work was published by Fiction House. Sheena shares some similarities with Tarzan of the Apes (such as white skin, the ability to communicate with animals, and a propensity for swinging on vines), but the comic is iconic in its own right for inspiring a series of similar heroines throughout the history of comics, for frequent reintroductions across media over many years, and for synthesizing particular Western beliefs about race, gender, colonialism, and tribalism at various moments in history. Sheena is also the first heroine to have her own comic book series, predating *Wonder Woman* #1 by three years.

HISTORY

Sheena debuted in the British tabloid *Wags* in 1937 (Markstein 2011). Her appearance in *Wags* and her first several strips in *Jumbo Comics* (starting with issue #1) were in black and white, though the majority of appearances—including the 18-issue run of the standalone series *Sheena, Queen of the Jungle* from 1942 to 1953—were published in full color.

Sheena has had several different origin stories. Initially, the character was raised by an African tribesman named Koba, a witch doctor who accidentally caused the death of his friend, Sheena's explorer father. In later instantiations of the character, her parents were missionaries, business tycoons, or, as in the 1984 film, geologists. In all instances, tragedy befell her or her parents, and in the course of growing up with natives Sheena learned how to communicate with animals, wield a knife and spear with expertise, swing on vines, and

(The Digital Comic Museum)

otherwise develop the various jungle skills that she would need to foil villains from issue to issue.

In most comics, Sheena appears alongside her mate Bob Reynolds, a "white man, young, clean, strangely out of place in such a poor setting" in the "depths of the dark continent" (*Wags* #46, 1937). Bob, an oil man who first encountered Sheena while doing research on "a woman leading a pack of those powerful howling savages" on the "last outposts of white man's civilization" (*Wags* #46), eventually becomes Sheena's near-constant companion. He is also her frequent object of rescue, as most stories in the *Sheena* series focus on how Bob gets into trouble and how Sheena saves him. In some issues of the series, Bob is transformed "into a less inept character sometimes named Rick Thorne and sometimes not" (Markstein n.d.). In addition to Bob, Sheena is sometimes accompanied by a helpful and playful chimp named Chim. Furthermore, several of the native tribal people, villains, and animals also recur through the series. Sheena's narratives in *Jumbo Comics* and in the standalone series were often self-contained, nonserial stories.

Though Sheena is widely recognized as the first jungle heroine to appear in comics, she clearly belongs to a character archetype found in literature dating back to the late 19th and early 20th centuries (e.g., Ayesha from H. Rider Haggard's *She: A History of Adventure*, Rima the Jungle Girl from W. H. Hudson's *Green Mansions*, or Queen La of Opar from Edgar Rice Burroughs's *The Return of Tarzan*). Also predating the Sheena comics were silent films such as *The Jungle Goddess* (1922) and *Lorraine of the Lions* (1925), both of which featured jungle queens and were inspired by much of the same literature that grounded Sheena's creation (Wickham n.d.).

Sheena, as a fair-skinned, transplanted "native," frequently surprises both other tribes as well as various European and American explorers. Furthermore, she uses her position of power and her knowledge of jungle life to thwart villains physically, mentally, and (occasionally) politically; as a result, Sheena is frequently shown to be revered by tribal people throughout her region. Indeed, most characters who encounter Sheena in the series comment on her beauty, strength, prowess, and femininity—often contrasting her qualities with those of the native peoples she leads.

The popularity of the character has led to a number of appearances in other media, most notably in a television series from 1955 to 1957 starring Irish McCalla in the titular role, a 1984 film starring Tanya Roberts, a 1999 animated web series, and a 2000–2002 television series starring Gena Lee Nolin. Since Fiction House Comics folded in 1953, Sheena has only appeared sporadically in comic book form. There were a number of copyright-violating single issues of Sheena in the 1960s and 1970s, a two-issue tie-in to the 1984 film produced by **Marvel Comics**, several reprints of issues from *Jumbo Comics* in the 1980s and early 1990s, a 1998 reboot created by London Night Studios (which placed Sheena in South America and drastically changed the character), and another reboot in 2007 by Devil's Due Publishing, a company that also republished two volumes' worth of Sheena comics taken from *Jumbo Comics*. Many liberties were taken with Eisner and Iger's original conceptualization of Sheena across these various reboots and reimaginings, and none proved as popular with audiences as the original series did to readers in the middle of the 20th century.

IMPACT ON COMICS

Sheena, Queen of the Jungle was a pioneering comic for several reasons. For one, her appearances in *Wags* and *Jumbo Comics* marked her as the first in what would become a long line of jungle heroines to appear in comics throughout the middle decades of the 20th century. Second, Sheena's pioneer status is bolstered by her being the first female character to have her own dedicated title. However, both of these early achievements also foreshadowed what would eventually become the cause of Sheena's long disappearance from comics.

Sheena's success in *Jumbo Comics* (she was featured on all but a few covers of the over 150-issue run) created competition from other comic creators, who often tried to reproduce or surpass *Sheena*'s level of sexual appeal, violent action, or other factors that they believed contributed to Sheena's success. Some of this competition, such as *Tiger Girl* and *Camilla, Jungle Queen* came from in-house artists and writers at Fiction House. Others, such as *Rulah, Jungle Goddess*; *Princess Pantha*; *Tegra, Jungle Empress*; and *Tygra of the Flame People* were produced by competing publishers. This archetype of a character saw further expression after Fiction House Comics closed. Marvel Comics was quick to capitalize on Sheena's absence, publishing comics *Lorna, the Jungle Queen* (later renamed *Lorna, the Jungle Girl*), and *Jann of the Jungle* both within a year after the last issue of *Jumbo Comics*. In the 1970s, **DC Comics** published the series *Rima, the Jungle Girl* (based loosely on Hudson's novels) and Marvel introduced *Shanna, the She-Devil*. All of these comics feature a central Caucasian (and often blonde) female character who holds a position of power or strength in a jungle environment. Many of these characters, like Sheena, were orphaned, could speak with animals, and had expertise with pointed weapons. As Mike Madrid notes in *Supergirls*, Sheena was an "archetype that would define the female superhero" (2009, 31) for many years to come. And though the jungle princess trope has faded in recent years, its long legacy in comics is echoed in such contemporary characters as Ya'Wara in the *Aquaman* series.

Part of the reason for the decline in Sheena-inspired comics in the latter part of the 20th century probably stems from widespread industry disavowal of what is now recognized as some racially insensitive or offensive content that marked Eisner and Iger's work. However, for a very different reason, controversy dogged *Sheena* almost since its inception: the revealing outfits worn by the protagonist and the violent action that takes place in every story were viewed by watch groups of the era as harmful to children. In the introduction to *The Best of the Golden Age Sheena, Vol. 1*, Stephen Christy remarks that Sheena's popularity declined in postwar years, forcing Fiction House to republish Sheena stories in edited form to appeal to a more censorship-enamored public; comics were "censored with a fine-toothed comb to remove any and all overtly sexual or violent references. . . . [the] damage the censors caused on Sheena in the 1950s . . . [and] their crusade against the comic led to its eventual cancellation" (Christy, quoted in Webb et al. 2008, 115). This legacy of censorship is also part of Sheena's impact on the industry, as the Comics Magazine Association of America, which eventually went on to create the Comics Code, formed the year after her cancellation.

THE MANY INCARNATIONS OF SHEENA

Sheena's various reboots have seen her go through some significant changes, mostly in an attempt to shed some of the more antiquated aspects of the original stories or to reproduce the same sense of titillation for more modern audiences. For example, the 1984 film *Sheena*, starring Tanya Roberts, recasts the Bob Reynolds character as a television news reporter instead of an oil man and ups the ante for provocativeness by featuring several scenes of Sheena bathing (complete with prolonged full frontal nudity in a PG film released just prior to the adoption of the PG-13 rating). The later 1998 comic book series would transport Sheena to South America, transform her from a blonde into a redhead, suit her up in black leather, place her in both rural and urban settings (such as boardrooms), and make her fight corporations bent on destroying the environment with a team of like-minded friends (Wickham). The 2000 TV series gave Sheena shape-shifting abilities that allowed her to transform into other animals and emphasized the sexual tension between her and her mate (now named Matt). The most recent 2007 reboot by Devil's Due Publishing combines several of these prior ideas (such as putting her in urban settings and giving her some supernatural abilities), but gave back to the character her blonde hair and revealing leopard skin outfit. The 2007 series also made the character younger and thinner than her earlier incarnations, while depicting Bob (now an environmentalist) as more self-sufficient.

IMPACT ON AMERICAN CULTURE

As evidenced by both the popularity of the initial run of *Sheena* comics and the relative poor quality and obscurity of her later appearances in comics and other visual media, Sheena's impact on American culture has varied greatly from decade to decade.

During the run of *Jumbo Comics* and *Sheena, Queen of the Jungle*, Sheena was not only Fiction House's most popular character but also one of the most popular characters in all of comics, inspiring many knock-offs and copycats. Her success and cultural impact at this time can be attributed to a number of factors. For example, since Sheena was inspired by turn-of-the-century adventure literature and pulp fiction, many of the themes that pervaded popular books and magazines in the era preceding the early days of the comic book industry were subsequently found in the pages of *Jumbo Comics* and other Eisner and Iger publications. That is, many of the tropes of pulp fiction serials and short stories of the 1920s and 1930s—crime fighting, savagery, social taboos, sexuality, violence, etc.—were reproduced in comics like

Sheena, Queen of the Jungle. This connection is clearest in those issues of *Jumbo Comics* that featured both Sheena comics as well as nonillustrated short fiction starring Sheena. These short stories were often used to flesh out her character, elaborate on her relationships, provide background, or otherwise inform readers about parts of Sheena's world that were not as easily conveyed in images. In other words, Sheena was popular not only because she represented a particular male fantasy, but also because the narratives that she took part in were consistent with the appetites of readers who were coming to a new medium. It is not surprising, then, that Sheena was one of the few comic book heroes of her era to also inspire standalone pulp novels based on her character.

Furthermore, Sheena was able to speak to both pre–World War II American values and postwar public controversy. Mike Madrid argues that the stories in *Sheena* were indicative of an isolationist ideology that was popular in a pre–Pearl Harbor United States (2009, 41), and though her stories are rife with colonial-era stereotypes, Sheena is decidedly an anticolonialism comic. Sheena's exploits almost always involved setting things right for tribal villages by returning everything to a status quo when it was threatened by outside (often colonizing) forces. Here, *Sheena* had to tread a fine line, as no doubt many readers probably found the idea of adventuring into the "dark continent" enthralling, and so *Sheena* had to both entertain that fantasy while also thwarting the plans of explorers who wished to exploit the land and its people.

Contemporary readers of the original run of *Sheena, Queen of the Jungle* will almost immediately notice that the comic's portrayal of Africa and its people, while consistent with much of the media of the era, is today understood to be disparaging to those of African descent. Sheena's character is represented as a naturally intelligent, beautiful, feminine Caucasian woman who stands in stark contrast to those she leads. The native people are often characterized in such a way as to fit colonial-era stereotypes of Africans as simple or feeble-minded, grotesque (with exaggerated features and stereotypical adornments), and primitive and backward (cannibalistic, pagan, etc.). Even though the people Sheena protects are native to their environments, none of them seem to have her command over the nature that surrounds them or her physical prowess. Sheena's top physical form and quick wits are always able to save her, whereas natives who lack those abilities are often the victims of villainous white explorers. It is worth noting that the comic's initial run in the United States predated the civil rights movement, and in many of the subsequent Sheena reboots efforts were made to change the portrayal of the natives she lived with so as to be more reflective of actual tribal culture. In some cases, these reboots tried to avoid the issue altogether by moving Sheena into contexts like the city, where race was less of a significant factor in the story.

SIEGEL & SHUSTER

Jerry Siegel   Joe Shuster

(Photofest Digital Library)

immigrants from the Netherlands and Russia, respectively. In Toronto, Shuster showed an early love for drawing, tracing out the funny pages onto the bedroom walls of their apartment. The Shusters moved to Cleveland when Joe was 10. While at Alexander Hamilton Junior High School, Joe had several cartoons published in the student newspaper, the *Federalist*. The family moved to Glenville, where Joe began attending high school. At Glenville, he became active in the Art Club and also painted sets for the Drama Club. He became successful as an amateur artist by winning a Cleveland poster contest for high school football and by having a cartoon about Thanksgiving placed on the front page of the *Torch*. Short and skinny, Joe was also obsessed with physical fitness, and followed many of the important figures of the movement, including Bernarr Macfadden, the outspoken publisher of *Physical Culture*. Shuster sent away for self-training manuals and enrolled in correspondence strength programs in an attempt to make himself stronger.

When Jerry Siegel was 17, his father was working in the clothing store he operated downtown when three men entered just before closing time. They grabbed a suit of clothes and ran off. Michel Siegel tried to stop them, but was overcome and died of a sudden heart attack. Having lost his father and faced with an uncertain future after graduation, Siegel poured all of his attention to his writing. After two failed attempts at starting a science fiction magazine by himself, Siegel turned to Shuster and they published five issues of a stapled, mimeographed magazine called *Science Fiction*. These issues, which circulated to a few science fiction fans such as Forrest Ackermann and Julius Schwartz, were filled mostly with short stories that Siegel had tried selling to the pulps, in addition to some smaller pieces illustrated by Shuster in a bold, deco style. Subscriptions did not rise, however, so they ceased publication.

At the same time, Siegel and Shuster started to work on a comic strip that they hoped to submit for syndication. They worked on "Interplanetary Police," as well as a series of short cartoon strips that they packaged together as *Popular Comics*. They found a local publisher in the *Cleveland Shopping News* for these comics, but the deal fell through.

In 1934, they both graduated from high school. Siegel was hard at work on revising an earlier character idea. In the third issue of *Science Fiction*, he and Joe did a story called "Reign of the Super-man" that featured a bald mad scientist who turns a poor man into a sociopath with mental powers (Siegel and Shuster 1933). Siegel kept the name, but began work on a more heroic version of the character. He and Shuster worked up a crude version for Consolidated Publishing, but it was also eventually turned down. Frustrated, Siegel took his burgeoning idea to other artists. Russell Keaton, who had drawn the Sunday newspaper comic *Buck Rogers*, was interested and worked up a few prototype strips. This version of the character was very different—this young Superman arrives via time travel, not from outer space, and has a different suit. But Keaton's interest waned, and Siegel was again left without an artist for an idea that was still evolving.

Teaming with Shuster again, the two turned the character into more of a strongman capable of acts that stretched the boundaries of believability, but at the same time was somewhat feasible within the realm of modernist science fiction. Shuster designed a much more interesting costume with a cape, and they changed his origin to one where he is sent here by his parents from a doomed alien world. Influenced by fitness, the high levels of crime in Cleveland, the movies of the 1930s, and their own lives as frustrated teenagers, Siegel and Shuster created Superman over time, using elements of their own lives to make it more indelible. Realizing they had a special character, they began work on turning it into a daily newspaper strip.

While working on Superman, they were hired by Major Malcolm-Wheeler Nicholson to do comics for his new publication of all-new comics material called *New Fun*, published by his National Allied Comics company. Siegel and Shuster's first published comics as a partnership occurred in *New Fun* #6 with "Henri Duval," a French Musketeer-like swashbuckler, and "Doctor Occult," a supernatural detective. The major was impressed with their work and assigned them more stories in his other magazines *More Fun*, *New Comics*, and *New Adventure Comics* with the features "Radio Squad," "Federal Men," and "Spy." Though no longer in print, these comics are highly accomplished in terms of Shuster's character art and architecture. They also all deal with social justice by addressing a great many real, Depression-era ills.

In addition to their work for the major, Siegel and Shuster worked continually on Superman: drafting, tweaking, and sending it out to newspaper syndicates. Seeing the need for a female lead, they answered an ad in the newspaper and met Jolan Kovacs (later Joanne Carter), who became the first model for the character of **Lois Lane**. She posed for Shuster several times before moving out of the area in search of stardom. She entered their lives again in 1948, after which she and Siegel were married and later had a daughter, Laura. Siegel had previously been married to Bella Lifshitz, with whom they had a son, Michael. Joe Shuster was married only once in the 1970s to Judy Calpini.

Comic books were doing fairly well on the newsstands in the mid-1930s, so the major was preparing to launch a new book, *Detective Comics*. *Detective* featured Siegel and Shuster's longest feature to date: "Slam Bradley," starring a ham-fisted adventurer detective who, paired with his nebbish partner Shorty Morgan, provided both adventure and comedy.

But the major was stretched thin and in debt, having already brought in outside financial partners such as publisher Harry Donenfeld, who ran the distribution firm Independent News. The major was sued by Donenfeld, who quickly claimed the company for himself. Donenfeld was eager to get into comics himself, and editor Vin Sullivan informed Siegel and Shuster that they might have a place in their planned new book, *Action Comics*.

In late 1937, Sullivan expressed specific interest in the Superman character, which by this time had been sent to nearly every company in the country. Siegel and Shuster were much more interested in getting it syndicated as a newspaper strip, not as a comic book. But Donenfeld's business accountant Jack Liebowitz assured them that if they would publish Superman in the new *Action Comics*, a syndicate deal with the powerful McClure Company might be around the corner. Siegel convinced Shuster that this was a good idea, and they sold the story for *Action* #1—and all subsequent rights to the character—for $130. Soon after, they were signed for newspaper syndication in a three-part deal between Siegel and Shuster, McClure, and Donenfeld himself.

Action Comics went on sale April 18, 1938, and within a few issues was an unqualified success. The character began to be merchandised to food products, toys, and was transformed into a successful radio program and a series of high-quality Fleischer cartoons distributed by Paramount Pictures. In 1940, the World's Fair in New York held Superman Day, highlighted by physical contests for children judged by Charles Atlas and a parade led by an actor dressed as Superman.

Though they were not sharing in the enormous merchandising and radio profits to the extent that Donenfeld was, Siegel and Shuster were making over $20 per page, providing content for *Action Comics*, *Superman* (which debuted in 1939), and the daily and Sunday strips. To help Shuster, they hired a stable of artists for their Cleveland studio. Among them were Wayne Boring and Fred Ray, who would both become definitive Superman artists. Meanwhile, Jerry was also scripting other characters, including the Spectre, Robotman,

AWARD-WINNING CREATORS

Siegel and Shuster were inducted, as a duo, into the Science Fiction, Horror and Fantasy Hall of Fame (1976), the Will Eisner Award Hall of Fame (1992), and the Jack Kirby Hall of Fame (1993). Siegel was awarded the Bill Finger Award for Excellence in Comic Book Writing (2005). Shuster was inducted into the Canadian Comic Book Creator Hall of Fame (2005). There are streets named after both of them (and Joanne Carter) in Cleveland and Toronto. Public art sculptures containing biographical information and images of *Action Comics* #1 mark the sites of their former homes in Cleveland.

and the Star-Spangled Kid. Of these characters, the Spectre, a grim supernatural avenger, would remain a fixture of the DC Universe with ties mostly to the Justice Society (Siegel 2003). But World War II interrupted the daily work of comics creators just as it did for every other profession. Jerry Siegel was drafted into the army in 1943 where he served a noncombat role in Hawaii. Shuster, who had been designated 4-F because of his bad eyes, continued to do layouts and supervise the studio back home. When Siegel returned from duty, he found that National had published the character Superboy, a teenaged version of Superman whom Siegel had proposed years earlier, in *More Fun Comics* #101 (1945). Furious that the company had used his character without his consent, Siegel instigated a lawsuit in 1947 and won a financial settlement, but not a return of copyright. They were consequently terminated. Siegel and Shuster attempted to return to the comic spotlight as a duo once more with *Funnyman*, a comic book and newspaper strip about a hero who solved crimes using pranks and gags, but it was unsuccessful (Andrae and Gordon 2010).

The 1950s were a dark period for the pair. Joe Shuster began teaching comic art part time in New York before anonymously (as "Josh") illustrating a series of under-the-counter erotica magazines called *Nights of Horror*, a job he took to give his sister enough money to be married (Yoe 2009). Siegel, on the other hand, was made comics editor of Ziff-Davis and supervised a wide variety of horror and science-fiction comics. He wrote some of these titles as well, including *Lars of Mars*. But sales of the new comics were not strong, and growing national distrust over horror comics made the line dissolve. Siegel did some subsequent work for **Stan Lee** at **Marvel** as "Jerry Ess" in short comics stories in *Marvel Tales*. Siegel also wrote television scripts for a Captain America–hosted kids' television show in Boston.

In 1959, Siegel went quietly back to Mort Weisinger and was rehired. Siegel wrote dozens of stories for *Superboy*, *Supergirl*, *Superman*, and *Adventure Comics*. These stories, some of the best work of Siegel's career, went mostly uncredited due to the parameters of his contract. During this time, Siegel created many of the key members of the Legion of Super-Heroes and much of their back story (Siegel 2007). He also wrote a number of outrageous stories about Bizarro, Superman's imperfect clone, which can also be read as ironic criticisms of Superman himself (Siegel 2000). Siegel also helped reimagine **Lex Luthor** (whom they created in 1940) as a slightly more sympathetic character. In 1967, Siegel again sued DC to regain the Superman copyright, and once again lost his job.

Siegel did some work for Archie Comics, organizing new versions of Golden Age characters into a Marvel-like team comic called *The Crusaders* (Siegel 2003). He also wrote *The Owl* for Gold Key. Overseas, he worked on British and Italian comics, including "The Shadow" and **Carl Barks**'s "Junior Woodchucks."

In the 1970s, after missing a deadline to once again file for copyright reclamation, Siegel wrote an open, angry letter cursing **DC Comics** for their mistreatment of Shuster and him: Siegel sent his letter to every media outlet he could find. It was finally picked up by editor/cartoonist Phil Yeh for *Cobblestone*, a small West Coast periodical. Their plight—that the creators of Superman were broke while Warner Brothers was readying a multimillion-dollar Superman movie—spread quickly. Siegel and Shuster made appearances on the *Late Show*, the *Today Show*, the *CBS Evening News*, and others. Pressured by the public as well as several famous comics artists such as Jerry Robinson and **Neal Adams**, Warner Brothers finally awarded Siegel and Shuster a lifelong annual pension and restored their byline to every Superman publication.

Revitalized by the public outpouring of support, Siegel and Shuster, both now living near Los Angeles, began to do a few select interviews and made appearances at conventions. Shuster worked on putting together an art show and a cartoon while Siegel did some writing, including the Starling for Eclipse, which was more of an adult retelling of the Superman story. Joe died on July 30, 1992, and was mourned in full-page ads in DC Comics and in newspapers across the country. Jerry Siegel died on January 28, 1996, and received the same outpouring of sympathy from the comics community. Siegel's wife Joanne died in 2011. After their deaths, their families continue to pursue their copyright options to Superman.

IMPACT ON COMICS

The creation of Superman literally changed the appearance of the medium. Until Superman, the comics in newspapers were generally Westerns, funny animals, kids, spies, or awkward Flash Gordon rip-offs. Superman was unlike any character you could read about in the newspaper, which drove demand and interest to these new types of "comic book" magazines. Without

Superman's success, it is difficult to gauge how long comic books would have been sustainable by these existing genres. The superhero characters that came after Superman, from **Batman** to **Spider-Man**, all copy at least portions of his costume, secret identity, origin, and moral nature. He is the iconic template—visually and categorically—of the superhero.

The most important addition to the genre made by Siegel is the trope of the secret identity. Though other genre protagonists such as the Shadow had secret identities before Superman, no writer capitalized on it as Siegel did. The Clark Kent-Lois Lane-Superman triangle is the core of the ongoing narrative of Superman, more so than the threat of alien invaders or bald tycoons. For while enemies and supervillains change in the serial format, the love triangle is what creates a more ongoing tension. And it is a tension that the reader—in 1938, young and male—could truly understand. Not only are readers in on the secret, but they can identify with it in the sense of feeling that others (in this case Lois) ignore them because they don't see the "real me." This is the genius of Superman.

Siegel's work is also very culturally topical, from quoting hit songs in early issues of *Action Comics* to referring to actual senators in *Spy*. Though Superman is an extraordinary creature, Siegel is very careful in his Golden Age adventures to tie him to reality so as not to become too unbelievable.

Shuster also championed many artistic techniques, one being his use of Craftint, which allowed artists to apply chemicals to bring shading patterns into their work. Shuster also experimented with using larger panels to convey a greater sense of scale, most notably in invasion scenes or tall panels meant to show the heights of buildings in his impossible cities. Siegel would claim that this was to save time. He also was one of the first American artists to really use speed-lines in the background to indicate the high velocities of cars, planes, and trains. Shuster also, in using physical fitness photos and real-life models—brought a level of realism that would not often be matched by other Golden Age comics. And his famous squinted eyes—in homage to the comic strip character Captain Easy and perhaps reflective of his own poor vision—are the definitive look of the Golden-Age superhero. To this day, whenever the Golden Age Superman is invoked, it is almost always the Shuster version.

IMPACT ON AMERICAN CULTURE

Superman's impact on American culture since 1938 is bordering on immeasurable. Not only has the character remained the archetype for the image of the superhero, but Superman also signifies a moral character that is continually employed by all manner of Americans from soldiers to talk show hosts to make a point—any point—about human goodness, justness, or even meekness. Unlike Mickey Mouse, Superman is a concept that has more of an ethical

"K-METAL"

The archives of DC Comics, housed in giant metal cabinets within its vast library, are filled with forgotten, illuminating details regarding Superman's history. In 1988, as a young DC editor, I myself unearthed a dusty, disremembered cardboard box filled with manuscript carbons. Excitedly, I realized they were all by Jerry Siegel, copies of his scripts from the very earliest years of Superman that hadn't seen the light of day for decades. Carefully matching the scripts to the published comics, the real find became the believed-lost script to an unpublished tale from 1940. What I found within its pages stunned me. By the end of the story, Siegel had foreseen, as "K-Metal," a prototype of Superman's legendary weakness (Kryptonite, radioactive fragments from his destroyed home world) three years before it would officially debut in the *Adventures of Superman* radio series. Moreover and far more significantly, Siegel took it upon himself to permanently alter the status quo of the series by revealing to Lois Lane the secret of Superman's dual identity once and for all, turning her into Clark Kent's confidante and Superman's "secret weapon," a development that would have changed the direction of the strip forever. Unsurprisingly, Superman's publishers ultimately rejected the story, ostensibly to protect the direction of "their" property; it was undoubtedly a blow to Siegel and to any illusions he might still have fostered regarding how much control he would ultimately be allowed over that which he and Shuster created.

Mark Waid

and moral dimension—the character has a meaning that is known, somehow, by most people all over the world. And unlike actors or politicians to whom the culture assigns a larger meaning, Superman does not age or change very much. And when he does, he eventually returns to his baseline iteration. Like one of the heads on Mt. Rushmore, the character, even though it is completely fictional, contains solid moral, patriotic, and symbolic meaning.

The impact Siegel and Shuster have had in the area of comics creators' rights is also important and ongoing. Their legal actions over the past decades have been crucial in defining the conversation about what happens when an author or artist sells a work to a comics publisher. Unless otherwise noted, these cases normally constitute "work for hire," meaning that the creators merely work on the characters for a fee, but the company still controls all of the rights. Siegel and Shuster came up with Superman several years before National bought it, making any claim of work for hire somewhat nebulous and thus, in their eyes, contestable. The opposing view is that they signed a standard contract for a property that was a gamble for both parties. Though the Siegel-Shuster cases have not resulted in any new laws, they have inspired many similar Golden Age comics creators and their families to instigate parallel lawsuits in an attempt to reclaim their own copyrights. For this reason alone, Siegel and Shuster remain very popular figures among comics creators who see themselves increasingly as underdogs working for colossal corporations. In a strange way, Siegel and Shuster have become, in many peoples' eyes, very much like their creation, a symbol not of concise facts, but of a morally based notion of "doing what's right."

Within 40 years of both of their families' arrival in North America, Siegel and Shuster owned their own homes, Siegel was married, Shuster was providing for his parents, and they were writing and illustrating comics as professionals—something they had no training in whatsoever. This is surely the American dream, but it was not one borne of lucky accidents. Siegel would often share the tale that he came up with the idea for Superman on a sleepless night, got up and ran over to Joe's, they drew it all down—and that was it. Though he did have such an idea one night, the actual execution of it took almost eight years. In other words, they worked very hard at making it work; they changed it, adapted it, then erased it and started over again. This effort and optimism that they learned through the urgings of Franklin D. Roosevelt's New Deal to "get to work," the endless pulp ads that promised a better "You!" if you worked hard enough, and Joe's training manuals that assured him he could become bigger and stronger was tempered with the ethically suspect world they saw outside and by Jerry's father's death in the presence of three common thieves. Siegel and Shuster combined a Puritan American morality with the Depression requirement of a healthy, contributing individual not only to work harder, but to create Superman.

SUMMARY

Siegel and Shuster symbolize, in most cases, the very act of creating comics: a writer works with an artist to produce a series of images and words that tell a story. Siegel and Shuster not only embody the incredibly imaginative results that can come of such an artistic relationship, but the difficulties as well. Though often spoken of only in tandem, they were two different men who brought different skills, literally, to the table. They shared one common wavelength—the desire to turn their imagination into something real. Without the benefit of formal education in art or writing, they taught themselves—Siegel through the pulps he absorbed and Shuster through the people he saw in his fitness manuals. Because they drew on the materials around them, they created a character who in some ways was already there. People already wanted and needed a symbol of justice; Siegel and Shuster just put him on paper. They wanted to be rich and famous, to escape Cleveland, and they did it while listening to the imaginative urges of childhood. It is absolutely no coincidence that teenagers invented the first comic book superhero.

It was their hard work, their status as underdogs in an underdog medium, eventually creating an immensely powerful corporate symbol—an icon that is recognizable all over the world—that makes them icons, just as much as Superman, for far more human reasons.

See also DC Comics; Lex Luthor; Lois Lane; Superman

ESSENTIAL WORKS

Andrae, Thomas, and Mel Gordon. *Siegel and Shuster's* Funnyman: *The First Jewish Superhero*. Port Washington, WA: Feral House, 2010.

Siegel, Jerry (w), John Forte (p), Wayne Boring (p), and Curt Swan (p). *Superman: Tales of the Bizarro World*. New York: DC Comics, 2000.

Siegel, Jerry (w), and Paul Reinman (p). *The Mighty Crusaders* (2003), Archie Comics.

Siegel, Jerry (w), and Joe Shuster (p). "Reign of the Super-Man." *Science Fiction* #3 (1933). http://ufdc.ufl.edu/UF00077088/00001.

Siegel, Jerry (w), and Joe Shuster (p). *Superman Chronicles, Vols. 1–8*. New York: DC Comics, 2006.

Siegel. Jerry (w), and Curt Swan (p). *Showcase Presents: Legion of Super-Heroes, Vol. 1*. New York: DC Comics, 2007.

Yoe, Craig. *Secret Identity: The Fetish Art of Superman's Co-creator Joe Shuster*. New York: Abrams ComicArts, 2009.

FURTHER READING

Andrae, Thomas. *Creators of the Superheroes*. Neshannock, PA: Hermes Press, 2011.

Daniels, Les. *Superman: The Complete History*. San Francisco: Chronicle Books, 2004.

DeHaven, Tom. *Our Hero: Superman on Earth*. New Haven, CT: Yale University Press, 2011.

Jones, Gerard. *Men of Tomorrow: Geeks, Gangsters, and the Birth of the Comic Book*. New York: Basic Books, 2005.

Brad J. Ricca

Spider-Man

Marvel Comics' flagship personality, "your friendly neighborhood Spider-Man," is probably the most beloved superhero of all time. Since 1962, "Ol' Webhead" has inspired a host of lively variations including the classic red-and-blue persona, the black-and-white 1980s Alterna-Gothic makeover, a cyberpunky 2099 variation, the provocative Scarlet Spider clone, and a plethora of more recent multicultural upgrades. All this drama and diversity make Spidey amazing indeed, considering the premise on which he is based "at first seemed absurd and ridiculous" (Weist 2004, 39). Marvel publisher Martin Goodwin initially balked at **Stan Lee**'s pitch for a wimpy teen "super-schnook" who never really triumphs, but Spider-Man now leads the upper echelon of phenomenally successful comic book properties (Lee quoted in Murray 2002, 30).

"Golden Age" predecessors **Superman** and **Batman** may have more than 20 years on the web-head, and recent megahits like Deadpool and Wolverine exude trendier "badass" attitudes, but Spidey's gregarious heroism, ambivalence towards his powers, and the extraordinary interconnectedness of his dynamic supporting cast speak more fluently to contemporary American anxieties.

Over the years, Spider-Man comics have inspired some of Marvel's most compelling achievements and set new standards for superhero genres. Influential archvillains like Doctor Octopus, the **Punisher**, the Kingpin, Venom, Carnage, and, of course, the variously gruesome Goblins have all spun out from Spidey's web. Corporate manipulation of Marvel's marquee property has also inspired notable publicity stunts and gimmicky revamps. The most controversial examples include the greatly embellished back story for Peter Parker's parents, developing the mysteries of his Secret Wars–inspired alien costume, the prolonged narrative hijinks of the Clone saga, saturating the press with Peter Parker and Mary Jane's overhyped marriage, and the rise of a mixed-race teen Spider-Man in the parallel *Ultimate* universe in 2011. Today, Spider-Man's many incarnations remain plentiful, and the enthusiasm with which fans subscribe to his travails remains truly extraordinary.

HISTORY

It is difficult to discern which is more often told: Spider-Man's origin or the tales told around that origin. All reveal fascinating aspects of a teenage loner fatefully "bitten by a radioactive spider" to find himself with "the proportionate strength and agility of an arachnid." Stan Lee frequently recites the story of Spidey's development thus: publisher Martin Goodman was worried that readers would be repulsed by "the decided 'ick' factor" of a hero "sticking to walls" and spewing webs, but Lee was bored with the schlocky monster tales Marvel purveyed and persevered in his personal quest to revolutionize the teen sidekick as a more vigorous hero (David and Greenberger 2010, 13).

Lee had the ferocious pulp avenger, the Spider, in mind when he first dreamed up his "inversion of every other comic-book hero out there," and the original concept may have been influenced by a neglected **Jack Kirby** and Joe Simon prototype, the Silver Spider (David and Greenberger 2010, 12). Sources vary as to whether Kirby or **Steve Ditko** first designed the iconic webbed costume, but the results were more exciting than anyone could have anticipated (Murray 2002, 29). The entire Spider-Man concept resonates with the primary attributes of many genres and traditions. Like a heady puree of Shelley's *Frankenstein*, **Bob Kane**'s Batman, and Franz Kafka's "Metamorphosis," Spider-Man's origin invokes gothic and crime fiction motifs like the ostracized genius, doomed loved ones, the misuse or misfiring of science, the gritty noir city, the driven vigilante, and the fateful "return of the repressed." Even his costume suggests a richly allusive mix of pulp hero fashions and vigilante masks, as well as a quirky fusion of Superman's primary colors and Batman's predatory metaphor.

The Lee-Ditko origin is also rife with poetic justice and personal torment. Spider-Man's refusal to stop the criminal who eventually murders his benevolent Uncle Ben argues that no matter how desperately we strive for fame or freedom, we are ensnared by forces beyond our estimation. In this sense then, Spider-Man's origin may owe more to the despondent first-person narratives of Edgar Allan Poe, Guy de Maupassant, Kafka, and H. P. Lovecraft than **Jerry Siegel** and **Joe Schuster**, Simon and Kirby, or C. C. Beck. In the final panel of his origin story, a devastated Spider-Man turns away from readers: "a lean and silent figure" fades "into the gathering darkness, aware at last that in this world, with great power there must also come—great responsibility!" (*Amazing Fantasy* #15, 1962). The omniscient narration emphasizes Spider-Man's plight as an object lesson in fate, humility, and love. Its closing moral also mirrors the familiar conventions of satiric 1950s and 1960s horror comics. Later reprisals attribute the famous line to Uncle Ben himself, increasing the intimacy of his patriarchal advice to young Petey, but the chilling original gloats over Peter Parker's wretched guilt. To become Spider-Man is to know only fleeting happiness and little hope as you fight on existentially against a "sea of

(Associated Press)

troubles." This sinister tone may arise from Steve Ditko's previous experience as a master of cynical, weird tales that focus on struggle, disappointment, and rejection. Ditko remains as secretive as Peter Parker about his role in Spider-Man's genesis, but his periodic comments on the collaboration suggest a fascinating alternative to Lee's more familiar version (Murray 2002, 27).

IMPACT ON COMICS

Spider-Man's arrival in *Amazing Fantasy* #15 (1962) and the launch of his own title *Amazing Spider-Man* #1 (1963) comprise pivotal moments in world comics. Since then, some of the most engaging ideas in comic book history have circulated through Marvel's longest running spider-title, *The Amazing Spider-Man*. Of its many high points, five influential runs by key creators deserve special mention. Foremost are the initial 38 issues developed by Stan Lee and

Steve Ditko, which remain very "deserving of their classic status," especially with regard to Ditko's stark mise-en-page and "exquisite use of shadow" to lend ironic atmosphere (Snowdon 2003, 603). The ingenuity and introspection of these early stories have made Lee and Ditko the inimitable Lennon and McCartney of Spidey myths, and in terms of narrative originality, the *Amazing Spider-Man* will always remain "Ditko's book" (Gross 2002, 21).

No other collaboration in mainstream comics has produced so consistently compelling reading with the "scope and brilliance of its concepts," especially with regard to "Spider-Man's rogues' gallery" (Gross 2002, 16). With their first 16 stories, Lee and Ditko introduce the Chameleon, the Vulture, Doctor Octopus, the Sandman, the Lizard, Electro, Mysterio, the Green Goblin, and Kraven the Hunter, not to mention slyly cross-marketed cameos by the Fantastic Four, the Human Torch, Dr. Doom, and Daredevil. By the middle of the following year, most original villains were reprised at least once, with fan favorites "Doc Ock" and the Green Goblin developing exciting sagas of enmity and evil. More memorable baddies would soon appear including the Scorpion, the Molten Man, and the first Spider-Slayers.

Two early episodes have particular aesthetic importance. The intricate "Crime Master" arc (*Amazing Spider-Man* #26–#27, 1965) amplified Spider-Man's conflict with ruthless archnemesis the Green Goblin, but the finest note in the Lee-Ditko symphony would arrive in "The Final Chapter" (*Amazing Spider-Man* #33, 1966). We find Spider-Man "trapped in a wrecked underwater stronghold" while "May Parker lies comatose in the hospital" (Olshevsky 1985, vol. 2, 4). With an exquisitely blocked five-panel, two-page spread, Ditko builds to one of the most memorable moments in superhero comics. As Spider-Man undergoes "the torment of a virtually indescribable ordeal," he ponders giving in, but ultimately resolves to fight on. In one of Ditko's greatest images, Spidey frees himself with a Herculean effort, then escapes to save Aunt May. As Lee's caption confirms, "From out of the agony—comes TRIUMPH!"

Such exhilarating scenarios explain why so many pay homage to the spirited Lee-Ditko Spider-tales. In fact, contemporary Spider-media can never escape the anxiety of their influence. Since the 1960s, they have been obsessively reprised or reincarnated in titles like *Untold Tales of Spider-Man*, *Spider-Man: Chapter One*, and most successfully with Brian Michael Bendis's recapitulation of the Lee-Ditko plots in contemporary settings through *Ultimate Spider-Man*. Ditko eventually abandoned Spider-Man projects for creative reasons, but Lee has always kept his hand in the material. In 1977, he began adapting Spidey for the newspaper market, and the strip remains in healthy syndication.

The less consistent but equally dynamic works of Lee and John Romita signify the second *Amazing* phase. Romita—a veteran of high-fashion romance comics—brought a clean, commercial line to Spider-Man that gave characters sumptuous presence. Most importantly, Romita introduced a chic new eroticism by hunking up Peter and cramming his panels with "jazzy" bomb-shells like Mary Jane Watson, Gwen Stacy, the Black Widow, and the Inhu-mans' Medusa. Key Romita tales include the infamous showdown where Spider-Man and the Green Goblin discover each other's identities (*Amazing Spider-Man* #39–#40, 1966), the revelation of Mary Jane Watson's wit and beauty (*Amazing Spider-Man* #42, 1966), and the arrival of the vicious mob boss, the Kingpin, who would become one of Marvel's most iconic villains (*Amazing Spider-Man* #50, 1967). Romita also assisted in developing the kindly Robbie Robertson, an early African American role model in Marvel comics and a sturdy foil for the hotheaded J. Jonah Jameson's tirades, but his single greatest contributions to Spider-Man's legacy are two iconic anniver-sary covers.

Perhaps the single greatest image in Spider-comics, Romita's "Spider-Man No More" (*Amazing Spider-Man* #50, 1967) depicts a martyred Peter Parker walking dejectedly towards us as an enormous Spider-Man looms over him against a red sunset. The masked hero peers over his shoulder at his more mundane self, seemingly unconcerned. The potent tragedy of "Spider-Man No More," and the complementary splash page that describes Parker "put-ting away his toys" by relegating his costume to a trash can, stand as suc-cinct expressions of the doubt and worry that plague Spider-Man's otherwise heroic persona. Romita's other masterstroke for *Amazing*'s "Great, Long-Awaited 100th Anniversary Issue" (1971) is equally witty in its description of an empowered Spider-Man, bathed in dramatic light as he crawls over a "web" of friends and enemies with the caption, "The Spider or the Man?" The very contexts that empower and elevate him also ensnare his associates and define the limits of his own glory. A similar pose had graced the inaugural issue of the short-lived *Spectacular Spider-Man* magazine in 1968, but after Romita's striking reprisal on the 100th anniversary issue the image became inordinately popular, and Romita himself would sculpt the iconic pose for a Macy's Thanksgiving Parade balloon in 1987 (Daniels 1987, 209).

Romita's work on *Amazing* would also initiate the first Spider-Man dynasty when his son, John Romita, Jr., illustrated the best Spidey-centered tales of the 1980s, 1990s, and early 2000s. His crisp action sequences lent crucial tension to the decade-spanning epic of "tooth and intrigue" surrounding the Hobgob-lin, a vivid heir to the original Goblin's legacy of malice (Snowdon 2003, 603). Like his father, Romita Jr. was a master of cover imagery and contributed numerous memorable designs to advertise the rise of a new Gobliny threat to Spidey's well-being. All told, both Romitas invested more Spider-Man tales with fun, excitement, and style than any other creators. Their works remain among the best pulse-pounding examples of each era.

A fourth major Spider-artist would bend the hero and the *Amazing* series in wild new directions in the late 1980s. **Todd McFarlane** dazzled fans with a hyperactive design so addictive, it led to Spider-Man's entrapment

A PERSONAL POINT OF VIEW: COMICS' NERVOUS BREAKDOWN

I came up with the idea for the return of Peter Parker's parents in the 1990s. I thought it was an avenue of Peter's life worth exploring. I still believe that. I greenlighted the Clone Saga because my writers were enthusiastic about it at a level that overrode my and my boss's hesitation. One likes to have enthusiastic writers. As my boss (and one of those writers) Tom DeFalco said, "Hey, the next guys after us will change it back, anyway."

Daniel Yezbick refers in his accompanying entry to the "the prolonged narrative hijinks of the Clone saga." That's fine. He's entitled to his opinion. But the danger in seeing this opinion stated in a scholarly reference book is that readers may get the impression that these opinions are statements of fact, as obvious as the sky's blueness. The millions of dollars and units of sales the storylines generated; the *rise* in sales of the Spider-Man titles they created, when those of other comics lines were sinking; the fact that talented people did outstanding work on many of the maligned stories; and the fact that many, many readers enjoyed the stories—all this needs to be noted. That many, if not all, of those stories have recently been collected and reprinted, and the plot and character elements in them are being used for new stories, again goes to demonstrate that many people got a genuine kick out of those stories.

My theory is that the comics industry was going through a collective nervous breakdown in the early and mid-1990s, with distribution crises and the unrealistic expectations of corporate interests putting pressure on staffers and freelancers alike to do anything and everything to keep sales climbing ever higher. When that proved unrealistic and the industry imploded, the Clone Saga, especially, became a convenient symbol for some people of what was "wrong" with comics. Buzz about that idea seeped into mainstream press such as the *Wall Street Journal*, where the Clone storyline made a convenient tie-in with Marvel's business woes.

Of course people were upset about the revelation that Peter was the clone and vice versa. That was the whole point: to get people thinking and talking about Spider-Man. It was also a strategy to get Peter back to an allegedly simpler time in his life. That the Clone storyline (and its lead-in, the return of Peter Parker's parents) came to be identified with a crisis period in comics is, in a way, a tribute to people's love of Spider-Man and his role as a character so many people identify with. At any other period in comics history, the story would have certainly been controversial, but not the lightning rod it became.

Were the "Parents" and "Clone" storylines great, terrible, average? That's for each individual reader to decide for him- or herself. Me, I think they were pretty good. But that's just my opinion. I could be wrong.

Danny Fingeroth,
Group Editor of Spider-Man comics line, 1983–1984; 1991–1995

within the speculators' bubble of the mid-1990s. Based on the appeal of his tight, eye-popping pencils, McFarlane was soon granted his own *Spider-Man* series. It was nearly blinding in its visual frenzy, and he too produced his share of iconic covers, especially the still striking 300th issue of *Amazing* (1988), but his most lasting contribution involves the introduction of Venom (*Amazing Spider-Man* #299, 1988), and the post-McFarlane spin-off, Carnage (*Amazing Spider-Man* #344, 1991). Both characters remain popular, but their primary interest derives from the black "symbiote" costume meant to Batmanify Spider-Man in the mid-1980s. Venom and Carnage have shared grisly triumphs and tragic angst, but in the long term, they are ragged metaphors for the way that Peter Parker's costumed self preys upon his private life. Much like the popular **Punisher** introduced by Gerry Conway and Ross Andru in 1974 (*Amazing Spider-Man* #129, 1974), Venom and Carnage present ruthless antitheses to Spider-Man's more enlightened quest for peace and satisfaction. As victims of cruelty and parasitism, all three tread a darker path whereas Spider-Man, who exhibits affinities with each, manages to locate humor, promise, and passion in his gallant response to fate and fortune.

After McFarlane's influence faded, *Amazing* was revitalized in the early 2000s when *Babylon 5* creator J. Michael Straczynski brought "originality and patience" to the plotting and restored the title to "heights not seen in eons" (Snowdon 2003, 603–4). Straczynski builds his tales carefully, working in the tragedies of 9/11 and the impact of the ruthless Morlun, a nasty addition to the already impressive parade of Spider-baddies. Most famously, he initiated the fresh "Spider-totem" arc that plays upon the animistic themes of Spider-Man's milieu. Straczynski suggests that, like Catwoman or Animal Man, there is some folkloric fulfillment at work as Spider-Man transmutes human virtues with bestial attributes.

Today, numerous creators add ambitious, new depth to Spider-Man's mythos, building powerfully on existing frameworks, especially in the *Ultimate* series, which has dared to replace Parker with Miles Morales, a Latino/African American teen whose predicaments will redefine key questions of power and responsibility for the 21st century. As the narrative center of Marvel's Spider-media, *Amazing* also incorporates the occasional political comment. In 1971, the title famously featured a trio of "drug awareness" Green Goblin stories commissioned by the U.S. Department of Health (*Amazing Spider-Man* #96–#98). Though trite by recent standards, the stories were memorable for their rejection by the Comics Code Authority. More contemporary "statements" include the somber 9/11 memorial cover (*Amazing Spider-Man* vol. 2, #36, 2001) and a variant commemorating President Barack Obama's inauguration (*Amazing Spider-Man* #483, 2009). Obama is the first president to campaign for office on his love of Spider-Man while his Republican opponent publicly preferred Batman. The presidential cover set off a media firestorm while reprints and imitations soon made it the most recognizable *Amazing* image in recent years.

Spidey's influence has also led to a thriving family of other "Spider-titles," experiments, and spin-offs. Our "webhead" has appeared in well over 200 comic books including limited series, graphic novels, one-shots, and spin-offs—over a third of which were launched in the last 20 years. Other estimable Spider-series have included *Peter Parker, the Spectacular Spider-Man*, later revamped as *Peter Parker, Spider-Man* (260 issues, 1975–1998). The title included an early Spider-Man/Daredevil pairing by Frank Miller, the arrival of the 1980s antidrug heroes Cloak and Dagger, numerous Hobgoblin and Punisher tales, Al Milgrom's offbeat stories surrounding the Spot, and the celebrated whodunit, "The Death of Jean DeWolff," which aided Peter David's rise to auteur status. From 1964 to 1994, reprint titles like *Marvel Tales* and *Spider-Man Classics* also provided affordable editions of significant stories while reiterations like Danny Fingeroth's *Marvel Saga* and the lavish Kurt Busiek-Alex Ross collaboration *Marvels* celebrated important episodes within Spider-Man's history. Much of the most playful material belongs to *Marvel Team-Up*, a series that paired Spidey with a different hero each month for 150 issues between 1972 and 1985. Other titles would follow including *Web of Spider-Man* (129 issues, 1985–1996), *Spider-Man Adventures* (15 issues, 1994–1996), *Spider-Man: The Manga* (31 issues, 1997–1999), *Spider-Man 2099* (46 issues, 1994–1996), *Spider-Man Unlimited* (27 issues, 1993–1999), and beginning in 2001, *Spider-Man's Tangled Web*, devoted to featurettes involving supporting characters (22 issues, 2001–2003). Of the many titles that arose during the mid-1990s, McFarlane's *Spider-Man* remains noteworthy for its first issue, "launched in a blaze of variant cover colourings, states of baggedness and a hot creator" to become "the number-one-selling comic book ever to that date" with print runs in the millions (Snowdon 2003, 602).

Even Spider-Man's feminine counterparts comprise a complex tradition of their own. The first Spider-Woman was introduced in 1977, appeared in several series, and graced two U.S. postage stamps in 2007. The first Spider-Girl also thrived for over 100 issues in various titles in the late 1990s and into the 2000s. More recently, the multicultural upgrading of the Spidey-verse has continued with Anya Sofia Corazon, a.k.a. Araña, a Puerto Rican–Mexican Spider-heroine developed by Straczynski, Mark Brooks, and Fiona Avery.

Not all great Spider-Man stories need to plumb the depths of his guilt, and his frequent pairing with other heroes from outside Marvel have led to odd but entertaining adventures. The most famous and enjoyable are the two oversized Spider-Man/Superman crossovers from 1976 and 1981, but Spider-Man has also partnered with Batman, Backlash, Gen13, the Savage Dragon, SNL's Not-Ready-for-Prime-time Players, and Ren and Stimpy's Powdered Toast Man, among many, many others.

IMPACT ON AMERICAN CULTURE

At its core, Spider-Man's appeal lies in the aching familiarity of his predicaments as a costumed superhuman and a rather kind, but bookish kid of average circumstances and low self-esteem: "Peter Parker put into words what many of his readers could not articulate: the turbulence of growing up and attempting to grapple with often cruel realities" (Gross 2002, 11). In fact, Stan Lee's interest in deconstructing the "teen sidekick" super-cliché would lend Spider-Man much of his crucial gravitas. John Romita links Parker's popularity to mediocrity and compassion: "He's a guy with misgivings, constantly wondering what the hell he's doing it all for—but he still feels if somebody's down a well and you can crawl down and save them, you have that obligation" (Romita 2002, 4). Parker's ethos is more familiar to us than the unique plights of Krypton's sole surviving son or Wayne Manor's brooding, vengeful heir. As a "kind of Charlie Brown of the high school set," he takes the myth of the withdrawn, 98-lb. weakling in startling directions (Weist 2004, 39, 71). Parker's youth echoes other alter egos like **Captain Marvel**'s Billy Batson, but his transformation from lonely orphan to courageous web slinger represents "one of the most complex personalities ever written into comics" (Weist 2004, 71).

For decades, two contrasting characters determined Parker's troubled path: Aunt May and J. Jonah Jameson. Aunt May remains the primary symbol of his workaday remorse: "Because he didn't act, he left his aunt a widow. She was a living reminder of his guilt" (Lee 2002, 4). Spider-Man's 1962 debut also coincided with the cultural upheavals of the period when "America was a country in the midst of redefining itself. . . . Yet through it all, one comic-book character, Spider-Man, seemed to reflect the times and the youth of the country better than any other" (Gross 2002, xi). Superman's allegorical adoption by Smallville and assimilation into Metropolis spoke to 1930s America, but Spider-Man became the most evocative of Marvel's supermartyrs. *Rolling Stone* and *Esquire* celebrated his campy outsider's perspective, and as "the quintessential hero of the 1960s . . . his turbulent life and his constant introspection and self-doubt captured what America itself would be going through during that decade" (Gross 2002, 11). How perfect an antagonist, then, is J. Jonah Jameson, the ultimate authoritarian hypocrite?

As the callous editor of *The Daily Bugle* and *Now Magazine*, Jameson's assault on Spider-Man's public image marks him as the typical middle-aged professional thriving on abuse of a young, idealistic hero. The antithesis of the *Daily Planet*'s upstanding Perry White and Radio WHIZ's Sterling Morris, Jameson abuses the power of his position and the responsibility of free speech to spread scandal and slander. Where Peter Parker's motivations are secret, noble, and steeped in tragedy, Jameson's lies are public, popular, and filled with scorn. At his most bloodthirsty, Jameson hires assassins and commissions robotic Spider-Slayers to liquidate the "menace" he finds so unnerving, but his character would eventually develop more positively. By the late 1960s, Jameson evolved into "a serious, even moving figure; a staunch advocate of personal liberties and crusader against organized crime" who also eventually comes to "care for Peter Parker as a second son" (Gross 2002, 15). His most famous moment arrived in 1964 (*Amazing Spider-Man* #10) when the self-aggrandizing editor offers an astonishing monologue, tricked out by Ditko's subtle use of progressively lonely compositions, canted angles, and noir backgrounds: "Spider-Man represents everything that I'm *not*! He's brave, powerful, and unselfish! The truth is, I *envy* him!"

Peter Parker himself is no stranger to self-reflection. Much of the "fun" of Spider-Man's tangled web involves the ironic contrast between Spider-Man's frivolous wisecracks and Parker's self-deprecating soliloquies. Stan Lee recalls how readers likened Spidey to "a superhero Hamlet, always soul-searching, always giving vent to his innermost thoughts and convictions" (Lee 1986, 25). Romita's visuals also emphasized Parker's messiah complex: "I would have him on the edge of a building with his head in his hands almost like Christ in the Garden" (Romita 2002, 4). Peter's earnest reflections remain even more compelling than his superstunts: "It is his simple humanity, rather than his exotic talent, that has won him millions of enthusiastic fans. He is one superhero who has not lost the common touch'" (Daniels 1991, 96).

Peter Parker also endures a troubled love life. The women who waft through his chaotic world take more than they give. From early teen crushes Liz Allen and Betty Brant to foxy jackpots like Mary Jane, Felicia Hardy (the Black Cat), and Silver Sable, women give Peter fleeting comfort. In tragic cases like Gwen Stacy, Jean DeWolff, and MJ's cosmically erased marriage, his intimacies are generally rewarded with more sorrow than sympathy. Even his relations to elder women and matriarchs like Aunt May and Madame Web can leave him anxious and uncertain. Close male associates like Harry Osborne (Green Goblin II), Ned Leeds (Hobgoblin), John Jameson (Man-Wolf), and Flash Thompson (a later version of Venom) are prone to troublesome bouts of addiction, deception, and supervillainy. To this day, Spider-Man's web of family, friends, and lovers remains deliciously sticky.

Such relationships would eventually inspire a seismic shift in Marvel superhero fiction when Gerry Conway and Gil Kane forever altered how superhero stories function with 1973's "The Night Gwen Stacy Died" and its companion tale, "The Goblin's Last Gasp" (*Amazing Spider-Man* #121–#122). Their two-parter brought the first glimpses of cynicism to Marvel's Pop Art parade by killing off the hero's girlfriend and archenemy: "From that point on, nothing was certain. The heroine could die. The superhero could fail. Order would not necessarily be restored. Evil could triumph" (Gross 2002, 25). More importantly for the Spider-Man saga, "perceptive fans" recognized that the circumstances surrounding Gwen Stacy's death were painfully uncertain (Gross 2002, 25).

When the Goblin tosses her from atop the Brooklyn Bridge, Spider-Man snags her with his webbing, but the impact snaps her neck and the desperate efforts of the tortured hero become forever implicated in her death. Years later, Kurt Busiek and Alex Ross would remount the pivotal death scene as their finale to *Marvels*, a lush homage to Marvel myth making: "The Marvel universe was changing and Gwen's death was a terrific symbol of that" (Busiek 2002, 4). Gwen's specter would haunt Peter with the same fateful insistence as Uncle Ben, but her legacy and the realities it suggested would also resonate throughout the Marvel Universe, influencing watershed moments and publicity stunts like the deaths of Jean Grey, Guardian, Elektra, Aunt May, **Captain America**, the Human Torch, and eventually, in 2011, even an *Ultimate* incarnation of Spider-Man himself.

Spider-Man's voluminous comic-book mythology has inspired a deluge of products, and he remains among the most broadly merchandised superheroes ever. Only Superman's chest sigil and the Bat-sign seem as pervasive as his signature blue and red mask. Since the early 1960s, its webby color scheme has spread across every conceivable market for clothing, food, media, and toys. Some novelties remain iconic in and of themselves. These include the Aurora model kits, Third Eye black light products, and Mego Spider-Man dolls of the 1960s and 1970s, as well as the still-popular Underoos from Fruit of the Loom. More recently, a host of action figures, fashions, and accessories have inundated homes, schools, and colleges, especially in response to multimedia adaptations and computer games.

The broad reach of Spidermanalia has also led to dramatic moments of resistance. In 2004, protests arose surrounding an agreement between Columbia Pictures and Major League Baseball advertising *Spider-Man 2* on MLB- game used bases during interleague play. Outrage from both sports and Spider-fans killed the deal almost overnight (Rovell 2004). Early negative buzz surrounding the much-maligned 2011 Broadway musical, *Spider-Man: Turn Off the Dark* comprises a more recent example. Marvel's collaboration with Julie (*Lion King*) Taymor and U2 suffered extensive injuries and rewrites with the highest production costs and longest run of previews in Broadway history. Since its official 2011 opening, however, it has had significant financial success. Other musical adaptations are more obscure but equally fascinating, such as the funk-laden 1972 slugfest, the *Amazing Spider-Man Rock-a-Comic: From Beyond the Grave* or the delightfully campy 1975 *Spider-Man: Rock Reflections of a Superhero*. Several dynamic read-along Power record sets appeared in the 1970s and a "hugely enjoyable" series of short BBC radio plays with music by Queen-veteran Brian May appeared in 1996 (Clifton 2007).

No adaptations have made as substantial an impact as Columbia Pictures' trilogy: *Spider-Man* (2002), *Spider-Man 2* (2004), and *Spider-Man 3* (2007). Though these productions "spent some fifteen years in developmental and legal hell," the first and third films broke opening weekend box office records and helped catapult the superhero genre to new commercial heights (Gross 2002, xii). A past master of bombastic horror-comedy, director Sam Raimi developed electrifying web-slinging sequences and paid thoughtful homage to Spidey's comic-book contexts. Though the 9/11 tragedies necessitated changes that compromised the first film's climactic battle with Willem DaFoe's Green Goblin, the trilogy boasts at least one iconic moment, the rainy upside-down arachnakiss between Tobey Maguire's Spider-Man and Kirsten Dunst's sultry Mary Jane. With Marc Webb's high profile relaunch in 2012, Spiderman's big screen legacy has been retooled with a hefty emo vibe for the post-*Twilight* era of paranormal teen drama.

Spider-Man also enjoyed multimedia adaptations years before Maguire and Dunst's soggy "snog." The first rung to TV stardom began as early as 1967 when the beloved Saturday-morning cartoon, ABC's *Spider-Man*, not only introduced Spidey and his signature villains to the small screen, but also allowed its young executive producer, Ralph Bakshi, to hire on maestros like **Joe Kubert**, **Jim Steranko**, and Wally Wood as production designers. Bakshi battled network execs over the show's maturity, but after three full seasons and 50-plus episodes, it remains a cherished example of early television animation. Of course, its most enduring legacy is Paul Francis Webster's catchy opening "Spider-Man theme" which puts the hero's predicaments in surprisingly funky terms with lines like "Is he strong?/ Listen, Bud./ He's got radioactive blood."

Later animated series include the odd, 26-episode *Spider-Man and His Amazing Friends* from 1981–1983 on NBC where Peter Parker fights evil alongside his roommates, Iceman and Firestar. Another fairly forgettable 26-episode *Spider-Man* program launched Marvel Productions in 1981 (David and Greenberger 2010, 170). Next came the top-rated *Spider-Man: The Animated Series* between 1994 and 1998 on Fox Kids, which enjoyed four seasons and 65 episodes. It was followed in 1999 by the "least successful" Spider-program, Fox's strange *Spider-Man Unlimited*, which pitted a futuristic Spider-Man against "Counter Earth" mutants. After only 13 episodes, the series died in medias res "with an unresolved cliffhanger" (David and Greenberger 2010, 173). With the success of Columbia's *Spider-Man* feature came 2003's MTV adaptation, *Spider-Man: The New Animated Series*. It boasted CGI production values, Brian Michael Bendis as executive producer, and voice work by Lisa Loeb as Mary Jane and Neal Patrick Harris as the titular Webhead for 13 episodes. The equally witty *Spectacular Spider-Man* ran for two popular seasons from 2008 to 2009 on both Kids' WB and Disney XD. More recently, a Spider-writer's dream team including Brian Michael Bendis, Joe Kelly, Paul Dini, Duncan Rouleau, and Steven T. Seagle has assembled to develop the next *Ultimate Spider-Man* program.

Spider-Man has also made periodic live TV appearances. One of the first involved the PBS educational series *The Electric Company* from 1971 to

1977. Portrayed by Danny Seagren, the strangely mute hero's vocabulary-enhancing battles taught kids courage and language. Marvel cross-marketed the series with a 57-issue young readers' comic, *Spidey Super-Stories* (1974–1982), which lasted five years longer than the TV sketches. Next came the brief 1977 single season CBS program starring Nicholas Hammond as an acrobatic, roof-leaping hero "with clunky wrist bracelets for web-shooters and an even clunkier utility belt around his waist" (David and Greenberger 2010, 168). The show ran for only 12 episodes, which were eventually recut to produce *Spider-Man: The Dragon's Challenge* for foreign markets. Live action Spider-Man fared somewhat better overseas. The bizarre Turkish 1973 action film, *Three Dev Adam* (*Three Giant Men*) includes numerous scenes of Captain America beating on a strangely villainous Spider-Man. Next came the equally weird but absorbing Japanese television series, *Supaidāman*, which ran for 41 episodes between 1978 and 1979. Somewhere between *Godzilla* and *Ultraman*, the show is a free-spirited hodgepodge of giant robots, motor-cross sports, martial arts, and conspiracy clichés all packed into one giant sushi roll of fun. Even in today's Spidey-saturated market, nothing else feels quite like it.

Lastly, it is all too easy to underestimate Spider-Man's importance in computer gaming. From the 1978 *Questprobe* comic book/video game hybrids to the dozens of options and apps now marketed for gaming systems, home computers, and smart phones such as Peter David's *Spider-Man: Edge of Time*, Spider-Man might be the most popular gaming hero of recent years with products designed for every age group across more than a dozen platforms. Filling multiplexes, Broadway stages, and 3D smart screens with the same verve with which he traverses comics panels, our friendly neighborhood Spider-Man remains a consistently cool, perpetually entertaining, and frequently spectacular superhero of global significance.

SUMMARY

Most superfolk possess some paradoxical elements of the Everyman and the *Übermensch*, but Spider-Man provides a poignant dichotomy between the free-spirited, wise-cracking web slinger and the alienated adolescent who negotiates "great power and responsibility" in school, at work, and in the home. Spider-stories play profoundly upon this vivid split between the seemingly carefree Spider-hero and his angst-ridden alter ego. The most substantial Spider-Man tales are loaded with almost Poe-like doublings, doppelgangers, clones, and mutations: quirky animistic villains and angry father figures in the Lee-Ditko tales, dueling blonde and redheaded love interests in the Romita years, contrasting—even parasitic—costumes in the revamps of the 1980s and 1990s, and the chronic onslaught of disappointments and failures that have plagued Peter Parker since his uncle's murder. This emphasis on split and multiple personae is well mirrored in the compulsive progression of multigenerational and now multicultural relaunches and "upgrades." Perhaps Spider-Man's appeal lies not only in his negotiation of psychological struggle and physical conflict, but also in his role as an ever-evolving arbiter of self, fate, and duty to those he loves. As the 1967 TV theme proclaims, "Wealth and fame he ignores./Action is his reward. /To him life is a great big bang up./ Wherever there's a hang-up, you'll find a Spider-Man!"

See also Ditko, Steve; Lee, Stan; Marvel Comics

ESSENTIAL WORKS

Bendis, Brian Michael (w), and Mark Bagley (p). *Ultimate Spider-Man: The Ultimate Collection Vol. 1*. New York: Marvel, 2007.

Lee, Stan (w), Steve Ditko (p), and John Romita (p). *Marvel Masterworks: The Amazing Spider-Man. Vols. 1–4, 10*, and *13*. New York: Marvel Comics Group, 2009–2011.

Stern, Roger (w), Tom Defalco (w), Bill Mantlo (w), John Romita Jr. (p), Ron Frenz (p), Mike Zeck (p), Marie Severin (p), and Al Milgrom (p). *The Amazing Spider-Man: The Origin of the Hobgoblin*. New York: Marvel, 2011.

Straczynski, J. Michael (w), and John Romita Jr. (a). *Amazing Spider-Man by JMS Ultimate Collection, Book 1*. New York: Marvel, 2009.

FURTHER READING

Comicboards.com. "Spiderfan.org: The Unofficial Spider-Man Home Page." http:// spiderfan.org/. Accessed on January 31, 2012.

David, Peter, and Robert Greenberger. *The Spider-Man Vault*. Philadelphia: Running Press, 2010.

Simpson, Paul, Helen Rodiss, and Michaela Bushell, eds. *The Rough Guide to Superheroes*. London: Penguin, 2004.

Daniel F. Yezbick

Spiegelman, Art

Art Spiegelman is the author and illustrator of *Maus*, which in 1992 was the first (and to date only) comic book to ever win a Pulitzer Prize. He has had a long and prolific career as a comics artist, writer, editor, and lecturer. Spiegelman is an iconic member of the underground comix movement from the 1970s, and his work broke boundaries of comics form, themes, values, and expectations. His work includes alternative comics: *Breakdowns* (1978), *Maus* (1986, 1991, 1996), and *In the Shadow of No Towers* (2004); and children's books: *Open Me . . . I'm a Dog* (1997) and *Jack and the Box* (2008). He co-founded and co-edited *RAW* magazine (1980–1991) with his wife Françoise Mouly, as well as *Little Lit*, an annual anthology of alternative children's comics still being produced. He has guest lectured across the globe on the aesthetics and history of comics with "Comix 101," a beginner's guide originally designed for museum curators.

Though autobiographical comics had been around in the decades before Spiegelman wrote *Maus*, it was his work and success that opened the medium up for memoir and biographical narratives in both the comics industry and in American culture. The commercial success of his alternative comics work and the boundaries they broke have marked Spiegelman as an innovator of the comics medium and an iconic member of the comics culture.

HISTORY

Spiegelman was born in Stockholm in 1948 and immigrated to America with his family in 1951. His parents, Vladik and Anya, were Polish Jews who had survived the concentration camps of the Holocaust, and it is their story that forms the basis of *Maus*. A young Spiegelman grew up in the Rego Park neighborhood of Queens, New York, and became inspired by *Mad* magazine as a youth. Spiegelman has one brother, Richieu, who perished as a child during the Holocaust. He attended but did not graduate from Harper College. In 1968 he suffered a nervous breakdown, his mother committed suicide, and he dropped out of college. However, 30 years later in 1995 he was awarded

(AFP/Getty Images)

an honorary doctorate by Binghamton University (previously Harper College) for his efforts in establishing comics as a literary form. From 1971 to 1975 Spiegelman lived in San Francisco and enjoyed the hippie, underground culture. In 1975 he moved back to New York to become a "rooted cosmopolitan" (*Towers* 2004, 1). He has taught classes at the School of Visual Arts in New York and lectured on comics history and aesthetics. He is renowned for smoking like a chimney and often still smokes on stage while giving lectures. Art Spiegelman came into marriage "kicking and screaming" (Spiegelman "Comix 9–11–101") when in 1977 he married Françoise Mouly. The couple have two children, Nadja and Dashiell, who frequently appear in Spiegelman's autobiographical work.

His career began at Topps Bubble Gum Company where he worked for 20 years creating comics, novelties, and collectibles including Garbage Candy, Wacky Packages, and the Garbage Pail Kids. In 1989, Spiegelman left Topps because the company refused to grant artists profit percentages and then proceeded to auction off his original work, which he could not afford to buy (Witek 2007, 259). Along with Topps, Spiegelman has worked commercially for major publications including the *New York Times*, *Playboy*, the *New Yorker*, and *Harper's* magazine. His most notable commercial works are his controversial cover contributions to the *New Yorker*, which include "The Kiss" in February of 1993 and the iconic black on black 9–11 World Trade Towers tribute. "The Kiss" was a Valentine's Day cover in response to the riots in Crown Heights, Brooklyn, between African Americans and Hasidic Jews in the neighborhood. The image is of a Hasidic Jew kissing a black woman, to which there were protests from both sides. However, the majority of his career has been in alternative, underground, or counterculture comics; either editing and contributing to *Arcade* and *RAW* or creating his own works *Breakdowns*, *Maus*, and *In the Shadow of No Towers*.

One of the most celebrated cartoonists of his time, Spiegelman has won dozens of awards including a Pulitzer Prize in 1992. His many honors for *Maus* include the Joel M. Cavior Award for Jewish Writing (1986); a National Book Critics Circle nomination (1986); the Urhunden Prize for Best Foreign Album in Sweden (1988); the Max & Moritz Prize in Erlangen, Germany (1990); the *Los Angeles Times* book prize (1992); the Before Columbus Foundation Award (1992); the Eisner Award for Best Graphic Album (1992); the Harvey Award (1992); the Prize for Best Comic Book at Angoulême International Comics Festival (1993); the Sproing Prize in Norway for Best Foreign Album (1993); and a second Urhunden Prize (1993).

In addition to the awards recognizing *Maus*, he has been honored with a *Playboy* Editorial Award for best comic strip (1982); the Yellow Kid Award in Italy for best comic strip author (1982); the regional design award in *Print* magazine (1983–1985); the Inkpot Award at the **Comic-Con International: San Diego** (1987); a Guggenheim fellowship (2004); and a *New York Times* Book Review Notable Book designation (2004) for *In the Shadow of No Towers*. He was inducted into the **Will Eisner** Hall of Fame in 1999 and named chevalier, Ordre des Arts et des Lettres in France in 2005. His many awards for a lifetime of work are international in scope and contribute to Spiegelman's iconic status.

Spiegelman is hesitant to name any one particular source as an influence, stating, "It becomes a problem when you talk about influences because I think there's lots of stuff that I just picked up as stray strands. . . . It's hard to know" (Monte Smith 2008). The strands that Spiegelman has cited over the years as influencing his work include literary authors like Franz Kafka ("The Metamorphosis"), William Faulkner (*The Sound and the Fury*), Vladimir Nabokov (*Lolita*), and Gertrude Stein (*The Mother of Us All*). He has pulled from avant-garde filmmakers including Ken Jacobs (*Window*), Ernie Gehr (*Serene Velocity*), and Stan Brakhage (*Cat's Cradle*), paying particular interest to nonnarrative experimental film. From popular culture he admired Charlie

Chaplin's (*The Great Dictator*) humor and *The Twilight Zone*'s twisting plot line. From comics he admires *Little Lulu* (Marjorie Henderson Buell), *Krazy Kat* (George Herriman), *Little Nemo* (Winsor McCay), and *Master Race* written and drawn by Bernard Krigstein, to whom he dedicated his first published book, *Breakdowns*. However, Spiegelman has most often cited **Harvey Kurtzman**, creator of *Mad* magazine, as an inspiration, and he has emulated Kurtzman, working as editor, artist, writer, and talent scout (Witek 2007, 154 and 182).

The majority of Spiegelman's works share common themes and methods with his three primary works: *Breakdowns*, *Maus*, and *In the Shadow of No Towers*, which are all autobiographical in nature. He has stated that "disaster is his muse" (Gross 2004). Each book focuses on different traumas in his life: a nervous breakdown, his mother's suicide, his parents' experience of the Holocaust, and the attacks on 9/11 and their aftermath. Themes of memory, ephemera, culture, and survival are addressed. All of his alternative comic books focus on the artist's attempt to "model a memory" (Pollie 2009). Spiegelman addresses issues of fidelity and does not attempt objectivity. Instead he acknowledges, in fact relishes, his subjective experience of the intersection of personal life and historical moments. The styles of these pieces vary greatly. *Maus* is fairly structured with standard comics layout and a clear animal cartoon metaphor. However, the aesthetic of *Breakdowns* and *Towers* is what Spiegelman refers to as "collage comic strips" (Mann et al. 1988). His works attempt to stretch comics form and conventions along with expanding Spiegelman's understanding of his own memory.

IMPACT ON COMICS

A long-time advocate of underground comix, Spiegelman was co-editor of *Arcade* with Bill Griffith in the 1970s. Upon the demise of *Arcade* and with the influence of Françoise Mouly (who would later become his wife) Spiegelman reluctantly agreed to co-edit *RAW*, "a graphix magazine." The publication had 11 issues in as many years (1980–1991), with the first eight issues in a large black-and-white format with slick packaging and "extras" like "City of Terror" trading cards and a flexi-disc of sampled sound. Spiegelman's support of the anthology brought emerging talent from America and Europe to produce work for independent bookstores and the coffee tables of "Damned Intellectuals" (subtitle for *RAW* vol. 2, 1980). Spiegelman believed that *RAW* was "in service of people's personal visions" and created "accessible precious objects" (Mann et al. 1988). *RAW* provided an outlet for artists to create a quality product and to disseminate their graphic work to an audience ready for complex, mature comics. *RAW* printed the serialized version of Spiegelman's *Maus*, which would in later form win a Pulitzer Prize. In the course of

IN THE SHADOW OF NO TOWERS

In the aftermath of the 9/11 attacks, Spiegelman found himself of no use digging through the rubble of the Twin Towers to locate bodies and instead worked on creating an image for the cover of the *New Yorker*. Along with his wife Françoise, he created the iconic black-on-black image that would later become the cover of his *In the Shadow of No Towers* book. Spiegelman talked of the uncanny feeling of walking around New York, continuously looking over his shoulders for the towers that were no longer a part of the skyline. He describes the cover as the shortest comic because in one light there are two towers "illuminated (in) blackness" and with the slightest tilt you are left only with the empty page. The image of the towers is "insisting on their presence as they faded out of view and into memory" (Spiegelman "Comix 9–11–101"). The towers, which were meant to last forever, have become ephemeral, and comics, which were designed to be transitional, have become permanent.

In a lecture entitled "Comix 9–11–101" for the Chicago Humanities Festival two months after the disaster, Spiegelman stated that the World Trade Towers falling was a "surreal, sublime, horrifying, awful, awe filled experience," that left him unable to cope (Spiegelman "Comix 9–11–101"). The first page of *Towers* highlights the "glowing bones" (Inskeep 2004) that haunted Spiegelman as he "was living in September twelfth for almost a year afterwards" (Callahan and Kaspar 2008). Later he would exclaim that "there is a danger in looking" (Spiegelman "Comix 9–11–101"). The image has more impact than the written word, and images can be seared into the memory. His experiences on 9/11 left him vowing to create more comics, which led to *In the Shadow of No Towers*. The book deals with Spiegelman's own issues of posttraumatic stress, paranoia, and disillusionment. The author stated, "From the time the Twin Towers fell, it seems as if I've been living in internal exile. . . . I no longer feel in harmony with American culture" (Witek 2007, 264) equally terrorized by Osama bin Laden and President Bush.

the magazine's run, *RAW* would include works by notable comic artists Sue Coe, Kim Deitch, Richard McGuire, **Alan Moore**, Jacques Tardi, and Yoshiharu Tsuge among many others. Spiegelman's contribution as an editor and artist to *RAW* continued the tradition of underground comix through to the trend of alternative comics.

Underground comix are generally self-published comics that take on social and satirical content and generally fly in the face of the Comics Code Authority (CCA) with explicit sex, violence, and drug use. Underground comix were at their height of popularity in the 1960s and 1970s, and alternative comics grew out of that tradition in the 1980s and beyond. Alternative comics acquired their genre name by being an "alternative" to mainstream comics that tend toward superheroes. Unlike underground comix, they are generally distributed by small presses and break fewer CCA regulations, but still maintain the social awareness of their predecessors. Spiegelman is a major player in the advent of "new wave" or "art comics" which are subgenres of the alternative comics movement. Spiegelman had the audacity to see "comics as a medium of self-expression" (Mann et. al. 1988) and to break the ultimate taboo of the comic industry: he took himself and his art seriously (Pollie 2009) in an age where superheroes were supreme. For his contributions to alternative comics at a time when the genre was under threat of dying, the iconic Spiegelman has made significant impact on the culture of comics.

Spiegelman joined the ranks of autobiographical comics artists alongside Justin Greene (*Binky Brown*) and Harvey Pekar (***American Splendor***) in 1978 with his comic *Breakdowns*, released by Belier Press to "resounding silence" (Gatti 2008). Though *Breakdowns* was not particularly successful in its early incarnation, it was reissued in 2008 with an additional comics introduction and prose afterword. Spiegelman's first book is comprised of collage comics and autobiographical vignettes of his brief nervous breakdown in 1968 and his experience after his mother's suicide the same year. However, the book is more recognized for its formal experiment with breaking down the comics form. The work is considered iconic; Paul Karasik (*City of Glass*) described *Breakdowns* as "the *Citizen Kane* of modern comics. It changed the way cartoonists built comics" (Gatti 2008). An example of this can be seen in the recurring squiggle, a formal motif in the work, in which Spiegelman uses a simple line for various coded functions throughout the comic's vignettes. Erin McGlothlin in her essay describes this formal breakdown as "autobioGRAPHICal re-visioning," with Spiegelman's act of sketching comics as "autobiographical performance" (Chaney 2011, 49). His purposeful manipulation of the comics form to present an ongoing discussion of autobiographical text was groundbreaking.

Breakdowns was Spiegelman's first memoir-style work published as a standalone book, but it was *Maus* that gave him iconic status in the culture of comics and in autobiographical work. *Maus* had a major effect on the reception of comics in the world of mainstream prose literature, awakening many to the potential of comics as a medium for serious subjects. The success of *Maus* opened doors for a new generation of autobiographical alternative comic artists including but certainly not limited to Howard Cruse (*Stuck Rubber Baby*), Seth (*Palookaville*), Marjane Satrapi (*Persepolis*), and Steve Peters (*Chemistry*). Art Spiegelman's work in alternative and autobiographical comics, successful financially and critically, changed the face of the comics industry, broadening the market from superheroes and slapstick to allow for serious and historical work.

In the Shadow of No Towers is Spiegelman's most recent autobiographical work, a memoir about his experience during and after September 11, 2001. It was released initially as "weekly" full-page installments overseas in *Die Zeit*, a German newspaper, and later, in the United States, *Forward* magazine published the series. The large-page book was published in 2004 on pressboard by Pantheon. It was Spiegelman's attempt to "sort out what I saw as opposed to the images from the TV that were replacing what I saw" (Gross 2004). The book is comprised of 10 double-page-spread comics, 7 plates, and 4 pages of prose, in full color. It explores Spiegelman's own experiences, paranoia, and dissatisfaction with the current political climate. Several of the comics use the collage aesthetic developed in *Breakdowns*, some the style of *Maus*, and finally the plates are selected early comics from the 1900s reprinted in a new context. These comics include *Bringing Up Father* (1913–2000) created by George McManus, *Little Nemo* (1905–1914) created by Winsor McCay, and *Kin-der-Kids* (1906) created by Lyonel Feininger. These old comics were a comfort to Spiegelman in the days after 9/11 and, when retextualized in *In the Shadow of No Towers*, form a unique political commentary bursting from our past.

IMPACT ON AMERICAN CULTURE

The ramifications of Art Spiegelman's work on American culture can be most notably seen through *Maus* and the Pulitzer Prize Spiegelman earned in 1992 for the work. *Maus* brought comics into regard as serious literature, giving the art form more credence in academic and popular circles. His work, particularly his long-form work, is noted as having set the bar for mature comics in current American society. Terry Gross of National Public Radio stated that "sophisticated, funny, adult comics are a given in American culture, book-length comics are a given." She asked Spiegelman, "What do you think about being one of the people to start that?" His response spoke to his discovery of a "wonderful moment for comics to find a different slot in American culture to live and breathe in" (Gross 2004). Though he is humble about any connection he may have to the current state of affairs of alternative comics in American culture, fellow artists and popular press attribute much of the success of this genre of comics to him. In 2005 Art Spiegelman was named one of *Time* magazine's 100 most influential people in the world. Spiegelman's entry in the article is written by Marjane Satrapi, author of *Persepolis*, who was inspired to become a cartoonist by *Maus*. She stated that Spiegelman "showed me that comics can be more than superhero stories" (2005, 57). Spiegelman's contributions to comic arts have changed the perceptions of comics in American culture.

THE SPECIAL OLYMPICS PULITZER

Art Spiegelman first believed the announcement for his 1992 Pulitzer Prize to be a joke. However, his selection for a Pulitzer was no mistake. Submissions for a Pulitzer Prize go through two committees. The first is the Nominating Committee made up of hundreds of jurors who whittle down thousands of submissions to no more than three nominations per category. Those nominations are then sent to the Pulitzer Prize Board for final selection. The board is comprised of 18 members from various backgrounds including a myriad of academic disciplines and professional journalists. The selection process is long and arduous, and earning a Pulitzer Prize is a great accomplishment.

Despite the magnitude of the award or maybe because of it, Spiegelman is often quoted as associating his Pulitzer *Special* Prize in Arts and Letters with winning the literary "Special Olympics" (Witek 2007, 33). The Special Award Pulitzer has been accorded to historic popular culture icons including: Alex Haley for *Roots* (1977); Theodore Seuss Geisel, more widely known as Dr. Seuss (1984); science fiction author Ray Bradbury (2007); and musician Bob Dylan (2008), a group of internationally known artists and icons in which Spiegelman is honored to be a member. His win changed the way the world looked at comics; it also changed the way Spiegelman looked at the world. Jules Feiffer, who won a Pulitzer in Political Cartooning in 1986 (a category introduced in 1922), told Spiegelman, "This is either going to ruin your life, or it's a license to kill" (Witek 2007, 247) and Spiegelman chose the latter. He has stated that the Pulitzer win has given him the latitude to "propose projects that would otherwise not be heard out . . . and that people take me seriously when I suggest an absolutely insane project" (Witek 2007, 162). The financial success of *Maus* has afforded Spiegelman the luxury of creative freedom.

A graphic novel winning a Pulitzer Prize had major ramifications for Spiegelman as well as American culture. According to Martin Rowson, "Comix, mostly thanks to Spiegelman's example, went from being exuberantly and experimentally childish and druggy to being often obsessively introspective. . . . Because that worked commercially, it has now become the established default setting for modern American graphic novelists" (2008, 25). *Maus*'s success, as seen in its Pulitzer win, is an iconic moment in the shifting trend of America's perception of the comic art form. *Maus* is a moment in comic history in which we take notice of comics growing up.

Through the years a variety of individuals have described Spiegelman's impact on American culture through his comics. Joseph Witek says, "Most observers agree that no single person has done more to achieve cultural repositioning of the comics medium than Art Spiegelman" (2007, ix). His work has opened up autobiographical comics as a form of literature in academia. Charles W. Hatfield states, "Arguably the most urgent and complex of autobiographical comics, and certainly the best known among American readers, is Art Spiegelman's celebrated *Maus*" (2005, 139). *Maus* changed the way academics and popular press viewed the comic industry, opening doors for later work and rereading of classic works.

His advocacy for comics as an educator in classrooms and in the public eye is well documented. He is an ambassador for the comics art form and has made a huge impact in the shift in the public opinion of comics, which was once under intense scrutiny for contributing to the delinquency of minors in the 1950s. Touted by many, "Art Spiegelman has almost single-handedly brought comic books out of the toy closet and onto the literature shelves" (The Barclay Agency 2009). Though the majority of the public praise and recognition are due to Spiegelman's alternative comics work like *Maus* and *Breakdowns*, his impact on American culture through his more commercial work cannot be forgotten. "Spiegelman has become one of *The New Yorker*'s most sensational artists, in recent years drawing illustrations for covers that are meant not just to be plainly understood but also to reach up and tattoo your eyeballs with images once unimaginable in the magazine of old moneyed taste" (Mitchell 1994). Even his oft-forgotten early work with Topps creating the Garbage Pail Kids molded a generation, much like his inspiration, *Mad* magazine.

Through *RAW* Spiegelman helped to disseminate underground comics. *RAW* also served comic and American culture by discovering new talents and providing established counterculture comic artists a place to publish their work. An advocate for comic artists and the medium itself, Spiegelman has spoken around the world about the history and aesthetics of comics in "Comix 101" and the state of comics as a cultural form in "What the %@&*! Happened to Comics" lectures. His own work has been the subject of an exhibit at the Museum of Modern Art in New York, several academic books, and countless articles. He has appeared on television as a guest star in several series including *The Simpsons* ("Husband and Knives," 2007) and documentary films including *Comic Book Confidential* (1988), *Will Eisner: Portrait of a Sequential Artist* (2007), *Comic Book Literacy* (2009), *Art Spiegelman, Traits de mémoire* (2010), and *Cartoon College* (2012). His advocacy and devotion to educating the general public to the possibilities of comics as an artistic form have contributed to America's changed perception of the comic industry as a whole, and alternative comics in particular.

Spiegelman's work spans decades with a variety of topics and themes; however, he is consistent in challenging many traditional American values and mores. His work generally focuses on the individual, whether that person is himself, as in *Breakdowns* and *In the Shadow of No Towers*, or Vladek, his father, in *Maus*. Despite the focus on individuality, which is consistent with American values, there is no celebration of the individual in his works. Instead the American focus on individuality is depicted as neurotic, even at the risk of painting Spiegelman himself as unstable. He bucks traditional puritan morality in the majority of his work, with no clearly marked good and evil. Even *Maus*, which is highly codified with mice for Jews and cats for Nazis, often muddles the distinction of good and evil, with characters on either side complicating the metaphor. Clearly, Spiegelman views the events of the Holocaust as evil, yet his work does not try to create a moral message. He finds it "a cheap shot to try to give any moral to it [the Holocaust]. It would be kind of diminishing what happened" (Witek 2007, 141). Instead he focuses on the subjective experience and memory of his father, complicating the world of black-and-white comics, sketching a moral grey on his pages.

Though the majority of his work bucks complacency among American readers, compliments of Spiegelman's own paranoid tendencies and his early comics education in *Mad* magazine and underground comics, his work does promote certain American values of ethical equality and pragmatism. *In the Shadow of No Towers* and *Breakdowns* are particularly susceptible to Spiegelman's own inherited paranoia; however, it is these two works that also encourage free thinking along with pragmatism. This can be seen with the recurring theme in the art of packing, learned from Spiegelman's father— a practical skill, ingrained with the need to flee that many minority groups feel. Spiegelman explores the metaphor of packing while addressing issues of inequality and oppression that are often whitewashed with the American ideal of ethical equality that is not yet achieved. *Maus* also inherently spends a great deal of time on issues of equality and pragmatism, given the nature of the work. It depicts a time in world history in which we are confronted with systemic prejudice, a reminder that we must continuously strive for the American ideal of ethical equality.

SUMMARY

Art Spiegelman is an iconic comics artist first and foremost for his Pulitzer Prize–winning opus *Maus*, in which he brings an alternative autobiography with a "metaphor meant to shed like a snakeskin" (Mann et al. 1988) to a mainstream audience. Through *Maus* Spiegelman changed the face of the comics industry as well as the perception of comics in American culture. His frank expression of complex, traumatic, and emotional experiences has changed the way in which Americans look at comics. As Spiegelman is fond of saying, he broke the oldest taboo of comics, "taking one's self seriously" (Pollie 2009), and likewise the American public has take him and comics in general, seriously.

His work with *RAW* has fulfilled a need for emerging alternative comics artists to publish their work, launching new voices into a medium growing with adult issues, themes, and styles. *RAW* is an iconic publication that changed the audience for underground comics. Spiegelman's additional work in *Breakdowns* and *In the Shadow of No Towers* has experimented with the comics form, condensing and breaking down comics conventions, creating a collage form that requires rereading to fully appreciate. His incorporation of lived history means that he is greatly influenced by the culture in which he lives, even if this culture is ultimately rejected.

In addition to his direct work in the comics medium, Spiegelman has been an advocate for comics in the media and in the classroom. Lecturing around the world with "Comix 101," a beginners' guide to alternative comics. Spiegelman has provided humor, humility, and a quirky charm to the public persona of comics. He has been a prominent voice in legitimizing comics as a field of study with a history, language, and aesthetic of its own, proving comics to be a medium with an impact on American culture and values.

See also Kurtzman, Harvey; *Mad*; *Maus*; *RAW*

ESSENTIAL WORKS

Spiegelman, Art. *Breakdowns: Portrait of the Artist as a Young %@&*!* New York: Pantheon Books, 1978.
Spiegelman, Art. *In the Shadow of No Towers*. New York: Pantheon Books, 2004.
Spiegelman, Art. *Maus: A Survivor's Tale*. New York: Pantheon Books, 1996.

FURTHER READING

Chaney, Michael A. *Graphic Subjects: Critical Essays on Autobiography and Graphic Novels*. Madison: University of Wisconsin Press, 2011.
Witek, Joseph. *Art Spiegelman: Conversations*. Jackson: University Press of Mississippi, 2008.

Tanya D. Zuk

Steranko, Jim

James (Jim) Steranko (November 5, 1938–) is an American comics writer/artist/historian best known for his work on **Marvel Comics'** *Strange Tales* and spin-off *Nick Fury: Agent of S.H.I.E.L.D.* series. His inclusion of modernist art techniques and contemporary graphic design was revolutionary for sequential storytelling at the time and has influenced a generation of writers and artists in the years since. Steranko's work has made an indelible impression on the development of the comics medium despite a brief body of comics work that is limited mostly to cover images and only a handful of complete stories.

HISTORY

Steranko was born into working-class Reading, Pennyslvania, the son of a coalminer and tinsmith and raised during the Great Depression. Despite Steranko's father having musical talent, the elder Steranko was never wholly supportive of his son's artistic talent, confused as to why his son would not want to work in a factory like the rest of his family. The younger Steranko, however, was determined to make a career in art, possibly as an architect, and collected recyclables, particularly newspapers, to pay for his art supplies. It was through this exposure that Steranko was influenced by the work of Sunday comic strip artists Milton Caniff (*Terry and the Pirates, Steve Canyon*), Alex Raymond (*Flash Gordon*), Hal Foster (*Prince Valiant*), and Chester Gould (*Dick Tracy*), all of whom he credits for inspiring his love for the medium and his storytelling techniques. Steranko also found a muse in Saturday matinees and comic books given to him by his uncle, in particular Frank Robbins's *Johnny Hazard* and Wayne Boring's *Superman*. While only in his midteens, Steranko began to draw simple (though highly advanced for his age) comics layouts.

After high school, Steranko's first work in illustration was as a freelance artist—sign painter, pamphlet illustrator, and later the art director for an ad agency—but his interest in comics led to a visit to **DC Comics'** New York offices and a chance meeting with Julie Schwartz, then the company's **Batman** group editor. Schwartz gave the full script and original artwork work for an

Adam Strange story to the aspiring artist, saying, "If you study this carefully and figure out how even one half of it was done, you'll be a pretty good comics artist" (Robertson 2009, 1). Steranko's first work came in 1966 through Harvey Comics' short-lived *Spyman*, a character whose adventures Steranko created, wrote, and drew.

The following year, Steranko visited Paramount Studios to pitch an animated television program based around another spy creation, "Special Agent X." After being turned down, Steranko modified the aborted proposal to shop around to comics publishers, but was turned down by several. Steranko then met with editor-in-chief Roy Thomas in the Marvel Comics offices. Thomas was impressed by the samples and introduced him to publisher **Stan Lee**. Lee, upon gauging the work himself, asked Steranko what book he wanted to work on. Already suited to the genre and a fan of both the book and its then-artist, **Jack Kirby**, Steranko requested the "Nick Fury: Agent of S.H.I.E.L.D." feature in *Strange Tales*, sharing page space with the adventures of Doctor Strange. Steranko did finishing pencils over Kirby's breakdowns for three issues before taking over with full art on issue #154 (1967).

Steranko continued on the adventures of Nick Fury, plotting stories with Roy Thomas scripting, eventually taking full writing and art chores, a rare handover of responsibility in the early days of Marvel. Steranko's experimentalism brought new popularity to the title as it outgrew its feature status to become a standalone title in 1968. Soon, however, clashes erupted between Steranko and Marvel editorial over various elements of the series direction, from costume changes and storyline direction to the very philosophies of its main character. Steranko quit the book entirely when a fill-in issue was inserted into the middle of the seminal "Who Is Scorpio?" story arc, a move that he felt severely disrupted the story's flow. After a three-issue run on *Captain America*, a handful of fill-ins on *The X-Men* (including designing their classic title logo) and a number of classic covers (notably *Hulk King-Sized Special* #1), Steranko's days with Marvel were over.

Steranko's career, however, found its focus again in freelance work. He had never truly left, having continued to do film and commercial artwork during his tenure in comics. It was this moonlighting that allowed Steranko the freedom to argue passionately without fear of reprisal against editorial changes in his work. His cover work continued, too, but in the realm of book-cover illustration for various fantasy and pulp publishers.

Over the past three decades, Steranko has continued to occasionally dip back into sequential storytelling, most notably in 1976 with the pulp-detective-inspired *Chandler: Red Tide*. The creator-owned story was meant to be the first mass-marketed graphic novel, but many academics consider *Red Tide* an illustrated novel instead (the quibbling point being the lack of comics' traditional balloons and captioning where *Red Tide* is prose-on-picture). *Red Tide* is most notable for Steranko's calculated use of the Golden Mean

ESCAPE ARTIST

Jim Steranko has also served as the inspiration for two comic-based characters. According to Jack Kirby biographer Mark Evanier (2011) and Pulitzer Prize–winning author Michael Chabon (Raymond 2011), both DC Comics' Mister Miracle and *The Adventure of Kavalier and Klay*'s the Escapist were inspired by Steranko's early career as an escape artist.

Steranko's father was an amateur magician and had a talent for sleight of hand tricks he had learned from books, which he would later share with his son. "Whenever I could, I'd dig out those books and read them and eventually began to do magic and that led into escapes. Escapes meaning that when I was 15, 16, and 17, I was breaking out of jails, out of strait jackets, and handcuffs, out of safes, and the bottom of a river. I did TV shows and Elks and the American Legion" (Green 1971, 26). His first escapes were inspired by the image of his father emerging from collapsed coal mines.

While in his late teens, Sterakno traveled the carnival circuit as an illusionist, performing tricks like fire eating and the Hindu bed of nails in addition to his escape artistry. His repertoire included being hung upside-down while straitjacketed, handcuffed, entombed, strapped to rotating Ferris wheels and submerged while tied in bags and locked into steamer trunks.

Steranko believes his comics work and escape artistry are connected in a profound way: "With some escapes . . . death is an imminent factor, bringing the metaphysics of eternity with it, especially if one has a philosophy of afterlife or reincarnation. Since comics frequently deal with their reality, not ours, metaphysics is part of the architecture. I've experimented many times with the concept of transcending that reality to explore ideas at a higher or more sophisticated level" (Von Busack 2002, 12).

in image-to-prose placement, a continuation of his experimentalism in the medium. Despite its lack of commercial success, *Red Tide*'s publisher, Pyramid Books, would go on to hire Steranko to do painted covers for reprints of *The Shadow*, a character close to the artist's heart.

From 1981 to 1982, Steranko enjoyed a year-long contract with the magazine **Heavy Metal**, serializing the adaptation of Peter Hyam's sci-fi adventure film *Outland*.

In 1984 and at the request of DC editor-in-chief Julie Schwartz, Steranko joined an all-star group of creators in contributing to the *Superman* title's 400th issue. The short story he both wrote and fully illustrated would influence a young Mark Millar who would later go on to write the highly successful *Red Son* reimagining of Superman, the ending of which paralleled Steranko's contribution.

He has maintained a rigorous working life, writing a two-volume history of comics that is considered by many to be the premier retelling of the industry's early period, published by his independent publishing venture, Supergraphics. Steranko has continued to serve as mentor and teacher to a generation of artists through his multiple publications on art technique and storytelling. A career retrospective co-authored with science-fiction guru Harlan Ellison, titled *STERANKO*, was released in November 2011.

IMPACT ON COMICS

Steranko has claimed influence by a variety of artists on the development of his work, in both the comics and contemporary art communities. Among his comics peers, Steranko has named Kirby, Frank Robbins, Joe Maneely, Wally Wood, Al Williamson and **Neal Adams** as those who both taught and challenged him. The work of painters Bernard Kirgstein (who also dabbled in comics), Peter Max, and Salavdor Dali would make their way into his work as well; Dali most noticeably in the formless, surrealist *Captain America* #111 (1969).

In Steranko's short tenure in comics work, he incorporated a jazzy, free-flowing style that often broke the traditional rules for sequential storytelling. He wrote the first wordless and captionless sequence in *Nick Fury, Agent of S.H.I.E.L.D.* #1 and in the following issue, creatively using montage to communicate a sex scene that got by the censors at the conservative Comics Code Authority. Inspired by Kirby's advent of the two-page spread, Steranko created the first four-page spread in *Strange Tales* #167 (1968). During a 2010 interview, Steranko summed up his style: "[W]hat I attacked were moldering, brittle, and fatigued anachronisms that should have been hacked away years before . . . because comics had become apathetic and had the stink of decay on them. Good or bad, I brought a volley of new ideas to the form and those ideas opened the door for others, such as [Bill] Sienkiewicz and [Dave] McKean" (Giles 2001, 15).

His influence on other comics creators is staggering in relation to his output of pure comics work. Those artists who have publicly described his work as being formative to their own styles include: J. H. Williams III (*Batwoman, Promethea*), Paul Gulacy (*Sabre, Batman*), Mario Hernandez (*Love and Rockets*), Jim Starlin (*Warlock, Dreadstar*), David Lloyd (*V for Vendetta*), David Mack (*Kabuki*), Jerry Ordway (*Superman*), Jimmy Palmiotti (*The Monolith*), Adam Kubert (*Uncanny X-Men, Superman*), and Andy Kubert (*Batman, 1602*), among numerous others.

Likewise, much of his work is so iconic that artists still pay homage to it. His covers for *Nick Fury: Agent of S.H.I.E.L.D.* (1968), *Captain America* #111 (1969), and *The Incredible Hulk Special* #1 (1968) have been so recycled that they have become, in their own way, memetic and self-referential. A compilation of Steranko's covers and their variations can be found at his official website *The Drawings of Steranko* (Robertson 2009, "Homages"). It was for his lifetime of contribution to the medium that Steranko was inducted as a member of the Will Eisner Comic Book Hall of Fame's Class of 2006.

IMPACT ON AMERICAN CULTURE

In addition to his comics work, Steranko has also worked as conceptual artist in Hollywood, for directors Steven Spielberg, George Lucas, and Francis Ford Coppola, among others. It was working for Spielberg and Lucas in the formative stages of *Raiders of the Lost Ark* that Steranko gave, perhaps, his most significant contribution to American pop culture. Lucas and Spielberg were both familiar with Steranko's work and invited the artist to illustrate several scenes from the script to help sell the movie to studio Paramount Pictures. "The function of a production illustrator," Steranko explains, "is to visualize the concepts, characters and key scenes. . . . That starting point . . . serves as a graphic guide to help the director stage powerful and memorable sequences" (Walentis 1981, 66)

Although Lucas suggested a number of key scenes for Steranko to illustrate, the director essentially gave the artist carte blanche to work in his own style. Steranko's contributions included the first image of Indiana Jones, with his whip, battered hat and leather jacket, and pouch belt across his chest. "The film had not yet been cast," Steranko said. "Indy's facial characteristics were left to me and . . . Harrison Ford appears almost exactly like the figure in the painting" (Walentis 1981, 69).

SUMMARY

Despite the fact that Jim Steranko's last complete work in the comics industry was published a quarter of a century ago, the dynamism and grace he brought to the page continue to resonate with today's generation of writers and artists. His sense of experimentalism challenged the traditional notions of what was possible, or even appropriate, in the comics medium. Scripting and illustrative techniques he pioneered during his all-too-brief tenure continue to be used today and, indeed, are now so prevalent in contemporary comics that their predominance in the canon belies the furor they originally inspired. If anything, Steranko's passion for the form and strict adherence to his own artistic ideals in the light of censorship are what makes him truly iconic.

See also Captain America; *Heavy Metal*; Marvel Comics

ESSENTIAL WORKS

Steranko, Jim (w, p), and Joe Sinnott (i). "If Death Be My Destiny!" *Strange Tales* #116 (1968), Marvel Comics. Reprinted in *Nick Fury: Agent of S.H.I.E.L.D.* New York: Marvel Comics, 2001.

Steranko, Jim (w, p), and Joe Sinnott (i). "Tomorrow You Live, Tonight I Die!" *Captain America* #111 (1968), Marvel Comics. Reprinted in *Essential Captain America, Vol. 2.* New York: Marvel Comics, 2010.

Steranko, Jim (w, p), Joe Sinnott (i), Frank Giacoia (i), Dan Adkins (i), and John Tartaglione (i). "Who Is Scorpio?" *Nick Fury, Agent of S.H.I.E.L.D.* #1–#3, #5 (1968), Marvel Comics. Reprinted in *Nick Fury: Who Is Scorpio?* New York: Marvel Comics, 2001.

FURTHER READING

Spurlock, J. David, Harlan Ellison, and Jim Steranko. *STERANKO*. Coral Gables, FL: Vanguard Productions, 2011.

Steranko, Jim. *Steranko Design: Hypertyp*. Coral Gables, FL: Vanguard Productions, 2011.

Steranko, Jim. *The Steranko History of Comics*. 2 vols. Seattle: SuperGraphics, 1972.

Jared Hegwood

Supergirl

The most iconic thing Supergirl ever did was die.

The *Crisis on Infinite Earths* is a watershed event in comic book history, and the iconic image from the *Crisis* is the cover to issue #7 (1985), **Superman** cradling his dead cousin Supergirl. This image symbolically announces the end of the DC continuity that had been in place since 1938.

The second most iconic thing Supergirl ever did was pop out of a rocket. This image adorned the cover of *Action Comics* #252 (1959), and it symbolized one of the most colorful and longest lasting eras in the history of Superman—the Weisinger expansion of the Superman mythos. Mort Weisinger was the editor of the Superman line of **DC Comics** from 1958 to 1970. He wanted to add some depth and variation to the world of Superman. Though Supergirl is only one aspect of this expansion, she is the most enduring and the most representative. By the mid-1970s, much of what Weisinger established had ceased to factor into Superman stories, but Supergirl persisted.

HISTORY

Like her cousin Superman, Kara Zor-El is a survivor of the destruction of Krypton. She grows up in Argo City, which luckily happens to be domed and even more luckily remains intact as Krypton explodes. When a meteor shower spells doom for Argo, Zor-El (brother to Superman's father Jor-El) builds a rocket to send his teenaged daughter to Earth. Kara's parents had been observing Earth for some time and know of Superman. They make her a costume, which derives from his so that he will accept her as Kryptonian.

For about 10 years *Supergirl* is a backup feature in *Action Comics*. These were light tales of Kara correcting relatively minor wrongs or getting herself out of trouble of her own making. Kara resides at Midvale Orphanage and takes on the guise of Linda Lee. She has many nonthreatening misadventures (which Supergirl herself eventually comes to describe as "mild") such as surreptitiously helping other kids get adopted, transforming into a superbaby, or dealing with Streaky, her supercat. The typical affected-by-kryptonite stories occurred as Supergirl found ways for Linda to *not* get adopted—because it would be harder to keep her identity a secret, and she does not want any loved ones as they could possibly be harmed. Eventually Supergirl gets tired of being cooped up in the orphanage, but Superman keeps insisting she stay there as his "secret weapon" ready to take over should something happen to him.

Perhaps keeping Linda Lee stuck in that orphanage meant story ideas had quickly dried up. Fred and Edna Danvers adopt her in *Action* #279 (1961), and she is henceforth known as Linda Lee Danvers. While her name changes, the nature of her adventures do not. Six months later in *Action* #285 (1962), Superman introduces Supergirl to the world after deciding she has learned to use her powers wisely. While this broadens the backdrop of her stories, they are much the same as before. The threats are mostly to Supergirl and not the world at large as they are primarily "How can this be?" types of stories. Supergirl is made to look as though she lost her powers, is either betrayed by or betraying her family, has suddenly become bad, or is victim of the traditional strange bodily transformation (becoming gigantic, developing an extra head, etc.). Eventually it is revealed her parents Zor-El and Alura survived Krypton's destruction. *Supergirl* develops a more genuine arc where Linda is torn between her adoptive parents and her birth parents. *Supergirl* also has the added element of love interests such as normal guy Dick Malverne, future boy Braniac 5 (of the Legion of Super-Heroes), half-fish Jerro of Atlantis, and all-horse Comet, when he was in the human form of Bill Starr.

Action #318 (1964) sees Linda graduate high school and move on to Stanhope College. Then in *Adventure Comics* #381 (1969) she graduates to lead into the feature. While *Adventure* is touted as Supergirl's book, she often shares it with lesser-known characters like Zatanna or Animal Man. Often there are two short Supergirl stories rather than an issue-length one. This gives the writers less opportunity to develop the character, and she battles the usual array of mad scientists, robots, and aliens as well as the omnipresent threats to her superpowers and secret identity.

Supergirl is given some villains of her own, namely, Black Flame and Starfire. Linda gets a nemesis too, when Nasthalthia (known as "Nasty"), the niece of Lex Luthor, is introduced. She is there to be a hypercompetitive, self-centered, vindictive thorn in Linda's side, as well as help Luthor carry out his schemes and occasionally attempt to prove Linda is Supergirl. During this time the editors attempt to create some interest with a series of different costumes, most of which were based on suggestions sent in by readers.

With *Adventure* #406 (1971), Linda graduates from Stanhope and starts a television career at station KSF in San Francisco. Finally Supergirl is a young adult, and the nature of her stories change. The stories have a stronger soap opera element than did most DC titles, and her adversaries are more potent and threatening at long last. Supergirl's gig headlining *Adventure* ends with issue #424 (1972) as Linda quits station KSF and enrolls as a graduate drama major

ALL IN THE FAMILY

Supergirl may be the most well-known member of the "Superman Family" to have her own feature, but she is not the only character in Superman's supporting cast to spin off into a series of one's own. Of course, all manner of Superman's friends have had their turn in the spotlight starting with *Superman's Pal Jimmy Olsen* in 1954. Others within "the House of El" with their own features include not only cousin Supergirl, but their shared cousin Van-Zee, who disguised himself as "Nightwing" and patrolled the Kryptonian city of Kandor. Even Superman's Kryptonian father, Jor-El, has had his own feature stories, as has the family pet, Krypto the Superdog.

at Vandyre University. Beginning in 1972, she stars in her own title, *Supergirl*. This too is structured like *Adventure* with multiple stories in one issue, limiting the chances for depth and development. The title is cancelled after 10 issues, and Supergirl goes on to co-star in *Superman Family*, where Linda promptly moves to Florida to be a counselor at a progressive school. About three and a half years later she moves to New York where she becomes the star of a soap opera. However, that career only lasts 15 issues, and eventually DC again tried Supergirl in her own title with *The Daring New Adventures of Supergirl* (1982). Linda moves to Chicago and once again becomes a graduate student, this time in psychology. Unfortunately, daring, new, or not, this *Supergirl* only lasts 23 issues. While Supergirl was thought of fondly and sustained regular appearances since 1959, it was clear she was not popular enough to hold her own in a series entitled *Supergirl*. The plentiful changes in jobs and cities suggest that after 25 years, DC did not really know what to do with this character. Perhaps this made what was soon to come an easier decision to reach.

In 1985, DC decided to consolidate its multiple Earths. The agent for this was the historic comic book maxiseries *Crisis on Infinite Earths*. In issue #7, Kara makes the ultimate sacrifice during an assault on the series' antagonist, the Anti-Monitor. No doubt fans of Supergirl were dejected and depressed over the loss of such a loveable character. Always the optimistic supporter of her older cousin, she came to represent the girl next door who just happened to be able to toss a battleship. This is best expressed by Superman in the aforementioned *Action* #285: "Physically she is the mightiest female of all time! But at heart she is as gentle and sweet and is [*sic*] quick to tears as any ordinary girl! I guess that's why everyone who meets her loves her!" The cover of issue #7 became the quintessential image of the *Crisis* and the most noteworthy event of Kara's existence. Readers had to get used to a DCU without a Supergirl.

For three years.

Other Supergirls

Although Supergirl had ceased to exist in DC continuity (as a result of the *Crisis*, history was changed; Kara Zor-El never existed), it did not take long for DC to decide to once again use the name "Supergirl." Time-Warner (the corporation that owned DC Comics) had lucrative deals involving products that featured their characters. T-Shirts, games, coloring books, and other products too numerous to count were marketed; as a brand, "Supergirl" needed to be kept "alive."

The first one shows up in *Superman*, volume 2, #21 (1988). She is known simply as "Matrix," so-called because she is created from the "life-matrix" of a human. When Matrix's home world is destroyed, she comes to Superman's Earth, meets him, and is sent to reside at the boot camp for virtuous living, the Kent farm in Smallville, where she takes the name Mae Kent.

After her initial appearances, Mae goes into a self-imposed exile. When she returns, she serves as part of Superman's supporting cast. Eventually, she is given her own monthly series written by Peter David (*Supergirl*, volume 4, 1996–2003). Here David introduces us to a different Linda Danvers. The use of the name is a tip of the hat to the original Supergirl. The "new" Linda Danvers is depressed and has become involved with a demonic cult. This cult turns out to have its eyes on Linda for a ritual sacrifice. Matrix discovers it and stops the ritual, but Linda is left dying. As the two touch, Matrix merges her biological protoplasm with Linda's. Linda is saved and, in a spiritual sense, so is Matrix. Matrix had always felt incomplete. She was not quite human, was not quite a Kent. But now she had found a literal soul-mate, and together they become Supergirl.

Soon they discover Matrix's sacrifice has caused Supergirl to gain the powers and the mantle of the Earth-Born Angel of Fire. This means not only is she superstrong and can fly, she can also project telepathic "psi-blasts" and when she really needs to be dramatic, she sports a pair of fiery wings.

Later still, Linda is separated from Matrix, and the character is depowered. A new costume is created for this iteration, designed to reflect the fashion sense of teenage girls (or at least an assumption of it). This meant a plain bare-midriff T-shirt, a short red cape, a blue skirt, white gloves, and a black hair band. Linda goes on a quest with her travelling companions, the former demon Buzz and Mary Marvel, to find the fallen Earth Angel. During the climactic battle, a different Earth-Angel merges with Matrix, and they give Linda the powers she and Matrix had before the split. Soon after, Linda meets the supposedly nonexistent Kara Zor-El. The story involves Linda trying to sacrifice herself instead of Kara, but to no avail. The last issue of *Supergirl* volume 4 was #80 (2003), making it the longest lasting Supergirl series to date.

As Linda/Supergirl was being phased out, DC introduced yet another permutation of Supergirl. This is Cir-El, the future daughter of Clark Kent, and she looks very different from all the other Supergirls (short, black instead of long, blonde hair). It turns out she is not really Clark's daughter but rather a human who has been infused with Kryptonian DNA by Brainiac. When she realizes her presence means a dystopian future for Earth, she sacrifices herself so that she will be removed from existence, history, and continuity.

Upon examining the tale of Cir-El, one sees there is a common occurrence in the sagas of all of the Supergirls. Most of them either did or attempted to sacrifice their lives. During the battle that erupted after Linda tracked down Matrix (*Supergirl* #74, 2002), Linda intends to sacrifice herself so a character named "Twilight" can live. Also, Linda plans to take Kara's role in the Crisis and die in her stead. Even though she does not die, she is willing to and takes actions that she thinks insure her death. Cir-El hurls herself into a "time portal" to prevent her very existence. It is Kara, though, who makes the most iconic sacrifice in DC Comics history, and it results in her death.

Could this be a coincidence? What is it about Supergirl that makes her such a candidate for noble sacrifice? The key word is *noble*. There is a nobility about Kara, Mae, Linda, and perhaps even Cir-El. While they possess kindness (Kara), naiveté (Mae), and youth (Linda), these qualities do not make any character inherently noble; however, they all have humanity and a strength of character that makes a sacrifice by someone with these qualities more moving and dramatic. Does an image of Superman cradling Wonder Woman have the same impact as one of him cradling Supergirl? The death of this innocent, cheerful, optimistic character simply packs more of a wallop.

Three years after Cir-El, a new Supergirl would debut in the pages of *Superman/Batman*. This too was Kara Zor-El of Krypton. Despite the appearance of the original Kara Zor-El in Peter David's comic, DC still insists she never existed, and this Kara is a separate entity from the original. She is noticeably different from the original in that she is feistier, more independent, and occasionally petulant. She lives in Metropolis with Lana Lang and poses as her niece, Linda. Kara is treated as more of a fish out of water, and much of the character development concerns her getting to know her powers and finding her place on Earth. This is a far cry from the "superheroes-for-girls" approach of the Weisinger era. Kara Zor-El II (as she is called in DC's Wikia) has given fans a Kara with more depth and complexity.

IMPACT ON COMICS

Unlike other comic book icons, Supergirl's impact is harder to ascertain. She is not the first teenage female hero, nor is she the first superpowered relative of a hero (Mary Marvel beats her on both counts). No genre-defining events happen in her solo stories. The only major historical event to occur in these is her arrival. With Supergirl, it is the role she fills—the seemingly ordinary girl who is extraordinary. She is the young woman who is simply nice, sweet, considerate, caring. No other female character in the DCU so completely and consistently reflects these qualities. The others tend to either be more serious, short-fused, spoiled, cynical, or smart-mouthed.

The qualities Kara possessed are how she put the *hero* in *superhero*. Her impact has been to be the presence that embodies those qualities. In *Crisis* #7 the second Doctor Light is inspired by Kara while witnessing her sacrifice: "Supergirl doesn't stop, she keeps hitting him, fighting him, as if she doesn't care about herself at all. She is a hero . . . totally selfless and concerned only with others, while I have wasted my life away my life with selfishness. No more, Supergirl, no more! Whatever happens here, you've shown me the truth!" When Kara dies, her absence is felt throughout the fictional superhero community and by many fans as well.

IMPACT ON AMERICAN CULTURE

There was a *Supergirl* movie in 1984 directed by Jeannot Swarc, starring Helen Slater, and produced by Alexander and Ilya Salkind, who had developed the popular *Superman* movie franchise. The spin-off was a commercial and critical failure. Laura Vandervoort portrayed Kara on *Smallville* (Season 7, 2007–2008, and guest appearances thereafter), but these made little to no impact. However, there is definitely a fan base to whom Supergirl speaks. Websites like *Maid of Might*, *Girl Wonder.org*, and *Supergirl Forever* show not only a devoted following to Supergirl but a devoted following to the original Kara. Some teens, tweens, and young women who do not read the comic nonetheless sport T-shirts with an "S-shield" or an image of Supergirl. The website *Supergirl.com* is not about the character but rather Olympic Gymnast Nastia Liukin's site to promote girls' sports, healthy living, and provide a positive role model. Supergirl is used to reflect this. Liukin refers to herself and the girls as "Supergirls," and the site is all about being a "Supergirl." Not only is the S-shield used heavily in the site's design but the illustrations used are of the original Kara. There is also the "Supergirl Jam," a televised surfing, skateboarding, and snowboarding competition for women in their late teens and twenties. Not only does the S-shield accompany every graphic superimposed on the screen, but the winners are draped in a pink cape featuring the iconic symbol.

SUMMARY

Whether it is simply DC protecting the name *Supergirl* or something deeper, there is a need for a Supergirl. Ever since the original Kara was allegedly wiped from existence, DC has not gone more than three years without giving us a Supergirl. It could be because there are enough female fans who respond to the idea of a supergirl; it could be because DC wants to keep Supergirl alive in the culture at large for both role modeling and merchandising purposes. Perhaps there is a subconscious question, "What if there were a woman just as strong as Superman?" that intrigues readers.

DC felt erasing Supergirl from continuity would improve their universe. It did not.

See also Batgirl; DC Comics; Superman; Wonder Woman

ESSENTIAL WORKS

Binder, Otto (w), Jerry Siegel (w), Jim Mooney (a), and Al Plastino (a). *Action Comics #252–#268* (May 1959–Sept. 1960), National Comics Publications [DC Comics]. Reprinted in *Supergirl Archives Volume 1*. New York: DC Comics, 2001.

David, Peter (w), Ed Benes (a), Alex Lei (i). "Many Happy Returns." *Supergirl #75–#80* (Dec. 2002–May 2003). DC Comics. Reprinted in *Supergirl: Many Happy Returns*. New York: DC Comics, 2003.

Gates, Sterling (w), Jamal Igle (a), Jonathan Sibal (i). *Supergirl: Who Is Superwoman?* New York: DC Comics, 2009.

Wolfman, Marv (w), and George Perez (p). *Crisis on Infinite Earths*. New York: DC Comics, 1998.

FURTHER READING

Girl-Wonder.org. *Super Girl*. http://girl-wonder.org/supergirl/. Accessed January 2, 2012.

Michelle. *Supergirl: Maid of Might*. http://maidofmight.net. Accessed January 2, 2012.

Brian Camp

Superman

Since his debut in *Action Comics* #1 (1938), Superman has grown from an American comic book character into something larger. Clearly Superman is a comic book icon having given rise to a slew of imitators, tributes, homages, and indeed the genre of superhero comics itself. Scholars such as Umberto Eco, the Italian theorist and novelist, have accorded him mythological status, as has his publisher, **DC Comics**. Superman has moved beyond a comic book icon to being an icon of American culture and a globally recognized icon of America. Superman began humbly enough as the creation of two Cleveland high school students, **Jerry Siegel and Joe Shuster**.

As an icon, not only of comic books but also of American culture in general, Superman has a complex history that plays into any consideration of his status. As a fictional character Superman has had so many iterations that probably no one has seen or heard every version. His media appearances include numerous comic books, a comic strip, radio serial, animated short features, movie serials, three live-action television series, five major films, and several animated television series. Superman's list of product endorsements extends from peanut butter to American Express and his public service announcements from buying War Bonds in World War II to antismoking campaigns. In addition to these instances of Superman, the 75-year history of the character includes media profiles in the *Saturday Evening Post*, *Time*, and many newspapers, court cases over copyright issues, fan discourse in letters pages, fanzines and conventions, scholarly articles and books, and truly encyclopedic websites. Superman is a sum of all these elements, and the way the character resonates with different audiences probably depends on what alignment of different incarnations they bring to their interaction with Superman.

HISTORY

So well known is the origin of Superman that in 2006, **Grant Morrison** and Frank Quitely could retell the story in *All-Star Superman* in eight words and four panels: "Doomed Planet; Desperate Scientists; Last Hope;

Kindly Couple." Their summation nicely captures Superman's origins on the doomed planet of Krypton and his mother Lara and father Jor-El's decision to send him in a rocket ship to Earth where he was taken in by the Kents. But this was not quite the Superman who appeared in *Action Comics* in June 1938. In that comic the story unfolds in a great rush as if Siegel and Shuster want to quickly get to the action and show off their Superman. The planet is unnamed, the Kents are simply "passing motorists" who turn the child "over to an orphanage," and far from being invulnerable to the sun and able to fly, as in Morrison and Quitely's version, Superman could merely hurdle a 20-story building and withstand ordnance up to a bursting shell. But other elements are there: he works for a newspaper, has an interest in **Lois Lane**, and wears his distinctive blue and red costume complete with cape and chest chevron. Indeed the Siegel family has argued in a copyright case that the key elements of Superman were present in *Action Comics* #1 (*Siegel v. Time Warner et al.* 2008, 23).

There is a certain temptation to look for essential qualities of Superman that explain his iconic status over time, and some scholars have engaged in that effort (Gordon 2001). By focusing on Superman at a specific time in his long history, it may be possible to see what made him iconic at that time, but the later the version of Superman, the harder it is to isolate the character in this fashion because the memory of him over time is to a certain extent what will have made him iconic, rather than any immediate factor. Existing histories of Superman tend to privilege some versions of the character over others. For instance, Umberto Eco's groundbreaking analysis, and those who have followed him, look at the comic book Superman in preference to the comic strip version. In Les Daniel's more or less official history of Superman, the radio serial is mentioned, but it and the 1950s television serial take up far less space than the comic book version. Likewise, Paul Levitz's celebration of 75 years of DC Comics focuses on the Superman comic books, with other instances presented as ancillary. Often the picking and choosing of which versions of Superman are relevant and which are not is somewhat equivalent to the councils of Nicaea and Trent delineating the lines of Christianity and its texts. For instance, in response to a reader's letter in *Superman* #252 (1972), E. Nelson Bridwell wrote that "we don't accept" a television animated series version of Superman's foe Brainiac's origins. And indeed DC Comics has several times attempted to sort out and delimit the nature of Superman and the rest of its gaggle of superheroes through continuity rectification texts like *Crisis on Infinite Earths*, indeed so much so that a division exists between those who want to canonize comics as texts with defined continuities and those who want the freedom of seeing all these stories, in the words of **Alan Moore**, as "imaginary tales" with not too much regard for contradiction (Moore 1986).

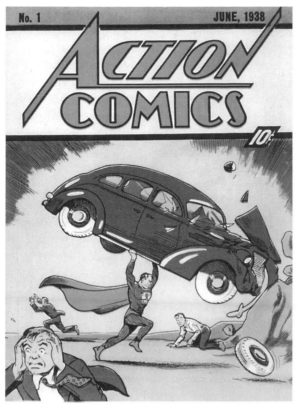

(Photofest)

IMPACT ON COMICS

Superman is the prototypical comic book superhero and the subject of much derivation, tribute, and homage from the original **Captain Marvel** to Alan Moore's *Supreme*. Indeed **Batman** was an attempt to replicate the success of Superman. The superhero genre of comics owes its existence to Superman.

The 1986 *Crisis* series led to a remaking of Superman in the hands of John Byrne. Although *Crisis*, Moore's "Whatever Happened to the Man of Tomorrow?" and Byrne's "The Man of Steel" were all part of an effort to sort out continuity, the latter two ultimately undermined such efforts and opened a space for multiple layers of storytelling. Byrne's imaginative retelling of Superman's origins, mixing elements from Richard Donner's film version to show Krypton as an emotionally cold planet and reworking tropes from early stories to position Superman as a product of America, demonstrated the possibilities of rebooting characters. To be sure infinite rebooting was not on the horizon in 1986, and other characters like the **Flash** had previously been reimagined, but Byrne's Superman took a long-running character and for the first time altered it significantly in one fell swoop. It took DC Comics some time to realize it, but this sort of reboot, when combined with Moore's notion of all stories being imaginary, opened the way for infinite storytelling.

Another, albeit unintended, influence on comics came in a Superman story arc, "The Death of Superman," that culminated in his "death" in *Superman* #75 (1993). DC Comics hyped the series so much that it sold millions of comics primarily through comic book stores, and many of the buyers, apparently unaware that the death of major comic book characters is seldom permanent, illogically felt they were making an investment that would one day return them a sum akin to the value of *Action Comics* #1 (De Haven 2010, 17). Chuck Rozanski, a comic book store owner, later argued that the resulting distrust by those unable to realize a profit on their purchase was a crucial element in the 80 percent decline of comic book sales and a decline in book stores and comic book companies in the 10 years following the issue.

IMPACT ON AMERICAN CULTURE

One way to gauge the iconic nature of Superman at a particular point in his history is to see how the media reported on the character. In June 1941, the *Saturday Evening Post*, then one of the most widely circulated magazines in America, carried a long feature article on Superman and his creators. The piece by John Kobler was somewhat snide in tone, referring to Jerry Siegel as a "short, plump, heavy spectacled young man" and given to cramming "four or five candy bars in his pockets at the cinema," among other barbs. Kobler nonetheless marveled at the way in which Superman had so quickly become an "all-around success," a "miracle man in fact as well as in fancy." The scope of Superman's activities by 1941 was indeed miraculous given the trouble Siegel and Shuster initially had in getting him into print. As Kobler noted, he appeared in the monthly *Action Comics* and the bimonthly *Superman* comic book, the radio serial aired three times a week, and 230 newspapers carried the comic strip to a combined circulation of 25 million readers. In Christmas 1940, 100,000 children paid 30 cents to view Macy's Superman exhibit, there were 250,000 members of the Superman of America Club, and Paramount Pictures was set to release 12 Fleisher animated adventures in October 1941. In the first six months of 1941, 33 licensed products had returned $100,000 to Superman's publishers. The tone of the piece suggested that somehow Siegel and Shuster, seeking "psychological compensation" through projecting infantile fantasies, in combination with the sharp business practices of Donenfeld and his general manager Jack Liebowitz had, at least according to the intellectuals, created "the first authentic cultural hero since Paul Bunyan." Little matter that Siegel and Shuster were boobs unable even to understand the

Nietzschean philosophy through which the *New Republic* magazine analyzed the character, Superman had such an appeal that a cockney boy in London during a heavy air raid scarcely noticed it, so engrossed was he in a Superman comic (Kobler 1941). But intense media presence and an array of licensed products do not alone turn a character into an icon.

With the world at war in 1941, and with America's forced entry into that war in December, for Superman to become an American icon he had to overcome the notion of a superman as racial ideology promoted by Nazis. The *Los Angeles Times* of December 5, 1941, carried a "Private Lives" panel (an illustrated feature similar to "Ripley's Believe It or Not," but about people) by Edwin Cox that made fun of the Nazi Field Marshal Wilhelm Keitel apparently nicknamed "Wittzblatt" or "comic strip general" by noting "and they don't mean Superman." Although this use clearly referred to Superman, the term still cropped up as a Nazi term, such as in a January 7, 1942, editorial in the *Los Angeles Times*, which wrote of Nazi "supermen," and in Westbrook Pegler's article in the *Washington Post* on January 11, 1942, referring to Hitler sarcastically as "the superman," clearly meaning it in its Nazi sense. In the *Washington Post's* report of December 10, 1941, about the Japanese invasion in the Philippines in which an American pilot declared that the Japanese were not the "supermen" that they might seem, the exact reference seems unclear, but increasingly when American newspapers referred to *superman* they meant Superman. These mentions might refer to individuals with sporting prowess being labeled Superman, as in a January 8, 1942, *Washington Post* snippet on champion bowler Tony Suess, or the sort of qualities required in pilots, good but not Superman, in a January 16, 1942, *Washington Post* article on the Army's recruitment criteria.

Indeed, headline writers very quickly started to associate the fighting ability of American service personnel with Superman. A headline in the February 16, 1942, *Washington Post* read: "One-Man Army Kills 116 Japs in Bataan, Lives to be Modest about It, Superman Fights for MacArthur." By September 1942, according to a report in the *Nation's Business* drivers in the U.S. Army called a six-ton truck "the Superman" (Corey 1942, 44). In early April 1942 the Navy Department decided that Superman comic books were "essential supplies destined for the Marine garrison at Midway Islands" according to a report in *Time* ("Superman's Dilemma"). As the war progressed, at one stage the Army Library Services distributed 100,000 copies of the *Superman* comic a month, before giving way to the PX store distribution (Gordon 1998, 140). Superman comics helped provide Americans with a unified vision of just what the war was about, the defense of a democracy often expressed as the right to consume an abundance of goods and services, something that had already begun to take shape as the American Way. Furthermore, *The Adventures of Superman* radio serial on September 7, 1942, introduced Superman for the first time as fighting for "Truth, Justice, and the American Way" (*Adventures of Superman*). Covers of *Action Comics* and *Superman* urged readers to buy war bonds, as did the radio serial. The stories in the comic books and elsewhere never had Superman directly confront the Axis powers; instead he served as a reminder of American values. In all these phenomena Superman was front and center, cementing his place as an icon of American culture forged in the heat of battle, in the good war, and a moment of American triumph, not so much as a warrior but rather as an exemplar of what America was fighting for.

Given the place of World War II in American culture and the way prominent individuals such as Dwight Eisenhower figured large in American life into the 1960s, it is not so surprising that Superman's iconic status established during the war helped the character survive the downturn in the comic book industry in the 1950s following the anti–comic book campaign of **Fredric Wertham** and the introduction of television. In part, the advent of television and *The Adventures of Superman* television series help explain the manner in which Superman could transcend his WWII iconic status and develop an even broader-based iconic status across generations. At one level this is a simple enough occurrence of expanding Superman's appeal and audience. But as with every iteration of Superman beyond comic books, it is a reminder that Donenfeld and Liebowitz, the key owners of the Superman copyright in these years, were in the business of business and not wedded to comic books. Superman did not become an icon through the execution of some master plan by DC. Rather in their desire to make money off what must have seemed like a craze, like so many other crazes, DC sold Superman everywhere they could in the late 1930s and 1940s. This took him in to other media, and whereas with some popular phenomena this would undermine the value of the product, in Superman's case it increased it over the long term. However, DC was not unmindful of protecting its asset even as they sold him everywhere they could. When critics like Sterling North attacked comics in 1940 for their violence and poor spelling and grammar, DC quickly hired an advisory board of educators and child psychologists to protect their brand (Gordon 1998, 136). Likewise, in 1954 when Wertham's campaign threatened comic books, DC participated in the establishment of the Comics Code Authority. In the case of the television series, the original episodes had a hard edge somewhat in keeping with film noir and the crime comic books popular in the early 1950s. By the time the first season of the series aired on ABC, some of this edge had reportedly been toned down at the insistence of Kellogg's, the sponsor (Hayde 2009).

Just as it is possible to analyze Superman's iconic status at any given time through what the press wrote, it is also possible to ascertain something of his standing by what they did not write. From the end of World War II through to the 1960s, few negative items appeared in the press. In October 1945 social theorist and seminarian Walter Ong accused Superman, along with **Wonder Woman**, of being fascist. Although reported on by *Time* magazine, no major newspapers picked up the story ("Are Comics Fascist?"). Again although several papers and *Time* reported the success of the Superman movie serial starring Kirk Alyn between 1948 and 1952, only the *Los Angeles Times* ran the potential negative story for Superman that Alyn's wife divorced him for being a wife beater, something that Superman fans would immediately have recognized as being ironic given Superman's intervention in just such a domestic dispute in *Action Comics* #1 ("Singer Virginia O'Brien"). And despite the anti–comic book campaign waged by Wertham, who included Superman among his targets, most press accounts that mentioned Superman in this context referred to him as one of the wholesome comic characters alongside the likes of Mickey Mouse. Even the Superman television series that came under some attack received at best scant attention, with a few articles here and there criticizing the show as eroding family values or for the level of violence (Remenih March 1953; Remenih August 1953). DC could use Superman's status to undercut such criticism. In August 1953 producers announced that at the end of each show Superman would "lecture youngsters on good health habits, safety hints, good eating habits etc." And in 1956 the *New York Times* reported that 40 comic books published by DC carried a page devoted to "a socially constructive purpose" including in one instance Superman taking children to the public library (Corrigan 1956). All this suggests that such was the status of Superman that he could shrug off some of the criticism directed at comics and violence on television simply because he was Superman.

Superman as Icon of America

In the late 1940s and early 1950s Superman's status as an American icon extended so that globally he became an icon of America. One manner in which Superman spread to the world was through the hands of U.S. service personnel. A photograph in the July 1945 issue of *National Geographic* showed a young Burmese boy with a large pile of comics he had received from troops. In 1947 publishers in Australia and Brazil began local editions of Superman, and other countries such as Mexico and Denmark followed soon after. In early 1949 the Soviet Union launched the opening salvos of the propaganda war that accompanied the Cold War, declaring in the Soviet *Literary Gazette* that Superman promoted the sort of "gangster" attitude towards others that life under capitalism entailed (Schwartz 1949). In October that year the *Gazette* made this criticism a little more explicit. Korny Chukovsky, based on his survey of American comic books, charged Superman with the "mass fascsization" of American children who apparently "all" read the comic starting at age eight ("Russian Says"). In February 1949 when France passed legislation setting up a special commission of the minister of justice to exercise control over the content of comics, and indeed all children's publications, and limiting foreign content to 25 percent, American comics were a clear target with the suggestion that they were responsible for delinquency among French youth. The daily newspaper *Le Monde* editorialized against this notion, stating, "Tarzan, Red Rider and Superman would have to have big shoulders to carry all that blame" and laying the cause at the door of the German occupation (Barry 1949).

A similar situation occurred in 1957 when the highly educated and pugnacious television critic for the *Manchester Guardian* Bernard Levin lambasted the Superman television series. For Levin it was "the crudest, shoddiest, and most uncompromisingly cretinous programme" that he had seen on the Independent Television Network (Levin 1957). Such was the force of his venom that the following day the *New York Times* noted his criticism ("TV Show Scored"). Later that year the *Times* carried another article worrying about the effect of seething resentment about American shows being shown in the United Kingdom (Gander 1957). Again Superman was front and center in this concern. Levin's continued dismay with Superman as "not only the worst thing I have ever seen on television, but the worst thing I have ever encountered in any form" notwithstanding, the Superman television series was one of the American shows driving the global growth of television and proved popular around the world including in Japan, where it was dubbed (Levin 1958; Falk 1959; Gordon 1960). Other instances of Superman's global reach in the 1950s included a locally produced radio series in Australia and the availability of Superman comic books in India in these years (Gordon 2001). In this way, albeit not always favorably, the world experienced Superman, and he solidified his global iconic status.

America Falls Apart—Superman Keeps It Together

As an icon Superman embodies the tensions of American culture. Because he represents all of America, sometimes this embodiment becomes a means of smoothing out those tensions. The Vietnam War is a good case in point. From time to time in the 1960s, *Action Comics* and *Superman* printed letters from service personnel in Vietnam. *Superman* #216 (1969) carried a very rare story, by Robert Kanigher, in which Superman intervened in the Vietnam War. Prior to this occurrence Superman had not ever intervened in real wars in the pages of DC Comics, save for some action against fifth columnists in the United States during World War II. In this Vietnam story, a key plot point had troops writing to the *Daily Planet* complaining that Superman was not helping the troops. Clark Kent then joins troops working as a medic and encounters a nefarious communist plot by a dragon-lady-like Dr. Han, who has turned a soldier into a giant with superstrength and invulnerability who attacks his own side. Superman intervenes, repulses a communist attack, and restores the GI to normal, and all without killing anyone, in keeping with his code (or to

LETTER TO THE EDITOR

Superman has . . . forged a whole new American mythology around himself. . . . One sees Superman and his efforts in every phase of American life. Professor Max Lerner, in *America as a Civilization*, cites Superman as a contemporary folk hero [akin to] . . . King Arthur and Robin Hood . . . [and] Paul Bunyan. . . . The greatest compliment is imitation. *Superman* has been satirized and borrowed from for over thirty years. He is a legend, and every bit as rich as the legends of the past. *Superman* is replete with the values of his contemporaries and their weaknesses—humanity that will not be admitted to under an exterior of strength—a social conscience—reverence for human life—power and the daring to explore the unknown, the assertion of omnipotence. This is the legend of the *Superman*. . . .

[From *Superman*] came my imagination, my own social conscience and reverence for human life, my own daring to dream. It is time that I, and a generation like me, thanked National Periodicals for *Superman*. He has helped to make us *dream*.

Elliot S! Maggin, Superman #238 (1971)

be more correct, the Comic Code). As stories go, it was a fairly standard piece of propaganda about the righteousness of the American cause and the pitilessness of the communist Vietnamese.

Later that year *Action Comics* #382 carried a letter from a Marine in Vietnam who praised Superman for fighting "valiantly against crime as we do against Communist oppression." The editors thanked the anonymous author for his letter and went on to say, "We sure wish you dodge those speeding bullets!" In this context of Superman lending support for the Vietnam War at a time when the tide of public opinion had turned after the Tet Offensive, Brandeis student Elliot S. Maggin's letter to the editor a year or so later (see sidebar), in which he showered praise on Superman as an inspiration for doing what is right in the world and as a harbinger of his social conscience, might seem a little odd given Maggin's decisive liberal tone. The point here is not to accuse Kanigher of being a propagandist for the war or Maggin of being a liberal, but that Superman's appeal transcended these differences and held them together as American. For Maggin Superman stood for all that is best about America, so much so that in 2007 he thought of running for Congress on the slogan "Truth, Justice, and the American Way" (Maggin 2007)

During the 1976 bicentennial celebration of the American Revolution, Maggin, by then a writer for DC, worked on the equally celebratory 300th issue of

THIS LOOKS LIKE A JOB . . .

When the *Superman* movie opened in cinemas in late 1978, a sight gag caught the attention of some journalists. Christopher Reeve as Clark Kent had trouble finding a place to change into Superman because telephone booths no longer existed, having been replaced by nonenclosed pay phones. It was but a whimsical moment in the film, but it helped cement the notion that Superman always or often changed into his costume in a phone booth. But this simply was not the case in the comic books, the 1950s television series, the comic strip, and the radio serial. This notion garnered its common acceptance prior to the film through an intersection of popular cultural texts and fan intervention in shaping the character.

Mort Weisinger related a possible origin of the story in the letters column of *Action Comics* in May 1967. Apparently *Candid Camera* set up a gag in which "Superman" asked people coming out of a phone booth if they had found his civilian suit in there. In the letters column of *Superman* in July 1970 George Brooks a reader enquired: "When did Superman start (as Maxwell Smart would say) 'the old switching to the super-costume in the phone booth trick'?" To which the editors mistakenly replied he only started after the quip on *Get Smart*. A fan, Mark Woldt, hastily corrected this error in the November 1970 issue noting Superman's use of a phone booth in the March–April issue of 1951. In April 1971 Nick Van Hoogstraten and Robert Leardo both pointed out a September–October 1949 occurrence. In the meantime in the January 1971 issue Denny O'Neil had Clark Kent, in his new role as a television reporter, joke that he could use a dust cloud as cover to change rather than "ducking into a phone booth." By 1973 *Action Comics'* letter page used a splash panel showing Clark changing into Superman in rapid motion but with a phone booth as the location of the shift from Clark to Superman. By 1978 and the movie version of Superman changing in a phone booth had become part of Superman's shtick.

Superman. Writing with Cary Bates, Maggin imagines what Superman would be like if he arrived on Earth in 1976 and what the world would be like in 2001 when he reached maturity as Superman. The story used the device of having Superman forgo his identity for some time and contemplate living simply as Clark Kent. Humans being humans, Superman eventually has to fulfill his destiny and defeat a false claimant to the title of savior of humanity. In the climax to the story Superman informs an angry mob that they had been saved from destruction not by his android opponent but by "someone who wanted you to look not to heroes and false gods for salvation . . . someone who has enough faith to know your salvation is within you . . . all of you!" Superman declaims all this standing triumphantly on the wrecked shell of the android with arms outstretched, messiah-like. Impressed by Superman's humility, the crowd looks on and individuals exclaim: "That man, power runs through his very being! Unlimited power! Who was he? Where did he come from? He's shown us what we all can be if we try! Yes he was a SUPERMAN!" And these citizens then erect a statue of him, as the narrative voice in the book puts it, "the man who surely is the greatest hero of all." In this story DC was of course celebrating a milestone of the character. The story also served as a means of denoting that Superman and what he stood for were timeless, tied Superman's own celebration to the bicentennial through emphasizing the importance of self-reliance as a means of resisting tyranny and the necessity for heroes (or leaders) to be humble, and reminded those who would follow mindlessly to instead be self-reliant. Superman is essentially American because, despite his power, he demands that people not worship false heroes and gods but choose instead to think and act for themselves.

SUMMARY

Constant cross-referencing between stories and media platforms has increased Superman's iconic status. In 1978 *Superman* movie director Richard Donner felt a need to make reference to the origins of Superman in comic books and to pay tribute to the movie serial and television versions. The movie opens with a cinema curtain parting, complete with a soundtrack incorporating the noises of a curtain being drawn. Then to the sound of film running through a projector the words "June, 1938," appear on the screen followed by the fade-in of a comic book cover that reads *Action Comics* and that has an illustration of two rocket ships fleeing an exploding planet (not of course the cover to the real *Action Comics* #1). A hand turns the page and a boy's voice says: "In the decade of the 1930s even the great city of Metropolis was not spared the ravages of the worldwide depression. In the times of fear and confusion, the job of informing the public was the responsibility of the *Daily Planet*, a great metropolitan newspaper, whose reputation for clarity and truth had become a symbol of hope for the city of Metropolis." The scene then dissolves from the comic book to a live scene of the *Daily Planet* building and the spinning globe on top, pans to the night sky and stars, and the opening credits roll as the camera sweeps through space over the stirring John Williams score. Later in the film Kirk Alyn and Noel Neill (Lois Lane in the serial and from season 2 onward of the television series) made cameo appearances as Lois Lane's parents. Since that movie, this referencing of Superman's history as a means to evoke his iconic status in a story has become yet another way of building and strengthening that status by constant playful reference to it. For instance, the television series *Smallville*, which focused on Clark Kent's development into

Superman and in which he only appeared in costume in the last minutes of the final episode of 10 seasons, fixed the series as part of the Superman mythos by constant reference to other earlier versions of Superman (Gordon 2011). Such is the iconic status of Superman that 10 seasons of television could be carried on the back of that status with never a sight of him in full kit going about his business as Superman.

See also Lex Luthor; Lois Lane; Siegel, Jerry and Joe Shuster; Supergirl

ESSENTIAL WORKS

Byrne, John (w, p), Dick Giordano (i), and Tom Ziuko. *Superman: The Man of Steel*. New York: Ballantine Books, 1988.

Moore, Alan (w), Curt Swan (p), and George Perez (i). "Whatever Happened to the Man of Tomorrow?" *Superman* #423 (September 1986). DC Comics.

Siegel, Jerry (w), and Joe Shuster (p). *Superman Chronicles, Vols. 1–8*. New York: DC Comics, 2006–2010.

FURTHER READING

Daniels, Les. *Superman: The Complete History*. San Francisco: Chronicle Books, 1998.

De Haven, Thomas. *Our Hero: Superman on Earth*. New Haven, CT: Yale University Press, 2010.

Eco, Umberto. "Il mito di Superman e la *dissoluzione* del tempo," in *Demitizzazione e imagine*, edited by E. Castelli. Padua: Cedam, 1962. Translated by Natalie Chilton. "The Myth of Superman." *Diacritics* 2 (1972): 14–22.

Hayde, Michael J. *Flights of Fantasy: The Unauthorized but True Story of Radio & TV's Adventures of Superman*. Duncan, OK: BearManor Media, 2009.

Ian Gordon

Swamp Thing

Swamp Thing (**DC Comics**) emerged from the 1970s "monster boom" as the industry's most popular original monster, transcending the "swamp monster" archetype via the original 10 issues of the series and the second series in the 1980s. Swamp Thing offered a contemporary and emotionally resonant incarnation of the venerable "Green Man" archetype in myth, folklore, and religion: an iconic, usually inarticulate, nonhuman elemental being linked with pagan beliefs, agrarian culture, and the vegetable kingdom. By the mid-1980s, Swamp Thing personified countercultural and ecological philosophies contrary to America's swing to the Right in the Reagan era, briefly making this horror comic an unlikely outpost for alternative, even radical concepts, visions, and voices.

HISTORY

Writer Len Wein and artist Berni Wrightson introduced "Swamp Thing" as a self-standing eight-page story in *House of Secrets* #92 (1971). *Swamp Thing* debuted as its own title later that year. Wein and Wrightson brought something unique to the archetype; strong as Wein's scripting was for its era, it was Wrightson's vision that propelled the comic into long-forbidden turf. Inspired by pen-and-ink artist Franklin Booth, **EC Comics**'s Graham "Ghastly" Ingels, Frank Frazetta, and the rich imagery of the original 1930s Universal monster movies, Wrightson's atmospheric pen, brush, and ink artwork set "Swamp Thing"—the story and the subsequent series—above and beyond all precursors and contemporaries.

The original *House of Secrets* "Swamp Thing" was set in the early 20th century. When scientist Alex Olsen is murdered, the titular plant being forms around Olsen's remains to exact revenge against his murderer (friend and partner Damian Ridge), only to be spurned by his beloved wife, Linda. Wrightson patterned the characters of Ridge and Linda after Mike Kaluta and Louise Jones (now Louise Simonson), and Olsen after himself, lending a semiautobiographical component to the imagery. For the series, Wein and Wrightson

ROOT OF THE MATTER

Predecessors to Swamp Thing included Theodore Sturgeon's short story "It" (published in *Unknown*, 1940), in which a sentient plant creature mysteriously congeals over a skeletal corpse. Sturgeon's story inspired writer Harry Stein and artist Mort Leav's introduction of the Heap in *Air Fighters* #3 (1942)—a sentient plant creature that congealed around the body of a downed World War I flying ace. The Heap was the backup co-star of *Airboy Comics*, establishing the comic book swamp monster archetype. Marvel Comics' swamp monster, Man-Thing, debuted as an 11-page story in Marvel's black-and-white comic magazine *Savage Tales* #1 (1971), as Skywald revived the Heap to complete the 1971 swamp monster rally.

revamped the origin into a contemporary setting: an act of espionage detonates the lab of scientist Alec Holland, saturating Holland with his biorestorative formula before hurling his flaming body into the Louisiana bayou. The plant monster Swamp Thing emerges to discover his wife Linda was also murdered, leaving the forlorn creature alone to pursue a series of adventures involving many horror/science-fiction archetypes (Frankenstein, lycanthropy, Lovecraftian beings, robotics, aliens, voodoo, etc.). During their collaborative run, Wein/Wrightson introduced Swamp Thing's nemesis Anton Arcane, who surgically created the monstrous "Un-Men" and resurrected his murdered brother Gregori as the Patchwork Man (note, too, Gregori's orphaned daughter, Abigail a.k.a. Abby, would become the series heroine). The Wein/Wrightson collaboration lasted only 10 issues, during which the team established a multiple-award-winning high-water mark for the genre and comics.

Subsequent Swamp Thing series and the spin-off title *John Constantine: Hellblazer* (and other DC/Vertigo titles) revisited Swamp Thing's origin, creating a deep back story for Alec and Linda Holland, friend Lt. Matthew Cable (later becoming Matt the Raven in **Neil Gaiman**'s **Sandman**), and more, retroactively folding characters introduced in the 1980s into extensive, revisionist prequel narratives.

After Wrightson's departure, Wein stayed to script 13 more issues, working with artist Nestor Redondo. Wein's involvement waned, as Swamp Thing's obsession with avenging Linda's murder and restoring himself to human form became the primary focus; Redondo also lost interest, as his initial stellar work gave way to increasingly lackluster issues credited to Redondo Studios. With Wein's departure, David Michelinie and Gerry Conway scripted the series conclusion (with Fred Carillo drawing and David Anthony Kraft coplotting the finale, #24, in 1976) with Holland restoring his humanity. Wein, Michelinie, and Conway invested the series with fuller characterizations of the evil Arcane, heroic Matt Cable, and Arcane's niece Abigail, along with an expanded rogues' gallery.

Orphaned from his cancelled series, Alec Holland unceremoniously transformed back into his mossy self, stranded amid vaguely connected appearances of ever-dwindling import in Conway's run on *Challengers of the Unknown* #81–#87 (1977–1978), a particularly freakish role in Steve Englehart's *DC Comics Presents* #8 (1979), and a guest appearance penned by future *Swamp Thing* writer Marty Pasko in *The Brave and the Bold* #176 (1981). The nadir was an appearance in *Super Friends* #28 (1980) as one of five nondescript enemies the superheroes fought. Clearly, DC Comics no longer knew what to do with Swamp Thing, nor did they care. The character was licensed to film producers Benjamin Melniker and Michael Uslan in a deal DC executive vice-president Paul Levitz later characterized as "the worst deal DC ever made" (Levitz 1988). The licensing agreement gave all but the comic book publishing rights to the producers, including rights to adapt any elements past, present, or future from the comic for all media without further clearances from or payment to DC.

The pending release of Melnicker/Uslan's *Swamp Thing* (1982) prompted DC to resurrect the character via a new series, *The Saga of the Swamp Thing* (1982–1985). Len Wein edited the new series, guiding writer Martin Pasko and artist (and Joe Kubert School pioneer class graduate) Tom Yeates. The rush to get the comic series out in conjunction with the movie's theatrical release immediately created enormous deadline pressures that never lifted for the entirety of Yeates's run and Pasko's tenure, prompting Yeates to engage Kubert School classmates John Totleben, Stephen Bissette, and Cara Sherman-Tereno to assist on art chores. Pasko's initial narrative arc reunited Swamp Thing, Matt Cable, Abby Arcane, and supervillain Anton Arcane, adding a new supporting cast: TV journalist Liz Tremayne, ally Dennis Barclay, and the malignant General Sunderland (whom Yeates patterned after then secretary of state Alexander Haig). Pasko exiled Swamp Thing from the Louisiana bayou and plunged him and his entourage into a cross-country and (eventually) global sojourn culminating in a confrontation with a possible Anti-Christ to avert Armageddon. En route, Pasko and Yeates indulged their own revisionist takes on classic horror archetypes, including punk vampires, an island populated by projected fantasies, and the Golem. Fan reaction was mixed, and sales slumped as Pasko was increasingly spread thin juggling comics writing with more lucrative television scripting, and Yeates—whose devotion to adventure comics did not extend into monster/horror comics—chose to depart, prompting editor Wein to engage a new art team. Wein went with Yeates's suggestion of former Kubert School classmates Stephen Bissette and John Totleben, who had worked/ghosted on the title since *SOTST* #2. Totleben in particular had a strong affinity for, and devotion to, the character—Swamp Thing and Wrightson were formative influences for Totleben, and he had already (via Yeates) proposed a more plantlike Swamp Thing character design that Wein rejected as "too radical." The new team began working from Pasko's scripts with *SOTST* #16's *Twilight Zone* homage (1983), but Pasko departed after the horrific Anton Arcane/Un-Men revamp for *SOTST* #19 (1983). Wein hired **Alan Moore**, a British writer who had never written for a "colonial" American publisher, to assume scripting duties with *SOTST* #20 (1984). Already fans of Moore's British *2000 AD* and *Warrior* scripts, Bissette and Totleben celebrated the news, and this new team forged a bold new direction for the series.

For readers, the transformation started with Moore's collaboration with guest penciller Dan Day and inker John Totleben on *SOTST* #20, which ruthlessly resolved every loose end from the Pasko/Yeates tenure. For the Moore/Bissette/Totleben team (assisted from the beginning by Kubert School pioneer class graduate Rick Veitch), the transformation began an exchange of voluminous letters, including detailed plot and character suggestions from the artists, and Moore's current and future plans for the series. *SOTST* #21's (1984) "The Anatomy Lesson" introduced Moore's radical rethink of the Alec Holland/Swamp Thing origin, revealing Swamp Thing was never a human/plant hybrid, but that Holland had died and Swamp Thing was in fact a sentient, wholly vegetable elemental that only thought he was once a man. Editor Len Wein eagerly sanctioned this, though it echoed Totleben's previously rejected redesign of Swamp Thing into a more plantlike being (the first of many plot concepts Totleben and Bissette brought to the table, including original characters like Nukeface and the involvement of DC characters like **Jack Kirby**'s Demon). The redefinition of the character and series galvanized a growing readership. While Bissette and Totleben were intent on the horror elements of their collaboration with Moore—making a concerted, conscious effort to elevate Swamp Thing and horror comics to emulate the efforts of genre contemporaries in other media, like Stephen King, George Romero, Peter Straub, David Cronenberg, and Ramsey Campbell—Moore was also orchestrating an ambitious revamp of the entire DC Universe, using Swamp Thing as his springboard. To keep the peace, Moore and Wein told Bissette the intrusion of DC superheroes was an editorial edict, but the fact was that Moore was eager to play in that universe, incorporating characters from the Golden Age Spectre into the Silver Age Justice League, Jason Woodrue/the Floronic Man, and the Phantom Stranger.

Len Wein departed with *SOTST* #24 (1984), and Karen Berger assumed editorial duties with *SOTST* #25 (1984). Under Berger's guidance, the team expanded to include aesthetically consistent collaborations with new hands, including Shawn McManus—drawing a celebrated ode to Walt Kelly's **Pogo** in *SOTST* #32 (1985)—inker Alfredo Alcala, and Rick Veitch becoming a full team partner who would, eventually, take over as writer/penciller (with *Swamp Thing* #65 in 1987). Abby Cable was elevated to full co-star status,

TWISTED TAKE

Before the comic book Swamp Thing existed, Arkansas-born rockabilly musician Sleepy LaBeef played a bigfoot-like monster named Swamp Thing in Ron Ormond's horror/sex film *The Exotic Ones* (a.k.a. *The Monster and the Stripper*, 1968), filmed on location in Nashville, Okefenokee Swamp Park in Georgia, and on Louisiana's famed Bourbon Street in New Orleans's French Quarter.

culminating in *SOTST* #29 (1984), an issue that cost the series the Comics Code seal of approval. This was followed by a double-sized issue's descent into Hell to rescue Abby. Free of the Comics Code, the creative team returned the series to a full Gothic horror title, en route redefining Swamp Thing as a powerful elemental being capable of growing multiple bodies, changing size and form, and traveling the planet while experiencing a rich emotional life, eventually marrying Abby and psychedelically consummating their relationship in *SOTST* #34's (1985) "The Rites of Spring." The team also created the botanical realm of the Green (the elemental plant universe) and its rulers, the Parliament of Trees, along with the wholly new character John Constantine, prompted by Bissette/Totleben's insistence on drawing the Police's Sting as a background character (in *SOTST* #25, 1984) and threat to continue doing so.

The Bissette/Totleben art team departed with the rechristened *Swamp Thing* #50 (1986), the conclusion of the epic "American Gothic" arc reinterpreting traditional genre archetypes (vampirism, lycanthropy, voodoo, serial murderers, etc.), after which Rick Veitch and Alfredo Alcala took over the art chores. Veitch's love for science fiction, fantasy, and superheroes rather than horror inspired Moore to construct an Odysseus-like exile-and-return-to-Earth arc that sent Swamp Thing into space, incorporating DC characters like Adam Strange and Jack Kirby's New Gods. With Moore's departure with *Swamp Thing* #64 (1987), Veitch scripted and penciled through #87 (1989) without missing a beat (or deadline).

Veitch sustained the poetic threads Moore established, further exploring the relationship between Abby and Swamp Thing, and Chester Williams and Liz Tremayne (a Marty Pasko character Moore reintroduced), and introducing Cajun Gene "Labo" LaBostrie, the fetal elemental Sprout (created by the Parliament of Trees to supplant Swamp Thing when they believed him dead), and others. The latter development resulted in Swamp Thing convincing John Constantine to impregnate Abby to spawn an infant host for Sprout, culminating in the birth of their child. Veitch also initiated a time-travel excursion through the DC Universe, incorporating Merlin, Tomahawk, Jonah Hex, Enemy Ace, and other DC characters—an expansive saga abruptly terminated before the publication of *Swamp Thing* #88 (1989) in which Swamp Thing would have met Jesus Christ prior to the Crucifixion. Outraged, Veitch left the title for good and DC's employ for over a decade.

After Veitch's departure, *Swamp Thing* continued well into the 1990s. Despite the efforts of writer Doug Wheeler, scripting almost 30 issues in the wake of Veitch's departure, many readers bailed after the *Swamp Thing* #88 debacle. Wheeler took considerable heat even as he resurrected Arcane, introduced many new characters (including many of Swamp Thing's elemental forefathers and a shaman protector for his offspring), and named Abby and Swamp Thing's daughter Tefe. Alas, he also adopted guest scripter Stephen Bissette's concept for Matango (based on the 1962 Toho film released stateside as *Attack of the Mushroom People*) and fungal elementals in the Gray, an arc that alienated many before its conclusion in "Quest for the Elementals," *Swamp Thing* #104–#109 (1991). Fans demanded a new direction, and editor Karen Berger complied, engaging horror novelist Nancy Collins (author of *Sunglasses after Dark*, etc.), based in part on Collins living in Louisiana (the only Swamp Thing creator ever to do so). Collins tapped her Southern roots to revitalize the horror quotient with a cast of Cajun characters (including the legendary Las Perdu) and reinvigorating the family ties across the board with an elemental nanny for Tefe, Lady Jane. Collins also delineated Constantine's lineage, orchestrated the arrival of Sunderland's daughter and the return (again) of Arcane, and more, making her run (#110–#138, 1991–1993) memorable. Lady Jane shattered Swamp Thing and Abby's marriage and spirited Tefe to the Parliament of Trees in Collins's finale, ensuring Swamp Thing's return to lone "champion of Earth" status—which has essentially defined the character since.

Since Collins's tenure, the character has limped along, never recovering urgency or traction. The psyche of the shattered, embittered Swamp Thing was laid bare in a remarkable two-issue crossover scripted by Alan Moore compadre Dick Foreman (*Black Orchid* #5 and *Swamp Thing* #139, 1994), followed by writer Mark Millar's run that opened with human Alec Holland finding out he had dreamed everything. Shorn of his roots, Holland/Swamp Thing were cast adrift again—only to have Millar reveal this, too, was a sleight-of-mind concocted by three magicians fulfilling an ancient prophecy. Reestablishing the known Swamp Thing mythos, Millar revamped the tapestry: the Parliament of Trees became dangerous foes, one of a plethora of elemental parliaments; Swamp Thing shed his illusory humanity to become a devastating elemental force, overwhelming each of the Parliaments of Earth (Vapors, Waves, Stones, etc.) and threatening to exterminate mankind. The series became volatile, sexualized, and unpredictable; in this, at least, there was a return to the spirit of the Moore/Bissette/Totleben/Veitch run. Having learned the truth behind his appointed mission from the Parliament of Worlds, Swamp Thing spared humanity, and the series ended with #171 (1996).

Swamp Thing sporadically reappeared in various DC titles. Vertigo relaunched Swamp Thing with a short-lived third series (2000–2001) charting the adventures of Swamp Thing and Abby's daughter Tefe. Writer Andy Diggle and artist Enrique Breccia resurrected Swamp Thing for a fourth series (2004–2006); Breccia stayed on when new writer Josh Dysart took over, but their ongoing narrative was terminated before it reached its final act, leaving fans to wonder what might have been.

Swamp Thing returned in *Brightest Day* (2010–2011), corrupted by Green Lantern/Blackest Night crossover series villain Nekron to yet again jeopardize all life on Earth. The White Lantern mobilized other DC heroes to reconstruct a new Swamp Thing body/incarnation to successfully defeat the demonic Swamp Thing, spawning the three-issue *Search for the Swamp Thing* (2011) in which John Constantine tracks Swamp Thing and his transformation. A fifth *Swamp Thing* series (2011–) brings back Alec Holland in human form, a new Swamp Thing, and a renegade Abby—initially facing a variation of Doug Wheeler's much-maligned Matango—to what end, only time will tell.

IMPACT ON COMICS

Any lasting impact of the 1970s Swamp Thing stemmed from the initial *House of Secrets* one-shot story and the first 10 issues by Wein and Wrightson. Wrightson's art in particular fueled the horror comics revival of the decade, influencing a new generation of creators (including John Totleben). Swamp Thing won both Wein and Wrightson industry Shazam awards in 1972 (Best Writer, Best Penciller, Best Individual Story), and a 1973 Shazam for Best Continuing Series. Alas, after Wrightson's departure, little of the original Wein/Wrightson Swamp Thing impetus informed what followed. Domestic and foreign reprints and collected editions of the key Wein/Wrightson issues kept the character in the public eye even as the series ended and the character essentially vanished. Parodies of Swamp Thing appeared in Dave Sim's *Cerebus*, **Marvel Comics'** *Alf*, and the *2000 AD* strip "Zombo," among others.

Any impact after the 1970s sprang from the Moore/Bissette/Totleben/Veitch (1984–87) run on the series, heralding a new era for the character and a new movement within DC Comics. Building on the bedrock laid at Marvel Comics in the 1970s by British artist Barry Windsor-Smith and at the turn of the 1970s to 1980s by artist John Bolton, the arrival at DC of Brian Bolland (drawing *Camelot 3000* and covers on many titles) and Alan Moore (initially scripting *Swamp Thing*, but quickly accepting jobs from other editors for other characters) heralded the 1980s British Invasion. The redefinition of the character, title, series, horror comics, and the DC Universe began with *Saga of the Swamp Thing* #21 (1984), arriving when horror comics were almost nonexistent in the marketplace.

SEEDS OF A GOOD IDEA

In preparation for Neil Gaiman and Jamie Delano's planned takeover of the second series after Veitch completed his tenure, Gaiman submitted "Note towards a Vegetable Theology" to editor Karen Berger, proposing a unifying continuity for the DC elemental universe. As noted, Gaiman and Delano abandoned their plans after the *Swamp Thing* #88 debacle. Gaiman finally sanctioned its publication in *Prince of Stories: The Many Worlds of Neil Gaiman* (St. Martin's Press, 2008).

SOTST reinvigorated horror comics even as Moore used the title as a beachhead for greater plans beyond the boundaries of genre. Moore's ambitions were only partially realized before his eventual falling-out with DC in 1986–1987. Until then, Moore/Bissette/Totleben/Veitch dramatically redefined the character, series, and genre with lasting impact on the DC Universe and the industry. Previously staid DC proved surprisingly receptive to reinventions of fallow characters, matching and eclipsing Marvel's sales for the first time since 1966–1967. Moore's arrival, invention, and productivity were perfectly attuned to the publisher's appetite for change, paralleling and arguably encouraging DC's willingness to indulge similarly radical experimentation from Moore's immediate contemporary **Frank Miller** and seasoned pros like Howard Chaykin. The success of *Swamp Thing* and the rapid rise of Moore's star made possible previously unthinkable adventures—including Moore and Dave Gibbons's **Watchmen** (1986–1987), which arguably would not have existed without *Swamp Thing*. The team and series won numerous industry awards, including the U.K. Eagle Awards (Favorite Comic Cover, Favorite Comic Book, Favorite Writer, Favorite Supporting Character, 1984) and U.S. Jack Kirby Awards (Best Writer, 1985, 1986; Best Single Issue, 1985; Best Continuing Series, 1985–1987).

The team infused the 1980s mainstream comics industry with an extension of the visionary 1960s and 1970s American and British underground comix movement, manifesting a core devotion to philosophical and psychedelic aspects of the counterculture. This was most vividly embodied in the psychotropic properties given Swamp Thing's peyote-like "tubers" (another Totleben invention, embellished by Veitch, adopted by Moore) central to the celebrated "Rites of Spring" interspecies consummation of plant and human conjugal relations via a literal "trip." The team dedicated an issue to late underground cartoonist Greg Irons, introduced the hippie character Chester Williams (based on U.K. underground/alternative comix creator Bryan Talbot's character Chester P. Hackenbush), and embraced ecological themes, feminist concerns, and eruptions of Eastern and alternative religions, symbols, and iconography, profoundly redefining the series and what was possible in mainstream comics. Rick Veitch was a living link to underground comix, having first published in the late 1960s/early 1970s via underground comix collaborations with older brother/poet Tom Veitch before his 1980s and 1990s solo miniseries and graphic novels, including *Abraxas and the Earthman* for *Epic Illustrated*, *Heartburst*, *The One*, and *Brat Pack*.

SOTST #29's (1984) loss of the Comics Code was another major turning point, an unexpected event initially resisted by DC, forced to publish sans Code by the ever-crushing schedule demands; there simply was not time to make changes the Code deemed necessary. When the uncensored issue earned instant acclaim and sales skyrocketed, DC removed the series entirely from newsstand distribution and made it their first ongoing, unrated, direct market "Mature Readers/Sophisticated Suspense" title. This launched an experiment helmed by editor Berger that became the official Vertigo Comics line in 1993, allowing unfettered creative freedoms never available to the *Swamp Thing* creative teams.

Above all, Moore and his creative partners codified a poetic, expansive narrative canvas for the character and series that was the catalyst for the entire Vertigo universe and much that followed. Moore established basic narrative templates that a number of Vertigo series and miniseries emulated, as well as initiating DC's willingness to extensively retool, reboot, and completely reinvent past DC characters and properties, as long as the trademark (i.e., the name) remained the same (see Neil Gaiman's *Sandman*). The seminal Moore tenure has remained in print, domestically and overseas; any lasting momentum and impact Swamp Thing enjoys is still primarily due to the fact that the original 1970s Wein/Wrightson and 1980s Moore/Bissette/Totleben/Veitch runs continually reach a new and ever-widening readership. The ongoing popularity of horror comics since *SOTST* #21's debut is due in part to the availability of the key *Swamp Thing* issues. Bissette, Totleben, and Moore also fueled the genre's evolution with the anthology *Taboo* (10 volumes, 1988–1993), which Bissette and Totleben founded and Bissette edited and co-published, debuting Moore and Eddie Campbell's serialized **From Hell** and Moore and Melinda Gebbie's *Lost Girls*, among others.

It must be noted, too, that DC's censorship of Veitch's *Swamp Thing* #88 (1989) had a lasting negative impact on the series, the publisher, and the industry. Veitch's *Swamp Thing* #88 proposal and script and Michael Zulli's pencils had been vetted and accepted by DC editorial, and the inks by vet Tom Sutton were underway when DC balked and pulled the plug before Sutton finished the inks. With Veitch's immediate departure, the team that had been groomed to follow Veitch (writers Neil Gaiman and Jamie Delano) also left the title in solidarity with Veitch. The story broke in the mainstream press, reported in the *Wall Street Journal* and *Time* magazine. Thus, while Vertigo blossomed with ever-adventurous, taboo-breaking new titles, its founding title, *Swamp Thing*, was publicly neutered.

Arguably, the series and character never recovered from the debacle; it certainly never regained traction after the Nancy Collins run. Mark Millar's *Swamp Thing* opened with a four-issue arc co-scripted with **Grant Morrison** adopting the celebrated gag finale of the TV series *Newhart* (in which Bob Newhart awoke in bed with his wife from his former series, *The Bob Newhart Show*, to realize the entire *Newhart* series had been a dream): human Alec Holland awakens in bed, having dreamed—well, everything. Despite occasionally interesting story arcs, the ongoing series waned and was eventually canceled. After its demise, Swamp Thing sporadically reappeared in various DC titles, much as he had in his late-1970s limbo. Matt Cable (in human form) and Abby returned in the *Sandman* spin-off *The Dreaming* (#22–#24 in 1998, and #42–#43 in 1999), ending with Matt's lasting demise. Vertigo also offered the Jon J. Muth one-shot *Swamp Thing: Roots* and writer Tom Peyer's V2K entry *Totems*, and the Bissette/Totleben team reunited for one last Swamp Thing story, "Jack-in-the-Green," scripted by Neil Gaiman (in Neil Gaiman's *Midnight Days*, 1999), which was Bissette's farewell to mainstream American comics.

The third series starred Abby's daughter Tefe; the fourth series (29 issues, 2004–2006) reduced a soulless Swamp Thing (his elemental and human "halves" having been separated earlier in the mythos) to a sort of DC incarnation of Theodore Sturgeon's almost mindless, shambling "It," sentience minus soul. Still, there were high points: writer Will Pfeifer and artist Richard Corben concocted an homage to real-life cryptozoologist Loren Coleman (*Swamp Thing* #7–#8), followed by writer Josh Dysart and artist Breccia's lively end run through to #29. The team resurrected Arcane, introduced a new beau for Abby (shepherding Abby and Tefe back to Louisiana for another stab at domestic bliss), outed Tefe as a lesbian, thereafter reempowering Swamp Thing only to pitch him against a resurrected and utterly homicidal Jason Woodrue/Floronic Man. As noted, Dysart and Breccia's run was aborted, and readers now find themselves into a fifth series still too new to summarize or assess.

Outliving Swamp Thing, without a break, has been John Constantine, star of the popular spinoff title *Hellblazer* (debuting January 1988 and remaining the longest lasting of all the Vertigo titles—the only Vertigo launch title still standing). The original creative team Jamie Delano and John Ridgeway were succeeded by writers Garth Ennis, Mike Carey, Paul Jenkins, Warren Ellis, Neil Gaiman, Grant Morrison, Peter Mulligan, and others, and a steady procession of top-drawer artists. There has been one feature film, *Constantine* (2005), to date.

IMPACT ON AMERICAN CULTURE

It was the production and pending release of Melnicker and Uslan's *Swamp Thing* (1982), directed by Wes Craven (*A Nightmare on Elm Street, Scream,* etc.), that prompted DC to resurrect Swamp Thing in 1982. Among the promotional merchandizing were an art portfolio illustrated by Paul Gulacy (published by Eclipse Comics) and a movie novelization. Compromised by a change in the distributor's management, the film floundered theatrically, but became a staple of 1980s cable television programming and video store inventory, gaining cult stature.

Amid the volatile changes in the comic following Alan Moore's and Rick Veitch's departures, a second low-budget film was produced, *Return of the Swamp Thing* (1989), which lifted narrative and character fragments from the series but none of its wit, impact, or imagery; the movie novelization was written by Peter David. Even less derivative of the 1980s series was a cable TV series *Swamp Thing* (1990–1993). Both films and the series starred Dick Durock, who also played Swamp Thing as a guest on a British TV quiz show hosted by Jonathan Ross and as an elemental environmental activist in American TV public service spots, briefly supplanting Smokey the Bear.

A short-lived cartoon series (1991) spawned two video games and merchandizing, including Kenner Toy action figures, puzzles, games, and fuzzy Swamp Thing children's slippers. Only after the licensing rights reverted to DC Comics later in the 1990s did DC begin to license and manufacture limited-edition figures, posters, and so on more closely aligned with the comic book character's maturation, beginning with a DC Direct figure designed by artist Michael Zulli. A DC role-playing game, busts, statues, an action figure line, and more followed.

Swamp Thing cameoed in the Cartoon Network *Justice League* TV show episode "Comfort and Joy" (2003). A character named "Swamp Thing" (played by M. C. Gainey) figured in the action movie *Con Air* (1997). Novelist Thomas Gavin featured the Moore/Bissette/Totleben Swamp Thing in his novel *Breathing Water* (1994) as one of the obsessions of a central character, the 12-year-old asthmatic Paul, son of a gifted cartoonist passing the boy off as a long-lost heir; Gavin erroneously cites Totleben as the penciller and Bissette as the inker in one passage, but otherwise makes evocative use of the comic.

Musicians have also adopted Swamp Thing for occasional outings. Malcolm McClaren's fourth album *Swamp Thing* (1985) initiated the trend, followed by a 1980s Madison, Wisconsin–based pop rock band named Swamp Thing (Bob Appel, Mike Kashou, and Biff Blumfumgagnge), and others. The Grid (David Ball and Richard Norris) tune "Swamp Thing" was "a million seller" hit in the United Kingdom (according to the band's MySpace page) and appeared in the soundtrack for the John Waters movie *Pecker* (1998), and the lyrics of "Swamp Thing" by U.K. band The Chameleons clearly echoed the comic. Most recently, Gary Lucas & Gods and Monsters recorded "Swamp T'ing" for their album *The Ordeal of Civility* (2011).

SUMMARY

The 1971–1972 Wein/Wrightson *Swamp Thing* was a bracing crash course in traditional horror genre tropes. In the context of mainstream comics of the era, such a concentrated resurrection of archetypes—only two years after the Comics Code relaxed restrictions forbidding lycanthropy, vampirism, and so forth—seemed fresh and exciting, especially as delineated by Wrightson's lush Gothic artwork, fusing the illustrative strengths of EC Comics' Graham Ingles and Frank Frazetta. In just 10 issues, Wein and Wrightson reestablished a grand tradition banished from four-color comic books for nearly two decades.

The 1980s Moore/Bissette/Totleben/Veitch *Swamp Thing* was something else altogether, an at times extreme revamp of the character, series, and genre as a transformative, even apocalyptic work. Moore's uncanny ability to retain fidelity to established continuities even as he wholly redefined and reinvented much of the DC Universe found great favor. At its best, the 1980s Swamp Thing kept pace with the radical evolution of the horror genre in literature (i.e., Ramsey Campbell and Clive Barker, both of whom were fans of the series) and film, plucking nerves while expanding the possibilities of what seemed possible and permissible in mainstream comics. Consciously evocative of underground comix, psychedelia, Carlos Castaneda, John C. Lilly, Joseph Chilton Pearce, Brian Eno, and more, Moore and his creative partners laid the bedrock for the entire Vertigo line in four short years. After the departure of Rick Veitch from the series at the end of the 1980s, the salad days were over.

See also EC Comics; Gaiman, Neil; Moore, Alan; Morrison, Grant; Pogo; *Sandman*; Warren, Jim

ESSENTIAL WORKS

Moore, Alan (w), Stephen Bissette (p), Rick Veitch (p), John Totleben (i), and Alfredo Alcala (i). *Saga of the Swamp Thing, Volumes 1–6*. New York: DC Comics/Vertigo, 2009–2011; reprints *Saga of the Swamp Thing* #20–#64, including *Swamp Thing Annual* #2.

Wein, Len (w), Berni Wrightson (a), and Nestor Redondo (a). *Roots of the Swamp Thing*. New York: DC Comics/Vertigo, 2011; reprints *House of Secrets* #92 and *Swamp Thing* #1–#13.

FURTHER READING

Handley, Rich. "Roots of the Swamp Thing." http://swampthingroots.com/time line_01.html. Accessed February 8, 2012.

Irvine, Alex. *The Vertigo Encyclopedia*. New York: DK Publishing, 2008.

Whitted, Qiana J. "Of Slaves and Other Swamp Things: Black Southern History as Comic Book Horror." In *Comics and the U.S. South*, edited by Brannon Costello and Qiana J. Whitted, 187–213. Jackson: University Press of Mississippi, 2012.

Stephen R. Bissette

Tales from the Crypt

Tales from the Crypt, along with its companion titles *The Vault of Horror* and *The Haunt of Fear*, ushered in the first major wave of horror comics starting in the early 1950s. Though initially plagued by controversy and paranoia, through reprints and adaptations *Crypt* has enjoyed a long, healthy afterlife following its premature death.

HISTORY

In 1947, Max Gaines—founder of Educational Comics—died as a result of a fatal boating accident. His company passed to his son, William, who initially wanted nothing to do with **EC Comics**. The younger Gaines had never been a fan of comics, especially not the innocuous titles his father had published: *Picture Stories from the Bible*, *Tiny Tot Comics*, and *Animal Fables* among them. Eventually, though, Bill Gaines gave comics a chance. Western, crime, romance, and teenage comics like *Archie* had exploded in popularity in postwar America, and Gaines was quick to follow the trend. He hired a young artist by the name of Al Feldstein, who immediately got to work on an *Archie* knockoff, *Going Steady with Peggy*. When the teenage comic market declined, Gaines canceled *Peggy* before it even hit newsstands.

Gaines was not averse to following other trends. He changed the name of his company—from Educational Comics to Entertaining Comics—and he changed the names of the comics themselves: *International Comics* became *International Crime Patrol* and *Happy Houlihans* became *Saddle Justice*, then *Saddle Romances*. Soon, though, Gaines grew interested in innovating. Discovering that Feldstein and he shared a love of classic suspense radio shows like *Lights Out*, Gaines began introducing horror stories into his crime comics. The first "Crypt of Terror" story, "Return from the Grave," appeared in issue #15 of *Crime Patrol* (Dec. 1949–Jan. 1950), along with a macabre host—the Crypt-Keeper. In the tradition of Raymond, the sardonic host of the horror anthology radio show *Inner Sanctum*, the Crypt-Keeper was a wisecracking, pun-spewing counterpoint to the tales of terror he narrated.

Soon after, a second host, the Vault-Keeper, appeared with the story "Buried Alive," on the pages of the comic *War Against Crime* #10 (Dec. 1949–Jan. 1950). These new stories were immediately popular, and once again Gaines decided to change the name of his comics to suit the emerging trends, the difference being that Gaines was now *creating* the trend. After *Crime Patrol* #16, the comic became *The Crypt of Terror*. Three issues later, the title changed again, and with issue #20, *Tales from the Crypt* was born. Not long after, *War Against Crime* became *The Vault of Horror*, and a third title, *The Haunt of Fear*, replaced the EC Western comic, *Gunfighter*. *The Haunt of Fear* debuted a new narrator, the Old Witch, in its second issue; the three narrators collectively were known as the GhoulLunatics. While the Crypt-Keeper's origins were revealed in *Tales from the Crypt* #33 ("Lower Berth") and the Old Witch's "A Little Stranger" explained her beginnings in *The Haunt of Fear* #14, the Vault-Keeper never received an origin story.

The three GhoulLunatics shared space in each of their comics, with that title's associated character taking the lead story. For example, a normal issue of *Tales From the Crypt* would feature the Crypt-Keeper narrating the first tale, the Vault-Keeper narrating a second, and the Old Witch telling a third. There was often a fourth story with a rotating host, plus a text-only story, a letters page, and later an "Artist of the Issue" feature. Gaines had an amazing stable of artists, and he knew it. Beyond Feldstein, future comic-art legends such as **Harvey Kurtzman**, Jack Kamen, Wally Wood, "Ghastly" Graham Ingels, and Joe Orlando were among the *Tales* contributors, and Gaines took great pains to compensate, reward, and spotlight them. He encouraged artists to explore their own style, and paid on delivery, generally at $25 a page—higher than the industry standard (Hadju 2008, 184).

Story was just as important. Gaines, who was constantly dieting, took a supplement called Dexedrine, a psychostimulant that kept him awake nights. He would fill his late hours by reading horror and science fiction stories, then distill the plots down to broad concepts he called "springboards." Each morning, Gaines would go through a proposal process with Feldstein, by then his head writer, trying to "sell" him on his springboards. After whittling Gaines's ideas down to something viable, Feldstein would get to work writing—a story a day. Feldstein's output was fecund bordering on lunatic: for a time in 1953, he was writing four stories a week, editing seven magazines (the three horror comics, plus *Crime SuspenStories*, *Shock SuspenStories*, *Weird Science*, and *Weird Fantasy*), and illustrating many of the covers.

While details changed, *Crypt* and its companion titles' stories usually followed a fairly standard pattern: despicable character does awful things, and pays for them, often in grisly, ironic ways. "If someone did something really bad," Gaines later said, "he usually 'got it.' And of course the EC way was he got it the same way he gave it" (Diehl 1996, 36). As the years marched on, however, it became increasingly difficult to inject originality

Tales from the Crypt of Terror was an anthology published
by Entertaining Comics in 1954 that featured stories from the
publisher's popular horror comics, *Tales from the Crypt* and
The Vault of Horror. (Photofest)

into the stories. Gore, which had been left to readers' imaginations early
in *Crypt*'s run, became standard, making *Crypt*, *Vault*, and *Haunt* show-
cases for O. Henry irony mixed with Grand Guignol splatter-horror. Work
like that of "Ghastly" Graham Ingels—who earned his nickname through
his depictions of decomposition and "dripping" horror—took center stage.
Gaines himself grew a little leery of the more gruesome art, self-censoring
the Johnny Craig cover of *Vault of Horror* #32 to remove a cleaver from a
living corpse's head.

But gory art was not all that was giving Gaines pause. His springboards
were running out, and Feldstein's manic writing pace was taking its toll. In
a 1954 *Writer's Digest* article titled "Madman Gaines Pleads for Plots," Bill
Gaines put out a call to freelancers: "For five years my editors and I have been

writing an average of a comic book every six days: five a month, sixty a year. Each magazine contained four stories. That's 240 plots a year; 1,200 in five years. Now we're written out. Bone dry" (Gaines 1954, 18).

IMPACT ON COMICS

Tales from the Crypt, *The Vault of Horror*, and *The Haunt of Fear* were breakaway successes almost at once. Though horror comics had existed since 1947's *Eerie Comics*, *Tales from the Crypt* heralded a renaissance. Titles like *Haunted Thrills*, *Startling Terror Tales*, and *Terror of the Jungle* appeared from rival companies, crowding the marketplace and providing real competition for EC. Most of the readers—54 percent, according to one study—were adults, and by 1953, horror and horrific crime made up roughly a quarter of all comics being published. More Americans were reading horror comics than *Reader's Digest* or the *Saturday Evening Post* (Skal 2001, 230).

EC's horror titles remained leaders in the field, both in terms of profitability and originality. "The racks grew top-heavy with imitators," Gaines said, "[but] the EC approach in all these books is to offer better stories than can be found in other comics" (Gaines 1954, 20). Dedication to quality work paid off. Lyle Stuart, EC's business manager, stated, "Break even [for sales] was thirty-six or thirty-seven percent. . . . Our magazines were coming in at eighty-nine percent . . . ninety-three percent. . . . even *Life* wasn't doing that" (Diehl 1996, 76).

Unfortunately, being the leader also meant being the lightning rod for criticism. In a March 27, 1948, *Collier's* article, Dr. **Fredric Wertham** declared reading comic books was "definitely and completely harmful and was a distinct influencing factor in every single delinquent or disturbed child we studied" (Crist 1948, 22). In 1954, Wertham published *Seduction of the Innocent: The Influence of Comic Books on Today's Youth*. The book eviscerated horror and crime comics, drawing a link between them and juvenile delinquency. Under attack from the media, Gaines volunteered to appear before the Senate Subcommittee to Investigate Juvenile Delinquency, featuring the popular presidential hopeful, Senator Estes Kefauver. The hearings went badly, and sales of *Crypt*, *Vault*, and *Fear* plummeted. In a multilateral effort, Gaines called a meeting of representatives from other comics publishers, intending they work together to decide whether comics really were harmful to children, and to present a united front against Kefauver and Wertham's charges. Instead, the other companies banded together in opposition to Gaines—at his own meeting—and became the Comics Magazine Association of America. Under the new Comics Code Authority, they banned "all scenes of horror," specifically targeting "depravity, lust, sadism, and masochism" and the "walking dead, torture, vampires, ghouls, cannibalism and werewolfism" (Senate Committee on the Judiciary 1955). In short, almost everything from the pages of *Tales from the Crypt*. "This isn't what I had in mind," Gaines said, abruptly leaving the meeting (Diehl 1996, 93). On September 14, 1954, Gaines announced that his horror and crime comics would cease publication.

Killing the comics, however, did not kill the influence. The impact of *Crypt* would reverberate long past its demise. In 1964, editor Russ Jones and Warren Publishing introduced *Creepy* (and its later sister publications *Eerie* and *Vampirella*). In his "Creepy and Eerie Confidential," Jones explained his idea to revitalize the EC spirit in new publications—black-and-white magazines that fell outside the Comics Code purview. *Eerie*, *Creepy*, and *Vampirella* all featured horror hosts, like *Crypt* and its sister publications.

Major publishers also tried their hand at EC-flavored horror anthologies. **Marvel** went on to publish *Supernatural Thrillers*, *Chamber of Darkness*, and *Tower of Shadows*, each with a horror host; **DC**'s *House of Mystery* and *House of Secrets*, hosted by Cain and Abel respectively, were more successful.

The comics industry was not the only thing affected by *Crypt* and its ilk. In 1953, Gaines and company created a fan club called the National EC Fan-Addict Club, with an ongoing newsletter called the *Fan-Addict Bulletin*; by March of 1954, the club boasted 17,700 members. A number of celebratory fanzines cropped up, among them *Good Lord!*, *Potrzebie*, and *Hoohah!* Much later, after the collapse of EC's horror lines, new—now nostalgic—fanzines began to appear: *Spa Fon*, *Seraphim*, and what "remains by reputation the best second-generation fanzine," *Squa Tront* (Diehl 1996, 152). These fanzines featured original art, interviews, creator profiles, and occasional reprints of EC stories.

Eventually, reprints of EC tales were not limited only to fan publications. Only a decade after *Tales from the Crypt* disappeared from magazine racks, Ballantine Books revived the comics in a series of mass-market paperbacks collecting several EC stories each. Between 1964 and 1966, the anthologies *Tales From the Crypt* and *The Vault of Horror* were published, in addition to two collections of Ray Bradbury EC adaptations, *The Autumn People* and *Tomorrow Midnight*. Other reprints followed. In 1978, former EC "Fan-Addict" Russ Cochran introduced the Complete EC Library, which collected every issue of every EC comic in oversized black-and-white hardcovers, with *Crypt*, *Vault*, and *Haunt* comprising five volumes each.

Actual comics reprints followed: in the early 1990s, both Gladstone Publishing and Russ Cochran Publisher released series of double-sized (64-page) comics combining two full issues each. In 1992, Cochran teamed with Gemstone Publishing to release every issue of *Tales from the Crypt*, *The Vault of Horror*, and *The Haunt of Fear* almost exactly as they originally appeared, but with each title beginning at #1. Finally, a whole new generation was

TALES FROM RAY BRADBURY

One of the writers from whom Gaines borrowed plots was science fiction and horror master Ray Bradbury, whose "The Handler" appeared uncredited in *The Haunt of Fear* as "A Strange Undertaking." Not long after, Gaines springboarded Bradbury's "The Emissary" into *Vault of Horror #22* under the title "Look What the Dog Dragged In" . . . again uncredited. Presumably upset about the plagiarism but interested in how they were adapted, Bradbury wrote Gaines to let him know he had inadvertently forgotten to pay him for the adaptations, and requested a sum of $50. "I pretended they took my stories inadvertently," Bradbury later said. "They had read them, and then subconsciously stole them" (Bradbury 2005, 187). He further suggested that he and Gaines work together in the future, a prospect that thrilled Gaines. Official interpretations of Bradbury stories proliferated; by the time EC stopped publishing comics, over two dozen adaptations had been spread across the company's horror, science fiction, and crime lines.

now able to buy comics their parents (and grandparents) had been forbidden to read.

IMPACT ON AMERICAN CULTURE

In 1971, Amicus Films concocted the first official film version of *Tales from the Crypt*. Like the comics, it was an anthology piece, comprised of five stories based on EC's terror tales. Directed by Academy Award–winner Freddie Francis, *Tales from the Crypt* starred Joan Collins, Peter Cushing, and Ralph Richardson as the Crypt-Keeper (in a departure from the comics, this Crypt-Keeper appeared as a sort of abbot in a spooky monastery). *The Vault of Horror*, a sequel film directed by Roy Ward Baker, followed in 1973. Gaines, ever concerned with fairness, distributed the proceeds of both films among the writers and artists who had worked at EC during that period.

Novelist Stephen King, long a champion of EC's horror comics, released *Creepshow* in 1982. Both a movie and a companion graphic novel (illustrated by comics legend Berni Wrightson), *Creepshow* emulated *Tales from the Crypt*'s humor and style, with King's Crypt-Keeper doppelganger, the Creep, providing puns and color commentary. A year later, director Walter Hill, producer David Giler, and producer Joel Silver conceived of a *Tales from the Crypt* anthology picture; not an homage, but a direct adaptation. Bill Gaines sold them the rights and gave his blessing, but delays and scheduling interfered. Eventually, directors Richard Donner and Robert Zemekis came into the project, and it morphed from a feature film into an anthology series that debuted in 1989 on the cable channel HBO.

A critical and popular hit, *Tales from the Crypt* enjoyed seven seasons on HBO, winning a CableACE Award for Best Dramatic Series (1990) and attracting big name talent, both as actors and directors. Each episode was bookended by the Crypt-Keeper, a sophisticated puppet voiced by John Kassir. The show, too, kept the comics' fear-with-fun attitude, remaining playful and horrific at the same time.

Spinoffs kept *Tales* alive on TV. *Tales from the Cryptkeeper*, an animated children's program, debuted in 1993, and for the first time, the Vault-Keeper and the Old Witch joined the Crypt-Keeper onscreen. In 1996, the kids' game show *Secrets of the Cryptkeeper's Haunted House* appeared, and in 1999 *New Tales from the Cryptkeeper* debuted.

Three full-length films followed. Both *Demon Knight* (1995) and *Bordello of Blood* (1996) were released theatrically; *Ritual* arrived on domestic DVD in 2006. In 2007, a documentary directed by filmmaker Chip Selby titled *Tales from the Crypt: From Comic Books to Television* told the entire history of EC's horror titles, and featured interviews with horror luminaries such as John Carpenter and George A. Romero.

Tales from the Crypt was also adapted as a radio program. In 2000, Seeing Ear Theatre produced eight episodes, all executive-produced by the five producers of the HBO series. Both Danny Elfman's opening score and John Kassir's voice talents made the move to radio, with the Crypt-Keeper now singing lyrics to the theme song. Initially conceived as a comic-book version of radio programs like *Suspense* and *Lights Out*, *Tales from the Crypt* had at last come full circle.

SUMMARY

Tales from the Crypt and its sister titles emerged in the early 1950s, and its initial success might have had a great deal to do with the time period. World War II had ended, and in its wake the United States seemed a calm, even cheerful place. But the horrors—death camps and atom bombs among them—lingered. America became a paranoid country, exemplified by air raid drills, fallout shelters, and McCarthyism. Bill Gaines and company externalized those horrors in *Crypt*, *Vault*, and *Fear*, making them more easily understandable . . . and perhaps more easily disposable. *Tales from the Crypt* is timelessly relevant—mutable enough to be adapted for modern times yet still viscerally affecting in its original form. It is iconic because its basic tenets are as comforting today as they were for the Baby Boomers who first read these stories: no matter what terrible things happen, the bad guys will almost certainly be punished, and justly.

See also EC Comics; Warren, Jim; Wertham, Fredric

ESSENTIAL WORKS

Gaines, William (s), Al Feldstein (w), and Bill Elder (i). "Lower Berth." *Tales from the Crypt* #33 (Dec.–Jan. 1953), Entertaining Comics [EC Comics].
Gaines, William (s), Al Feldstein (w), and George Evans (i). "Strictly from Hunger!" *The Vault of Horror* #27 (Oct.–Nov. 1952), Entertaining Comics [EC Comics].
Gaines, William (s), Al Feldstein (w), and Graham Ingels (i). "Thump Fun!" *The Haunt of Fear* #20 (August 1953), Entertaining Comics [EC Comics].

FURTHER READING

Diehl, Digby. *Tales from the Crypt*. New York: St. Martin's Press, 1996.
Hadju, David. *The Ten-Cent Plague: The Great Comic-book Scare and How It Changed America*. New York: Farrar, Straus and Giroux, 2008.
von Bernewitz, Fred, and Grant Geissman. *Tales of Terror!* New York: Harper, 2000.

Kevin Quigley

Teenage Mutant Ninja Turtles

The Teenage Mutant Ninja Turtles were created by Kevin Eastman and Peter Laird in 1984. Best known for the animated series, the characters were a pop culture phenomenon in the late 1980s. *Teenage Mutant Ninja Turtles*' original print run was only a few thousand, but by the peak of their popularity, there were 700,000 copies of each issue and 90 percent of all American boys between ages 3 and 8 owned at least one Teenage Mutant Ninja Turtles action figure.

Between 1987 and 1992, it would have been hard to find a boy in America who was not a fan of the Teenage Mutant Ninja Turtles. The cartoon, action figures, and movies had kids acting out their favorite adventures, either by pretending to be their favorite Turtle or with the large assortment of action figures, all while yelling out catchphrases like "Turtle Power" or "Cowabunga!"

Leonardo, Michelangelo, Donatello, and Raphael were icons within a few years of their creation, with top-grossing feature films and a cartoon with a catchy theme song every boy in America had memorized. The "Heroes in a Half-Shell" were not just the most famous independent comic book ever; at one point, they were the biggest thing in popular culture.

HISTORY

Eastman and Laird's Mirage Studios published the original *Teenage Mutant Ninja Turtles* comic book series. Eastman's uncle Quentin loaned the two guys $1,000 to publish that first issue. The characters were conceived to parody popular comic books at the time, notably the teenagers in *Teen Titans* and the mutants in *X-Men*. Meanwhile, Daredevil and **Wolverine** were frequently fighting and standing on top of piles of ninjas, and Dave Sim's *Cerebus* featured an anthropomorphic barbarian aardvark. All these concepts were thrown together into a black-and-white tongue-in-cheek satire of the comics of the time.

The Turtles' origin was the stuff of Silver Age superheroes: four ordinary turtles and a rat came in contact with "mutagen ooze" that mutated them into humanoid figures. The rat became their "Master Splinter" and, because he had been owned by a cultured ninja, named the turtles after Renaissance painters and taught them ninjitsu. Their archnemesis in the cartoon was Shredder, who was the man who killed Splinter's owner. However, Shredder was killed off early on in the comics.

The Turtles were helped by not just their Master Splinter, but also their reporter friend April O'Neil, probably influenced by the fact that **Superman, Spider-Man, Flash,** and **Batman** all had love interests who were reporters.

Another popular supporting character was Casey Jones, a hockey-masked vigilante who fought crime with a baseball bat, hockey stick, and other sporting equipment. As a parody of vigilantes like the **Punisher** as well as the hockey-mask-wearing Jason Voorhees from the *Friday the 13th* film franchise, Casey Jones gained his own cult following. He has starred in his own comic book miniseries and was played by actor Elias Koteas in the first and third *Teenage Mutant Ninja Turtles* movies.

Archie Comics began publishing *Teenage Mutant Ninja Turtles Adventures* in 1989. The first handful of issues featured direct adaptations of episodes of the cartoon show, but the comic then went in its own direction. The stories became darker, striking a tone somewhere between the show and the original comic series. For instance, supporting characters actually died, April was trained as a ninja by Splinter, and Raphael wore the black outfit he wore in the Mirage series. The series spawned the spin-off series *The Mighty Mutanimals* about a team made up of the Turtles' humanoid animal friends and former villains. In 1991, the Ninja Turtles even met **Archie Andrews** and his friends in the *Teenage Mutant Ninja Turtles Meet Archie* one-shot.

In 1995, the Turtles were redesigned by the extremely popular comic book artist Jim Lee. The new iteration, with their more muscular build, never quite caught on with fans, and Eastman and Laird have gone so far as to say it is not a part of the official comic book canon.

In 2003, Dreamwave published a short-lived line of Teenage Mutant Ninja Turtles comics with stories written by popular comic book author Peter David. In 2011, IDW began publishing a new *Ninja Turtles* comic book series following the original Mirage continuity. Besides the ongoing series, the heroes also took part in the *Infestation* crossover, where they fought Cthulu monsters along with other 1980s icons Transformers and G. I. Joe.

IMPACT ON COMICS

Teenage Mutant Ninja Turtles was one of the comic series that started the comic book boom in the early 1990s and in particular is credited with starting a boom in black-and-white do-it-yourself comics. Many creators jumped

DAREDEVIL

Not only were the Teenage Mutant Ninja Turtles a parody of Daredevil comics, they basically share an origin with him. So close, in fact, that a case could be made that the Ninja Turtles operate within the Marvel Universe.

When young Matt Murdock saw a big truck was about to run over an old man who was crossing the street, he selflessly ran into the street to push the old man out of the way. As a reward, a can of radioactive waste that was in the truck's cargo fell out and splashed in Murdock's eyes, blinding him, but heightening his other senses, enabling him to fight crime as the superhero Daredevil.

The effects that substance would have on animals was never addressed in the Marvel comics, but it was the linchpin for the Turtles' origin, which also involves a young man pushing an old man out of the way, implying that the Turtles and Daredevil got their powers from the same incident.

Matt Murdock was later trained by Stick, while the Teenage Mutant Ninja Turtles were guided by Splinter. The Shredder's ninja henchmen were called the Foot, while the name of the clan of ninjas who were frequently ganging up on Daredevil is the Hand.

While Daredevil is a popular character, and has had mainstream exposure in the 2003 *Daredevil* film, he has never quite been a phenomenon. The Teenage Mutant Ninja Turtles might be a rare case of the parody being more famous than the original concept.

at the chance to make small-press books hoping to hit the multimedia jackpot that Eastman and Laird had with their property.

Kevin Eastman was heavily influenced by **Heavy Metal**, an adult sci-fi fantasy comic magazine, and especially the artwork of Richard Corben. He bought the magazine in 1991 and is now publisher and editor. Eastman's wife, model and actress Julie Strain, even voiced the main character in *Heavy Metal 2000*, a sequel to the cult animated film based on stories from the magazine.

In 1992, David Laird established the Xeric Foundation, which grants money to comic book creators in order for them to self-publish. Notable winners of this grant have been Jason Lutes (*Jar of Fools*), Adrian Tomine (*Optic Nerve*), Linda Medley (*Castle Waiting*), James Sturm (*The Revival*), Jai Nitz (*Paper Museum*), Fred Van Lente and Ryan Dunlavey (*Action Philosophers!*), and Jeff Lemire (*Lost Dogs*).

IMPACT ON AMERICAN CULTURE

The Ninja Turtles craze really started when the toy company Playmates bought the license to make action figures. Not much later, a syndicated cartoon series debuted, which changed the characters from grim and gritty vigilantes with **Frank Miller**-esque dialogue into wise-cracking, pizza-loving crime fighters with California surfer accents. Each turtle now had not just a specific weapon of choice, but also a different colored mask, making it easier for kids to distinguish between them.

In the cartoon, the Teenage Mutant Ninja Turtles' leader is Leonardo, who uses a katana sword and wears a blue mask. He is the leader and the serious one of the group. Donatello wears purple and fights with a bo staff. He is the smart one of the group and, as the theme song says, he "does machines." Raphael's favorite color is red, and his primary weapons are the sais or daggers. He is the most sarcastic one in the cartoons, but was perhaps the darkest in the comics, eventually wearing all black. Michelangelo, the "party dude," wears orange and uses a pair of nunchakus. He also uses the most surfer slang, such as "totally radical" and the word that became the turtles' main catchphrase, "Cowabunga!"

The cartoon portrayed the characters as somewhat goofy but lovable, angering some fans of the original comic books. Even though they fought villains in each episode, the stakes were never too high, and there were some moralizing and environmental messages thrown in to the show. Due to the violent connotations associated with the word *ninja*, the cartoon was titled *Teenage Mutant Hero Turtles* in many European markets. By the time the cartoon ended in 1997, it was the longest running animated show ever, until *The Simpsons* surpassed it just two years later.

The first *Teenage Mutant Ninja Turtles* movie was released on 1990. The film told the Turtles' origin story and featured both men in Ninja Turtle costumes as well as puppetry by Jim Henson's Creature Shop. Produced on a budget of $14 million, it earned $134 million at the box office, making it the fourth highest grossing movie of that year and the biggest independent film ever at the time. It was followed a year later by *Teenage Mutant Ninja Turtles II: The Secret of the Ooze*. As part of promotion for *Teenage Mutant Ninja Turtles II*, the Turtles were interviewed for a Barbara Walters special that aired before the Academy Awards. She asked them about their lack of nominations at the Oscars and then, in true Barbara Walters fashion, she made the Turtles cry when she asked them about their parents. *Teenage Mutant Ninja Turtles III* came out in 1993, and sent the heroes back in time 400 years, but by then the Turtles craze had died down considerably.

Even when the Turtles were only known within the comic book fan community, they were subject to parody and copycats with long titles, such as the *Adolescent Radioactive Black Belt Hamsters*, published by Eclipse Comics, and the *Geriatric Gangrene Jujitsu Gerbils*. When the Turtles hit the big time, other cartoons got into the act by having their own versions. For instance, Plucky Duck and Hampton Pig, characters on *Tiny Toon Adventures*, took on the alter egos of the "Immature Radioactive Samurai Slugs."

One famous concept possibly inspired by the Teenage Mutant Ninja Turtles came in 1993 in the form of the Japanese TV series *Mighty Morphin' Power*

Rangers, who were also youthful martial artists who were easily identified by the color of their outfit. When the concept was imported from Japan to America, the Power Rangers became a phenomenon in their own right, basically filling the role in the early 1990s that the Ninja Turtles had in the late 1980s. The team went through many permutations and has starred in two motion pictures. This all came full circle in 1997 when the production company behind the Power Rangers, Saban Entertainment, produced *Ninja Turtles: The Next Mutation*, a live-action television series that added Venus DeMilo, the Turtles' sister. The two teams even teamed up in a two-part crossover episode.

In 2002, Warner Bros attempted to reignite the film franchise with a CGI-animated film simply titled *TMNT*. The quasi sequel to earlier films caught up with the Turtles after they had drifted apart and had to reunite to face new threats. It featured voice work by Sarah Michelle Gellar as April O'Neil and Chris Evans as Casey Jones.

A second *Teenage Mutant Ninja Turtles* animated series hit the airwaves in 2003. This version was much more like the Mirage comic book, with some storylines being close adaptations of those in the comics. In 2009, the series ended with a 90-minute movie called *Turtles Forever*, in which the team was sent to a parallel universe and the Turtles were forced to team up with the iteration from the 1980s version. In scenes reminiscent of **DC Comics'** *Crisis on Infinite Earths*, a white wall of nothingness was erasing the different realities, and the Turtles get a glimpse of the other versions of themselves, including Turtles from the movies. The "1987" and "2003" Turtles are tasked with protecting the "Turtles Prime." When they are sent to the "prime" reality, it is the black-and-white world of the 1984 comic book. After the comic book Turtles refer to the cartoon Turtles as sell-outs (echoing what fans of the dark, satirical comic book said of the cartoon geared toward young children), the twelve Turtles team up and save the day. The movie ended with a quick scene of young Eastman and Laird drawing the Turtles for a comic they are hoping will sell and then taking a break to get some pizza.

The movie would serve as the end of an era, since that same year media conglomerate Viacom would buy the global rights of the Teenage Mutant Ninja Turtles from Mirage Studios with plans to produce a CGI-animated series on Nickelodeon.

SUMMARY

With the arguable exception of **Todd McFarlane's** Spawn, no comic book property has been created since the Ninja Turtles that has been as iconic as they are. While there have been numerous revivals and reboots of the Teenage Mutant Ninja Turtles over the years, they have never had the mania around them that existed around the time of the first movie. The Turtles are still icons, not just for the impact they had on pop culture, but for the inspiration they

USAGI YOJIMBO

While the Turtles have crossed over with other properties in the comics such as Archie, one of the most unique comic book crossovers ever actually happened on the *Teenage Mutant Ninja Turtles* animated series. Usagi Yojimbo was a ronin who also happened to be a talking rabbit that guest-starred on two episodes of the 1980s cartoon. Most of the target demographic of the show would merely think he was a new animal sidekick, not unlike the mutant frogs and other humanoid animals that would occasionally help the Turtles fight other mutated animals. Older viewers might catch that his name is a reference to the Akira Kurosawa film *Yojimbo*, but few would know that he was actually the star of his own independent comic series by cartoonist Stan Sakai. One clue a young fan might have was that Usagi Yojimbo's action figure had the word "Sakai" stamped on his foot, while all the all the others had the word "Mirage" on theirs. *Usagi Yojimbo* is still being published by Dark Horse. In 1999, it won an Eisner Award for the story arc "Grasscutter."

Another action figure in the Teenage Mutant Ninja Turtles line was Panda Khan, who was an armored anthropomorphic panda bear. The action figure was released even though the planned episode of the cartoon featuring Panda Khan never came to fruition. The character originated in Colleen Doran's independent comic series *A Distant Soil*.

provide to any comic book creator for how rich and famous one can possibly become from an idea that first manifests as a black-and-white comic book.

See also Heavy Metal; McFarlane, Todd; Miller, Frank

ESSENTIAL WORK

Eastman, Kevin, and Peter Laird. *Teenage Mutant Ninja Turtles: The Ultimate Collection*. San Diego, CA: IDW Publishing, 2011.

FURTHER READING

Sabin, Roger. *Comics, Comix, and Graphic Novels: A History of Comic Art*. London: Phaiden, 1996.
Wiater, Stanley, and Stephen R. Bissette. *Comic Book Rebels: Conversations with the Creators of the New Comics*. New York: D. I. Fine, 1993.

Tommy Cash

The Thing

The Thing is one of the first superheroes of **Marvel Comics'** Silver Age and is one of the company's most iconic characters. An original member of the **Fantastic Four**, the Thing (Benjamin Grimm) was created in 1961 by writer **Stan Lee** and artist **Jack Kirby**. Since then, he has been featured in most issues of that series (1961–present), as well as *Marvel Two-in-One* in the 1970s and 1980s, various miniseries, and two solo series, from 1983–1986 and in 2006. Although his appearance has changed over the years, his characterization has remained remarkably consistent since the early 1960s. With his famous catch phrase "It's clobberin' time!" Thing is perhaps the quintessential Marvel superhero.

HISTORY

The Thing first appeared in the pages of *Fantastic Four* #1 (1961). Along with the rest of the team, he received his powers from exposure to cosmic rays during an experimental space flight. For Ben, his powers were as much of a curse as they were a blessing. After their rocket crashed, he found himself changing. He became bigger and stronger, and his skin became thicker and tougher, almost like lumpy orange leather. Soon, Ben realized that he would be stuck as a "thing" apparently for the rest of his life.

In the beginning, Thing was bitter about his situation and angry at the rest of humanity that cowered in fear at his appearance. Although he never completely lost this feeling of anger and isolation, Ben soon began to accept his fate. His appearance began to evolve as well, as his leathery skin morphed into a more clearly defined rockiness. Through all this, Reed Richards, his best friend and the man who organized the ill-fated space flight that created the Fantastic Four, continued to try to find a way to cure the Thing. His experiments worked for the first time in *Fantastic Four* #78, but one issue later Ben himself decided to turn back into the Thing so he could save his friends. This would emerge as a recurring story for the Thing: losing his powers and then gaining them back again a few issues later. In *Marvel Two-in-One* #50, Ben took matters into his own hands by going back in time to give a cure to his past self. It worked, but instead of changing the Thing of the present, it created an alternate timeline where Ben Grimm is completely normal.

Over the years, Thing has been involved with a number of different women, the most prominent being the blind sculptress Alicia Masters. She loves Ben because she can sense the good and gentle man underneath his gruff exterior. Due to his own insecurities, Thing frequently has doubts about their relationship, though. For a time in the 1980s, Thing left the team to sort out his feelings for Alicia. Shortly after this, Thing became involved with Sharon Ventura, a female wrestler who eventually joined the Fantastic Four and became transformed into a monstrous She-Thing. In 2008, Ben began dating Debbie Green, a school teacher, and the couple planned on getting married. Before the wedding, though, he was reminded of all the women lost by other heroes. Although Debbie tells Ben that she is prepared for the risks involved with life with a superhero, Ben explains to her, "I ain't as strong as them guys. I couldn't go on if somethin' happened to you." As a result, in *Fantastic Four* #569 (2009), he decides to call the wedding off.

IMPACT ON COMICS

The Thing's status as an iconic character comes from four qualities that make him the perfect Marvel superhero. Like most of the first wave of Silver Age Marvel heroes, the Thing essentially is a metaphor that helps readers understand different aspects of human behavior. **Spider-Man** represents responsibility; **Captain America** represents patriotism; the **Hulk** represents anger; the **X-Men** represent difference. The Thing, meanwhile, symbolizes loyalty. He demonstrates this throughout his career, beginning with his first appearance in 1961. Spurred on by the success of the Soviet Union in space, Reed Richards prepares to launch his experimental rocket into outer space. His friend, pilot Ben Grimm, is skeptical, warning Richards (as well as Susan and Johnny Storm) that the cosmic rays the ship might encounter could kill them or have some other kind of devastating effect. But Reed, Sue, and Johnny have their minds set on going, so Ben decides that he will not abandon them despite his misgivings. His loyalty to Reed wins him over, but unfortunately he turns out to be right about the cosmic rays. They penetrate the hull of the ship and cause it to crash. When the foursome emerge from the wreckage, they have been transformed, and Ben gets the worst of it. "He's turned into a—a—some sort of a thing!" cries Susan.

Over the years, Thing's loyalty to his friends has remained his primary motivation. He is not interested in meting out justice in the way that **Batman** or even Spider-Man is. He enjoys a good scrape, but generally he seems to adhere to more of a "live and let live" philosophy—that is, unless his friends are threatened or need his help. In those situations, he is willing to sacrifice anything. Thing's ultimate act of loyalty is demonstrated in a story from 2004

A MAN OF FAITH

The Thing is one of the few superheroes with a recognized and believable religious affiliation. In 2002, a story in *Fantastic Four* #56 reveals that the Thing is Jewish. While visiting his old neighborhood on the Lower East Side of Manhattan, he helps an old pawnshop owner named Hiram Sheckerberg. When Ben thinks that the old man has died, he recites a Hebrew prayer over the body. The man sits up and asks Thing if the fact that he did not publicly announce his religion meant that he was ashamed of it. No, Ben explains, he just did not want "people thinkin' Jews are all monsters" like him. Later, in *The Thing* #8 (2006), while preparing for his bar mitzvah, Ben is shown talking with his rabbi and attending Hebrew school to learn the Torah.

(*Fantastic Four* #509–#511). After the Thing is killed, the rest of the Fantastic Four, convinced that it is not his "time" yet, decide that they will travel to heaven to bring him back. Seeing his friends convinces Ben that he would rather go back to Earth than spend the rest of eternity in heavenly bliss. Reed wonders, "What kind of friend would ask you to give up heaven?" Ben replies, "What kinda friend wouldn't do it? You need me, I'm there. B'sides, somebody's gotta keep you knotheads t'gether, right?" Thing's loyalty is so powerful that it even rubs off on people pretending to be the Thing. In the classic story "This Man . . . This Monster!" from *Fantastic Four* #51 (1966), a mysterious scientist kidnaps the Thing and takes away his powers to duplicate them in himself as part of an effort to destroy Reed Richards. Instead of doing this, the doppelganger realizes that Reed is a brave and sincere man. When Reed gets himself trapped in the Negative Zone, the scientist decides that Richards deserves to be saved, and in the end he sacrifices himself in the process of rescuing the team's leader—just as the original Thing would have done. As Reed explains it to Ben, "Somehow, at the last minute, some of your own heroism reached out through the endless void—and touched him!"

The second quality that has established the Thing as the quintessential Marvel character is his attitude toward being a superhero. Often, he does not want to be one. Peter Coogan, author of *Superhero: The Secret Origin of a Genre* (2006), argues that Thing is the first superhero for whom his powers were a burden. He is trapped in a body that is misshapen, ugly, bulky, and awkward. People look at him with fear and revulsion, and that makes him depressed. "It ain't no bowl a' Fruit Loops lookin' like Mount Everest on a bad day," he explains in *Marvel Two-in-One* #29 (1977). His body isolates him from average people and makes him feel alone. For many years, Thing worried that his girlfriend Alicia was only able to put up with his ugliness because she was blind. At the same time, he was often concerned that she would leave him for someone better-looking. When Alicia meets the Silver Surfer, there is some connection between the two of them, and Thing thinks that she prefers the alien to him. His reaction in *Fantastic Four* #50 (1966) is one of disappointment and resignation. "I can't even git mad! . . . If I wuz Alicia . . . who would I pick?? A gleamin' gladiator like him . . . or an ape like . . . me? Face it, ugly! It ain't no contest!"

Within the superhero genre, this was a true innovation. Earlier heroes like Superman, Batman, and Captain America were matinee idols; they were strong, masculine, and handsome; they were outgoing and popular. Thing changed that, and in doing so he created a nuance for the genre that deepened its ability to connect with audiences. Now the kid who felt ugly, or thought he was overweight, or was afraid that her acne turned her into a monster that no one wanted to be around had someone powerful and heroic with whom to identify. Underneath his thick, orange skin, underneath his surface ugliness, Ben Grimm is gentle and good—perhaps the best human being in the Marvel Universe—and the people who really know him are able to look beyond the surface Thing to see the real person in his heart. This is the same kind of identification that would help to establish the popularity of the X-Men, but it started with the Thing. In addition, the idea of the unlikely hero, the man or woman whose powers are as much a curse as they are a blessing, has since become a cliché of the Marvel Universe and can be seen in the stories of characters ranging from Spider-Man and the Hulk to **Wolverine**. Thing, though, can never escape or even hide his curse, making his story especially tragic.

This adds an emotional depth to Thing that most other superheroes lack. On multiple occasions, for example, he is shown crying. In *Fantastic Four* #300 (1987), he cries when Alicia marries Johnny Storm. Three issues later, he cries again when he realizes he still loves Alicia. As he watches Johnny's death in *Fantastic Four* #587 (2011), Thing is clearly in agony, especially since he realizes that he cannot do anything to help his friend. Tears roll down his rocky cheeks, but the most powerful image of the story shows the Thing comforting Franklin and Valeria, the children of Reed Richards and Susan Storm. It is this sentimental side combined with his loyalty to friends and family that has made him into a strong uncle figure. This first emerges with the birth of Franklin. Initially, when he is introduced to the child in *Fantastic Four* #94 (1970), he is reluctant to hold him, but when he finds out that his middle name is Benjamin he asks Sue to "hand 'im over to his Uncle Benjy!" Soon, Thing has tears in his eyes, because now he feels that he is "part of a family . . . instead of a freak show!" He has also taken on the role of uncle with other characters. In *Marvel Two-in-One*, Thing was forced to "adopt" a superpowerful alien with the mind of a child called Wundarr, and as he gains the ability to speak he calls Thing his "uncle." When his former teammate Crystal asks the Thing to help her protect her daughter from her husband Quicksilver in *The Thing* #3 (1983), he refers to himself as her "Uncle Benjy."

Like any good uncle, Thing is also funny, and this humorous side of the character helps to make him so quintessentially Marvel. Part of what helped Marvel develop its brand in the 1960s was its particular sense of humor, with characters like Spider-Man cracking jokes while battling criminals. The Thing was on the forefront of this, but he was more involved in physical comedy. For example, in *Fantastic Four* #102 (1970), Thing has a cold, which is not itself funny, but seeing a large orange monster blowing his nose and wearing a bathrobe and slippers is. Frequently, Thing is more like the straight man, as other characters put him into humorous situations through pranks. Many of these have come at the hands of the Yancy Street Gang in a running gag that began back in *Fantastic Four* #15 (1963). Ben used to be the leader of the gang, but now its main goal seems to be to playfully torment the Thing. Of course, the motivation for this repeated razzing is the sense of pride they have in one of their own becoming a famous superhero. Ben's teammate Johnny is also known for playing pranks on him. One classic story, published in *Marvel Fanfare* #15 (1984), details a long series of pranks that Johnny has planned for Thing on April Fools' Day. The joke is on Johnny in the end, though, when Thing lets him know that he is early, that it is actually March 31. The pranks are clearly signs of affection between the two teammates, and Ben realizes this when he looks back at the huge effort Johnny put into the production.

IMPACT ON AMERICAN CULTURE

With the rest of the Fantastic Four, Thing has appeared in a variety of other media. The first *Fantastic Four* animated series appeared on television from 1967–1968, to be followed by series in 1978, 1994–1996, and 2006. The Thing appeared without the rest of the Fantastic Four in a series called *Fred and Barney Meet the Thing*, from 1979. In this series, characters from the Flintstones were featured in half of each episode with the Thing starring in the other half. The animated series made some changes to the character, though. This version of the Thing is a teenager named Benjy Grimm who wears two rings that, when touched together, allow him to take on the rocky form of the Thing. "Thing rings, do your thing," he shouts during the transformation. Played by Michael Chiklis, Thing also appeared in the films *The Fantastic Four* (2005) and *Fantastic Four: Rise of the Silver Surfer* (2007).

SUMMARY

The Thing is the quintessential Marvel superhero and the soul of the Marvel Universe. His rock-like appearance mirrors his characterization: he is loyal, dependable, and strong. He is willing to stand by his friends and family no matter what, frequently sacrificing his own desires (especially his desire to be "normal" again) to help those in need. The Thing is sentimental and can take a joke (even when it is on him), but he also likes a good brawl, which is why his catch phrase "It's clobberin' time!" is always said with a sense of fun and anticipation. Because he is so well liked within the Marvel Universe, his words carry a great deal of weight. For example, his criticism of both sides of the superhero registration debate that was at the core of Marvel's 2006 crossover event *Civil War* was one of the most poignant moments of that storyline. For fans, Thing is a character that has elicited a great deal of identification since he was created in 1961. The Thing often feels lonely and isolated because his monstrous body is ugly and frightening to many people, but his inherent goodness teaches fans who might feel the same way that they do not have to be defined by their appearance. Fans reading the Thing's adventures learn the lesson that the people who really know them will always care about them, no matter what they look like. In this way, Thing is iconic because of the lessons that he teaches readers. Of course, his strength, his sense of fun, and his ability to "clobber" his enemies help, too.

See also Fantastic Four; Kirby, Jack; Lee, Stan; Marvel Comics

ESSENTIAL WORKS

Byrne, John (w, p), and Joe Sinnott (i). "Remembrance of Things Past." *Marvel Two-in-One* #50 (April 1979), Marvel Comics. Reprinted in *Essential Marvel Two-in-One, Volume 2*. New York: Marvel Comics, 2007.

Lee, Stan (w), Jack Kirby (p), and Joe Sinnott (i). "This Man . . . This Monster!" *Fantastic Four* #51 (June 1966), Marvel Comics. Reprinted in *Essential Fantastic Four, Volume 3*. New York: Marvel Comics, 2007.

Slott, Dan (w), and Kieron Dwyer (a). "Last Hand." *The Thing* #8 (August 2006), Marvel Comics.

FURTHER READING

Coogan, Peter. *Superhero: The Secret Origin of a Genre*. Austin, TX: MonkeyBrain Books, 2006.

Jones, Gerard, and Will Jacobs. *The Comic Book Heroes*. Rocklin, CA: Prima Publishing, 1997.

Matthew Pustz

Toth, Alex

Alexander (Alex) Toth (June 25, 1928–May 27, 2006) was an American cartoonist and animator best known for his tenure with Hanna-Barbera Productions. His character designs were seen on numerous Hanna-Barbera properties, but most famously *Space Ghost, Sealab 2020, Jonny Quest, Birdman, Thundarr the Barbarian*, and various iterations of the *Super Friends* franchise. Toth was influenced by the newspaper comic strip greats and brought their economic sense of storytelling and highly polished line work to both comic books and animation. Despite a career that was wrought with personal conflict and brief stays at employment, Toth's fingerprints can be found on an entire generation of comic book artists. For his contributions to the field, he was inducted into the Jack Kirby Hall of Fame in 1990.

HISTORY

Toth was born in New York City, the only son of Sander and Mary Elizabeth Toth, an amateur musician and artist, respectively. Toth's efforts at art were encouraged by his parents, his mother specifically, who would often draw profiles while her son watched. Drawing since the age of three, Toth would spend hours lying on the floor, listening to radio serials, re-creating the scenes as he imagined them happening and forming the characters as he imagined they might look. Later, he found inspiration in the slick, illustration-heavy magazines (*Saturday Evening Post, Colliers*, and *Liberty*) and newspaper comic strips of the time.

Like many of his contemporaries, Toth was greatly influenced by the work of Milton Caniff (*Terry and The Pirates, Steve Canyon*), Alex Raymond (*Flash Gordon*), Noel Sickles (*Scorchy Smith*), and Hal Foster (*Prince Valiant*). While enrolled at the famed Manhattan High School of Art and Design (formerly the High School of the Industrial Arts), Toth began taking assignments from Stephen A. Douglas, the art editor of *Famous Funnies* and *Heroic Comics*, who also helped launch the careers of Frank Frazetta and John Romita, Sr. During World War II, many of the regular artists working on Douglas's publications had been drafted, opening the door for young talent such as the then 15-year-old Toth. In an interview with *Comic Book Artist*, Toth recalls: "[I]t was a wonderful training ground. It was 'on-the-job training,' is what it was . . . an after school-hours thing for me, which was far better than . . . some of the . . . odd delivery kid jobs I had. It was terrific, the ego thing, to see one's name in print" (Cooke 2001, 25).

After graduating in 1947, Toth was hired by Sheldon Myer (creator of *Sugar and Spike*), then an editor for **DC Comics**, where he worked for the next five years on Golden Age incarnations of Dr. Midnight and **Green Lantern** in addition to various romance, Western, and science fiction titles. Working with Myer was instrumental in the young comic strip devotee's move into the comic book medium: "Shelly was . . . highly intelligent [and] he taught me a lot in tough and telling ways. He . . . taught me . . . how to tell a story to the exclusion of all else. It became my Holy Grail, I don't think I've learned it all yet!" (Hitchcock 1991, 3).

Eventually Myer would leave editing to return to his own art pursuits, leaving Toth in the hands of editor Sol Harrison. Where Myer worked with Toth on his story-telling technique, it was Harrison's devotion to pared-down layouts that inspired Toth's clean, minimalist style. Toth would later be fired by DC editor-in-chief Julie Schwartz over a disagreement. This would not be the first time where Toth and his employer ended their relationship on less-than-pleasant terms.

Toth would not lack for work as he had long aspired to move out of comics and into the more respected and lucrative daily newspaper strips that had originally inspired him. In 1950, he would move out to San Jose, California, as a dream of his would be fulfilled when he was hired to do ghost work on Warren Tuft's *Casey Ruggles* feature. Creative differences caused the two to clash, and Toth moved back to New York to take new work at DC. That return was brief, however, as Toth quit DC and moved to Los Angeles, taking assignments from Standard Comics.

In 1954, Toth was drafted into the U.S. Army and stationed in Japan. Where any other artist might have found his output significantly reduced, Toth revived an old idea of his for the Tokyo Quartermaster's *Depot Diary* and found an enthusiastic audience. *Jon Fury* was an adventure serial starring an Apache newsman and his charter pilot brother. Toth had complete creative control over *Jon Fury*, his first time enjoying such freedom. Each episode was presented in Sunday-page format. Toth would later be awarded a service commendation for the strip.

Upon returning to the States two years later, Toth moved to California and began doing anonymous work (company policy at the time) for the Beverly Hills–based Whitman/Western Comics, working even-numbered panel page layouts for their **Dell Comics** adventure and funny cartoon character lines. Toth initially felt restricted by the editorial guidelines, but soon came

TOTH'S INFLUENCE

What is most impressive about Toth's legacy is that despite his legendary demeanor, his devotees are so many and so varied. But as Howard Chaykin has said, "A lot of his difficulty was forgiven for the brilliance of his work" (Hunt, Clark, and Johnson 2009). Those artists and animators not included in the main entry who have publicly described his work as being formative to their own styles are legion: Toby Cypress (*Rodd Racer*), Jamie Hernandez (*Love and Rockets*), Grant Alexander (Pixar artist), Klaus Janson (inker, *The Dark Knight Returns*), Dave Gibbons (*Watchmen*), Scott Morse (*Spaghetti Western*), Joe Quesada (*Daredevil: Father*, former editor-in-chief of Marvel Comics), David Mazzucchelli (*Batman: Year One*), Steve Lieber (*Whiteout*), Darwyn Cooke (*The New Frontier*), Paul Smith (*Uncanny X-Men*), Tim Sale (*The Long Halloween*), Ronnie del Carmen (Pixar artist), Mark Chiarello (painter, art director for DC Comics), Tommy Lee Edwards (*Marvel:1985*), Jean Paul Leon (*Static*), Bruce Timm (*Batman: The Animated Series*), Glen Murakami (*Batman: The Animated Series*), and many others.

to enjoy the challenge of composing each static panel's information in an interesting way. His success at Dell led to TV (*The Danny Thomas Show, The Real McCoys, 77 Sunset Strip*) and film adaptations (*The Wings of Eagles, The Land Unknown, Oh! Susanna*). While at Dell, Toth did what is perhaps his most beloved comics work, the adaptation of the Disney television show, *Zorro*.

Toth soon found work at West Hollywood–based animation shop Cambria Studios. He was already friends with animator Warren Tufts and took the reins as the art director of *Space Angel* from 1960 to 1962. Toth left near the end of the first season after creative differences, but soon found himself at Hanna-Barbera working on *Jonny Quest*, created by his friend and former Cambria partner Doug Wildey. He then spent the next few years doing character model sheets and storyboards for *Space Ghost*, *Scooby-Doo*, *Josie and the Pussycats*, and *Herculoids*. In 1969, Toth left Hanna-Barbera over creative differences, this time citing their tendency towards low-quality, simplistic stories. He would return in 1973 to produce *Super Friends* and would work intermittently with the studio until 1982.

During this time, Toth continued to work in comics, drawing a single issue of *X-Men* (#12, 1965, "Where Walks the Juggernaut!") for **Marvel Comics**, writing as well as drawing stories for Pete Millar's *CARtoons* and *DRAGtoons* magazines, and collaborating with Archie Goodwin at Warren Publishing on *Creepy* and *Eerie*. Between 1964 and 1974, Toth would have contracts at DC Comics and Archie Comics (on the Red Circle stable of superheroes) and would return to *Creepy* for Warren.

As with most of his career, Toth would bounce from one employer to the next, doing both long and short stints in both comics and animation until 1985, when the deaths of his wife, Guyla, and shortly after, his mother, sent Toth into a deep depression and the artist became a recluse, ending all regular output. He did draw sporadically over the next 21 years, but mostly one-shots or doodles for fans. He died in 2006 of a heart attack while working at his drawing table.

IMPACT ON COMICS

"He was known to draw an entire comic book page—I saw him do this— decide it was too cluttered and then rip it to shreds and do it over with fewer lines. There was nothing wrong with the first version other than that Alex thought he could do it better. He usually could" (Evanier 2006).

While most contemporary fans are aware of the ever-present shadow that **Jack Kirby, Jim Steranko,** and John Romita, Sr., cast over today's artists, they are less aware of Toth's influence in that the lessons he brought to the forefront of the craft were less of verisimilitude and more of a strict economy to every panel. John Paul Leon says, "I read an interview with him and he said, 'The first half of your career you learn to put in, the second half you learn what to take out.' There's not a line [in *Torpedo: 1939*] that's superfluous. It's a perfect balance" (Hunt, Clark and Johnson, 2009). DC Comics art director Mark Chiarello echoes the sentiment: "His stuff was so bizarrely complex, but so simple. Every single panel he thought out . . . every aspect of it. He was a thinking man's genius when it came to storytelling" (Hunt, Clark, and Johnson 2009).

While the work he produced would be legacy enough, Toth was a tireless student of the form and served as a mentor to many young artists. Gil Kane once said of him, "He was the finest artist that comics ever had [and] next to Eisner, he was its most important educator" (quoted in Toth 1977, 3). Though he never taught formally, Toth was an endless advocate for his influences, and he passed on the lessons he had taken from them. "To be around Alex was to be with the ultimate fan," says writer/historian Mark Evanier. "He collected . . . studied . . . , wrote long essays (usually crammed onto postcards) to friends about them. It was always fascinating to hear a Toth analysis because he understood other artists from the inside" (Evanier 2006). John Romita, Sr., remembers, "I think he had hundreds of daily strips photostatted. He went from just another DC artist to a creative genius just by studying" (Keefe 2008). Toth was an accomplished critic who wrote scores of essays on comic book art and the comics industry for publications such as *Comic Book Artist* and *Alter Ego*.

In addition to that, artists such as Steve Rude, Paul Pope, and Michael Avon Oeming had regular mail correspondence with their hero. While still in art school and inspired by hearing of someone else who had written the reclusive master, Pope eagerly sought out Toth's advice: "His scope of knowledge was impressive and attractive to the young artist I was. But he didn't go out of his way to praise me as a student. He was so diligent and so focused about the responses he gave [to my art]" (Hunt, Clark, and Johnson 2009). Oeming recalls the influence his teacher had on him: "[For me], obviously, his love of shadows. There's a lot of guys who put black on the page but they aren't always saying much with it. Toth always did. His straightforward storytelling can be seen in my *Powers*" (Hunt, Clark, and Johnson 2009).

But as long-time friend John Hitchcock remembers, Toth was often reticent in handing out advice. "If somebody asked Alex's opinion, if somebody requests criticism, he'd fight it, but you'd get this brutal truth" (Hunt, Clark, and Johnson 2009). The irascibility that was often coupled with his critique is best seen in a well-circulated breakdown of several *Jonny Quest* pages that Rude sent Toth during the height of their exchanges. The pages are notorious for Toth's keen dissection of each panel, but more so for their condescending tone.

As Howard Chaykin would later say, "He was a seminal figure in comics. He is an astonishingly talented artist, and you cannot overstate how important an artist Alex is for comics and for me, personally. [But] all our meetings were confrontational. He was a difficult man" (Hunt, Clark, and Johnson 2009).

However, as another former DC art director, the legendary Carmine Infantino, once said, "Oh, to me, he's the best in the business. . . . That's my opinion, then and now" (Groth 2010, 25).

IMPACT ON AMERICAN CULTURE

Alex Toth's impact on the comic industry cannot be overstated, but most Americans are untouched by it. His work in animation, however, influenced millions of children through the 1970s and 1980s. His legacy continues even today in that the reimagining of those cartoons has inspired a revival for animated programming.

Adult Swim, the Cartoon Network's block of adult-fare programming, debuted in 2001 with *Space Ghost: Coast-to-Coast*, a satirical spoof of the talk-show format casting Toth's cowled space policeman as host. The show paired animation cels from the original cartoon against pretaped celebrity interviews. Already an established cult hit for Cartoon Network, *SGCC* was joined by other send-ups of Toth's work: underwater-adventure *SeaLab*

2020 became the broad comedy *SeaLab 2021* and the titular hero of *Birdman and the Galaxy Trio* traded in his superhero costume for a suit and tie as *Harvey Birdman: Attorney at Law*. While Toth had publicly admitted to the ridiculous nature of the source material, the send-ups reportedly irritated the artist. Still, the creative talent behind the material only saw Toth as one of their heroes.

Adult Swim was given one year to succeed, but soon turned the poorly performing Cartoon Network into an almost overnight cash cow. In 2004, bolstered by a trio of shows almost entirely made up of Toth's original work, Cartoon Network surpassed CNN in overall revenues (Dempsey 2004). Adult Swim has also been a guardian angel for animation that, despite critical acclaim, had been cancelled for low ratings or controversy. *Family Guy* and *Futurama*, both cancelled by Fox, were later revived by Adult Swim. The overwhelming success of both has led to a comeback for primetime animation, something all attributable to a handful of animators inspired by the imagination of Alex Toth.

SUMMARY

While Alex Toth never reached the popularity of the comic book masters he worked alongside, or even those whom he would later influence, his fingerprints are found all over their work and, in turn, their devotees. His style was not flashy, but focused on panel and page composition, crisp, clean line work, and character design. Students of the medium recognize the unquantifiable impact he has made on two industries. Toth's deceptively simple work preached that the art serviced the story first and eschewed the experimentalism of the time. His fierce dedication to his craft and unwillingness to compromise came to cost him work and friendships in both fields, but the techniques and standards he is credited as popularizing in the art community are so pervasive that they might as well be invisible to the layman's eye. Toth's contributions to the field are incalculable.

See also DC Comics; Dell Comics; Marvel Comics; Warren, Jim

ESSENTIAL WORKS

Toth, Alex. *Edge of Genius*. New York: Pure Imagination, 2008.
Toth, Alex. *Setting the Standard: Comics by Alex Toth, 1952–1954*. Seattle: Fantagraphics Books, 2011.
Toth, Alex. *Zorro: The Complete Classic Adventures*. Berkeley, CA: Image Comics, 2011.

FURTHER READING

Alex Toth Estate. "Tothfans." http://www.tothfans.com. Accessed December 14, 2011.

Mefford, Jon, dir. "Simplicity: The Life and Art of Alex Toth." *Space Ghost & Dino Boy: The Complete Series*. DVD. Two discs. Disc Two. Turner Home Entertainment, 2007. Television episode.

Mullaney, Dean, and Bruce Canwell. *Genius, Isolated: The Life and Art of Alex Toth*. San Diego, CA: IDW Publishing, 2011.

Jared Hegwood

Uncle Scrooge

He acquired his signature silk topper from a Russian haberdasher offering "a free cane with every purchase" before haggling with the czar. The broadcloth coat was a swap from Scotland in 1902, and his webbed feet still sport the spats that exude the requisite affectation of the self-made multigajillionaire. From his penny-wise appearance to his persnickety moods, Scrooge McDuck remains the most iconic of the "Quackers" **Carl Barks** developed for Disney's Donald Duck comics in the 1940s, 1950s, and 1960s. After a few early appearances in one-shot specials, McDuck's cantankerous persona stole the show. Before long, Uncle Scrooge appeared regularly in Disney titles worldwide where he exhibited all of the tight-fisted qualities of his Dickensian namesake. Unlike most comedic cheapskates and millionaire adventurers, however, Scrooge draws enormous satisfaction from his "physical passion" for cash (Barrier 1987, 23). Barks himself described him as the "stingiest character ever to live in the realms of fiction."

HISTORY

Would you really care about spider bites, speeding bullets, or cosmic surfboards, if you had $500,000,000,000,000,000,000,000,000,000,000, 000,000,000,000,000,000,000,000,000,000,000,000,000.16 in a massive money bin? Thus goes the life of "Uncle" Scrooge, the most notoriously frugal fantasticajillionaire of the thrifty Clan McDuck.

Disney "Duck Man" Carl Barks first introduced Scrooge as a rank-and-file villain for 1947's "Christmas on Bear Mountain" in **Dell**'s *Four Color Comics* #178. As the tycoon's given name suggests, Donald's miserly uncle was conceived to suit a Christmas-themed allegory of beneficence, but McDuck's role in Donald's world soon grew to match the gargantuan proportions of his fortune. With recurring roles in subsequent *Four Color* tales including "The Old Castle's Secret" (*FC* #189, 1948), "Voodoo Hoodoo" (*FC* #238, 1949), and "The Pixilated Parrot" (*FC* #282, 1950), Scrooge's character acquired surprising depth and charisma. By 1952, he was seminal to Barks's globe-trotting adventures and, by the mid-1950s, McDuck was starring as the robust hero of his own title that "rose to the top of all newsstand comic-book sales" (Barks 1987, 12). Since that time, voluminous series of foreign-language translations have made Uncle Scrooge a mainstay of international media. In fact, the worldwide fascination with Scrooge McDuck is particularly unique among Disney properties in that he "was never a movie star like his noisy nephew Donald," but rather "a creature of the printed page" who achieved inordinate success (Barks 1987, 11).

Many creators have lent their talents to Scrooge's miscellany, but two auteurs, Carl Barks and Don Rosa, invested the multimillion-dollar drake with particularly evocative virtues. In their hands, Scrooge's urge to amass ever greater fortunes became an ideological inquiry into capitalist entrepreneurship, neurotic stinginess, and the conflicts of the global marketplace. Barks and Rosa celebrate Scrooge's dogged work ethic, emphasizing his attachment to "Old Number One," the first dime he ever earned, and his personal motto of always staying "tougher than the toughies and sharper than the sharpies." Yet, when Scrooge's drive overwhelms his reason or his ethics, he is plunged into embarrassing, *expensive* situations that expose his foolishness and punish his excess.

As scholar Thomas Andrae observes, Barks's Scrooge stories explore "the American dream and our preoccupation with wealth, power, and technological control. They reveal the ironies and contradictions of the myth of the self-made man and question the fetishism of money and success on which this myth is based" (Andrae 2006, 19). Rosa's Scrooge stories include similar themes, but also opt for more idealistic, Horatio Alger–esque views on the competitive American spirit. Examples include Rosa's "The Raider of Copper Hill," where an ambitious Scrooge contemplates the construction of the Statue of Liberty, or "The Invader of Fort Duckburg," where Scrooge and Teddy Roosevelt swap tall tales around the "presidential campfire." Both artists construct exciting, satiric worlds, and Rosa even opens up his mise-en-page to homage and allusion as when his Eisner-award-winning *The Life and Times of Scrooge McDuck* concludes with a dour riff on the Xanadu sequence from Orson Welles's *Citizen Kane*.

Regardless of who dresses Scrooge's sets, dynamic comedy remains central. More specifically, Barks and Rosa orchestrate intricate sequences of slapstick and parody. Barks's routines are frenetic, farces trimmed with smart-aleck wit. In only one episode in 1954's "The Secret of Atlantis" from *Uncle Scrooge* #5, McDuck and his nephews initiate a madcap, multipage pigeon chase that takes them from the Money Bin to the tops of skyscrapers and down again, but not before becoming embroiled in the grandest pie fight in comic book history.

The most famous Barksian escapades drop Scrooge and company into complex conflicts rife with xenophobia and postcolonial anxiety. These bizarre commentaries on American dominance of emerging nations and subaltern societies employ funny animal allegories as signs of Cold War capitalism and Caucasian privilege. They are as funny and thrilling in their emphasis on Ugly American arrogance as they are conflicted.

The broad racial caricatures in stories like "Voodoo Hoodoo" (*FC#* 238, 1949) and "Land of the Pigmy Indians" (*Uncle Scrooge* #18, 1957) may rankle politically correct 21st-century dispositions, but Barks's international adventures were conceived as armchair fantasies of world travel and multicultural exchange. As underground cartoonist Howard Cruse recalls, "Barks takes the appetites and insecurities of existence into heady realms of cartoon fantasy, but the adventures are rooted solidly in the textures of everyday emotion" (Cruse 1982, 23). Barks himself admitted, "I never had much love for a lot of the foolish customs we have in this world, and so I poked fun at a lot of that stuff" (Ault 2003, 6). Working in anonymity with only his wife, Garé, collaborating as colorist and letterer, Barks assembled research files on foreign cultures that lent crucial verisimilitude to the distant locales visited by Scrooge and his nephews. The results, as many have noted, were surprising in their multipronged attack on mainstream American ideals. Some foreign readers cared little for Scrooge's exploitation of other nations. The most startling response arose from the 1971 revolutionary socialist manifesto *How to Read Donald Duck: Imperialist Ideology in the Disney Comic* by Ariel Dorfman and Armand Mattelart, who threatened to "pluck and roast" Mr. Disney's ducks for their subjugation of the Chilean people (Dorfman and Mattelart 1971, 2). Citing several Scrooge and Donald stories, they argued that "grotesque folklorism" and "superficial and stereotyped prejudices" belittled otherwise proud cultures (Dorfman and Mattelart 1971, 48). Though flawed by factual errors and ideological limitations, Dorfman and Mattelart served *Uncle Scrooge* well by extending the critical discourse surrounding his and Barks's ambivalence to diversity and difference.

In the 1990s, Don Rosa would paint the same duck a different color, building equally mythic yarns upon Barksian formulas. By the 1980s, Barks was beginning to gain notoriety thanks to the dogged efforts of determined critics and devoted fans. The international market in *Scrooge* reprints boomed, and there was a popular hunger for new projects. What Barks rendered in rough patches of back story, Don Rosa would weave into a resplendent quilt of continuity. As a comedic epic that rivals anthropomorphic masterworks like Jeff Smith's **Bone** and Dave Sim's *Cerebus*, Rosa's *The Life and Times of Scrooge McDuck* overhauls previous allusions to the tycoon's glory days, lost loves, and vanquished rivals. The final mammoth tale would fill three full graphic novels, and every chapter retains the spunky comedy, blithe wit, and gutsy glory of Barks's originals.

Rosa also provided old Scrooge lovers with new thrills, incorporating a kind of trivial pursuit into his stories with hidden references peppered throughout each installment. His "Cowboy Captain of the Cutty Sark" features a

THE ROGUES' GALLERY

Scrooge McDuck requires frequent, excruciating lessons in charity and humility. He finds himself constantly embroiled in world-spanning races, chases, and donnybrooks that arise over little more than a shouting match with other moguls like Flintheart Glomgold from 1956's "The Second Richest Duck" (*Uncle Scrooge* #15). In other tales, he struggles against swindlers like Chisel McSue in 1953's "Trouble from Long Ago (the Horseradish Story)" (*FC* #495), or negotiates age-old clan feuds between the McDucks and the Whiskervilles as in 1994's "The Last of the Clan McDuck" and 1996's "The Billionaire of Dismal Downs." In fact, McDuck's rogues' gallery of "burglars, bamboozlers, sneak thieves, and legal loophole law-twisters" rivals any superhero's catalogue of gaudy villains (Barks 1987, 294). Alongside the likes of Porkman DeLardo, Bombie the Zombie, Soapy Slick, and Copperhead McViper, two major antagonists developed iconic personalities of their own: the "terrible, terrible" Beagle Boys, and the mysteriously seductive sorceress-cum-duck Fatale, Magica DeSpell. As "one of the great criminal families of all time, notable for their great resourcefulness and their great failures," the Beagle Boys signify the polar opposite of the McDuck ethos (Chalker 1974, 20). If Scrooge scoured the globe as a lonely bird to accumulate his legacy, the Beagle dynasty collaborates on crime. As hounds, they also instinctively relish the agony of waterfowl, and since 1952, the Beagles have used giant robots, gargantuan axes, bottled messages, gophers, x-rays, steam shovels, dream machines, riverboats, and conquistador costumes to bamboozle Scrooge.

The uncanny Magica DeSpell constitutes an entirely different problem. Disney's Duck family dramas remain fairly drake-centered, with sidebar females like Daisy and her nieces, Grandma Duck, Glittering Goldie, and later, Scrooge's sisters, Hortense and Matilda, providing small but pithy feminine color. The majority of Scrooge's rivals are masculine, but none compare to the slinky sorceress from Mt. Vesuvius. In Barks's words, Magica exemplifies "witchcraft at its perfidious, spell-casting worst" and her lifelong hunt for his Old Number One dime has become the most persistent of his wealth-centered castration anxieties. Scrooge scoffed at her magical prowess when she first appeared in 1964, but after years of "sure-enough, honest-to-god, unspurious, professional hex-throwing," McDuck "hasn't laughed since" and Magica's long-standing hold on the title of his most dangerous rival remains unchallenged (Barks 1987, 294).

dog-nosed parody of Gregory Peck's Captain Ahab and, in the fashion of Hirschfeld's famously encrypted "Ninas," Rosa frequently deploys what he would label "D.U.C.K" spoilers amidst the insane details of his compositions. Barks also toyed with hidden messages, but Rosa became Scrooge McDuck's James Joyce, flooding the already formidable action of steamboat races, gold rushes, cavalry charges, and desert chases with myriad kernels of playfulness and intrigue. Rosa also toned down the ethnic satires, amping up the struggle, competition, and stick-to-itiveness that made Scrooge a flustered miser. His potent combination of artistic homage, sequential puzzle, and devout continuity appears derivative at times, but Rosa's extension of Barks's Duckiverse is every bit as raucous, exciting, and side-splitting. Barks and Rosa also contributed to Scrooge's domestic misadventures centering around quasi-metropolitan Duckburg. These situational comedies lack the wild exoticism and derring-do of the international sojourns, but Scrooge's homebound stories are also profound critiques of midcentury capitalism, conformity, and conspicuous consumption. Many Duckburg features describe Scrooge's efforts to protect the cubic acres of cash he hordes in his Money Bin, but the most cherished of these is undoubtedly 1952's "Only a Poor Old Man" wherein the Great Duck ponders his compulsive love of currency.

The story appeared in the first issue of Dell's *Uncle Scrooge* title, and greatly revised Scrooge's motivations, to show that his money lust is not rooted in envy or avarice. McDuck's uniquely jolly relationship to cash is best illustrated by the money baths and swan dives he takes through his abundant ocean of greenbacks and coins. In simplest terms, he appreciates his money as a well-earned reward. Like Snoopy's dog house or **Pogo**'s nonsensical sing-alongs, Uncle Scrooge's money—despite the power, status, and privilege it allows him—is the stuff of personal dalliance and fantasy. At one point he confides to his nephews that "you would love it too if you earned it like I did." It is the responsibility and accomplishment that come from amassing his wherewithal from everywhere that so enthrall him.

All told, Uncle Scrooge's exploits have spanned the furthest backwaters of the Americas and the queerest corners of the Earth, not to mention other planets, mythical realms, and underground and undersea lost civilizations. As one of the most original action-comedy stars in comics, McDuck's extraordinary wealth, derived from "square deals" with big profits, still provides even bigger pay-offs of laughter and delight.

IMPACT ON COMICS

Uncle Scrooge and his "umptillion fabutillion" dollars have had as much impact on American cartooning as any caped crusader or canine flying ace. Among the highest watermarks in funny animal comics, Scrooge's exploits filled more than 400 issues of his own title, as well as numerous one-shot giants like *Daisy Duck and Uncle Scrooge Showboat* or *Uncle Scrooge Goes to Disneyland*, and later archival "library" compilations like the *Carl Barks Library* series. At one point in the mid-1990s, at least four separate Scrooge-centered series ran simultaneously in the United States alone. He would also star in more than 40 installments of *Walt Disney's Comics and Stories* and enjoy recurring roles in other Disney titles like *Huey, Dewey, and Louie Junior Woodchucks*, *Donald Duck*, and *Gyro Gearloose*. In fact, Scrooge's milieu remained popular enough in the 1960s and 1970s to support a 47-issue spin-off title featuring the Beagle Boys, another 12-issue series entitled *Uncle Scrooge vs. the Beagle Boys* in the early 1980s, and a *Walt Disney Showcase* devoted to Magica DeSpell. A single installment of Whitman's Top Tales series, 1960's *Uncle Scrooge the Lemonade King*, with illustrations by Barks and Norman McGary, comprises an important foray into children's books. As an odd coda, Barks also began a series of Scrooge- and Donald-based oil paintings and limited edition prints in the mid-1980s, and to much surprise, connoisseurs coughed up thousands for "arty" renderings of their favorite penny-pincher. These works inspired other high-end Scrooge collectables including fine china figurines that also fetch extraordinary prices, further confirming McDuck's cache as a feisty money-maker.

IMPACT ON AMERICAN CULTURE

Scrooge's fan base has always been ardent, as historian Michael Barrier confirms: "Two of the greatest adventure heroes in comic books stood about three feet tall, were covered in feathers, and had bright orange bills and feet.... They were unlikely heroes, but their adventures in the Walt Disney comic books of the 40s and 50s were much more exciting to me, and to millions of other children, than all the exploits of the costumed superdoers" (Barrier 1973, 211). Scrooge's globe-trotting explorership never lost its grip, though it was limited to print media for 50 years. McDuck has enjoyed few big screen appearances beyond the 1967 educational short, *Uncle Scrooge and Money*. Ironically, in 1983, he did a leading turn as his own namesake, in 1983's *Mickey's Christmas Carol*. Eventually, a good deal of Barks's Scrooge material was loosely adapted for the animated series *DuckTales*, which ran for 100 episodes from 1987 to 1990 and also spawned a fairly Scrooge-centric feature film and spin-off videogame. A number of figurines, toys, action figures, and, of course, piggybanks were also marketed between the 1960s and early 2000s. While films, toys, and TV series certainly aided Uncle Scrooge's reputation as an irascible miser, a plethora of foreign-language "albums" attests to his extraordinary popularity overseas.

At times, Scrooge's influence becomes quite absurd, even by Barksian standards. Perhaps his hippest, strangest moment of resonance involves Chloe Sevigny's name check during her seduction scene from Whit Stillman's 1998 indie comedy, *The Last Days of Disco*. After her crush for the evening reveals himself as an avid Barks collector, Sevigny's character slinks towards him, amorously purring, "There's something really sexy about Scrooge McDuck." Scrooge's unlikely links to high fashion and sexual politics have also included the YouTube–abetted Gay Marriage anthem "Sex with Ducks" and iconoclastic blog posts such as Brad Pike's "Scrooge McDuck and the Modern Elite" (Pike 2011). A more subtle but no less significant homage occurs throughout Art Spiegelman's Pulitzer Prize–winning Holocaust memoir *Maus*, wherein Art's irritably tight-fisted survivor father, Vladek, sports eyeglasses evocative of the "same optician" who fashioned "Uncle Scrooge's pince-nez" (Spiegelman and Mouly 2009, 9).

Emphasizing core ethical conflicts concerning success, profit, status, and greed, Scrooge McDuck provides distinct "perspective on American culture" because his persona encompasses a range of "readily recognizable characteristics" such as "ingenuity, integrity, determination, a kind of benevolent avarice, boldness, a love of adventure, and a sense of humor" (Lucas 1987, 9). As Hollywood icon and longtime Barks aficionado George Lucas observes, Uncle Scrooge's popularity has "something to say about the culture that produces it. . . . These comics are one of the few things you can point to and say: like it or not, this is what America is" (Lucas 1987, 9).

SUMMARY

As Donald Duck's estranged uncle of wealth and mystery, Scrooge leapt directly from Carl Barks's creative impulses towards high-flying adventure and sly mockery. Since then, Scrooge has changed the very landscape of "funny animal" art. It is argued that Donald Duck cinematically eclipsed Mickey Mouse in popularity because Disney Studios preferred to play it safe with their masthead character. Donald's films, filled with outrageous antics and tantrums, spoke to everyone's frustrations. The same dynamic applies to how Donald's ornery tycoon uncle upstaged his nephew from Christmas 1947 onward into the next century.

ESSENTIAL WORKS

Barks, Carl. *Uncle Scrooge McDuck: His Life and Times*. Berkeley, CA: Celestial Arts, 1987.

Rosa, Don. *The Life and Times of Scrooge McDuck*. Timonium, MD: Gemstone Publishing, 2005.
Rosa, Don. *The Life and Times of Scrooge McDuck Companion*. Timonium, MD: Gemstone Publishing, 2006.

FURTHER READING

Andrae, Thomas. *Carl Barks and the Disney Comic Book: Unmasking the Myth of Modernity*. Jackson: University Press of Mississippi, 2006.
Ault, Donald. ed. *Carl Barks: Conversations*. Jackson: University of Mississippi, 2003.
Barrier, Michael. *Carl Barks and the Art of the Comic Book*. New York: Lilien, 1981.

Daniel F. Yezbick

Ware, Chris

Cartoonist Chris Ware found widespread acclaim for his work on *Jimmy Corrigan: The Smartest Kid on Earth*. A complicated and avant-garde graphic novel, *The Smartest Kid on Earth* is considered a tremendous literary feat and regularly called a modern masterpiece. Ware's work pushed the limits of what graphic novels could be—ushering in a wave of intelligent and highly literary projects. Ware's unique approach to an image's composition has made him one of the most respected sequential artists working in the field.

HISTORY

Born in Omaha, Nebraska, in 1967, Ware was exposed to comic strips at an early age. His mother and grandfather worked for the *Omaha World-Herald* and familiarized him with the publication's art department. After high school, Ware attended the University of Texas in Austin and drew for the university's student newspaper. He has since disavowed much of this early work; however, it was the gestation period for a number of his characters. His most significant creations from the time included the duo Quimby the Mouse and Sparky the Cat, a nameless potato-shaped protagonist, and an early version of Jimmy Corrigan. These characters would later reappear in Ware's other works (Ball and Kuhlman 2010, xiii–xvi).

While Ware might now distance himself from his university drawings, they were significant enough to capture the attention of comics stalwart **Art Spiegelman,** who asked Ware to contribute to his anthology magazine *RAW*— which sought artistic works of sequential art. Ware published two pieces in the final two issues of the magazine in 1990 and 1991 (Ball and Kuhlman 2010, xvi).

After earning his undergraduate degree, Ware moved to Chicago in 1991 to pursue a master's degree in printmaking at the Art Institute of Chicago. He did not complete the degree because of a perceived bias against narrative art. His time at the institute, however, seemed to have impacted his work by deepening Ware's art history knowledge (Raeburn 2004, 12).

His move to Chicago was not without some success. Once there he began drawing a full-page comic strip for the alternative weekly newspaper *NewCity*, and based on his work in *RAW*, publisher **Fantagraphics** Books offered him an ongoing series. In 1993, Ware published *The ACME Novelty Library*. For an alternative comix series, *The ACME Novelty Library* was a major success, selling about 20,000 copies of each issue (Raeburn 2004, 9). The series contained a number of Ware's previously established characters, most importantly his ongoing Jimmy Corrigan narrative, which was completed in 2000's *The ACME Novelty Library* #14. The series also worked to highlight Ware's experimentation as many of the issues were published in irregular sizes ranging from pamphlets to oversized books. Ware's work on the series garnered him a cavalcade of awards, including the Harvey, Eisner, and Ignatz Awards, and a Reuben Award for Excellence. Fantagraphics published 15 issues of the anthology series before Ware took over all facets of the publishing process (Fantagraphic Books).

While Ware's work brought him industry attention, it was not until he completed his Jimmy Corrigan narrative that he received more mainstream acknowledgement. After seven years of work, Ware completed the Jimmy Corrigan story. In 2000, the narrative was edited and published as *Jimmy Corrigan: The Smartest Kid on Earth*, a 380-page hardback book. The graphic novel was released to critical acclaim and sold 80,000 copies. It is now considered one of the medium's most celebrated works—earning comparisons to Spiegelman's own Pulitzer Prize–winning Holocaust tale **Maus: A Survivor's Tale** (Raeburn 2004, 9).

The Smartest Kid on Earth's slim plot follows the titular character, a downtrodden, ineffectual, and friendless man, after he receives a letter from his long-absent father seeking to reconnect. What follows is a family story in which three generations of Corrigan men are each shown with similar qualities: sad, defeated men with rich fantasy lives. The book moves from 1890s Chicago to a small town in Michigan in the 1980s.

The book received "Best of the Year" mentions in several prominent media outlets such as *Time*, the *Village Voice Supplement*, and *Entertainment Weekly*. In 2005, *Time* magazine ranked the work as one of the 10 best English-language graphic novels written. The book's most significant accolades were the American Book Award and the 2001 Guardian First Book Award.

Ware has undertaken two other major long-form narrative projects that are expected to be collected in graphic novels. He is serializing these stories in various media outlets that he then collects in *The ACME Novelty Library* series—similarly to how he built his first book. The serialized stories are "Building Stories" and "Rusty Brown."

In 2004, Ware was chosen as the first cartoonist to regularly serialize an ongoing story in the *New York Times Magazine*. Between 2005 and 2006, Ware published "Building Stories," an ongoing project about the inhabitants of a three-story Chicago apartment building. The first full chapter of "Building

CLEAR LINE STYLING

In various interviews, Ware has stated that he drew inspiration from Hergé—the Belgian creator of the *Adventures of Tintin* comic series. Hergé used a specific drawing style known as *ligne claire*, or clear line, which gives equal weight to every line on a page. The end result is that the foreground and background in an image have equal depth of field. In an interview with the *Independent*, Ware stated that though he did not like the comic's content as a child, he took the idea of using naturalistic colors surrounded by a black line directly from Hergé.

In an interview with the Public Broadcasting Service, Ware said that he believes the black lines that surround his work represent approximations of the way adults see images. Ware believes that once people reach a certain age they stop "seeing" images and begin to classify and categorize them. One result of this way of compositing images is that some consider Ware's work antiseptic. In true Ware fashion, he has called this interpretation something of a failure on his part.

Stories" appeared in 2007's *The ACME Novelty Library* #18. "Rusty Brown" follows a similar pattern. Brown is a 30-something cantankerous man-child who lives with his mother and collects action figures and other pop culture trinkets.

Outside of sequential art and the publication of *The ACME Novelty Library*, Ware has found success in a number of areas. Ware has edited two significant works of comic books since the publication of *The Smartest Kid on Earth*. In 2004, he edited *McSweeney's Quarterly Concern* #13, an issue completely devoted to comic books, and the 2007 *Best American Comics*.

In 2006, Ware designed four "Thanksgiving" covers for the *New Yorker* that were published by the magazine simultaneously. The covers were collected and released with supplemental material in *The ACME Novelty Library* #18.5 in 2007.

In the following years, 2007 and 2008, Ware contributed animation to the short-lived *This American Life* television show, based on the radio program. One animation featured Quimby the Mouse.

There has been other design work as well. The *Huffington Post* reported in 2010 that Ware designed a cover for *Fortune* magazine's "Fortune 500" issue, which ranks the United States' top companies. Ware's cover featured a large "500" styled as a skyscraper, looming over the United States. The cover contained satirical social commentary related to the economic downturn of 2008. Among the depictions Ware drew was a sign for "Toxic Asset Acres," "401K Cemetery," and a house floating in the sea, a references to homes being "underwater," or worth less than the homeowner's mortgage.

IMPACT ON COMICS

Ware's impact on comic books is as a counterpoint to mainstream comic books. While comic books have matured, they are, for better or worse, still popularly associated with superheroes and youth. This is not necessary true, but prevailing thought remains. Ware's work strives to bring a maturity and literacy to the medium that is not explicitly tied to brightly colored costumes. With the achievement of *The Smartest Kid on Earth*, Ware has shown, as Spiegelman's *Maus* did, that graphic narratives can be highly literate works of art. This distinction places Ware in high company along with cartoonists such as **Daniel Clowes** (*Ghost World*), Jaime and Gilbert Hernandez (*Love and Rockets*), and Charles Burns (*Black Hole*).

Perhaps Ware's largest impact on the medium is his willingness to subvert typical beliefs about comic books, in design and subject matter. Ware's designs exhibit a number of convergent styles and themes. He has worked to move beyond what is typically expected of sequential art—easily defined panels of images—and brings a sophistication to the medium that helps buoy his stance as a critics' darling. Unlike traditional graphic novelists, Ware combines graphic design and other elements. His works are often filled with fake ads that mimic ones found in the 1950s, cut-outs, and foldout instructions. Frequently called geometric, Ware's illustrations are obsessively detailed and meticulously designed. One page might be crammed with numerous stamp-sized panels while the next is scant.

The best example of Ware's work is his Jimmy Corrigan narrative. The book represents a high point in proving comic books can be taken as serious art. While Spiegelman received a Pulitzer Prize in 1992 for the second volume in his *Maus* narrative, the award was not a traditional Pulitzer. Instead the award's committee gave a "special" award, finding *Maus* hard to classify in comparison to more traditional literature. Ware's American Book Award marked the first time a graphic novel was judged among other highly literary works and found superior (Raeburn 2004, 17).

Thematically, Ware's work is atypical of what is normally thought of as sequential art. He does not rely heavily on superhero adventure stories; neither does he rely on gags associated with newspaper comic strips. Ware fills his cartoons with nostalgia and melancholy; his work is sad, often dealing with everyday life and loneliness. This is perhaps an extension of his own inner demons. Additionally, his work often has semiautobiographical elements. Again, an example is *The Smartest Kid on Earth*. Like the key protagonist in the book, Ware's father disappeared from his life when he was young.

Noticeably absent from many of Ware's works are "punch lines" that accompany more traditional comic strips. His work can be mean-spirited, even cruel. He explains in "Apology and Souvenir Comic 'Strip'," part of the cumbersome *The Acme Novelty Library Final Report to Shareholders and*

Saturday Afternoon Rainy Day Fun Book, that "gags" do not happen in real life, and questioned why they should appear in art.

While aspiring cartoonists might point to Ware as a leader in the medium, he is also working to rewrite, or more appropriately redraw, sections of comic book history by reviving sequential art from the medium's early years. This dedication creates examples for budding sequential artists that help downplay the role of the superhero genre.

A fan of older comic strips, Ware champions the composition found in early works such as George Herriman's *Krazy Katz* and Frank King's *Gasoline Alley*—both of which he has worked to reprint in book form. Ware has stated that King's work heavily influenced his approach to comics; he learned that the emotional impact of a comic did not need to be tethered to either the words or images, but the overall composition. He frequently associates his method of cartooning to composing music. In this sense, he has said he does not use cinematic techniques to construct panels (Wivel 2011).

As a creator, Ware is notoriously self-eviscerating, often hedging his work with apologies. Like his characters, Ware seems to live in melancholy, aware of his achievements yet unsure if he deserves them. This self-flagellation comes through time and again in not only interviews and introductions but also his drawings. In fact, it can be difficult to read Ware's work without finding an apologia in some form. This rhetoric has been critiqued in a number of ways and called both a shield to hide Ware's beliefs and a means to create an outsider persona linked to literary success opposed to mass-market fame (Ball and Kuhlman 2010, 46). Regardless of the causes of Ware's self-loathing, his own criticism is another indication of the seriousness with which Ware takes his craft, and yet another example of attempts to hold the medium to a higher standard.

IMPACT ON AMERICAN CULTURE

Ware's life and work have been studied in an attempt to understand how he produces such dense art and what influenced him. At the moment there are two volumes that discuss both aspects. *Chris Ware (Monographics Series)* by Daniel Raeburn examines the cartoonist's life while making a case for Ware's concept that in order to rise to the level of literature, sequential art must tell worthwhile stories. The second book is more academic. *The Comics of Chris Ware*, edited by David M. Ball and Martha B. Kuhlman, is a collection of essays from a variety of academic fields that seek to unpack Ware's unique works. Taken together these two works indicate a growing academic interest in Ware's work and its impact on greater culture. It is likely that Ware's already formidable recognition will receive more academic study as his next two major narratives come to fruition.

Furthermore, scholar Douglas Wolk suggests that while Ware's initial creations worked by twisting the concept of a humorous comic strip into gagless comics, his drawings have themselves become something of a cliché, which spawned imitators, one example being Ivan Brunetti, similarly interested in comic strip history and subverting the joke formula (Wolk 2007, 351).

SUMMARY

In summation, Ware's impact on comic books and American culture stems from his attempts to create highly literary works of sequential art. Though he was something of an alternative comix celebrity prior to the publication of his first book, *Jimmy Corrigan: The Smartest Kid on Earth*, its publication moved him into mainstream culture. The awards this work gathered belie the cultural bias that sequential art is crude or of lesser value and indicate that comic books can be taken seriously by the general public.

Moreover, Ware's artistic approach is unique. He works to create a language of composition in which an artist views not just individual panels but the whole page as an image. In this manner he creates exceptionally detailed images. It has been suggested that this take on comic books can be traced to the medium's early comic strips. In this way, Ware has encouraged an alternate comic book history that downplays the role of superhero comics, while drawing on early newspaper strips.

See also Fantagraphics; *Maus*; *RAW*; Spiegelman, Art

ESSENTIAL WORKS

Ware, Chris. *Jimmy Corrigan: The Smartest Kid on Earth*. New York: Pantheon Books, 2000.
Ware, Chris. *Quimby the Mouse: Or Comic Strips, 1990–1991*. London: Jonathan Cape, 2010.

FURTHER READING

Ball, David M., and Martha B. Kuhlman, eds. *The Comics of Chris Ware*. Jackson: University Press of Mississippi, 2010.
Raeburn, Daniel. *Chris Ware (Monographics Series)*. New Haven, CT: Yale University Press, 2004.

David J. Cross

Warren, Jim

Modern comic book readers who delight at the grisly imagery of *Marvel Zombies*, reflect on the brutal political satire of Robert Kirkman's *The Walking Dead*, or are transfixed by the **Joker**'s transition from comic relief cartoon to his Puckish, bloodthirsty, sociopathic incarnation, owe an enormous debt to the work of one man: Jim Warren. In the 1950s, Warren's friend Hugh Hefner wanted to publish a horror comic anthology, and Warren wanted to publish an erotic magazine. Through a series of circumstances bizarre enough to be a plot twist in one of Warren's suspense magazines, Hefner went on to become the iconic, pajama-clad publisher of *Playboy* and Warren went on to publish what are inarguably some of the finest horror comics of all time. Yet unlike the Emperor of the Bunny Mansion, much of the significance of Jim Warren's iconic work appears lost to history. As the publisher of titles such as *Famous Monsters of Filmland*, *Eerie*, and *Vampirella*, Warren created a safe space for some of the finest artists in the world to tell compelling stories. His innovative marketing, creative strategies for skirting the Comics Code, and support for the distribution and preservation of historically significant works like **Will Eisner**'s *The Spirit* has rightfully earned Warren a place as an icon worthy of exploration and celebration.

HISTORY

James Warren was born on July 29, 1930, in Philadelphia. Despite his family's working-class roots, Warren received enthusiastic support from his parents and relatives for his interest in art. Growing up, Warren was fascinated by magazines of all types with a particular interest in comics. After serving in the Army at the outset of the Korean War, Warren decided to pursue work in comics and publishing.

Looking at successful magazine models, Warren was immediately attracted to the money being generated by "girlie" pictorial publications like *Playboy*. In what Warren himself acknowledges as a tawdry and badly produced *Playboy* knockoff, *After Hours* magazine was launched in 1957. Lasting only

(The Weird World of Eerie Publications)

four issues, production on *After Hours* was abruptly halted when Warren was arrested on obscenity and distribution of pornography charges stemming from an issue that prominently featured bare breasts and Bettie Page. Photographed in handcuffs and called a dangerous pornographer by the *Philadelphia Inquirer*, Jim Warren's career in the "girlie mag" industry was at an end (Langdon 2008). There were, however, two seminal events that emerged from his *After Hours* experience. First, Warren received experience in national magazine distribution. Second, Warren was introduced to writer and horror film enthusiast Forrest J. Ackerman.

Ackerman was a Hollywood literary agent with a keen enthusiasm for "men's magazines." After reading an issue of *After Hours*, he contacted Warren and offered to assist in developing a pictorial and story series entitled "Girls from Science Fiction Movies." Warren's arrest and the subsequent demise of *After Hours* halted further development of the series, but Warren was impressed with Ackerman's writing style and found the idea appealing, especially with renewed public interest in science fiction and horror.

In the late 1950s, Universal Studios began selling syndication packages of old horror movies to local television stations. On most Friday nights, local stations across America were showing films like *The Wolfman*, *Frankenstein*, and *Dracula* with a morbid but campy local performer (often a voluptuous woman) introducing the movies and goofing on them throughout the program. With an insight that would shape Warren's iconic contributions to comics, he noted a fundamental shift in audience perspective—the monster had turned into the hero for the kids watching (Cooke 1999). With this concept, Warren and Ackerman created what was intended to be a one-shot pictorial publication entitled *Famous Monsters of Filmland*. It featured black-and-white photos of famous movie monsters with tongue-in-cheek commentary. First published in February of 1958, the magazine sold out mere hours after its first printing.

With the successful launch of *Famous Monsters of Filmland*, Warren introduced monster comics with the book *Monster World*. Looking to further
diversify the scope of his publications, Warren launched *Spacemen* in 1960
and then began an audacious experiment in humor comics. The iconic founding editor of **Mad**, **Harvey Kurtzman**, launched *HELP!* magazine as *Mad* for
a collegiate audience. With a young Gloria Steinem as the magazine's first
employee, *HELP!* also featured a section called "The Public Gallery," which
allowed for open comic submissions. Contributions to *HELP!*'s "Public Gallery" included early works from **Robert Crumb**, **Art Spiegelman**, and Gilbert Shelton, making the book instrumental in the birth of the underground
comix movement of the late 1960s. Other contributors included acclaimed
film director and Monty Python member Terry Gilliam, who would go on to
become *HELP!*'s associate editor. Frequently courting controversy, Warren
also published the antiwar comic *Blazing Combat* from 1965 to 1966 before
opposition to Vietnam War had become mainstream.

Warren is most noted for horror books, and in 1966 Warren Publishing
launched *Creepy* and *Eerie*. Warren aspired to create psychological horror
that transcended the cheap devices associated with the genre. Horror comics
enthusiast and commentator Stephen R. Bissette argues that the time was ripe
for such works with events like the Kennedy assassination and the Vietnam
War forcing a young generation to consider both the nature of evil and their
own mortality (2010, xiii). Given the ambitious and potentially unsettling
approach Warren proposed with his publications, the most substantial barrier he would immediately face was the Comics Code. The Code was created
in 1954 in response to fears about indecency in comics, with horror comics
expressly forbidden.

In another move that would radically change the history of American comics, Warren hatched a plan to ensure distribution of his horror titles. Warren
had actually welcomed the Comics Code as a tool to bring stability to the
industry (Cooke 1999), but was keenly aware of the chilling effect it had on
content exploration. With this in mind, Warren established parameters on
the publication of his horror titles. Specifically, books like *Creepy* and *Eerie*
would be called "magazines," not "comic books." At newsstands, they would
be sold on magazine racks, not comics racks. Their paper size would be 8-1/2"
× 11", which was standard for magazines at the time. Finally, the books were
(at least ostensibly) stated as being for a mature audience. Satisfied that these
parameters exempted the books from the Comics Code and enthused about
the potential profit, distributors and vendors sold Warren publications without incident.

In addition to navigating around the Comics Code to ensure distribution,
Warren created a range of other significant marketing innovations. Warren
produced the famous horror artist Dick Smith's how-to guide on creating monster and horror make-up effects, which served as a touchstone for an entire

EERIE PUBLICATIONS: COPYCAT KILLERS

Warren Publishing's success in horror comics produced countless imitators, the most notorious of which was undoubtedly Eerie Publications. With a name that effectively served to confuse the public with Warren's flagship book *Eerie*, Eerie Publications resisted employing artists and writers with much talent. As such, Eerie Publications became adept at the bizarre and fairly unsavory practice of taking pre–Comics Code and early post–Comics Code comics, copying them directly (with little or no textual changes), and adding additional blood and gore in an attempt to boost sales (Howlett 2010). While this undoubtedly hurt the public's perception of quality in horror comics, the mercenary ugliness of Eerie Publication's work has spawned a small but enthusiastic collectors' market for their books.

generation of horror filmmakers (Roach and Cooke 2001). In 1974, Warren promoted the first "Monster Con" where enthusiastic fans could attend (frequently in costume) and meet the creators of horror films and comics.

With the success of *Creepy* and *Eerie* beginning to fade, Warren Publishing was in desperate need of a new book to recapture the popular imagination. In 1969, they found it in one of Warren's most memorable contributions to the medium: *Vampirella*. Much like buxom hostesses of Universal's "Shock Theater" packages airing on local television stations, Vampirella introduced stories in the book and frequently provided sarcastic commentary on events. Unlike the mascots for other Warren books, such as "Uncle Creepy" in *Creepy* magazine, Vampirella occasionally appeared as a character in stories. With vampy good looks and sexiness derived from the provocative Jane Fonda film *Barbarella* (Cooke 1999), Vampirella's visage became iconic, inspiring imitation from performers like "Elvira—Mistress of the Dark."

Cumulatively, Warren's horror titles provided a space for some unforgettable stories. Primarily drawn in black and white, stories frequently subverted traditional horror. For example, "Child" in *Eerie* issues #57–#60 retells the Frankenstein story from the childlike perspective of the monster. Jim Stenstrum's and **Neal Adams**'s "Thrillkill" in issue #75 of *Creepy*, however, is generally regarded as the finest work to appear in a Warren publication and one of the finest comic book stories ever printed. Visually, the book depicts a sniper shooting random pedestrians and commuters during rush hour in a metropolitan American city. The story's art is disturbingly realistic and entirely evocative of the Charles Whitman shootings at the University of Texas and the political assassinations of the 1960s. Rather than having the shooter reveal his motivations, the text of the story is told entirely through an interview with a defrocked clergyman who had served as the shooter's minister when he was young. The minister suggests that while horrific, the shooter's actions were not inconsistent with society's brutal, militarized, and exclusionary power structure. He goes on to argue that the shooter's upbringing in a house filled with guns and a hypermasculine father probably made his suicidal killing spree seem like an ascent to his version of heaven from the hell he had found on Earth.

Stories like these demonstrate the evolution of Jim Warren's publications from monster magazines aimed at kids to sophisticated fiction capable of offering social commentary. In their exhaustive compendium on the history of Warren Publishing, *The Warren Companion: The Definitive Compendium to the Great Comics of Warren Publishing* (2001), David Roach and Jon Cooke outline several specific periods in the history of Warren's work:

1958–1964: The Monster Era. Monster stories dominate the Warren titles in this period.

1965–1967: The Goodwin Era. With Larry Ivie and Archie Goodwin as principal writers, stories moved away from 1950s camp monsters towards more psychological horror.

1968–1970: The Dark Years. As the initial enthusiasm for horror comics waned, Warren's publication schedule became infrequent with many story reprints. Vampirella's popularity helped the company regain its footing.

1971–1976: Barcelona. With a renewed focus on realism, literary writing (with stories by a number of significant writers including Harlan Ellison), and a nearly complete break from traditional horror tropes, Warren published many of his most memorable works in this era. Particularly influential was the decision to utilize international talent from the Barcelona S. I. Agency as the primary artists for many of the books. Drawing on his childhood interest in Will Eisner, Warren restored prints of *The Spirit* that were exquisitely published alongside his regular titles.

1976–1980: The Louise Jones Years. With Louise Jones as an editor, this period was dominated by big science fiction projects; glossy, full-color editions of Vampirella; and tie-ins to other properties such as *Star Wars* and *Lord of the Rings*.

1980–1983: Decline and Fall. During this period, Warren became ill and was unable to provide the vision that had defined his tenure as head of the company. The company quietly folded and ceased operations in 1983.

IMPACT ON COMICS

Jim Warren's impact on comics was immeasurable. Probably his most significant contribution was the successful circumvention of the Comics Code to allow artists to tell mature stories that starkly contrasted the culturally approved, safe-for-kids material many houses were publishing in the 1960s.

Warren Publishing's frequent use of international artists furthered the status of comic books as a truly global art form. In Warren's era, the drugstores and newsstands that sold comics offered almost exclusively American content. Warren's efforts to seek out and display talent from all over the world furthered the American understanding that comics are a global medium.

A generation of talented artists were also inspired by Warren. As Sam Sherman, the president of Independent International Pictures, noted, "Jim Warren created a whole new world of images, words, designs and ideas that captivated an entire generation of baby-boomers who grew up to create their own scripts, stories, special-effects, make-up, and movies" (Langdon 2008). In fact, Stephen King recounts that Warren Publishing was one of his most significant early influences (Roach and Cooke 2001).

An accomplishment that both blessed and cursed Jim Warren was his success in reviving and developing the publication of horror comics. Clearly, Warren's success in publishing horror comics meant a great deal to the company's fortunes and his creative success. That said, the dozens of poorly developed, cheap imitators probably diminished horror comics in the public's imagination. Warren's success in the genre also meant that major publishers with far greater resources would develop excellent horror titles of their own. DC, for example, published a colossal 13 horror titles in the 1970s, hiring away many of Warren's best artists and writers (Roach and Cooke 2001). Additionally, the inspiration Warren provided to millions of kids in the 1950s and 1960s would create a generation of filmmakers, writers, and comic book artists who would capture the audience he previously held. In short, Warren's contributions to comics both raised his company to unprecedented heights and laid the foundation for its demise.

IMPACT ON AMERICAN CULTURE

As noted, Warren's impact on American culture was profound. Warren published the antiwar *Blazing Combat* at a time when war comics typically assumed American armed conflicts to be inherently just. Warren later upped his willingness to smite the morality of the period when he published the first interracial kiss in a mainstream publication, in 1972 with issue #43 of *Creepy*.

It is impossible to tell, however, whether Warren published with a concern for social justice or a keen understanding that controversy creates cash. His tendency towards self-promotion was evidenced by the large placard above his desk that stated "Someone has to make it happen" and the stern warning Gloria Steinem received from a colleague to "watch out for (Warren). He's laid everything except the Atlantic Cable" (Cooke 1999). Whether Warren

WARREN'S VAMPY ICON

Vampirella, a voluptuous raven-haired beauty wearing a tiny red sling suit, made her eye-catching debut in one of Warren's Code-avoiding magazines, *Vampirella* #1 (1969). In her original incarnation Vampirella was not technically a vampire, but one of the few surviving members of the Vampiri race from the planet Drakulon. She had all the powers of a vampire, but none of their weaknesses. She teamed with the famed vampire-hunting van Helsing family to oppose the evil vampires of Earth. When Harris Publications acquired rights to the character and began publishing Vampirella comics in 1991, they retooled her origin. Now she was the daughter of Lilith, Adam's first wife, and born in a region of Hell called Drakulon. Vampirella attempts to ensure her mother's redemption by killing all the demons and vampires born of Lilith. Whatever her origin, for more than 40 years Vampirella has been protecting mortals from evil vampires, and has looked ravishing doing so.

Randy Duncan

published with an eye towards profit or political change (perhaps both?), the instrumental effect of Warren Publishing at a time of cultural upheaval should not be overlooked.

Giving kids a steady diet of vampires and monsters would have been a reasonably profitable business strategy for Warren. Instead, Warren aspired to produce stories that moved beyond the "monster-as-antagonist" cliché. Oppressive social values almost always create the monster in Warren publications. Through a polysemic trick, evil in Warren's books often comes from the arbiters of evil rather than evil ones themselves. In that sense, one might argue that many of the stories Warren published are more Marxist in their approach to equality than the traditional American perspective of equality based on opportunity.

SUMMARY

By the late 1980s, Warren was presumed dead, despite being very much alive (Cooke 1999). In the time since, Warren books have been largely forgotten. They were typically not in color, they were not about superheroes, the publication size was wrong, and they weren't technically even "comics" to begin with. While controversial a generation ago, they're hardly shocking in the post–**Gaiman** and **Moore** era. There are almost no articles studying Warren in the popular or academic press. Nonetheless, in an era spanning nearly 25 years, Jim Warren published some of the most thought-provoking and meaningful comics ever created. Readers of honest and realistic comic books, horror enthusiasts, and those who appreciate the internationalization of popular culture would do well to consider the iconic contributions of Jim Warren. As a promotional badge distributed with an early book proclaims, "WARREN: WE'RE NOT BIG. WE'RE GOOD."

ESSENTIAL WORKS

McGregor, Don (w), and Luis Garcia (a). "The Men Who Called Him Monster." *Creepy* #43 (January 1972). New York: Warren Publishing. Reprinted in *Creepy Archives Volume 9*, Milwaukie, OR: Dark Horse, 2011.

Stenstrum, Jim (w), and Neal Adams (a). "Thrillkill." *Creepy* #75 (November 1975). New York: Warren Publishing. Reprint forthcoming in *Creepy Archives*, Milwaukie, OR: Dark Horse, 2012.

Warren, James, and Forrest Ackerman. *Famous Monsters of Filmland* #1 (February 1958). Philadelphia, PA: Warren Publishing. Reprinted in *Famous Monsters of Filmland: The Annotated #1*, Encino, CA: Movieland Classics, 2011.

FURTHER READING

Cooke, Jon. "The James Warren Interview." *TwoMorrows*. February 11, 1999. http://twomorrows.com/comicbookartist/articles/04warren.html.

Howlett, Mike. *The Weird World of Eerie Publications: Comic Gore That Warped Millions of Young Minds*. Port Townsend, WA: Feral House, 2010.

Langdon, Verne. "The Most Famous Monster of Them All." *Jim Warren Publishing*. 2008. http://www.jimwarrenpublishing.com/history.html.

Roach, David, and Jon Cooke. *The Warren Companion: The Definitive Compendium to the Great Comics of Warren Publishing*. Raleigh, NC: TwoMorrows Publishing, 2001.

Bond Benton

Watchmen

Watchmen was originally released as a 12-issue limited series by **DC Comics** in 1986–1987. Written by **Alan Moore**, drawn by Dave Gibbons, and colored by John Higgins, the series was an immediate success and has gone on to be one of the most influential comics ever created. Set in an alternate 1985, *Watchmen* has a radically novel take on the genre of superheroes and pushes the confines of the medium in every direction. Beginning by asking what would happen if superheroes really existed in the world, Moore and Gibbons created an entirely new approach to the genre, exploring the effects of super-powers on science, politics, psychology, and society. In the process, *Watchmen* revolutionized modern comics, bringing superheroes into the adult world and changing the medium permanently.

HISTORY

The idea for *Watchmen* grew out of DC's acquisition of Charlton Comics' stable of superhero characters, including Captain Atom, the Blue Beetle, and the Question. Alan Moore, at the time writing **Swamp Thing** for DC, had an idea for a new approach to these characters; after hearing about Moore's idea for the limited-run story, Dave Gibbons contacted Moore and was brought on board. However, in the end DC decided that Moore's project would be both too limiting for the Charlton characters and would change them too radically and permanently, and asked Moore and Gibbons instead to create their own characters modeled on the Charlton characters for the project (Gibbons 2008, 29).

This change turned out to be liberating. Since they were creating their own characters from scratch, Moore and Gibbons could design them to reflect the greater environment of the world of the comic without having to take into account years of character continuity. Furthermore, these characters could be superheroic archetypes, rather than specific iterations of those archetypes, and could therefore be used as a commentary on the nature of superhero comics more generally. Moore and Gibbons thus created the characters of *Watchmen* at the same time as they created its world: an alternate present reflecting the social and political changes that might have occurred had supermen and -women really come into being at the same time as their comic book versions.

Moore already had a history of incorporating real-world concerns into his comics. In particular, his work on *Marvelman* (*Miracleman* in the United States) and *Swamp Thing* took previously existing characters and radically altered them to make their stories both more realistic and more mature. In *Marvelman* specifically, Moore confronted the question of the impact of superheroes on their environment, showing a superhero questioning his role as the most powerful being on Earth. However, *Watchmen* takes these concerns a step further by projecting them into the past, in the process creating an entirely different geopolitical structure created as a result of the influence of superheroes. In *Watchmen*, as the back matter of issue #4 points out, not **Superman** but God exists, and he's American; hence the Cold War between the United States and the USSR has a wildly new dynamic. Furthermore, these social changes are not limited to global concerns; the existence of superheroes has affected everything from the comic book industry to automobiles, from cigarettes to fast food.

In fact, the world Moore and Gibbons created, while centering in part on the lives and actions of various superheroes, also focuses on the everyday characters who populate this world. Two of the most important characters in the series, the two Bernies, have no particular special powers at all; one is a newspaper vendor, the other a (nonpaying) customer reading a *Black Freighter* pirate comic—an invention of Moore and Gibbons, which forms an alternate narrative within *Watchmen*. However, the time spent with these characters in the course of the series gives these two men just as much weight as the heroes themselves, and perhaps one of the most poignant moments of the comic is when the two die in each other's arms. Furthermore, this level of detail does not only extend to characters but is also present in the environments themselves. The panels are laced with background messages, images, and symbols that resonate throughout the work. The end result is an ornately detailed, fully imagined, self-referential world that is just as complicated, confusing, and morally ambiguous as our own.

The basic plot of the comic is structured as a murder mystery. The story opens with the death of the Comedian, a superhero who has mostly been employed by the government in various unsavory and clandestine tasks. The primary detective for this story is **Rorschach**, who has refused to comply with the law outlawing all vigilantes not specifically government sanctioned. However, the plot rapidly adds layers of complication: the disintegrating relationship between Dr. Manhattan, the only true superpower in *Watchmen*, and Sally Jupiter/the Silk Spectre; Jupiter's nascent relationship with Dan Dreiberg/Nite Owl; an assassination attempt on Adrian Veidt/Ozymandias; and over all, the rapidly approaching threat of nuclear war. By the final issue,

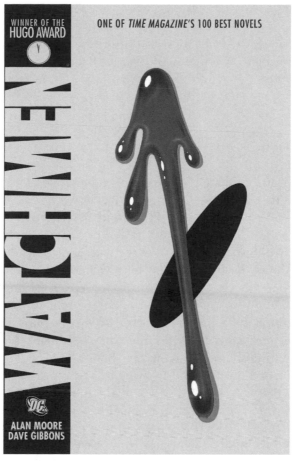

(AP Photo/DC Entertainment)

Watchmen is clearly not a murder mystery at all, but a story centered on the responsibility of superheroes to save the world not just from alien menaces and supervillains but from itself.

After the comic finished its run in 1987, DC republished it in one bound collection, marketing it as a "graphic novel." This kind of republishing was at the time largely unheard of in the comics industry; *Watchmen*, along with **Frank Miller**'s *The Dark Knight Returns*, were two of the first mainstream comics series to be issued in book form. These reprints brought even more attention to the series than the original comics had done. However, this attention had an unexpected side effect for Moore and Gibbons. Their original contract with DC—a fairly standard, even generous, one for the time—had specified that the rights to the story would revert to them after the comic had been out of print for three years. Before *Watchmen*, few if any comics had managed more than one or two reprints. However, due to its extreme popularity, *Watchmen* has never been out of print, and so the rights to it remain with DC. This ownership situation has led to the deterioration of the relationship between DC and Moore, as Moore feels that DC has violated the spirit of the agreement. When in 2009 Warner Brothers released a film adaptation of *Watchmen* directed by Zack Snyder, Moore refused to be associated with the project.

IMPACT ON COMICS

It is difficult to overestimate the impact *Watchmen* has had on the comics industry. Before its publication in book form, the series had won **Jack Kirby** Awards for Best New Series, Best Writer, and Best Writer/Artist, as well as nominations for Best Single Issue and Best Artist. The graphic novel dominated the 1988 **Will Eisner** Comic Industry Awards, winning Best Finite Series, Best Graphic Album, Best Writer, and Best Writer/Artist. And also in 1988, *Watchmen* became the first comic to win a Hugo Award from the World Science Fiction Society. *Watchmen* is also the only graphic novel to be included on *Time* magazine's 2005 list of the best 100 novels published since 1923. Along with *The Dark Knight Returns* and **Art Spiegelman**'s ***Maus***, *Watchmen* has been instrumental both in making the comic book medium more acceptable to mainstream audiences and in bringing that medium to new levels of complexity and maturity.

Watchmen was part of a larger movement in the industry to make comics more adult-themed; by the 1980s the Comics Code of the 1950s had lost much of its hold on the medium, and comics were no longer as limited in their content. However, *Watchmen* surpassed much contemporaneous work because of its innovations in the medium itself. *Watchmen* is not only novel in its placement of superheroes in a real-world context, but also because of the uses to which it puts the very nature of sequential art. **Scott McCloud** has pointed out the unique relationship of the comics medium to time (McCloud 1993, 94–117); Moore and Gibbons exploit that relationship, bringing it to the forefront and in the process making *Watchmen* a meditation on the nature of time itself.

Watchmen also put its back matter to a unique use; it used the space usually dedicated to readers' letters for further development of the *Watchmen* universe. While originally the excerpts from the first Nite Owl's autobiography were included simply because the comic had not existed long enough to generate letters of its own, Moore and Gibbons found the possibilities of those three pages so intriguing that they decided to continue to use them for other "archival" material. This back matter—excerpts from books, articles on pirate comics, psychological files, and more—interacts with the sequential art

FILMING *WATCHMEN*

Despite demand, for some time it seemed unlikely that a *Watchmen* film would ever be made; Terry Gilliam, the first director attached to the project, eventually admitted defeat, calling *Watchmen* unfilmable, and Moore has argued that the narrative of the comic is so tied to its medium that to make a film of it would be a waste of time. When Zack Snyder's version was released in 2009, it met with mixed critical reception, and some critics specifically attacked it for its faithfulness to the original graphic novel, arguing that what was innovative in one medium was untranslatable to another. However, other critics have suggested that the few changes Snyder did make indicate his intention to use the narrative of *Watchmen* to make the same kind of critique of the medium of film and the genre of action movies that Moore and Gibbons made of superhero comic books.

of the comic both to provide a background to these newly formed characters and to complicate the world of the comic.

That world itself is incredibly detailed, in large part because of Gibbons's art. Every panel seems to contain references to other panels, using tropes like spray-painted graffiti, posters, newspaper headlines, even hamburger wrappers. Furthermore, there is always more going on in one panel than is obvious, or even comprehensible for the first-time reader. For instance, while the context of one panel may be the conversation of the two Bernies at the newsstand, the art of the panel depicts neither character: in the foreground, a newspaper headline reminds the reader of the looming atomic threat; the word balloons contain both Bernie's commentary on his profession and an excerpt from the internal pirate comic, and the ironic resonances between them; and the background depicts a doomsday sandwich-board man, later revealed to be Rorschach, checking his trash-can mail-drop. This internal cohesiveness not only works to develop *Watchmen*'s universe but also to create a feeling of synchronicity around the comic: everything, everywhere, is somehow connected. The climax of the comic brings all the diverse characters of the previous issues together in one moment that has come to seem inevitable.

Although *Watchmen* is certainly approachable for a reader unfamiliar with the medium, as Richard Reynolds has pointed out, a complete reading requires a high level of comics literacy (Reynolds 1992, 109). In fact, the project of *Watchmen* is not just to create a world, but to create a world that directly reflects the history of comic books. As a result, there are continual references to specific tropes in superhero comics and in comics more generally. At the same time, *Watchmen* questions unspoken assumptions surrounding the medium. The series makes overt the subtext of fetishism associated with the tight, sexualized costumes of superheroes; it points out the absurdity of super-heroes in a world without corresponding supervillains; and it foregrounds one of the basic questions of the genre that had largely been left unspoken: what kind of person wants to put on tights to fight crime?

However, the immediate impact *Watchmen* had on the medium itself was not to encourage the creation of more complicated, more detailed, or more thoughtful stories. Instead, the lesson the industry learned from *Watchmen*'s success was that audiences wanted more sex and violence. Geoff Klock has pointed out that the comics that followed *Watchmen* emulated its mature, even pathological, approach to superheroes, but not its craft. Klock calls the period that followed the "Dark Age" of comics, a period filled with "a proliferation of dark, psychotic, violent loners with sexual dysfunctions who dismembered anyone who looked at them the wrong way" (Klock 2003, 80). This seems to have been the opposite of Moore and Gibbons's intention; while they meant to force a reevaluation of the assumptions of the medium, it took 10 years or more before comics began truly to engage with the larger questions raised by *Watchmen*, rather than just emulating its morally ambiguous and dystopic style.

IMPACT ON AMERICAN CULTURE

Watchmen reflects the times in which it was written in both its political and social concerns. At heart, it is a Cold War comic, meditating on the tensions between East and West and the threat of thermonuclear war. Although set in an alternate reality where Richard Nixon is still president, its engagement with the rhetoric of both the Right and the Left, its depiction of the brinkmanship of the time, and its preoccupation with commercialism and advertising all place *Watchmen* squarely in the United States in the 1980s. The very fact that the biggest threat in the book is not a supervillain but the possibility of nuclear apocalypse locates *Watchmen* as belonging to the final days of the Cold War.

Furthermore, the ethical questions with which *Watchmen* engages are 1980s concerns. *Watchmen* is to a large degree a treatise on the nature of heroism, and on what makes heroes in the modern era; it rejects the rhetoric employed, for instance, in the Reagan presidential campaign, which lauded a kind of superheroic cowboy individualism, in favor of praising the every-day heroisms of ordinary people. Furthermore, the division between hero and villain in *Watchmen* is blurry at best. Hence *Watchmen* echoes the growing beliefs in the 1980s that historical American values were perhaps too naïve for the postindustrial age.

But the fact that *Watchmen* places these ethical questions and concerns into a comic book, long considered a medium solely for children, itself had an enormous impact. *Watchmen* cleared a space for adult comics not only by containing sex and violence, but by going beyond simplistic moral structures to create a world in which it turns out the bad guys are no worse than the good guys. Moore and Gibbons, through the sophistication of their texts and their manipulations of the medium, proved that the ghettoized comic book could be an appropriate format for more than children's themes. *Watchmen* is now regularly taught not only in courses on comics but in courses on American literature, and is increasingly accepted as one of the most important American works of art of the post–World War II period, of whatever medium. In the process, *Watchmen* has opened the door for other carefully crafted, thoughtful works of sequential art to be recognized as more than just disposable entertainment.

SUMMARY

Watchmen was one of the first comics to put superheroes in the real world, to investigate the impact that beings with superhuman powers would have on their surroundings. Furthermore, *Watchmen* was one of the first comics to treat superheroes as real people rather than two-dimensional symbols of good and evil. What makes *Watchmen* unique, however, is the skill with which it approaches both these projects, taking a medium long considered childish and demonstrating its undeniable potential. *Watchmen* has become iconic in part because it is groundbreaking, but also because it is brilliant in its manipulation of the medium itself.

Watchmen calls the concept of the superhero itself into question, presenting the reader with a cast of vigilante crime fighters who are all somehow less than virtuous. At the same time, it lauds the superheroic actions of everyday men and women, who in brief moments are able to rise above their own concerns to make the world around them a slightly better place. The complexity of all its characters not only makes the work itself vibrant but also refuses a simplistic, four-color worldview, insisting that even the greatest acts of heroism sometimes stem from ulterior motives, and leading the reader to recognize that nothing in the world is black and white.

As a result, *Watchmen* permanently changed not only the standards of the comics medium but also the place of the comics medium in society, using the very tools and tropes of comic books to prove the power and legitimacy of sequential art.

See also Moore, Alan; Rorschach

ESSENTIAL WORK

Moore, Alan (w), Dave Gibbons (p. i), and John Higgins (c). *Watchmen*. New York: DC Comics, 1987.

FURTHER READING

Gibbons, Dave. *Watching the Watchmen*. London: Titan Books, 2008.
Klock, Geoff. *How to Read Superhero Comics and Why*. New York: Continuum, 2003.
Van Ness, Sara J. *Watchmen as Literature: A Critical Study of the Graphic Novel*. Jefferson, NC: McFarland, 2010.

Kathleen McClancy

Wertham, Fredric

Dr. Fredric Wertham (1895–1981) was a German-born Jewish psychiatrist who emigrated to the United States in 1922. In the mid-1940s, he began to study the effects of comic books on children, particularly the troubled children who visited the Lefargue Clinic he established in 1946 in Harlem for low-income individuals. He published his views in a number of articles written for popular magazines, and he became the best-known of the comic book critics in postwar America. Wertham's push for legislation to restrict the sales of comics culminated with the publication of his book *Seduction of the Innocent* in 1954. He also served as an expert witness, testifying before a New York State legislative hearing on comics in 1949 and before the U.S. Senate Subcommittee on Juvenile Delinquency about comic books in 1954. To counteract the bad publicity generated by Wertham and other critics, comic book publishers formed a trade association and instituted a self-regulatory code that would restrict the content of comics for nearly 60 years, until it was scrapped in 2011.

HISTORY

When Dr. Fredric Wertham came to America, he took a position at Johns Hopkins Hospital's psychiatric clinic as chief resident in psychiatry. In 1932, he left to become a senior psychiatrist in the Department of Hospitals in New York City. He established the Lefargue Clinic in 1946 in Harlem to provide psychiatric care to low-income individuals. It was there he began a systematic study of the effects of comic books on children. His conclusions were reported by Judith Crist in an article in *Collier's* magazine in March 1948, which marked Wertham's entry into the campaign against comic books.

Based on observations of and interviews with children, Wertham's studies employed a clinical method of investigation not embraced by the emerging paradigm of social science research to determine media effects. Wertham saw comic books as a contributing factor to juvenile delinquency because comics were part of the social world of children, conditioning them to accept violence. He wrote, "The very fact that crime comics are socially tolerated shows how much expression of hostility we tolerate and even encourage" (Wertham 1954, 241). In Wertham's view, it did no good to treat juvenile delinquents while ignoring the cultural environment that helped shape them.

He also discussed his findings in a professional symposium the same month, titled "The Psychopathology of Comic Books." That material was the basis for an article he wrote for the *Saturday Review of Literature* titled "The Comics . . . Very Funny!" published in May 1948 and republished in condensed form in *Reader's Digest* in August. The resulting publicity led comic book publishers to form the Association of Comics Magazine Publishers and adopt a self-regulatory code in July 1948. This action failed to mollify Wertham, who repeated his charges against comic books and also attacked the new code.

The psychiatrist's interest in comic books made him an obvious choice to testify before the New York Joint Legislative Committee to Study the Publication of Comics, created in March 1949. Legislation in 1949 resulting from the committee's work was vetoed by Gov. Thomas Dewey on the grounds it was unconstitutional.

Wertham turned his attention to other projects for a while, writing several books exploring the relationship between forensic psychiatry and the legal system. He became an expert witness and testified at high-profile murder trials. During this time, Wertham developed his ideas about social psychiatry, which focused less on the individual and more on broader social and cultural influences on behavior.

Comic books recaptured Wertham's attention again in the early 1950s, and he set to work on *Seduction of the Innocent*, an indictment of the comic book publishers and their comics, aimed at a popular audience. The *Ladies' Home Journal* published excerpts from several chapters in its November 1953 issue, just months after the creation of the U.S. Senate Subcommittee to Investigate Juvenile Delinquency. Although the subcommittee's staff had already begun collecting information on comic books for planned hearings, the publication of the article in November led to an outcry by readers who wrote to their legislators urging action.

The subcommittee's comic book hearings began April 21, 1954, in New York City with two days of testimony. Senators conducted a final day of hearings on June 4. Congressional staffers compiled a list of witnesses and finalized the list shortly before the start of the hearings. Wertham was scheduled to testify during the first day of the hearings. A background statement on the psychiatrist noted that Wertham was the author of *Seduction of the Innocent* and that his view of comic books was considered the "extreme" position among psychiatrists (Nyberg 1998, 369).

Key points in Wertham's testimony included the following: (1) he asserted that there was no question that comics had negative effects on children; the only question was how far-reaching those effects would be; (2) he felt the

SEAL OF APPROVAL

Spider-Man not only fought crime, he fought the Comics Code Authority. When Marvel Comics wanted to do an antidrug story, it requested permission from the Comics Magazine Association of America, whose code forbade any mention of drugs. The CMAA denied the request.

Marvel went ahead anyway, producing a three-issue story in which Spider-Man learns his roommate, Harry, is a drug addict. The issues, cover-dated May, June, and July 1971, did not carry the CMAA's Seal of Approval. The disagreement was one factor that led to the first revision of the regulatory code, in 1971.

However, Spider-Man's rebellion was short-lived. At a meeting, a Marvel representative assured the trade association that in the future, Marvel would abide by the code and not publish any issues without the seal of approval.

Senate subcommittee made a mistake in concentrating only on crime and horror comics, because violence was found in most genres; (3) he believed that the "normal" child was the most at risk from reading comics.

The subcommittee issued its interim report in March 1955. The senators did not call for federal censorship. Instead, they placed the responsibility for policing comic books primarily on publishers. The committee had no way to enforce this recommendation, but it did not have to. The publishers had formed the Comics Magazine Association of America in fall 1954 and implemented a self-regulatory code, which would last until 2011. The natural choice to head the association, publishers agreed, was Wertham, but he turned down the offer.

Wertham criticized the 1954 regulatory code, suggesting that the Senate subcommittee's conclusion that the industry could police itself was a disservice to the American public. The psychiatrist never completely dropped his campaign against comics, but as public interest waned, he turned his attention to media violence in other forms of popular culture, particularly television (Beaty 2005, 165, 171).

Wertham's final book, *The World of Fanzines*, was published in 1973 and has been characterized as a sociological study of fan magazines (Beaty 2005, 192).

IMPACT ON COMICS

Dr. Fredric Wertham's impact on the comic book industry is undeniable. To this day, comic book fans and creators alike cast Wertham as the villain who tried to destroy the comic book industry—and nearly succeeded in the mid-1950s.

Stan Lee, a longtime comic book writer and editor, typifies the position of many. In his autobiography *Excelsior!*, Lee ridiculed Wertham's position, calling his arguments "patently sophistic." He wrote: "[Wertham] was attacking my field, and worse, he was getting people all riled up. I never cease to be amazed at the gullibility of human beings" (Lee 2002, 92–93). Today, Lee's descriptions of Wertham and his arguments are always played for laughs when Lee speaks at comic book conventions and other fan venues. However, it was no laughing matter for the comic book industry in 1954. Wertham never achieved his goal—federal and/or state legislation restricting sales of comics—but he spurred publishers to adopt a self-regulatory code that would govern the content of most mass-market comics from 1954 to 2011. The enactment of a code successfully derailed the public's concerns, and the controversy over comic books died down.

The unlikely champion of the comic book industry during the 1954 hearings was publisher William Gaines, whose **EC** horror comics were fodder for the senators investigating comics. Gaines testified after Wertham; when backed into a corner in defense of comics, Gaines contended that an EC cover featuring a bloody ax and a severed head was in good taste, for a horror comic.

Recognizing his testimony was a public relations disaster for the industry, Gaines wanted the trade association to counteract the bad publicity comics had received by funding a study of effects and enlisting the support of the American Civil Liberties Union to fight censorship. Other publishers were not interested. They wanted a quick solution to the problem that would let them continue their lucrative publishing businesses. They held an organizational meeting for the Comics Magazine Association of America on August 17, 1954, and reviewed a draft of a regulatory code already prepared. Gaines, unhappy with the way he was treated by the CMAA, resigned in October 1955, discontinued his comics publishing business, and converted *Mad* to a magazine format, which did not fall under the jurisdiction of the CMAA. Other comics publishers, however, did have to abide by the code.

Modeled on the film Production Code of 1930, the Comics Code consisted of 41 specific regulations. The first section laid out guidelines for the publication of crime comics. This section emphasized portraying crime in a negative light, creating respect for established authority, depicting commission of crime in such a way that young readers would not be tempted to imitate what they read, and making sure that excess violence was purged. The second section effectively eliminated horror comics; its first provision read, "No comics magazine shall use the word horror or terror in its title."

The code went further than simply addressing crime and horror comics, however. It restricted language, stressed that comics should uphold the values of family and parental authority, and took a strongly moralistic tone regarding stories about romance and the depiction of the female body.

Gradually the type of comic book that had caused so much trouble for the industry disappeared, leaving mostly romance, teen, and funny animal comics. In the years following imposition of the Code, several comic book publishers went out of business. However, their demise could not be blamed wholly on the code. Television began to make inroads into the audience for comics, and the loss of the major distributor of comics, American News Company, left many publishers with no way to distribute their comics. "By 1957 there were 150 fewer titles on the stands than in 1954" (Duncan and Smith 2009, 40).

Imagine the film industry today being restricted to producing only "G-rated" films suitable for viewing by the youngest members of the audience. That was the nature of comic book publishing in the mid-1950s. Publishers became producers of a juvenile "subliterature" that appealed to a limited audience and drove creators not interested in stories for young children to apply their talents elsewhere (others simply lost their jobs as circulation decreased and companies folded).

The Comics Code underwent two revisions—in 1971 and in 1989—which liberalized the restrictive provisions of the original. In addition, changes in comic book distribution, known as the "Direct Market," allowed publishers to bypass the traditional magazine distribution system and meant comics could be distributed to retailers without the Code's seal of approval. This provided for the entrance of a number of so-called independent comics publishers whose output included more adult-oriented fare.

Despite these changes, there is no denying the Comics Code retarded the development of American comics as a storytelling medium for all ages and across all genres for decades. No one mourned the demise of the Comics Code in 2011, but in the minds of many, the damage was done. Even now, in the United States, comics readers, creators, and scholars struggle to legitimize their interest in comics. Superhero comics and Japanese manga dominate sales while other types of comics remain below the radar of the public.

IMPACT ON AMERICAN CULTURE

As Bart Beaty's study of Fredric Wertham points out, the psychiatrist has become "a nonentity as far as the history of communications is concerned." He was criticized by the professional psychiatric community of his time, by the American intellectuals of the 1940s and 1950s, and by the social scientists, who rejected his "reformist psychiatry and progressivist liberal political traditions" (Beaty 2005, 12). Wertham scholar James Reibman suggested that had the psychiatrist's argument been framed as a public health issue rather than one of censorship, his push for regulation might have been more successful (1999, 235).

Instead, Wertham's call for psychiatrists and others to become advocates for children by pressing for social policies dealing with media violence fell on deaf ears. Today, media regulation continues to be carried out by media producers. For example, the Supreme Court ruling in 2011 declared a California law aimed at violent video games unconstitutional, leaving the Entertainment Software Rating Board in charge of policing content.

Wertham's crusade against comics did affect the exportation of American culture—his war on comics had repercussions on the distribution of American comics in other countries, as well as the development of the comic book industry globally. In John Lent's *Pulp Demons: International Dimensions of the Postwar Anti-Comics Campaign* (1999) contributors trace the history of anticomics sentiment in Britain, Germany, Canada, Australia, the Philippines, Taiwan, South Korea, and Japan.

One arena in which Wertham inadvertently contributed to American culture and comics was the rise of the underground comics. Comics, seen as strictly for children, attracted a generation of creators who adopted the form for its transgressive possibilities. Graphic representation of sex, violence, and the counterculture lifestyle using a medium associated with children reflected the creators' challenge to an American system that repressed free expression.

Perhaps the best way to evaluate Wertham's impact on American culture is to consider what could have been. Film and television producers continue to mine comic book content for cinematic stories with broad public appeal. Independent comics such as **Art Spiegelman**'s Holocaust narrative *Maus* push the boundaries of storytelling. Who knows what contributions to American and global culture died or were never born because of the anticomics crusade in postwar America?

SUMMARY

Dr. Fredric Wertham, a psychiatrist who immigrated to the United States from Germany in 1922, led the anti–comic book crusade in America between 1948 and 1954. His criticism of comics reached the public through articles in popular magazines as well as the publication in 1954 of *Seduction of the Innocent*, his attack on comic books and their publishers. Although Wertham is dismissed by many as a fanatic with little scientific evidence, some modern scholars argue that his ideas merit a closer reading. They suggest he practiced a form of social psychiatry and targeted comic books because he felt their violence was symptomatic of a society that desensitized people—especially children—to social ills. The comic book publishing industry, fearing ongoing negative publicity as a result of the crusade against comics, created the Comics Code Authority to regulate content. The code, adopted in 1954, severely limited the artistic freedom and growth of comics. Although it collapsed in 2011, the code had an undeniable effect on the content and status of the American comic book.

ESSENTIAL WORKS

Crist, Judith. "Horror in the Nursery." *Collier's*, March 29, 1948, 22–23.

Wertham, Fredric. "The Comics—Very Funny!" *Saturday Review of Literature*, May 29, 1948, 6–7.

Wertham, Fredric. "It's Still Murder: What Parents Don't Know About Comic Books." *Saturday Review of Literature*, April 9, 1955, 11–12.

Wertham, Fredric. *Seduction of the Innocent*. New York: Rinehart, 1954. Reprint, Laurel, NY: Main Road Books, 1996.

Wertham, Fredric. *The World of Fanzines: A Special Form of Communication*. Carbondale: Southern Illinois University Press, 1973.

FURTHER READING

Beaty, Bart. *Fredric Wertham and the Critique of Mass Culture*. Jackson: University Press of Mississippi, 2005.

Gilbert, James. *A Cycle of Outrage: America's Reaction to the Juvenile Delinquent in the 1950s*. New York: Oxford University Press, 1986.

Hadju, David. *The Ten-Cent Plague: The Great Comic-Book Scare and How It Changed America*. New York: Farrar, Straus and Giroux, 2008.

Lent, John, ed. *Pulp Demons: International Dimensions of the Postwar Anti-Comics Campaign*. Madison, NJ: Fairleigh Dickinson Press, 1999.

Nyberg, Amy. *Seal of Approval: The History of the Comics Code*. Jackson: University Press of Mississippi, 1998.

Amy Kiste Nyberg

Wizard: The Guide to Comics

Wizard: The Guide to Comics was a comic fanzine and pricing guide published between 1991 and 2011 by Wizard Entertainment (later Wizard World, Inc.). Including exclusive interviews, a colorful pricing guide, and one-of-a-kind comic books, *Wizard* has served as a key mediator between fans and creators alike for two decades. With 20 years under its belt, the magazine has had a controversial impact in both the comics industry and popular culture.

It is important to note that Wizard World, Inc. is often confused with Wizards of the Coast, LLC. While *Wizard* magazine and the *Wizard World* conventions are properties of Wizard World, Inc., Wizards of the Coast, LLC, is a separate entity best known for its line of *Magic: The Gathering* trading card games.

HISTORY

In August 1990, **Marvel Comics** released **Todd McFarlane**'s *Spider-Man* #1 to a voracious public. Shipping with two different covers, in both bagged and unbagged editions, in both newsstand and direct sales editions, and with limited-edition "variant" covers in such unique colors as blue, gold, and "platinum," *Spider-Man* #1 sold an astounding 2.5 million copies. Just one year later, in October 1991, Marvel broke its own record with the publication of what the *Guinness Book of World Records* now considers the "best-selling comic book of all time": Jim Lee's *X-Men* (vol. 2) #1, which, featuring four different team covers and one "gate-folded" cover, sold over 8.1 million copies (Glenday 2011, 300).

Somewhat lost between these seminal events, however, was the debut issue of *Wizard: The Guide to Comics*, a fanzine created by a then 21-year-old New Yorker named Gareb Shamus. Released one month prior to *X-Men* #1, the first issue of *Wizard* featured Todd McFarlane's eye-catching rendition of **Spider-Man** in a wizard's outfit, an exclusive interview with McFarlane, previews of "new hot comics," and an all-new, color-coded pricing guide. With over 250 various issues and special editions having been subsequently published, *Wizard* and its parent company, Wizard Entertainment, have made an enduring impact across the many industries involved in the cultural production of the mass medium of comic books.

One of the immediate impacts *Wizard* had on the comics scene was due to its innovative aesthetic design. Beginning with the first issue, *Wizard* stood out—literally—from other comics publications on the shelf. A few centimeters both taller and wider than the traditional comic book, issues of *Wizard* also shipped "polybagged," or completely sealed in a light transparent bag, with words and images, often in color, printed on the bags themselves. These glossy covers immediately caught fans' eyes, and a steady introduction of new gimmicks increased both the magazine's visibility and its sales.

In addition to serving as a deterrent to reading the magazine in the comic book store (a common problem for any shop), polybagging allowed *Wizard* to include a range of special inserts, from targeted company advertisements to postcards to promotional trading cards. One of the most popular of *Wizard*'s innovations was an exclusive collector's series of specially numbered comic books. Generally designated with the issue numbers of "1/2," these mail-order comics required the reader to send in the original coupon along with a moderate fee for shipping and handling. In return, the reader received a limited-edition comic book along with a "certificate of authenticity." In other issues, however, *Wizard* often included these one-of-a-kind comics inside the magazine itself, usually in the form of 22-page "#0" issues. In both cases, these special issues sought to keep a modicum of continuity in the numbering of a given series while adding another rare issue for the collector's archive. Other popular promotions included full-color posters, multiple collectible covers, stickers, and dozens of various "anniversary" issues.

Another key feature of *Wizard* was its use of full color throughout the magazine, especially in its pricing sections. Most of the pricing guides to this point, including both the *Comics Buyer's Guide* and the *Overstreet Price Guide Update*, were black-and-white publications featuring hard-to-see thumbnail covers and even harder-to-read computer-generated text. *Wizard*'s pricing guides, on the other hand, emphasized the fluctuating popularity of various series by utilizing an immediately identifiable color-coded system: pink for comics whose value has decreased, yellow for comics whose value has increased and are "hot," and green for recently released publications. Sprinkled throughout the price guides were smaller features such as top-10 lists for writers, artists, and individual issues as well as humorous spotlights on specific issues from the comics vault.

Wizard also became known for its unique incorporation of readers' responses in their letters page. Prominently located at the beginning of each issue, the letters section included both unsolicited reader art as well as contests

NOT HELPING THE CASE

Other popular examples of Wizard's declining standards ranged from "ad[s] in *Wizard* that quote *Wizard* in an attempt to get you to buy something from *Wizard*" to asking creators in their interviews such questions as whether they would sleep with their own characters (Sims 2011). Further reinforcing popular stereotypes of the "average" comics reader (i.e., male, single, and generally lacking in social skills), typical articles in magazines like *Wizard* included "Dangerous Curves: How the Black Widow Stacks up against the New Breed of Bad Girls" (#103), "X-Posed: Sexy Secrets from the X-Men Movie Set" (#104), "The Hottest Girl in Comics—The Search Is On!" (#114), and "X Sells: Grant Morrison Spills All the Dirty Secrets of the X-Men . . . and X-Women!" (#129). Rather than the new *Overstreet*, *Wizard* became more like a *Cosmopolitan* for men.

like the best envelope of the month. Topics ranged from debates over specific issues in the industry, specific comics, and such classic comic book questions as "Who Is Stronger: The Thing or the Hulk?" and "Who Is Better: Batman or Superman?" *Wizard* also excelled in producing a number of popular "best of" lists, including "The Top 10 Greatest Slugfests" (#113), "The 50 Best Comic Movies Ever!" (#143), "The 25 Greatest Comic Movie Moments" (#151), and "The 100 Greatest Villains Ever" (#177). As argued by a wide variety of practitioners in the interdisciplinary field of cultural studies, such outlets can serve as a means for fans to actively participate in the construction of unique comics communities (Pustz 1999; Jenkins 2006). More recent contributions from the emerging field of critical comic book studies support such conclusions, with many scholars suggesting that such participation is a key means for such fans to develop what the late French sociologist Pierre Bourdieu has termed "cultural capital" (Brown 1997; Kleefeld 2009).

In addition to publishing *Wizard* magazine, Wizard World, Inc., has published a number of other popular fanzines, including *Toyfare* (1997–2011), a collectible action figure pricing guide; *InQuest Gamer* (1995–2007), a guide for collectible card games; and *Anime Insider* (2002–2009), devoted to Japanese manga. At its height, *Wizard* averaged 185,000 readers per month while the other titles constituted a combined circulation of around 238,000 (Gustines 2005). The success of *Wizard* also spawned a number of other collector's magazines, including the short-lived *Hero Illustrated* (1993–1995), and outlasted similar slick magazines like *Comic Buyer's Guide Price Guide* (1990–1994). Wizard World also published a number of hardcover works celebrating popular creators, as part of their "millennium" series, and as a popular series on *How to Draw* (2005–2007) comic books. In recent years, Wizard has further sought to expand their reach through the development of several new online ventures and nationwide comic book conventions.

With the advent of Free Comic Book Day (FCBD) at the dawn of the 21st century, *Wizard* returned to its roots, producing several free introductions to various aspects of comic collecting, including *The 100 Top Trade Paperbacks of All Time* (2006), *How to Draw Sampler* (2008), and *Hot List: The 50 Best Comic Movies* (2009). In addition to publishing special issue comics and hard covers, Wizard Entertainment's web site remains a popular source of industry news, exclusive art and stories, and high-end comic merchandise such as limited-edition convention comics, clothing, and designer statues and toys (*see* www.wizardworld.com).

With a cover date of March 1, 2011, the last issue of *Wizard Magazine* (#235), featuring Ryan Reynolds as the Green Lantern, was released in January 2011. As with other publishers in the industry, an unlucky combination of rising paper costs and declining sales helped contribute to *Wizard*'s demise (Phegley 2010). Even though Wizard tried to make their flagship title into a more business-friendly magazine format (Sidman 2006), the cover price— $5.99 for the final issue—proved to be too much in an era of $3.99 comic books. In February 2011, however, Wizard introduced a new, Internet-only fanzine, entitled *Wizard World: Pioneers of Pop Culture*, devoted to all aspects of the comic book business. Wizard has further attempted to expand its public presence through the reintroduction of an e-newsletter, an iPhone application, and a blog "where pop-fi comes to life."

With "the goal of leveraging Wizard World's intellectual property assets across the entertainment industry" ("WIZD Appoints Greg" 2011), the company is currently attempting to reconfigure itself as "a digital entertainment and event company" ("WIZD Appoints John" 2011). The primary means of accomplishing this is through the reincorporation of the company as a publicly traded business. As of this writing, Shamus, now president and CEO of the publicly traded Wizard World (WIZD), is building a board of directors, whose notable members include garment manufacturer John Macaluso, CW network chief operating officer John Maatta, management consulting company founder Greg Suess, and Michael Mathews, "a successful entrepreneur in guiding hyper-growth for companies in the digital marketing space" (Wizard World 2011), as chairman of the board. What these individuals have to do with comics is anyone's guess. But as Suess recently noted, "Wizard World has a deep database of loyal, engaged and passionate fans, sponsors, talent and media partners in a specifically defined, multi-billion dollar category. There is an opportunity to profitably mine that database to create new events, sponsors, content and applications, particularly via Wizard World's new digital platform" ("WIZD Appoints Greg" 2011).

With the cancellation of the long-running title in 2011, the rise and fall of Wizard provides a sobering example of how to remain relevant in such a volatile industry as comics. The company has recently announced plans for an expanded *Wizard World Comic Con Tour*, including the acquisition of such new destinations as Austin, Cincinnati, Miami, and Nashville. Shamus has also made a number of exclusive deals with such companies as Creation Entertainment, Certified Guaranty Company, and Diamond Comic Distributors. Such deals will include hospitality suites for retailers, VIP fan experiences, and reserved convention seating. Whether Wizard World will be able to continue to build on this new foundation will depend on a host of factors, including changing industry trends, rejuvenation of fan interest, and the economics of comics publishing itself.

IMPACT ON COMICS

Wizard's tenure, however, has not been without a number of controversies. Of the many debates involving *Wizard* magazine, one in particular continues to reverberate across the comic book community: the issue of pricing guides and the question of their authenticity.

One of the most enduring controversies has involved what many in the comics community have considered the inflation of comic prices, both over the short and long terms. In the short term, *Wizard*'s hype regarding specific issues, especially the popular variant issues, often led to drastic swings in the market and frustrated consumer demand. *Wizard*'s suggested prices were almost universally higher than any of the other pricing guides then in circulation, especially *The Overstreet Comic Book Price Guide*, which is considered to be one of the authoritative price guides in the industry. *Wizard*'s own attempt at producing a viable stand-alone price guide, the $14.99 *Wizard Comic Book Price Guide Annual* (1995–1996), lasted only two volumes.

While *Wizard* gave its readers a monthly sense of the market in contrast to *Overstreet*'s annual status, it also led to rampant speculation in the collectible market. Prices not only fluctuated greatly from month to month, but many comics sellers inflated prices even further in an attempt to increase their secondary profits, especially from the horde of naïve new fans brought into the market by such publicized titles as *Spider-Man* and *X-Men*. Since both collectors and sellers appreciated the higher values, *Wizard* became the go-to publication for comics news and pricing. As with the decimation of the sports card industry a few years before, the inflation of comic prices not only encouraged a record number of speculators into the market but also greedy publishers who began publishing an inexhaustible supply of special issues, variant covers, and signed and numbered editions. *Wizard*'s inclusion of popular sales of CGC (Comics Guaranty Corporation, now

Certified Guaranty Company) comics in their pricing guide inflated the market even further, as the guide serves as a benchmark for the exorbitant prices being paid by investors for "slabbed" comic books that have been encased in plastic.

These controversies came to a head when fan favorite **Frank Miller** spoke to a large crowd at the 2001 Harvey Awards. Of the many provocative statements he made, Miller said that not only was *Wizard* a "bible written by Satan," but also concluded that "cheap and stupid and trashy" magazines like *Wizard* "regularly cheapen and poison" the field of comics (Smith 2010). In subsequently ripping apart a copy of *Wizard* in front of the crowd, Miller continued his public criticism of the ongoing commodification of both comic books and comic communities.

IMPACT ON AMERICAN CULTURE

Perhaps the more damaging charge was in the questioning, both within and outside the comics industry, of the utility and authenticity of such "popular" trade publications as *Wizard*.

Now acutely self-aware of the highly unstable conditions of the comics market, many fans began to balk at what they saw as the rather crude stereotypes of comic book fans in popular publications throughout American culture (Brown 1997). As various media industries took notice of the popularity of comic books during the 1990s, *Wizard* itself morphed from a popular fanzine to "a self congratulatory hype machine" (Smith 2011) containing synergistic stories between various companies and their comic-related products. Again, fans and creators alike bristled at these characterizations. While Miller was destroying a copy of *Wizard* on stage, he stated not only that "this monthly vulgarity reinforces all the prejudice people hold about comics" but it also "cr[ies] to all the world that we're as cheap and stupid and trashy as they think we are" (Smith 2010).

In the contemporary conjuncture of mass consumption and corporate production, comic book fans remain upset with the dominant stereotypes around their fandom. In response to these concerns, fans continue to seek more authentic experiences that validate rather than denigrate their cultural status (Hills 2002; Lopes 2009). Building off of the works of Pierre Bourdieu and the cultural studies traditions, cultural scholars continue to illustrate how "fan cultures" leverage their "cultural capital" in order to acquire status within both the comic book and popular culture communities (Brown 1997; Beaty 2007). As scholar Jeffrey Brown writes, "Comic fandom allows its participants to achieve the social prestige and self-esteem that accompanies cultural capital without surrendering to the hegemonic rules of Official culture" (Brown 1997, 29).

SUMMARY

These criticisms continue to resonate throughout the comics community, especially now that such communities are back in the spotlight due to the significant number of popular films currently being made about a wide range of comic characters. If, indeed, *Wizard* promoted negative stereotypes in its magazines, then fans would be rightly upset at such attempts to co-opt their fandom by using such cultural stereotypes as a means of corporatizing the comics and related industries.

Despite these critiques, Wizard Entertainment continues to find some success within the industry. In recent years, Wizard has sponsored a number of popular comic book conventions across the United States. The initial four sites—Chicago, Philadelphia, Los Angeles, and Texas—proved to be extremely popular, especially as Wizard World produced limited numbers of a wide range of collectible merchandise in order to increase demand and attendance. As one store owner put it, a Wizard World convention is "a pop culture phenomenon" as "[i]t brings people out of their basements and creates community" (Shreffler 2009). But the recent cancellation of several of these conventions raises serious questions about Wizard's abilities to adapt to today's fluctuating comic markets.

See also Comic-Con International; Fanboy; McFarlane, Todd; Miller, Frank

ESSENTIAL WORKS

Goldstein, Douglas. *Wizard Millennium Edition*. New York: Wizard Entertainment, 2009.
McCallum, Pat. *Wizard Big Covers Book*. New York: Wizard Entertainment, 2004.
Wizard Entertainment. *How to Draw Heroic Anatomy*. New York: Wizard Entertainment, 2009.

FURTHER READING

Brown, Jeffrey A. "Comic Book Fandom and Cultural Capital." *Journal of Popular Culture* 30 (1997): 13–31.
Hills, Matt. *Fan Cultures*. New York: Routledge, 2002.
Pustz, Matthew J. *Comic Book Culture: Fanboys and True Believers*. Jackson: University Press of Mississippi, 1999.

J. Z. Long

Wolverine

He's "the best at what he does" and what he does often isn't very nice or pretty, but it has taken this **Marvel Comics** superhero from just being one of the **X-Men** to being an iconic character in his own right, appearing in several monthly titles—simultaneously being a member of both the X-Men and the Avengers as well as starring in his own solo adventures—not to mention being a popular guest star in many other titles. He is a mutant with enhanced senses—especially a heightened sense of smell that allows him to track people—and a healing factor that allows him to recover from extremely serious injuries. His bones are coated with the indestructible metal adamantium, which further protects him from harm and also covers claws that allow him to cut through almost anything. His past was secret for many years, not only to the readers but to himself as well. He is over a century old, with his power keeping him young. He has been a spy, a warrior, a lover, and a hero. He has been shown to have an animalistic nature and at times goes into a berserker rage that lets his instincts take over so that carnage can ensue. He has endured great triumphs and tragedies. He has made his way into television, movies, books, and games, as well as various forms of merchandise. He is Wolverine.

HISTORY

While Wolverine first appeared in 1974, information about him and his history were revealed in bits and pieces over the next three decades, with some of the information later being revealed as false memories. He first appeared in the final panel of *The Incredible Hulk* #180, with a full appearance in #181 (often reprinted as his "first" appearance). In this story written by Len Wein with art by Herb Trimpe, he had been dispatched by the Canadian government as their "Weapon X" to fight the **Hulk** who had previously caused damage there. While he did battle the Hulk, as well as the monstrous Wendigo, he failed to stop the Hulk in the allotted time and in #182 was called off by the government. Not much was revealed about Wolverine at the time except

(AP Photo/Marvel Comics)

that he was athletic, a good fighter, and had "claws forged of diamond-hard adamantium and the power to back them up."

Wolverine next appeared soon after in a slightly altered costume in the classic *Giant-Sized X-Men* #1 where he was recruited by Charles "Professor X" Xavier as part of his new team of X-Men. While Wein wrote that issue, it was Chris Claremont as chronicler of the team's adventures for nearly the next 20 years who told the readers more about Wolverine, including facts that were different from what Wein had intended. This included the ideas that Wolverine was a teenager and that his adamantium claws were housed in his gloves. *X-Men* #98 showed that not only was Wolverine several decades older than his teens but also that his claws were a part of him. Some sources have also revealed the planned idea that he was an actual Wolverine that had been mutated into human form (while this has also been contested, as some early stories hinted that there was something "different" about Wolverine).

The "maskless" appearance in *X-Men* #98 also established his iconic look of "pointy hair" on either side, mimicking the style of his mask.

Additional character background and traits were revealed by Claremont over the next few years. In *X-Men* #103, readers learned that his real name was "Logan," though there was no indication if that was his first or last name. Even though he told it to certain people in later issues, his own teammates only knew him as Wolverine until Nightcrawler learned his name in *Uncanny X-Men* #139. When he questioned Wolverine as to why he never told his teammates, Wolverine's reply was simply, "You never asked." Wolverine became an important part of the X-Men over the next few years and also increased in popularity with the fans. In 1982 he starred in a self-titled four-issue limited series by Claremont and **Frank Miller**. This was one of Marvel's earliest limited series and the first with a "solo" character.

While during the rest of the 1980s Wolverine was active with the X-Men, simultaneous solo stories were also showcased in an ongoing and long-running *Wolverine* series beginning in 1988. In the earlier issues of the series Wolverine spent his time on the Southeast Asian island of Madripoor, where, under the alias of Patch, he co-owned a bar in the more lawless section of the country. Of course everyone saw through his disguise (an eye patch), but figured if Wolverine wanted to pretend to be someone else, they were not going to argue. Some stories in *Wolverine* also crossed over into the other X-Men titles. It was also around this period that Wolverine was first shown fighting Sabretooth, a similarly powered character who was revealed to have a long history with Wolverine, both as an ally and as an antagonist. Many aspects of their joint history were revealed over the next several years, and there was some speculation that a familial relationship may exist as well. Also starting in the late 1980s, Wolverine began to be a popular guest star in other characters' comics as well as the star of many other limited series and one-shots.

More of Wolverine's past was revealed in 1991 in Barry Windsor-Smith's now-classic "Weapon X" story in *Marvel Comics Presents* #72–#84, which told of how Wolverine got the adamantium bonded to him by the Weapon X Project. Two years later in *X-Men* (vol. 2) #25, the villain Magneto used his abilities to pull the adamantium out of his body. It was then revealed that he had bone claws all along and that the adamantium had just coated them as it did his bones. Over the next five years both the loss of the adamantium and failed attempts to restore it negatively affected Wolverine, and it was eventually restored to him by the villain Apocalypse who wanted Wolverine as one of his "Horsemen."

The 2000s continued to unravel the mysteries of Wolverine's background. In 2001 the limited series *Origin* by Paul Jenkins, Joe Quesada, Bill Jemas, and Andy Kubert revealed to readers Wolverine's true past. He was born James Howlett in Alberta in 1882 and was the son of a plantation owner. His powers first revealed themselves when he saw his father murdered. "Logan" turns out to be the name that he used while on the run with the woman who was falsely accused of the murder. However, due to various mental tampering over the years and his own healing factor removing "traumatic" memories, Wolverine had no memory of this part of his history until the events of *House of M* (2005) restored them.

Now with his memory intact, Wolverine went on other solo adventures in which he redressed matters from his past including the fact that he had a son, Daken, who had similar abilities (and would later become the "Dark" Wolverine). His time was further split up when he became a member of the Avengers and helped to deal with the "Secret Invasion," "Dark Reign," and other major events that they went through. In addition, the X-Men's later leader, Cyclops, put Wolverine in charge of the new X-Force, a "black ops" team of mutants who take care of threats to mutantkind in a way that the other teams are unable or unwilling to do. In 2011, events in the X-Men titles led to a schism between the two teams, with Wolverine becoming the leader of one faction. Wolverine left Utopia, the San Francisco Bay island where most of the X-Men were based, and returned to Westchester County, New York (former site of the Xavier School for Gifted Youngsters), where he became the headmaster of a new school for young mutants, as chronicled in the *Wolverine and the X-Men* series that began in 2011.

IMPACT ON COMICS

When introduced as one of the "All-New All-Different X-Men" Wolverine was one of several multinational characters, many of whom were older than their predecessors. Wolverine brought conflict to the team, and his attitude would often cause conflict with Professor X and the team field leader, Cyclops (as well as his successor Storm). Wolverine's "wild" nature was also something new. Here was a hero who went into berserker rages, sometimes striking out at friend and foe alike with razor-sharp claws at the ready (one notable example was in *Fantastic Four* #374 [1993], where he severely damaged **The Thing**'s face). Even without that element of his nature, he was shown to have a "rougher" style than his teammates, smoking cigars, riding motorcycles, drinking beer, and getting into brawls just for the sake of "getting into a good scrap." He was also shown to have an opposite nature from Cyclops, and there have been times where Cyclops's girlfriend Jean Grey (a.k.a. Marvel Girl/Phoenix) found that she may be as attracted to Wolverine as he was attracted to her.

Wolverine found himself fitting in well with the "Grim and Gritty" period that developed in comics in the mid- to late 1980s, and starting in that period he was a common guest star in other comic books, teaming up with everyone from the gun-wielding **Punisher** to the more innocent child-superteam,

---

SUPERPOWER

Wolverine's secret mutant power may be the ability to appear in a large number of comics simultaneously. Besides his appearances in the various X-Men titles—including 2011's *Wolverine and the X-Men*, *X-Force* (2008–2010), and *Uncanny X-Force* (2010–)—and in several Avengers titles since 2005, he has starred in the three ongoing *Wolverine* series (1988–2003, 2003–2009, 2010–), *Wolverine: Origins* (2006–2010), *Wolverine: Weapon X* (2009–2010), and *Wolverine: The Best There Is* (2011–2012). An additional title, *Wolverine: First Class*, was published from 2008 to 2010 and took place at an earlier period in Wolverine's time with the X-Men (generally equivalent to the issues published in the early 1980s), often teaming him up with the teenaged X-Men Kitty Pryde. Wolverine has also appeared in a large number of limited series and specials, both as a member of the X-Men and in a solo or team-up adventure. Many of Wolverine's appearances have been collected into bound editions.

Power Pack. One notable guest appearance was in *Fantastic Four* #348–#349 (1990–1991) in which he teamed up with **Spider-Man**, the Hulk, and Ghost Rider, all of whom were also frequently making guest appearances in many titles. His appearances in these titles tended to increase sales, and may also have appealed to the "speculator" market. His popularity in Marvel is such that a "nicer" version of Wolverine has appeared in comics aimed at younger readers. Wolverine was even popular outside of Marvel Comics and has his imitators and parodies, including "Wolveroach" in the popular title *Cerebus*. DC's alien bounty hunter Lobo has also been written as a parody of Wolverine-like characters, and the two even battled in 1995–1996's *DC vs. Marvel* limited series (Wolverine won).

IMPACT ON AMERICAN CULTURE

While many people, especially non-comics readers, may be familiar with the X-Men in general, Wolverine may be the team member most familiar to the general public. Wolverine has been with the X-Men for almost all of their television and film appearances, starting with a 1982 episode of *Spider-Man and His Amazing Friends* and followed by "Pryde of the X-Men," a 1989 pilot for a proposed animated X-Men series. For some reason, Wolverine was portrayed with an Australian accent in both programs. He also appeared in the three actual X-Men animated programs—*X-Men* (1992–1997); *X-Men: Evolution* (2000–2003), where, while several characters were portrayed as teens, he was both an adult and a teacher; and *Wolverine and the X-Men*

(2008–2009) in which he got top billing. *X-Men* and *X-Men: Evolution* also had comic book series based on them. A version of Wolverine also appeared in another cartoon, *The Super Hero Squad Show* (2009–), as well as a series of short anime adventures in 2011.

But it was in movies where Wolverine's popularity increased significantly, even among non-comics readers, beginning with 2000's *X-Men*. Played by Australian actor Hugh Jackman (though, unlike the early cartoons, without an Australian accent), he was one of the main characters in the film, with one of the major plotlines being how he first met the team. Besides raising the profile of Wolverine, the film also brought fame to Jackman, who was relatively unknown. Interestingly the role had originally gone to Scottish actor Dougray Scott, but he had a conflict with his schedule, so Jackman was brought in. Jackman received a Saturn award for his work as Wolverine, and soon was given lead roles in several films. Wolverine also had major roles in the 2003 sequel, *X2*, in which the villain of the film, Colonel Stryker, had ties to Wolverine and his history, and in 2006's *X-Men: The Last Stand*.

Wolverine was popular enough to get his own film with 2009's *X-Men Origins: Wolverine*. Based on a number of comic book sources including *Origin* and *Weapon X*, the film told Wolverine's background from his childhood to relatively recent times including his history with Sabretooth (Liev Schreiber), his encounters with other characters from the X-Men universe including Stryker, how he got the adamantium, and the source of the memory loss that he displayed in the other films. He has a cameo in *X-Men: First Class*, and as of this writing, a second solo film, *The Wolverine*, is in the works.

Besides television and films, Wolverine has appeared in original novels and in various video games both solo and as part of the X-Men. He has also appeared in various aspects of pop culture including toys, statues, games (including educational games), dolls, Halloween costumes, posters, and much, much more. He is among the X-Men portrayed by actors at Universal Studios Orlando. He has also been referenced in other films and television programs, including a 2007 *Simpsons* episode in which Bart looks at "The infamous Wolverine comic with pop-out claws," which, when opened, rakes the face of his friend Milhouse. It is notable that Wolverine is shown in name and appearance (with a mention of his "iconic sideburns") while in the same episode the Thing and Hulk are referred to as the "Thung" and the "Mulk."

While he has been a member of several superhero teams and has even taken on the role of leader or mentor when the need arises, Wolverine is, at heart, a loner, a "rugged individual" who chooses to make his own way and fight his own battles. He has his own moral code and does his best to live by it. In the past he has even bemoaned the fact that while "scrappin's second nature," thanks to his adamantium skeleton, claws, and healing factor there was "no such thing as a fair fight," and that he was "turned into a killing machine" and he did not like it. He may not be concerned with what is legal, but he is always on the side of what is right. With that, he joins many other characters from fiction both in and out of comics.

SUMMARY

Starting off with an appearance in a Hulk comic, Wolverine has grown to become one of Marvel Comics' best-known characters. Even without his mask his appearance is well known, including his distinctive hairstyle. He is always ready for a fight, be it a simple brawl or something in which his razor-sharp claws are needed, but he is certainly on the side of the good guys. He is often a loner, but when needed he is always there for his teammates and even willing to partner with other heroes if circumstances demand it. He has even taken on the role of mentor and teacher, taking younger mutants like Kitty Pryde or Jubilee under his wing. He can be rough, he can be tough, he can be crude—but there is no doubting that he is the best at what he does.

See also X-Men

ESSENTIAL WORKS

Claremont, Chris (w), Frank Miller (p), and Josef Rubinstein (i). *Wolverine* #1–#4 (Sept.–Dec. 1982), Marvel Comics. Collected in *Wolverine, Best of Wolverine Vol. 1, Wolverine by Miller and Claremont, Wolverine Omnibus Vol. 1*, and elsewhere.

Jenkins, Paul (w), Andy Kubert (p), Joe Quesada (i), and Richard Isanove (i). *Wolverine: The Origin* #1–#6 (Nov. 2001–July 2002), Marvel Comics. Collected in *Wolverine: The Origin.*

Windsor-Smith, Barry (w, p, i). "Weapon X." *Marvel Comics Presents* (vol. 1) #72–#84 (March–Sept. 1991), Marvel Comics. Collected in *Wolverine: Weapon X, Best of Wolverine Vol. 1, Wolverine Omnibus Vol. 1*, and elsewhere.

FURTHER READING

Manning, Matthew. *Wolverine: Inside the World of the Living Weapon.* New York: Dorling Kindersley, 2009.

Sanderson, Peter. *Ultimate X-Men: The Ultimate Guide* (Updated Edition). New York: Dorling Kindersley, 2006.

David S. Serchay

Wonder Woman

Born on a lost island of Amazons, Wonder Woman came to America during World War II to help fight the Nazi menace. Upon her arrival in the United States, she adopted the identity of army nurse Diana Prince and took on a war job to remain close to her sweetheart, Colonel Steve Trevor. Privy to the latest developments in the U.S. Army's efforts in their battles home and abroad, she was able to swiftly react to threats to the nation. In the course of her Golden Age adventures, she has fought enemies as varied as Axis powers; Mars, the god of war; intergalactic imperialists; and many other crazy and colorful foes. Wonder Woman was created by Harvard-educated psychologist William Moulton Marston, and the superheroine thrived during comics' Golden Age. After the death of her creator, however, she struggled to find a substantial audience, and she has since been subject to frequent and varied overhauls. It is her original Golden Age incarnation that has had the most impact and that has been utilized in a myriad of different ways, including her adoption as a feminist icon by Gloria Steinem in the 1970s. Wonder Woman was a trailblazer, the first prominent female superhero, and her comic has remained continually in publication since her Golden Age debut. Only **Superman** and **Batman** share a similar endurance, and together they form the cornerstone of the DC Universe, as manifest in the 2008–2009 series *Trinity*.

HISTORY

Wonder Woman was an experiment of sorts; a product of psychologist William Moulton Marston (May 9, 1893–May 2, 1947), who published the comic books under the pseudonym Charles Moulton, in order to distance them from his academic work. "Charles Moulton" was a synthesis of two names: those of her creator and of the comic's editor Charles Gaines. Marston's comics were clearly extensions of his theoretical work, and a means of influencing a generation of young American comic readers. Marston was convinced of the educational potential of comics, and his comic book superheroine enacts his theories of human behavior. Marston's theories are explained in his study

(Getty Images)

Emotions of Normal People (first published in 1928), which proves to be a useful tool in shedding light on Wonder Woman. The work details his model of human response, which is divided into four categories: dominance, submission, inducement, and compliance. What is perhaps most interesting, in light of Wonder Woman, is his call for the "emotional re-education of women to become love leaders" (1979, 394).

Marston's comics appear to be a key to this process of reeducation; an attempt to normalize female dominance, and to make this authority appealing to men. Marston writes, "Men dislike intensely the idea of submitting to women" (1979, 396), and he later proposes a means of addressing this hurdle in an article in *The American Scholar*, "Why 100,000,000 Americans Read Comics" (1944). In this article, he introduces Wonder Woman to a readership skeptical of comics, and proposes a solution to the male resentment of female superiority: "Give them an alluring woman stronger than themselves to submit to and they'd be proud to become her willing slaves!" (43). It is his superheroine, Wonder Woman, who is this alluring figure and a means of reeducating his young American audience; in this way, his comic books become extensions of his academic work, or the means of putting his theories into play. Marston

MYTHIC GODS AND HEROES

Princess Diana comes from a distant age of mythic gods and heroes. Her relatives are taken from Homeric legend, from the tales told in Classical Greece. Her mother, Hippolyte, is the Queen of the Amazons: a mythical race of barbarian warrior women who lived on the distant fringes beyond the boundaries of Greek cities. The Amazons made their entry into Greek myth as opponents of the greatest Greek heroes. Heracles, Theseus, and Achilles all engaged in battles with Amazons, battles that were inevitably won by the Greek heroes. Amazons were powerful enemies (the "supervillains" of the age), and their role in Greek myth was to prove the valor of the Greek heroes they fought.

selected Harry G. Peter to illustrate his comics, purportedly because of the "simplicity" of his art (Daniels 2000, 24); Peter's illustrations have a quaint quality, which imparts a certain innocence upon Marston's work.

Wonder Woman comes from a lost island of Amazons, a female-only paradise concealed from the world outside. Marston's Amazons are governed by peace and love, which is, incidentally, a marked departure from the Amazons of Greek myth. Marston's Amazons remain bound by the principle of loving submission: their strength is tempered by obedience to loving authority. The peace and tranquility of the Amazonian utopia, Paradise Island, are thrown into turmoil when the plane of U.S. Army Officer Steve Trevor crashes on their shores. The Amazons are suddenly confronted with the conflict of World War II and the injustice that rages in the outside world. Their goddesses, Aphrodite and Athena, decree that the strongest and wisest Amazon should return with Steve Trevor and remain in America to help fight the war against the Axis forces. A contest is held, and the winner is a masked contestant; an unknown Amazon whom no one recognizes. To the Amazon queen's dismay, the mysterious winner turns out to be her daughter, and thus, it is the Amazon princess, Diana, who leaves Paradise Island for America's shores (*All-Star Comics* #8, 1941).

When Wonder Woman leaves for America, she takes several Amazonian inventions with her: bullet-deflecting bracelets, a golden lasso that compels anyone bound by it to tell the truth, and her means of long-distance travel, an invisible plane. After reaching America, the Amazon princess adopts a false identity, one purchased from Diana Prince (a nurse who looks uncannily like herself, and who needs the money to travel abroad to be with her sweetheart). Wonder Woman's new alter ego, Diana Prince, takes a job as an Army nurse in order to remain close to the injured Steve, and subsequently gains employment at the war office in which he works (*Sensation Comics* #1, 1942; *Sensation Comics* #3, 1942). Her alter ego is the antithesis of the Amazonian superheroine: bespectacled, demure, meek, frail, and unassuming. This cover proves to be a success, and, undetected, she remains close to Steve. Even though she is often caught in compromising positions, no one really believes that Diana Prince and Wonder Woman could be one and the same.

The Amazon Princess turns out to be a wonderful novelty in man's world, and she overwhelms crowds with feats of Amazonian strength. Steve quickly falls in love with Marston's alluring superheroine; however, the Amazon princess remains focused on her fight against injustice, and lovelorn Steve is left to trail behind. Wonder Woman proves to be invaluable to America's war efforts, and the superheroine frequently defeats Nazis, the Japanese, and their various allies. The superheroine's battles, however, are not restricted to those of World War II, and she also fights fantastic and colorful enemies, including underground mole men, conquerors from out of space, animal-human hybrids, mythic gods, and common thieves. Wonder Woman is fiercely protective of her adoptive homeland, and she uses her Amazonian strength to help fight its wars. She is a powerful female role model, one who submits to a higher cause; in this way, she is a manifestation of her creator's psychological theories, an alluring example of a "love leader," or a figure whose strength is tempered by submission and love.

After Marston's death, the superheroine was subject to frequent overhauls; however, despite the continual changes, the first volume of her comic continued uninterrupted until 1986. After the last issue of volume 1, which coincided with **DC Comics**'s company-wide crossover event, *Crisis on Infinite Earths*, writer and artist George Pérez (together with co-writers Greg Potter and Len Wein) updated the Amazon princess's origin story for a relaunch of *Wonder Woman*. Pérez's revamped origin story reflects a greater degree of mythical accuracy, and the Amazons become known in man's world for their warlike ways; nonetheless, volume 2 did not divert too far from Marston's Golden Age origin, as the Amazons' reputation for hostility is revealed as a fabrication invented by those in power (due to the threat that the Amazons pose to the prevailing patriarchal ways). The Amazons are forced into seclusion, demonized because they are different, and Paradise Island becomes a refuge from a world that seeks to destroy them (*Wonder Woman* #1, 1987). Pérez's origin story is an amalgamation of Marston's original tale, together with a noticeable dose of classical scholarship. Wonder Woman is given a more solid mythical base; however, this comes at the expense of a playing down of Marston's psychological theories. In Wonder Woman's later incarnations, the symbolism of Marston's tales all but disappears, and the shift toward greater mythical accuracy supplants much of the novel charm of the Golden Age comics.

Wonder Woman's first comic book appearance was in *All-Star Comics* #8 (1941), and after the character's initial success, she found a regular home in *Sensation Comics* (1942), before being given her very own comic, titled *Wonder Woman*, several months later in the summer of 1942. The comic has spanned four volumes, and has run continuously since its debut: volume 1

(1942–1986), volume 2 (1987–1998), volume 3 (2006–2010), a return to the numeration of volume 1 (2010–2011), and volume 4, which commenced in 2011. At the height of her popularity, during World War II, Wonder Woman also featured in a daily newspaper strip (1944–1945). The superheroine has many group affiliations, and has been a regular feature in many other comics: she has served as a secretary to the Justice Society of America (from *All-Star Comics* #11), and remains a full-fledged member of their successor, the Justice League of America, in their self-titled comic and their various renamed series, which include *JLA*, *JLA: Classified*, *Justice*, and *Justice League*. Wonder Woman became a central figure in the DC series *Trinity*, and has featured in many DC crises and events. Most notably, perhaps, in *Crisis on Infinite Earths* (which marked the end of her first comic book series), Wonder Woman is seemingly killed after finally marrying her long-suffering sweetheart, Steve Trevor. Wonder Woman continues to remain a prominent figure in DC events, and has featured in countless crossovers and spin-offs throughout her 70 years in print.

IMPACT ON COMICS

Following Marston's death, Wonder Woman went through a prolonged period of frequent changes; her comic endured many major overhauls, and she was continually reinvented. In the 1950s, the superheroine became a romance editor, and she fielded readers' romantic quandaries while the handsome Steve Trevor affectionately looked on. In the 1960s, Wonder Woman was split into three differently aged versions of herself: Wonder Tot, Wonder Girl, and the Wonder Woman of the then present day. All three characters went on weird and wonderful adventures together, despite the curious illogicality of it all. In the late 1960s and early 1970s, Wonder Woman became a fashion-conscious mod: she donned a white jumpsuit and, under the instruction of her Karate sensei I-Ching, she took a brief turn toward James Bond–style spy escapades. Subsequently, Wonder Woman returned to a characterization more consistent with Marston's comics of the Golden Age, but this return to the past was eventually overhauled in *Wonder Woman*'s second volume. Wonder Woman's drastically changing persona has been linked to the comic book's poor sales, as writers constantly reinvented her in the hope of capturing a larger market share.

Wonder Woman has had a significant impact in the world outside comics, but she has been fraught with much disinterest within the comic world itself. The following quote, taken from the superhero Aquaman, would serve to demonstrate this reaction to the superheroine: "I think you're a little vapid and boring—and often more than a little Pollyannaish" (*Amazing Adventures of the JLA* 2005, 10). In an effort to increase interest in her character, during the mid-2000s Wonder Woman was given a harder edge: in a controversial moment in her character development, she killed the villain Maxwell Lord by snapping

THE CHEETAH AND THE ENEMY WITHIN

It is the Cheetah who is, perhaps, Wonder Woman's most prominent and enduring villain, and like the superheroine herself, she is a character that has taken many different forms. Marston's Cheetah debuts as a cruel and fiendish huntress living a double life. She switches between dual personalities, "changing like Jekyll and Hyde from aristocratic beauty to modern medusa" (*Wonder Woman* #6 1943, 1a). One half is good; the other half is bad, and she switches between the two: glamorous debutant Priscilla Rich and a predatory cheetah in a cat suit. This split consciousness may seem like a well-worn theme to modern comic readers; however, in Marston's era of comics, this dual characterization was quite unique. The Cheetah remained a prominent villain within *Wonder Woman*, and she becomes, in Pérez's run (1987–1992), more prominently a beast. In an interesting character turn, the beast that is the Cheetah becomes a reflection of the inner beast within Wonder Woman herself. As demonstrated in a vicious battle with the Cheetah, Wonder Woman takes on the properties of the villainess she fights: "All Diana can hear is her own raging heart . . . and finally, she hears one thing more—the roar of a mad animal. . . . she hears herself" (*Wonder Woman* #31, 1989, 19). It is Wonder Woman that now must fight for control of her soul, just as Marston's Cheetah did in the comic's early years.

his neck (*Wonder Woman* #219, 2005). This turn toward a darker side is continued in the miniseries *Amazons Attack* (2007), as her Amazonian sisters wage a bloody war against the United States. Amazons have become a liability, or an enemy force to be reckoned with, and as the Amazon princess's characterization becomes increasingly violent, she moves further away from Marston's "love leader" ideal. The diversity of her past characterizations endows the superheroine with a certain depth, and in more recent years, in *Wonder Woman*'s third volume (2006–2010), the complexity of her history becomes a prominent theme. Wonder Woman becomes a synthesis of the various different personas from her past, and in the words of Wonder Woman, from this period of self-exploration: "At the moment, I am not sure who I am . . . Princess, diplomat, superhero, spy" (*Wonder Woman Annual* #1, 2007, 1).

IMPACT ON AMERICAN CULTURE

At its peak in the 1940s, the *Wonder Woman* comic sold "around two and a half million copies" (Robbins 1996, 7), but in more recent decades, her comic book has not been the main source of her influence. Wonder Woman's comic has gone through expansive periods of poor sales, but, nonetheless, it has remained continually in print: the speculation surrounding its continual publication has centered upon a rumored contract between the Marston estate and her publisher, DC Comics. Marston reportedly made a strict stipulation that if the publisher failed to keep the title in print, they would lose the licensing rights. Overall, Wonder Woman is a very profitable character; she appears on a wide range of merchandise including clothing, figurines, and collectables. It is rumored that in order to maintain a hold on Wonder Woman's licensing rights, the publication of her comic endured, despite frequent poor sales; furthermore, the comic's longest hiatus, a yearlong break between series 1 and 2, was filled with the miniseries *The Legend of Wonder Woman* (1986) in order to fulfill the stipulations of the contract. This contract, nonetheless, is rumored to be no longer valid: according to writer Kurt Busiek (in a post on DC's online forum), the publisher eventually bought the character outright from the Marston estate (Busiek in Cronin 2005).

Wonder Woman has continued to remain an influential character despite periods of poor comic book sales, and it is perhaps, most famously, Wonder Woman's 1975–1979 television series that has exposed the superheroine to her largest audience in more recent decades. Former Miss World USA, Lynda Carter, starred in the series as Wonder Woman, and to use the words of Carter, it is the role she will be "forever identified with" (*Wonder Woman* #600, 2010, 1). The TV series was initially set in 1940s World War II, but due to the high costs of producing a period piece and the limitations of featuring Nazi villains, the setting of the TV series was shifted to the then present day. In more recent years, an animated film was released in 2009, featuring a plot based on Pérez's revamped origin story. Wonder Woman has also been a staple in animated adaptations of DC Comics, including the various *Super Friends* series through the 1970s into the 1980s, and in Bruce Timm's *Justice League* series for Cartoon Network in the early 2000s.

Sex, Bondage, and Wertham

Fredric Wertham's infamous attack on the gory comics of the 1950s, *Seduction of the Innocent*, presents a noteworthy addition to the controversy surrounding Wonder Woman. Wertham criticizes the superheroine's supposedly "homosexual" connotations and her "extremely sadistic hatred of all males" (1954, 192–93). To continue in the words of Wertham, "For boys, Wonder Woman is a frightening image. For girls she is a morbid ideal" (193). Wonder Woman's entourage of co-eds, the Holliday girls, are interpreted as "gay party girls" who are preoccupied with mutually rescuing each other from the "machinations of male enemies" (193). It is this very theme of capture and escape that has continued to plague Wonder Woman; most notably, perhaps,

TRUTH LASSOS AND LIE DETECTORS

William Moulton Marston is the self-proclaimed inventor of the lie detector test (otherwise known as the polygraph); however, his actual role in its creation is more ambiguous (Daniels 2000, 12–15). The lie detector does draw a striking parallel to one of Wonder Woman's own crime-fighting tools: namely, the lasso of truth. In a manner similar to the lie detector, the lasso of truth is strung around the speaking subject; however, this is where a more simple analogy ends. While the lie detector indicates truth or fallacy in the subject's reactions to his or her own words, the lasso of truth compels the subject to speak only the truth.

in Les Daniel's *Wonder Woman: The Complete History* (2000, 59–72), which includes a comprehensive account of the reaction to Marston's preoccupation with bondage. The prevalence of bondage in Marston's comic is undeniable, and to reiterate in the words of Marston's Wonder Woman: "How tiresome— I spend all my time tonight getting tied up!" (*Sensation Comics* #33, 1944, 10). Despite the frequent use of bondage within Marston's comics, it is only one manifestation of power in a text that recurrently enacts dominance and submission. The sensationalization of bondage alone removes one element from a wider context of power: one in which authority, imperialism, and colonialism take on equally significant roles. The narrative of superhero comics, more broadly, depends upon dominance and submission: most evidently, in the struggle between hero and villain. Furthermore, the Amazon princess's mythical heritage is certainly well suited to tales of domination: classical Amazons are renowned for their continual subjugation at the hands of Greek heroes (Kleinbaum 1983), and in this light, perhaps it does not seem so out of character for an Amazon to be recurrently bound.

Emancipation, Feminism, and Steinem

Moving on from bondage to emancipation, Wonder Woman has also been a prominent icon for female liberation, one drawn upon by many feminist writers from the late 1960s to the present day. Wonder Woman has inspired adulation from many feminist writers including, most prominently, Gloria Steinem, who offered a tribute to the superheroine in the form of an edited book of Golden Age reprints. To understand why the superheroine was adopted as a prominent feminist icon, the atmosphere of the comic's heyday should be considered: male superheroes abounded in comics that were, to quote Marston, full of "blood-curdling masculinity" (1944, 42), or alternatively, in the words

QUEER AS FOLKLORE

Many call Wonder Woman a "feminist icon," although I tend to consider her a queer icon as well, which may in and of itself be enough to horrify those who desperately need to make money off of her to prevent me from ever touching that character again.

And I mean queer in its broadest sense—antiassimilationist, antitradition, and defiantly ambiguous. As the ultimate "other," the original Wonder Woman came from a world where women were more powerful than men, and from a culture where women—Amazons, reimagined not as a tribe of fearless warrior women but as a highly evolved, technologically advanced race whose mental acuity gave them fantastic powers—dominated.

Sex and gender were powerful tools to subordinate the hypermasculine. Rather than kill her enemies, Wonder Woman worked most often to rehabilitate them. The now-infamous scenes of bondage spoke deeply about rechanneling aggressive, violent impulses into loving, sexual ones. Domestically, Wonder Woman could not imagine sublimating her passion for her work for the love of oafish Steve Trevor. Most notably, Wonder Woman, coupled with a tendency toward the bizarre and surreal in her stories, embodied the spirit of fun, hope, and joy; she was an utterly uncynical character, proud of her body, her gender, her sex, and her mission in "Man's World."

What was wonderful about the original Wonder Woman was that she represented a way of seeing the world, one that defied patriarchal norms. But I believe such defiance has played a heavy role in making Wonder Woman a sales conundrum in modern times.

As decades have passed, Wonder Woman has been reimagined as an often-militant warrior/soldier from a land not of cultural savants but savage brutes. Today, it remains the most commercially viable iteration of the character, partly because it plays into the fantasies and culturally sanctioned fears of anything overtly feminine of the predominately straight male audience the comic industry serves instead of reshaping them. She is *familiar* in this incarnation, and buttresses the conventional wisdom as opposed to bucking it. Here, her otherness, her queerness, is all but erased. And money is made.

Even many female comic readers (but not necessarily fans from other mediums) often prefer Wonder Woman to be less like "the other" and more like the norm, i.e., the male: deadly serious, morally conflicted, and thus "real." And when even women embrace an utterly patriarchal version of Wonder Woman, I cannot help but ponder—what happened?

But as the ultimate queer character, Wonder Woman is at her strongest and most unique when she challenges her readers and asks us why we believe what we do, suggesting that looking at the world through a completely different lens might not be such a bad idea. For she shows us how to live our lives better, not just live them, period.

But that can be a hard sell in a world that rewards the admittedly superlative but desperately grim *Batman* franchise with billions of dollars worldwide. What chance does a woman celebrating queer concepts like joy, love, peace, hope, the pleasures of sex, female power, liberation from norms and tropes, and otherness have against a cultural zeitgeist like that?

A lot, I say—because she *is* Wonder Woman, after all.

Phil Jimenez

of Steinem, "the "POW!" and "CRUNCH!" style" (1969, 1). Wonder Woman offered an alternative to the glut of brutally violent comics, and the love that she promoted proved to be a welcome respite. Steinem, by her own account, "was rescued" from a heroine-less childhood by Wonder Woman (1969, 1), and this sentiment has been repeated by Trina Robbins, who argues that at the time of Wonder Woman, "girl readers could find little in the way of heroic role models in the pages of comic books" (1996, 3).

Wonder Woman has become a suitably political figure, as evident, most notably, on the 1972 debut cover of *Ms.* magazine. The magazine in question, which was edited by Steinem, pictures a giant-sized Wonder Woman straddling a road that divides the chaotic bloodshed of the Vietnam War from a sleepy, peaceful American town; "Wonder Woman for President," the cover boldly declares, and the superheroine is heralded as a potential solution to the problematic political atmosphere of the day. She is a figure of liberation; however, she is not an unproblematic one. Her fight, which is in the name of her adoptive home America, serves to complicate her imposition of power: when she wins a battle or a war, just whom is she winning it for? It is understandable to see why she was so ardently taken up as a figurehead by several American feminists, but to take Wonder Woman as a universal figure, or one who fights for all of womankind, does carry a tinge of imperialism (or, as is evident in the period of *Trinity*, the globalization of "the American Way" for which she fights).

American Identity

Clad in an American flag, Wonder Woman wears her allegiance on her sleeve (figuratively speaking); however, in the mid-1980s, her American identity becomes a little more problematic than her costume would suggest. In the United States, Wonder Woman is an immigrant: she came from a faraway island and settled in this new world in order to help fight for "freedom and democracy" during World War II (*Sensation Comics* #6, 1942, 1). She quickly assimilates to its values and becomes "America's guardian angel" (*Sensation Comics* #12, 1942, 5), and the politics of this process of acculturation is discussed in Matthew J. Smith's "The Tyranny of the Melting Pot Metaphor: Wonder Woman as the Americanized Immigrant" (2001). It is in the second volume of *Wonder Woman*, Smith argues, that her immigrant status starts to be explored: writer Pérez, who grew up in a Spanish-speaking household, significantly develops this aspect of her characterization. Wonder Woman starts a process of acculturation, one that distances her from her homeland, or to reiterate using the words of Pérez's Wonder Woman, "I am no longer like my sister Amazons!" (*Wonder Woman* #9, 1987, 8). In the process of discussing Wonder Woman's assimilation, Smith draws upon an interesting plot development in *Wonder Woman* #73 (1993). In what is perhaps the strangest plot turn of the series, the Amazon princess takes a job in the cheap fast-food outlet Taco Wiz. This may seem like a curious thing for a superpowered princess to do, but in the tight job market, it is the only employment she can find. It is interesting to consider, Smith argues, that in order to become an assimilated Americanized immigrant, Wonder Woman must go through the process of working in a minimum-wage job.

The Trinity of Truth, Justice, and the American Way

Over the years, Wonder Woman has come to be associated with the battle cry of DC's central hero, Superman: "Truth, Justice and the American Way." It is Wonder Woman's pivotal role in the DC series *Trinity* that links her most explicitly with these ideals. To quote Kurt Busiek's 2008–2009 series *Trinity*, Wonder Woman embodies all three. First, "truth sustains her, drives her," and she was briefly a goddess of truth. Second, she fights "a war for justice," for the freedom to speak and to be heard. Third, even though she is not American, she stands for that which is associated with the American way, "strength, readiness, power tempered by ideals, the hand of peace backed by the willingness to fight" (*Trinity* #6, 2008, 10). Busiek draws upon aspects of her characterization that have long been evident, and her later incarnations have been driven by an unshakable certainty of beliefs. In the words of Wonder Woman, "I am simple because I wish to see things simply. Because I do not care for shades of gray. Either the blade is true or it isn't. Either the action is right, or it is wrong. Either the heart is pure . . . or it is corrupt" (*Wonder Woman* #222, 2005, 6). Wonder Woman is a character driven by absolute ideals, and her certainty in her conviction, appropriately, coincides with the uncertainty of the times. In a time of insecurity, and of social and political unrest, she is a throwback to the seeming certainty of comics' Golden Age.

SUMMARY

In over seven decades of publication, Wonder Woman has undergone many changes, but it is, undoubtedly, William Moulton Marston's original super-heroine that has had the greatest impact. It was Marston's background in psychology that made her comics so unique: she was a manifestation of his psychological theories, and she captured a large audience with her symbolically charged exploits. Wielding bullet-deflecting bracelets and a truth-compelling lasso, Wonder Woman promoted submission to loving authority; however, after Marston's death, this original ideal became obscured. Wonder Woman has, nonetheless, remained a character driven by conviction: she has been a Goddess of Truth, a United Nations delegate, and a linchpin in DC's Trinity. Wonder Woman has become an iconic figurehead, as her appropriation by American feminist Gloria Steinem demonstrates; she has served as a role model for girls at a time in which there were few, and it is, perhaps, this pioneering spirit that serves to make her an American icon. Wonder Woman is a trailblazer, and the runaway success of Marston's Golden Age comic served to open up the way for other superheroines to follow.

See also Batgirl; DC Comics; Supergirl

ESSENTIAL WORKS

Busiek, Kurt (w), Fabian Nicieza (w), Mark Bagley et al. (p), and Mark Farmer et al. (i). *Trinity Vols. 1–3*. New York: DC Comics, 2009.

Heinberg, Allan (w), Terry Dodson (p), Gary Frank (p), Rachael Dodson (i), and Jonathan Sibal (i). *Who Is Wonder Woman?* New York: DC Comics, 2008.

Moulton, Charles (w), and Harry G. Peter (a). *Wonder Woman Archives Vols. 1–6*. New York: DC Comics, 1998–2010.

FURTHER READING

Daniels, Les. *Wonder Woman: The Complete History*. San Francisco: Chronicle Books, 2000.

Fleisher, Michael L. *The Original Encyclopedia of Comic Book Heroes: Volume Two, Wonder Woman*. New York: DC Comics, 2007.

Clare Pitkethly

X-Men

The X-Men are a team of superheroes in the **Marvel Comics** Universe. Members of the team, with a few exceptions, are mutants, each with an inborn power. Over the course of five decades, the team has expanded from five "students" in school to dozens of characters on an artificial island. Characters have joined, left, and often rejoined. Some have "died," only to come back one way or another. Even those who once fought the team have sometimes become members in good standing. Stories have run the gambit from simple "good guys vs. bad guys" to "loss and betrayal," and have spanned the globe, the galaxy, and even extended into the future. The X-Men are major characters of the Marvel Universe, the focus of popular films and animated television programs, and there have been many months in which there have been over a dozen comic books that feature the team, one of its members, or a title that is a spin-off from an existing X-Men title. In addition, since the 1970s, many of the "X-Books" have been among the best-selling American comics titles. Besides their superheroic adventures, the X-Men have also served as a metaphor for people faced with prejudice, with it often being said that the X-Men are trying to save "a world that hates and fears them."

HISTORY

The X-Men first appeared in *X-Men* #1 (1963) in a story by **Stan Lee** and **Jack Kirby**. Gathered together by Charles Xavier, a.k.a. Professor X, are Scott "Cyclops" Summers, Hank "Beast" McCoy, Bobby "Iceman" Drake, Warren "Angel" Worthington III, and joining the team in this issue, the telekinetic Jean "Marvel Girl" Grey. The five are all teenagers with the cover story that they are students at the professor's "School for Gifted Youngsters" in upstate New York. Dressed in matching blue and gold costumes, the team fights a number of villains, most notably their very first foe, Magneto. Other early antagonists included Magneto's Brotherhood of Evil Mutants, the Vanisher, the Blob, the Juggernaut (who was not a mutant but was Xavier's stepbrother), and the robotic, mutant-hunting Sentinels.

(Photofest)

Over the next few years changes to the team included more individualized costumes, improved powers, new members (e.g., Cyclops's brother Havok), and the first of many seeming "deaths" of team members who later turned up alive (something repeated often over the following decades). The team made appearances in other Marvel titles, and the characters' origins were revealed in backup stories. Roy Thomas took over from Lee as writer, while Kirby's successors included such notables as Werner Roth (as Jay Gavin), **Jim Steranko,** Sal Bucema, Barry Windsor-Smith, and **Neal Adams.** Despite such talent, *X-Men* was not a very good seller in those early days, and the series was briefly canceled after #66 (1970). The series was brought back by reprinting earlier stories while the characters made appearances elsewhere, most notably the Beast, who took on a more "bestial" form in his solo series in *Amazing Adventures.* The team's hiatus lasted until 1975, with publication of *Giant-Size X-Men* #1.

In this famous story by Len Wein and Dave Cockrum, the original team is captured, and Xavier puts together a new team of mutants to rescue them. This new team consists of new and existing characters from around the world including the African Storm, the German Nightcrawler, the Russian Colossus, the Irish Banshee, the Apache Thunderbird, and, most notably due to his later popularity, the Canadian **Wolverine**. After this adventure the original members, except for Cyclops, leave and the new team's further adventures began with *X-Men* #94, written by Chris Claremont, who would write the series for the next 16 years. This new team of X-Men was different than their predecessors as several of them were older and more experienced. While this new team would fight old foes like the Sentinels and Magneto, their adventures also began to be a little more cosmic.

In one of their earliest missions, the new team is aboard a space shuttle that is saved from destruction by the recently returned Jean Grey. The others think that she has sacrificed herself when the ship lands in the water, but she instead flies out as the "Phoenix." In this form she is much more powerful. However, the power begins to corrupt her to the point where she becomes the planet-destroying "Dark Phoenix." She regains control for a while, but various events make it harder to keep in control. When it looks as if Dark Phoenix will reemerge, Jean commits suicide in order to stop it and save the universe. Years later it is revealed that Jean is still alive and that the Phoenix, a cosmically empowered duplicate, had taken her place all along. "The Phoenix Saga," co-written by Claremont and artist John Byrne, remains one of the most pivotal in X-Men history and added to the title's increasing popularity.

The team continued in the 1980s with even more new members joining, including Kitty Pryde, Rogue, Jubilee, and Gambit. Even Magneto joined for a time, modifying his views on mutant superiority. New villains emerged including Mystique (along with her own Brotherhood of Evil Mutants), Mr. Sinister, and Apocalypse. Spin-off teams like the New Mutants and X-Factor (composed of the X-Men's founding members) would find themselves caught up in some of the same adventures as the X-Men, including "The Mutant Massacre" and "Inferno." This was the inauguration of crossover storylines that still permeate the X-titles today.

The early 1990s brought more changes to the team. The members of X-Factor rejoined, and with the size of the team having increased, they were often divided into two squads, one of which was the focus of the new, best-selling *X-Men* comic (the original title having added "*Uncanny*" to its name years earlier). New X-Men were introduced, including the time-traveling Bishop, and new enemies included Magneto's zealous "Acolytes" and antimutant forces such as "Friends of Humanity." A new group of students were put together as Generation X and taught by former X-Man Banshee and former villain Emma Frost. One major X-Men story of the 1990s occurred when a time traveler inadvertently created the alternate timeline known as "The Age of Apocalypse." Writers like Fabian Nicieza and artists such as Jim Lee, John Romita, Jr., and Marc Silvestri helped to shape this era.

The 21st century brought even more changes to the team with stories created by **Grant Morrison,** Mike Carey, Joss Whedon, the returned Claremont, and others. Professor Xavier publicly revealed himself as a mutant and expanded the team's image. Many more students were brought to the school, now known as the "Xavier Institute." Along with all the new characters, several existing characters had their appearances or abilities altered. The team had triumphs and tragedies including, once again, the death of Jean Grey. The world of the X-Men changed significantly during the *House of M* limited series, when the Scarlet Witch exercised her reality-warping abilities so that out of the millions of mutants worldwide, all but 198 lost their powers. Among the upheavals that followed, the team has moved to California, first based in San Francisco and later on an artificial island called Utopia. Times have grown darker for the team and mutantkind in general, and as team leader, Cyclops has made some hard decisions that led to a schism among those calling themselves X-Men.

IMPACT ON COMICS

Along with **Spider-Man,** the **Fantastic Four,** and the Avengers, the X-Men were among the first Marvel Comics superheroes and teams of the 1960s to have their own title. They were shown to be a part of the Marvel Universe, encountering other characters in both their own book and those of the other characters. However, the readership was not always there, with low sales, and even the fan-made Alley awards named it "strip most needing improvement." As mentioned earlier, the series was even canceled for a time, and, when relaunched, did not print new stories. But with the rise of the new X-Men, reaction improved. Sales greatly increased, with directly distributed copies alone breaking 100,000 copies in the fall of 1980. The 1991 premiere of *X-Men* vol. 2 holds a record for sales (due in part to the multiple covers), and even in the 1980s sales increased to the point that multiple comics titles were commercially viable. In recent years, the "X-Books" have won awards (including numerous Eisners) for both the individual titles and for the various creators. The X-Men and related teams continue to be a major presence in the Marvel Universe, and they have often been involved in the company-wide events such as the "Secret Invasion" and "Dark Reign."

IMPACT ON AMERICAN CULTURE

The X-Men have made many appearances on film and television and have appeared in many other forms of entertainment and merchandise. The film and television versions have often featured certain members of the team, with the line-up not always in sync with the comics. The first onscreen appearance by the X-Men was in a 1966 "Sub-Mariner" segment of the animated television series *The Marvel Superheroes*. The original team was shown, though not identified by the name. They next appeared in a 1982 *Spider-Man and His Amazing Friends* episode. Spider-Man's "friends" were Iceman and a new character Firestar (later incorporated into the Marvel Universe), and in the episode they attended a reunion of their old team, the X-Men. They made one more appearance on the show, and there was an attempt to give the X-Men their own animated series in 1989 with the pilot "Pryde of the X-Men." The series was not picked up, although the pilot was occasionally seen as part of the syndicated *Marvel Action Universe*.

The team finally got its own animated, self-titled show in 1992. It lasted five seasons, and besides the "core characters," it occasionally featured others from the "X-Universe." Several notable *X-Men* storylines were adapted for the series including "The Phoenix Saga" and "Days of Future Past," an alternate future story from 1981. The X-Men from this series also appeared in other Marvel-based cartoons. The X-Men returned to television from 2000 to 2004 with the animated *X-Men: Evolution*. This series changed certain aspects of the comics, with Professor X, Storm, and Wolverine as adults, with the others, including Cyclops and Jean, as students who also attended nearby Bayville High. The one-season *Wolverine and the X-Men* (2008) had the team briefly disband after the disappearance of Professor X, but soon reform to fight new threats.

While there was a 1996 television movie based on *Generation X*, the X-Men proper made their live-action debut with the 2000 film *X-Men*, which included in its cast Patrick Stewart (Professor X), Hugh Jackman (Wolverine), Halle Berry (Storm), Anna Paquin (Rogue), and Ian McKellen (Magneto). The story told of how Wolverine and Rogue joined the team and helped to defeat the plans of Magneto. The 2003 sequel *X2* was loosely based on the classic X-Men story "God Loves, Man Kills" from *Marvel Graphic Novel #5* (1982), with the antimutant Reverend Stryker being replaced by General Stryker (Brian Cox), who had ties to Wolverine's past. This was followed by 2006's *X-Men: The Last Stand*, which saw the deaths of several characters, brought others including the Beast (Kelsey Grammer) and Kitty Pryde (Ellen Page) to the forefront, and was loosely based on both the Phoenix Saga and the first storyline from *Astonishing X-Men* (2004).

The next two X-Men films both took place in the past. While 2009's *X-Men Origins: Wolverine* was primarily about that character, 2011's *X-Men: First Class* provides an early history of the team, though one inconsistent with the comic book stories. Primarily set in 1962, it features the young Xavier and Magneto (James McAvoy and Michael Fassbender) and told of how the X-Men were formed. The *X-Men* films have generally been successful, with

THE X-PANDING X-MEN UNIVERSE

Besides all of the spin-offs featuring new teams and solo adventures of members, as well as many limited series, the team itself has starred in a number of ongoing series. The three "main" titles are *X-Men* volume 1, now called *Uncanny X-Men* (1963–2011, restarted in 2011 with a new first issue); volume 2, also called *New X-Men* and *X-Men Legacy* (1991–present); and volume 3 (2010–). Other ongoing series that took place alongside the other titles are *X-Treme X-Men* (2001–2004), *Astonishing X-Men* (2004–), *X-Force* (2008–2010), *Uncanny X-Force* (2010–), and *Wolverine and the X-Men* (2011–). In addition to these titles, there have been a number of additional series that chronicled new stories set in the team's past and others based on the various animated series. Also notable is *X-Men Forever* (2009–2010, 2010–2011) which was written by Claremont and featured an alternate continuity based on what was happening when he first stepped down as writer in 1991.

the first three being among the highest grossing films in the years that they were released.

Besides their film and television appearances, the X-Men have appeared in other forms, including dolls and action figures, statues, posters, and clothing. They have also appeared in original novels including one in which they team up with the characters of *Star Trek: The Next Generation*. One of the more interesting ways the X-Men appear in popular culture is at Universal Orlando Resort's "Islands of Adventure," whose Marvel Superhero Island features a Storm Force Acceleration ride and has performers dressed as various X-Men walking around the park.

The writers of X-Men have often tried to reflect society and current events, even going so far as having the students enjoy a coffee shop with a beatnik poet in the early days. Almost from the beginning, the X-Men have used mutants as a metaphor for any group that has been facing prejudice, ranging from African Americans to homosexuals. While from the start antimutant feeling was shown, it started to grow with *X-Men* #14 (1965) when anthropologist Bolivar Trask began to warn people of the "Mutant Menace" and unleashed the first of the mutant-hunting robotic Sentinels.

Over the years the antimutant feeling varied in intensity as well as its source. Sometimes it was the government who financed projects like Operation: Zero Tolerance and attempted to force mutant registration. In other instances the X-Men were persecuted by organized groups—both political and paramilitary—such as the Friends of Humanity. Some of these were supervillain-like teams, but others had some parallel to various real-life supremacist movements. Examples of antimutant sentiment ranged from terrorist to protests, to basic discrimination. One notable example of the latter was in *Uncanny X-Men* #427 (2003), in which the body of mutant hero Skin, killed by an antimutant group, had to be removed from the cemetery where it was buried due to its antimutant policy. This is reminiscent of the real-life past examples of segregated cemeteries. Like persecuted homosexuals, some mutants conceal their abilities (basically staying "in the closet") to be able to "pass" and avoid discrimination. Another parallel is found in the film *X2* in a scene in which Iceman "comes out" to his parents, and his mother asks him if he has tried not being a mutant. Another parallel is that in the classic story "Days of Future Past" (*Uncanny X-Men* #141–#142) and in other portrayals of possible futures, mutants have been rounded up and put into camps. In the future of the X-Man Bishop they have also had an "M" branded onto their faces, similar to the tattooing of Jews in concentration camps. In addition, there have also been parallels to various "separatist" movements among persecuted minorities and a desire for a "mutant homeland" that has been shown in several ways including the fictional islands of Genosha and Utopia, both depicted as mutant sanctuaries.

Over the years, stories with the simple theme of "good guys stop the bad guys" have been replaced with more complex tales, and even the issue of "good vs. evil" itself has changed. Magneto was a recurring villain, but his portrayal changed over time, and with revelations of his background as a Holocaust survivor, he seemed less of a villain than someone who wanted to protect his people "by any means necessary," even if that involved violence. This set up a dualistic opposition to Xavier's "peaceful coexistence and equality" stance, and the parallels between the real-world Malcolm X and Martin Luther King, Jr., in terms of their philosophies seem evident. He has even been an ally of the X-Men on many occasions, and other former foes such as Rogue and Emma Frost have become vital members of the team as well. Other past enemies such as Mystique, Juggernaut, and Sabretooth have also worked with the team, though at times reluctantly. Some return as antagonists, while others remain trustworthy teammates and have even been in leadership positions.

On the other side of the coin, over the years Professor X has been shown as not being morally "pure." Even at the start he was shown using his powers to affect minds and keeping secrets from the team even to the point of faking his own death. But in recent years other secrets have come to light, such as his hiding of the deaths of a secret X-Men team between the old and the new, and keeping secret the knowledge that their high-tech "Danger Room" had become sentient. Even the X-Men have grown a little darker in a reaction to troubled times, including Cyclops's setting up the "black ops" X-Force team. Some of these changes may be due in part to the fact that over the years, the average age of readers of the X-Men's adventures has increased and that comic books are being written to reflect that.

SUMMARY

They've been called uncanny, amazing, astounding, and astonishing. They have been a metaphor for victims of prejudice and discrimination, a major force for good in the Marvel Universe, and they and their spin-off characters have been the stars of dozens of titles. They are the X-Men.

See also Adams, Neal; Kirby, Jack; Lee, Stan; Morrison, Grant; Wolverine

ESSENTIAL WORKS

Claremont, Chris (w), John Byrne (w, p), and Terry Austin (i). "The Dark Phoenix Saga." *X-Men* (vol. 1) #129–#137 (Jan.–Sept. 1980), Marvel Comics. Collected in *X-Men: Dark Phoenix Saga*. New York: Marvel, 2010.

Claremont, Chris (w), John Byrne (w, p), and Terry Austin (i). "Days of Future Past." *X-Men* (vol. 1) #141 (Jan. 1981) and *Uncanny X-Men* (vol. 1) #142 (Feb. 1981), Marvel Comics. Collected in *X-Men: Days of Future Past*. New York: Marvel, 2011.

Wein, Len (w), and Dave Cockrum (p, i). "Second Genesis." *Giant-Size X-Men* #1 (May 1975), Marvel Comics. Collected in *Essential X-Men Vol. 1*. New York: Marvel, 2008.

FURTHER READING

Irwin, William, ed. *X-Men and Philosophy: Astonishing Insight and Uncanny Argument in the Mutant X-Verse*. Hoboken, NJ: Wiley, 2009.

Sanderson, Peter. *Ultimate X-Men: The Ultimate Guide*. New York: Dorling Kindersley, 2006.

Wein, Len, and Leah Wilson, eds. *The Unauthorized X-Men: SF and Comic Writers on Mutants, Prejudice, and Adamantium*. Dallas: Benbella Books, 2006.

David S. Serchay

Zap Comix

Zap Comix #1 by **Robert Crumb** is in one of the most important comic books ever published. *Zap* caused a sea change in the industry regarding creator-owned, royalty-paying comic books as well as revamped a declining magazine distribution system that no longer cared about the lowly and much maligned comic book.

HISTORY

While there are various valid claimants to being the "first" underground comic book of the modern era, *Zap Comix* was the first to grab the attention of the comics creator and the reader communities as it rippled across America in those early months of 1968. This seminal comic book was printed on a hand-fed press by Charles Plymell, with able assistant Don Donahue, in the last week of February 1968 in San Francisco. Many friends contributed to the comic book's grassroots production, helping to hand-collate the stacks, trim them up, then saddle stitch two staples on by hand. The original edition acknowledges Plymell's role, noting on the lower back cover "Printed by Charles Plymell."

Zap Comix first began to be sold on the street on February 25, 1968, in the Haight-Ashbury neighborhood by Robert Crumb's very pregnant wife, Dana, pushing a baby carriage with some copies piled in it. Contrary to a popular myth, Robert Crumb never stood at the corner of Haight & Ashbury huckstering *Zap Comix* that day, or ever. Dana was accompanied by Don Donahue and another friend, Marylin "Mimi" Jones McGrew. One of many street fairs was going on that day. They also got some *Zaps* placed into a few Haight-Ashbury stores such as In Gear. Selling at 25 cents a copy, the first day sales totaled only $20.50.

The next day a small distribution company called Third World Distribution, financed by Moe Moskowitz, purchased approximately 500 copies. These copies were distributed a few copies per account on consignment into some 200 outlets along the San Francisco peninsula down to around San Jose

(Photofest)

State University. They also went to head shops (stores that sold drug paraphernalia) and progressive book stores inside Berkeley near the University of California campus. *Zap Comix* #1 was the fifth publication, along with the *Berkeley Barb*, *San Francisco Oracle*, *East Village Other*, and *Rolling Stone*, that Third World nursed along in its infancy. Third World soon discovered, during the following week's distribution run, *Zap* was sold out everywhere. Some of these stores ringing the bay were calling, asking for more copies. Lucky souls who had purchased one had shown it to their friends. Stories like "Meatball," with their less-than-subtle references to getting high, were enthusiastically received by the nation's growing population of readers seeking to expand their collective unconscious.

Zap's conservative first print run of less than 3,500 copies was exhausted in a little over a month. Moskowitz then special-ordered another run of 5,000 prepaid copies. (Copies in this second printing have "Printed by Don Donahue" on their lower back cover.) Inside two months, that printing had sold out as well. In the meantime, Crumb encountered fellow comic creators S. Clay Wilson as well as famed concert poster artists Victor Moscoso and Rick

Griffin. Crumb had fairly recently taken close notice of Griffin's iconic comic strip poster for the Avalon Ballroom headliners Quicksilver Messenger Service. Griffin and Moscoso were by then world famous for their numerous contributions to the Bay Area concert poster scene. Griffin's "flaming eyeball" Jimi Hendrix poster is reputed by many collectors worldwide as the most famous rock art concert poster of all time. He invited the trio into what became *Zap Comix* #2, published in late August 1968, sans Donahue as printer.

Donahue had by this time purchased Plymell's printing press in exchange for a $200 tape recorder. Around July 1968, Donahue printed up an estimated 5,000 copies of another all-Crumb issue, which is titled *Zap Comix* #0. Despite his best intentions, Donahue could not keep up with the growing demand. The hand-fed printing press proved to be too slow with feeding it one page at a time. The older, business-savvy Moscoso convinced the other creators to trademark the name *Zap Comics* and *Comix*. He also agreed to front $10,000 to an emerging printer called Print Mint. This deal enabled the new publisher of comic books to front estimated royalties in advance. When Print Mint issued its reprints done on a professional modern web press, four more pages were added, thus making it easy to distinguish first printings from all later editions.

It was around the same time that Gary Arlington opened one of the first comic book stores in the country, the San Francisco Comic Book Company. This time-honored establishment became a mecca for the comics creator community soon to descend upon the Bay Area as well as those seeking to buy and read *Zap* and other underground comix.

That summer Crumb fled the Bay Area. Suddenly Crumb was getting more attention than he wanted—both for *Zap Comix* and as the designer of the *Cheap Thrills* album cover for Janis Joplin's group Big Brother and the Holding Company. A number of hucksters flocked to the Bay Area with promised "deals," all guaranteeing Crumb riches beyond imagination. Crumb balked at the offers and left the Bay Area. He landed briefly in Chicago, where he joined up with Jay Lynch, Skip Williamson, and a much younger Jay Kinney to birth another significant anthology in the burgeoning underground comix movement, *Bijou Funnies*.

Still, *Zap Comix* #2 arrived by late summer sporting a cover by Rick Griffin and containing work by Crumb, Griffin, Moscoso, and Wilson. Donahue had just started trying to print covers to #2 when he found out about an expanded Print Mint deal, which saw *Zap* go national in scope. *Zap*'s popularity was still unquestioned, as an initial print run of 500 copies got eaten up at an art show at the Light-Sound Dimension Gallery on August 20, 1968.

In December 1968 *Zap Comix* #3 was issued with an initial print run of upwards of 50,000 copies. This issue included Gilbert Shelton doing a rather intense Wonder Warthog story along with Crumb doing a two-pager, "Daze," which contained overt warnings about needles and "speed kills" directed right at fellow cartoonist Rory Hayes (who later died of his drug problem). Rick Griffin, Victor Moscoso, and S. Clay Wilson also contributed more intense, mind-bending stories.

In early 1969 *Zap Comix* #4 appeared, containing a story called "Joe Blow," a satire on the nuclear family that contained multiple and graphically depicted acts of incest and was meant to push the boundaries of the law. It pushed too far, and many retailers were busted for obscenity for stocking the offensive material. The most infamous case involving *Zap* #4 was *People v. Kirkpatrick* (1970), which went to the Court of Appeals of the State of New York.

Most of Print Mint's cash flow began being diverted to defense attorneys. Despite the legal woes, other underground presses, including Rip Off Press (publishers of the **Fabulous Furry Freak Brothers**) and Last Gasp (publisher of *It Ain't Me Babe*, the first all-female-produced comic), began to garner a larger portion of the underground comix market by pushing boundaries all of their own.

Zap #5 debuted in May 1970, but *Zap* #6 did not arrive until 1973. Its arrival came within a month or so of "Berkeleycon 73" during April 1973. This seminal event was the first alternative underground comix convention, co-hosted by John Barrett, Robert Beerbohm, Jon Campbell, Clay Geerdes, Mike Manyak, Nick Marcus, Scott Maple, Bud Plant, and assorted other helpers on the University of California–Berkeley campus.

Even as artists and fans were celebrating their art form at Berkeleycon, the storm clouds were gathering. In some ways 1973 was the beginning of the end for the underground comix movement. Just a month before Berkeleycon, the New York Court of Appeals upheld the obscenity conviction of Charles Kirkpatrick for selling *Zap* #4. This encouraged more vigorous prosecution of head shops and record stores selling underground comix. More devastating was the *Miller v. California* case that was decided by the United States Supreme Court in June 1973. Miller did not involve comic books, but it established a new nationwide test for determining obscenity. The court rejected the vague standard that a work had to be shown to be "utterly without redeeming social value" in favor of a three-pronged test that hinged on "the average person, applying contemporary community standards." The Miller test provided greater latitude for obscenity prosecution for content such as that found in *Zap* and many other underground comix.

Despite the efforts to crack down on underground comix, *Zap* continued publication. Spain Rodriguez, Robert Williams, Gilbert Shelton, and later, Paul Mavrides joined the regular contributors. After issue #6, *Zap* appeared more infrequently, yearly for a time and then with years between issues. *Zap* #15 in 2005 is the most recent issue published. **Fantagraphics Books** intends to reprint the entire run as *The Complete Zap Comix* beginning in fall 2012.

POSTER ART TO COMIC ART

Griffin's "flaming eyeball" Jimi Hendrix poster for shows held at the Fillmore and the Winterland for Bill Graham Presents #105, February 1–4, 1968, is reputed by many collectors worldwide as the most famous rock art concert poster of all time. Noted poster historian Eric King has said, "Rick Griffin was a religious mystic who saw a vision of the all-seeing eye of God the father, the Old Testament 'jealous and angry God' before whom Rick felt we are all wanting, all guilty, all unworthy sinners doomed to burn forever on a lake of fire. Consequently he sought something to intermediate between him and that awful eye. This poster image represents to millions of people worldwide a gateway between religious thought and a human's ability to comprehend such matters."

IMPACT ON COMICS

Comic books labored under heavy constraints in the 1960s. The Comics Code established in 1954 established guidelines that effectively sanitized all comics for children's consumption and consequently forbade adult content. Although over 90 percent of American youth were regular readers of comics prior to that, comics were blamed for problems in youth culture. An inflammatory book called *Seduction of the Innocent* by Dr. **Fredric Wertham** and public bonfires of comic books helped feed the paranoia, which only seemed to abate when publishers agreed to clear out anything objectionable from their pages. *Zap* challenged that long-standing expectation by introducing all manner of adult themes and images back into mass-marketed comic books.

Consequently, *Zap* helped to usher in the underground comics movement. It inspired Gilbert Shelton and Jack "Jaxon" Jackson to drive out to Berkeley to connect with Print Mint and get Shelton's seminal underground comic, *Feds 'N' Heads*, to wider distribution. This brought characters like the Fabulous Furry Freak Brothers to a wider audience.

IMPACT ON AMERICAN CULTURE

The backlash against *Zap Comics* #4 ended up creating much grief for many a head shop owner nationwide. The material was considered obscene and thus illegal. More than 70 busts were recorded nationwide. Ironically, the very distribution system that had enabled the underground comics scene to flourish was later responsible for undoing the very shops that had promoted them.

One person busted for selling *Zap* was high school teacher Phil Seuling, arrested by an undercover NYPD police officer. He was led out in handcuffs during one of the many comic book conventions he hosted, and soon he was in the process of losing his teaching job in Brooklyn. However, within months he made lemonade out of this lemon by bringing **DC**, **Marvel**, Warren, and other publishers into his growing distribution system. He further expanded what soon became known as the Direct Market, which redefined the way comics were distributed and helped spawn comic book specialty shops across the nation.

One of Crumb's key creations, **Mr. Natural**, went on to appear in his own comic book series as well as merchandising on posters and prints, postal and trading cards, buttons, coffee mugs, T-shirts, and more. For some years he was an iconic image of the counterculture with his "Twas Ever Thus Sez Mr. Natural."

SUMMARY

Zap Comix had a seminal influence in the annals of American comic book history. It tested the outside parameters of essential aspects of the First Amendment to the United States Constitution. Hundreds of comics creators who could not or would not work within the confines of an overly restrictive Comics Code of what was "proper" were introduced to the possibilities of "alternative" comics. *Zap Comix* also inspired creator-owned, royalty-paying comic books to enter the consciousness of the industry, a change that has been essential to the development, in particular, of the graphic novel market.

See also Crumb, Robert; Fabulous Furry Freak Brothers; Mr. Natural

ESSENTIAL WORKS

Crumb, Robert. *The Complete Crumb Comics, Vol. 4: Mr. Sixties!* Seattle: Fantagraphics, 2009.

FURTHER READING

Danky, James, and Denis Kitchen. *Underground Classics: The Transformation of Comics into Comix*. New York: Abrams, 2009.
Rosenkranz, Patrick. *Rebel Visions: The Underground Comix Revolution 1963–1975*. Seattle: Fantagraphics Books, 2002.

Robert Beerbohm

Bibliography

Adams, Sam. "Interview: Joe Sacco." *A. V. Club*. http://www.avclub.com/articles/joe-sacco,57360/. Accessed June 10, 2011.

The Adventures of Superman. Producer Whitney Ellsworth. Starring George Reeves, Phyllis Coates, Noel Neill, and Jack Larsen. 1952–1958. Film.

The Adventures of Superman. September 7, 1942. Available at http://www.archivc.org. Radio serial.

Alexander, Mark. *Lee & Kirby: The Wonder Years*. Raleigh, NC: Two Morrows Publishing, 2011.

Alexrossart.com. "Alex Ross Biography." http://www.alexrossart.com/bio.asp. Accessed May 15, 2011.

Alexrossart.com. "Chicago-area Artist Raises Money for Twin Towers Fund with Some Help from Wonder Woman: Spccial Online Auction to Benefit the Twin Towers Fund." http://www.alexrossart.com/article_twintowers.asp. Accessed Junc 11, 2011.

Alexrossart.com. "FAQ." http://www.alexrossart.com/faq.asp. Accessed May 15, 2011.

Ali, Barish, "The Postcolonial Gothic: Haunting and Historicity in the Literature after Empire," PhD diss., State University of New York, 2005.

Amash, Jim. "You Two Ought to Do Something Together: Charles Sinclair on His Partnership–and Friendship–with Bill Finger, Co-creator of Batman." *Alter Ego* 84 (2009): 35–49.

Andrae, Thomas. *Carl Barks and the Disney Comic Book: Unmasking the Myth of Modernity*. Jackson: University Press of Mississippi, 2006.

Andrae, Thomas. *Creators of the Superheroes*. Neshannock, PA: Hermes Press, 2011.

Andrae, Thomas, and Mel Gordon. *Siegel and Shuster's Funnyman: The First Jewish Superhero*. Port Washington, WA: Feral House, 2010.

Alter, Robert. "Scripture Picture." *New Republic*, October 19, 2009. http://www.tnr.com/article/books-and-arts/scripture-picture.

"Are Comics Fascist?" *Time*, October 22, 1945. http://www.time.com/time/magazine/article/0,9171,778464,00.html. Accessed August 1, 2011.

"Arkham Asylum." *DC Database*. http://dc.wikia.com/wiki/Arkham_Asylum. Accessed May 4, 2011.

Arnold, Mark. "A Family Affair: The Harvey Comics Story." *Comic Book Artist* 19 (2002): 18–38.

Arnold, Mark. "Harvey Comics History." *The Harveyville Fun Times!* http://web.archive.org/web/20080724205323/http://home.att.net/~thft/harveyhist.htm. Accessed December 26, 2011.

Aronsohn, Lee, and Steven Molaro. "The Psychic Vortex." *The Big Bang Theory*. CBS: January 11, 2010. Television episode.

Art of Frank Miller. http://www.Artoffm.com. Last revised September 1, 2007.

"Artist Bio—Chris Ware." Fantagraphic Books. http://www.fantagraphics.com/index.php?option=com_content&task=view&id=272&Itemid=82. Accessed July 18, 2011.

Associated Press. "Post-relaunch, DC Sells More than 5M Copies." http://www.businessweek.com/ap/financialnews/D9QBHM2O0.htm. Accessed October 15, 2011.

Ault, Donald, ed. *Carl Barks: Conversations*. Jackson: University Press of Mississippi, 2003.

Azzarello, Brian (w), and Joe Kubert (a). *Sgt. Rock: Between Hell and a Hard Place*. New York: DC Comics, 2004.

Baker, Bill. *Alan Moore Spells It Out*. Milford, CT: Airwave Publishing, 2005.

Baker, Bill. *Alan Moore's Exit Interview*. Milford, CT: Airwave Publishing, 2007.

Bakunin, Mikhail. "The Reaction in Germany." In *Bakunin on Anarchy*, edited and translated by Sam Dolgoff, 55–57. New York: Vintage Books, 1971.

Ball, David M., and Martha B. Kuhlman, eds. *The Comics of Chris Ware*. Jackson: University Press of Mississippi, 2010.

Barclay Agency. "Art Spiegelman Biography." 2009. http://www.barclayagency.com/spiegelman.html. Accessed July 16, 2011.

Barks, Carl. "Introducktion." In *Uncle Scrooge McDuck: His Life and Times*, edited by Edward Summer, 11–12. Berkeley, CA: Celestial Arts, 1987.

Barnes, David. "Time in the Gutter: Temporal Structures in Watchmen." *KronoScope* 9 (2009): 51–60.

Barr, Mike W. (w), and Jerry Bingham (p). *Batman: Son of the Demon*. New York: DC Comics, 1987.

Barrier, Michael. *Carl Barks and the Art of the Comic Book*. New York: Lilian, 1981.

Barrier, Michael. "The Duck Man." In *The Comic-Book Book*, edited by Don Thompson and Dick Lupoff, 210–27. Carlstadt, NJ: Rainbow Books, 1973.

Barrier, Michael. "On Wings of Ducks." In *Uncle Scrooge McDuck: His Life and Times*, edited by Edward Summer, 13–25. Berkeley, CA: Celestial Arts, 1987.

Barry, Joseph. "Juvenile Books and French Politics." *New York Times*, February 13, 1949: BR5.

Batchelor, Bob. "Brain versus Brawn." In *The Man from Krypton: A Closer Look at Superman*, edited by Glenn Yeffeth, 199–210. Dallas: BenBella Books, 2005.

Bates, Cary, Otto Binder, Curt Swan, Kurt Schaffenberger et al. *Superman's Girlfriend, Lois Lane*. New York: DC Comics, 1958–1974.

"Batman." *Box Office Mojo*. http://boxofficemojo.com/movies/?id=batman .htm. Accessed March 29, 2012.

Beaty, Bart. *Fredric Wertham and the Critique of Mass Culture*. Jackson: University Press of Mississippi, 2005.

Beaty, Bart. *Unpopular Culture: Transforming the European Comic Book in the 1990s*. Toronto: University of Toronto Press, 2007.

Beauchamp, Monte. "Behind the Eightball: The Daniel Clowes Interview." In *Daniel Clowes: Conversations*, edited by Ken Parille and Isaac Cates, 12–26. Jackson: University Press of Mississippi, 2010.

Beauchamp, Monte, ed. *The Life and Times of R. Crumb: Comments from Contemporaries*. Northampton, MA: Kitchen Sink Press, 1998.

Bell, Blake. *Strange and Stranger: The World of Steve Ditko*. Seattle: Fantagraphics, 2008.

Bender, Hy. *The Sandman Companion*. New York: DC Comics, 1999.

Benson, John. *Confessions, Romances, Secrets and Temptations: Archer St. John and the St. John Romance Comics*. Seattle: Fantagraphics Books, 2007.

Benson, John. *Romance without Tears*. Seattle: Fantagraphics Books, 2003.

Benton, Mike. *The Comic Book in America: An Illustrated History*. Dallas, TX: Taylor Publishing Company, 1989.

Benton, Mike. *Super Hero Comics of the Golden Age*. Dallas, TX: Taylor Publishing Company, 1992.

Berger, Arthur Asa. *The Comic-Stripped American: What Dick Tracy, Blondie, Daddy Warbucks and Charlie Brown Tell Us about Ourselves*. Baltimore: Penguin Books, 1974.

Berger, Marilyn. "G.T. Delacorte, Philanthropist, 97, Dies." *New York Times*, May 5, 1991.

Bernard, Mark, and James Bucky Carter. "Alan Moore and the Graphic Novel: Confronting the Fourth Dimension." *ImageTexT* 1 (2004). http://www .english.ufl.edu/imagetext/archives/v1_2/carter/index.shtml.

Bernewitz, Fred, and Grant Geissman. *Tales of Terror! The EC Companion*. Seattle: Fantagraphics Books, 2000.

"Bio." Accessed November 23, 2011. http://www.artofmikemignola.com/Bio.

"Biography—Stan Lee: ComiX-Man." *A&E Biography*, 1995. Television episode.

Bissette, Stephen. The Stephen R. Bissette Collection. HUIE Library, Henderson State University, Arkadelphia, AR.

"Blade Box Office." *Box Office Mojo*. http://www.boxofficemojo.com/movies/?id=blade.htm. Accessed July 16, 2011.

"Blade II Box Office." *Box Office Mojo*. http://www.boxofficemojo.com/movies/?id=blade2.htm. Accessed July 16, 2011.

"Blade: Trinity Box Office." *Box Office Mojo*. http://www.boxofficemojo.com/movies/?id=blade3.htm. Accessed July 16, 2011.

Blake, Brandy Ball. "Watchmen: The Graphic Novel as Trauma Fiction." *ImageTexT* 5 (2009). http://www.english.ufl.edu/imagetext/archives/v5_1/blake/. ISSN: 1549–6732.

Blumberg, Arnold T. "The Night Gwen Stacy Died: The End of Innocence and the Birth of the Bronze Age." *Reconstruction: Studies in Contemporary Culture* 3, no. 4 (2003). http://reconstruction.eserver.org/034/blumberg.htm.

Blumberg, Arnold T. "Wesley Snipes Talks Blade 2." *Mania: Beyond Entertainment*. 2002. http://www.mania.com/wesley-snipes-talks-blade-2_article_33594.html. Accessed July 15, 2011.

Bolland, Brian. "On Batman: Brian Bolland Recalls *The Killing Joke*." In *DC Universe: The Stories of Alan Moore*, 256. New York: DC Comics, 2006.

Boneville.com. "BONE to Warner Brothers." http://www.boneville.com/2008/03/13/bone-to-warner-bros. Accessed October 23, 2011.

Boneville.com. "The History of Bone." http://www.boneville.com/bone/bone-history. Accessed October 28, 2011.

Booker, M. Keith. *"May Contain Graphic Material": Comic Books, Graphic Novels, and Film*. Westport, CT: Praeger, 2007.

Brady, Matt. "The Simone Files I: Birds of Prey—Updated." *Newsarama*. http://forum.newsarama.com/showthread.php?t=98825. Accessed January 24, 2007.

Bridwell, E. Nelson. "In Memoriam Otto Binder." *Amazing World of DC Comics* 3 (1974): 30.

Brown, Jeffrey A. *Black Superheroes, Milestone Comics, and Their Fans*. Jackson: University of Mississippi Press, 2001.

Brown, Jeffrey A. "Comic Book Fandom and Cultural Capital." *Journal of Popular Culture* 30, no. 4 (1997): 13–31.

Brown, Joshua. "Of Mice and Memory." *Oral History Review* 16 (1988): 91–109.

Buell, Marge Henderson. "A Little Lulu Chronology." *The Little Lulu Library*, 12. Marceline, MO: Another Rainbow Publishing, 1992.

Buhle, Paul. "Comic Book Heroes." In *Jews and American Comics: An Illustrated History of an American Art Form*, edited by Paul Buhle, 52–68. New York: New Press, 2008.

Bureau of Justice Statistics. "Crime-State Level: State by State and National Trends." http://bjsdata.ojp.usdoj.gov/dataonline/Search/Crime/State/Run CrimeStatebyState.cfm. Accessed July 5, 2011.

Burr, Ty. "Hey Buddy!" *Entertainment Weekly*, May 21, 1993: 23.

Burton, Tim. *Burton on Burton*. Edited by Mark Salisbury. London: Faber and Faber, 2005.

Byrne, John, and Dick Giordano. *Superman: The Man of Steel*. New York: DC Comics, 1991.

Byrne, John (w, p), Dick Giordano (i), and Tom Ziuko. *Superman: The Man of Steel*. New York: Ballantine Books, 1988.

Cabarga, Leslie, ed. *The Harvey Girls*. Milwaukie, OR: Dark Horse Books, 2009.

Callahan, Nathan, and Mike Kaspar. "Art Spiegelman Interview." *KUCI: Weekly Signals*, October 14, 2008.

Canterbury, Mike. "An Interview with the Man of Mystery," *Marvel Main 1*. 1968. http://www.vicsage.com/wp/interviews/interview-with-ditko-from-marvel-main-4/. Accessed February 7, 2012.

Capitanio, Adam. "'The Jekyll and Hyde of the Atomic Age': The Incredible Hulk as the Ambiguous Embodiment of Nuclear Power." *Journal of Popular Culture* 43 (2010): 249–70.

Carlin, John, Paul Karasik, and Brian Walker, eds. *Masters of American Comics*. New Haven, CT: Yale University Press, 2005.

Carney, Sean. "The Tides of History: Alan Moore's Historiographic Vision." *ImageTexT* 2 (2006). http://www.english.ufl.edu/imagetext/archives/v2 _2/carney/.

Carter, Bill. "A Match Made in Heaven." *New York Times*. http://www .nytimes.com/2010/04/19/business/media/19conan.html. Last modified April 18, 2010.

Carter, Gary M., and Pat S. Calhoun. "Journey into the Unknown World of Atlas Fantasy." In *The Overstreet Comic Book Price Guide*, edited by Robert M. Overstreet, A-87–103. New York: Avon Books, 1992.

Castiglia, Paul, ed. *The Shield: America's First Patriotic Comic Book Hero*. New York: Archie Comic Publications, 2002.

Caswell, Lucy Shelton, and David Filipi. *Jeff Smith: Bone and Beyond*. Columbus: Ohio State University Press, 2008.

CCBeck.com. http://www.ccbeck.com/. Accessed March 29, 2012.

Chalker, Jack L. *An Informal Biography of Scrooge McDuck*. Baltimore, MD: Mirage Press, 1974.

Chaney, Michael A. *Graphic Subjects: Critical Essays on Autobiography and Graphic Novels*. Madison: University of Wisconsin Press, 2011.

Chris @ Ridiculously Awesome. "30 Things I Like about Comics." http://
    ridiculouslyawesome.wordpress.com/2011/07/07/30-things-i-like-about-
    comics%e2%80%9414-lobo/. Last modified July 7, 2011.

"Chris Ware's REJECTED Fortune Cover Paints Honest, Dismal Picture of
    American Capitalism." *Huffington Post*, http://www.huffingtonpost
    .com/2010/04/23/chris-wares-rejectedemfor_n_550341.html#s84460
    &title=Chris_Wares_Fortune. Accessed October 28, 2011.

Chute, Hillary. "Joe Sacco [Comics Journalist]." *The Believer*. http://www
    .believermag.com/issues/201106/?read=interview_sacco. Accessed June 1,
    2011.

Cioffi, Frank L. "Disturbing Comics: The Disjunction of Word and Image in
    the Comics of Andrzej Mleckzko, Ben Katchor, R. Crumb, and Art Spie-
    gelman." In *The Language of Comics: Word and Image*, edited by Robin
    Varnum and Christina T. Gibbons, 97–122. Jackson: University Press of
    Mississippi, 2001.

Claremont, Chris (w), John Byrne (p), and Terry Austin (i). "Fist to Fist with
    the Savage Fury of Wed-Di-Go!" *X-Men* #140 (1980). Marvel Comics.

Claremont, Chris (w), John Byrne (p), and Terry Austin (i). ". . . Something
    Wicked This Way Comes!" *X-Men* #139 (1980). Marvel Comics.

Clark, John, and Bruce Hamilton. "Life with Lulu: An Interview with Marge."
    The Little Lulu Library #1, 13–16. Marceline, MO: Another Rainbow
    Publishing, 1992.

Clifton, Peter. "Spider Fan Look Back: Sound of the Times." *Spider-Fan.org*.
    http://spiderfan.org/lookback/sound_of_the_times.html. Last modified
    June 20, 2007.

Comic Book Awards Almanac. "Will Eisner Comic Industry Award: Summary
    of Winners." http://www.hahnlibrary.net/comics/awards/eisnersum.php.
    Accessed June 7, 2011.

Comic Book Confidential. Directed by Ron Mann, Martin Harbury, Charles
    Lippincott, and Don Haig. 1988. Santa Monica: Pacific Arts, 2002. Film.

Comic Book Database. "Neal Adams." http://comicbookdb.com/creator
    .php?ID=374. Accessed August 1, 2011.

Comic Books Page. "The Platinum Age 1897–1938." http://www.thecomic
    books.com/old/Platinum.html. Accessed August 19, 2011.

Comics Creators Guild. "About the CCG." http://www.comicscreatorsguild
    .co.uk/welcome/about. Accessed August 1, 2011.

"Complete Works of Frank Miller." *Moebius Graphics*. http://moebiusgraph
    ics.com. Accessed Nov. 2, 2007.

Continuity Studios. "Neal Adams Biography." http://www.nealadamsenter
    tainment.com/pages/ infocontact.html. Accessed August 1, 2011.

Coogan, Peter. *Superhero: The Secret Origin of a Genre*. Austin, TX: Monkey-
    Brain Books, 2006.

Cooke, Jon B. *Comic Book Artist Collection Volume 2*. Raleigh, NC: Two-Morrows Publishing, 2002.

Cooke, Jon B. *The James Warren Interview*. http://twomorrows.com/comic bookartist/articles/04warren.html. Last modified February 11, 1999.

Cooke, Jon B. "A Talk with Alex Toth." *Comic Book Artist* 11 (2001): 25.

Corey, Herbert. "Your Son's a Better Soldier Than You Were." *Nation's Business*, September 1942: 42–44.

Corrigan, Faith. "'Superman' Plays Librarian as Comics Go Social-Minded." *New York Times*, May 16, 1956: 32.

Costello, Matthew J. *Secret Identity Crisis: Comic Books and the Unmasking of Cold War America*. New York: Continuum International Publishing, 2009.

Couch, N. C. Christopher, and Stephen Weiner. *The Will Eisner Companion*. New York: DC Comics, 2004.

Coville, James. "The History of Superhero Comic Books." 2011. http://www .psu.edu/dept/inart10_110/inart10/cmbk2fungold.html. Accessed August 20, 2011.

Cowsill, Alan, Alex Irvine, Matthew K. Manning, Michael McAvennie, and Daniel Wallace. *DC Comics Year by Year: A Visual Chronicle*. New York: DK Publishing, 2010.

Crist, Judith. "Horror in the Nursery." *Collier's*, March 27, 1948.

Cronin, Brian. "Comic Book Legends Revealed #183" http://goodcomics .comicbookresources.com/2008/11/27/comic-book-legends-revealed-183/. Accessed October 30, 2011.

Cronin, Brian. "Comic Book Urban Legends Revealed #1." *Comics Should Be Good*. http://goodcomics.blogspot.com/2005/06/comic-book-urban-leg end-revealed-1.html. Accessed December 18, 2011.

Cronin, Brian. "Comic Book Urban Legends Revealed #21." http://goodcom ics.comicbookresources.com/2005/10/20/comic-book-urban-legends-revealed-21/. Accessed July 7, 2011.

Cronin, Brian. "The Superhero Trademark FAQ." 2006. http://www.comic bookresources.com/?page=article&id=6738. Accessed August 1, 2011.

Cronin, Brian. *Was Superman a Spy?* New York: Plume, 2009.

Cronin, Brian. "When We First Met #32." http://goodcomics.comicbook resources.com/2011/06/30/when-we-first-met-32/. Accessed July 7, 2011.

Crumb, R. *The Complete Crumb, Volume 5: Happy Hippy Comix*. Edited by Gary Groth with Robert Fiore and Robert Boyd. Seattle: Fantagraphics Books, 2005.

Crumb, R. *The Complete Crumb, Volume 7: Hot 'N' Heavy*. Edited by Gary Groth and Robert Boyd. Seattle: Fantagraphics Books, 2009.

Crumb, R. *The Complete Crumb, Volume 11: Mr. Natural Committed to a Mental Institution*. Edited by Mark Thompson and Gary Groth. Seattle: Fantagraphics Books, 2008.

Crumb, R. "I'm Taking You to See My Old Man." *Zap Comix* #6. Apex Novelties, 1973.

Crumb, R. "The Origins of Mr. Natural." *Mr. Natural #1*. Apex Novelties, 1970.

Crumb, R. "The Saints." *Mystic Funnies* #1. Alex Wood, 1997.

Cruse, Howard. "Ducks and a Legacy." *Comics Scene*. September 1982: 22–24.

Daniels, Bradley J. "Arkham Asylum." In *Psychology of Superheroes: An Unauthorized Exploration*, edited by Robin S. Rosenberg, 201–12. Dallas: BenBella Books, 2008.

Daniels, Les. *Batman: The Complete History*. San Francisco: Chronicle Books, 1999.

Daniels, Les. *Comix: A History of Comic Books in America*. New York: Outerbridge & Dienstfrey, 1971.

Daniels, Les. *Marvel: Five Fabulous Decades of the World's Greatest Comics*. New York: Harry N. Abrams, 1993.

Daniels, Les. *Superman: The Complete History*. San Francisco: Chronicle Books, 1998.

Daniels, Les. *Wonder Woman: The Complete History*. San Francisco: Chronicle Books, 2000.

"Dark Knight." *Box Office Mojo*. http://boxofficemojo.com/movies/?id=darkknight.htm. Accessed March 29, 2012.

Dauber, Jeremy. "Will Eisner's American Jewish History." In *The Jewish Graphic Novel: Critical Approaches*, edited by Samantha Baskind and Ranen Omer-Sherman, 22–42. New Brunswick, NJ: Rutgers University Press, 2010.

David, Peter, and Robert Greenberger. *The Spider-Man Vault*. Philadelphia: Running Press, 2010.

Dean, Michael. "Image Story: A Four-Part Series." *Comics Journal*, October 25, 2000. http://archives.tcj.com/3_online/n_image1.html. Accessed August 4, 2011.

DeFalco, Tom. *Comics Creators on Spider-Man*. London: Titan Books, 2004.

DeFalco, Tom, and Matthew K. Manning. *Hulk: The Incredible Guide*. New York: DK Publishing, 2008.

DeFalco, Tom, Peter Sanderson, Tom Brevoort, Michael Teitelbaum, Daniel Wallace, and Andrew Darling. *Marvel Encyclopedia*. New York: DK Publishing, 2009.

De Haven, Thomas. *Our Hero: Superman on Earth*. New Haven, CT: Yale University Press, 2010.

Delich, Craig. "The Many Oaths of the Green Lantern." *Alter Ego 7* (2001): 36–39.

Dempsey, John. "Toons Get the Bugs Out." *Variety*. http://www.variety.com/article/VR1117908191. Last modified July 24, 2004.

Deppey, Dirk. "Comic Book Culture: Eddie Campbell Interview." *Comics Journal* 273 (2006): 66–115.

Deppey, Dirk. "The Fog Hollow Memorial Address." *Comics Journal*, November 10, 2002. http://archives.tcj.com/index.php?option=com_content&task=view&id=190&Itemid=70. Accessed August 4, 2011.

Diehl, Digby. *Tales from the Crypt: The Official Archives Including the Complete History of EC Comics and the Hit Television Series*. New York: St. Martin's Press, 1997.

Dietrich, Bryan D. "The Human Stain: Chaos and the Rage for Order in Watchmen." *Extrapolation* 50 (2009): 120–44.

Dini, Paul, and Chip Kidd. *Batman: Animated*. New York: Harper Entertainment, 1998.

Doherty, Thomas. "Art Spiegelman's Maus: Graphic Art and the Holocaust." *American Literature: A Journal of Literary History, Criticism and Bibliography* 68 (1996): 69–84.

Dorfman, Ariel, and Armand Mattelart. *How to Read Donald Duck: Imperialist Ideology in the Disney Comic*. New York: International General, 1971.

Duin, Steve, and Mike Richardson. *Comics: Between the Panels*. Milwaukie, OR: Dark Horse Comics, 1998.

Ecke, Jochen. "'Solve and Coagula': Alan Moore and the Classical Comic Book's Spatial and Temporal Systems." *Studies in Comics* 2, no. 1 (2011): 105–19.

Eco, Umberto. "The Myth of Superman." *Diacritics* 2 (1972): 14–22.

Edgar, Joanne. "Wonder Woman Revisited." *Ms. Magazine* 1 (1972): 52–55.

Eisner, Will. Letter to Mark Estren, October 10, 1973.

Eisner, Will. Preface to *The Contract with God Trilogy: Life on Dropsie Avenue*, xiii–xx. New York: W. W. Norton, 2006.

Eisner, Will. *Shop Talk*. Milwaukie, OR: Dark Horse Comics, 2001.

Eisner, Will, and Frank Miller. *Eisner/Miller*. Edited by Charles Brownstein. Milwaukie, OR: Dark Horse Books, 2005.

Elliott, Brad. "The Punisher Preview." *Amazing Heroes* 114 (1987): 26–32.

Elliot, Fievell. "May the Source Be with You: Comparing New Gods and Star Wars." In *The Collected Jack Kirby Collector, Volume 2*, edited by John Morrow, 87–89. Raleigh, NC: TwoMorrows Publishing, 2004.

Ellis, Doug, John Locke, and John Gunnison. *The Adventure House Guide to the Pulps*. Silver Spring, MD: Adventure House, 2000.

Englehart, Steve. "Captain America II: 169–186." http://www.steveenglehart.com/Comics/Captain%20America%20169–176.html. Accessed June 22, 2011.

Entertainment Weekly. "Cool Cult Favorites: 'Sandman.'" http://www.ew
    .com/ew/article/0,,302789,00.html. Accessed July 30, 2011.

Estrada, Jackie. "Special Section: Comic-Con 40." *Comic-Con Souvenir Book*
    40 (2009): 39–121.

Eury, Michael, and Dick Giordano. *Dick Giordano: Changing Comics, One
    Day at a Time*. Raleigh, NC: TwoMorrows, 2009.

Eury, Michael, and Michael Kronenberg. *The Batman Companion*. Raleigh,
    NC: TwoMorrows, 2009.

Evanier, Mark. "Alex Toth." *POVOnline*. http://www.newsfromme.com/
    archives/2006_05_28.html. Last modified May 28, 2006.

Evanier, Mark. "The Jack FAQ." *POVOnline*. Accessed August 17, 2011.
    http://www.povonline.com/jackfaq/JackFaq1.htm.

Evanier, Mark. *Kirby: King of Comics*. New York: Abrams, 2008.

Evanier, Mark. *Mad Art: A Visual Celebration of the Art of MAD Magazine and
    the Idiots Who Created It*. New York: Watson-Guptill Publications, 2002.

Evanier, Mark. "What Was the Relationship between Dell Comics and Gold
    Key Comics?" http://www.povonline.com/iaq/IAQ07.htm. Accessed on
    August 24, 2011.

"Everything You Ever Wanted to Know About Arkham Asylum." http://www
    .comicsbulletin.com/bobro/103585005565655.htm. Accessed May 4,
    2011.

Ewert, Jeanne C. "Reading Visual Narrative: Art Spiegelman's *Maus*." *Narra-
    tive* 8 (2000): 87–103.

Falk, Ray. "Tokyo TV Report." *New York Times*, August 9, 1959.

Fantaousakis, Kotas. "Wesley Snipes: His Martial Arts Training." *Fighting-
    Master.com*. http://www.fightingmaster.com/actors/snipes/training.htm.
    Accessed July 15, 2011.

"Fantastic Four." *Marvel*. http://www.marvel.com/universe/Fantastic_Four.
    Accessed July 31, 2011.

"Fantastic Four on TV." IGN. http://www.ign.com/articles/797130. Accessed
    July 31, 2011.

"Father of Tintin: Hip Hip Hergé!" *The Independent*. http://www.indepen
    dent.co.uk/news/people/profiles/father-of-tintin-hip-hip-hergeacute-
    427505.html. Accessed July 18, 2011.

Fawcett, Billy. *Capt. Billy's Whiz Bang*. Thousand Oaks, CA: About Comics,
    2008.

Feiffer, Jules. *The Great Comic Book Heroes*. Seattle: Fantagraphics Books,
    2003. First published 1965 by Dial Press.

Feldstein, Al. "The EC Publisher of the Issue William Gaines—Alias Melvin."
    Mad 5 (1953): cover verso.

Field, Tom, and Gene Colan. *Secrets in the Shadows: The Art and Life of Gene
    Colan*. Raleigh, NC: TwoMorrows Publishing, 2005.

Fiene, Don. *The R. Crumb Checklist*. Cambridge, MA: Boatner Norton Press, 1981.

Fingeroth, Danny, and Roy Thomas, eds. *The Stan Lee Universe*. Raleigh, NC: TwoMorrows Publishing, 2011.

Fishbaugh, Brent. 1998. "Moore and Gibbons's *Watchmen*: Exact Personifications of Science." *Extrapolation* 39 (3): 189–98.

Fox, Julia R., and Byungho Park. "The 'I' of Embedded Reporting: An Analysis of CNN Coverage of the 'Shock and Awe' Campaign." *Journal of Broadcasting and Electronic Media* 50 (2006): 36–51.

"Franchises: Marvel Comics." *Box Office Mojo*. http://www.boxofficemojo.com/franchises/chart/?id=marvelcomics.htm. Accessed July 13, 2011.

"Frank Miller." *Lambiek*. http://lambiek.net/artists/m/miller.htm. Last modified July 13, 2011.

"Frank Miller: Biography." *Answers.com*. http://www.answers.com/topic/frank-miller. Accessed March 30, 2012.

"The Freak Brothers Top Thirty." http://www.freaknet.org.uk/pages01/p03/tt01.html. Accessed June 6, 2011.

"Frequently Asked Questions." Imagecomics.com. http://www.imagecomics.com/faq/. Accessed August 4, 2011.

"From the Ashes: Charlton and Harvey to Resume Publishing This Spring." *Comics Journal* 97 (1985): 15–16.

Frus, Phyllis, and Christy Williams, eds. *Beyond Adaptation: Essays on Radical Transformations of Original Works*. Jefferson, NC: McFarland, 2010.

Gabillict, Jean-Paul. *Of Comics and Men: A Cultural History of American Comic Books*. Translated by Bart Beaty and Nick Nguyen. Jackson: University Press of Mississippi, 2010. [Original 2005]

Gagliardo, Aaron. "The American Academy of Art." *Illustration* 7, no. 27 (2009): 88–104, 106–9.

Gaiman, Neil, et al. *Preludes and Nocturnes*. New York: DC Comics, 1991.

Gaiman, Neil, et al. *Season of Mists*. New York: DC Comics, 1992.

Gaiman, Neil, et al. *The Wake*. New York: DC Comics, 1997.

Gaines, William. "Madman Gaines Pleads for Plots." *Writer's Digest*, February 1954.

Gander, L. Marsland. "British TV and Anglo-American Relations." *New York Times*, September 22, 1957.

Gatti, Tom. "Exclusive Interview with Art Spiegelman." *London Times*, November 21, 2008.

Gavin, Thomas. *Breathing Water*. New York: Arcade Publishing, 1994.

Geissman, Grant. *Foul Play! The Art and Artists of the Notorious 1950s E.C. Comics!* New York: Harper Design, 2005.

Gelb, Jeff. "The Animated Little Lulu." *The Little Lulu Library* #1, 11. Marceline, MO: Another Rainbow Publishing, Inc., 1992.

Genter, Robert. "'With Great Power Comes Great Responsibility': Cold War Culture and the Birth of Marvel Comics." *Journal of Popular Culture* 40 (2007): 953–78.

George, Milo, ed. *The Comics Journal Library, Volume One: Jack Kirby.* Seattle: Fantagraphics, 2002.

George, Milo, ed. *The Comics Journal Library, Volume Two: Frank Miller.* Seattle: Fantagraphics, 2003.

Gersh, Lois H., and Robert E. Weinberg. *The Science of Supervillains.* Hoboken, NJ: John Wiley & Sons, 2005.

Gibbons, Dave. *Watching the Watchmen.* London: Titan Books, 2008.

Giddins, Gary. "Seduced by *Classics Illustrated.*" In *Give Our Regards to the Atomsmashers!*, edited by Sean Howe, 78–94. New York: Pantheon Books, 2004.

Giles, Keith. "Jim Steranko Interview." *Comic Book Resources.* 2001. http://www.comicbookresources.com/?page=article&id=477. Accessed August 17, 2011.

Gilmore, Mikal. "Introduction." In *The Wake* by Neil Gaiman et al., 10. New York: DC Comics, 1997.

Gilson, Dave. "Joe Sacco: The Art of War." *Mother Jones*, July/August 2005: 80–81.

Glenday, Craig, ed. *Guinness World Records 2011.* New York: Bantam Books/Random House, 2011.

Glicksohn, Susan Wood. *The Poison Maiden & the Great Bitch: Female Stereotypes in Marvel Superhero Comics.* Baltimore, MD: T-K Graphics, 1974.

Gold, Mike. "The Joker's Dozen." In *The Greatest Joker Stories Ever Told*, edited by Mike Gold, 6–10. New York: DC Comics, 1988.

"Golden Legacy (1966)." http://comicbookdb.com/title.php?ID=10024. Accessed November 18, 2011.

Goldstein, Hilary. "Xavier vs. Magneto: A Philosophical Debate." http://comics.ign.com/articles/705/705136p2.html. Accessed October 18, 2010.

Gordon, Ian. *Comic Strips and Consumer Culture, 1890–1945.* Washington, DC: Smithsonian Institution Press, 1998.

Gordon, Ian. "Nostalgia, Myth, and Ideology: Visions of Superman at the End of the American Century." In *Comics and Ideology*, edited by Matthew McAllister, Edward Sewell, and Ian Gordon, 177–93. New York: Peter Lang, 2001.

Gordon, Ian. "Smallville: Superhero Mythos and Intellectual Property Regimes." In *The Smallville Chronicles: Critical Essays on the Television Series*, edited by Lincoln Geraghty, 89–108. Lanham, MD: Scarecrow Press, 2011.

Gordon, Mitchell. "TV Abroad." *Wall Street Journal*, October 20, 1960.

Goulart, Ron. *Comic Book Encyclopedia: The Ultimate Guide to Characters, Graphic Novels, Writers, and Artists in the Comic Book.* New York: HarperCollins, 2004.

Goulart, Ron. *Ron Goulart's Great History of Comic Books.* Chicago: Contemporary Books, 1986.

Grayson, Devin. "A DCU:NG Email Interview with Devin Grayson." *DCU: The Next Generation.* 1998. http://teensdc.tripod.com/grayson.htm. Accessed March 3, 2010.

Green, Robin, "Face Front! Clap Your Hands, You're on the Winning Team!" *Rolling Stone* 91 (1971): 26–29.

Gresh, Lois H., and Robert Weinberg. *The Science of Superheroes.* Hoboken, NJ: John Wiley & Sons, 2002.

Grid, The. http://www.myspace.com/gridmusic. Accessed March 30, 2012.

Grimes, William. "Harvey Pekar, 'American Splendor' Creator, Dies at 70." *New York Times*, July 12, 2010.

Gross, Edward. *Spider-Man Confidential.* New York: Hyperion, 2002.

Gross, Terry. "Art Spiegelman." *Fresh Air*, September 16, 2004. Radio show.

Gross, Terry. "A 'Handbook' to Robert Crumb." *Fresh Air*, May 2, 2005. Radio show.

Grossman, Lev. "Top Ten Graphic Novels." *Time.* http://entertainment.time.com/2009/03/06/top-10-graphic-novels/. Last modified March 6, 2009.

Grossman, Lev. "Top Ten Graphic Novels of 2007." *Time.* http://www.time.com/time/specials/2007/article/0,28804,1686204_1686244_1692006,00.html. Last modified December 9, 2007.

Groth, Gary. "An Interview with THE Artist . . . Jim Steranko." *Fantastic Fanzine* 11 (1970): 25. Republished by Ken Meyer, Jr., in "Ink Stains 23: Fantastic Fanzine 11." *Comic Attack.* http://comicattack.net/2010/10/is-23-fantastic-fanzine-11.

Groth, Gary, "Interview with Carmine Infantino." *Comics Journal* 191 (2010): 25.

Groth, Gary. "Joe Sacco, Frontline Journalist: Why Sacco Went to Gorazde." *Comics Journal: Interviews.* 2001. http:www.tcj.com/aa02ws?i_sacco.html. Accessed March 10, 2008.

Gustines, George Gene. "Where Superheroes Go for Industry News." *New York Times*, August 2, 2005: E4.

Gustines, George Gene. "Writer of the Undead Is Reborn as a Partner at Image Comics." *New York Times*, July 22, 2008.

Hajdu, David. *The Ten-Cent Plague: The Great Comic Book Scare and How It Changed America.* New York: Farrar, Straus and Giroux, 2008.

Handley, Rich: "Roots of the Swamp Thing." http://swampthingroots.com/timeline_01.html. Last modified 2007.

Haney, Bob (w), and Bruno Premiani (p). "The Thousand-and-One Dooms of Mr. Twister." *The Brave and the Bold* #54 (July 1964), DC Comics.

Hare, R. D. *Manual for the Hare Psychopathy Checklist* (2nd ed. rev.). Toronto: Multi-Health Systems, 2003.

Harper, David. "Multiversity Comics Presents: Eric Stephenson." http://www .multiversitycomics.com/2011/01/multiversity-comics-presents-eric.html. Last modified January 31, 2011.

Harris, Neil. *Cultural Excursions: Marketing Appetites and Cultural Tastes in Modern America*. Chicago: University of Chicago Press, 1990.

"Harvey Loses $50 Million Ghostbusters Suit to Columbia Pictures." *Comics Journal* 117 (1987): 21.

"Harvey Sues Marvel Star Comics, Charges Copyright Infringement." *Comics Journal* 105 (1986): 23–24.

Harvey, Robert C. *Meanwhile . . . A Biography of Milton Caniff*. Seattle: Fantagraphics, 2007.

Harvey, Robert C. "Will Eisner's Vision and the Future of Comics." In *Will Eisner: Conversations*, edited by M. Thomas Inge, 176–84. Jackson: University Press of Mississippi, 2011.

Hatfield, Charles. *Alternative Comics: An Emerging Literature*. Jackson: University Press of Mississippi, 2005.

Hatfield, Charles. *Hand of Fire: The Comics Art of Jack Kirby*. Jackson: University Press of Mississippi, 2012.

Hayde, Michael J. *Flights of Fantasy: The Unauthorized but True Story of Radio & TV's Adventures of Superman*. Duncan, OK: BearManor Media, 2009.

Heer, Jeet. "Jack Kirby and Stan Lee." *National Post*, October 11, 2003. http:// www.jeetheer.com/comics/kirbylee.htm.

"Hellboy." http://hellboy.wikia.com/wiki/Hellboy. Accessed November 23, 2011.

Hersey, George L. *The Evolution of Allure: Sexual Selection from the Medici Venus to the Incredible Hulk*. Cambridge, MA: MIT Press, 1996.

Hignite, Todd. *In the Studio: Visits with Contemporary Cartoonists*. New Haven, CT: Yale University Press, 2006.

Hills, Matt. *Fan Cultures*. New York: Routledge, 2002.

Hitchcock, John. "Twenty Questions with Alex Toth." *TVParty*. 1991. http:// www.tvparty.com/comics/toth1.html. Last modified May 26, 2006.

Ho, Oliver. "Dylan Dog vs. Hellboy: A Study of Pulp and Pop Pastiche." 2009. http://www.popmatters.com/pm/feature/109764-dylan-dog-vs.- hellboy-a-study-of-pulp-and-pop-pastiche. Accessed November 23, 2011.

Holm, D. K. *The Pocket Essential Robert Crumb*. North Pomfret, VT: Trafalgar Square Publishing, 2005.

Holtz, Allan. "Dell Publishing's 'The Funnies' Part 16." 2008. http://strippers guide.blogspot.com/search/label/Dell%27s%20The%20Funnies. Accessed on August 29, 2011.

Hoskin, Michael, Chad Anderson, Anthony Flamini et al. *Origins of Marvel Comics*. New York: Marvel, 2011.

Howlett, Mike. *The Weird World of Eerie Publications: Comic Gore That Warped Millions of Young Minds*. Port Townsend, WA: Feral House, 2010.

Hughes, Jamie A. "'Who Watches the Watchmen?': Ideology and 'Real World' Superheroes." *Journal of Popular Culture* 39 (2006): 546–57.

Hull, Norman. "Monsters, Maniacs and Moore." *England Their England*. Central Independent Television, 1986. Television episode.

Hunt, Swain, Dwight Clark, and Adrian Johnson. "Bravo for Alex Toth." 2009. *Sidebar*. http://sidebar.typepad.com/my_weblog/2009/09/alex-toth .html. Accessed October 15, 2011. Podcast.

Iaccino, James F. *Jungian Reflections within the Cinema: A Psychological Analysis of Sci-Fi and Fantasy Archetypes*. Westport, CT: Praeger, 1998.

The Ice Storm. Directed by Ang Lee. Fox, 1997. Film.

Incredible Hulk Library, The. Accessed November 22, 2011. http://www .thehulklibrary.com.

Inskeep, Steve. "Morning Edition–Art Spiegelman: *In the Shadow of No Towers*." *National Public Radio*. September 10, 2004. Radio show.

Itzkoff, Dave. "It's Never Really Dead in Zombieland." *New York Times*, October 9, 2011.

Jacob, Kathryn Allamong. "Little Lulu Lives Here." *Radcliffe Quarterly* (2006). http://www.radcliffe.edu/print/about/quarterly/s06_lulu.htm.

Jenkins, Henry. *Fans, Bloggers, and Gamers: Exploring Participatory Culture*. New York: New York University Press, 2006.

Jensen, Jeff. "*Watchmen*: An Oral History." 2005. http://www.ew.com/ew/ article/0,,1120854,00.html. Accessed July 25, 2011.

Jimenez, Phil (w & a). "A Day in the Life . . ." *Wonder Woman* #170 (2001), DC Comics.

Johnston, Rich. "Lying in the Gutters." *Comic Book Resources*. http://www .comicbookresources.com/?page=article&id=15187. Last modified March 12, 2007.

Jones, Gerard. *Men of Tomorrow: Geeks, Gangsters, and the Birth of the Comic Book*. New York: Basic Books, 2004.

Jones, Russ. "Creepy and Eerie Confidential." *PopFiction*. http://www.popfic tion.com/hotad/html/monstermania/creepy/. Accessed November 5, 2011.

Jones, Steve. "Marvel Heroes: Back to Drawing Board." *USA Today*, September 13, 1996.

Jones, William B., Jr. *Classics Illustrated: A Cultural History, Second Edition.* Jefferson, NC: McFarland, 2011.

Jones, William B., Jr. *Classics Illustrated: A Cultural History, with Illustrations.* Jefferson, NC: McFarland, 2002.

Jones, William B., Jr. "Forty-Eight Pages and Speech Balloons: Robert Louis Stevenson in *Classics Illustrated.*" In *Robert Louis Stevenson Reconsidered: New Critical Perspectives*, edited by William B. Jones, Jr., 228–37. Jefferson, NC: McFarland, 2003.

Jones, William B., Jr. "'Hello Mackellar': *Classics Illustrated* Meets *The Master of Ballantrae.*" *Journal of Stevenson Studies* 4 (2007): 247–69.

Kane, Bob (w), Bill Finger (p), and Jerry Robinson (i). *Detective Comics* #38 (April 1940), DC Comics.

Kane, Bob, and Tom Andrae. *Batman & Me: An Autobiography.* Forestville, CA: Eclipse Books, 1989.

Kanigher, Robert (w), and Joe Kubert (a). *The Sgt. Rock Archives, Vol. 1.* New York: DC Comics, 2002.

Kanigher, Robert (w), and Joe Kubert (a). *Sgt. Rock Archives, Vol. 2.* New York: DC Comics, 2003.

Kanigher, Robert (w), and Joe Kubert (a). *Sgt. Rock Archives, Vol. 3.* New York: DC Comics, 2005.

Kartalopoulos, Bill. "A RAW History: The Magazine." http://64.23.98.142/indy/winter_2005/raw_02/index.html. Accessed October 19, 2011.

Kartalopoulos, Bill. "A RAW History: Part One." http://64.23.98.142/indy/winter_2005/raw_01/index.html. Accessed October 19, 2011.

Katz, Jack. "Correspondence from Jack Katz, August 7, 1974." Ohio State University Billy Ireland Cartoon Library & Museum, Will Eisner Collection, Box WEE1, Folder 22.

Keefe, Jim. "Interview with John Romita." JimKeefe.com. http://www.jimkeefe.com/studio/romita/interview.htm. Last modified June 24, 2008.

Keltner, Howard. *Golden Age Comic Books Index 1935–1955.* Gainesville, TX: privately published, 1998.

Khoury, George. "Alex Ross Interview." *Jack Kirby Collector* 27 (1999). http://twomorrows.com/kirby/articles/27ross.html. Accessed July 8, 2011.

Khoury, George. *The Extraordinary Works of Alan Moore.* Raleigh, NC: TwoMorrows Publishing, 2003.

Khoury, George. *The Extraordinary Works of Alan Moore: Indispensable Edition.* Raleigh, NC: TwoMorrows Publishing, 2008.

Khoury, George. *Image Comics: The Road to Independence.* Raleigh, NC: TwoMorrows Publishing, 2007.

Khoury, George. *Kimota! The Miracleman Companion.* Raleigh, NC: TwoMorrows Publishing, 2001.

Kidd, Chip, and Geoff Spear. *Shazam! The Golden Age of the World's Mightiest Mortal*. New York: Abrams ComicArts, 2010.

Killjoy, Margaret. "Alan Moore." *Mythmakers and Lawbreakers: Anarchist Writers on Anarchism*. Oakland, CA: AK Press, 2009.

Kirby, Jack. "Kirby on Survival." *New Gods* #6 (Nov. 1984), DC Comics.

Kirkus Reviews. *Supergods*. http://www.kirkusreviews.com/book-reviews/grant-morrison/supergods/#review. Accessed June 1, 2011.

Kitchen, Denis, and Paul Buhle. *The Art of Harvey Kurtzman: The Mad Genius of Comics*. New York: Abrams ComicArts, 2009.

Kleefeld, Sean. *Comic Book Fanthropology*. Hamilton, OH: Eighty Twenty Press, 2009.

Kleinbaum, Abby Wettan. *The War against the Amazons*. New York: New Press, 1983.

Klingman, Jim. "Sgt. Rock of Easy Company in 'The Longer Shadow.'" *Back Issue 37* (2009): 3–8.

Klock, Geoff. *How To Read Superhero Comics and Why*. New York: Continuum, 2002.

Knight, Stephen. *Jack the Ripper: The Final Solution*. New York: McCay, 1976.

Kobler, John. "Up, Up and Away! The Rise of Superman Inc." *Saturday Evening Post*, June 21, 1941: 14–15, 70–78.

Kouf, Will. "Captain America." 2007. http://www.archive.org/details/CaptainAmerica. Accessed May 14, 2011.

Kowalski, Jesse. *Heroes and Villains: The Comic Book Art of Alex Ross*. Andy Warhol Museum. http://www.warhol.org/ArtBlogsDetail.aspx?id=2870&blogid=199. Accessed June 10, 2011. Art exhibit.

Krutnik, Frank. *In a Lonely Street: Film Noir, Genre, Masculinity*. New York: Routledge, 1991.

Kubert, Joe. *Yossel: April 19, 1943*. New York: ibooks, 2003.

Kuijsten, Marcel, ed. *Reflections on the Dawn of Consciousness: Julian Jaynes's Bicameral Mind Theory Revisited*. Henderson, NV: Julian Jaynes Society, 2007.

Kuldell, Heather, and Curt Holman. "Midnight Munchies with Adult Swim." *Creative Loafing Atlanta*. http://clatl.com/atlanta/midnight-munchies-with-adult-swim/. Last modified November 10, 2004.

Kunzle, David. "Dispossession by Ducks: The Imperialist Treasure Hunt in Southeast Asia." *Art Journal* (1990): 159–66.

Kurtzman, Harvey. *From Aargh! to Zap!: Harvey Kurtzman's Visual History of the Comics*. New York: Prentice Hall Press, 1991.

Kurtzman, Harvey. *Frontline Combat, Vol. 1*. Timonium, MD: Gemstone Publishing, 2008.

Kurtzman, Harvey. *Playboy's Little Annie Fanny, Vols. 1–2*. Milwaukie, OR: Dark Horse Comics, 2000–2001.

Kurtzman, Harvey. *Two-Fisted Tales, Vols. 1–2*. Timonium, MD: Gemstone Publishing, 2006–2007.

Kurtzman, Harvey, ed. *Humbug, Vols. 1–2*. Seattle: Fantagraphics Books, 2009.

Lambert, Josh. "'Wanna watch the grown-ups doin' *dirty* things?': Jewish Sexuality and the Early Graphic Novel." In *The Jewish Graphic Novel: Critical Approaches*, edited by Samantha Baskind and Ranen Omer-Sherman, 43–63. New Brunswick, NJ: Rutgers University Press, 2010.

Langdon, Verne. "The Most Famous Monster of Them All." *Jim Warren Publishing*. Last modified 2008. http://www.jimwarrenpublishing.com/James.html.

Langer, Lawrence L. "A Fable of the Holocaust." *New York Times*, November 3, 1991. http://www.nytimes.com/books/98/12/06/specials/spiegelman-maus2.html.

Langley, Travis, and Robin Rosenberg. "Reflections on the Psychopathy of the Joker: A Comic-Con Panel Report." *International Journal of Comic Art* 13 (2011): 654–76.

Lawrence, Novotny. *Blaxploitation Films of the 1970's: Blackness and Genre*. New York: Routledge, 2008.

Lee, Stan. *The Amazing Spider-Man*. New York: Simon and Schuster, 1979.

Lee, Stan. *The Best of Spider-Man*. New York: Ballantine, 1986.

Lee, Stan. "Deposition." *Comics on Trial, Vol. 2*. New York: Pure Imagination, 2011.

Lee, Stan. "Introduction." In *The Invincible Iron Man, Vol. 1*, by Stan Lee (w), Larry Lieber (w), Don Heck (a) et al., vi–vii. New York: Marvel Comics, 2000.

Lee, Stan. "Introduction." In *Marvels*, by Kurt Busiek (w), Alex Ross (p), and Richard Starkings (l), n.p. New York: Marvel, 2008.

Lee, Stan. *Origins of Marvel Comics*. New York: Simon and Schuster, 1974.

Lee, Stan. *Secrets behind the Comics*. New York: Famous Enterprises, Inc., 1947.

Lee, Stan. "Spider Friends." *Starlog Movie Magic Presents Spider-Man and Other Comics Heroes* 1 (2002): 4–5.

Lee, Stan (w), and Gil Kane (p). *Amazing Spider-Man* #96–#98 (May–July 1971), Marvel Comics.

Lee, Stan, Larry Lieber, Don Heck, and Jack Kirby. *Tales of Suspense* #39 (1963), Marvel Comics.

Lee, Stan, and George Mair. *Excelsior! The Amazing Life of Stan Lee*. New York: Simon & Schuster, 2002.

Lee, Stan (ed.), and Martin Nodell (p). "The Red Skull Strikes Again." *Captain America's Weird Tales* #74 (October 1949), Timely [Marvel Comics].

Lee, Stan (ed.), and John Romita (p). "The Betrayers." *Captain America Comics* #76 (May 1954), Atlas [Marvel Comics].

Lee, Stan (ed.), and John Romita (p). "His Touch Is Death." *Captain America Comics* #78 (September 1954), Atlas [Marvel Comics].

Lent, John, ed. *Pulp Demons: International Dimensions of the Postwar Anti-Comics Campaign.* Madison, NJ: Fairleigh Dickinson Press, 1999.

Levin, Bernard. "Achievement in the Field of Drama." *Manchester Guardian*, January 4, 1958.

Levin, Bernard. "A Moronic 'Superman.'" *Manchester Guardian*, May 9, 1957.

Levitz, Paul. Telephone conversation with Steven R. Bissette. 1988.

Levitz, Paul. *75 Years of DC Comics: The Art of Modern Mythmaking.* Cologne, Germany: Taschen, 2010.

Lieck, Ken. "Has He Really Grown Up?" *Austin Chronicle*, September 8, 2000. http://www.austinchronicle.com/books/2000–09–08/78514/.

Lilley, Wayne. "Drawing Power: Calgary Native Todd McFarlane Leads a Vanguard of Canadian Artists Who Are Rising to Prominence in North America's Hotly Competitive Comic-Book Trade." *Globe and Mail*, October 29, 1993.

Loeb, Jeph (w), and Jim Lee (p). *Batman: Hush.* New York: DC Comics, 2009.

Lois & Clark: The New Adventures of Superman. Developed by Deborah Joy Levine. Starring Teri Hatcher and Dean Cain. 1993–1997. Television series.

Lopes, Paul Douglas. *Demanding Respect: The Evolution of the American Comic Book.* Philadelphia, PA: Temple University Press, 2009.

Lucas, George. "An Appreciation." In *Uncle Scrooge McDuck: His Life and Times*, edited by Edward Summer, 9. Berkeley, CA: Celestial Arts, 1987.

Lynch, Stephen. "Pulp Affliction." *Orange County Register*, April 14, 2000.

MacDonald, Heidi. "Image Takes a 'Chance.'" *Publisher's Weekly*, September 16, 2002.

Mad Archives, Vol.1. New York: DC Comics, 2002.

"*Mad* Magazine: A Semi-Secret History." http://www.life.com/gallery/60151/mad-magazine-a-semi-secret-history#index/0. Accessed July 25, 2011.

Madrid, Mike. *The Supergirls: Fashion, Feminism, Fantasy, and the History of Comic Book Heroines.* Ashland, OR: Exterminating Angel Press, 2009.

Maggin, Elliot S!. *The Universe According to Elliot S! Maggin.* http://www.maggin.com. Accessed October 1, 2007.

Malan, Dan. *The Complete Guide to Classics Collectibles, Volume One: The U.S. Series of Classics Illustrated and Related Collectibles.* St. Louis, MO: Malan Classical Enterprises, 1991.

Malan, Dan. *The Complete Guide to Classics Illustrated, Volume Two: Foreign Series and Related Collectibles*. St. Louis, MO: Malan Classical Enterprises, 1993.

Markstein, Don. "Alfred E. Neuman." 2001. http://www.toonopedia.com/alfred_e.htm. Accessed July 25, 2011.

Markstein, Don. *Don Markstein's Toonopedia*. 2008. http://www.toonopedia.com. Accessed December 26, 2011.

Markstein, Don. "Julius Schwartz." 2001. http://www.toonopedia.com/schwartz.htm. Accessed August 1, 2011.

Markstein, Don. "Lobo." http://www.toonopedia.com/lobo1.htm. Accessed November 18, 2011.

Markstein, Don. "Sheena, Queen of the Jungle." http://www.toonopedia.com/sheena.htm. Accessed August 1, 2011.

Marshall, Monica. *Joe Sacco*. New York: Rosen Publishing Group, 2005.

Marston, William Moulton. *Emotions of Normal People*. Minneapolis, MN: Personal Press, 1979.

Marston, William Moulton. "Why 100,000,000 Americans Read Comics." *American Scholar* 13 (1944): 35–44.

Matzer, Marla. "Blade Suit Seeks Slice of the Action for Its Creator." *Los Angeles Times*, August 21, 1998.

McCabe, Joseph. "Speeding Bullets and Changing Lanes." In *The Man From Krypton: A Closer Look at Superman*, edited by Glenn Yeffeth, 161–74. Dallas: Smart Pop, 2006.

McCloud, Scott. "Destroy!!" *Scott McCloud Journal*. 2011. http://scottmccloud.com/2-print/older/destroy/index.html. Accessed March 31, 2012.

McCloud, Scott. E-mail message to author, July 2, 2011.

McCloud, Scott. "Inventions." *Scott McCloud Journal*. 2011. http://scottmccloud.com/4-inventions/index.html. Accessed March 31, 2012.

McCloud, Scott. *Reinventing Comics*. New York: Perennial, 2000.

McCloud, Scott. *Understanding Comics: The Invisible Art*. New York: Harper Perennial, 1993.

McConnell, Frank. "Introduction." In *The Kindly Ones*, by Neil Gaiman et al., 9. New York: DC Comics, 1996.

McConnell, Frank. "Introduction." In *The Sandman: Book of Dreams*, by Neil Gaiman et al., 4. New York: HarperTorch, 1996.

McLaughlin, Jeff, ed. *Stan Lee Conversations*. Jackson: University Press of Mississippi, 2007.

McLaughlin, Jim. *2000–2001 Year in Review: Fanboys and Badgirls: Bill and Joe's Marvelous Adventures*. New York: Marvel, 2002.

Meltzer, Brad (w), and Rags Morales (p). *Identity Crisis* #1–#7 (June–Dec. 2004), DC Comics.

Merino, Ana. *Fantagraphics: Creadores del Canon*. Gijón, Spain: Semana Negra, 2003.

Merrill, Jonathan A. "Those Elusive Four Colors!" *The Little Lulu Library* #1, 5–9. Marceline, MO: Another Rainbow Publishing, Inc., 1992.

Miller, Frank, and Lynn Varely. *300*. Milwaukee, OR: Dark Horse Publishing, 1999.

Miller, Frank. "The Dark Knight Falls." *Batman: Dark Knight Returns* #4. DC Comics, 1986.

Miller, Jack (w), Robert Bernstein (w), George Kashdan (w), Bob Haney (w), Nick Cardy (a), and Romana Fradon (a). *The Aquaman Archives, Volume 1*. New York: DC Comics, 2003.

Miller, Jerome G. "The Debate on Rehabilitating Criminals: Is It True That Nothing Works?" http://www.prisonpolicy.org/scans/rehab.html. Accessed July 5, 2011.

Miller, Raymond. "The Timely Comics Story." *Rocket's Blast Special 1* (1967): 1–8.

Millidge, Gary Spencer. *Alan Moore Storyteller*. Lewes, UK: ILEX, 2011.

Misiroglu, Gina, and David Roach, eds. *The Superhero Book*. Detroit: Visible Ink, 2004.

Mitchell, Elvis. "Film Review: Snuffing Out Vampires When a Stake Won't Do." *New York Times*, 2002. http://movies.nytimes.com/movie/review?res=9407E0D61138F931A15750C0A9649C8B63&scp=1&sq=blade%202%20film%20review%202002&st=csc. Accessed July 26, 2011.

Mitchell, Sean. "Now, for a Little Hedonism: From His Holocaust Saga in Which Jewish Mice Are Exterminated by Nazi Cats, to the New Yorker Covers Guaranteed to Offend, to a Wild Party That Ends in Murder: Art Spiegelman's Cartoons Don't Fool Around." *Los Angeles Times*. http://articles.latimes.com/1994–12–18/entertainment/ca-30486_1_art-spiegelman. Last modified December 18, 1994.

Moldstad, Frank. "Six Things That Made Mid-lifers Who We Are." http://work.lifegoesstrong.com/mad-magazine. Accessed July 25, 2011.

Monte Smith, Christopher. "Art Spiegelman Interview." *IndieBound*. 2008. American Booksellers Association. http://www.indiebound.org/author-interviews/spiegelmanart. Accessed July 12, 2011.

Moore, Alan. *Alan Moore's Writing for Comics*. Urbana, IL: Avatar Press, 2003.

Moore, Alan. Contribution to *The Life and Times of R. Crumb*, edited by Monte Beauchamp, 71–82. New York: St Martin's Griffin, 1998.

Moore, Alan. "Stan Lee: Blinded by the Hype, an Affectionate Character Assassination, Part One." *Daredevils* 3 (1983): 45–46.

Moore, Alan. "Whatever Happened to the Man of Tomorrow?" *Superman* #423 (September 1986), DC Comics.

Moore, Alan (w), and Brian Bolland (a). *Batman: The Killing Joke*. New York: DC Comics, 1989.

Moore, Alan (w), and Brian Bolland (a). *The Killing Joke: The Deluxe Edition*. New York: DC Comics, 2008.

Moore, Alan (w), and Eddie Campbell (a). *From Hell: Being a Melodrama in Sixteen Parts*. London: Knockabout Comics, 2000.

Morales, Robert (w), Kyle Baker (p), and J. D. Smith (c). *The Truth: Red White and Black*. New York: Marvel, 2004.

Morrison, Grant (w), and Andy Kubert (p). *Batman and Son*. New York: DC Comics, 2008.

Morrison, Grant. *Supergods*. New York: Spiegel & Grau, 2011.

Morrow, John, ed. *The Jack Kirby Collector*. Raleigh, NC: TwoMorrows Publishing, 1994–present.

Muir, John Kenneth. *The Encyclopedia of Superheroes on Film and Television*. Jefferson, NC: McFarland, 2004.

Murray, Chris. "Interview with the Magus." *Studies in Comics* 2 (2011): 7–19.

Murray, Chris. "Signals from Airstrip One: The British Invasion of American Mainstream Comics." In *The Rise of the American Comics Artist, Creators and Contexts*, edited by Paul Williams and James Lyons, 31–45. Jackson: University Press of Mississippi, 2010.

Murray, Will. "The Eternal Green Lantern: An Overview of the Emerald Gladiators of *Two* Comic Book Ages." *Alter Ego* 102 (2011): 3–14.

Murray, Will. "Spider Time." *Starlog Movie Magic Presents Spider-Man and Other Comics Heroes* 1 (2002): 26–27.

Murray, Will. "Strange Origins of Spider-Man." *Starlog Movie Magic Presents Spider-Man and Other Comics Heroes* 1 (2002): 28–30.

Myer, Peter L. "Introduction." In *The Plastic Man Archives, Volume 1*, by Jack Cole, 7–9. New York: DC Comics, 1999.

National Public Radio. "Intersections: Of *Maus* and Spiegelman: *Mad* Inspired Comic Book Look at the Holocaust." http://www.npr.org/templates/story/story.php?storyId=1611731. Accessed July 25, 2011.

"New Centurions: Eight Men and Women Whose Achievements Have Made Chicago a Better Place." *Chicago Magazine* 51, no. 1 (2002): 52–59.

Nguyen, Kevin. http://www.amazon.com/Supergods-Vigilantes-Miraculous-Mutants-Smallville/dp/1400069122/. Last modified July 2011. Amazon.com Review.

Noer, Michael. "The Forbes Fictional 15." *Forbes*. http://www.forbes.com/2007/12/11/fictional-characters-wealth-oped-books-fict1507-cx_de_mn_1211 fictionalintro.html. Last modified December 11, 2007.

Nolan, Michelle. *Love on the Racks: A History of American Romance Comics*. Jefferson, NC: McFarland, 2008.

Nyberg, Amy K. *Seal of Approval: A History of the Comics Code*. Jackson: University of Mississippi Press, 1998.

Nyberg, Amy. "Seal of Approval: The Origins and History of the Comics Code." PhD diss., University of Wisconsin-Madison, 1994.

Offenberger, Rik. "Neal Adams: Renaissance Man." http://www.comicsbulletin.com/features/111086279993605.htm. Accessed August 1, 2011.

Olshevsky, George. *The Official Marvel Index to The Amazing Spider-Man*. 9 vols. New York: Marvel Comics Group, 1985.

Olshevsky, George. "Origins of Marvel Comics." In *The Comic Book Price Guide 1980–1981*, edited by Robert Overstreet, A-46–73. Cleveland, TN: Crown Publishers, 1980.

O'Malley, Bryan Lee. *Official Bryan Lee O'Malley Website*. Accessed July 31, 2011. http://radiomaru.com/.

O'Malley, Bryan Lee. *Scott Pilgrim & The Infinite Sadness*. Portland, OR: Oni Press, 2006.

O'Malley, Bryan Lee. *Scott Pilgrim Gets It Together*. Portland, OR: Oni Press, 2007.

O'Malley, Bryan Lee. *Scott Pilgrim vs. The Universe*. Portland, OR: Oni Press, 2009.

O'Malley, Bryan Lee. *Scott Pilgrim vs. The World*. Portland, OR: Oni Press, 2005.

O'Malley, Bryan Lee. *Scott Pilgrim's Finest Hour*. Portland, OR: Oni Press, 2010.

O'Malley, Bryan Lee. *Scott Pilgrim's Precious Little Life*. Portland, OR: Oni Press, 2004.

O'Neil, Denny. "Introduction." In *A Contract with God, and Other Tenement Stories*, by Will Eisner, 9–11. Princeton, WI: Kitchen Sink Press, 1985.

O'Neil, Dennis. "Postscript." In *Batman: A Death in the Family*, by Jim Starlin (w), Jim Aparo (p), and Mike DeCarlo (i), 143–44. New York: DC Comics, 1988.

Ortved, John. *The Simpsons: An Uncensored, Unauthorized History*. New York: Faber & Faber, 2009.

Overstreet, Bob. *The Official Overstreet Comic Book Price Guide, 40th Edition*. Timonium, MD: Gemstone, 2010.

Patrick, Christopher J., and Sarah K. Patrick. "The Incredible Hulk." In *The Psychology of Superheroes*, edited by Robin S. Rosenberg and Jennifer Canzoneri, 213–28. Dallas: Benbella Books, 2008.

Peeples, Gustav. "God, Communism, and the WB." In *The Man from Krypton*, edited by Glenn Yeffeth, 77–92. Dallas: BenBella Books, 2005.

Pekar, Harvey. *American Splendor: The Life and Times of Harvey Pekar*. New York: Ballantine Books, 2003.

Pekar, Harvey. *Best of American Splendor*. New York: Ballantine Books, 2005.

Pekar, Harvey. *How I Quit Collecting Records and Put Out a Comic Book with the Money I Saved*. New York: Ballantine Books, 2003.

Petrovic, Paul. "The Culturally Constituted Gaze: Fetishizing the Feminine from Alan Moore and Dave Gibbons's *Watchmen* to Zack Snyder's *Watchmen*." *ImageTexT* 5, no. 4 (2010). http://www.english.ufl.edu/imagetext/archives/v5_4/petrovic/.

Phegley, Kiel. "CBR's Top News Stories of 2010." *Comic Book Resources.* 2010. http://www.comicbookresources.com/?page=article&id=30112. Accessed December 31, 2011.

Phegley, Kiel. "Inside Ian Churchill's New Style." *Comic Book Resources.* 2009. http://www.comicbookresources.com/?page=article&id=23165. Accessed August 4, 2011.

Phillips, Charles. *Archie: His First 50 Years.* New York: Abbeville Press, 1991.

Pike, Brad. "Scrooge McDuck and the Modern Elite." http://thoughtcatalog.com/2011/scrooge-mcduck-and-the-modern-elite. Accessed May 4, 2011.

Pisani, Joseph. "The Smartest Superheroes." *Business Week*, June 1, 2006. http://www.businessweek.com/investor/content/may2006/pi20060531_495737.htm.

Plexico, Van Allen. "And There Came a Day." In *Assembled 2*, edited by Van Allen Plexico, 21–27. Lexington, KY: White Rocket Books, 2009.

Plowright, Frank, ed. *The Slings & Arrows Comic Guide* (2nd ed.). Eastbourne, UK: Slings & Arrows, 2003.

Pollie, Robert. "A Mirror Held Up to Spiegelman." *7th Avenue Project.* http://www.podcastdirectory.com/podshows/6029828. Last modified October 26, 2009.

Powers, Thom. "Joe Sacco Interview." *Comics Journal* 176 (1995): 88–109.

Pratchett, Terry. "Foreword." In *Prince of Stories: The Many Worlds of Neil Gaiman*, edited by Hank Wagner, Christopher Golden, and Stephen R. Bissette, xii. New York: St. Martin's Press, 2008.

"The Press: Ace Harlem to the Rescue." *Time*, July 17, 1947. http://www.webcitation.org/5zsn4kPc8.

Public Broadcasting Service. "Interviews: On Cartooning." http://www.pbs.org/pov/tintinandi/sfartists_ware.php. Accessed July 18, 2011.

Pustz, Matthew J. *Comic Book Culture: Fanboys and True Believers.* Jackson: University Press of Mississippi, 1999.

Quattro, Ken. "The Comics Detective." http://thecomicsdetective.blogspot.com/2010/04/return-to-wonderful-wags-of-oz.html. Last modified April 25, 2010.

Raeburn, Daniel. *Chris Ware.* New Haven, CT: Yale University Press, 2004.

Randall, Jon. *Slack or Bust: An Interview with Paul Mavrides.* 1996. http://sonic.net/~goblin/fbros.html. Accessed June 6, 2011.

Raphael, Jordan, and Tom Spurgeon. *Stan Lee and the Rise and Fall of the American Comic Book.* Chicago: Chicago Review Press, 2003.

Rausch, Barb. "Katy Keene: A Not-So Distant Mirror." *Katy Keene Magazine* 17 (1985): 21.

Ravi, Dan. *Comic Wars: How Two Tycoons Battled over the Marvel Comics Empire and Both Lost*. New York: Broadway Books, 2002.

Raymond, Nate. "The Real Kavaliers and Clays." *The Amazing Website of Kavalier & Clay*. http://www.sugarbombs.com/kavalier. Accessed August 17, 2011.

Regalado, Aldo. "*Unbreakable* and the Limits of Transgression." In *Film and Comic Books*, edited by Ian Gordon, Mark Jancovich, and Matthew P. McAllister, 116–36. Jackson: University Press of Mississippi, 2007.

Reibman, James E. "Fredric Wertham: A Social Psychiatrist Characterizes Crime Comic Books and Media Violence as Public Health Issues." In *Pulp Demons: International Dimensions of the Postwar Anti-Comics Campaign*, edited by John Lent, 234–68. Madison, NJ: Fairleigh Dickinson Press, 1999.

Reidelbach, Maria. *Completely Mad: A History of the Comic Book and Magazine*. Boston: Little, Brown and Company, 1991.

Remenih, Anton. "Television News and Views." *Chicago Daily Tribune*, March 24, 1953: A7.

Remenih, Anton. "Television News and Views." *Chicago Daily Tribune*, August 4, 1953: 16.

Reynolds, Richard. *Super Heroes: A Modern Mythology*. Jackson: University Press of Mississippi, 1992.

Rhoades, Shirrel. *A Complete History of American Comic Books*. New York: Peter Lang, 2008.

Richards, Dave. "Waxing Shellhead, Part 1: Brevoort Talks Iron Man." *Comic Book Resources*. http://www.comicbookresources.com/?page=article&old=1&id=12174. Last modified October 22, 2007.

Ro, Ronin. *Tales to Astonish: Jack Kirby, Stan Lee, and the American Comic Book Revolution*. New York: Bloomsbury, 2004.

Roach, David, and Jon Cooke. *The Warren Companion: The Definitive Compendium to the Great Comics of Warren Publishing*. Raleigh, NC: Two-Morrows Publishing, 2001.

Robertson, Tony. "Homages." *The Drawings of Steranko*. http://www.thedrawingsofsteranko.com/Ster_hmgs/ster_homages_pg.html. Last modified November 1, 2009.

Robertson, Tony. "Steranko Recognizes the Power of Kindness." *The Drawings of Steranko*. http://www.thedrawingsofsteranko.com/kindness.html. Last modified June 8, 2009.

Robbins, Trina. *From Girls to Grrrlz*. San Francisco: Chronicle Books, 1999.

Robbins, Trina. *The Great Women Cartoonists*. New York: Watson Guptill Publications, 2001.

Robbins, Trina. *The Great Women Superheroes*. Northampton, MA: Kitchen Sink Press, 1996.

Rogers, Vanetta. "Geoff Johns Talks Aquaman Ongoing Series." *Newsarama*. http://www.newsarama.com/comics/geoff-johns-talks-aquaman-110329 .html. Last modified March 29, 2011.

Romita, John. "*Spider Friends*." *Starlog Movie Magic Presents Spider-Man and Other Comics Heroes* 1 (2002): 4–5.

Rosen, Alan. "The Language of Survival: English as Metaphor in Spiegelman's *Maus*." *Prooftexts* 15, no. 3 (1995): 249–62.

Rosenkranz, Patrick. "The ABCs of Autobio Comix." *Comics Journal*, March 6, 2011. http://www.tcj.com/the-abcs-of-auto-bio-comix-2/. Accessed May 15, 2011.

Ross, Alex. "Introduction." In *Kimota! The Miracleman Companion*, by George Khoury, 5. Raleigh, NC: TwoMorrows Publishing, 2001.

Ross, Alex, Jim Kreuger, and Bill Reinhold. *Earth X Trilogy Companion*. New York: Marvel, 2008.

Ross, Jonathan. "Jonathan Ross Meets Jim Steranko, His Comic-book Hero." *Guardian*, July 21, 2010: G2.

Rossen, Jake. *Superman vs. Hollywood: How Fiendish Producers, Devious Directors, and Warring Writers Ground an American Icon*. Chicago: Chicago Review Press, 2008.

Rovell, Darren. "Baseball Scales Back Movie Promotion." *ESPN Sports Business*. 2004. http://sports.espn.go.com/espn/sportsbusiness/news/story?id =1796765. Accessed October 10, 2011.

Rowson, Martin. "Master of the Dark Arts: Art Spiegelman, Grandfather of the Graphic Novel, Was a True Revolutionary." *Observer*, November 30, 2008.

Rozanski, Chuck. "'Death of Superman' Promotion of 1992." http://www .milehighcomics.com/tales/cbg127.html. Accessed October 21, 2011.

"Russians Says Comic Books 'Fascisize' U.S. Children." *New York Times*, October 16, 1949: 33.

Sabin, Roger. *Adult Comics: An Introduction*. New York: Routledge, 1993.

Sacco, Joe. "Down! Up! You're In the Iraqi Army Now!" *Harper's Magazine* (April 2007): 47–62.

Sacco, Joe. *Palestine*. Seattle: Fantagraphics Books, 2001.

Sacco, Joe. *Palestine, The Special Edition*. Seattle: Fantagraphics Books, 2007.

Sacks, Ethan. "Captain America Killed!" *New York Daily News*, 2007. http:// www.nydailynews.com/entertainment/arts/2007/03/07/2007–03–07 _captain_america_killed.html. Accessed May 17, 2011.

Sacks, Jason. "Panther's Rage: The First Marvel Graphic Novel." http://www .fanboyplanet.com/comics/js-panthersrage.php. Accessed October 30, 2011.

Sadowski, Greg, ed. *The Comics Journal Library, Volume 7: Harvey Kurtzman*. Seattle: Fantagraphics Books, 2006.

Sager, Christian. "Does DC Comics' 'New 52' Win Over New Readers?" http://geekout.blogs.cnn.com/2011/09/29/does-dc-comics-new-52-win-over-new-readers/. Last modified September 29, 2011.

Sanders, Clinton R. "Icons of Alternate Culture: The Themes and Functions of Underground Comix." *Journal of Popular Culture* 8 (1975): 836–52.

Sanders, Joe, ed. *The Sandman Papers*. Seattle: Fantagraphics Books, 2006.

Sanderson, Peter. "Pro2Pro Roundtable Discussion: The Fantastic Four." *Back Issue* 7 (2004): 47–61.

Sanderson, Peter. *Ultimate X-Men: The Ultimate Guide* (Updated Edition). New York: Dorling Kindersley, 2006.

San Diego Comic Convention, Inc. *Comic-Con: 40 Years of Artists, Writers, Fans & Friends*. San Francisco: Chronicle Books, 2009.

Satrapi, Marjane. "The 2005 *Time* 100: The Lives and Ideas of the World's Most Influential People." *Time*, April 18, 2005.

Savage, William W. Jr. *Commies, Cowboys, and Jungle Queens: Comic Books and America, 1945–1954*. Hanover, NH: Wesleyan University Press, 1998.

Saxon, Wolfgang. "Helen Honig Meyer, Who Led Dell Publishing, Dies at 95." *New York Times*, April 24, 2003.

Schelly, Bill. *The Golden Age of Comic Fandom*. Seattle: Hamster Press, 1999.

Schelly, Bill. *Man of Rock: A Biography of Joe Kubert*. Seattle: Fantagraphics Books, 2008.

Schelly, Bill. *Worlds of Wonder: The Life and Times of Otto Binder*. Seattle: Hamster Press, 2003.

Schumacher, Michael. *Will Eisner: A Dreamer's Life in Comics*. New York: Bloomsbury, 2010.

Schwartz, Harry. "What Russians Read in Their Newspapers." *New York Times*, January 9, 1949: E10.

Schwarz, Rachel. "Tattoos and Body Art of Blade." *ReLache Body Art*. http://www.relache.com/tattoo/movie/blade/index.html. Accessed July 15, 2011.

Scott Pilgrim. http://www.scottpilgrim.com. Accessed July 31, 2011.

"The Secret Origins of Elvis and Captain Marvel Jr." *Dial B for Blog*. http://www.dialbforblog.com. Accessed March 29, 2012.

Senate Committee on the Judiciary. *Comic Books and Juvenile Delinquency*. Interim report pursuant to S. Res. 89, 83d Cong., 1st sess., and S. 190, 83d Cong., 2d sess., a part of the investigation of juvenile delinquency in the United States. Washington: U.S. G.P.O., 1955.

Sharrett, Christopher. "Batman and the Twilight of the Idols: An Interview with Frank Miller." In *The Many Lives of the Batman*, edited by Robert E. Pearson and William Uricchio, 33–46. New York: Routledge, 1991.

Shprintz, Janet. "Snipes Throwing Legal Blade at Trinity Team." *Variety*, April 20, 2005.

Shreffler, Brion. "Wizard World." *Philadelphia City Paper*, June 18, 2009: 33.

Sidman, Ray. "Wizard Dumps Comics Size for Magazine Format." *CBG Xtra*. Last modified May 15, 2006. http://cbgxtra.com/comics-news-and-notes/wizard-dumps-comics-size-for-magazine-format.

Siegel, Jerry, and Joe Shuster. "Superman." *Action Comics* #1. New York: National Allied Publications, 1938.

Siegel, Jerry (w), and Joe Shuster (p). *Superman Chronicles, Vols. 1–8*. New York: DC Comics, 2006–2010.

Siegel, Jerry, Joe Shuster et al. *Superman: Daily Planet*. New York: DC Comics, 2006.

Siegel v. Time Warner et al., United States District Court—Central Division of California—Eastern Division. Case Nis. CV 04–8400 SGL (RZx), Plaintiff's Submission, July 21, 2008.

Sigal, Mark, David Rubin, Paul Hock, and Mark Bigley. "The Kind and the Director: 1971 Interview with Jack Kirby and Carmine Infantino." *Comic Book Artist 1* (1998): 64–67, 80.

Siklos, Richard. "The Caped Avenger Keeps His Enemies at Bay: Comic Book Artist Todd McFarlane Refuses to Give In to the Corporate 'Dark Army.' Despite the Odds, He Survives—Very Well—and with Principles Intact." *Financial Post*, April 29, 1995.

Siklos, Richard. "Spoiler Warning: Comic Books Are Alive and Kicking." 2010. http://money.cnn.com/2008/10/10/news/companies/siklos_marvel.fortune/. Accessed August 1, 2011.

Simon, Joe. "My Bulletin Board." *Captain America* #600 (August 2009), Marvel Comics.

Simon, Joe, and Jim Simon. *The Comic Book Makers*. Lebanon, NJ: Vanguard Productions, 2003.

Simpsons, The. "Husbands and Knives." Directed by Nancy Kruse. 2007. Los Angeles: 20th Century Fox. Television episode.

Sims, Chris. "10 of 'Wizard' Magazine's Dubious Moments." *Comics Alliance*. http://www.comicsalliance.com/2011/03/03/wizard-magazine-worst-terrible/. Last modified March 3, 2011.

Sinclair, Ian. *Lud Heat: A Book of the Dead Hamlets: May 1974 to April 1975*. Uppingham, UK: Goldmark, 1987.

"Singer Virginia O'Brien Tells Blows, Gets Decree." *Los Angeles Times*, June 25, 1955: A5.

Skal, David J. *The Monster Show: A Cultural History of Horror*. New York: Norton, 1993.

Smallville. Created by Alfred Gough and Miles Millar. Starring Tom Wells, Alison Mack, and Erica Durance. 2001–2011. Television series.

Smith, Andy. "Pressing Issues: Wizard Press and the Trapeze of '90s Fan Culture." *PopMatters*. August 25, 2010. http://www.popmatters.com/pm/feature/129883-pressing-issues-wizard-press-and-the-trapeze-of-90s-fan-culture.

Smith, Jeff, and Eric Nolen-Weathington. *Modern Masters Vol. 25: Jeff Smith*. Raleigh, NC: TwoMorrows Press, 2011.

Smith, Matthew J. "The Tyranny of the Melting Pot Metaphor: Wonder Woman as the Americanized Immigrant." In *Comics & Ideology*, edited by Matthew McAllister, Edward Sewell, Jr., and Ian Gordon, 129–50. New York: Peter Lang, 2001.

Smith, Zack. "Op/Ed: WIZARD Magazine: A Eulogy to Days Good and Bad." *Newsarama*. http://www.newsarama.com/comics/wizard-eulogy-op-ed-110125.html. Last modified January 25, 2011.

Snowdon, Adrian P. "Amazing Spider-Man." In *The Slings & Arrows Comic Guide: A Critical Assessment*, edited by Frank Plowright, 602–9. Eastbourne, UK: Slings & Arrows, 2003.

Spelling, Ian. "Night Hunter." *Starlog*, October 1998: 48.

Spiegelman, Art. "Comix 9–11–101." *Chicago Humanities Festival*. http://www.chicagohumanities.org/Genres/Arts-And-Architecture/Art-Spiegelman-Comix-911–01.aspx. Last modified May 12, 2010.

Spiegelman, Art. *The Complete Maus: A Survivor's Tale*. New York: Pantheon Book, 1996.

Spiegelman, Art, and Chip Kidd. *Jack Cole and Plastic Man: Forms Stretched to Their Limits!* San Francisco: Chronicle Books, 2001.

Spiegelman, Art, and Françoise Mouly, eds. *Read Yourself Raw*. New York: Pantheon, 1987.

Spiggle, Susan. "Measuring Social Values: A Content Analysis of Sunday Comics and Underground Comix." *Journal of Consumer Research* 13, no. 1 (1986): 100–113.

Stafford, Richard Todd. "Toward an Epistemological Theory of Comics Journalism: Case Studies in Joe Sacco's War Reportage." *Public Knowledge Journal* 2, no. 1 (2011). http://pkjournal.org/?page_id=1490.

Starlin, Jim (w), Jim Aparo (p), and Mike DeCarlo (i). *Batman: A Death in the Family*. New York: DC Comics, 1988.

Steele, Edward D., and W. Charles Redding. "The American Value System: Premises for Persuasion." *Western Speech* 26 (1962): 83–91.

Steinem, Gloria. "Introduction." In *Wonder Woman*, edited by Gloria Steinem, 1–6. New York: Bonanza Books, 1969.

Steranko, Jim. "1970 Jim Steranko Portfolio." http://comicattack.net/2010/12/is-25-jim-steranko. Accessed August 17, 2011.

Stevenson, Daniel R. *Year by Year Title Listing, 1939 to 1989*. July 24, 2008. Unpublished.

Stewart, Tom. "The Blackest Panther: Don McGregor in the Jungles of Wakanda." *Back Issue* 27 (2008): 57–61.

Stiles, Steve. "The Groundbreaking Neal Adams: A Pivotal Figure in the Field." http://steve stiles.com/adams.htm. Accessed August 1, 2011.

"Strange Tales #154: Steranko Bibliography." *The Comic Book Database.* http://www.comicbookdb.com/issue.php?ID=72840. Accessed August 17, 2011.

Stuller, Jennifer K. "Feminist Analysis: Second Wave Feminism in the Pages of Lois Lane." In *Critical Approaches to Comic Books: Theories and Methods*, edited by Matthew J. Smith and Randy Duncan, 235–51. London: Routledge, 2011.

Stuller, Jennifer K. *Ink-Stained Amazons and Cinematic Warriors: Superwomen in Modern Mythology.* London: I. B. Tauris, 2010.

"Superman's Dilemma." *Time*, April 13, 1942. http://www.time.com/time/magazine/article/0,9171,766523,00.html#ixzz1XRzeNznh. Accessed August 1, 2011.

Superman: The Movie. Director Richard Donner. Starring Margot Kidder and Christopher Reeve. 1978. Film.

Superman II: The Richard Donner Cut. Director Richard Donner. Starring Margot Kidder and Christopher Reeve. 2006. Film.

Theakston, Greg Allen, ed. *The Neal Adams Treasury.* Detroit, MI: Pure Imagination, 1976.

Thomas, Roy. "A Fantastic First! The Creation of the Fantastic Four—And Beyond!" *Alter Ego* 2, no. 2 (1998): 4–9.

Thomas, Roy. "Deposition." *Comics on Trial, Vol. 2.* New York: Pure Imagination, 2011.

Thompson, Maggie. "Introduction." In *Archie: The Complete Daily Newspaper Comics 1946–1948*, 291–301. San Diego: IDW Publishing, 2010.

Thompson, Maggie. "Marge." *The Little Lulu Library* #18, 641–44. Marceline, MO: Another Rainbow Publishing, Inc., 1992.

Thomson, Iain. "Deconstructing the Hero." In *Comics as Philosophy*, edited by Jeff McLaughlin, 100–129. Jackson: University Press of Mississippi, 2005.

"Todd McFarlane Complete Biography." *Spawn.com.* http://spawn.com/info/todd/bio.long.aspx. Accessed July 31, 2011.

Toth, Alex. *The Art of Alex Toth.* New York: Feature Associates, 1977.

Tucci, Billy. *Sgt. Rock: The Lost Battalion.* New York: DC Comics, 2008.

"TV Show Scored." *New York Times*, March 10, 1957.

"Twenty-Eight People Who Count." *Esquire*, September 1965: 97.

United States. *Juvenile Delinquency (Comic Books): Hearings before the Subcommittee to Investigate Juvenile Delinquency.* Washington, DC: U.S. G.P.O., 1954.

Uslan, Michael. *The Boy Who Loved Batman*. San Francisco: Chronicle, 2011.

Valdes, Robert. "Adapting *Hellboy*." http://entertainment.howstuffworks .com/arts/comic-books/hellboy3.htm. Accessed November 23, 2011.

Van Ness, Sara J. *Watchmen as Literature: A Critical Study of the Graphic Novel*. Jefferson, NC: McFarland, 2010.

Versace, Rocco. *This Book Contains Graphic Language: Comics as Literature*. New York: Continuum, 2007.

Von Busack, Richard. "Escape Artist." *Metro*, December 12–18, 2002.

Wagner, Hank, Christopher Golden, and Stephen R. Bissette. *Prince of Stories: The Many Worlds of Neil Gaiman*. New York: St. Martin's Press, 2008.

Waid, Mark. "Stacking the Deck: The Other Joker Stories." In *The Greatest Joker Stories Ever Told*, edited by Mike Gold, 278–83. New York: DC Comics, 1988.

Walentis, Al. "Steranko Helped Sell Raiders." *Reading Eagle*, June 14, 1981: 66, 69.

Webb, Bob, Bob Powell, Matt Barker, et al. *The Best of the Golden Age of Sheena, Volume 1*. Chicago: Devil's Due Publishing, 2008.

Webb, Bob, Bob Powell, Matt Barker, et al. *The Best of the Golden Age of Sheena, Volume 2*. Chicago: Devil's Due Publishing, 2009.

Wein, Len (w), Herb Trimpe (a), and Jack Abel (i). "And Now . . . The Wolverine." *Incredible Hulk* #181 (Nov. 1974), Marvel Comics.

Weiner, Robert G. *Marvel Graphic Novels and Related Publications: An Annotated Guide to Comics, Prose Novels, Children's Books, Articles, Criticism and Reference Works, 1965–2005*. Jefferson, NC: McFarland, 2008.

Weiner, Stephen. "How the Graphic Novel Changed American Comics." In *The Rise of the American Comics Artist*, edited by Paul Williams and James Lyon, 3–13. Jackson: University Press of Mississippi, 2010.

Weinstein, Simcha. *Up, Up and Oy Vey! How Jewish History, Culture, and Values Shaped the Comic Book Superhero*. Baltimore: Leviathan Press, 2006.

Weist, Jerry. *100 Greatest Comic Books*. Atlanta, GA: Whitman, 2004.

Weller, Sam. *The Bradbury Chronicles: The Life of Ray Bradbury*. New York: William Morrow, 2005.

Wells, Earl. "Once and For All, Who Was the Author of Marvel?" In *The Comics Journal Library, Volume 1: Jack Kirby*, edited by George Milo, 74–87. Seattle: Fantagraphics, 2002.

Wertham, Fredric. *Seduction of the Innocent*. New York: Rinehart and Co., 1954. Reprint, Main Road Books, 1996.

Wertham, Fredric. *Seduction of the Innocent*. London: Museum Press, 1955.

"Wesley Snipes Returns as Vampire Warrior in Action-Thriller Blade 2." *Jet*, April 1, 2002: 58–61.

Wiater, Stanley, and Stephen R. Bissette. *Comic Book Rebels: Conversations with the Creators of the New Comics*. New York: Donald I. Fine, 1993.

Wickham, Paul. "Sheena Intro Page." http://terrororstralis.com/sheena.htm. Accessed August 1, 2011.

Williams, J. P. "All's Fair in Love and Journalism: Female Rivalry in *Superman*." *Journal of Popular Culture* 24 (1990): 103–12.

Williams, Kristian. "The Case for Comics Journalism: Artist-reporters Leap Tall Conventions in a Single Bound." *Columbia Journalism Review* 43, no. 6 (2005): 51–55.

Williams, Paul, and James Lyons, eds. *The Rise of the American Comics Artist: Creators and Contexts*. Jackson: University Press of Mississippi, 2010.

Winton, Ezra. "Picking through the Rubble of Memory: A Conversation with Comics Journalist Joe Sacco—Part Two." *Art Threat*. http://artthreat.net/2010/12/joe-sacco-interview-2/. Last modified December 13, 2010.

Witek, Joseph. *Art Spiegelman: Conversations*. Jackson: University Press of Mississippi, 2007.

Witek, Joseph. *Comic Books as History: The Narrative Art of Jack Jackson, Art Spiegelman, and Harvey Pekar*. Jackson: University Press of Mississippi, 1989.

Witterstaetter, Renee. "Interview with Steven Grant." *David Anthony Kraft's Comics Interview* 72 (1989): 5–13.

Wivel, Matthias. "Interview with Chris Ware Part 1 of 2." *Comics Book Journal*. http://classic.tcj.com/alternative/interview-with-chris-ware-part-1-of-2/. Accessed July 18, 2011.

Wizard World. "Wizard World, Inc. (WIZD) Appoints Michael Mathews as Chairman of the Board!" Press Release, March 23, 2011. http://www.wizardworld.com/wiwoinwapmim.html.

"WIZD Appoints Greg Suess to Its Board of Directors." *Entertainment Newsweekly*, May 27, 2011: 159.

"WIZD Appoints John D. Maatta to Its Board of Directors." *Technology and Business Journal*, June 7, 2011: 2575.

Wolfman, Marv (w), George Perez (p), Jim Aparo (p), and Tom Grummett (p). *Batman: A Lonely Place of Dying*. New York: DC Comics, 1990.

Wolfman, Marv (w), George Perez (p), and Dick Giordano (i). "The Judas Contract: Book Three—There Shall Come a Titan!" *Tales of the Teen Titans* #44 (July 1984), DC Comics.

Wolk, Douglas. *Reading Comics: How Graphic Novels Work and What They Mean*. Cambridge, MA: Da Capo, 2007.

Wright, Bradford W. *Comic Book Nation: The Transformation of Youth Culture in America*. Baltimore, MD: Johns Hopkins University Press, 2003.

Yronwode, Cat. "Will Eisner Interview." In *Will Eisner Conversations*, edited by M. Thomas Inge, 47–78. Jackson: University Press of Mississippi, 2011.

Zimmerman, Dwight Jon. "Interview with Mike Baron." *David Anthony Kraft's Comics Interview* 63 (1988): 4–19.

Zombeatles_Fan. "Swamp Thing Returns to Play Club D, O'Cayz+Rev Cycle." *The Daily Page.* http://www.thedailypage.com/forum/viewtopic.php?t=49938. Last modified on August 12, 2010.

About the Contributors

Kane Anderson earned his PhD from the University of California at Santa Barbara in theater studies and holds an MFA in theater performance (acting) from Arizona State University. His dissertation, "Truth, Justice and the Performative Way!" examines superheroes through the lenses of theater and performance studies in addition to comics studies. His research includes superhero-themed gay parties, the fan reaction to DC Comics' "New 52" initiative and the phenomenon of "Super-Obama," as well as manga adaptations of Shakespearean plays and the performance of *kamishibai*, Japanese "paper theater." He continues his ethnographic research into cosplay at Wondercon and Comic-Con International. Look for him as the red-headed Captain Marvel and Mr. Incredible. He also won the Inge Award for Comics Scholarship for his analysis of *V for Vendetta* and the Occupy Movement, which appears in the *International Journal of Comics Art*.

Thomas Andrae (PhD, University of California, Berkeley) teaches in the Sociology Department at California State University, East Bay. He is cofounder and senior editor of *Discourse: Journal for Theoretical Studies in Media and Culture*. He is the author of *Carl Barks and the Disney Comic Book: Unmasking the Myth of Modernity* (University Press of Mississippi, 2006), *Creators of the Superheroes* (Hermes Press, 2011), *TV Nation: Prime Time Television and the Politics of the Sixties* (forthcoming), and coauthor of Bob Kane's autobiography, *Batman and Me* (Eclipse Books, 1989), (with Mel Gordon) *Siegel and Shuster's Funnyman: The First Jewish Superhero* (Feral House, 2010), and (with Carsten Laqua) *Walt Kelly: The Life and Art of the Creator of Pogo* (Hermes Press, 2012). He is also the editor of the 30-volume collection, *The Carl Barks Library* (Another Rainbow Publishing, 1983–1988) and producer of the documentary *The Duck Man: An Interview with Carl Barks* (1997).

Robert Beerbohm began mail order sales of comic books at age 14 by placing his first advertisement in *Rocket's Blast ComiCollector* #47 (1966) published by Gordon B. Love, and then set up at his first comicon in Houston, turning 15 at that show. More than a thousand comicons later, he is one of just four persons left alive who has sold comics at every San Diego Comic-Con since 1970. He was a co-founder of *Comics & Comix* on Telegraph Avenue near the University of California–Berkeley campus in 1972, the seminal legendary first multicounty chain store operation merchandizing comic books in America. He also co-hosted Berkeleycon '73, the first comics show devoted to creator-owned, royalty-paying comics publishing. Mr. Beerbohm can be found in the acknowledgments dating back a few decades in more than 200 comics history books supplying data and lore. A life-long student of the sequential comic strip book in all its myriad formats and genres since reading his first ones in the 1950s, he is currently working on *Comic Book Wars*, a history of the rise of the direct sales market and comic book stores. These days one can find him on the internet at www.BLBcomics.com.

Bond Benton joined the State University of New York Fredonia Communication Department in 2010 as a professor of public relations. His doctorate is from the University of Vienna in Austria with his dissertation focusing on the influence of culture on meaning. A particular focus of his research is the interaction of media, popular culture, and cross-cultural communication as it relates to the values and decisions of constituencies. As popular culture is frequently viewed as a foundation for shared social meaning, his research also reflects an interest in pop cultural artifacts such as graphic novels, including a forthcoming book chapter he has written on the death of Captain America. The peculiar space of *The Fabulous Furry Freak Brothers* as both an icon and critique of their own iconography is informed by his work on how texts shape and are shaped by subcultures.

Stephen R. Bissette, a pioneer graduate of the Joe Kubert School, teaches at the Center for Cartoon Studies (since its launch in 2005). He is renowned for his work on *Swamp Thing*, *Taboo* (launching *From Hell* and *Lost Girls*), *1963*, and *Tyrant*; co-creating John Constantine; and creating the world's second "24-Hour Comic" (initially invented by Scott McCloud for Bissette). He writes, illustrates, and has co-authored many books; his latest is *Teen Angels & New Mutants: Rick Veitch's Brat Pack and the Art, Karma, and Commerce of Killing Sidekicks* (2011); his short story "Copper" appears in *The New Dead* (2010), and he illustrated *The Vermont Monster Guide* (2009).

Stergios Botzakis is an assistant professor of adolescent literacy at the University of Tennessee–Knoxville. His areas of expertise are content area literacy, media literacy, and popular culture. His research is about using alternative texts and media in school, and he is a big fan of graphic novels and comics. He has read the Black Panther's adventures from the time he was with the Avengers and has followed them over multiple limited series and cartoon shows. Since he was a toddler he has been surrounded by DC Comics, including his Superman action figure and lunch box, the Adam West *Batman* television show, the *Super Friends* cartoons, and of course thousands of comic books. Not only can he remember reading the first Hellboy limited series with great interest and following his adventures since, he has also seen both movies.

Jeffrey A. Brown received his doctorate in anthropology from the University of Toronto in 1997. He is currently an associate professor and the graduate coordinator with the Department of Popular Culture at Bowling Green State University in Ohio. He has also been a curator with the Royal Ontario Museum and a guest curator for the Toledo Museum of Art and the Canadian Museum of Civilization. Dr. Brown is the author of two books, *Black Superheroes: Milestone Comics and Their Fans* and *Dangerous Curves: Gender, Fetishism and the Modern Action Heroine* (both with the University of Mississippi Press). He is also the author of over a dozen academic articles about gender, ethnicity, and sexuality in contemporary media that have appeared in journals such as *Screen, Cinema Journal, African American Review, Feminist Review, Differences, Men and Masculinities,* and the *Journal of Popular Film and Television.*

Brian Camp received his master of arts in communication studies from Memphis State University in 1991. Although an independent scholar, he has contributed to *The Greenwood Encyclopedia of Comics and Graphics Novels,* was quoted in both *Superhero: The Secret Origin of a Genre* and *The Power of Comics,* and appeared on a panel at the Comics Arts Conference. Being a lifelong fan of comics, he has studied not only the content but the history of the medium, its creators, and most importantly, its characters.

Rod Carveth is an assistant professor of public relations at Morgan State University in Baltimore, Maryland. He earned his PhD in communication studies from the University of Massachusetts–Amherst. He is the co-editor of two books, *Media Economics: Theory and Practice* and *Mad Men and Philosophy.* He primarily teaches courses in advertising and public relations, but also has taught an interdisciplinary course on *The Simpsons.*

Tommy Cash graduated from Henderson State University, a school he chose partly because of a curriculum that included courses involving comic books. This allowed him to call reading the copy of *Fantastic Four* he had been reading anyway "homework." Comic books have been a part of his life since he was three years old when his mother bought him a copy of *Tom and Jerry* at a used book store. He has been reading and sharing comic books ever since.

He now works with adults with developmental disabilities in Arkadelphia, Arkansas.

Charles A. Coletta earned both his BA and MA in literature from John Carroll University and his doctorate in American cultural studies from Bowling Green State University, where he has taught in the Department of Popular Culture since 2000. He organized the "Comic Book as Culture" conference at BGSU in 2008. In 2006, he assisted Eva Marie Saint in preparing for her role as "Martha Kent" in *Superman Returns*.

Corey K. Creekmur is an Associate Professor of English and Film Studies at the University of Iowa; his research concentrates on American and South Asian cinema as well as comics, and he is the general editor of the Comics Culture series for Rutgers University Press.

David J. Cross is a lifelong comic book fan. He graduated from Ohio State University and worked as a journalist before returning to school. Currently, he is completing a master's degree in communications and media studies from Florida State University. His thesis project is concerned with Superman comic books and their responses to historical events.

Keith Dallas is an instructor of English at Hofstra University, where he received his MA in 1993. Besides creating and writing the comic book series *Omega Chase* (Th3rd World Studios) and *The Argonauts* (Timeless Journey Comics), Dallas also co-wrote the *Ghostbusters: Con-Volution* one-shot for IDW. For TwoMorrows Publishing, Dallas co-wrote and edited *The Flash Companion*, a comprehensive examination of DC Comics' the Flash and the writers, artists, and editors who produced the characters' stories since their inceptions. His forthcoming TwoMorrows project, *American Comic Book Chronicles*, will provide a year-by-year account of the events of the comic book industry during the 1980s.

Randy Duncan is professor of communications at Henderson State University. He is co-author of *The Power of Comics: History, Form and Culture* (Continuum, 2009) and *Critical Approaches to Comics: Theories and Methods* (Routledge, 2012), both with Matthew J. Smith. He is a co-founder (with Peter Coogan) of the Comics Arts Conference and serves on the editorial board of the *International Journal of Comic Art* and the board of directors of the *Institute for Comics Studies*.

Lance Eaton is a visiting lecturer at Emerson College, University of Massachusetts, and North Shore Community College. His areas of research include comics, gender and sexuality, horror, film, and popular culture. He regularly teaches a course on monsters and another on comics in American culture. He has presented on comics at national conferences and published entries in *September 11 in Popular Culture: A Guide* and *Encyclopedia of Comic Books and Graphic Novels* from Greenwood Press.

Steve Englehart has been the lead writer for both Marvel and DC Comics on several occasions, and a founding father of Malibu's Ultraverse. His redefinition of the Batman and the Joker as mature adults completely changed both comics and the films made from them for the last three decades, not to mention his contributions to Captain America, Silver Surfer, Doctor Strange, Coyote, the Justice League of America, and dozens of others, all labeled "definitive" by the readers. He created Kilowog of the Green Lantern Corps and the Night Man, who got a TV series. The San Diego Comic-Con said he has "more hits with more characters at more companies than any other writer." These days, he explores all these different realities in novels. Said *Shelf Awareness*: "Englehart never takes his hand off the throttle."

Danny Fingeroth was a longtime writer and executive editor at Marvel Comics, where he ran the Spider-Man line. He has lectured on comics at venues including Columbia University, the Smithsonian Institution, and the Metropolitan Museum, and has publicly interviewed figures including Jules Feiffer, Al Jaffee, Jerry Robinson, and Harvey Pekar. Fingeroth has taught comics writing and appreciation at the New School, New York University, the MiMaster Institute in Milan, and the Museum of Comic and Cartoon Art (MoCCA), where he is senior vice-president of education. He serves on MoCCA's board of advisors and on the board of directors of the Institute for Comics Studies. Fingeroth is the author of *Superman on the Couch: What Superheroes Really Tell Us About Ourselves and Our Society*; *Disguised as Clark Kent: Jews, Comics, and the Creation of the Superhero*; and *The Rough Guide to Graphic Novels*. With Roy Thomas, he co-edited *The Stan Lee Universe*, a compendium of rarities from Lee's personal archives and elsewhere. Fingeroth's website is www.dannyfingeroth.com.

Ian Gordon is an associate professor of history at the National University of Singapore. His books include *Comic Strips and Consumer Culture: 1890–1945* (Smithsonian, 2002), *Comics & Ideology* (Peter Lang, 2001), and *Film and Comic Books* (University Press of Mississippi, 2007). His 2001 essay "Nostalgia, Myth, and Ideology: Visions of Superman at the End of the American Century," is in the *Cultural Studies* anthology edited by Michael Ryan.

Maggie Gray completed a PhD in the history of art at University College London in 2010, with a thesis entitled "'Love Your Rage, Not Your Cage': Comics as Cultural Resistance: Alan Moore 1971–1989." Her work has been published in the journals *Studies in Comics*, *Journal of Graphic Novels and Comics*, and *Kunst und Politik*, as well as the forthcoming collection *Alan Moore and the Gothic Tradition* edited by Matt Green. She has taught comics, the history of art and design, and aesthetics at Middlesex University, University College London, and Central St. Martins College of Art and Design.

Diana Green holds a BFA in comic book illustration from Minneapolis College of Art & Design (MCAD), where she teaches comic art history and related courses, and a master's in liberal studies from Hamline University. She has been presenting academic papers on comics since 2007 and has two papers and 10 reference entries pending publication. Currently she is coordinating MCAD's annual anime and manga conference *Schoolgirls and Mobile Suits*. Her primary focus in comic studies is the representation of cultural similarities and distinctions in comic narratives, and dealing with concepts of "the other" as portrayed in comics. In this context, the work of Robert Crumb is pertinent. Future projects include a book on Concrete and a volume on the history of GLBT representations in comics. The life of Joe Kubert is an integral part of the history of American comics, and Kubert is featured prominently in Ms. Green's coursework on the subject.

Michael W. Hancock (PhD, University of Kansas) teaches English and graphic novels at the Illinois Mathematics and Science Academy. He has written on Art Spiegelman, Bryan Talbot, and Jim Woodring and is a contributor to M. Keith Booker's *Encyclopedia of Comic Books and Graphic Novels* (Greenwood, 2010) and the forthcoming *Comics through Time: A Historical Encyclopedia* (ABC-CLIO).

Jared Hegwood has a doctorate in English from the University of Southern Mississippi and currently serves as faculty at Augusta State University. Dr. Hegwood regularly teaches classes on graphic narratives in relation to both contemporary and world literature. While at Southern Mississippi, he helped develop a pilot graduate emphasis in the academic study of graphic narratives, which included discussion on Jim Steranko's work.

David Heineman (PhD, University of Iowa) is an assistant professor of communication studies at Bloomsburg University of Pennsylvania. His research and teaching interests include rhetorical theory and criticism, new media technologies, visual communication, and popular culture. His most recent scholarship has focused on politics in new media, identity in gaming culture, and the rhetoric of public memory. He has long had a personal interest in comics, prompting recent research on the representation of gender and sexuality in graphic novels, manga, and Golden Age comics.

Crag Hill is currently an assistant professor of English education at Washington State University, where he has been instrumental in integrating young adult literature and graphic novels into the curriculum. For 18 years he taught English language arts for grades 9–12. In Fall 2011, he taught a graduate seminar titled "Sequential Art: Comics as Ensembles of Productive Mechanisms of Meaning." This seminar examined the theory of sequential art, the synergy of text and image (text as image/image as text), tapping into the exponentially growing body of comics theory and criticism, in print and online. He was a major contributor to the project *Rationales for Teaching Graphic Novels* (Maupin House, 2010), writing 10 of the 108 rationales, including rationales for *V for Vendetta*, *The Sandman: Preludes & Nocturnes*, *Pride of Baghdad*, *Safe Area Goražde*, and *The Adventures of Jimmy Corrigan*.

Shawn Hill has been reviewing art in the Boston area since 1990. His education combines an MA in art history and a BA in studio art. He generally strives to empathize with the goals of artists. Currently an assistant professor at Montserrat College of Art, he teaches art history surveys, with a special interest in photography and 20th-century art. His first comic purchase was in 1975, and was probably *Superboy* (featuring the Legion of Super-Heroes). He enjoys the drama afforded by superteam dynamics.

Alec R. Hosterman is senior lecturer and area coordinator of communication studies in the Ernestine M. Raclin School of the Arts at Indiana University South Bend. He regularly teaches courses in visual communication, understanding comics and graphic novels, new media studies, and theories of popular culture. Mr. Hosterman has a BA from Aquinas College and an MA from Ball State University. Currently, he is finishing his PhD through Texas Tech University, writing his dissertation on the relationship between graphic narratives and Jean Baudrillard's concept of hyperreality. In the spring of 2010, he had the pleasure of bringing Scott McCloud to IUSB to speak about the relationship between visual communication and comics. In addition to his teaching interests, Mr. Hosterman is a self-confessed new media junkie and an avid photographer of all things natural.

Bill Jennings joined the University of Cincinnati faculty in 2004 and has specialized in teaching courses on rhetoric, persuasion, and communication theory. His dissertation is from the University of Texas and concentrates on how political language and meaning are deployed in different arenas of popular culture and civic life. This area of study led to the publication of *Political Keywords* (Oxford University Press, 2004), a book that considers how a mere handful of words are put to radically different tasks depending on political affiliation and ideology. In many ways, the word *comics* shares the same fate as some of the most contested political expressions in that the use of the term reveals more about the assumptions of the speaker than it does about the fundamental nature of comics. As a lifelong reader of comics, he knew that it was a complex and diverse area of study. But it was only later as manager of a retail comic chain store that he experienced the problematic that *comics* means different things to different people. Trained as a historian as well, he considers how words and ideas are being pushed and pulled over time, and it is this worldview that shapes his entry on Dell Comics.

Phil Jimenez is an award-winning writer and artist who has worked for DC Comics and Marvel Comics for over 20 years. Well known for his work on pop culture icons like the X-Men and Spider-Man, he remains most popular for his work on Wonder Woman, creating over two years of the character's in-print adventures and co-authoring a voluminous encyclopedia about her world. Phil has also worked for television, film, museums, and as a teacher and mentor at the School of Visual Arts and the Cooper-Hewitt Design Museum in New York City.

William B. Jones, Jr., is a writer, teacher, and lawyer who lives in Little Rock, Arkansas. He received a BA in English from Rhodes College, an MA in English literature from Vanderbilt University, and a JD from the Bowen School of Law, University of Arkansas at Little Rock. Mr. Jones has written about popular culture for a number of newspapers, magazines, and journals since 1986. The author of *Classics Illustrated: A Cultural History, with Illustrations* (McFarland, 2002), he revised and expanded the book, which was published as *Classics Illustrated: A Cultural History, Second Edition* (McFarland, 2011). Jones has been invited to speak on *Classics Illustrated* at the Library of Congress, at literary conferences in New York and California, and at comics art exhibits in Arkansas and Tennessee. He currently writes introductions for the revived *Classics Illustrated* series published by Jack Lake Productions. Jones is also the editor of *Robert Louis Stevenson Reconsidered: New Critical Perspectives* (McFarland, 2003).

Jarret Keene (PhD, English, Florida State University, 2001) is a regular book critic for *Tucson Weekly* and *Vegas Seven* magazine, and his reviews have appeared in publications like the *Denver Post* and *Spin*. His essays and scholarship on pop culture, especially comic books, have been published in academic journals and fanzines. In 1995, he began teaching at FSU one of the very first classes devoted to alternative comics, assigning his students stories like Grant Morrison's eerie homage to the Warner Brothers–produced Wile E. Coyote/Road Runner cartoons, "The Coyote Gospel." His course packet was consistently jammed with Fantagraphics, Drawn & Quarterly, and Alternative Comics material, as well as mainstream works by Morrison,

Alan Moore, Garth Ennis, and Neil Gaiman. Currently, Keene serves on the editorial board of *Popular Culture Journal*, published by the English department at the University of Nevada, Las Vegas. He shops for comics in the greatest specialty shop on Earth-One, Alternate Reality Comics in Las Vegas.

Nathaniel Kosslyn is an undergraduate at New York University who has read and loved comics from a very young age. He has an extremely good memory of the comics he has read, and therefore is a resource on individual issues or storylines.

David Kunzle was educated at Cambridge and London Universities and served as Professor of the History of Art at the University of California Los Angeles beginning in 1977 (currently Distinguished, Emeritus). His books include a two-volume *History of the Comic Strip* (1456–1825, 1826–1896); *World Conquest from Duck Perspective* (on the Disney comic, in German); and an updated edition of his *Fashion and Fetishism: The Corset, Tight-lacing and Other Forms of Body-Sculpture* (History Press, 2004). His recent books are *Father of the Comic Strip, Rodolphe Töpffer* and a facsimile edition, with English translation and critical apparatus, *Rodolphe Töpffer, The Complete Comic Strips*, both with the University Press of Mississippi (2007). He has written an additional 130 articles on various aspects of political, protest, cartoon, mass-medium, and public art, from the early modern period to the present, published in six different languages. His current project is called *CHESUCRISTO: The Fusion in Word and Image of Jesus Christ and Che Guevara*.

Derek Lackaff, PhD, is an assistant professor of communications at Elon University. He studies the ways in which digital technologies have enabled expanded creative production and enhanced access to audiences.

Travis Langley, superherologist, received his PhD in psychology from Tulane University. He is a professor of psychology at Henderson State University where he teaches classes on crime, mental illness, social behavior, and media, including a course titled *Batman*. He and his students investigate the behavior of comic book fans for their ongoing ERIICA Project: Empirical Research on the Interpretation & Influence of the Comic Arts. An organizer of the Comics Arts Conference, he regularly presents panels analyzing superheroes at conventions such as San Diego Comic-Con International, WonderCon, and New York Comic Con, including one panel on the psychopathy of the Joker that turned into an article for the *International Journal of Comic Art*. He has authored *Batman and Psychology: A Dark and Stormy Knight*, the definitive text on the psychology of Batman (John Wiley & Sons, 2012).

Paul Levitz is a comic book fan (editor/publisher of *Etcetera* and *The Comic Reader*), historian (member of the editorial board of the first edition of *Who's Who in American Comic Books*), writer (*Legion of Super-Heroes* and many other titles), editor (*Batman* and other titles), and publisher (formerly president and publisher of DC Comics). His book, *75 Years of DC Comics: The Art of Modern Mythmaking*, won an Eisner Award for "Best Comics Related Publication" in 2011.

J. Z. Long is an interdisciplinary scholar who holds a PhD in cultural studies from George Mason University. J. Z. currently works in the Gray Research Center of the Library of the Marine Corps in Quantico, VA. During the late 1980s and into the 1990s, he had the pleasure of serving as the assistant manager of two independent comic book stores, where he vividly remembers the hype around *Spider-Man* #1, *X-Men* #1, and, of course, *Wizard* #1.

Kathleen McClancy is a visiting assistant professor at Wake Forest University. She studied American literature with an emphasis on cultural and media studies at Duke University, where she received her PhD in 2009. She is presently involved in a study of the representations of Vietnam veterans in popular culture, and has published on Ted Kotcheff's *First Blood* and Neal Stephenson's *The Diamond Age*. She has written on Alan Moore's *Miracleman* and *V for Vendetta*, and is the co-chair of the Comics Arts Conference.

Patrick McLaughlin, PhD, received his bachelor's and master's degrees from Clarion University of Pennsylvania and his PhD in literature and criticism from Indiana University of Pennsylvania. Dr. McLaughlin is a professor of composition, language, and literature at Lakeland Community College, located 23 miles east of Cleveland, OH. In that capacity he teaches fantasy literature, science fiction, and graphic fiction. The graphic fiction course is unique in that the team-taught class (involving a writing and art teacher) enables students to complete their own original work of graphic fiction that is published in an anthology at the end of the semester. For eight years, Dr. McLaughlin has hosted a Comics Symposium that regularly features locally, regionally, and nationally prominent individuals in the fields of comics and graphic fiction. Past special guests have included Denny O'Neil, Harvey Pekar, and Marc Sumerak.

Ana Merino is an associate professor of creative writing and cultural studies and the director of the MFA in Spanish creative writing at the University of Iowa. Merino works on comics and graphic novels criticism. She has written a scholarly book on Hispanic comics, a critical monograph on Chris Ware, and numerous articles and essays about comics. She is a member of the board of directors at the Center for Cartoon Studies. She has served as curator for four comics exhibitions, one of them dedicated to Fantagraphics for La Semana Negra in Gijón, Spain.

Andrei Molotiu is Senior Lecturer in the Department of History of Art at Indiana University, Bloomington. He holds an MA and a PhD from New York University and is the author of *Fragonard's Allegories of Love* (Getty Museum, 2007), *Abstract Comics: The Anthology* (Fantagraphics, 2009), and *Nautilus* (Fahrenheit, 2009), a collection of his own abstract comics. He is currently writing a monograph on Lee and Ditko's *Amazing Spider-Man*.

Kim Munson is an art historian and a partner in Comic Art Productions and Exhibits (CAPE), a company that develops and curates comics-themed museum exhibitions. Kim earned an MA in art history from San Francisco State University after a long career as an art director and scenic artist in Los Angeles, including two seasons of the George Romero series *Tales from the Darkside* and the feature film *Nightmare on Elm Street 3*. In 2004, she worked with the law offices of Marc Greenberg to develop a historical background of the Blade character for the *Snipes v. New Line Cinema* lawsuit.

Jacque Nodell is an American independent scholar residing in Denmark. Jacque's main interests lie in comic book industry history and the history of nonsuperhero comic genres, primarily that of romance and monsters. Jacque runs the popular blog *Sequential Crush*, which is dedicated to preserving the memory of romance comics from the 1960s and 1970s. Jacque's undergraduate degrees are in history and anthropology from the University of Wisconsin–Milwaukee, and she holds a master of arts in history from the University of Missouri–St. Louis.

Michelle Nolan is a pop culture historian and author of the McFarland books *Love on the Racks: A History of American Romance Comics* (2008) and *Ball Tales: A Study of American Baseball, Basketball and Football Fiction from the 1930s through 1960s* (2010). She has published more than 10,000 newspaper and magazine feature and news articles over a span of more than 45 years and has contributed to dozens of books. She lives in Bellingham, WA.

Amy Kiste Nyberg is an associate professor of media studies in the Department of Communication and the Arts at Seton Hall University, South Orange, NJ. She joined the Seton Hall faculty in 1993 and teaches introductory and advanced-level journalism courses. She earned her doctorate in mass communication from the University of Wisconsin–Madison and has more than 20 years' experience as a journalist. The author of *Seal of Approval: A History of the Comics Code* (University Press of Mississippi, 1998), she also has written conference papers, journal articles, and book chapters on comics journalism.

Her course "The Journalistic Tradition," a study of influential works of journalism, uses Joe Sacco's *Palestine* as a key text.

David B. Olsen is a PhD candidate in the Department of English at Saint Louis University, where he has taught courses in literature, writing, poetry, science fiction, and graphic novels. He is also a graduate of the Cornell University School of Criticism and Theory. Since 2006, he has presented papers on comics and graphic novels at the International Comic Arts Forum, the Festival of Cartoon Art at the Ohio State University, San Diego Comic-Con International, and the Modern Language Association national convention, as well as a number of other papers on contemporary and experimental fiction.

Robert N. O'Nale, Jr. is a graduate of Henderson State University's Master of Liberal Arts program with an emphasis in art history. His master's thesis was on gestalt psychology as it applies to reading and composition of comic books and sequential art. He has also contributed articles to *The Encyclopedia of Comic Books and Graphic Novels* (Greenwood, 2010), edited by M. Keith Booker.

Clare Pitkethly is completing her PhD at the University of Melbourne, Australia. She has published various articles and chapters on comics, including "Recruiting an Amazon: The Collision of Old World Ideology and New World Identity in Wonder Woman" in the volume edited by Angela Ndalianis, *The Contemporary Comic Book Superhero* (Routledge, 2008), and "The Pursuit of Identity in the Face of Paradox: Indeterminacy, Structure and Repetition in Superman, Batman and Wonder Woman" in the *Journal of Graphic Novels and Comics*.

Matthew Pustz is the author of *Comic Book Culture: Fanboys and True Believers*, published in 2000 by the University Press of Mississippi, and the editor of the anthology *Comic Books and American Cultural History*, published by Continuum Books in 2012. He is also a frequent presenter at the Popular Culture Association annual meetings where he has discussed a variety of comics-related topics, including the politics of superheroes, the ability of comics to teach history, and the ways in which the 1970s are reflected in the comics of the period. Pustz teaches history and American Studies at Fitchburg State University and at Endicott College in Massachusetts.

Kevin Quigley's first experience with comics was the *Tales from the Crypt* reprints in the 1980s and 1990s. A novelist and nonfiction writer, Mr. Quigley has published several works with the small press Cemetery Dance. His chapter in the book *Drawn into Darkness* focused exclusively on horror comics from the early 1980s through modern publications like *American Vampire*. His critical study of the graphic collection *J. N. Williamson's Illustrated Masques* was part of an ongoing column for the horror website *FEARnet.com*, which tackles contemporary horror in every medium, including comics.

David N. Rapp is an associate professor in the School of Education and Social Policy and the Department of Psychology at Northwestern University. His research focuses on reading comprehension, with particular interest in the underlying mechanisms responsible for successful discourse experiences. To date, his work has investigated the ways in which prior knowledge, unfolding text information, and comprehension goals interactively influence the processes and products of reading activities. This work has been funded by the National Science Foundation, the U.S. Department of Education, and the National Institute on Aging. He is an associate editor at *Discourse Processes* and the *Journal of Educational Psychology*, and serves on the editorial boards of the *Journal of Experimental Psychology: Applied* and *Scientific Study of Literature*. He is also on the board of directors of Reading with Pictures, a nonprofit organization that provides comics advocacy and research support for integrating comics into classroom literacy curricula.

Brad J. Ricca is a SAGES Fellow and full-time lecturer in English at Case Western Reserve University. He has given talks about comics at the Comic Arts Conference, the Modern Language Association, and the Popular Culture Association. He has published essays on comics historiography in *Critical Approaches to Comics* (Routledge, 2012) and on Superman in *Alan Moore and the Gothic Tradition* (Manchester University Press, forthcoming). He directed a documentary about Siegel and Shuster titled *Last Son* (2010), which won a Silver Ace Award from the Las Vegas Film Festival. His book about Superman's creators, *Super Boys*, is forthcoming from St. Martin's Press.

Phil Rippke, MA in rhetoric, and **Ruth Beerman**, PhD candidate in rhetoric at the University of Wisconsin–Milwaukee, both have interests in popular culture, especially comics. Phil is a life-long comics reader and fan, and edited John Sheridan and Kit Wallis's comic *Breathe* (from Markosia Enterprises). Ruth published "The Body Unbound: *Empowered*, Heroism, and Body Image" in the *Journal of Graphic Novels and Comics* (December 2012), about the role of female superheroes and Adam Warren's graphic novel *Empowered*.

Trina Robbins, historian and writer, has been producing graphic novels, comics, and books for over 30 years, since she produced the first all-woman comic book, *It Ain't Me, Babe*, in 1970. Her subjects have ranged from Wonder Woman and the Powerpuff Girls to her own teenage superheroine, *GoGirl!*, and from female cartoonists and superheroines to women who kill. She is considered the expert on the subject of early-20th-century female cartoonists, and is responsible for rediscovering many brilliant but previously forgotten women, including Golden Age Fiction House cartoonist Lily Renee and the great Nell Brinkley. Her full-color book, *The Brinkley Girls: The Best of Nell Brinkley's Cartoons from 1913–1940* (Fantagraphics, 2009), was nominated for an Eisner Award and a Harvey Award. In 2011 Robbins edited *Tarpe Mills and Miss Fury* (IDW), collecting five years of previously unreprinted Sunday strips, and she scripted *Lily Renee: Escape Artist*, a graphic novel biography of the 1940s woman cartoonist who, as a Jewish teenager in Vienna, escaped the Nazis in 1939. She is currently editing a collection of Lily Renee's comic book art.

Robin S. Rosenberg is a clinical psychologist and author who writes about superheroes and the psychological phenomena their stories reveal. She was editor of and contributor to *Psychology of Superheroes* (Smart Pop, 2008), series editor of the Oxford University Press *Superhero* series, author of *What's the Matter with Batman? An Unauthorized Clinical Look under the Mask of the Caped Crusader*, and *Psychology Today*'s superhero blogger. She has been featured speaking about psychological aspects of superheroes in various media, including the History Channel, NPR, the *Financial Times*, *Psychology Today*, the Canadian Broadcast Company, and on documentaries and special features of superhero DVDs. She is also co-author of three college-level psychology textbooks. Rosenberg uses superhero characters and stories to reveal psychological phenomena.

Julia Round lectures in the Media School at Bournemouth University, UK, and edits the academic journal *Studies in Comics*. She has published and presented work internationally on cross-media adaptation, television and discourse analysis, the application of literary terminology to comics, the redefinition of "graphic novel," and the presence of Gothic and fantastic motifs and themes in this medium. She has written extensively on the work of Alan Moore (*Blackwell New Companion to the Gothic*, 2012; *Alan Moore and the Gothic Tradition*, 2011; *The Rise and Reason of Comics and Graphic Literature*, 2010; *International Journal of Comic Art* 10, no. 1, 2008), and is currently working on a monograph on Gothic graphic novels (*Ghosts in the Gutter*, McFarland, forthcoming) that analyses the impact of the English Gothic tradition on contemporary British and American comics. Further details at www.juliaround.com.

Cord A. Scott is an adjunct instructor in the Chicago area, specifically Loyola University Chicago and Triton College. His dissertation was on war comics as a reflection of cultural history in America. His academic focus is on cultural aspects of American history with an emphasis on comics. He has written several articles for academic journals such as the *Journal of Popular*

Culture, the *International Journal of Comic Art*, and the *Journal of the Illinois State Historical Society*. He has also contributed to an academic book on Captain America entitled *Captain America and the Struggle of the Superhero* (McFarland, 2009, edited by Rob Weiner), as well as a forthcoming book on Spider-Man, entitled *Spider-Man, Spider-Women, and Webspinners: Critical Perspectives*, edited by Rob Weiner and Robert Moses Peaslee.

David S. Serchay has been a librarian with the Broward County (Florida) Library System since 1998, and his duties have included ordering graphic novels for the collection. He has a BA in communications from Florida Atlantic University and an MLS from the University of South Florida. He is the author of *The Librarian's Guide to Graphic Novels for Children and Tweens* (Neal-Shuman, 2008) and *The Librarian's Guide to Graphic Novels for Adults* (Neal-Shuman, 2009) and has written and lectured about comics and graphic novels.

Matthew J. Smith is a professor of communication at Wittenberg University where he teaches courses in media studies, including one in graphic storytelling. He holds a PhD from Ohio University and is a past president of the Ohio Communication Association. Along with Randy Duncan, he is co-author of *The Power of Comics: History, Form and Culture* (Continuum, 2009) and co-editor of *Critical Approaches to Comics: Theories and Methods* (Routledge, 2012).

Jennifer K. Stuller is a writer, critic, pop culture historian, and the author of *Ink-Stained Amazons and Cinematic Warriors: Superwomen in Modern Mythology* (I. B. Tauris, 2010). She has contributed to several books including *Gotham City 14 Miles: 14 Essays on Why the 1960s Batman TV Series Matters* (CreateSpace, 2011), and *Critical Approaches to Comics and Graphic Novels: Theories and Methods* (Routledge, 2012) for which she wrote the feminist analysis chapter using 1970s Lois Lane comic books. Stuller's interests focus on what popular culture can tell us about social mores, particularly regarding gender and sexuality in a given time or place. She is a public speaker—regularly presenting at the Comics Arts Conference and the Slayage Conference on the Whedonverses. Stuller provides expert opinion for radio, documentaries, and newspapers, and is a contributor to *Bitch* magazine. Having graduated with honors from the Program in the Comparative History of Ideas at the University of Washington, she lives in Seattle with her husband, Ryan Wilkerson, and their two Malteses, Giles and Wesley. More information at www.ink-stainedamazon.com.

Craig S. This, BA and MA in history, is a lecturer at Sinclair Community College in Dayton, OH. He teaches a popular culture course entitled Comic

Books and American Culture. He has published articles on "Ecofeminism in *The Strange Disappearance of Miss Finch*" and "Captain America Lives and So Do the Nazis: Nazisploitation in Comic Books after 9/11" in *Nazisploitation: The Nazi Image in Low-Brow Cinema and Culture* (Continuum Books, 2011). He is currently working on a historical essay on Ghost Rider (*Comics through Time*, ABC-CLIO, forthcoming).

Mark Waid is a full-time writer and comics historian who, for the past 25 years, has divided his time between scripting for comics publishers and studying and cataloguing their history. He has authored more than 50 graphic novels, chief among them *Kingdom Come* (DC Comics), the best-selling Superman graphic novel of all time.

Dave Wallace is a journalist who has been writing about comics for more than a decade. Born in the United Kingdom, he grew up reading weekly issues of the *Beano*, *Asterix* collections, and *Tintin* books before discovering American comics as a teenager. Having also been raised on a diet of 1980s and 1990s indie rock and video games, he instantly warmed to Scott Pilgrim on reading the first book of the character's adventures. This led him to thoroughly enjoy every volume of the series, as well as the 2010 movie and video game adaptations.

Hames Ware is founding co-editor of the *Who's Who of American Comic Books* (four volumes)—considered the benchmark comic book reference for comic book historians. He also served as art reference editor for the AC Comics reprint series and as a regular columnist for *Animato* (writing columns on animated cartoon voice providers of 1930s–1950s theatrical animated cartoons) and *Alter Ego* (columns with Jim Vadeboncoeur, Jr., on Golden Age comic book artists). For about 40 years, he contributed hundreds of character voice-overs to many radio, television, and film projects, including the narration for the Emmy-winning documentary *Precious Memories, The American Experience*, among others.

Robert G. Weiner is an associate humanities librarian for Texas Tech University. He has graduate degrees in history and library science and has written on numerous popular culture topics from comics to film and music. He is the author of the reference book *Marvel Graphic Novels: Annotated Guide* (McFarland, 2008) and the editor of *Captain America and the Struggle of the Superhero* (McFarland, 2009). He also has an article related to Captain America in the edited volume *The Gospel According to Superheroes* (Peter Lang, 2005).

Candace E. West holds a PhD in religious studies from Stanford University, where she has taught seminars on Dante, religious storytelling, introductory religious studies, religion and literature, and religious ethics in speculative fiction. For her doctoral work, she explored the relationship between selfhood and storytelling in the short stories of Isak Dinesen. She has written on the connection between heroism and humanism in the shows of Joss Whedon and, in her current work, examines how contemporary storytellers like Whedon and Neil Gaiman have taken up and transformed a range of religiously charged ideas (e.g., hope, heroism, and spiritual crisis) in new narratives and new narrative forms.

Robert Westerfelhaus earned his MA and PhD from Ohio University. He is currently an associate professor in the Department of Communication at the College of Charleston, where his teaching focuses upon American popular culture. In 2009–2010, Westerfelhaus taught courses on comic books, film, and television as a Fulbright recipient at the Instytut Anglistyki at the Uniwersytet Marii Curie-Skłodowskiej in Lublin, Poland. His research has appeared in *Critical Studies in Media Communication, Text and Performance Quarterly*, and other peer-reviewed journals. He has contributed several encyclopedia entries concerning comic books.

Kent Worcester is a professor of political science at Marymount Manhattan College, where he teaches courses on contemporary war, democratic theory, Plato's *Republic*, and graphic literature. He is the co-editor (with Jeet Heer) of *Arguing Comics: Literary Masters on a Popular Medium* (University Press of Mississippi, 2004) and *A Comics Studies Reader* (University Press of Mississippi, 2009), as well as the author of *C.L.R. James: A Political Biography* (SUNY Press,1996) and *The Social Science Research Council, 1923–1998* (Social Science Research Council, 2001). He has been reviewing comics and interviewing cartoonists for the *Comics Journal* since the mid-1990s. His recent articles include "Editorial Cartoons and the 2010 British General Election" (Paul Baines et al., *Explaining Cameron's Coalition: How It Happened, The 2010 General Election*), and "New York City, 9/11 and Comics" (*Radical History Review*, no. 111).

Daniel F. Yezbick is associate professor of English and international education coordinator at Forest Park College in St. Louis, MO, where he teaches comic art, film, literature, and writing. He received his dual BA (1995) in English and film/video studies from the University of Michigan's Residential College and his MA (1998) and PhD (2004) in English from the University of Illinois at Urbana-Champaign. He has lectured and published on diverse topics including comics and sequential art, stereoscopic narrative, radio drama, and New Deal Shakespeare. He served as an editor of *Meanwhile* (Fantagraphics, 2011), R. C. Harvey's critical biography of Milton Caniff, and is currently at work on Fantagraphics Press's *Perfect Nonsense: George Carlson's Comics* *and Children's Art*. Originally from Detroit, Dan grew up on a steady diet of Shakespeare, Orson Welles, and Spider-Man and has been addicted to stage, screen, and sequential narrative ever since.

Tanya D. Zuk recently earned her master of arts in media arts from the School of Theatre, Film & Television at the University of Arizona, Tucson. She has presented work at the Comic Arts Conferences in San Diego and San Francisco. Her primary research method is social history, incorporating elements of fan ethnography, industrial analysis, and textual analysis. She studies the cultural impact of popular culture on minority groups through "artifacts" including comics, television programs, and film.

Index